Lecture Notes in Computer Science 1929

Edited by G. Goos, J. Hartmanis and J. van Leeuwen

T0189802

Springer

Berlin
Heidelberg
New York
Barcelona
Hong Kong
London
Milan
Paris
Singapore
Tokyo

Robert Laurini (Ed.)

Advances in
Visual
Information Systems

4th International Conference, VISUAL 2000
Lyon, France, November 2-4, 2000
Proceedings

 Springer

Series Editors

Gerhard Goos, Karlsruhe University, Germany
Juris Hartmanis, Cornell University, NY, USA
Jan van Leeuwen, Utrecht University, The Netherlands

Volume Editor

Robert Laurini
Claude Bernard University of Lyon
LISI - 502, INSA de Lyon
69621 Villeurbanne Cedex, France
E-mail: Robert.Laurini@lisi.insa-lyon.fr

Cataloging-in-Publication Data applied for

Die Deutsche Bibliothek - CIP-Einheitsaufnahme

Advanced in visual information systems : 4th international conference,
VISUAL 2000, Lyon, France, November 2 - 4, 2000 ; proceedings /
Robert Laurini (ed.). - Berlin ; Heidelberg ; New York ; Barcelona ; Hong
Kong ; London ; Milan ; Paris ; Singapore ; Tokyo : Springer, 2000
  (Lecture notes in computer science ; Vol. 1929)
  ISBN 3-540-41177-1

CR Subject Classification (1998): H.3, H.5, H.2, I.4, I.5, I.7, I.3

ISSN 0302-9743
ISBN 3-540-41177-1 Springer-Verlag Berlin Heidelberg New York

Springer-Verlag Berlin Heidelberg New York
a member of BertelsmannSpringer Science+Business Media GmbH
© Springer-Verlag Berlin Heidelberg 2000
Printed in Germany

Typesetting: Camera-ready by author
Printed on acid-free paper   SPIN 10722905   06/3142   5 4 3 2 1 0

Preface

Presently, in our world, visual information dominates. The turn of the millenium marks the age of visual information systems. Enabled by picture sensors of all kinds turning digital, visual information will not only enhance the value of existing information, it will also open up a new horizon of previously untapped information sources. There is a huge demand for visual information access from the consumer. As well, the handling of visual information is boosted by the rapid increase of hardware and Internet capabilities. Advanced technology for visual information systems is more urgently needed than ever before: not only new computational methods to retrieve, index, compress and uncover pictorial information, but also new metaphors to organize user interfaces. Also, new ideas and algorithms are needed which allow access to very large databases of digital pictures and videos. Finally we should not forget new systems with visual interfaces integrating the above components into new types of image, video or multimedia databases and hyperdocuments.

All of these technologies will enable the construction of systems that are radically different from conventional information systems. Many novel issues will need to be addressed: query formulation for pictorial information, consistency management thereof, indexing and assessing the quality of these systems.

Historically, the expression Visual Information Systems can be understood either as a system for image information or as visual system for any kind information. The invited speakers were selected from both directions: SK Chang from the University of Pittsburgh and Chamei Chen from Brunel University. SK Chang will present the sentient map for education purposes, that is to say, a novel way to use and to understand visual information systems. Chaomei Chen will summarize the new possibilities of visualizing information issued from databases.

In this fourth conference, emphasis was given to structuring image and video information systems and retrieval, especially ones based on color and shape. For this purpose, indexing is the key issue. To conclude the conference, some papers on benchmarking will be presented.

September 2000   Robert Laurini

VISUAL 2000 Conference Organization

General chair
Robert Laurini   Claude Bernard University of Lyon, France.

Steering committee
Shi Kuo Chang   University of Pittsburgh, USA
Ramesh Jain   University of California at San Diego, USA
Tosiyasu Kunii   The University of Aizu, Japan
Clement Leung   Victoria University of Technology, Australia
Arnold Smeulders   University of Amsterdam, The Netherlands

Program co-chairs
William Grosky   Wayne University, USA, American PC co-chair
Clement Leung   Victoria University, Australia, Australasian PC co-chair
Arnold Smeulders   U. of Amsterdam, The Netherlands, European PC co-chair

Program committee
Marie-Aude Aufaure   University of Lyon I, France
Josef Bigun   Halmstad U. and Chalmers U. of Technology, Sweden
Patrice Boursier   University of La Rochelle, France
Patrick Bouthemy   IRISA, France
Selcuk Candan   Arizona State University, USA
Shi Kuo Chang   University of Pittsburgh, USA
Liming Chen   Ecole Centrale de Lyon, France
Tat-seng Chua   National University of Singapore
Maria Franca Costabile University of Bari, Italy
Isabel Cruz   Worcester Polytechnic Institute, USA
Alberto Del Bimbo   University of Florence, Italy
Nevenka Dimitrova   Philips, USA
André Flory   INSA of Lyon, France
Borko Fuhrt   Florida Atlantic University, USA
Theo Gevers   University of Amsterdam, The Netherlands
Athula Ginige   University of Western Sydney, Australia
Luc van Gool   Catholic University of Leuven, Belgium
Jiawei Han   Simon Fraser University, Canada
Nies Huijsmans   University of Leiden, The Netherlands
Horace Ip   City University of Hong Kong, China
H.V. Jagadish   University of Michigan, USA
Jean-Michel Jolion   INSA of Lyon, France
Tosiyasu Kunii   Hosei University, Japan
Inald Lagendijk   Delft University of Technology, The Netherlands
Jinhua Ma   University of Aizu, Japan
Rajiv Mehrotra   Kodak, USA
Mario Nascimento   University of Alberta, Canada

Kingsley Nwosu	Lucent Technologies, USA
Stelios Orphanoudakis	University of Crete, Greece
Fernando Pereira	Institute of Telecommunications, Portugal
Masao Sakauchi	University of Tokyo, Japan
Simone Santini	Praja, USA
Raimondo Schettini	CNR-Milan, Italy
Timothy Shih	Tamkang University, Taiwan
John Smith	IBM, USA
Uma Srinivasan	Macquarrie University, Australia
Peter Stanchev	Wayne State University, USA
Claude Trépied	University of Tours, France
Remco Veltkamp	Utrecht University, The Netherlands
Marcel Worring	University of Amsterdam, The Netherlands

External reviewers

Michael Buckley	Macquarrie University, Australia
Patrick Gros	IRISA-Rennes, France
Fabrice Heitz	ENSPS, Strasbourg, France
Alessandra Lisi	University of Bari, Italy
Donato Malerba	University of Bari, Italy
Tat-Hieu Nguyen	University of Amsterdam, The Netherlands
Stéphane Pateux	IRISA-Rennes, France
Renato O. Stehling	State University of Campinas, Brazil
Jeroen Vendrig	University of Amsterdam, The Netherlands

Local organization committee

Patrick Prévôt	INSA of Lyon, France, Chair
Marie-Aude Aufaure	Claude Bernard University of Lyon, France
Stephane Bres	INSA of Lyon, France
Liming Chen	Ecole Centrale de Lyon, France
Jean-Michel Jolion	INSA of Lyon, France
Robert Laurini	Claude Bernard University of Lyon, France
Jean-Yves Ramel	INSA of Lyon, France

Table of Contents

Guest Speaker

The Sentient Map and Its Application to the Macro-University E-Learning
Environment...1
    S.-K. Chang

Image Information Systems

An Image Data Model. 14
    W.I. Grosky, P.L. Stanchev

Interaction in Content-Based Image Retrieval: The Evaluation of the
State-of-the-Art Review...26
    M. Worring, A. Smeulders, S. Santini

Video Information Systems

Automatic Video Summary and Description...37
    S.-Y. Lee, S.-T. Lee, D.-Y. Chen

Relevance Ranking of Video Data using Hidden Markov Model Distances and
Polygon Simplification. 49
    D. DeMenthon, L.J. Latecki, A. Rosenfeld, M. Vuilleumier Stückelberg

Video Clustering Using SuperHistograms in Large Archives..........................62
    L. Agnihotri, N. Dimitrova

3D Camera Movements Tracking and Indexing Based on 2D Hints Extraction.......74
    M. Ardebilian, W. Mahdi, L. Chen

Main Mobile Object Detection and Localization in Video Sequences.................84
    G. Tsechpenakis, Y. Xirouhakis, A. Delopoulos

Statistical Motion-Based Retrieval with Partial Query...................................96
    R. Fablet, P. Bouthemy

Experiments in Using Visual and Textual Clues for Image Hunting on the Web....108
    Y. A. Aslandogan, C. T. Yu

Guest Speaker

Visualising Information: A Mosaic of Perspectives......................................120
    C. Chen

Visual Querying

Spatial/Temporal Query Processing for Information Fusion Applications............127
    S.-K. Chang, G. Costagliola, E. Jungert

Metaphors for Visual Querying Spatio-Temporal Databases...........................140
    C. Bonhomme, M.-A. Aufaure-Portier, C. Trépied

About Ambiguities in Visual GIS Query Languages: A Taxonomy and Solutions..154
    F. Favetta, M.-A. Aufaure-Portier

Visualization of Dynamic Spatial Data and Query Results Over Time in a GIS
Using Animation...166
    G. S. Iwerks, H. Samet

Color

Upgrading Color Distributions for Image Retrieval: Can We Do Better?.............178
    C. Vertan, N. Boujemaa

Color Normalization for Digital Video Processing.....................................189
    J. M. Sánchez, X. Binefa

Multimedia Content Filtering, Browsing, and Matching Using MPEG-7 Compact
Color Descriptors...200
    S. Krishnamachari, A. Yamada, M. Abdel-Mottaleb, E. Kasutani

Shape-Based Retrieval

Shape Description for Content-Based Image Retrieval................................212
    E. Ardizzone, A. Chella, R. Pirrone

Wavelet-Based Salient Points: Applications to Image Retrieval Using Color and
Texture Features...223
    E. Loupias, N. Sebe

Matching Shapes with Self-Intersections..233
    S. Abbasi, F. Mokhtarian

Image Databases

A Novel Approach for Accessing Partially Indexed Image Corpora...................244
    G. Duffing, M. Smaïl

Show Me What You Mean ! Pariss: A CBIR-Interface that Learns by Example.....257
    G. Caenen, G. Frederix, A.A.M. Kuijk, E.J. Pauwels, B.A.M. Schouten

Scale Summarized and Focused Browsing of Primitive Visual Content..............269
   X. Zabulis, J. Sporring, S. C. Orphanoudakis

Integrated Browsing and Searching of Large Image Collections......................279
   Z. Pecenovic, M. N. Do, M. Vetterli, P. Pu

A Rich Get Richer Strategy for Content-Based Image Retrieval......................290
   L. Duan, W. Gao, J. Ma

MRML: A Communication Protocol for Content-Based Image Retrieval............300
   W. Mueller, H. Mueller, S. Marchand-Maillet, T. Pun, D. McG. Squiré.
   Z. Pecenovic, C. Giess, A. P. de Vries

An Integrated Multimedia System with Learning Capabilities..........................312
   G. Ciocca, I. Gagliardi, R. Schettini, B. Zonta

Video Indexing

Global Motion Fourier Series Expansion for Video Indexing and Retrieval..........327
   E. Bruno, D. Pellerin

Feature Driven Visualization of Video Content for Interactive Indexing.............338
   J. Vendrig, M. Worring

Conceptual Indexing of Television Images Based on Face and Caption Sizes and
Locations..349
   R. Ronfard, C. Garcia, J. Carrive

Image Databases

SIMPLIcity: Semantics-sensitive Integrated Matching for Picture Libraries.........360
   J. Z. Wang, J. Li, G. Wiederhold

Semantic Indexing for Image Retrieval Using Description Logics....................372
   E. Di Sciascio, F. M. Donini, M. Mongiello

An Iconic and Semantic Content-Based Retrieval System for Histological Images.384
   R. W. K. Lam, K. K. T. Cheung, H. H. S. Ip, L. H. Y. Tang, R. Hanka

Image Retrieval

Image Retrieval by Colour and Texture Using Chromaticity Histograms and
Wavelet Frames...397
   S. Liapis, G. Tziritas

Adaptive Multi-class Metric Content-Based Image Retrieval.........................407
   J. Peng

Integrating Visual and Textual Cues for Image Classification.......................419
    T. Gevers, F. Aldershoff, J.-M. Geusebroek

Benchmarking

Evaluating the Performance of Content-Based Image Retrieval Systems............430
    M. Koskela, J. Laaksonen, S. Laakso, E. Oja

Benchmarking for Content-Based Visual Information Search........................442
    C. H. C. Leung, H. H. S. Ip

Posters

Video Content Representation Based on Texture and Lighting.......................457
    I.S. Radev, G. Paschos, N. Pissinou, K. Makki

Shape Similarity Measures, Properties and Constructions.............................467
    R.C. Veltkamp, M. Hagedoorn

Leaf Image Retrieval with Shape Features...477
    Z. Wang, Z. Chi, D. Feng, Q. Wang

A Software Framework for Combining Iconic and Semantic Content for Retrieval
of Histological Images..488
    K.K.T. Cheung, R.W.K. Lam, H.H.S. Ip, L.H.Y. Tang, R. Hanka

A Ground-Truth Training Set for Hierarchical Clustering in Content-Based Image
Retrieval...500
    D.P. Huijmans, N. Sebe, M.S. Lew

Query Models and Languages for Geographical Information Systems...............511
    M. Mainguenaud

Content-Based Image Retrieval by Relevance Feedback.............................521
    Z. Jin, I. King, X. Li

Chinese Cursive Script Character Image Retrieval Based On An Integrated
Probability Function..530
    I.King, Z. Jin, D. Y.-M. Chan

Author Index...541

The Sentient Map and Its Application to the Macro University E-Learning Environment

Shi-Kuo Chang
Department of Computer Science
University of Pittsburgh
Pittsburgh, PA 15260 USA
Chang@cs.pitt.edu

Abstract. The sentient map is a new paradigm for visual information retrieval. It enables the user to view data as maps, so that gestures, more specifically c-gestures, can be used for the interaction between the user and the multimedia information system. Different c-gestures are then dynamically transformed into spatial/temporal queries, or σ-queries, for multimedia information sources and databases. An e-learning environment called the Macro University serves as a test bed to evaluate this approach.

1. Introduction

Maps are widely used to present spatial/temporal information to serve as a guide, or an index, so that the viewer of the map can obtain certain desired information. Often a map has embedded in it the creator's intended viewpoints and/or purposes. For example, the map shown in Figure 1 has a viewpoint centered in Asia, and the purpose of the creator of the map is to emphasize that viewpoint.

Maps are often used as guides or indexes to convey information. A typical example is shown in Figure 2. It conveys not only the areas, but also the approximate quantities, of steel production.

A web page can also be regarded as a map, with the URLs as indexes to other web pages. In fact, any document can be regarded as a map in a multi-dimensional space. Moreover, with associated scripts, the maps can also be made active [1].

These two notions, that data can be viewed as maps and that maps can be made active, led us to propose a new paradigm for visual information retrieval -- the **sentient map**. In practice, the sentient map is a gesture-enhanced multimodal interface between the user and the multimedia information system.

The natural way to interact with a sentient map is by means of gestures. In this paper we will use the word "gesture" in the general sense. That is, gestures can range from the traditional mouse clicks and keyboard strokes, to hand gestures, facial expressions, the body language, and even collective gestures of a group of people. More specifically, simple gestures called **c-gestures** consisting of mouse clicks and keyboard strokes are used to interact with a sentient map.

R. Laurini (Ed.): VISUAL 2000, LNCS 1929, pp. 1-13, 2000.

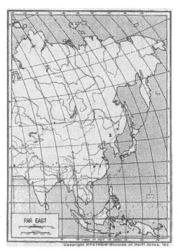

Fig. 1. Map of Asia.

This paper is organized as follows. To motivate the proposed approach, Section 2 describes the information access problem in e-learning. The sentient map and the three basic gestures are introduced in Section 3. Section 4 presents the underlying σ-query language, and Section 5 defines a simple gesture query language, the c-gesture language. A prototype sentient map system is described in Section 6. For empirical study, an e-learning environment called the Macro University serves as a test bed to evaluate this approach, and a preliminary user study is reported in Section 7. An extension of the c-gesture query language is described in Section 8.

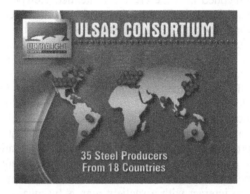

Fig. 2. A map showing world steel production.

2. Information Access in E-Learning

Nearly every academic institution these days has set up a web site and is in the process of starting, or has already started, a distance learning program on the Internet.

Coupled with a digital library, many an academic institution is experimenting with the virtual university. In some countries the local government has taken the initiative to form a consortium of universities offering online courses from each institution.

In spite of its promises, e-learning also presents many challenging pedagogical and technical problems. We will discuss the technical problem of information access to motivate the sentient map approach.

In a distributed e-learning environment, the user (student, instructor, educator, etc.) often is unaware of the existence and whereabouts of information items. Databases and data sources are constantly changing, making information access difficult.

It is therefore very confusing for a user to formulate queries, especially if the user has no idea whether such information items exist and where the information items might be located. Different databases and data sources may also require different ways to query them, and the user does not know what is the appropriate way to request information.

For a novice user, spatial/temporal queries are also not easy to formulate. The user needs a more natural way of interaction, so that seemingly complex queries can be broken down into simpler queries that are easy to express.

To overcome these difficulties in searching and accessing information, we propose the following approach:

(a) There should be a simple way to search for information, regardless of the information space to be queried. The *sentient map* described below provides a uniform presentation of real space/time, or virtual space/time. This uniform presentation in turn enables the user to use the *same gestures* in dealing with both real space/time and virtual space/time consistently.

(b) There should be a way to automatically transform such search requests into queries according to the structure of the information space. The transformation of a gesture query into a σ-query serves this purpose. An important characteristic of the σ-query is that depending on the structure of the information space, the transformation can be different.

(c) There should be a way to dynamically present the retrieved information to the user according to the user's current interest. Transcoding provides a way to accomplish this purpose. With a variety of transcoding schemes, the user can receive the appropriate amount of information at the proper level of details, depending upon the query and the user's interests.

In what follows we describe in detail the sentient map approach to deal with the information access problem. It should be mentioned however that the information access problem is present not only in e-learning, but also in numerous situations where information is distributed and constantly changing.

3. The Sentient Map

The *sentient map* is a map that can sense the user's input gestures and react by retrieving and presenting the appropriate information. We use the term "map" here in the general sense. Geographical maps, directory pages, list of 3D models, web pages, documents, still images, video clips, etc. are all considered maps, as they all may serve as indexes and lead the user to more information. In practice, a sentient map is a gesture-enhanced interface for an information system.

A sentient map *m* has a *type*, a *profile*, a *visual appearance*, and a set of *teleactivities*.

m=(type, profile, v, IC)

A sentient map's *type* can be geographical map, directory page, web page, document and so on.

A sentient map's *profile* consists of attributes specified by its creator for this map type.

A sentient map's *visual appearance* is defined by a visual sentence *v*, which is created according to a visual grammar or a multidimensional grammar.

The *teleactivities* of a sentient map is defined by a collection of *index cells IC*. Each index cell *ic* may have a visual appearance, forming a *teleaction object*. These teleaction objects are usually overlaid on some background.

Ignoring the type and profile, a sentient map is basically a collection of teleaction objects including a background object.

A *composite sentient map* is defined recursively as a composition of several sentient maps.

As said before, in practice the sentient map is a novel user interface that combines the features of the map, the browser, and the index. Furthermore, the sentient map is accessed and manipulated using gestures.

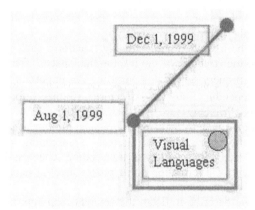

Fig. 3. The three basic gestures.

In our approach we begin with the three basic gestures shown in Figure 3: (a) a *finger gesture* to **point** at an object on the sentient map, (b) a *moving finger gesture* to indicate a **time-line**, and (c) a *moving finger gesture* to draw a boundary for a **space** on the map. Any gesture query is composed of these three basic gestures for *point*, *time-line* and *space*.

These basic gestures are sufficient to express spatial/temporal queries [3]. For the user's convenience, the basic gestures can be augmented by other auxiliary gestures to add more constraints to the query, for example, indicating yes or no by clicking on a yes/no menu (c-gesture), making a circle/cross (finger gesture) or nodding/shaking the head (head gesture).

The three basic gestures are also not just restricted to point, time and space. As to be discussed in Section 8, the time-line gesture and space gesture can be replaced by other dimensions for maps whose types are document, web page, etc. The three basic gestures can be represented by mouse clicks: a double-click to select an object, a click and a double-click at both end points to specify a time-line, and multiple clicks to specify an area. We will call gestures represented by mouse clicks and keystrokes **c-gestures** (see Section 5). Color can be used to highlight these basic c-gestures.

By combining the basic gestures with other auxiliary gestures the user can specify the spatial/temporal relationship between two objects on the sentient map.   For example, *finger gestures* can be used to add/change certain attributes of objects on the map.   *Head movement gestures* can be used to indicate yes (nodding head), no (shaking head), etc. *Motion-assisting speech gestures* can also be used to augment finger gestures, hand gestures and head gestures.

4. The σ-Query

We use the σ-query [3] as the intermediate representation in the transformation from gestures to queries. As described in previous sections, the user can utilize the three basic gestures to point at objects, draw time-lines, and indicate the boundary of search space. The combined gestures are then transformed into a σ-query.

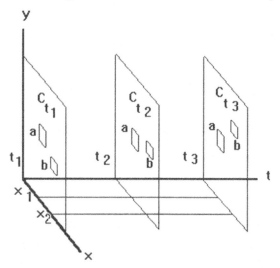

Fig. 4. Example of extracting three time slices (frames) from a video source.

An example of a σ-query is illustrated in Figure 4. The video source R consists of time slices of 2D frames. To extract three pre-determined time slices from the source R, the query in mathematical notation is: σ_t (t_1, t_2, t_3) R. The meaning of the σ–operator in the above query is to *select*, i.e. we want to select the three frames (time slices) along the time axis. The subscript t in σ_t indicates the selection of the time axis. In the SQL-like language ΣQL, a σ–query is expressed as:

> SELECT t
> CLUSTER t_1, t_2, t_3
> FROM R

In the above a new keyword "CLUSTER" is introduced, so that the parameters for the σ–operator, such as t_1, t_2, t_3, can be listed. The word "CLUSTER" indicates that objects belonging to the same cluster must share some common characteristics, such as having the same time parameter value. A cluster may have a sub-structure specified in another (recursive) query. Clustering is a natural concept when dealing with spatial/temporal objects. The result of a σ–query is a string that describes the relationships among the clusters.   This string is called a *cluster-string* [2].

The clause "CLUSTER *" means default clustering. For example, if the time axis is selected for a video source, the default clustering is to sample all time slices.

With the notation described above, it is quite easy to express a complex, recursive query in the ΣQL language. For example, to find the spatial relationship of two objects 'a' and 'b' from the three time slices of the video source R, as illustrated in Figure 8, the σ–query in mathematical notation is: σ_x $(x_1, x_2)($ σ_t $(t_1, t_2, t_3$ $)$ R). In the ΣQL language the query can be expressed as:

> SELECT x
> CLUSTER x_1, x_2
> FROM
> > SELECT t
> > CLUSTER t_1, t_2, t_3
> > FROM R

The query result is a cluster-string describing the spatial/temporal relationship between the objects 'a' and 'b'. How to express this spatial/temporal relationship depends upon the (spatial) data structure used.

5. The C-Gesture Query Language

The c-gesture query language uses mouse clicks to represent gestures. The basic syntax is defined below:

```
<point> ::= <double-click>
<time-line> ::= <single-click> <double-click>
    <begin-time-value> <end-time-value>
<space> ::= <single-click> <single-click><single-click>
    <double-click>
```

Example 1: The user double-clicks on a video icon to **point** at it as the source. The user then single-clicks followed by a double-click to specify a *time-line*, and enters the values for a time interval such as [10, 34]. The σ-query *Query 1* is:

> SELECT t
> CLUSTER [10,34]
> FROM video-source

The query result is the set of video frames in the time interval [10, 34] from the video source.

Example 2: The user double-clicks on the objects retrieved by *Query 1* to point at them as the source. The user then single-clicks twice followed by a double-click to specify a rectangular *space*. Since three points specify a triangle, the rectangle is defined as the triangle's minimum enclosing rectangle. For example, if the three points are (1,3), (6,2), (2,5), the rectangle is [(1,2), (6,5)]. The σ-query *Query 2* is:

> SELECT x, y
> CLUSTER [(1,2), (6,5)]
> FROM   *Query 1*

   The query result is the rectangles from the video frames in the time interval [10,34] from the video source.

Example 3: The user double-clicks on the objects retrieved by *Query 2* to point at them as the source. Using the extended c-gesture to be explained in Section 8, the user then single-clicks followed by a double-click followed by a click on an attribute name such as *type* in a pull-down menu to specify a *type-line*, and enters the value for a type such as `person'. The σ-query *Query 3* is:

> SELECT type
> CLUSTER `person'
> FROM *Query 2*

   The query result is the objects of type `person' in the rectangular areas from the video frames in the time interval [10,34] from the video source.
   Combining the three queries *Query 1*, *Query 2* and *Query 3*, the overall σ-query is:

> SELECT type
> CLUSTER `person'
> FROM
>   SELECT x, y
>   CLUSTER [(1,2), (6,5)]
>   FROM
>   SELECT t
>   CLUSTER [10,34]
>   FROM video-source

A data model is the user's conceptualization for organizing and understanding the information space. In the above examples, the data model is assumed to be: $t \rightarrow x,y \rightarrow$ **type**. A data model for databases, video-sources, web-base and so on is the representation of the logical structure of the information space. For the web-base, the data model is a virtual logical structure.

If a unique data model is specified for an information space, that data model dictates the query translation in the following sense: when a user enters a gesture query, the query is translated into a σ-query according to that unique data model. On the other hand, the information space may be ill structured so that there are several plausible data models, i.e., the information space can be organized and understood in several different ways. When the user enters a gesture query, the query is translated into different σ-queries, and the optimal σ-query is selected based upon some criteria.

6. A Prototype Sentient Map System

The basic design approach of the prototype sentient map system is illustrated in Figure 5.

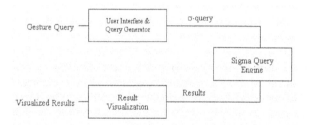

Fig. 5. Design approach of the sentient map system.

The User Interface & Query Generator translates a gesture query into a σ-query according to the data model. If there are multiple data models, there will be multiple translated queries and the optimal query is selected and sent to the Sigma Query Engine, which searches the data bases and data sources to retrieve the results. The Result Visualization module transforms the retrieved results into visual representations. For example, tabular data are transformed into graphs

The current prototype runs on any PC. In the virtual conference room -- developed by Dr. T. Chen at Carnegie Mellon University [6] -- several users represented by their *avatars* are engaged in a discussion, as shown in Figure 6. When they need information they may turn their attention to the sentient map on the wall, as illustrated by Figure 7. In the current demo the user can select one of the three major maps: World map, Earthquake map and Star map.

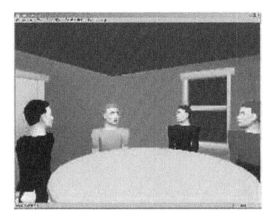

Fig. 6. A virtual conference room [6].

Suppose the Earthquake map is selected, as shown in Figure 8. Next, the user can click twice followed by a double-click to define an area such as Japan. Then, when the user clicks once followed by a double click, a message will be displayed: "use right button to choose time". The user can choose the time (date) from a pull-down menu. The first choice is the start time, next choice the end time.

Fig. 7. A virtual conference room with maps.

For example, if the user chooses the Earthquake map, then chooses Japan area, finally chooses time interval 1993-1995, the sentient map will display the earthquake frequency graph in Japan from 1993 to 1995, as illustrated in Figure 9. The translated query is as follows:

```
SELECT t
CLUSTER *
WHERE  t≥1993 AND t≤1995
FROM
      SELECT x, y
      CLUSTER  Japan
      FROM EarchQuakeMap
```

Fig. 8. The Earthquake map is selected.

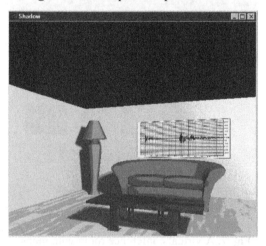

Fig. 9. The earthquake frequency graph is displayed.

The data model used in this scenario is: **type (map type) → area → time-line.** There are maptype, timetype, areatype, sublinks, mapfile in the structure, which leads to the translated query as shown above.

7. An Application to the Macro University

One application of the sentient map is the Macro University [5], a consortium of universities and research groups interested in e-learning. It disseminates enabling technologies for e-learning, develops tools and contents for adaptive e-learning such as the cross-lingual courseware and provides a test bed for e-learning projects. Currently the Macro University has fourteen members that cooperate in research, development and e-learning courseware design.

For this e-learning environment, we implemented two versions of the sentient map user interface: a *PC version* implemented in Visual C++ and a *Web version* implemented in JavaScript. As described in Section 6, the PC version of the sentient map implemented in Visual C++ is integrated into the NetICE environment for virtual teleconferencing. Students and instructors can use this environment as a virtual classroom. When the user's surrogate (the user's *avatar*) points at the sentient map on the wall, more information becomes available and is also visible to all the participants of the virtual teleconference.

The Web version of the sentient map implemented in JavaScript is independent of NetICE With a browser, a user can use c-gestures to query e-learning courses offered anywhere in the world by a member university of the Macro University Project. An example is illustrated in Figure 10, where the point c-gesture is used to select a query about instructor, subject or course title. A time line c-gesture or an area c-gesture, as shown in Figure 11, is used to formulate the query.

Fig. 10. A point c-gesture is used to select a query.

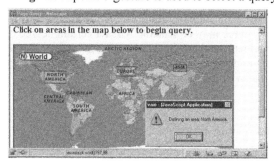

Fig. 11. An area c-gesture is used to formulate a query.

A preliminary user study was carried out. Questionnaires were provided for the initial evaluation by a small group of users. Their responses suggest that the sentient map paradigm is easy to understand and that the Web version of the sentient map user interface is also easy to use, but more expressive power in formulating c-gesture queries and better feedback in the form of SQL queries are recommended. The feedback feature was added to the sentient map. The two versions of the sentient map user interface were also integrated, so that the user can start in the virtual teleconference environment, and then go to the web to obtain more information from the e-learning universe.

8. Extended C-Gesture Query Language

We can expand the capability of the sentient map interface so that c-gesture queries are applicable to any document, any web page or any sensor. In order to do so, the c-gesture query language is extended. The extended syntax is defined below:

> **<attribute-line> ::= <attribute_name><single-click> <double-click>**
> **<attribute_value_1> <attribute_value_2>**
> **<attribute-space> ::= <attribute_name> <single-click>**
> **<single-click> <single-click> <double-click>**

In addition to the *time-line* and *space* c-gestures, we introduce *attribute-line* and *attribute-space* c-gestures by prefixing the c-gestures with *attribute-names* which can be represented, for instance, by an icon or by color coding. For each document, web page or sensor, a number of characteristic attributes are defined so that the user can use attribute-line and attribute-space c-gestures to formulate a gesture query. The customization of c-gestures can be done either before a session or dynamically during a session. The user can then formulate c-gesture queries in a real space, or a virtual space, or a hybrid space composed of real space and virtual space.

9. Discussion

To go beyond mouse clicks and key strokes as c-gestures, we need a system that understands more powerful human gestures. Real-time identification of finger gestures from a video source may be feasible when a certain degree of imprecision in determining spatial and temporal attribute values is acceptable. The use of contextual information in gesture understanding, and the inverse problem of interpreting context from gestures, should also be explored [4].

Acknowledgment

I would like to thank my three students – Lily Zhao, Kim Balley and Yekaterina Goldina -- who implemented both versions of the Sentient Map system.

References

[1] S. K. Chang, "Towards a Theory of Active Index", Journal of Visual Languages and Computing, Vol. 6, No. 1, March 1995, 101-118.

[2] S. K. Chang and E. Jungert, *Symbolic Projection for Image Information Retrieval and Spatial Reasoning*, Academic Press, 1996.

[3] S. K. Chang and E. Jungert, "A Spatial Query Language for Multiple Data Sources Based Upon Sigma-Operator Sequences", *International Journal of Cooperative Information Systems*, Vol. 7, No. 2&3, 1998, 167-186.

[4] A. Chever et al., "A Unified Framework for Constructing Multimodal Experiments and Applications", CMC'98, Tilburg, The Netherlands, 1998, 63-69.

[5] Macro University project's home page, www.cs.pitt.edu/~chang/cpdis/macro-u.html, 2000.

[6] NetICE project's home page, http://amp.ece.cmu.edu/proj_NetICE.htm, 1999.

An Image Data Model

William I. Grosky and Peter L. Stanchev

Department of Computer Science, Wayne State University
Detroit, MI 48202
{grosky, stanchev}@cs.wayne.edu

Abstract. In this paper, we analyze the existing approaches to image data modeling and we propose an image data model and a particular image representation in the proposed model. This model establishes a taxonomy based on a systematization over existing approaches. The image layouts in the model are described in semantic hierarchies. The representation is applicable to a wide variety of image collections. An example for applying the model to a plant picture is given.

1 Introduction

Images are becoming an essential part of the information systems and multimedia applications. The image data model is one of the main issues in the design and development of any image database management system. The data model should be extensible and have the expressive power to present the structure and contents of the image, their objects and the relationships among them. The design of an appropriate image data model will ensure smooth navigation among the images in an image database system. The complexity of the model arises because images are richer in information than text, and because images can be interpreted differently, according to the human perception of the application domain.

There are different models for representing the semantic richness of an image, but most of them are more or less dependent on the image application domain. In this paper, we analyze some existing tools and approaches to image data modeling and we propose a new image data model. It can be applied to a wide variety of image collections. The model employs multiple logical representations of an image. The logical image representation can be viewed as a multiple-level abstraction of the physical image view. The model is based on the analysis of different image application domains such as: medical images, house furnishing design plans [27], electronic schema catalogues, and geographical information systems [28]. The proposed model could be used as a frame for designing and building a wide range of image database systems and could be proposed as a standard to the MPEG committee. It can be treated as an extension of the general image database model [25, 26]. A particular representation based on this model is also discussed.

R. Laurini (Ed.): VISUAL 2000, LNCS 1929, pp. 14-25, 2000.

2 Image Data

Before we analyze the various existing approaches to image data modeling and the proposed tools, we introduce some of the basic methods using for description of the image and the image contents. The image data can be treated as a physical image representation and their meaning as a logical image representation. The logical representation includes the description of the image, image-objects characteristics, and the relationships among the image objects. In the following sections some of the main techniques for image representation are shown.

2.1   Physical Image Representation

The most common form of the physical image representation is the *raster form*. It includes the image header and image matrix. The *image header* describes the main image parameters such as image format, image resolution, number of bits per pixel, and compression information. The *image matrix* contains the image data.

2.2   Logical Image Representation

An *image object* is a meaningful portion (consisting of a union of one or more disjoint regions) of an image, which we have called a *semcon* [6]. The image description includes meta, semantic, color, texture, shape, and spatial attributes. In the proposed image representation we use the concept of *object-based point feature maps* [31]. In 2-D space, many of the image features can be represented as sets of points. These points can be tagged with labels to capture any necessary semantics. Each of the individual points representing some feature of an image object we call a *feature point*.

Meta attributes are attributes related to the process of the image creation. These attributes can be image acquisition date, image identification number and name, image modality device, image magnification, etc.

Semantic attributes contain subjective information about the analyzed image. A specialist in the field of the specific image collection gives the values of such attributes.

Color attributes could be represented as a histogram of intensity of the pixel colors. Based on a fixed partition of the image, an image could be indexed by the color of the whole image and a set of inter-hierarchical distances, which encode the spatial color information. The system Color-WISE is described in [24], and it partitions an image into 8*8 blocks with each block indexed by its dominant hue and saturation values. A histogram refinement technique is described in [23] by partitioning histogram bins based on the spatial coherence of pixels. A pixel is coherent if it is a part of some *sizable* similar-colored region, and incoherent otherwise. In [12] a statistical method is proposed to index an image by color correlograms, which is actually a table containing color pairs, where the k-th entry for $<i, j>$ specifies the probability of locating a pixel of color j at a distance k from a pixel of color i in the image.

A point placed at the center-of-mass of the given region and labeled with the descriptor **color histogram**, the histogram itself, as well as the region's identifier can represent a color histogram of that region. For the proposed representation, each image object is evenly divided into equal non-overlapping blocks, and the representation captures the spatial distribution of the dominant hue and saturation values for each block. This spatial distribution is captured by our previously devised **anglogram** data structure [32]. In more detail, the hue component of each pixel is quantized to 24 values, the saturation component of each pixel is quantized to 12 values, and the feature point anglogram is computed with a bin size of 10°. Therefore, an image index consists of 24 feature point histograms for the sampled hue constituents, and 12 feature point histograms for the sampled saturation constituents, each feature point histogram consisting of a sequence of 18 integers. We note that the size of our image indices depends only on the quantization of color components, and is independent of the image-partitioning scheme.

Texture attributes. According to Amadasun and King [2]: "Literally, texture refers to the arrangement of the basic constituents of a material. In the digital image, texture is depicted by the spatial interrelationships between, and/or spatial arrangement of the image pixels. Visually, these spatial interrelationships, or arrangement of image pixels, are seen as changes in the intensity patterns, or gray tones". The most used set of texture features is Haralick's gray level co-occurrence features [11]. This is based on the calculation of the co-occurrence matrix $P_{d,\alpha}(g, g')$, which counts the number of pixel pairs in an image that have values g and g' and are separated by a pixel distance d in a relative direction α. Using $\alpha = 0°$, 45°, 90°, and 135°, we get the so-called 4 neighbors of a pixel. Using the co-occurrence matrix, the following coefficients are calculated: angular second momentum, contrast, correlation, sum of squares, inverse difference moment, sum average, sum variance, sum entropy, entropy, difference variance, difference entropy, information measures of correlation, maximum correlation coefficient. Other often-used texture measurements are (1) Tamura features [29]. He suggested six basic textural features; namely, coarseness, contrast, directionality, line-likeness, regularity, and roughness; (2) Unser's sum and difference histogram [33]. He proposed 32 features based on calculations over different sums and histograms of the pixel gray levels; (3) Galloway's run-length based features [5]. He calculated 20 coefficients on the basic on run-length matrixes; (4) Chen's geometric features form binary image sequences [4]. He proposed 16 coefficients, based on threshold images; (5) Laine's texture energy from Daubechies wavelet [15]. He suggested 21 features, based on Daubechies wavelet transformed image; (6) Gabor's filter. Wagner [34] summarized 18 different methods including 318 different features and gave the exact formulas for every single such feature.

For the proposed representation, for each image object, the Tamura features [28] of coarseness, contrast, directionality, line-likeness, and regularity, are calculated as texture object characteristics. These values are normalized.

Shape attributes techniques can be represented in two distinct categories: **measurement-based methods** ranging from simple, primitive measures such as **area** and *circularity* [21] to the more sophisticated measures of various *moment invariants* [19]; and *transformation-based methods* ranging from functional transformations such as *Fourier descriptors* [18] to structural transformations such as *chain codes* [17] and *curvature scale space feature vectors* [20]. An attempt to compare the various shape representation schemes is made in [18]. Those features, which characterize the shape of any image object, can be classified into the following two categories.

- *Global shape features* are general in nature and depend on the characteristics of the entire image object. *Area, perimeter,* and *major axis* direction of the corresponding image region are examples of such features.
- *Local shape features* are based on the low-level characteristics of image objects. The determination of local features usually requires more involved computation. *Curvatures, boundary segments,* and *corner points* around the boundary of the corresponding image region are examples of such features.

For the proposed representation, an object shape is represented by the spatial distribution of its *corner points* [1], again using our *anglogram* data structure [30].

Spatial attributes could be presented in different ways: (1) as a *topological set of relations* between two image-objects, containing the relations *in, disjoint, touch,* and *cross;* (2) as a *vector set of relations* which considers the relevant positions of the image-objects. These include E, S, W, N, SE, SW, NW, NE in terms of the four world directions East, South, West, North; (3) as a *metric set of relations* based on the distance between the image-objects, containing the relations *close, far, very close, very far;* (4) 2D-strings [3]. Each image is considered as a matrix of symbols, where each symbol corresponds to an image object. The corresponding 2D-string is obtained by symbolic projection of these symbols along the horizontal and vertical axes, preserving the relative positions of the image objects. In order to improve the performance of this technique, some 2D-string variants have been proposed, such as the extended 2D-string [14], 2D C-string [16], and 2D C$^+$-string [13]; (5) geometry-based *θR-string* approach [8]; (6) the *spatial orientation graph* [7], (7) the *quadtree-based spatial arrangements of feature points* approach [1].

For the proposed anglogram representation, the global description of the feature maps is obtained by constructing a Delaunay triangulation [22] of all relevant feature points. This feature point histogram is obtained by discretizing the angles produced by this triangulation and counting the number of times each discrete angle occurs in the image object of interest, given the selection criteria of which angles will contribute to the final feature point histogram. For example, the feature point histogram can be built by counting the two largest angles, the two smallest angles, or all three angles of each individual Delaunay triangle. An O(*max(N, #bins)*) algorithm is necessary to compute the feature point histogram corresponding to the Delaunay triangulation of a set of N points. The shape and color description of the object-based point feature maps with the help of these techniques are described in [30, 31].

3 Image Data Models

An *Image Data Model* is a type of image data abstraction that is used to provide a conceptual image representation. It is a set of concepts that can be used to describe the structure of an image. The process of image description consists of extracting the global image characteristics, recognizing the image-objects and assigning a semantics to these objects. Approaches to image data modeling can be categorized based on the views of image data that the specific model supports.

Some valuable proposals for image data models are: VIMSYS image data model, model, where images are presented as four plane layers [10]; EMIR^2- an extended model for image representation and retrieval [18]; and AIR - an adaptive image retrieval model [9].

The *AIR (Adaptive Image Retrieval) model* claims that it is the first comprehensive and generic data model for a class of image application areas that coherently integrates logical image representations. It is a semantic data model that facilitates the modeling of an image and the image-objects in the image. It can be divided into three layers: physical level, logical level and semantic or external level representation. There are two kinds of transformations that occur in the model. The first is the transformation from the physical to the logical representation, such as a spatial oriented graph. The second transformation involves the derivation of the semantic attributes from the physical representation.

The *VIMSYS (Visual Information Management System) model* views the image information entities in four planes. This model is based on the image characteristics and the inter-relations between those characteristics in an object-oriented design. These planes are the *domain objects and relations* (DO), the *domain events and relations* (DE), the *image objects and relations* (IO) and the *image representations and relations* (IR). An object in this model has a set of attributes and methods associated with them. They are connected in a class attribute hierarchy. The attribute relationships are spatial, functional and semantic. The *IO plane* has three basic classes of objects: images, image features and feature organizations. These objects are related to one another through *set-of, generalization (is-a)*, and relations. Image feature is further classified into texture, color, intensity and *feature-of* geometric feature. The *DO plane* consists of a semantic levels specification of domain entities, built upon the two previous levels. The *DE plane* has been included in the model to accommodate the event definition over image sequences. The *IR plane* is clearly functional.

The *EMIR^2 (Extended Model for Image Representation and Retrieval) model* combines different interpretations of an image in building its description. Each interpretation is presented by a particular view. An image is treated as a multiple-view object and is described by one physical view and four logical views: structural, spatial, perceptive and symbolic. For the description of the view, a context-free grammar formalism is used. The *structural* view defines the set of image objects. The *spatial* view of an image object is concerned about the shape of the image objects (contour) and their spatial relations (far, near, overlap, etc.), which indicates their relative positions inside the image. The *perceptive* view includes all the visual attributes of the image and/or image objects. In this model, these attributes describe color, brightness and texture. The *symbolic* view associates a semantic description to an image and/or image object. In this model, two subsets of attributes are used: one associated with the image, e.g. size, date, author, etc., and the other associated with the image objects, e.g. identifier, name, etc.

4 The Image Model

The proposed model establishes a taxonomy based on a systematization of the existing approaches. The main requirement to the proposed model could be summarized as: (1) powerfulness - to be applicable to a wide variation of image collections; (2) efficiency - the obtained image description to be easy used for image retrieval in an image database.

The image is presented at two levels - logical and physical. The logical level contains the global description and content-based sublevels. The global description level consists of the meta and the semantic attributes of the image. The content-based layout contains the object features connected with color, texture, shape, and spatial object characteristics. The physical level contains the image header and the image matrix. A semantic schema of the proposed model is shown in Figure 1.

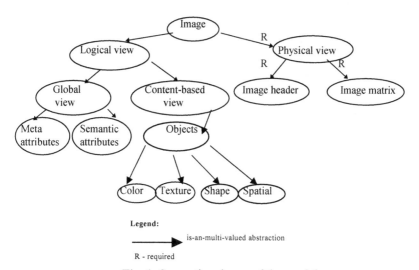

Fig. 1. Semantic schema of the model

In the proposed representation the contents based view is given with the help of the Delaunay triangulation. Our experiments confirm that this technique is very useful for color, shape and spatial distribution. Theoretically, from the definition of the Delaunay triangulation, it is easily shown that the angles of the resulting Delaunay triangles of a set of points remain the same under uniform translations, scalings, and rotations of the point set. An example is illustrated in Figure 2 as follows: Figure 2b shows the resulting Delaunay triangulation for a set of 26 points shown in Figure 2a for a airplane image; Figure 2(c) shows the resulting Delaunay triangulation of the transformed (translation, rotation, and scaled-up) set of 26 points in Figure 2a; Figure 2d shows the resulting Delaunay triangulation of the transformed (translation, rotation, and scaled-down) set of 26 points in Figure 2a.

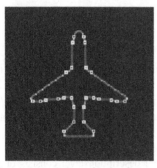

Figure 2a – A Set of 26 points

Figure 2a – Delauney Triangulation

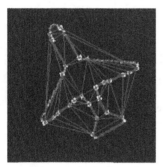

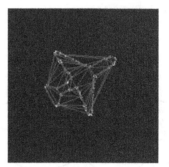

Figure 2c and Figure 2d – Other Delauney Triangulations

4.1 Image Retrieval

The images are searched by their image description representation, and it is based on similarity retrieval. Let a query be converted through the image data model in an image description $Q(q_1, q_2, ..., q_n)$ and an image in the image database has the description $I(x_1, x_2, ..., x_n)$. Then the retrieval value (RV) between Q and I is defined as: $RV_Q(I) = \Sigma_{i = 1, ..., n} (w_i * sim(q_i, x_i))$, where w_i ($i = 1,2, ..., n$) is the weight specifying the importance of the ith parameter in the image description and $sim(q_i, x_i)$ is the similarity between the ith parameter of the query image and database image and is calculated in different way according to the q_i, x_i values. They can be: *symbol, numerical* or *linguistic* values, *histograms, attribute relational graphs, pictures or spatial representations characters.*

5 Applying the Model Via an Example

Let's consider the used in the following plant picture 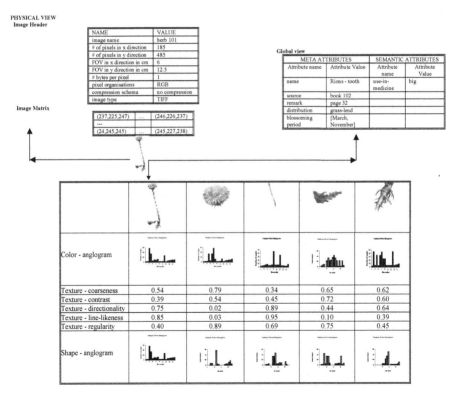 . After the segmentation procedure the image is partitioned in the following image-objects: blossom {   },

stalk {   }, leaf {   }, and root {   }. The model manipulation capabilities are realized in the Detroit Image Database Management System. A possible view as a result of applying the suggested representation to the example image is given in Figure 3. A possible definition of the proposed representation in the IDBMS Detroit is given in Figure 4.

PHYSICAL VIEW
Image Header

NAME	VALUE
image name	herb 101
# of pixels in x direction	185
# of pixels in y direction	485
FOV in x direction in cm	6
FOV in y direction in cm	12.5
# bytes per pixel	1
pixel organisations	RGB
compression schema	no compression
image type	TIFF

Global view

META ATTRIBUTES		SEMANTIC ATTRIBUTES	
Attribute name	Attribute Value	Attribute name	Attribute Value
name	Rions - tooth	use-in-medicine	big
source	book 102		
remark	page 32		
distribution	grass-lend		
blossoming period	[March, November]		

Image Matrix

(237,225,247)	...	(246,226,237)

(24,245,245)	...	(245,227,238)

Color - anglogram					
Texture - coarseness	0.54	0.79	0.34	0.65	0.62
Texture - contrast	0.39	0.54	0.45	0.72	0.60
Texture - directionality	0.75	0.02	0.89	0.44	0.64
Texture - line-likeness	0.85	0.03	0.95	0.10	0.39
Texture - regularity	0.40	0.89	0.69	0.75	0.45
Shape - anglogram					

Fig. 3. Image representation through the proposed model

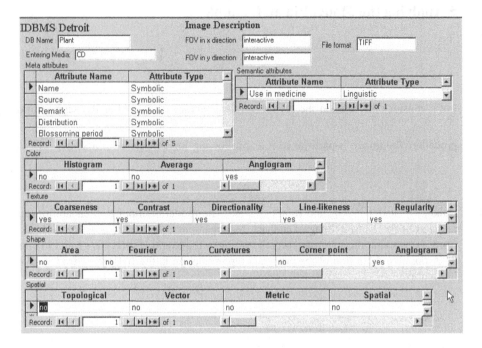

Fig. 4. The application domain definition in the IDBMS Detroit

6   Conclusions

The main advantages of the proposed model and particular image representation could be summarized as follows:

- Generality. The model uses the main techniques from the existing image data models and it is applicable to a wide variety of image collections;
- Practical applicability. The model can be used as a part of image retrieval and image database system;
- Flexibility. The model could be customized when used with a specific application;
- Robustness of the proposed representation. The chosen methods for image description allow similar descriptions again minor variation on the image.

The proposed image representation is very easy to be implemented and is very convenient for image retrieval in an image database system.

References

1. Ahmad, I., and Grosky, W., 'Spatial Similarity-based Retrievals and Image Indexing By Hierarchical Decomposition,' *Proceedings of the International Database Engineering and Application Symposium (IDEAS'97)*, Montreal, Canada, (August 1997), pp. 269-278.
2. Amadasun, M., and King, R., 'Textural Features Corresponding to Textural Properties,' *IEEE Transactions on Systems, Man, and Cybernetics,* 19 (1989), pp. 1264-1274.
3. Chang, S., Shi Q., and Yan, C., 'Iconic Indexing by 2-D Strings,' *IEEE Transactions on Pattern Analysis and Machine Intelligence*, Volume 9, Number 3 (May 1987), pp. 413-428.
4. Chen, Y., M. Nixon, and Thomas, D., 'Statistical Geometrical Features for Texture Classification,' *Pattern Recognition*, 28 (1995), pp. 537-552.
5. Galloway, M., 'Texture Analysis Using Gray Level Run Lengths,' *Computer Graphics and Image Processing*, 4 (1975), pp. 172-179.
6. Grosky, W., Fotouhi, F., and Jiang, Z., Using Metadata for the Intelligent Browsing of Structured Media Objects, *Managing Multimedia Data: Using Metadata to Integrate and Apply Digital Data,* Sheth A., and Klas W., (Eds.), McGraw Hill Publishing Company, New York, (1997), pp. 67-92.
7. Gudivada V. and Raghavan, V., 'Design and Evaluation of Algorithms for Image Retrievals By Spatial Similarity,' *ACM Transactions on Information Systems*, Volume 13, Number 1 (January 1995), pp. 115-144.
8. Gudivada, V., 'θR-String: A Geometry-Based Representation for Efficient and Effective Retrieval of Images By Spatial Similarity,' *IEEE Transactions on Knowledge and Data Engineering*, Vol. 10, No. 3, (May/June 1998), pp. 504-512.
9. Gudivada, V., Raghavan, V., and Vanapipat, K., 'A Unified Approach to Data Modeling and Retrieval for a Class of Image Database Applications,' *IEEE Transactions on Data and Knowledge Engineering,* (1994).
10. Gupta, A., Weymouth, T., and Jain, R., 'Semantic Queries with Pictures: The VIMSYS Model,' Proceedings of the 17th Conference on Very Large Databases, Palo Alto, California (1991), pp. 69-79.
11. Haralick, R., Shanmugam K., and I. Dinstein, H., 'Texture Features for Image Classification,' *IEEE Transactions on Systems, Man, and Cybernetics,* SMC-3 (1973).
12. Huang J., Kumar, S., Mitra, M., Zhu, W., and Zabih, R., 'Image Indexing Using Color Correlograms,' *Proceedings of the IEEE Conference on Computer Vision and Pattern Recognition,* San Juan, Puerto Rico, (June 1997), pp. 762-768.
13. Huang, P. and Jean, Y., 'Using 2D C[+]-Strings as Spatial Knowledge Representation for Image Database Systems,' *Pattern Recognition*, Volume 27, Number 9 (September 1994), pp. 1249-1257.
14. Jungert E. and Chang, S., 'An Algebra for Symbolic Image Manipulation and Transformation,' *Proceedings of the IFIP TC 2/WG 2.6 Working Conference on*

Visual Database Systems, Elsevier Science Publishing Company, Amsterdam, The Netherlands (1989), pp. 301-317.

15. Laine A. and Fan, J., 'Texture Classification by Wavelet Packet Signatures,' *IEEE Transactions on Pattern Recognition and Machine Intelligence*, 15 (1993).

16. Lee, S. and Hsu, F., '2D C-String: A New Spatial Knowledge Representation for Image Database System,' *Pattern Recognition*, Volume 23, Number 10 (October 1990), pp. 1077-1087.

17. Lu, G., 'An Approach to Image Retrieval Based on Shape,' *Journal of Information Science*, Volume 23, Number 2 (1997), pp. 119-127.

18. Mechkour, M., 'EMIR^2. An Extended Model for Image Representation and Retrieval,' in Revell, N. and Tjoa, A. (Eds.), *Database and Expert Systems Applications,* Berlin, (Springer -Verlag, 1995), pp. 395-414.

19. Mehtre, B., Kankanhalli, M., and Lee, W., 'Shape Measures for Content Based Image Retrieval: A Comparison,' *Information Processing & Management,* Volume 33, Number 3 (June 1997), pp. 319-337.

20. Mokhtarian, F., Abbasi, S., and Kitter, J., 'Efficient and Robust Retrieval by Shape Content through Curvature Scale Space,' *Proceedings of the International Workshop on Image Database and Multimedia Search*, Amsterdam, The Netherlands, (August 1996), pp. 35-42.

21. Niblack, W., Barder, R., Equitz, W., Flickner, M., Glasman, E., Petkovic, D., Yanker, P., Faloutsos, C., and Yaubin, G., 'The QBIC Project: Querying Images by Content Using Color, Texture, and Shape,' *Proceedings of SPIE Storage and Retrieval for Image and Video Databases*, Volume 1908, (January 1993), pp. 173-181.

22. O'Rourke, J., *Computational Geometry in C,* Cambridge University Press, Cambridge, England, 1994.

23. Pass, G. and Zabih, R., 'Histogram Refinement for Content-Based Image Retrieval,' *IEEE Workshop on Applications of Computer Vision*, (1996), pp. 96-102.

24. Sethi, I., Coman, I., Day, B., Jiang, F., Li, D., Segovia-Juarez, J., Wei, G., and You, B., 'Color-WISE: A System for Image Similarity Retrieval Using Color,' *Proceedings of SPIE Storage and Retrieval for Image and Video Databases*, Volume 3312, (February 1998), pp. 140-149.

25. Stanchev, P., 'General Image Database Model,' *Visual Information and Information Systems, Proceedings of the Third Conference on Visual Information Systems,* Huijsmans, D. Smeulders A., (Eds.) Lecture Notes in Computer Science, Volume 1614 (1999), pp. 29-36.

26. Stanchev, P., 'General Image Retrieval Model,' *Proceedings of the 27th Spring Conference of the Union of the Bulgarian Mathematicians,* Pleven, Bulgaria, 1998, pp. 63-71.

27. Stanchev, P., and Rabitti, F., GRIM_DBMS: a GRaphical IMage DataBase Management System,' in T. Kunii (Ed.), Visual Database Systems, (North-Holland, 1989), pp. 415-430.

28. Stanchev, P., Smeulders, A., and Groen, F., 'An Approach to Image Indexing of Document,' in E. Knuth and L. Wegner (Eds.), Visual Database Systems II, (North Holland, 1992), pp. 63-77.

29. Tamura, H., Mori, S., and Yamawaki,, T., 'Textural Features Corresponding to Visual Perception,' *IEEE Transaction on Systems, Man, and Cybernetics,* SMC-8 (1978), pp. 460-472.
30. Tao Y. and Grosky, W., 'Image Indexing and Retrieval Using Object-Based Point Feature Maps,' Journal of Visual Languages and Computing, To Appear
31. Tao Y. and Grosky, W., 'Shape Anglograms for Image Object Representation: A Computational Geometry. Submit.
32. Tao Y. and Grosky, W., 'Spatial Color Indexing using Rotation, Translation, and Scale Invariant Anglograms,' *Multimedia Tools and Applications,* To Appear.
33. Unser, M., 'Sum and Difference Histograms for Texture Classification,' *IEEE Transactions on Pattern Analysis and Machine Intelligence*, PAMI-8 (1986), pp. 118-125.
34. Wagner T., 'Texture Analysis,' in Jahne, B., Haussecker, H., and Geisser P., (Eds.), *Handbook of Computer Vision and Application*, Academic Press, San Diego, (1999), pp. 275-308.

Interaction in Content-Based Image Retrieval: An Evaluation of the State-of-the-Art

Marcel Worring[1]*, Arnold Smeulders[1], and Simone Santini[2]

[1] Intelligent Sensory Information Systems
University of Amsterdam, The Netherlands
{worring,smeulders}@wins.uva.nl
http://carol.wins.uva.nl/~worring
[2] University of California San Diego

Abstract. The paper presents a panoramic view of the work carried out in the last few years in the area of interactive content-based image retrieval. We define a unifying framework based on *query space* in which exisiting methods are described. The framework allows to evaluate methods in their proper context. An important part of the framework is a classification of different query types which helps in bridging the gap between desired functionality and efficient support in an actual system. Having put methods in a common framework gives way to indentify promising research directions that have not yet been sufficiently explored.

1 Introduction

At the current stage of content-based image retrieval research, it is interesting to look back towards the beginning and see which of the original ideas have blossomed, which haven't, and which were made obsolete by the changing landscape of computing. In February 1992, the NSF organized a workshop in Redwood, CA, to "identify major research areas that should be addressed by researchers for visual information management systems that would be useful in scientific, industrial, medical, environmental, educational, entertainment, and other applications" [10]. In hindsight, the workshop did an excellent job in identifying unsolved problems that researchers should have undertaken. In particular, the workshop correctly stated that "Visual Information Management Systems should not be considered as an application of the existing state of the art [in computer vision and databases] to manage and process images," and that "computer vision researchers should identify features required for *interactive image understanding,* rather than their discipline's current emphasis on automatic techniques".

In this paper we review the role of interaction in state-of-the-art content based image retrieval. It forms an integral part of the review covering content based image retrieval in [24].

---

* This work was supported in part by the ICES Multimedia Information Analysis Project (MIA)

R. Laurini (Ed.): VISUAL 2000, LNCS 1929, pp. 26–36, 2000.
Springer-Verlag Berlin Heidelberg 2000

Interaction of users with a data set has been studied most thoroughly in categorical information retrieval [14]. These techniques need rethinking when used for image retrieval. Most prominent problem is the *semantic gap* between the pictorial properties a system can derive automatically from the image on the one hand and the lingual interpretation of the image the user has in mind. Due to the semantic gap, the meaning of an image can only be defined in context. As a consequence, image retrieval requires active participation of the user to a much higher degree than categorized querying [20]. In content-based image retrieval, interaction is a complex interplay between the user, the images, their features, and their semantic interpretation. In this paper we explore the relations and provide a framework which unifies existing methods. The order of the sections follows the time line corresponding to a user interacting with the system.

2   Query space: definition and initialization

As the baseline of the review of methods, we define a new framework for interactive content based retrieval based on *query space*.

Consider a user who is going to interact with some selection of images $\mathcal{I}_Q$, from a large image archive $\mathcal{I}$. An abundance of features $\mathcal{F}$ could be derived from the images in $\mathcal{I}_Q$. A goal-dependent set $\mathcal{F}_Q \subset \mathcal{F}$ should be selected. In practice, the user is not always capable of selecting the features fit to reach the goal. For example, how should a general user decide between shape description using moments or Fourier coefficients? The user should, however, be able to indicate the feature class like shape or texture, relevant for the task. In addition to the feature class, [6] has the user indicate the required invariance. For example, the user can specify to be interested in color, that images might have varying viewpoint, but the illumination is white in all cases. The appropriate features can then automatically be selected by the system.

The user should also select a similarity function for comparison of images. As in realistic datasets the number of image pairs is too large to store explicitly all similarities, the proper choice for similarity is a goal dependent function $\mathcal{S}_Q$ expressed in the features. To adapt to different datasets and goals, $\mathcal{S}_Q$ should be a parameterized function. In most cases $\mathcal{S}_Q$ is Euclidean distance in $\mathcal{F}_Q$ parameterized by the vector weighting the different features [5, 8].

In systems that have a knowledge module, a set of labels $\mathcal{Z}$ can be employed to capture semantics. Then, in the initialization of query space, a set of goal and domain dependent semantic labels $\mathcal{Z}_Q \subset \mathcal{Z}$ can be selected.

Given the above, we define:

Definition 1. *The query space Q is the goal dependent 4-tuple* $\{\mathcal{I}_Q, \mathcal{F}_Q, \mathcal{S}_Q, \mathcal{Z}_Q\}$

The query space is an abstract model only. To define an instantiation $Q = \{I_Q, F_Q, S_Q, Z_Q\}$, the user should start by selecting the subset I_Q of images from the archive on which to work. Typically, the choice is based on factual descriptions like the name of the archive, the owner, date of creation, or website address. Any standard retrieval technique can be used for the selection. When no knowledge about preceding or anticipated use of the system is available, the initial query space Q^0 should not be biased towards specific images, or make some image pairs a priori more similar than others. Therefore, most methods normalize the features of F_Q based on the distribution of the feature values over I_Q e.g. [5,18]. To make S_Q unbiased over F_Q, the parameters should be tuned, arriving at a *natural distance measure*. Such a measure can be obtained by normalization of the similarity between individual features to a fixed range [28,18].

Let $z \in \mathcal{Z}_Q$ be a semantic label that could be attached to any image. When the user is annotating the imageset by hand the system can assign the user supplied meaning to the image. Having the user annotate all images explicitly with semantic labels is cumbersome and in practice incomplete. Hence, the need for interactive annotation. However, due to the semantic gap, labels cannot be assigned automatically with full certainty. The instantiation Z_Q of $\mathcal{Z}_Q$ therefore stores for each $i \in I_Q$ the probability $P_i(z)$. Clearly for user annotation we can set $P_i(z) = 1$.

The query space forms the basis for specifying queries, display of query results, and for interaction. An overview of the framework is presented in figure 1.

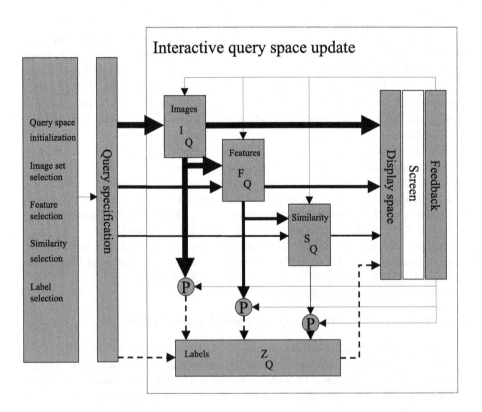

Fig. 1. *The framework for interactive content based image retrieval.*

3   Query specification

For specifying a query in Q, many different interaction methodologies have been proposed. They fall in one of two major categories:

- *exact queries*: a request for all images in I_Q satisfying a set of criteria
- *approximate queries*: a request for a ranking of the images in I_Q with respect to the query, based on S_Q.

Within each of the two categories, three subclasses can be defined depending on whether the queries relate to the

- *spatial content of the image*
- *the global image information*
- *groups of images*

The queries based on spatial content require segmentation of the image. In the following we need to make a distinction between:

- *strong segmentation*: a division of the image data such that the result contains the pixels of the silhouette of an object in the real world.
- *weak segmentation*: a grouping of the image data in regions internally homogenous according to some criterion.
- *sign location*: localization of a fixed shaped object.
- *partioning*: a division of the data array regardless of content of the data.

For exact queries, the three subclasses are based on different predicates the result should satisfy:

- *Exact query by spatial predicate* is based on the absolute or relative location of silhouettes, homogeneous regions, or signs.

Query on silhouette location is applicable in narrow domains only. Typically, the user queries using an interpretation $z \in \mathcal{Z}_Q$. To answer the query, the system then selects an appropriate algorithm for segmenting the image and extracting the domain-dependent features. In [7, 22] the user interactively indicates semantically salient regions to provide a starting point and sufficient context to derive z. Implicit spatial relations between regions sketched by the user in [26] yield a pictorial predicate. Other systems let the user explicitly define the predicate on relations between homogeneous regions [1]. In both cases, to be added to the query result, the homogenous regions as extracted from the image must comply with the predicate. In [19], users pose spatial-predicate queries on geographical signs located in maps in an extended version of SQL. The query can contain absolute or relative positions of signs and distances between signs.

- *Exact query by image predicate* is a specification of predicates on global image descriptions, often in the form of range predicates.

Due to the semantic gap, range predicates on features are seldomly used in a direct way. In [17], ranges on color values are pre-defined in predicates like "MostlyBlue" and "SomeYellow". Learning from user annotations of a partitioning of the image allows for feature range queries like: "amount of sky>50% and amount of sand>30%"[16].

- *Exact query by group predicate* is a query using an element $z \in \mathcal{Z}_Q$ where $\mathcal{Z}_Q$ is a set of categories that partitions $\mathcal{I}_Q$.

Both in [25] and [27] the user queries on a hierarchical taxonomy of categories. The difference is that the categories are based on contextual information in [25] while they are interpretations of the content in [27].

In the following types of query specifications the user specifies a single feature vector or one particular spatial configuration in $\mathcal{F}_Q$. As a consequence they are all approximate queries as no image will satisfy the query exactly.

- *Approximate query by spatial example* results in an image or spatial structure corresponding to literal image values and their spatial relationships.

Pictorial specification of a spatial example requires a feature space such that feature values can be selected or sketched by the user. Color pickers, or selections from shapes and texture examples [5, 8] have been used with limited success, as users find it difficult to specify their needs in low-level features. Kato [12] was the first to let users create a sketch of global image composition which was matched to the edges of the images in $\mathcal{I}_Q$. Sketched object outlines in [13] are first normalized to remove irrelevant detail from the query object, before matching it to objects segmented from the image. When specification is by parameterized template [4, 21] each image in $\mathcal{I}_Q$ has to be processed to find the best match with edges of the images. The segmentation result is improved if the user may elaborate the template with specification of salient details like color corners and specific textures. Pre-identification of all salient details in images in $\mathcal{I}_Q$ can then be employed to speed up the search process [23]. When weak segmentation of the query image and all images in $\mathcal{I}_Q$ is performed, the user can specify the query by indicating example regions [1, 26].

- *Approximate query by image example* feeds the system a complete array of pixels and queries for images most similar to the example.

Most of the current systems have relied upon this form of querying [5, 8]. The general approach is to use a S_Q based on global image features. Query by example queries are in [28] subclassified into *query by external image example,* if the query image is an image which is not in the database, versus *query by internal image example.* The difference in external and internal example is minor for the user, but affects the computational support as for internal examples all relations between images can be pre-computed. Query by image example is suited for applications where the target is an image of the same object or set of objects under different viewing conditions [6]. In other cases, the use of one image cannot provide sufficient context for the query to select one of its many interpretations [20].

- *Approximate query by group example* is specification through a selection of images which ensemble defines the goal.

The rationale is to put the image in its proper semantic context to make one of the possible interpretations $z \in \mathcal{Z}_Q$ preponderant. One option is that the user selects $m > 1$ images from a palette of images presented to find images best matching the common characteristics of the m images [3]. Such a query set is capable of more precisely defining the target and the admissable feature value variations therein. At the same time, a large query set nullifies the irrelevant variance in the query. This can be specified further by negative examples [2, 15]. If for each group in the database a small set of representative images can be found it can be stored in a visual dictionary from which the user can create its query [20].

Of course, the above queries can always be combined into more complex queries. For example, both [1, 26] compare the similarity of regions using features and in addition they encode spatial relations between the regions in predicates. Even with such complex queries, a single query is rarely sufficient to reach the goal. For most image queries, the user must engage in an active interaction with the system on the basis of the query results as displayed.

4   Query space display

There are several ways to display the query result to the user. In addition, *system feedback* can be given to help the user in understanding the result. We define

Definition 2. *The display space D is a space with perceived dimension d for visualization of query results.*

Note that d is the intrinsic dimensionality of the query result or d is induced by the projection function if the query result is of too high a dimension to visualize directly. In both cases d is not necessarily equal to the 2 dimensions of the screen.

When the query is exact, the result of the query is a set of images fulfilling the predicate. As an image either fulfills the predicate or not, there is no intrinsic order in the query result and $d = 0$ is sufficient.

For approximate queries, the images in I_Q are given a similarity ranking based on S_Q with respect to the query. In spite of the 2D rectangular grid for presenting images that many systems [5, 25] use, we should have $d = 1$. If the user refines its query using query by example, the images displayed do not have to be the images closest to the query. In [28], images are selected that together provide a representative overview of the whole active database. An alternative display model displays the image set minimizing the expected number of total iterations [3].

When images are described by feature vectors, every image has an associated position in feature space F_Q. The space spanned by the features is high dimensional. Both in [20, 9] F_Q is projected onto a display space with $d = 3$. Images are placed in such a way that distances between images in $\mathcal{D}$ reflect S_Q. To improve the user's comprehension of the information space, [9] provides the user with a dynamic view on F_Q through continuous variation of the 3D viewpoint. The display in [11] combines exact and approximate query results. First, the images in I_Q are organized in 2D layers according to labels in Z_I. Then, in each layer, images are positioned based on S_Q.

As system feedback in exact queries backprojection can be used, indicating which parts of the image fulfill the criteria. For example, in [16] each tile in the partition of the image shows the semantic label like sky, building, or grass the tile received. For approximate queries, in addition to mere rank ordering, in [1] system feedback is given by highlighting the subparts of the images that contributed most to the ranking result.

5   Interacting with query space

In early systems, the above process of query specification and display of query result would be iterated, where in each step the user would revise its query. This often is still appropriate for *exact queries*. For *approximate queries*, however, the interactive session as a whole should be considered. In the course of the session the system updates the query space, attempting to learn from the feedback the user gives on the relevance of the query result presented the search goal the user has. The query specification is used only for initializing the display.

Definition 3. *An interactive query session is a sequence of query spaces* $\{Q^0, Q^1, ..., Q^{n-1}, Q^n\}$ *such that* Q^n *bounds as close as possible what the user was searching for.*

The characteristics of Q^n depend on the goal of the user. Here we should make a distinction between the following three goals:

- *target search*: a search for one specific image
- *category search*: a search for images from a specific class.
- *associative search*: a search with no other goal than interesting findings.

For each of these classes, various ways of user feedback have been used. All are balancing between obtaining as much information from the user as possible and keeping the burden on the user minimal. The simplest form is to indicate which images are relevant [3], assuming "don't care" values for the others. In [2, 15] the user in addition indicates non-relevant images. The system in [18] considers five levels of significance, which gives more information to the system, but makes the process more difficult for the user. When dim ≥ 2, the user can manipulate the projected distances between images, putting away non-relevant images and bringing relevant images closer to each other [20]. The user can also explicitly bring in semantic information by annotating individual images, groups of images [20], or regions inside images [16] with a semantic label.

The interaction of the user with the display thus yields a relevance feedback A_i in every iteration i of the session. Combining this with definition 1 and 3 we have

$$\{I_Q^i, F_Q^i, S_Q^i, Z_Q^i\} \xrightarrow{A_i} \{I_Q^{i+1}, F_Q^{i+1}, S_Q^{i+1}, Z_Q^{i+1}\} \qquad (1)$$

Different ways of updating Q are possible as described now.

In [28] the images displayed correspond to a partitioning of I_Q. By selecting an image, one of the sets in the partition is selected and the set I_Q is reduced. Thus the user zooms in on *a target or category*. The method follows the pattern:

$$I_Q^i \xrightarrow{A_i} I_Q^{i+1} \qquad (2)$$

In current systems, the feature vectors in F_Q, corresponding to images in I_Q are fixed. When features are parameterized, however, feedback from the user could lead to optimization of the parameters. To our knowledge this has not been explored in image retrieval. It would correspond to the pattern:

$$F_Q^i \xrightarrow{A_i} F_Q^{i+1} \qquad (3)$$

For *associative search* users typically need to interact to learn the system the right associations. Hence, the system should update the similarity function:

$$S_Q^i \xrightarrow{A_i} S_Q^{i+1} \qquad (4)$$

In [2, 18] S_Q is parameterized by a weight vector on the distances between individual features. The weights in [2] are updated by comparing the variance of a feature in the set of positive examples, to the variance in the union of positive and negative examples. If the variance for the positive examples is significantly smaller, it is likely that the feature is important to the user. The system in [18] first updates the weight of different feature classes. The ranking of images according to the overall similarity function is compared to the rankings corresponding to each individual feature class. Both positive and negative examples are used to compute the final weight. The weights for the different features in the feature class, are taken as the inverse of the variance of the feature over positive examples.

The feedback A_i in [20] leads to new user desired distances between some of the pairs of images in I_Q. The parameters of the continuous similarity function should be updated to match in optimal way the new distances. The optimization problem is ill-posed usually. A regularization term is introduced which limits the departure from the natural distance function.

The system in [16] pre-computes a hierarchical grouping of images[1] based on the similarity for each individual feature. The feedback from the user is employed

---

[1] In fact, [16] is based on a partitioning rather than on images. It does, however, equally apply to whole images.

to create compound groupings corresponding to a user given $z \in \mathcal{Z}_Q$. The compound groupings are such that they include all of the positive and none of the negative examples. Images that were not yet annotated falling in the compound group receive the label z. The update of probabilities P is based on different partionings of I_Q, formalized as:

$$P^i(Z_Q|I_Q) \xrightarrow{A_i} P^{i+1}(Z_Q|I_Q) \tag{5}$$

For category and target search a system can also refine the likelihood of particular interpretations. Either updating the label based on the features of images, or on the similarity between images. The former has the generic form:

$$P^i(Z_Q|F_Q) \xrightarrow{A_i} P^{i+1}(Z_Q|F_Q) \tag{6}$$

The method in [15] falls in this class and considers *category search*. The single label in $\mathcal{Z}_Q$ is {relevant} with respect to the user query. In the limit case, where only one relevant image remains, it boils down to *target search*. All images indicated by the user as relevant or non-relevant in the current or previous iterations are collected. A Parzen estimator is incrementally constructed to find an optimal separation of the two classes.

The similarity based generic pattern is given by:

$$P^i(Z_Q|S_Q) \xrightarrow{A_i} P^{i+1}(Z_Q|S_Q) \tag{7}$$

This is the form used in [3] for target search with $\mathcal{Z}_Q = \{\text{target}\}$. In the reference an elaborate Bayesian framework is derived to compute the likelihood of any image in the database to be the target, given the history of actions A_i. In each iteration, the user selects an image from the set of images displayed. The crucial step then is the update of the probability for each image in I_Q of being the target, given that among the images displayed, the user decided to make this explicit selection. In the reference, a sigmoidal shaped update function is used, expressed in the similarity between the selected image and the remaining images on display.

6   Conclusion

Although in 1992 interactive image understanding was put forward as one of the spearpoints in content-based image retrieval, it is only recently that interaction and feedback have moved into the focus of attention. Putting the user in control has always been a leading principle in information retrieval research. It is expected that more and more techniques from traditional information retrieval will be employed, or worse reinvented, in content-based image retrieval.

User interaction in image retrieval has, however, quite different characteristics from text retrieval. Those deviating characteristics should be identified and catered for. In addition to the standard query types, six essentially different image based types have been identified in this paper. Each require their own user interface tools and interaction patterns. Due to the semantic gap, visualization of the query space in image retrieval is of great importance for the user to navigate the complex query space. While currently 2- or 3-dimensional display spaces are mostly employed in query by association, target search and category search are likely to follow. In all cases, an influx of computer graphics and virtual reality is foreseen in the near future.

As there is no interactivity if the response time is frequently over a second. The interacting user poses high demands on the computational support. Indexing a data set for interactive use is a major challenge as the system cannot anticipate completely on the user's actions. Still in the course of the interaction the whole query space i.e. the active image set, the features, the similarity, and the interpretations can all change dynamically.

References

1. C. Carson, S. Belongie, H. Greenspan, and J. Malik. Region-based image querying. In *Proceedings of the IEEE International Workshop on Content-Based Access of Image and Video Databases*, 1997.
2. G. Ciocca and R. Schettini. Using a relevance feedback mechanism to improve content-based image retrieval. In *Proceedings of Visual Information and Information Systems*, pages 107–114, 1999.
3. I. J. Cox, M. L. Miller, T. P. Minka, and T. V. Papathomas. The bayesian image retrieval system, PicHunter: theory, implementation, and pychophysical experiments. *IEEE Transactions on Image Processing*, 9(1):20 – 37, 2000.
4. A. del Bimbo and P. Pala. Visual image retrieval by elastic matching of user sketches. *IEEE Transactions on PAMI*, 19(2):121–132, 1997.
5. M. Flickner, H. Sawhney, W. Niblack, J. Ashley, Q. Huang, B. Dom, M. Gorkani, J. Hafner, D. Lee, D. Petkovic, D. Steele, and P. Yanker. Query by image and video content: the QBIC system. *IEEE Computer*, 1995.
6. T. Gevers and A. W. M. Smeulders. Pictoseek: combining color and shape invariant features for image retrieval. *IEEE Transactions on Image Processing*, 9(1):102 – 119, 2000.
7. S. Ghebreab, M. Worring, H.D. Tagare, and C.C. Jaffe. SCHEMed : a visual database tool for definition and entry of medical image data. In R. Jain and S. Santini, editors, *Proceedings of Visual Information Systems*, pages 189–196. Knowledge Systems Institute, 1997.
8. A. Gupta and R. Jain. Visual information retrieval. *Communications of the ACM*, 40(5):71–79, 1997.
9. A. Hiroike, Y. Musha, A. Sugimoto, and Y. Mori. Visualization of information spaces to retrieve and browse image data. In D.P. Huijsmans and A.W.M. Smeulders, editors, *Proceedings of Visual 99, International Conference on Visual Information Systems*, volume 1614 of *Lecture Notes in Computer Science*, pages 155–162, 1999.
10. R. Jain, editor. *NSF Workshop on Visual Information Management Systems*, Redwood, CA, 1992.
11. T. Kakimoto and Y. Kambayashi. Browsing functions in three-dimensional space for digital libraries. *International Journal of Digital Libraries*, 2:68–78, 1999.
12. T. Kato, T. Kurita, N. Otsu, and K. Hirata. A sketch retrieval method for full color image database - query by visual example. In *Proceedings of the ICPR, Computer Vision and Applications, The Hague*, pages 530–533, 1992.

13. L.J. Latecki and R. Lakämper. Contour-based shape similarity. In D.P. Huijsmans and A.W.M. Smeulders, editors, *Proceedings of Visual Information and Information Systems*, number 1614 in Lecture Notes in Computer Science, pages 617–624, 1999.

14. M. Lee M. L. Pao. *Concepts of Information Retrieval*. Libraries Unlimited, Englewood, Colo, 1989.

15. C. Meilhac and C. Nastar. Relevance feedback and category search in image databases. In *IEEE International Conference on Multimedia Computing and Systems*, pages 512–517, 1999.

16. T. P. Minka and R. W. Picard. Interactive lerning with a "society of models.". *Pattern Recognition*, 30(4):565–582, 1997.

17. V. E. Ogle. CHABOT - retrieval from a relational database of images. *IEEE Computer*, 28(9):40 – 48, 1995.

18. Y. Rui, T.S. Huang, M. Ortega, and S. Mehrotra. Relevance feedback: a power tool for interactive content-based image retrieval. *IEEE Transactions on circuits and video technology*, 1998.

19. H. Samet and A. Soffer. MARCO: MAp Retrieval by COntent. *IEEE Transactions on PAMI*, 18(8):783–798, 1996.

20. S. Santini, A. Gupta, and R. Jain. Emergent semantics through interaction in image databases. *IEEE Transactions on Knowledge and Data Engineering*, (in press).

21. S. Sclaroff. Deformable prototypes for encoding shape categories in image databases. *Pattern Recognition*, 30(4):627 – 641, 1997.

22. C-R. Shyu, C.E. Brodley, A.C. Kak, and A. Kosaka. ASSERT: a physician in the loop content-based retrieval system for HCRT image databases. *Image Understanding*, 75(1/2):111–132, 1999.

23. A.W.M. Smeulders, S.D. Olabariagga, R. van den Boomgaard, and M. Worring. Interactive segmentation. In R. Jain and S. Santini, editors, *Proceedings of Visual Information Systems*, pages 5–12. Knowledge Systems Institute, 1997.

24. A.W.M. Smeulders, M. Worring, S. Santini, A. Gupta, and R. Jain. Content based retrieval at the end of the early years. Submitted to Pattern Analysis and Machine Intelligence.

25. J. Smith and S-F. Chang. Visually searching the WEB for content. *IEEE Multimedia*, 4(3):12–20, 1997.

26. J. R. Smith and S-F. Chang. Integrated spatial and feature image query. *Multimedia systems*, 7(2):129 – 140, 1999.

27. A. Vailaya, M. Figueiredo, A. Jain, and H. Zhang. Content-based hierarchical classification of vacation images. In *IEEE International Conference on Multimedia Computing and Systems*, 1999.

28. J. Vendrig, M. Worring, and A.W.M. Smeulders. Filter image browsing: exploiting interaction in retrieval. In D.P. Huijsmans and A.W.M. Smeulders, editors, *Proceedings of Visual Information and Information Systems*, volume 1614 of *Lecture Notes in Computer Science*, 1999.

Automatic Video Summary and Description

Suh-Yin Lee, Shin-Tzer Lee, and Duan-Yu Chen

Department of Computer Science And Information Engineering, National Chiao Tung
University 1001 Ta-Hsueh Rd, Hsinchi, Taiwan
{sylee,szlee,dychen}@csie.nctu.edu.tw

Abstract. Multimedia technology has been applied to many kinds of
applications and the amount of multimedia data is growing dramatically.
Especially the usage of digital video data is very popular today. Thus, content-
based indexing and retrieval in video is getting more important in the future. In
this paper, we investigate an efficient and reasonable solution to describe video
contents, and propose an automatic generation of the summary of video
contents with as least manual interaction as possible. Based on the summary of
video contents, we extract the key features of the summary to represent its
content and produce the description of the video content in MPEG-7 format
using XML. We illustrate our approach by developing a system that can support
content-based browsing and querying on the WWW.

1   Introduction

The need for efficient methods for searching, indexing and managing multimedia data
is increasing due to the recent rapid proliferation of multimedia content. Therefore,
content-based queries and indexing is getting more important in the future. The
MPEG group recently establishes the MPEG-7 effort to standardize the multimedia
content interface. The proposed interface will bridge the gap between various types of
content meta-data, such as content features, annotations, relationships, and search
engines.

Digital video is becoming the rising tide of multimedia. The amount of video data is
growing tremendously. Thus indexing and cataloging of digital videos are more and
more important for retrieval. The best way for indexing and cataloging video data is
based on content. In the past, we usually describe and annotate the content of video
manually. However this traditional solution is not suitable for the enormous amount
of video data. We must find a mechanism that can generate the summary and
description automatically and provide an efficient and flexible solution to illustrate
video content for users.

In this paper, our system is divided into two parts. The first part extracts a summary
of video contents. We use video processing technologies, especially the information
of motion vector to get more meaningful summary about the video content. We use
MPEG-2 video streams as video sources and get meaningful abstracted summary
conveying significant information of the original video streams. At the same time, we
use the important features of the extracted summary to represent this summary. In the

R. Laurini (Ed.): VISUAL 2000, LNCS 1929, pp. 37-48, 2000.

second part, we use XML technology to generate extensible description schemes (**DSs**) in MPEG-7 [13]. Following the **DSs**, we can generate the descriptors (**Ds**) of the summary. When these descriptors are produced, we can use these descriptors to index and to catalog these videos. The characterizing indexing and cataloging results are more meaningful for video contents. A prototype system is implemented that can provide browsing and querying functions for users. Users can browse a video summary from WWW and download these videos that they are interested in. We aim to combine summarization and description procedures together, and generate the summary and descriptors concurrently. Figure 1 illustrates the framework of description generation flowchart. This paper is organized as follows. First, in Section 2, we present the summarizing procedure and discuss the classification of story units. In Section 3, we specify the description that we have developed in our prototype system. The applications of such video content description will be presented and reviewed in Section 4. Finally, further research direction is pointed out and conclusion is made in Section 5.

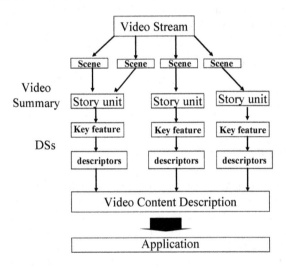

Fig. 1. The flowchart introduces the description generation.

2   Video Summary

The proposed system is a framework for using the summary of video content as the basis of descriptors in MPEG-7 to represent videos. Thus whether the summary is meaningful or not will affect the effectiveness of the system. The more significant the summary is, the more meaningful the descriptors of a video are generated. For this purpose, we must first extract useful and representative video clips from videos [2]. The summarization procedure is illustrated in the following steps. First, we dissect a video into scenes, and then cluster related scenes into story units. Finally we identify the types of story units and use the information to describe video contents.

2.1   Scene Change Detection

Video data is dissected into meaningful segments to serve as logical units called "shots" or "scenes". We use GOP-based scene change detection approach [3] to segment video data. By this approach, first we detect possible occurrences of scene change GOP by GOP (inter-GOP). The difference in each consecutive GOP-pair is calculated by comparing first I-frames in each consecutive GOP-pair. If the difference of DC coefficients between these two I-frames is higher than the threshold, then there may have scene change between these two GOPs. Then, the actual scene change frame within the GOP is located. We further use the ratio of forward and backward motion vectors to find out the actual frame of scene change within the GOP [4].

2.2   Scenes Clustering

After the procedure of scene change detection, a lot of scenes from the video are obtained. However, they are too many and are not suitable to describe the video content. Those related scenes belonging to the same story unit (**SU**) should be clustered together. A story unit is composed of consecutive and related scenes. For example, a segment of a video is about two persons discussing. This segment is composed of several different scenes, but those different scenes should belong to a dialog story unit in a video [6][7][8][9].

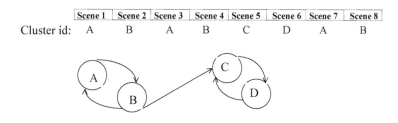

Fig. 2. This figure illustrates the scene transition graph in a story unit.

Figure 2 illustrates the scene transition graph about a story unit. A, B, C and D are four different scenes, but they appear alternately and closely in a sequence. According to our definition of a story unit, these four scenes should be grouped into the same story unit. The scenes are clustered into story units and then their types are identified. We illustrate our clustering procedure by two steps. First, we have to extract the key features to represent each scene. In this paper, we select the key frame of each scene. Secondly we cluster the scenes into story units.

Extracting the Key Frame of Scene
We extract the first I-frame of each scene as the key frame (**KFS**), since a scene is composed of consecutive similar frames and the first I-frame is qualified to represent this scene. Furthermore, we extract the low-level information of each **KFS**, such as luminance histogram and DC coefficients, to represent this key frame.

Clustering Related Scenes into Story Unit

After selecting the key frame of each scene, we compare these key frames of each scene pair, and each scene will be compared with those scenes before itself within a range **R** (**R**=20 scenes here). The smallest difference value between these **R** scenes and this target scene is computed. If the smallest difference is lower than a predefined threshold, the two scenes are similar, and they will be assigned the same cluster ID (**CID**) and story unit ID (**SUID**). At the same time we will set all the scenes in between these two identified similar scenes to the same **SUID**. However, if the smallest difference is over the threshold, they are assigned different **CID** and **SUID**. All scenes are scanned sequentially, and their own **CID**s and **SUID**s are assigned. Then the scenes with the same **SUID** are clustered into the same story unit. Figure 3 illustrates the clustering procedure.

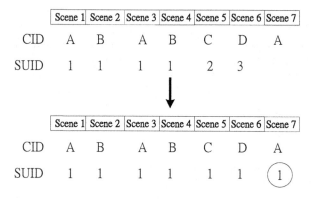

Fig. 3. These scenes that are related will be assigned the same SUID.

Difference between key frames

After extracting the representative key frame of each scene, we can measure the difference between two scenes. First, we generate the DC image of each key frame. Each key frame is composed of many macro-blocks (MB) in (Y, Cr, Cb) color space. We calculate the average of the DC coefficients, as the MB's DC coefficient.

The difference (**Diff**) between two scenes KFS_i and KFS_j is measured by their DC images as Eq. (1).

$$Diff(i,j) = \sum_{\substack{All\ Blocks\ of\ DC\ Image}} KFS_i(MB_k) - KFS_j(MB_k) \tag{1}$$

MB_k is block k in a DC image. Each video scene can be represented by a key frame of scene KFS. We measure the difference (*Diff*) of every pair of KFS in a story unit. Then we select the KFS that has the smallest difference with other KFS in a story unit as the key frame of this story unit (*KFSU*).

Feature Extraction from the Key Frame

The DC coefficients of KFSU
We extract the DC coefficients of every macro blocks of the *KFSU* and use the average of these DC coefficients to represent key frame. We can organize these DC coefficients as a DC Image. The amount of DC coefficients can be reduced.

The luminance histogram of KFSU
We can extract the luminance information from *KFSU*. The luminance information is an important feature of an image, because it can roughly present the content of an image.

The motion trajectory of SU
Motion information is the most prominent property of a video. The most intuitive specification of motion features for human being is motion trajectory. Many new technologies can extract the motion trajectory from a video [10]. In this paper, we define the extraction of motion trajectory. It is a simple description of the region motion trajectory in SU. Figure 6 shows the motion vectors of a macro-block in a scene sequence.

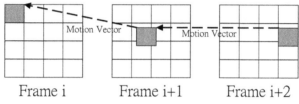

Frame i   Frame i+1   Frame i+2

Fig. 4. The motion vectors of a macroblock in a scene.

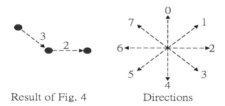

Result of Fig. 4   Directions

Fig. 5. Macro-Block Trajectory and directions.

In Figure 4, we can get the motion vector information from a scene sequence. Then we can use these motion vectors to generate simple MB trajectory in a scene.
Figure 5 shows the macro-block motion directions and the MB trajectory in Figure 4. We will record all macro-blocks' trajectory by a sequence of directions and the first macro-block position. If the direction sequence is long enough, then we keep this information in video description. The information can present the trajectory of a macro-block in a scene. It could be used to trace the trajectory of scenes in **SU**.

2.3   Story Unit Type Identification Rules

After the related scenes are clustered into a story unit, then we can distinguish the type of each story unit as action, dialogue, variation, still and default shot type [3][6]. The definition of each story unit type is described below.

Dialogue Story Unit
A dialogue story unit is composed of several scenes with people conversation and always presents the basic structure as "ABAB", in which A and B are scenes of type A and B, respectively. A dialogue story unit is defined as several dominant scenes appear alternatively among a short time period of video.

Action Story Unit
An action story unit is a series of short-term scenes with large variance. We try to detect an action story unit by finding a sequence of short scenes in which each scene has large image variance. When the variance is larger than the threshold and this story unit is not too long, then we say this story unit is an action story unit.

Still Story Unit
A still story unit is a series of long-term scenes with not much variance. We detect the still story unit by searching the long sequential scenes that have slight image variance in this story unit. When the variance of a story unit is less than the threshold and is long enough, then we say this story unit is a still story unit.

Variation Story Unit
A variation story is a long-term story unit with much variance. The definition of variation story unit is that the story unit is long enough and each scene in this story unit is different from other scenes.

Unidentified Story Unit
If a story unit does not belong to the above four story unit types, we set it to an unidentified story unit.

2.4 Grouping Story Units

We have implemented the prototyping system testing the extraction of **SU** using a 2-hour long video. The 2hr video contains about 1000 **SU**. There are too many to show all **SU**. We have to group similar **SU** together to reduce the amount of data we show to users firstly. Then we present pictorial representation of SU using a **SU** poster.

Poster of SU
The construction of a video poster relies on the compaction of dominance measure within each video scene.

$$Dom(i) = 16 * \frac{The\ number\ of\ scenes\ in\ SU_i}{\sum\limits_{k=1}^{M} The\ number\ of\ scenes\ in\ SU_k}\ , 1 \le i \le M \quad (2)$$

The parameter M is a predefined number that how many **SU** we want to group in one. Depending on the dominance, we can map each *KFSU* onto a layout pattern. Each poster is made up of 16 primary rectangles (more primary rectangles and more precise).

We measure the dominance of SU_i. Dominance measure is based on the number of scenes in this SU_i. Thus, if the amount of scenes in SU_i is more than in SU_j, then the dominance of SU_i will be greater than or equal to SU_j. Figure 6 shows the original scenes in a video sequence.

Scene 1	Scene 2	Scene 3	Scene 4	Scene 5	Scene 6	Scene 7	Scene 8	Scene 9	Scene 10

Fig. 6. The scenes in a video sequence.

Figure 7 shows the clustering of related scenes into story units. The scenes that contain the story key frames of SU are shadowed in gray color.

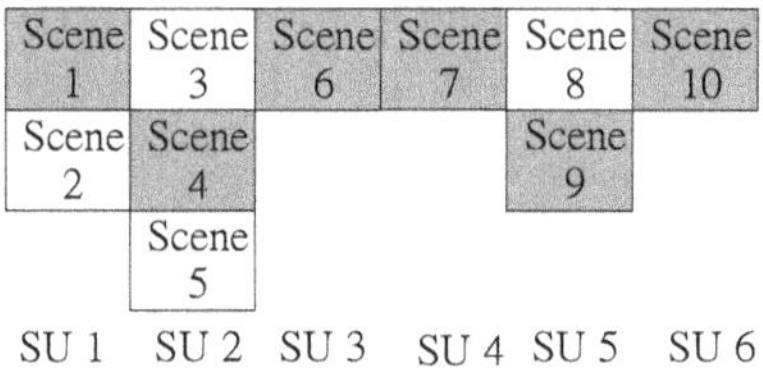

Scene 1	Scene 3	Scene 6	Scene 7	Scene 8	Scene 10
Scene 2	Scene 4			Scene 9	
	Scene 5				
SU 1	SU 2	SU 3	SU 4	SU 5	SU 6

Fig. 7. Clustering Scenes into Story Units.

Figure 8 shows the compaction of a video poster (**P**) after grouping story units into a video poster (**P**). **SU2** has the most dominance among these M **SU**, then its *KFSU* will occupy more space in **P**. Taking the dominance of scenes in a **SU** as a weight, we will allocate different space to each **SU**. The more number of scenes is, the more space of **SU** is allocated. We put the more important **SU** in top-left to bottom-right order.

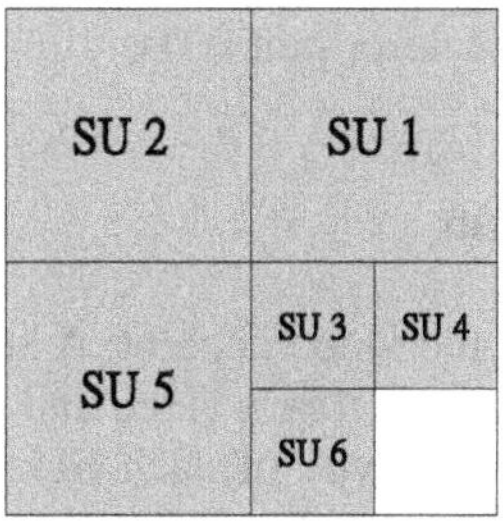

Fig. 8. Layout of Key Frame after Compaction.

Poster of Posters

One level grouping may not reduce the amount of **P** to be small enough. Thus we can reduce the number of **P** in further levels continuously. We can group several posters (**P**) into a Poster of Posters (**PP**). We select the most dominant **SU** to be the key **SU** of this poster (**KSU**) and use **KSU** to present this poster (**P**). Then we group these **KSU** into one poster (**PP**). Figure 9 illustrates the hierarchical structure of a POSTER.

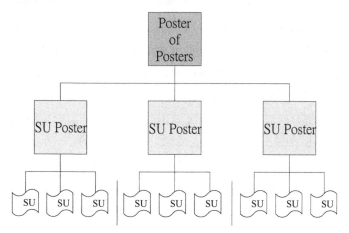

Fig. 9. The hierarchical structure of POSTERs.

3   Description of Video Content

MPEG-7 is formally named as "Multimedia Content Description Interface". It will extend the limited capabilities of current solutions in identifying multimedia content, by including more data types and specifying a standard set of description schemes and descriptors that can be used to describe various types of multimedia information. We follow MPEG-7 framework and provide a flexible description scheme of video content. We use summary as a basis for the description of the video content. The summary is a meaningful sub-stream of video content and using the features of summary to describe the video content is more reasonable and meaningful. We illustrate the video description by three steps. First, we illustrate the description definition language (**DDL**) used. Secondly we specify the description schemes (**DSs**) defined. Finally we describe the descriptors (**Ds**).

3.1   Grouping the Story Units

We use summary to represent the video content. A summary is generated by the **SU** mentioned above. **SU** are extracted from a video and more important **SU** are selected to compose into a summary. The type of each **SU** is characterized and assigned a priority. The higher priority **SU** are included in the summary of a video. Table 1 lists the priority of **SU** types.

Table 1. The priority of each story unit type

Story unit type	Predefined Priority
Dialogue	4
Action	3
Still	2
Variation	1
Unidentified	0

The summarizing rule is that unidentified type will never be used in a summary. The priorities of other four types will be adjusted depending on video content. Eq. (3) shows the function used to adjust the priority of SU types:

$$P_{new} = P_{pre} * \frac{NUM_T}{NUM_{SU}} \tag{3}$$

P_{new}: the adjusted priority of SU type in current video.

P_{pre} : the predefined priority of SU type.

NUM_T : the total number of SU type T in a video.

NUM_{SU} : the total number of SU in a video

Then we can get new priority of each SU type and we use these new priorities in the generation of our summary. The SU type with higher priority will have higher proportion in a video summary.

3.2   Description Definition Language (DDL)

To support content-based retrieval in the browsing system and applications, we develop a standard set of video content descriptor primitives, a framework for extending the content descriptors, and a process for representing, publishing, and transmitting the content descriptors using XML. We use the extensible Markup language, or XML [11][12][13][14], as the description definition language. XML is a tagged markup language for representing hierarchical, structured data. XML is easily readable by both machines and humans. Additionally, XML is portable and extensible. Thus the content descriptions will be defined, in general, from an extensible set of content description data types.

3.3   Descriptor Scheme (DS)

We use summary and its hierarchical structure to be the basis of description of video content. As shown in Figure 10, we define the description scheme that a story unit consists of six descriptors.

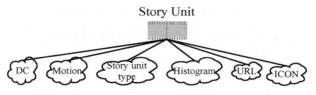

Fig. 10. Definition of Description Scheme.

We declare six attributes in the descriptor scheme. Each of the attributes is a descriptor (**D**). Depending on the above definition of **DS**, we can get these descriptors (**Ds**) from a video stream. Then we can use these **Ds** to describe the content of the original video, and to provide searching and browsing function in our system. ICON is the 64x64 pixels down-sampled image. We use this ICON to represent the original key frame image. Attribute URL indicates the location where users can download video summary.

4   Application

We are utilizing the description and summary of video content in the development of a web-based video content browsing system. The objective of this system is to catalog the video content and allow users to browse the video content by catalog. Content descriptors are used to represent the videos. Summary and descriptors can be automatically and concurrently generated. Two agents are supported in the system. First agent is text-based query service. Users can query these annotation descriptors which are movie type, director, and actor information. In addition, users can also key in a motion direction or a motion direction sequence as input and the server will find

Fig. 11. Browse and Advanced Query Interface.

out those story units which contain similar motion sequence. Moreover, users can search for an overall view or information in a video. For example, as shown in Figure 11, users can find out dialogue type video or action type video. Second agent provides the browsing function for users. Users can hierarchically browse the video content by posters. These two kinds of agents support the function that users can download the summaries that they are interested in for viewing.

5   Conclusion

In this paper, a mechanism for automatic extraction of more representative and significant scenes in the video content is proposed. We cluster the related scenes into story units. To accomplish the meaningful description, we first applied a summary technique to video content in order to obtain descriptors more suitable for representing video content. We implement a MPEG-7 like description by video summary and use XML to make the description scheme more flexible and extensible. Furthermore, the purposed system provides a convenient and fast method for users to browse and query the video content.

6   References

[1] ISO/IEC JTC1/SC29/WG11 N2966. "MPEG-7 Generic AV Description Schemes (V0.7)", Melbourne October 1999

[2] Nikolaos D. Doulamis, Anastasios D. Doulamis, Yannis S. Avrithis and Stefanos D. Kollias, "Video Content Representation Using Optimal Extraction of Frames and Scenes," IEEE conference on Image processing, Vol. 1, pp. 875-879, 1998.

[3] J. L. Lian, "Video Summary and Browsing Based on Story-Unit for Video-on-Demand Service," Master thesis, National Chiao Tung University, Dept. of CSIE, June 1999.

[4] J. Meng, Y. Juan, and S. F. Chang, "Scene Change Detection in a MPEG Compressed Video Sequence", IS&T/SPIE's Symposium on Electronic Imaging: Science & Technology, Vol. 2417, San Jose, CA, Feb. 1995.

[5] B.L. Yeo and B. Liu, "Rapid Scene Analysis on compressed Video", IEEE Transactions on Circuits and Systems for Video Technology, Vol. 5, No. 6 pp.533-544, 1995.

[6] M. M. Yeung and B. L. Yeo, "Video Content Characterization and Compaction for Digital Library Applications", In IS&T/SPIE Electronic Imaging'97: Storage and Retrieval of Image and Video Database, VI SPIE 3022, pp. 310-321, 1997.

[7] M. M. Yeung and B. L.Yeo, "Video Visualization for Compact Presentation of Pictorial Content", IEEE Transactions on Circuits and Systems for Video Technology, Vol. 7, No. 5, pp. 771-7785, Oct. 1997.

[8] M. M. Yeung, B. L. Yeo, and B. Liu, "Extracting Story Units from Long Programs for Video Browsing and Navigation," Proc. IEEE Conf. on Multimedia Computing and Systems, pp. 296-305, 1996.

[9] M. Yeung, B. L. Yeo, and B. Liu, "Video Browsing using clustering and scene transitions on compressed sequences," Proc. IEEE Conf. on Multimedia Computing and Systems, 1996.

[10] Man-Kwan Shan, Shh-Yin Lee, "Content-Based Retrieval of Multimedia Document Systems", PHD thesis, National Chiao Tung University, Dept. of CSIE, June 1998.

[11] W3 Consortium, RDF Schema Working Group, RDF schemas specification, http://www.w3.org/TR/WD-rdf-schema/, 1998.

[12] W3 Consortium, XML 1.0 Specification. http://www.w3.org/TR/REC-xml.

[13] W3 Consortium, XML Linking Language (Xlink). http://www.w3.org/TR/WD-xlink..

[14] Extensible Markup Language (XML), W3C Working Draft, http://www.w3.org/TR/WD-xml, November, 1997.

Relevance Ranking of Video Data Using Hidden Markov Model Distances and Polygon Simplification

Daniel DeMenthon[1], Longin Jan Latecki[2], Azriel Rosenfeld[1]
and Marc Vuilleumier Stückelberg[3]

[1] Center for Automation Research, University of Maryland
College Park, MD 20742, USA
{daniel,ar}@cfar.umd.edu
[2] Department of Applied Mathematics, University of Hamburg
Bundesstr. 55, 20146 Hamburg, Germany
latecki@math.uni-hamburg.de
[3] Computer Science Department, CUI, University of Geneva
24, rue Général Dufour, CH-1211 Geneva 4
Marc.VuilleumierStuckelberg@cui.unige.ch

Abstract. A video can be mapped into a multidimensional signal in a non-Euclidean space, in a way that translates the more predictable passages of the video into linear sections of the signal. These linear sections can be filtered out by techniques similar to those used for simplifying planar curves. Different degrees of simplification can be selected. We have refined such a technique so that it can make use of probabilistic distances between statistical image models of the video frames. These models are obtained by applying hidden Markov model techniques to random walks across the images. Using our techniques, a viewer can browse a video at the level of summarization that suits his patience level. Applications include the creation of a smart fast-forward function for digital VCRs, and the automatic creation of short summaries that can be used as previews before videos are downloaded from the web.

1 Motivation

People joke that a video tape is a "Write-Only Memory" (WOM). Indeed, in many homes, hours of TV programs and family memories get videotaped and pile up, yet very little is ever viewed again. One of the reasons is that, with only fast-forward viewing as a browsing tool, it is so painfully inefficient and time-consuming to review previously recorded material or search for specific footage that it is not worth the bother. Similarly, thousands of hours of video data are becoming available online, but there is no way to quickly preview this material before committing to a complete and often lengthy download.

However, the example of text search on the web demonstrates that even imperfect search tools can be very useful and successful. These tools attempt to

R. Laurini (Ed.): VISUAL 2000, LNCS 1929, pp. 49–61, 2000.
Springer-Verlag Berlin Heidelberg 2000

rank the relevance of the search results, so that the user can focus his attention initially on material that has a higher probability of being relevant to his query.

This paper describes our approach to applying this insight to video data. We propose to summarize videos by a method that ranks frames by relevance. The proposed mechanism will let the user say "I only have the patience to download and go over the $x\%$ most useful frames of this video before I decide to download the whole video".

We would like to select frames with the highest usefulness. At first, it seems that this is hopeless, unless we can understand the semantic contents of frames and videos. For example, there might be a shot that scans over books on a shelf and stops at the title of a book that is important for understanding the story.

However, in many cases there are syntactic clues, provided by techniques that the cameraman may use to convey the importance of the shot to the story. In many cases the camera motion corresponds to the motion of the eyes of a surprised viewer. The surprised viewer's gaze is attracted to a strange part of the scene, the gaze scans the scene to "zero in" on it, zooms in on it, and dwells on it for a while, until the new information has "sunk in". These changes in the image stream can be detected without understanding the content of the stream.

In this connection, *predictability* is an important concept. Frames that are predictable are not as useful as frames that are unpredictable. We can rank predictable frames lower, since the viewer can infer them from context. Frames of a new shot cannot generally be predicted from a previous shot, so they are important. (Cuts and transitions in image streams have similarities to image edges.) On the other hand, camera translations and pans that do not reveal new objects produce frames that are predictable.

We would like to detect when the camera stops (the viewer's gaze stopping on a surprising object). Note that what is unpredictable in this case is the camera motion, not the image content. As the camera slows down, the image content stops changing, so is quite predictable. Therefore, we can consider frames in which the motion field changes as more relevant than frames in which it does not.

We turn to a signal-theoretic view of video summarization. We can assume that the original image stream signal has tens of thousands of dimensions (color components of each pixel). We apply two filtering operations. The first operation can take the form of a dimension reduction that finds a feature vector for each frame and transforms the image stream into a feature vector trajectory, a signal that has many fewer dimensions than the original signal (e.g., 37 in one of the methods described below). Alternatively, we can represent each frame by a statistical model that captures average characteristics of colors, and possibly texture and motion, as well as contiguity properties. In this method too, we can view the original image stream as being filtered into a new signal in some (non-Euclidean) space, where we define the distance between frames as the distance between their statistical models. Both of these methods are described in the next section.

As a result of the first filtering step, we would like the output signal to be a straight line, or to remain in approximately the same position in the space, when nothing of interest happens, and to have a detectable curvature, a step or a roof, when a noteworthy event takes place.

Noise in this context is not the same as pixel noise. The image stream generated by a fixed camera looking from a window at a crowd milling around in the street may be considered to have a stationary component and a visual noise component, due to the changing colors of people's clothes. The passing of a fire truck would be an example of a signal over this fluctuating but monotonous background.

We apply a second filtering step, with the goal of detecting regions of high curvature along the trajectory, and we rank the filtering results. Since we expect the video signal to be noisy in the sense described above, we need the second filtering step to enhance the linear parts as well as the parts with significant curvature. In the non-Euclidean feature space of statistical frame models, projections cannot be computed; thus this filtering step should use only distance measures between models. It should allow for hierarchical output, so that the user can specify the level of detail (or scale) at which he wants to view the frames that show noteworthy events.

We can attempt to optimize both the first filtering step (mapping to the feature vector trajectory) and the second filtering step (edge-roof detection).

2   Mapping an Image Stream into a Trajectory

We begin with our proposal for the first filtering step, motivated in the previous section. We present two mappings of an image stream into a trajectory such that the trajectory is highly bent when events of interest occur in the stream. We assign a point on the trajectory to each frame in the stream.

For the first mapping, we define four histogram buckets of equal size for each of the three color attributes in the YUV color space of MPEG encoding. Each bucket contributes three feature vector components: the pixel count, and the x and y coordinates of the centroid of the pixels in the bucket. This yields 36 components, and we add the frame number (time) to obtain 37 components. Thus, the trajectory in this case is a polygonal arc in $\mathbb{R}^{37}$. (We are investigating an alternate scheme in which the number and sizes of the buckets are selected according to the color distribution over the video sequence.)

When the camera translates or pans smoothly without seeing new things, the centroid components change linearly and the feature vector trajectory is linear. If the camera suddenly decelerates (or accelerates), the trajectory has a high curvature, because the centroids decelerate.

As an alternative mapping, we generate a statistical model for each frame using a hidden Markov model (HMM) technique. We obtain sequences of pixels by taking random walks across each frame, moving either to the north, east, south or west neighbor with equal probability. When we hit the border of the image, we jump randomly to another pixel of the image, and start another sequence. We model our observations by counting the number of times we step to a pixel of a certain color, given that we come from a neighbor of the same color or of a different color (colors are the same if they are quantized to the same value; the quantization method is described below). Numbers representing the counts of transitions from one color to another color can be stored in a 2D table. Note that this table is a cooccurrence matrix [6] for the quantized colors, except for the fact that some pixels my be visited twice and other pixels may be missed.

To make this information independent of the number of steps taken, we can normalize each row so that the row numbers sum to 1. For large numbers of observations, this table is a color transition probability matrix, as it describes the probability of arriving at a certain color at the next step, given that we are at a certain color at the present step. In addition, we keep track of the values of the pixels at the first step of each new walk to compute a histogram of the colors of the image.

To avoid excessive model size, the colors must be quantized. Using HMM terminology, this operation can be called a *state assignment* of the pixels, since we are saying that when a color is in a certain interval, the pixel belongs to a given bin, or state. After quantization, we can describe the image by a histogram of the states and a state transition matrix. To compensate for the reduced descriptive power of a statistical model using fewer states, the HMM describes the distribution of each color within each bin/state. In our experiments, we modeled the color distribution within each state by three Gaussians, i.e. a total of six numbers. HMM techniques (described in the next paragraph) allow us to compute a quantization of the color space such that in each bin/state, the color distributions are well represented by Gaussians. The labeling of pixels into states is hidden, in the sense that only actual pixel values are observed, not their quantized values, and a computation assigns the best states as follows.

A state assignment is obtained in two steps in an iteration loop. In the first step, we compute the sequences of states that have the highest probabilities, given the observation sequences along the random walks. We obtain these maximum probabilities and the corresponding state sequences by a dynamic programming technique called the Viterbi algorithm [12], using the state transition matrix and the probability distribution of observations within each state (obtained at a previous iteration). In the second step, now that each pixel has been labeled with a specific state, we can recompute the most likely state transition matrix by tallying the transitions from state to state along the random walks. Also, we can recompute the most likely Gaussian probability distributions of observations within each state by finding the means and variances of the colors of the pixels labeled with that state. These two steps are repeated alternatingly until there is no significant improvement. This is the so-called segmental K-means approach to computing a Hidden Markov model from sequences of observations [12]. (The slower-converging Baum-Welch algorithm can be used instead with similar results.) The resulting statistical description of the image consists of a state transition matrix, which is essentially a cooccurrence matrix for quantized colors, together with a description of the color distributions within each bin, and the probability distribution of the states of the starting pixels of each random walk, which is a histogram of the quantized colors of the image.

Once we have obtained HMM models for the video frames, we are able to compute distances between frames. The idea behind a distance calculation between two images using HMMs is to find how well the HMM of one image can model the other (and vice versa), in comparison to how well each HMM can model the image on which it was trained. To measure the modeling ability of an HMM for any image, we can obtain an observation sequence from that image by a random walk, and compute the probability that this sequence could be produced by the HMM. When images are visually similar, this probability is high.

In other words, a distance measure between two images I_1 and I_2 with HMM models λ_1 and λ_2 is constructed by combining the probability that the observation sequences $\mathbf{O}_2$ obtained by random walks through image I_2 could be produced by the probabilistic model λ_1 of image I_1, and a similar probability where the roles of I_2 and I_1 are reversed. This quantity is normalized by the number of observations, and compared to how well the HMMs can model the images on which they were trained:

$$d(I_1, I_2) = -\frac{1}{N_2}\log P(\mathbf{O}_2|\lambda_1) - \frac{1}{N_1}\log P(\mathbf{O}_1|\lambda_2) + \frac{1}{N_1}\log P(O_1|\lambda_1) + \frac{1}{N_2}\log P(O_2|\lambda_2)$$

$$(1)$$

Quantities of the form $\log P(\mathbf{O}_i|\lambda_j)$ are computed by applying the classic Forward Algorithm [12] to the observation sequences $\mathbf{O}_i$ using the transition matrix and probability distributions prescribed by the HMM model λ_j.

This distance function defines a *semi-metric space*, because it satisfies
positivity: $d(x, x) = 0$ and $d(x, y) > 0$ if x is distinct from y,
symmetry $d(x, y) = d(y, x)$,
but not the triangle inequality, i.e., there can exist z's such that

$$d(x, y) > d(x, z) + d(z, y).$$

For this mapping, the trajectory describing a sequence of video frames is also a polygonal arc (in the sense that it is a finite, linearly ordered sequence of points) but it is not contained in Euclidean space; it is contained in a non-linear semi-metric space. This means that the points on the trajectory cannot be assigned coordinates, and we can only measure a semi-distance between any two points.

Distances based on image statistics (histogram, co-occurrence, HMM) are quite insensitive to image translation, and therefore produce points that are in approximately the same positions in space when the camera motion is a pan or a translation.

3   Trajectory Filtering by Polygon Simplification

Our first filtering operation, described in the previous section, maps a video sequence into a trajectory that is a polygonal arc, i.e., a polyline. The polyline may be noisy, in the sense that it is not linear but only nearly linear for video stream segments where nothing of interest happens (i.e., where the segments are predictable). Furthermore, the parts of high curvature are difficult to detect locally. Therefore, it is necessary to apply a second filtering operation, which we describe in this section.

The goal is to simplify the polyline so that its sections become linear when the corresponding video stream segments are predictable, which also means that the vertices of the simplified polyline are key frames of the non-predictable video stream segments. We achieve this by repeated removal of the vertices that represent the most predictable video frames. In the terms of the geometry of the polyline trajectory, these vertices are the most linear ones. While it is clear what "linear" means in a linear space, we need to define this concept for semi-metric non-linear spaces.

A polyline is an ordered sequence of points. Observe that even if the polyline is contained in Euclidean space, it is not possible to use standard approximation techniques like least-square fitting for its simplification, since the simplified polyline would then contain vertices that do not belong to the input polyline. For such vertices, there would not exist corresponding video frames. Thus, a necessary condition for a simplification of a video polyline is that a sequence of vertices of the simplified polyline be a subsequence of the original one.

Our approach to simplification of video polylines is based on a novel process of discrete curve evolution presented in [9] and applied in the context of shape similarity of planar objects in [11]. However, here we will use a different measure of the relevance of vertices, described below.

Aside from its simplicity, the process of discrete curve evolution differs from the standard methods of polygonal approximation, like least square fitting, by the fact that it can be used in non-linear spaces. The only requirement for discrete curve evolution is that every pair of points is assigned a real-valued distance measure that does not even need to satisfy the triangle inequality. Clearly, this requirement is satisfied by our distance measure, which is a dissimilarity measure between images.

Now we briefly describe the process of discrete curve evolution (for more details see [10]). The basic idea of the proposed evolution of polygons is very simple:

- At each evolution step, a vertex with smallest relevance is detected and deleted.

The key property of this evolution is the order of the deletion, which is given by a relevance measure K that is computed for every vertex v and depends on v and its two neighbor vertices u, w:

$$K(v) = K(u, v, w) = d(u, v) + d(v, w) - d(u, w) \qquad (2)$$

where d is the semi-distance function. Intuitively, the relevance $K(v)$ reflects the shape contribution of vertex v to the polyline.

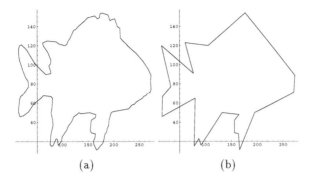

(a)   (b)

Fig. 1. Fish silhouette with 124 vertices (a) and a simplified curve with 21 points (b)

Fig. 1 illustrates the curve simplification produced by the proposed filtering technique for a planar figure. Notice that the most relevant vertices of the curve and the general shape of the figure are preserved even after most of the vertices have been removed.

We will demonstrate with the experimental results in the next section that the discrete curve evolution based on this relevance measure is very suitable for filtering polylines representing videos.

4   Experimental Results

We illustrate our techniques using an 80-second clip from a video entitled "Mr. Bean's Christmas". The clip contains 2379 frames. First, we applied the feature vector approach described above, in which a 37-dimensional feature vector derived from centroids and pixel counts in histogram bins is computed for each frame. A perspective view of the 3D projection of the video trajectory is shown in Fig. 2a. The two large black dots are the points corresponding to the first and last frames of the video. Curve simplification using the method described in Section 3 was then applied to this trajectory. Fig. 2b shows a simplification result in which only 20 points have been preserved (a method for automatic selection of the smallest point count that can still provide an appropriate level of summarization is presented at the end of next section).

Finally, HMM models were computed for every 5 frames, and curve simplification was performed using the probabilistic distance measure described in Section 2. For comparison with the feature vector method, we chose to also preserve 20 key frames with the HMM curve simplification. Since this method does not provide frame coordinates, we plotted the 20 points that correspond to these 20 frames along the trajectory found by the feature vector approach, in order

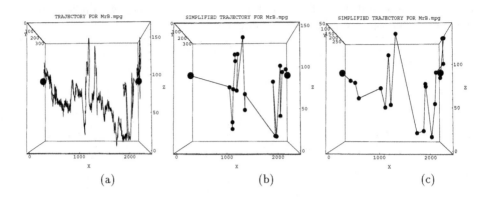

Fig. 2. Video trajectory (a) and curve simplification producing 20 relevant frames (black dots) for Mr. Bean's Christmas, using (b) the feature vector method, and (c) the HMM method.

to give an idea of the locations of the 20 frames in the video (Fig. 2c). Clearly, the HMM method located its key frames on segments of sudden change of that trajectory, i.e. in regions of significant change in the video clip.

Next we discuss the quality of the summaries produced by curve simplification using the feature vector and HMM methods. Knowing the content of each shot of the clip is helpful for this comparative evaluation.

1. Frames 1 to 996: Mr. Bean carries a raw turkey from a kitchen counter to a table. He cuts a string that tied the legs, brings a bowl of stuffing closer and starts pushing stuffing inside the turkey.
2. Frames 997 to 1165: He notices that his watch is missing.
3. Frames 1166 to 1290: He looks inside the turkey, then pulls stuffing out of the turkey to retrieve his watch.
4. Frames 1291 to 1356: He keeps removing stuffing.
5. Frames 1357 to 2008: He tries to look inside, then uses a flashlight to try to locate his watch inside the turkey. Finally, he bends toward the turkey to explore more deeply by putting his head inside the turkey.
6. Frames 2009 to 2079: The lady friend whom he invited for Christmas dinner rings his doorbell.
7. Frames 2080 to 2182: Hearing the bell, Mr. Beans stands up with his head stuck inside the turkey. He vainly attempts to remove the turkey.
8. Frames 2183 to 2363: He walks blindly toward the door with the turkey over his head, bumping into things.
9. Frames 2364 to 2379: His lady friend waits outside for the door to open...

Fig. 3 shows two storyboards obtained by curve simplification. Storyboard (a) results from the curve simplification obtained by the feature vector method. The frames correspond to the vertices of the simplified polyline in Fig. 2b. Storyboard

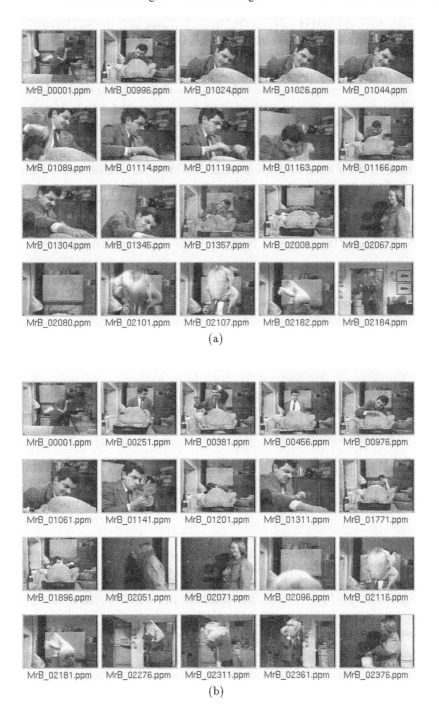

Fig. 3. Storyboards obtained by curve simplification of the video trajectory obtained by the feature vector method (a) and by the HMM method (b)

(b) results from the HMM method. The frames correspond to the vertices of the simplified polyline in Fig. 2c.

Both storyboards seem to be reasonable summarizations of the short video clip. The feature vector method misses Shot 9 (the last shot), and oversamples Shot 2 (where he notices that his watch is missing) with 8 frames. The HMM method represents each shot with at least one frame, and selects frames that tell more of the story, such as the string cutting of frame 381 and the flashlight episode of frame 1771. The slightly better performance of the HMM method for this example is not very significant, as we can think of several ways of improving each method. After these improvements are completed, we need to compare the outputs of our methods with ground-truth provided by humans who view the clips and select small numbers of frames as most descriptive of the stories.

5   A Video Player with Smart Fast-Forwarding

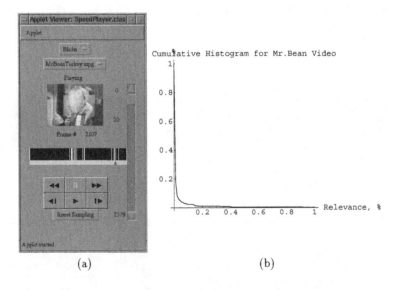

(a)   (b)

Fig. 4. (a): Video player with vertical slider for control of summarization level. (b): Cumulative histogram giving proportion of frames with relevances larger than a given number, used to determine default summarization level.

An interesting application of video summarization is to the design of a smart VCR fast-forwarding that samples only the most relevant frames. We have developed a Java video player that plays video clips in MPEG format, and can play the whole video at the normal rate, or show only the frames of highest relevance(Fig. 4a). A vertical *relevance slider* on the right-hand side of the window lets the user define the number of frames that he has the patience to watch.

For example, the "Mr. Bean's Christmas" video clip contains 2379 frames, so that playing it takes around 80 seconds. The user may choose to watch only the 20 most relevant frames and moves the slider up until the box at the left of the sliding elevator indicates 20. Then the player skips all but the 20 most relevant frames. The buttons at the bottom of the player window define VCR-type functions: Play, Pause, Fast-Forward, Fast-Backward, frame-by-frame forward stepping, and backward stepping. In all these modes, only the relevant frames, as defined by the relevance slider, are played.

A horizontal *sampling stripe* located under the image display panel shows the positions of the relevant frames within the video. It is a black stripe that shows a white vertical tick mark for each displayed frame. A triangular *frame marker* slides below the sampling stripe as the video clip is being played, and indicates which frame is being displayed. Navigation through the video can also be performed by dragging this triangular frame marker. This mode of navigation is called "scrubbing" by video editing practitioners. It is set to let the user visit all the frames, not just the relevant frames.

Video clips are selected from a pop-up menu. The user can also select different types of relevance measures from a second pop-up menu. The relevances presently available in the video player have been precomputed from Euclidean distances between feature vectors from histogram bins and from HMM distances, both described above, as well as from Euclidean distances between motion feature vectors, described in [16]. We plan to add other filtering choices, such as relevances based on the presence of faces, music and talk content in the sound track.

When a new video is selected for viewing, the vertical relevance slider is initially positioned at a default position which shows only a small number of relevant frames. This number is precomputed for each available type of relevance measure using a histogram slope technique. Cumulative histograms that represent, for any given relevance, the number of frames that have larger relevance, are found to have similar shapes (Fig. 4 (b)): most of the frames have small relevances; these frames have small variations with respect to their neighbors. Very few frames have large relevances. The two regions are separated by a sudden slope change. We wish to ignore the many frames with small relevances and show the few frames with large relevances, therefore we select the cutoff relevance at the slope break between the two regions, around slope -1. For the histogram of Mr. Bean's video, this corresponds to around 27 frames. After exploring the video at several relevance slider positions, the user can return the slider to its default position by clicking the button labeled "Reset Sampling".

This prototype uses MPEG-decoding Java source code written by J. Anders [1].

6   Related Work and Discussion

Huang et al. [8] showed that using more descriptive statistical models of images such as correlograms significantly improves retrieval performance of images, in comparison to simple statistical descriptions such as histograms. However, they do not have a method for selecting the right balance between the size of the correlogram and the discriminative power of the model. Second, they apply Euclidean distances to their statistical models. Consequently, they have to give different weights to the Euclidean coordinates depending on the situation. In our view, the use of hidden Markov models of images elegantly addresses these issues, by (1) supplementing coarse color quantization with a description of color distributions within each bin, while automatically adjusting each bin size to make this description optimal, and (2) addressing the distance issue by allowing an intuitive probabilistic definition of image distance.

In [3], we described how the Ramer-Douglas-Peucker method of polygon simplification [13] could provide effective summarizations of videos. This method is a binary curve splitting approach that at each step splits the arc at the point furthest from the chord, and stops when the arc is close to the chord. However, for N video frames it has time complexity N^2, which is prohibitive for large videos and complex distance measures. Variants that reduce the complexity to $N \log N$ cannot be applied to multidimensional video trajectories, as they make use of planar convex hulls [7]. In addition, the computation of the distance between an arc and its chord requires the use of Euclidean distances. The curve simplification technique we have proposed can be shown to be of order $N \log N$ and can accommodate non-Euclidean distances. These two features make the use of probabilistic image distances practical for video summarization.

The reader interested in video browsing research can refer to [14, 15, 17] and to the recent work of Foote [5].

7   Conclusions and Future Work

In this work, we have proposed and implemented a system for automatically providing summaries of videos whose size can be controlled by the user. The method applies a novel fine-to-coarse polyline simplification technique that computes for each vertex a relevance measure based on its two neighbors and at each step removes the least relevant vertex and updates the relevances of the affected neighbors. The proposed relevance measure is valid for non-metric spaces. This allows us to compute relevances using a probabilistic distance measure between hidden Markov models of the video frames. We produce reasonable summaries by showing the most relevant frames in temporal order. We have implemented a video player that incorporates this technology to let the user perform a smart fast-forwarding that skips the more predictable frames. A vertical slider lets the user define the number of relevant frames he has the patience to watch. We are currently investigating improved random sampling of images for the HMM calculation using quasi-random walks [2], as well as summarization results for a 2D HMM technique [4]. We are also improving our video player to let the user select a region of a frame and retrieve the frames that have the shortest HMM distances to that region.

References

1. Anders, J., Java MPEG page,
   http://rnvs.informatik.tu-chemnitz.de/~ja/MPEG/MPEG_Play.html
2. Coulibaly, I., and Lécot, C.,"Simulation of Diffusion Using Quasi-Random Walk Methods", Mathematics and Computers in Simulation, vol. 47, pp. 154–163, 1998.
3. DeMenthon, D.F., Kobla, V., M., and Doermann, D., "Video Summarization by Curve Simplification", Technical Report LAMP-TR-018, CAR-TR-889, July 1998; also ACM Multimedia 98, Bristol, England, pp. 211-218, 1998.
4. DeMenthon, D.F., Vuilleumier Stückelberg, M., and Doermann, D., "Hidden Markov Models for Images", Int. Conf. on Pattern Recognition, Barcelona, Spain, 2000.
5. Foote, J., Boreczky, J., Girgensohn, A., and Wilcox, L. (1998), "An Intelligent Media Browser using Automatic Multimodal Analysis", ACM Multimedia 98, Bristol, England, pp. 375-380, 1998.
6. Haralick, R.M., "Statistical and Structural Approaches to Texture", *Proceedings of the IEEE*, vol. 67, pp. 786–804, 1979.
7. Hershberger, J., and Snoeyink, J. "Speeding up the Douglas-Peucker Line-Simplification Algorithm", http://www.cs.ubc.ca/cgi-bin/tr/1992/TR-92-07.
8. Huang, J., Kumar, S.R., Mitra, M., Zhu, W-J., and Zabih, R., "Image Indexing Using Color Correlograms", IEEE Conf. on Computer Vision and Pattern Recognition, pp. 762–768, 1997.
9. Latecki, L.J., and Lakämper, R., "Convexity Rule for Shape Decomposition based on Discrete Contour Evolution", Computer Vision and Image Understanding, vol. 73, pp. 441–454, 1999.
10. Latecki, L.J., and Lakämper, R., "Polygon Evolution by Vertex Deletion", in M. Nielsen, P. Johansen, O.F. Olsen, and J. Weickert, editors, Scale-Space Theories in Computer Vision (Int. Conf. on Scale-Space), LNCS 1682, Springer, 1999.
11. Latecki, L.J. and Lakämper, R., "Shape Similarity Measure Based on Correspondence of Visual Parts", IEEE Trans. on Pattern Analysis and Machine Intelligence, to appear.
12. Rabiner, L.R., and Juang, B.-H., "Fundamentals of Speech Processing", Prentice Hall, pp. 321–389, 1993.
13. Ramer, U., "An Iterative Procedure for the Polygonal Approximation of Plane Curves", Computer Graphics and Image Processing, vol. 1, pp. 244–256, 1972.
14. Smith, M.A., and Kanade, T., "Video Skimming for Quick Browsing Based on Audio and Image Characterization", IEEE Conf. on Computer Vision and Pattern Recognition, 1997.
15. Yeung, M.M., Yeo, B-L., Wolf, W. and Liu, B.,"Video Browsing using Clustering and Scene Transitions on Compressed Sequences", SPIE Conf. on Multimedia Computing and Networking, vol. 2417, pp. 399–413, 1995.
16. Yoon, K., DeMenthon, D.F., and Doermann, D., "Event Detection from MPEG Video in the Compressed Domain", Int. Conf. on Pattern Recognition, Barcelona, Spain, 2000.
17. Zhang, H.J., Low, C.Y., Smoliar, S.W., and Wu, J.H., "Video Parsing, Retrieval and Browsing: An Integrated and Content–Based Solution", ACM Multimedia, 1995.

Video Clustering Using SuperHistograms in Large Archives

Lalitha Agnihotri and Nevenka Dimitr

Philips Research, 345, Scarborough Road,

Briarcliff Manor, NY-10510

(lalitha.agnihotri, nevenka.dimitrova)@philips.com

Abstract. Methods for characterizing video segments and allowing fast search in large archives are becoming essential in the video information flood. In this paper, we present a method for characterizing and clustering video segments using cumulative color histogram. The underlying assumption is that a video segment has a consistent color palette, which can be derived as a family of merged individual shot histograms. These merged histograms (SuperHistograms) are clustered using a Nearest Neighbor-clustering algorithm. Given a query video, in order to find similar videos, the SuperHistogram of the video will be generated and compared to the centers of the Nearest Neighbor clusters. The video clips in the cluster with center nearest to the query, can be searched to find video clips most similar to the query video. This method can be used in a variety of applications that need video classification and retrieval methods such as video editing, video archival, digital libraries, consumer products, and web crawling.

1 Introduction

With the advent of digital television (DTV), the increasing popularity of the World Wide Web (WWW) and consumer electronics components such as CD recordable and DVD, the amount of multimedia information available to consumers continues to grow. As content becomes readily available and products for accessing such information reach the consumer market, searching, indexing and identifying large volumes of multimedia data will become even more challenging. This requires adding additional feature characterization and retrieval components to the growing body of research in the areas of video indexing and classification [1, 3, 4, 9, 11].

The idea of video representation using SuperHistograms was introduced in [6]. The focus of the paper was to describe a method for extraction of *SuperHistograms*, the distance measures and the data structure representation within a video program. Briefly, the method computes color histograms for individual shots and then merges the histograms into a single cumulative histogram called a family histogram based on

R. Laurini (Ed.): VISUAL 2000, LNCS 1929, pp. 62-73, 2000.

© Springer-Verlag Berlin Heidelberg 2000

a comparison measure. This family histogram represents the color union of the two shots. As new shots are added, the family histogram accumulates the new colors from the respective shots. However, if the histogram of a new frame is different from the previously constructed family histograms, a new family is formed. In the end, there will be a few families of histograms to represent the entire television program. This set of families is ordered with respect to the length of the temporal segment of video that they represent. The ordered set of family histograms is called *SuperHistogram*.

In this paper, we present the video retrieval using clustering techniques for large video archives based on the SuperHistogram representation introduced in [6]. Video classification and searching in large video archives is implemented and the results are discussed. A nearest neighbor clustering method will be used to cluster the SuperHistograms for fast retrieval. The important issues addressed in this paper are: (a) color quantization for chosen color space, (b) methods to compare video segments based on SuperHistograms in order to perform the clustering, and (c) the number of clusters to be used for clustering, and (d) the appropriate content set.

The paper is organized as follows. In Section 2, we describe the method that will be used for computing SuperHistograms. In Section 3, we present the clustering algorithm using SuperHistograms for classification and retrieval. In Section 4 we present the results, and in Section 5 we present concluding remarks.

2 Computing SuperHistograms

SuperHistograms for video representation were introduced in a previous publication and here we will briefly present the definition and extraction of SuperHistograms so that we can focus on video retrieval. For further details the reader is referred to [6]. A histogram is a one-dimensional vector representing the color values and the frequency of their occurrence in an image [7]. For video content analysis based on color, the histograms need to be computed and stored along with the differences between two histograms.

The SuperHistogram computation algorithm consists of keyframe detection, color quantization, histogram computation, histogram family comparison and merging, and ranking of the histogram families to extract a SuperHistogram. In the following subsections we will present details of the steps involved in the SuperHistogram computation. We will use keyframes as a representative for shots, because within a shot there is usually only incremental change in the colors.

2.1 Quantization

The first step in the computation of video super-histograms is color quantization. In the literature there are methods for color quantization [12]. The problem is multifaceted: which color space to use, how many colors to choose, and how to subdivide the color space. We explored multiple color quantization schemes are to determine the best color space for classification. In this paper we use the YUV color space.

We experimented with the following quantization for the histograms:

1) 64 bins (64 Y): In this quantization, the U and V were ignored and the Y space was mapped from 0-255 to 0-64.
2) 128 bins (128 Y): Same as above, except the mapping of Y was from 0-128.
3) 256 bins (256 Y): Y was not scaled down.
4) 288 bins (8Y, 6U, 6V): The U and V were considered in this quantization. Y was scaled from 0-255 to 0-8. U and V were scaled non-linearly as follows
   if x is U or V value ranging from 0-255 and x' is the quantized value
   $x < 64, x' = 0$
   $64 < x < 192, x' = 1$-5
   $x > 192, x' = 6$
   The range between 64 to 192 was uniformly scaled to a value between 1-5.
5) 576 bins (16Y, 6U, 6V): Same as above except, Y was scaled down from 0-255 to 0-16.

The goal is to see how discriminating the above quantizations are. Nearest neighbor clustering is performed for each quantization. If the clusters generated have good spread of videos across clusters and one cluster does not "monopolize" all videos, then the corresponding quantization is good for video clustering and retrieval.

2.2 Computing Histogram Differences

For each keyframe we compute the histogram and then search the previously computed family histograms to find the closest family histogram match. The comparison between the current histogram, H_c, and the previous family histograms, H_p, can be computed using various histogram comparison methods. In tour experiments we tried the following two methods for calculating histogram difference D.

(1) Histogram difference using **L2** distance measure is computed by using the following formula:

$$D = \sqrt{\sum_{i=1}^{N} (H_C(i) \quad H_P(i))^2} \tag{1}$$

(2) **Histogram intersection** is computed using the following formula:

$$I = \frac{\sum_{i=1}^{N} \min(H_C(i), H_P(i))}{\sum_{i=1}^{N} H_C(i)} \tag{2}$$

2.3 Computing Family Histograms

A family histogram is a cumulatively averaged histogram derived from histograms representing frames, also called keyframes, from consecutive frames or from shot boundaries. In our experiments we will use frames extracted from scene breaks. The histogram of the first encountered frame is taken to be the family histogram for the first "family." Starting from the second keyframe and for each new encountered keyframe there should be a decision whether the new frame should be merged with an existing family histogram or if the current frame is substantially different and start a new family. Given two histograms extracted from two keyframes, the difference between these two histograms is computed. If the difference is less than a certain threshold, then the current histogram is merged into the family histogram. The family histogram is a data structure consisting of: (1) pointers to each of the constituent histograms and frame numbers, (2) a merged family histogram, and (3) a variable representing total duration that is initialized to the duration of the scene represented by the current histogram. Merging of family histograms is performed according to the following formula:

$$H_{fam}(\ell) = \sum_i \frac{T_i}{\sum_j T_j} H_i(\ell) \qquad (1)$$

(3)

In this formula l is a variable representing the bin number, fam is an index for this particular family and H_{fam} is a vector representing the family histogram, i is an index representing the shot number in the family histogram, T_i is a variable representing the duration of scene i. $H_i(l)$ is the numerical value indicating the number of pixels in bin l for keyframe numbeı of all scenes already in the family.

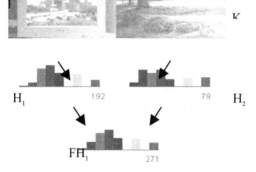

Fig. 1. An example of a family histogram.

An example of an extracted family histogram for a nine-bin histogram is given in Figure 1. Given the keyframes K_1 for a shot of 192 frames (dur_1), and K_2 representing 79 frames (dur_2), two histograms H_1 and H_2 are generated, which are then merged into cumulative family histogram FH_1 (H_{fam}) shown at the bottom of Figure 1, which represents a total of 271 frames $(total\_dur_{fam})$.

3 Program Classification and Comparison

We propose to use the SuperHistograms for classifying and searching large video archives. The important tasks are to find the color quantization for the histogram, the method to compare the distance between the SuperHistograms of video segments, and the clustering method. We decided to use nearest neighbor clustering method with fixed number of clusters.

3.1 Distance between SuperHistograms

In order to compare two video segments using SuperHistograms an appropriate distance measure should be defined. A SuperHistogram consists of m family histograms, each of which is represented by a histogram vector that is derived from non-contiguous sections of video. The challenge is to compare the SuperHistograms while remembering the fact that subsections of videos could resemble each other. For example, different episodes of a sitcom, such as Seinfeld, have different focus on the location where they are shot. So, comparing the families in the order of importance is not necessarily desired for video retrieval. Furthermore, the length of the families may be different and when comparing two family histograms and this should be taken into account. When the largest family of the video V1 and the smallest family of the video V2 are similar, the weight should convey the similarity while not overemphasizing it.

After program families are determined, let us say that program S is characterized by three family histograms SH = (SH_1, SH_2, SH_3) and let us say that program T is characterized by three family histograms, TH= (TH_1, TH_2, TH_3). Then the difference between two programs can be calculated according to the following formula:

$$\text{(4)}$$

$$Diff(SH,TH) = \frac{1}{w_i} \sum_j (w_i + w_j) D\left(SH_i, TH_j\right)$$

where,

$$D\left(H_i, H_j\right) = \sum_i \left| H_i(k) * w_i - H_j(k) * w_j \right| \quad \text{(5)}$$

and, $H_i(k)$ is the value in bin k of histogram H_i. The w_i and w_j are weights proportional to the duration of video that they represent. The distance measure in equation 5 is L1, however, this distance measure could be any of the presented distance measures in section 2.1. Further, w is the normalizing coefficient and is calculated as follows:

$$w_{i_j} = (w_i + w_j) \tag{6}$$

The important thing to remember is that if two video segments are partially similar then it is possible that the largest family histogram of one is similar to the smallest family histogram of the other. By using a cross histogram comparison method and weighting them suitably, we should be able to find partially similar videos also. Figure 2. shows the SuperHistograms for two episodes of Seinfeld. It can be seen that the two SuperHistograms look very similar.

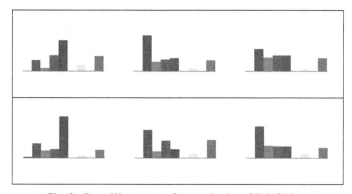

Fig. 2. SuperHistograms of two episodes of Seinfeld.

3.2 Nearest Neighbor Clustering

We perform video classification using Nearest Neighbor clustering on SuperHistograms extracted from video segments. In this process, we generate a few representative clusters, which are then used for fast retrieval. A compilation of literature on Nearest Neighbor classification can be found in [5]. A hierarchical clustering algorithm was used for fast image retrieval in [8].

The representation of SuperHistograms for nearest neighbor clustering consists of the three largest family histogram vectors followed by their weights defined as the duration of the corresponding shots. In general, *n-bin* SuperHistogram consisting of *m* families is represented by a vector of length: *(n+1)*m*. For example, in case of a SuperHistogram consisting of three families that use 64 bin histograms we obtain a vector of length $(64 + 1)*3 = 195$.

The SuperHistogram nearest neighbor (SNN) clustering algorithm consists of
1. Find the SuperHistograms for each video segment in the content archive.
2. Find and store the distances between all videos in an array.

3. Start with random SuperHistograms as seeds for centers of Nearest Neighbor Clusters. The number of clusters is predefined for each experiment.
4. For each of the rest of the SuperHistograms, find the closest seed and add it to the cluster.
5. Find the center of the clusters, i.e. the vector with the least distance to the rest of the vectors in a cluster.
6. Go to step 4. Perform steps 4 thorough 6 until there is no change in the center or number of changes is less than 2% or the number of iterations reaches maximum number of iterations.

As mentioned in the introduction there are several issues associated with the SNN clustering. We calculate the Standard Deviation (SD) of the cluster occupancy (number of videos in a cluster) for each quantization for a cluster size. The SD can be used to judge the uniformity of videos across clusters. A low SD implies well-populated clusters. However, a high SD means that too many vectors were placed in one cluster and too few in others. By favoring low SD will help us eliminate color quantizations that do not have good discriminating power for a given number of clusters. Additionally, we varied the number of clusters from 5-10 to find the number of clusters that gives the best spread for a given *good* quantization.

3.3 Retrieval of Video Segments

In our experiments we used a large number of videos from the web and generated their SuperHistograms. The SuperHistograms are clustered using the method described in section 2. The clusters generated using the method described in section 3.2 are used to retrieve videos of similar color palette. For a given a query video, we computed its SuperHistogram. This SuperHistogram is compared to the SuperHistograms that represent centers of all the clusters. The cluster whose center is closest to the SuperHistogram of the query video is searched further for similar videos. The top five matches for the query video are retrieved.

4 Experimental Results

For the experimental results we used a content set with 450 video segments which range from home video, TV programs, advertising videos for products on the Web, and medical videos. In this section we presents the experimental results for clustering in section 4.1 and retrieval in section 4.2.

4.1 Clustering

In the experiments the following considerations were taken into account:
1)   *The choice of experimental video content set*: We experimented with 41 video segments downloaded from different Web sites (Web videos) including home videos,

medical, sports, promotional videos and 41 digitized video segments from TV broadcast (TV videos) including soap, sitcom, commercial and news videos. For the results presented in the items 2) through 5) we used both content sets.

2)   *The method and threshold for comparison of histograms for finding Super-Histogram:* We experimented with L2 and Histogram Intersection comparison methods. We used the same method for generating SuperHistograms and for clustering. Using four clusters and 64 bins of the Y-space, Histogram Intersection had 70% in one cluster as opposed to 90% using L2 method. For Histogram intersection with the threshold at 25, 64 bins in Y space gave a better distribution than 8Y4U4V space. Five clusters had better distribution than three clusters.

3)   *The number of bins in the histogram used:* The best spread of the clusters was achieved for 16Y, 6U and 6V quantization for the TV videos using five clusters and the number of segments in each of the clusters were: 13, 8, 7, 7, 6. The best spread for the Web videos was achieved for 256 Y quantization (U and V are not considered) and the number of videos in the five clusters were: 18, 7, 7, 5, 4. This could be explained by the fact that the Web videos contained skiing events, car racing and outdoor imagery with lot of green and blue colors.

4)   *Number of clusters in the SuperHistogram Nearest Neighbor clustering:* In order to determine the best number of clusters, we varied the number of clusters and found the standard deviation (SD) of the number of videos in each cluster. A SD close to zero implies that the vectors were uniformly distributed across clusters. However, a high SD means that too many vectors were placed in one cluster and too few in others. This will also help us to eliminate quantization that do not have good discriminating power for a given number of clusters and a given histogram comparison method. Further, the number of clusters used for clustering the videos can be varied to experimentally find the number that gives the best spread. We varied the number of clusters to be 3, 5, 7, and 9. Tables 1 through 4 show the distribution of number of videos in each cluster for a given quantization level and given number of clusters for TV videos and Web videos.

Tables 1 and 2 present the results from clustering TV videos. In table 1 we present the results from clustering in the quantization space with 128 Y bins while U and V were ignored. With predefined number of clusters being 3, 5, 7, and 9 the number of videos in each cluster is given in each column. The last column presents the standard deviation (SD) i.e. how spread the clusters are. In this case the best distribution is achieved in the case of 9 clusters where the SD is 4.77. In table 2 we present the results from clustering in the quantization 576 bins which consisted of 16Yx6Ux6V. The best distribution is achieved in the case of 5 clusters were the SD is 2.78.

Tables 3 and 4 present the results from clustering videos downloaded from the Web. In table 3 we present the results from clustering in the quantization space with 128Y bins. In this case the best distribution is achieved in the case of 7 clusters were the standard deviation is 5.01. In table 4 we present the results from clustering in the quantization 576 bins which consisted of 16Yx6Ux6V. In this case, the best distribution is achieved in the case of 9 clusters were the standard deviation is 5.47.

Figure 3. gives a graphical representation of the standard deviation of five clusters in all the quantizations for 128 Y space for the TV videos. The X axis presents the color space, the Y axis presents the standard deviation. We notice that the cluster space with 576 bins (16Yx6Ux6V) gave the best spread for five clusters, i.e. 2.78.

No. of clust	Cluster 1	Cluster 2	Cluster 3	Cluster 4	Cluster 5	Cluster 6	Cluster 7	Cluster 8	Cluster 9	SD
3	32	6	3							15.95
5	16	13	10	1	1					6.91
7	14	10	8	5	2	1	1			5.01
9	13	12	6	3	2	2	1	1	1	4.77

Table 1. Clustering for TV videos for 128Y quantization.

No. of clust	Cluster 1	Cluster 2	Cluster 3	Cluster 4	Cluster 5	Cluster 6	Cluster 7	Cluster 8	Cluster 9	SD
3	24	11	6							9.29
5	13	8	7	7	6					2.78
7	13	8	7	6	3	2	2			3.97
9	14	7	7	6	2	2	1	1	1	4.39

Table 2. Clustering for TV videos for 576 (16Y, 6U, 6V) quantization.

No. of clust	Cluster 1	Cluster 2	Cluster 3	Cluster 4	Cluster 5	Cluster 6	Cluster 7	Cluster 8	Cluster 9	SD
3	23	9	9							8.08
5	22	10	6	2	1					8.49
7	14	10	8	5	2	1	1			5.01
9	16	9	6	4	2	1	1	1	1	5.12

Table 3. Clustering for Web videos for 128Y quantization.

No. of clust	Cluster 1	Cluster 2	Cluster 3	Cluster 4	Cluster 5	Cluster 6	Cluster 7	Cluster 8	Cluster 9	SD
3	25	10	6							10.01
5	27	5	4	4	1					10.61
7	24	5	3	3	2	2	2			8.07
9	18	8	4	3	2	2	2	1	1	5.47

Table 4. Clustering for Web videos for 576 (16Y, 6U, 6V) quantization.

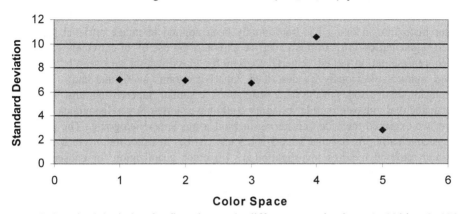

Fig. 3. Standard deviation for five clusters in different quantizations. 1: 64 bins, 2: 128 bins, 3: 256 bins, 4: 288 bins, 5: 576 bins.

4.2 Retrieval

From the content set of 450 video segments we chose 10 segments as queries for retrieval. We clustered the 440-video segments using various color quantization methods and into various numbers of clusters. The SuperHistogram of each of the query segment was compared to the SuperHistograms that represent centers of the clusters. The cluster whose center was closest to the SuperHistogram of the query video was searched further for similar videos. The top five matches for the query video were retrieved in this manner. Further, for measuring the performance, we retrieved the top five matches for the query video in all of the videos in the database. This is similar to performing an exhaustive 5 Nearest Neighbor (5NN) search for all the videos in the database. The percentage of the videos that are retrieved in both clustering retrieval and 5NN in the whole database (overlapped videos) will give an estimate of the clustering representativeness. For all the videos in the content set, we varied the number of clusters from 5 to 30 and we tried three different quantization methods: 128, 256, and 576 bins. Table 5 presents the percentage of overlapped videos in each of the cases. The best results were obtained when 7 clusters were used in the 576 bins (16Yx6Ux6V) quantization resulting in 78% overlap in retrieved video segments.

Table 5. Percentage of overlapped videos in Retrieval of Videos using multiple number of clusters and quantizations versus exhaustive Nearest Neighbor search of all the videos

Quantiza-tion	5 clusters	7 clusters	10 clusters	15 clusters	20 clusters	25 clusters	30 clusters
128 Y	36	36	26	32	48	36	34
256 Y	54	42	18	24	50	66	34
16Y6U6V	40	**78**	28	30	44	26	62

5 Concluding Remarks

Color histogram indexing has traditionally been applied to image retrieval [2] and video segmentation [10]. In this paper we explored the use of an extremely compact video representation called SuperHistogram for classification and search in large video archives. Previously we described SuperHistograms in [6] and had a general conclusion that episodes of the same program have similar SuperHistograms. We also speculated that videos of similar category could have similar SuperHistograms. In this paper we explored the video clustering method using SuperHistograms. The process of systematically proving that SuperHistograms can be instrumental in video clustering and retrieval requires investigation of: (a) color quantization for chosen color space, (b) methods to compare video segments based on SuperHistograms in order to perform the clustering, and (c) the number of clusters to be used for clustering, and (d) the appropriate content set. Our investigation proved that the choice of quantization can effectiveness of representation and retrieval. The best quantization was 16Yx6Ux6V colors (total 576 bins) achieving an overlap of 78%. The experiments showed that Histogram Intersection comparison measure for extraction of SuperHistograms and clustering resulted in a better cluster spread than L2 method. The number of clusters depends on the quantization scheme used, however in general 7 clusters worked best. In our investigations we used two vastly different content sets: TV videos with highly varied colors and Web videos with poor quality and dull colors (medical videos, home videos etc.) In the case of TV videos using all three components, Y, U and V with 576 bins gave better results. In the case of Web videos only using the Y color component and 128 bins gave the best results. This is intuitively satisfying because for highly colorful TV videos more bins and all color components are needed to characterize and cluster the videos, while for Web videos with dull colors fewer bins and just Y component is enough. Our conclusion is that systematic analysis of thematic visual elements such as color can assist in defining highly compact and richer characterization of video content using cumulatively averaged histograms, or Super-Histograms for video clustering.

6 Acknowledgements

We would like to thank Santhana Krishnamachari from Philips Research for his contribution to the SuperHistogram Nearest Neighbor clustering.

References

1.   M. Abdel-Mottaleb, N. Dimitrova, R. Desai and J. Martino, "CONIVAS: Cotent-based Image and Video Access System," Proc. of ACM Multimedia, 1996, pp 427-428
2.   M. Abdel-Mottaleb and R. Desai, "Image Retrieval by Local Color Features," The Fourth IEEE Symposium on Computers and Communications, Egypt, July 1999.

3. S-F. Chang, W. Chen, H. E. Meng, H. Sundaram and D. Zong, "VideoQ: An Automated Content Based Video Search System Using Visual Cues," *Proc. ACM Multimedia*, pp. 313-324, Seattle, 1997.

4. M. Christel, T. Kanade, M. Mauldin, R. Reddy, M. Sirbu, S. Stevens and H. Wactlar, "Informedia Digital Video Library," *Comm. of the ACM*, Vol. 38, No. 4, 1995, p57-58.

5. Belur V. Dasarathy, "Nearest Neighbor (NN) Norms: NN Pattern Classification Techniques," IEEE Computer Society Press, 1991.

6. N. Dimitrova, J. Martino, L. Agnihotri, and H. Elenbaas, "Color SuperHistograms for Video Representation," Int. Conf. on Image Processing, Japan, 1999.

7. R.C. Gonzalez and R.E. Woods, *Digital Image Processing*, Addison-Wesley Publishing Co., Inc., 1992.

8. Santhana Krishnamachari, and Mohamed Abdel-Mottaleb, "Heirarchical Clustering Algorithm for Fast Image Retrieval," *Proc. IS&T SPIE, Storage and Retrieval for Image and Video Databases VII,* Volume 3312, pp. 427-435, San Jose, 1999.

9. M.K. Mandal and T. Aboulnasr and S. Panchanatan, "Image indexing using moments and wavelets," *IEEE Transactions on Consumer Electronics*, Vol. 42, No. 3, August 1996.

10. A. Nagasaka and Y. Tanaka, "Automatic Video Indexing and Full Video Search for Object Appearances," *Visual Database Systems II*, Elsevier Sci. Pub., 1991, pp. 113, 127.

11. W. Niblack, X. Zhu, J.L. Hafner, T. Bruel, D. B. Ponceleon, D. Petkovic, M. Flickner, E. Upfal, S.I. Nin, S. Sull, B.E. Dom, "Updates to the QBIC System," *Proc. IS&T SPIE, Storage and Retrieval for Image and Video Databases VI,* Volume 3312, pp. 150-161, San Jose, 1998.

12. M. T. Orchard and C. A. Bouman, "Color Quantization of Images," *IEEE Trans. Signal Proc.*, Vol 39, No. 12, 1991.

3-D Camera Movements Tracking and Indexing Based on 2-D Hints Extraction

M. Ardebilian, W. Mahdi, L. Chen

Laboratoire ICTT, Département Mathématiques-Informatique
Ecole Centrale de Lyon, 36 avenue Guy de Collongue, BP 163 – 69131 Ecculy, Cedex – France
e-mail: {Mohsen.Ardabilan,Walid.Mahdi,Liming.Chen}@ec-lyon.fr

Abstract. Objects and camera movements are important clues which can be used for a better video and image understanding for content-based image and video indexing. In this paper, we propose a new general technique for 3-D camera movement tracking based on 2-D hints extracted from 2-D images. Our approach consists of extracting first 2-D hints based on object contours and calculating their different order derivatives. We then apply our pattern matching method to obtain objects movement vectors, and with help of 3-D projection theory, we detect the camera movement description in the 3-D space. The experiments that we have conducted on two video sequences show that our technique characterizes accurately the 3-D camera movement. The further work we have been undertaking shows that 2-D and 3-D hints combined with movement vectors can lead to 3-D scene description.

1. Introduction

Besides representative shot frames, further possibility to indexing a shot is its motion properties. The aim of motion detection is to be able to retrieve a ranked set of sequences, which have object motions similar to that specified by the query. This enables new content-based retrieval capabilities, which are particularly valuable to postproduction activities such as video editing. For instance, an editor may need to select, among a set of shots already retrieved for instance based on a query image, those that have been recorded with a particular camera operation such as zoom in. Moreover, automatic camera motions detection can be used for video clips production aiming at a nice visual impact, complying with a number of rules so as to the concatenation of shots which limits the use of successive zooms.

The motion detection has been the focus of many researchers working in the image-processing field. Ioka and Kuroka [1] have presented a method for retrieving sequences using motion information as a key. Although this technique does not address the problem of correspondence of trajectories, it can be incorporated as a low level tool into a complete video data management system for raw feature-based retrieval. Dimitrova and Golshani [2] have proposed a technique based on the motion compensation component of the MPEG video encoder, while Lee and Kao [3] have presented a video indexing approach based on the motion representation for the track of a motion object using optical flow for motion extraction.

R. Laurini (Ed.): VISUAL 2000, LNCS 1929, pp. 74–83, 2000.
Springer-Verlag Berlin Heidelberg 2000

In this paper, we focus particularly on 3-D camera motion tracking based on 2-D hints from the video frames. To achieve this, we first extract 2-D hints from successive frames of the video, setting up the matching between them ; Then using properties of the projective geometry we compute the 3-D camera motion trough the video sequence.

The rest of the paper is organized as follows : we define the various camera operations and give an overview of related work in section 2 ; section 3 summarizes our 2-D hints extraction technique which has also been used for shot detection in a previous work ; In section 4 we introduce in detail our 3-D camera movement tracking method, depicting the algorithm ; Some experimental evidence is presented in section 5 ; Finally, we conclude our work by a summary of our technique and indication to future direction.

2. Camera operations and related work

The seven basic camera operations are fixed, panning (horizontal rotation), tracking (horizontal transverse movement), tilting (vertical rotation), booming (vertical transverse movement), zooming (varying the focus distance), and dollying (horizontal lateral movement) as shown in figure.1. Camera operations include the basic operations and all the different possible combinations [4].

Akutsu and al. [4] have used motion vectors and their Hough transform to identify the seven basic camera operations. We note this technique based on motion vectors is noise sensitive and has a high computational complexity. Srinivasan et al. [5] have proposed a technique based on optical flow in order to distinguish tracking from panning and booming from tilting. An alternative approach in detecting camera operations is to examine what are known as the X-ray images [6]. A comprehensive survey of motion and camera operations detection techniques has been proposed by Idris and Panchanathan [7] and in [8].

We can note that all these approaches just provide a global indication of camera motion instead of an accurate estimation in the 3-D space as our technique will enable.

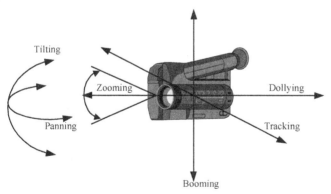

Fig. 1. Camera operations.

3.   2-D motion calculation based on 2-D hints

The first step of our 3-D camera movement tracking technique is the extraction of some 2-D hints from the video sequence and characterizing their 2-D motion. The same clues have been used in our previous work for efficient shot detection [9][10]. The extraction of these 2-D hints is followed by their motion tracking, giving birth to a set of feature points which are the input of our 3-D camera motion tracking method as we will explain in the next section.

3.1   2-D hints extraction

As the most of image processing and vision analysis techniques, our method is based on contour images. The basic way to obtain contour images consists of applying a contour filter to successive images of a video sequence. In our implementation we have used Canny edge detector filter. Once the contour image obtained, the next step is the contour matching which gives us 2-D motion through the video stream. However information of contour pixels only is not sufficient to lead to a robust matching algorithm. We have to add other geometrical information to contour pixels. For this purpose, we perform a fast connective Hough Transform on each n successive pixels to find the orientation of the contour (first derivative) and we label each contour portion. The Connective Hough Transform appears as a classification method, which groups pixels into a class by their connectivity. Then to each contour pixel is associated a label, which encodes the pixel position, its edge label which also gives the local edge orientation and its length. The binary contour image is thus transformed into a more consistent image which makes the contour and pixel matching easier.

3.2   2-D motion tracking

Once all possible contour pixels are labeled, two successive frames are superimposed and nearest contour pixels are matched with respect to their respective label. The *Euclidean Distance* is a suitable metric to express the similarity of two corresponding pixels as all possible information about a contour pixel and its neighborhood is already encoded in its label.

The matching procedure above is repeated for all images from the video sequence and contour pixels having the longest lifetime are selected for 3-D camera movement processing. We can note that the above approach is a general algorithm for feature points extraction and tracking. Other specific approaches have been proposed to achieve this. For sake of simplicity, we assume that there is no large moving object dominating the visual field in the video sequence. Otherwise, motion clustering and compensation can be used to reduce the effect of large moving objects.

4.   3-D camera tracking based on 2-D and 3-D hints

From points or lines moving in a scene as observed in a sequence of images, can we compute their 3-D motion, which leads to 3-D camera motion ?

This problem is known as *structure from motion* or *shape from motion* [11] [12] that we develop in this section. We have paid special attention to robustness of the method because solution resulted from the computation not only must be exact when all data are accurate but also give a good approximation of 3-D camera motion in the presence of noise as this always occurs, especially in compressed video. To achieve this, we first present a computational formalism that deals with 2-D plane from the stand point of projective geometry [13].

A point in the image represents a possible line of sight of an incoming ray. Any 3-D point along the ray projects a same point on the image. Thus only the direction of the ray is relevant. The image plane is regarded as a 2-D projective space, and points and lines represented by their homogeneous coordinates. That is, we suppose that the camera is at the origin, and a point is designated by a triplet (x_1, x_2, x_3) of real numbers, not all of them being 0, and defined up to a scale factor. These three numbers are called *homogenous coordinates*. If $x_3 \quad 0$, point (x_1, x_2, x_3) is identified with the point $(f \dfrac{x_1}{x_3}, f \dfrac{x_2}{x_3})$ on the image plane. Therefore, the coordinates of an image point p corresponding to a scene point $X = (x_1, x_2, x_3)$ is:

$$p = (f \frac{x_1}{x_3}, f \frac{x_2}{x_3}) \tag{1}$$

where f is the focal length in the camera model. Figure.2 illustrates the camera model.

This representation is called image coordinates or *inhomogeneous coordinates*. We can assume that $f = 1$ as different values of f only give different scalings of the image. Thus any image point can be represented by its homogenous coordinates.

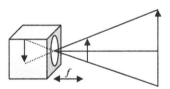

Fig. 2. Camera model

A full pinhole camera model incorporates intrinsic parameters and is described by some matrix A such as the whole image production in homogenous coordinate can be written by:

$$p = \begin{bmatrix} x_1/x_3 \\ x_2/x_3 \\ 1 \end{bmatrix} \quad \begin{bmatrix} x_1 \\ x_2 \\ x_3 \end{bmatrix} = A \begin{bmatrix} 1 & 0 & 0 & 0 \\ 0 & 1 & 0 & 0 \\ 0 & 0 & 1 & 0 \end{bmatrix} \begin{bmatrix} x_1 \\ x_2 \\ x_3 \\ 1 \end{bmatrix}, \quad A = \begin{bmatrix} s_x & s & u_0 \\ 0 & s_y & v_0 \\ 0 & 0 & 1 \end{bmatrix} \tag{2}$$

where s_x and s_y stand for the scalings along $\vec{x}$ and $\vec{y}$ axes of the image plane, s gives the skew between axes, and (u_0, v_0) are the coordinates of the intersection of the principal axis and the image plane.

A set of image points extracted by the technique described in the previous section can now be considered in their homogenous coordinates. The 3-D camera movement can be deduced from the 3-D movement of a rigid object. That is, viewed from the camera, we observe a moving scene which is considered as a moving rigid object. We compute the 3-D motion of the rigid object and we deduce the camera motion by taking exactly the opposite motion.

Let $\{p\}$, $= 1,...,N$, be a set of image points corresponding to a set of feature points. By a camera motion $\{R, h\}$ where R is a rotation and h a translation, image points move to other positions on the image plane, so $\{p\}$ move also into other positions $\{p\}$. The Euler's theorem proves that every rotation matrix represents a rotation around an axis by some angle. Thus, respective points and camera motion parameters satisfy:

$$p \ A^{T} h \ R A^{1} p \ = p \ F p \ = 0, \qquad = 1,...,N. \tag{3}$$

where the matrix F is called *fundamental matrix*.

To solve the above equation we use the approach named *essential matrix* and *eight-point algorithm* [14] where the *essential matrix* E is defined as:

$$E = h \ R \tag{4}$$
$$= (h \ r_1, h \ r_2, h \ r_3)$$

and r_i and h are column vectors. The relation between the *essential* and *fundamental matrix* can be expressed as:

$$F = A^{T} h \ R A^{1} \tag{5}$$

In our approach, as a first step, the coordinates in both images are translated (by a unique translation) so as to bring the centroid of the set of all points at the origin, then all coordinates are scaled so that the average distance from the origin is equal to $\sqrt{2}$, giving birth to what we call *Normalized Images*. The advantage of this scaling is twofold: First we do not need to compute the intrinsic parameters and second motion parameters R and h can be directly processed from such normalized images. The results obtained by a simple algorithm such as 8-point algorithm on normalized images are comparable to the best iterative algorithms.

The essential matrix E can be robustly estimated, up to sign, by the following least-square optimization [15] of the epipolar equation:

$$\sum_{=1}^{N} \frac{1}{N} (p' , E p) \quad min, \qquad \|E\| = \sqrt{2}, \qquad rank(E) = 2 \tag{6}$$

However, the solution is difficult to obtain analytically, so we introduce an "engineering compromise": we regard the nine element of E as "independent variables". Let $p_{(i)}$ and $p'_{(i)}$ be the ith components of vectors p and p', respectively. Then, the sum of squares of eq.6 is written in elements as:

$$\sum_{=1}^{N} \frac{1}{N} (p' , E p)^2 = \sum_{i,j,k,l=1}^{3} \sum_{=1}^{N} \frac{1}{N} p'_{(i)} p_{(j)} p'_{(k)} p_{(l)} E_{ij} E_{kl} \tag{7}$$

If tensor $M = (M_{ijkl})$ is defined by

$$M_{ijkl} = \sum_{=1}^{N} \frac{1}{N} p'_{(i)} p_{(j)} p'_{(k)} p_{(l)}, \tag{8}$$

The minimization is written in the form:

$$(E, M E) = \sum_{i,j,k,l=1}^{3} M_{ijkl} E_{ij} E_{kl} \quad min \quad \|E\|^2 = \sum_{i,j=1}^{3} E_{ij}^2 = 2, \quad rank(E) = 2 \tag{9}$$

We define a nine dimensional vector $\hat{E} = (\hat{E}_k)$ by renaming indices (i,j) of E_{ij} as $k = 3(i-1) + j$. Similarly, we define a nine dimensional matrix $\hat{M} = (\hat{M}_{\mu\nu})$ by renaming two pairs of indices (i,j) and (k,l) of M_{ijkl} as $(\mu, \nu) = (3(i-1) + j, 3(k-1) + l)$. Now the minimization above reads:

$$(\hat{E}, \hat{M}\hat{E}) = \sum_{\mu,\nu=1}^{9} \hat{M}_{\mu\nu} \hat{E}_{\mu} \hat{E}_{\nu} \quad min, \quad \|\hat{E}\|^2 = \sum_{\mu=1}^{9} \hat{E}_{\mu}^2 = 2, rank(\hat{E}) = 2. \tag{10}$$

The minimum is attained by the nine dimensional eigenvector $\hat{E}$ of norm $\sqrt{2}$ of matrix $\hat{M}$ for the smallest eigenvalue. The nine dimensional matrix $E = (E_{\mu})$ is then rearranged into a three dimensional matrix by renaming the index $:i = (\mu - 1) \, div \, 3 + 1, \, j = (\mu - 1) \, mod \, 3 + 1$. Nevertheless, the essential matrix will not in general have rank 2, and we should take steps to enforce this constraint. A convenient method of doing this is to use the Singular Value Decomposition (SVD). In particular, let $E = UDV^T$ be the SVD of E, where D is a diagonal matrix $D = diag(r, s, t)$ satisfying $r \geq s \geq t$. We let $E = U \, diag(r, s, 0) V^T$.

Once the essential matrix E is computed, motion parameters $\{R, h\}$ are deducted by the decomposition of E. To achieve this, we compute the unit eigenvector of $E E^T$ for the smallest eigenvalue. Then, we define the correlation matrix $K = h\ E$, and compute a rotation matrix R such that:

$$trace\left(R^T K\right) \quad max \tag{11}$$

and a four dimensional matrix $\hat{K}$ from K components as:

$$\hat{K} = \begin{matrix} k_{11}+k_{22}+k_{33} & k_{32}\ k_{23} & k_{13}\ k_{31} & k_{21}\ k_{12} \\ k_{32}\ k_{23} & k_{11}\ k_{22}\ k_{33} & k_{12}\ k_{21} & K_{31}\ k_{13} \\ k_{13}\ k_{31} & k_{12}\ k_{21} & k_{11}+k_{22}\ k_{33} & k_{23}+k_{32} \\ k_{21}\ k_{12} & K_{31}\ k_{13} & k_{23}+k_{32} & k_{11}\ k_{22}+k_{33} \end{matrix} \tag{12}$$

Let $\hat{q}$ be the four dimensional unit eigenvector of $\hat{K}$ for the largest eigenvalue. $trace\left(R^T K\right)$ is maximized by the rotation R represented by $\hat{q}$. The axis l and angle of the rotation are represented by $\hat{q}$ and deducted as :

$$= 2\cos^{-1} q_1, \qquad l = (q_2, q_3, q_4)\left(q_2^2 + q_3^2 + q_4^2\right)^{\frac{1}{2}}, \qquad if\ q_1\ 0,$$

$$= 2(\quad \cos^{-1} q_1), \qquad l = (q_2, q_3, q_4)\left(q_2^2 + q_3^2 + q_4^2\right)^{\frac{1}{2}}, \qquad if\ q_1 < 0. \tag{13}$$

Algorithm 1 summarizes the different steps of our method.

1.	Image normalization.
2.	Compute the tensor matrix M from two set of points p and p , $= 1,..., N$.
3.	Process all eigenvalues of M and the nine dimensional eigenvector corresponding to the smallest eigenvalue.
4.	Rearrange the eigenvector of step2 into a three dimensional matrix E.
5.	Enforce the singularity constraint.
6.	Process the eigenvector h corresponding to the smallest eigenvector of the matrix EE^T.
7.	Deduce the matrix $\hat{K}$ from the correlation matrix $K = h\ E$.
8.	Process the four dimensional eigenvector $\hat{q}$, corresponding to the largest eigenvalue of $\hat{K}$.
9.	Compute the rotation axis l and angle from $\hat{q}$.
10.	Return $\{l,\ ,h\}$.

Algorithm 1

Once the frame to frame camera motion estimation accomplished, we can generate the camera operation parameters through the entire video shot. These parameters can be used as indices for the video sequence retrieval. To achieve this, the most convenient way is to separate the several camera movement stemming from a video shot in case camera operations can be concatenated.

5.   Experimental results

To show the effectiveness of our method,   we have applied our 3-D camera tracking technique on two video sequences. As illustrated by Figure.3. (a) and (b), the first sequence is extracted from the movie "Talons Aiguilles". Figure 3.(c) shows the eight feature points extracted from each frame while Figure.3.(d) presents different views of the rotation axis which have been computed by our algorithm. The following table gives the computed three 3-D camera motion (is the rotation angle, l is the rotation axis and h is the translation axis). From these results one can straightforward deduce the camera movements such as camera rotation or translation direction in a video sequence while zoom in or zoom out are detected as forward or backward translations.

Motion parameters	Computational Results
(degree)	1.76383989564260
l	0.26859160954663 -0.88916392693631 -0.37046735121513
h	0.25621933702021 0.29271919643769 -0.92123130829005
smallest eigenvalue	8.366070956052572e-018

Table 1. The result of camera motion calculation.

Figure.4 illustrates 5 images extracted from another video shot. The results of the camera movement segmentation are shown in (f) for the translation and (g) for the rotation. From these results we can conclude that the camera makes an increasing translation along the $\bar{y}$ axis combined with a dominant rotation along the $\widehat{z o y}$ axis until the frame 10 and then $\bar{y}$ axis.

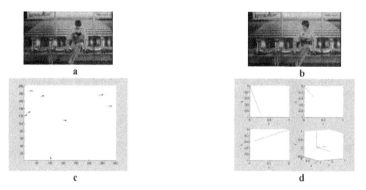

a   b

c   d

Fig. 3. Two frames extracted from a video sequence (a), (b);   (c) illustrates feature points obtained from images (a) and (b); (d) illustrates the rotation axis processed.

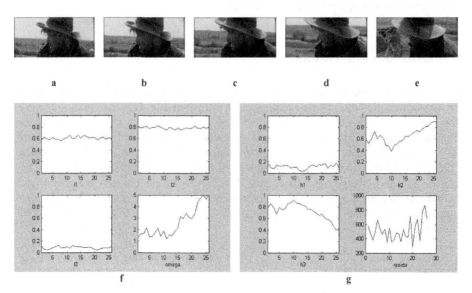

Fig. 4. Five frames from a second video shot (a-e). (f) Illustrates the dominant translation and (g) the rotation movements.

6.   Conclusion

In this paper we have described a new technique for 3-D camera movement characterization for content-based video indexing. We have first summarized a fast connective Hough transform based 2-D hints extraction technique which has also been used for shot detection. The motion assessment of these 2-D hints has also been introduced. We have then developed 3-D camera motion detection technique which makes use of projective geometry theory and least-square optimization.

Experimental results conducted on two real video sequences shows the effectiveness of our method characterizing accurately the 3-D camera movements. Future expansion of our work will include the depth estimation of all feature points extracted from the video frame and ultimately 3-D scene reconstruction.

References

1. M. Ioka and M. Kuroka, *A method for retrieving sequences of images on the basis of motion analysis, Proc. SPIE: Integration Issues Large Commercial Media Delivery Systems* **2615**, 1995, 2-16.

2. N. Dimitrova and F. Golshani, *Method for semantic database retrieval, ACM Multimedia 94*, 1994, 219-226.
3. S. Y. Lee and H. M. Kao, *Video indexing –An approach based on moving object and track, Proc. SPIE : Storage Retrieval Image Video Databases*, 1993, 25-36.
4. A. Akutsu, Y. Tonomura, H. Hashimoto, and Y. Ohba, *Video indexing using motion vectors, Proc. SPIE : Visual Commun. Image Process.* 92 **1818**, 1992, 1522-1530.
5. M. V. Srinivasan, S. Venkatesh, and R. Hosie, *Qualitative Estimation of Camera Motion Parameters from Video Sequences.*
6. A. Akutsu and Tonomura, Video Tomography: *An efficient method for camerawork extraction and motion analysis, Acm Multimedia94*, 1994, 349-356.
7. F. Idris and S. Panchanathan, *Review of Image and Video Indexing, Techniques Journal of Visual Communication and Image Representation* Vol. 8. No. 2, June, 1997, 146-166.
8. *Visual Information Retrieval*, A. Del bimbo, Morgan Kauffman Edition, 1999.
9. M. Ardebilian, X.W. Tu, L. Chen, *Video Segmantation Using 3-D Hints Contained in 2-D Images, Proc. SPIE : Multimedia Strage and Archiving Systems I*, Boston, USA, 1996.
10. M. Ardebilian, X. W. Tu, L. Chen, *Improvement of Shot Detection Methods Based-on Dynamic Threshold Selection, Proc. SPIE : Multimedia Strage and Archiving Systems II*, Dallas, USA, 1997.
11. O. D. Faugeras and S. Maybank, *Motion from point matches : Multiplicity of solutions, International Journal of Computer Vision*, **4**, 1990, 118-121.
12. E. Hildreth, *The Mesurement of Visual Motion*, MIT Press, 1983.
13. K. Kanatani, Geometric *Computation for Machine Vision, Oxford Engineering Science Series . 37, Oxford Science Publications*, 1993.
14 . R. Hartley, *In defence of the 8-point algorithm , Proc. ICCV, Cambridge MA USA*, 1995, 1064-1070.
15. G. H. Golub and C. Reinsch, *Singular value decomposition and least-squares solutions, Numerische Mathematik*, **14**, 1970, 404-420.

Main Mobile Object Detection and Localization in Video Sequences

Gabriel Tsechpenakis, Yiannis Xirouhakis and Anastasios Delopoulos

Image, Video and Multimedia Systems Laboratory,
Dept. of Electrical and Computer Eng.,
National Technical University of Athens,
Zographou Campus, 15773 Athens, Greece,
{gtsech,jxiro,adelo}@image.ntua.gr

Abstract. Main mobile object detection and localization is a task of major importance in the fields of video understanding, object-based coding and numerous related applications, such as content-based retrieval, remote surveillance and object recognition.
The present work revisits the algorithm proposed in [13] for mobile object localization in both indoor and outdoor sequences when either a static or a mobile camera is utilized. The proposed approach greatly improves the trade-off between accuracy and time-performance leading to satisfactory results with a considerably low amount of computations. Moreover, based on the point gatherings extracted in [13], the bounding polygon and the direction of movement are estimated for each mobile object; thus yielding an adequate representation in the MPEG-7 sense.
Experimental results over a number of distinct natural sequences have been included to illustrate the performance of the proposed approach.

1 Introduction

The detection of mobile objects in video sequences has been one of the major tasks in computer vision and video understanding. However, until lately, its use has been limited to specific applications such as traffic scenes monitoring and intrusion detection. During the last decade, the rapidly growing ideas of object-based video coding and content-based video retrieval, and the guidelines of the respective MPEG-4 and MPEG-7 standards, have emerged for successful mobile object detection and localization.

For a sequence acquired by a moving camera, the proposed approaches can be categorized into two classes: the first considering $3D$ camera motion as known and deriving constraints for objects' $2D$ motion parameters [9,1], and the second constructing a $2D$ parametric motion model for the background *dominant* motion [7]. Based on the obtained motion estimation results, mobile objects are then extracted using a variety of motion segmentation algorithms. Most such implementations for mobile object detection have been reported to either yield inadequate results or more often lead to not satisfactory execution times. For the special case of static cameras, the approaches can be divided again in two

R. Laurini (Ed.): VISUAL 2000, LNCS 1929, pp. 84–95, 2000.
Springer-Verlag Berlin Heidelberg 2000

main categories: the feature-based depending on the extraction of sequences' general characteristics [10] and the pixel-based examining the differences between successive frames using pixels as input features. Among pixel-based methods, luminance-based [3] and edge-based [4–6] approaches have been proposed, with the latter being reported as more robust.

A rather common consideration in mobile object localization is the trade-off between accuracy and time-efficiency. For instance, the MPEG-4 standard requires a relatively accurate mask containing only the mobile object, while for the MPEG-7 standard suffices having the bounding polygon (or even the bounding rectangle). In the general case, aside from the coding standards, different accuracy/performance trade-offs are acceptable by different applications; different levels of detail are for example required for content-based retrieval in terms of low level features [12] or semantics [2]. This trade-off is not so crucial in the static camera case, as it is when a mobile camera is utilized and thus requiring complex operations such as motion estimation and segmentation. Exploiting this fact, the method proposed in [13] extended an existing algorithm for static cameras [5] to the mobile camera case. Compared to existing techniques on mobile object detection with moving cameras [7, 9], the algorithm proposed in [13] was proved to be significantly faster, while the obtained accuracy was worse but comparable to the algorithms employing motion segmentation ideas.

The present work revisits the particular algorithm [13] and proposes a number of additions/modifications that substantially improve the accuracy of the obtained results. In contrast to [13], where the intruder was described as a gathering of points/pixels on image transient edges, in this work the latter are utilized to define the bounding polygon of the moving object. The direction of image transient edges is also estimated using a binary search criterion enabling clustering of the edges into separable moving objects. In this way, more than one main mobile objects can be localized and extracted from the sequence, accompanied by the respective 'direction of movement' attribute.

In [13], it is assumed that between successive frames background motion can be well approximated by a simple translation. Although, this may be true, at the same time, background updating can fail due to misfit of the compensated frames, leading to an increased set of transient edges, some of which belong in fact to the background. In this work, background updating is greatly enhanced by imposing another criterion before determining whether a certain edge is transient: the preservation of gradient direction through time. In general, stationary image portions (e.g. compensated background) preserve the direction of their gradient, whereas transient portions (e.g. object boundary and occluded background) do not. Finally, in the presence of severe temporal clutter, median filtering is proved inadequate for noise reduction, whereas a certain category of thinning filters performs better.

Since the main advantage of the proposed approach is its reduced time-complexity, significant attention has been paid so that most operations are reduced to their binary counterparts, given that they are performed on the edge maps and not the images themselves. Experimental results on natural sequences have been included to verify the efficiency of the algorithm. As it will be seen, the bounding polygon extracted in the present work can be often directly compared to the object contour extracted by other methods in the area. The latter holds true, since extracted contours are in most cases so noisy, that poorly describe the object physical boundary; commonly unsuitable for shape-based recognition or retrieval purposes [2, 11].

2   The proposed approach

2.1   The background compensation module

In order to eliminate background motion due to camera egomotion, a motion estimation scheme has to be employed. Parametric motion estimation schemes, while slightly improve the obtained motion field, dramatically increase computational load. At the same time, for successive (or nearly successive) frames in an image sequence, background motion can be assumed to be translational. In this sense, a simple non-parametric non-iterative block-matching scheme would be adequate. Still though, supposing that background motion is translational and that main mobile objects cover only a portion of the background, we can avoid dense motion field estimation and save computational time. In this work, an exhaustive-search block-matching motion estimation scheme is performed for a subset of every frame's pixels. The three-step logarithmic-search employed in [13], although faster, was proved not trustworthy for certain experiments.

Let $N \times M$ denote the input frame dimensions and p_N, p_M denote the percentage of pixels on each column and row of the image respectively, for which motion estimation is performed. These pixels are considered to be equally spaced on a column/row, having no prior knowledge for the location of the mobile object on the particular pair of frames. Since main mobile objects cover only a portion of each frame, it is expected that most of the obtained $(p_N N) \times (p_M M)$ motion estimates belong to the background and thus share similar values. Background motion is chosen as the most frequent vector in the set $\mathbf{U}$ of the motion estimates, or

$$\delta(f) = m(\mathbf{U}(f)) \,, \tag{1}$$

where $m()$ denotes the 'majority' operation (which equals a histogram operation with pre-determined bins), f denotes the current frame and $\delta(f)$ background motion from frame f-1 to frame f.

In this sense, given a pair of successive frames, $\delta(f)$ is obtained. In terms of such consecutive motion estimation processes, background motion is derived for any $\mathbf{I}(f_1)$ and $\mathbf{I}(f_2)$ at time instances f_1 and f_2. Let $\mathbf{d}(f_1, f_2)$ denote the corresponding background motion. Then, current frame $\mathbf{I}(f)$ is motion-compensated with reference to $\mathbf{I}(f_r)$ by $\mathbf{d}(f_r, f) \equiv [d_i \ d_j]$ as,

$$\mathbf{I}^c(i, j, f) = \mathbf{I}(i + d_i, j + d_j, f_r) \,, \tag{2}$$

where $\mathbf{I}(i, j, f)$ generally denotes the intensity value of a pixel with spatial coordinates (i, j) on frame f, and exponent (c) denotes the compensated frame counterpart.

2.2   The background updating module

The basic concept of background updating techniques is the slow insertion of the changed areas of the observed scene into a reference background image. Thus, a changed area of the observed scene (which then remains unchanged for a certain amount of time) is interpreted as a newly detected static feature of the scene and, consequently, is inserted into the reference background image. Otherwise, the observed alteration is considered as either a moving object or noise. In the particular background updating module, we implement the edge-based method of [5], which is proved to be remarkably robust for both indoor and outdoor scenes. The method's main advantage is its ability to distinguish and reject changes, which occur due to the existence of excessive temporal clutter in an observed scene, even due to objects (i.e small trees and plants) whose small but still noticeable motion proves rather confusing for other methods.

In order to update the reference background image, the particular algorithm uses a frame counter, whose increment depends on the following criterion,

$$\mathbf{C}_e(i, j, f) \;=\; \mathbf{C}_e(i, j, f-1) + \mathbf{E}(i, j, f) \,, \tag{3}$$

where $\mathbf{E}(i, j, f)$ is the edge map at pixel (i, j) at time instance f corresponding to frame pixel $\mathbf{I}(i, j, f)$, and $\mathbf{C}_e(i, j, f)$ is the respective frame counter value. Every edge pixel (i, j) that appears in the current input frame f raises pixel (i, j) of the frame counter, while the absence of an input edge in this location results in a respective decrease. Thus, static edges produce high values, whereas transient edges result in lower values of the frame counter. The reference background image is obtained by thresholding the counter,

$$\mathbf{B}(i, j, f) \;=\; \begin{cases} 1, & \text{if } \mathbf{C}_e(i, j, f) > \tau_a \\ 0, & \text{if } \mathbf{C}_e(i, j, f) \le \tau_a \end{cases}, \tag{4}$$

where threshold τ_a is the adaptation time or insertion delay of the background updating module.

Although such a criterion may be suitable for static cameras, background updating in the mobile case can fail due to misfit of the compensated frames, leading to an increased set of transient edges. In this work, background updating is enhanced by imposing another criterion before determining whether a certain region is transient or static. It is clear that we are at most interested in transient edges belonging to the object's contour rather than to its interior. At the same time, the contour of a moving object covers/uncovers parts of the background between time instants. In this context, the intensity change can quite reliably indicate the location of the moving contour.

Let $\nabla \mathbf{I}(i, j, f)$ denote the gradient at an image pixel and $\mathbf{G}(i, j, f)$ denote its direction,

$$\mathbf{G}(i, j, f) \;=\; \angle\, \nabla \mathbf{I}(i, j, f) \,. \tag{5}$$

By employing a similar counter $\mathbf{C}_g(i, j, f)$ to determine whether a pixel should be inserted in the background, we would increase the counter when $\mathbf{G}(i, j, f) \equiv$

$\mathbf{G}(i, j, f - 1)$. In short,

$$\mathbf{C}_g(i, j, f) = \mathbf{C}_g(i, j, f - 1) + (\Delta\mathbf{G}(i, j) < t_g) , \tag{6}$$

where t_g is a small angle. Then, the background is updated w.r.t.

$$\mathbf{B}(i, j, f) = \begin{cases} 1, & \text{if } \mathbf{C}_g(i, j, f) > \tau_b \\ 0, & \text{if } \mathbf{C}_g(i, j, f) \leq \tau_b \end{cases} , \tag{7}$$

where threshold τ_b is the corresponding adaptation time.

It has been experimentally verified that the two conditions together perform better than each one of them. Clearly conditions (4) and (7) can then be written in one decision module; if moreover we choose $\tau_a \equiv \tau_b$, one counter can be updated for both criteria.

2.3   Extracting the transient edges

Since both the current frame and the resulting reference background are binary edge images, the extraction of transient edges at pixel (i, j) is accomplished through a logical operator that isolates the input edges which are absent in the updated reference background image:

$$\mathbf{T}(i, j, f) = \mathbf{E}(i, j, f) \wedge \overline{\mathbf{B}(i, j, f)} , \tag{8}$$

where $(\wedge)$ and $(\bar{\ })$ denote the logical operators AND and NOT respectively.

The use of the logical operators AND/NOT results in a bilevel edge image $\mathbf{T}$, consisting of both the gradient edges of the mobile object present in the observed scene (if any) and the sparse remnants of the background edges, due to temporal clutter. In [13] median filtering is utilized to suppress noise, since mobile objects edges are spatially coherent, while the background remnants due to temporal clutter are spread randomly over extensive areas of the input frames.

However, it can be seen that median filtering in bilevel images in fact is equivalent to binary 'majority' filtering, leading to inadequate results for excessive temporal clutter. In other words, such a filtering scheme neglects the edge connectivity properties. On the other hand, unlike temporal clutter, mobile objects' boundaries consist of thick transient edges. In this context, convolution with a thinning kernel seems most appropriate.

2.4   Estimating direction of movement

Along the lines of the previous subsections, one has managed to come up with gatherings of pixels on transient edges, which themselves imply the position and size of the mobile object [13]. However, in the general case, more than one main mobile objects may be present in the scene, relatively close to each other (or even occluding one another) so that clustering the pixels into objects is essential. At the same time, it is interesting to estimate the direction of movement for each mobile object; such a task is mandatory in remote surveillance with the cameras tracking the intruder, and in content-based retrieval systems allowing queries such as 'a red object moving south-east'.

For that purpose, a block matching module is incorporated in the system. However, the time complexity involved by this process is negligible, since motion estimation is performed only for pixels belonging to transient edges. Moreover, the block matching scheme is applied to the bilevel images, reducing all computations to logical operations. In our implementation, we even chose to count the edge pixels included in each block to decide for the best matching block, instead of computing for example the mean absolute difference. For very complex images, it may be appropriate to perform motion estimation between the compensated frames, instead of their bilevel counterparts. However, even in this case the subset of pixels at hand is not by any means comparable to the total number of pixels in the frame.

Having available the motion information for the edge pixels, a motion-clustering scheme (e.g a self-organizing map) determines their classification in mobile objects. Another, not so obvious, property of this process is that it permits the rejection of edge pixels not obeying to some criteria, for example forming a small insignificant object.

2.5   Extracting the bounding polygon

In the final module, for each mobile object, its bounding polygon is extracted. Since more than one polygons may contain every mobile object (point set), we estimate the convex hull (the smallest convex polygon containing the point set). Indicatively, we utilize the Graham Scan method, which is computationally inexpensive, in particular when the points' coordinates are integers as in our case (see [8] for an implementation).

The particular shape representation is closely related to the alarm/detection decision module. For example, in [5], alarm decision was taken when edge points exceeded a certain threshold. In our case, maybe the area of the bounding polygon is the most secure choice. As in [5], the use of a temporal min-filter ensures that the detection module is not vulnerable to abrupt illumination variations.

Table 1. Open parameters

Parameter	Description	Constraints-Dependencies
r	frame-rate	relative camera velocity
a	motion estimation search area	relative camera velocity
τ_u	reference frame updating time	relative camera velocity
τ_a	background adaptation time	illumination changes
τ_l	min-filter length	illumination changes
t_d	detection decision threshold	bounding polygon area

2.6   Setting the open parameters

The proposed algorithm involves a number of open parameters, whose successful tuning ensures the algorithm's performance for different types of sequences.
Table 1 summarizes the aforementioned parameters.

The camera velocity relative to background, affects the motion compensation
process, thus large velocities require higher frame-rates (r) and larger block-
matching search areas (a). Large camera velocities towards a certain direction,
mandate for frequent reference background updating (τ_u). The background adaptation time (τ_a) and the min-filter length (τ_l) account for the algorithm's immu-
nity to abrupt/gradual illumination changes; τ_a is set well above the duration
of such a change while generally $\tau_a < \tau_l < 2\tau_a$. The detection decision threshold
(t_d) equals the area of the smallest object deemed as a main mobile one. The
threshold t_g indicating significant gradient-angle change and a similar threshold
t_e for the edge detection module are of minor contribution to the algorithm's
performance.

3   Experimental results

The proposed algorithm's performance was tested on a large number of natural sequences obtained using a hand-held camera. The employed frames were
initially available in PAL format and then appropriately subsampled so as to
derive their non-interlaced counterparts. In Figures 1(a)-(c) three frames of an
indoor sequence acquired by a static camera are depicted. In this convenient
case, the Makarov's algorithm yields adequate results for both successive and
non-successive frames of the sequence. In Figures 1(d)-(f) and 1(g)-(i) the results of the background updating and the motion detection scheme are illustrated. The algorithm was proved to be robust despite the varying lightening
conditions imposed during capturing.

In Figures 2(a)-(c) three non-successive frames of an outdoor sequence acquired by a mobile camera are illustrated. Camera motion was normal in speed,
however trembling and small $3D$ rotations were imposed. The compensated
frame counterparts w.r.t. a previous reference frame are depicted in Figures 2(d)-
(f). Despite the complex background, the considerable temporal clutter and the
relatively complex camera movement, the estimated transient edges are accurate
(Figures 2(g)-(i)).

Figure 3 was obtained from a TV news program. A single mobile object
is successfully extracted for an outdoor capture by means of a hand-held video
camera. Since a slight rotation is imposed to the camera during capturing for this
sequence, we test the assumption for nearly translational background movement
between successive frames. Figures 3(d)-(f) depict the extracted edge maps, while
in Figures 3(g)-(i), the transient edges of the main mobile object along with the
estimated bounding polygon are illustrated.

Figure 4 illustrates the performance of the algorithm in the presence of significant temporal clutter. In this case, even the mobile object moves in a par-

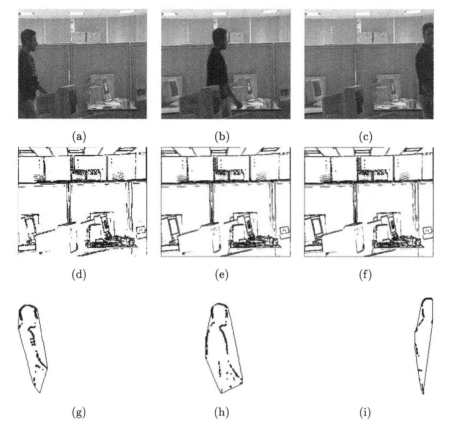

Fig. 1. Mobile object detection for a complex object (human body) in an indoor sequence acquired by a static camera (a case of partial occlusion), (a,b,c) three of the available frames, (d,e,f) background updating results, (g,h,i) obtained transient edges and bounding polygon.

ticularly noisy environment, being surrounded/occluded by deformable objects (vegetation), its bounding polygon is again adequately localized.

Finally, in Figures 5(a)-(c) three non-successive frames of the 'interview' sequence are depicted. The bounding polygons although failing to describe shape (Figures 5(d)-(f)), accurately localize the mobile object. At the expense of computational time, in this case, a segmentation approach is expected to do better in terms of accuracy.

The proposed algorithm has been tested against popular algorithms in the field of mobile object detection and localization; however, a thorough review is beyond the scope of this work. Compared to algorithms performing advanced motion estimation schemes (such as multiresolution or iterative probabilistic techniques) to obtain dense motion fields for every transition, the proposed method relies on simple block matching and edge detection, thus being of particularly

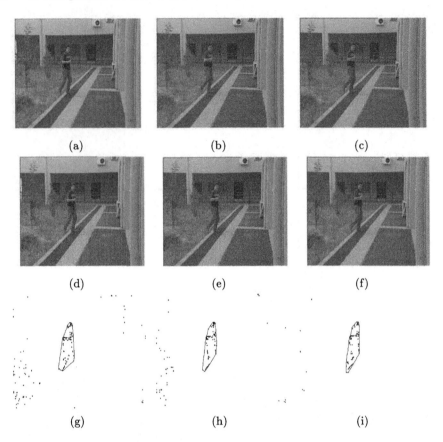

Fig. 2. Mobile object detection in an outdoor sequence acquired by a mobile hand-held slightly rotating camera, (a,b,c) three non-successive frames, (d,e,f) corresponding frames compensated w.r.t. a reference, (g,h,i) transient edges and bounding polygon obtained.

low computational cost. In addition, in contrast to motion segmentation and motion vector clustering schemes, the proposed method relies only on background updating, which in turn simply computes edge pixel differences, a binary operation of no significant cost. In this way, the presented method is verified to be particularly faster. Compared to schemes which rely on motion tracking or object following to avoid dense motion field estimation for all transitions, the method proves superior in cases of significant mobile object deformation or partial occlusion, since background updating is performed on a small aperture moving over the time-line. By considering the theoretical establishment of the algorithm, one would expect that the algorithm is likely to fail when rotations are imposed on the mobile camera. However, it has been experimentally shown that the algorithm fails only in the case of large rotations, where even the algorithms employing parametric motion models are proved to fail.

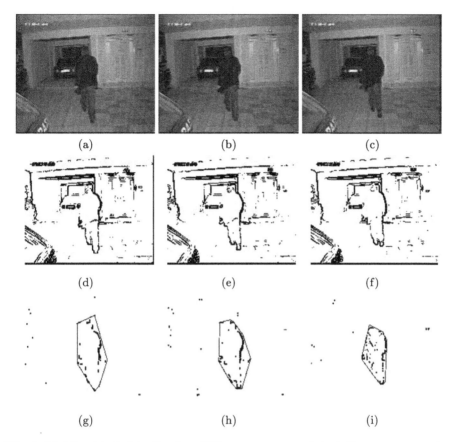

(a)   (b)   (c)

(d)   (e)   (f)

(g)   (h)   (i)

Fig. 3. Mobile object detection in a TV news program, (a,b,c) three non-successive frames, (d,e,f) corresponding edge maps, (g,h,i) transient edges and bounding polygon obtained.

On the other hand, the proposed method is not appropriate when seeking for exact object contours, instead of the bounding polygon or rectangle, in the MPEG-4 sense. In this case, any algorithm performing motion segmentation is more convenient. However, given the results presented over the last decade, it seems that the latter is an open subject for future research, so that the extracted contours are appropriate for shape modeling and object recognition.

4   Conclusions

In this work, a fast and relatively accurate algorithm for mobile object detection and localization is proposed. The proposed approach constitutes immediate extension of the algorithm proposed in [13] for mobile object localization using edge-based background updating.

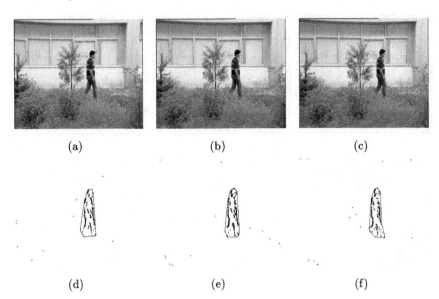

(a)   (b)   (c)

(d)   (e)   (f)

Fig. 4. Mobile object detection in the presence of temporal clutter, (a,b,c) three non-successive frames, (d,e,f) transient edges and bounding polygon obtained.

The proposed method seems superior in terms of time complexity of all algorithms involving costly motion estimation and/or segmentation schemes. At the same time, the accuracy in shape representation, succeeded through the bounding polygon extracted in the present work, is directly comparable to the object contours extracted by segmentation schemes.

The algorithm's performance has been tested over a large number of indoor/outdoor natural sequences and can be suitable for a variety of applications, such as surveillance and content-based indexing.

Acknowledgements: This work is supported by the National Program YPER-1997: "Efficient Content-Based Image and Video Query and Retrieval in Multimedia Systems" of the General Secretariat of Research and Development of Greece.

References

1. Ayer, S., Sawney, H.S., Gorkani, M.: Model-based 2d and 3d Dominant Motion Estimation for Mosaicing and Video Representation. In: Proc. Int'l Conf. on Computer Vision, Boston (1995) 583–590
2. Avrithis, Y., Xirouhakis, Y., Kollias, S.: Affine-Invariant Curve Normalization for Shape-Based Retrieval. In: Proc. Int'l Conf. on Pattern Recognition. Barcelona, Spain. September 2000
3. Hepper, D., Li, H.: Analysis of Uncovered Background Prediction for Image Sequence Coding. Picture Coding Symposium (1987) 192–193

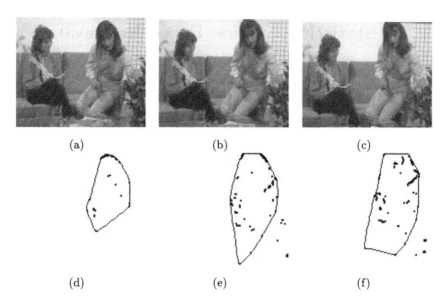

(a)   (b)   (c)

(d)   (e)   (f)

Fig. 5. Mobile object detection in the sequence 'interview', (a,b,c) three non-successive frames (compensated), (d,e,f) transient edges and bounding polygon obtained.

4. Makarov, A.: Comparison of Background Extraction Based Intrusion Detection Algorithms. In: Proc. of Int'l Conf. on Image Processing. Lausanne, Switzerland. September 1996, p. 521–524

5. Makarov, A., Vesin, J.M., Reymond, F.: Intrusion Detection Robust to Slow and Abrupt Lighting Changes. Real-Time Imaging, SPIE-2661 (1996) 44–54

6. Ngan, P.M.: Motion Detection in Temporal Clutter. Technical Report 693, Industrial Research Limited. Auckland, New Zealand (1997)

7. Odobez, J.M., Bouthemy, P.: Separation of Moving Regions from Background in an Image Sequence Acquired with a Mobile Camera. In: Video Data Compression for Multimedia Computing. Kluwer Academic Publisher (1997) 238–311

8. Sedgewick, R.: Algorithms. Addison-Wesley Publishing Co. (1983)

9. Thompson, W.B., Lechleider, P., Stuck, E.R.: Detecting Moving Objects Using the Rigidity Constraint. IEEE Trans. Pattern Analysis and Machine Intelligence $2(15)$ (1993) 162–166

10. Paragios, N., Perez, P., Tziritas, G., Labit, C., Bouthemy, P.: Adaptive Detection of Moving Objects Using Multiscale Techniques. In: Proc. of Int'l Conf. on Image Processing. Lausanne, Switzerland. September 1996, p. 593–596

11. Xirouhakis, Y., Avrithis, Y., Kollias, S.: Image Retrieval and Classification Using Affine Invariant B-Spline Representation and Neural Networks. In: Proc. IEE Colloquium Neural Nets and Multimedia. London, UK. October 1998

12. Xirouhakis, Y., Tirakis, A., Delopoulos, A.: An Efficient Graph Representation for Image Retrieval based on Color Composition. In: Proc. IMACS/IEEE Conf. on Circuits, Systems, Communications and Computers. Athens, Greece. July 1999

13. Xirouhakis, Y., Mathioudakis, V., Delopoulos, A.: An Efficient Algorithm for Mobile Object Localization in Video Sequences. In: Proc. Visual, Modeling and Visualization Workshop. Erlangen, Germany. November 1999

Statistical Motion-Based Retrieval
with Partial Query

Ronan Fablet[1] and Patrick Bouthemy[2]

[1]IRISA / CNRS   [2]IRISA / INRIA
Campus universitaire de Beaulieu, 35042 Rennes Cedex, France
e-mail : rfablet@irisa.fr, bouthemy@irisa.fr
http://www.irisa.fr/vista

Abstract We present an original approach for motion-based retrieval involving partial query. More precisely, we propose an unified statistical framework both to extract entities of interest in video shots and to achieve the associated content-based characterization to be exploited for retrieval issues. These two stages rely on the characterization of scene activity in video sequences based on a non-parametric statistical modeling of motion information. Areas comprising relevant scene activity are extracted from an ascendant hierarchical classification applied to the adjacency graph of an initial block-based partition of the image. Therefore, given a video base, we are able to construct a base of samples of entities of interest characterized by their associated scene activity model. The retrieval operations is then formulated as a Bayesian inference issue using the MAP criterion.

We report different results of extraction of entities of interest in video sequences and examples of retrieval operations performed on a video base composed of a hundred samples.

1 Introduction

Efficient use of video archives is of growing importance in various application fields and requires to index and retrieve visual documents based on their content. In particular, one challenging task is to retrieve samples in a video base from a query formulated by the user.

Three main schemes can be distinguished for video retrieval issues: retrieval using textual query, retrieval with query by sketch, retrieval with query by example. These three procedures for query formulation are also associated to different description schemes of visual documents from semantic characterization to low-level feature extraction. Textual query simply consists in using natural language to express a query [9, 15, 17]. It indeed requires to assign a list of key-words to each document of the video base. However, manual annotating cannot cope with the tremendous amount of video data to be analyzed, and automatic semantic characterization of videos from visual content is still beyond reach for video bases involving non specific types of content [9, 14]. For example, it remains impossible to deal with queries such as "retrieving red cars going to the right". To introduce

R. Laurini (Ed.): VISUAL 2000, LNCS 1929, pp. 96–107, 2000.
Springer-Verlag Berlin Heidelberg 2000

more flexibility in the retrieval process, a sketch drawn by the user to express his query can be considered [4]. For instance, an arrow can be used to indicate the direction of the displacement of the object corresponding to the drawn sketch. Nevertheless, this scheme does not allow to express a wide range of queries. For insatnce, how to sketch a query such as "retrieve rugby game samples"? The third class of retrieval schemes consists in handling queries formulated as video samples. Query by example then relies on the computation of a set of descriptors from the video query. These descriptors are compared to the features extracted and stored for each element of the video base. The latter retrieval approach currently appears more suited to deal with the variety of dynamic contents involved in non-dedicated video bases. In addition, it can benefit from the great deal of research devoted to the definition of tools for content-based video indexing based on the extraction of numerical features [1, 3, 5–7].

As far as retrieval with query by example is concerned, the proposed approaches mainly consider global queries [5–7, 16]. They exploit a global characterization of video content, considering static (color, texture) or dynamic content (motion). However, from user point of view partial query appears more flexible since it supplies the user with the opportunity of focusing on specific entities in the scene. As a consequence, the video analysis and indexing process should automatically perform both the extraction of some meaningful entities and the associated content-based characterization.

In this paper, we propose an original contribution to this issue. A non-parametric probabilistic modeling of motion information is exploited to design an appropriate scheme for the extraction of relevant entities in video sequences in terms of scene activity, and to simultaneously supply their motion-based characterization. Then, we can design an efficient statistical framework for motion-based retrieval involving partial query. The remainder of this paper is organized as follows. Section 2 outlines the general ideas underlying our work. In Section 3, the non-parametric statistical modeling of motion information is described. Section 4 is concerned with the scheme for automatic extraction of entities of interest related to scene activity. Section 5 deals with motion-based retrieval using partial query. Experiments are reported in Section 6, and Section 7 contains concluding remarks.

2   Problem statement

In order to handle video retrieval with partial query, the key issue is, on the one hand, to extract entities of interest (i.e., areas), and, on the other hand, to supply their associated characterization. As far as the former point is concerned, motion information represents an important cue to extract entities of interest in video sequences. In particular, motion segmentation techniques [8] can supply the complete partition of the image into regions of homogeneous motion, mainly in terms of 2D parametric motion models. However, they remain highly computationally expensive and not reliable enough to deal with large video sets. Besides, in case of complex dynamic scenes such as articulated motions, a single object may be divided into several different regions. Grouping them into a meaningful entity remains a difficult issue. On the other hand, motion detection techniques [8, 13] separate moving objects from the background but no further characterization of the associated areas is available.

Using the latter approaches based on 2D parametric motion models, the description of motion content attached to the extracted entities of interest mainly consists in the computation of their 2D trajectories. Even if it reveals relevant for query by sketch for instance, it may not appear general enough to handle various types of motion content such as areas including several moving objects (sport videos) or temporal texture samples (falls, crowd). Therefore, we aim at supplying a characterization of motion information expressing scene activity in a more flexible way. Scene activity will indeed be described using the non-parametric probabilistic modeling approach that we have recently introduced in [6]. This framework also provides a statistical similarity measure between video samples in terms of motion properties. The latter point makes feasible the extraction of areas comprising relevant scene activity from an ascendant hierarchical classification applied to the adjacency graph of an initial partition of the image into blocks.

To cope with retrieval using partial query, we exploit this segmentation scheme to build a base of entities of interest extracted within the key-frames of the elementary shots of the processed video set. We indeed store each extracted entity and its associated statistical scene activity model. Given a query (video sample), we similarly extract entities of interest in the proposed sample. The user selects one of these entities as the partial query. Since our motion characterization relies on a probabilistic framework, we can formulate the motion-based retrieval process as a Bayesian inference issue [6, 14].

3   Statistical modeling of scene activity

3.1   Local motion-related information

To characterize motion content within a given region, our approach relies on an analysis of the distribution of some local measurements. Two kinds of local motion-related quantities can be exploited. On the one hand, one can resort to dense optic flow fields [7, 16]. In our context, their use reveals time consuming and we may cope difficult situations which reveal complex for these approaches. As a consequence, we prefer considering local motion-related quantities directly derived from the spatio-temporal derivatives of the intensity function [5, 6, 11].

Since our goal is to characterize the actual dynamic content of the scene, we have first to cancel camera motion. To this end, we estimate the dominant image motion between two successive images and we assume that it is due to camera motion. To cancel camera motion, we then warp preceding and following images in the shot onto the selected key-frame.

Dominant motion estimation: To model the global transformation between two successive images, we consider a 2D affine motion model (a 2D quadratic model could also be considered). The six affine motion parameters are computed with the gradient-based incremental estimation method described in [12]. The use of a robust estimator ensures the motion estimation not to be sensitive to secondary motions due to mobile objects in the scene. The minimization is performed by means of an iterative reweighted least-square technique embedded in a multiresolution framework.

Local motion-related quantity: To describe the residual motion in the compensated image sequence, the following local motion-related quantity is considered:

$$
v_{obs}(p) = \left(\sum_{s \in \mathcal{F}(p)} \|\nabla I^*(s)\| \cdot |I_t^*(s)| \right) / \max \left(\eta^2, \sum_{s \in \mathcal{F}(p)} \|\nabla I^*(s)\|^2 \right) \tag{1}
$$

where $I^*(p)$ is the intensity function at point p in the warped image, $\mathcal{F}(p)$ is a 3×3 window centered on p, η^2 a predetermined constant related to the noise level in uniform areas (typically, $\eta = 5$), and I_t^* is the temporal derivative of the intensity function I^*. $I_t^*(p)$ is approximated by a simple finite difference. Whereas the normal flow measure $\frac{I_t^*(p)}{\|\nabla I^*(p)\|}$ turns out to be very sensitive to noise attached to the computation of spatio-temporal derivatives of the intensity function, the considered motion-related measurement forms a more reliable quantity, still simply computed from the intensity function and its derivatives. This local motion-related quantity was already successively used for motion detection issues [13], and for motion-based video indexing and retrieval [5, 6].

Our scene activity modeling approach relies on the evaluation of cooccurrence measurements to characterize the distribution of v_{obs} quantities. This requires to quantize the continuous variables v_{obs}. We apply a quantization on a predefined interval. It indeed appears relevant to introduce a limit beyond which these local measures are no more regarded as usable since gradient-based motion measurements are known to correctly handle velocity of rather small magnitude. In practice, sampling within $[0, 4]$ on 16 levels proves accurate enough. Let Λ be the discretized range of variations for $v_{obs}(p)$.

3.2   Temporal Gibbs modeling of scene activity

In order to characterize the scene activity in an area of interest of a key-frame, we exploit the probabilistic framework presented in [6] which relies on nonparametric scene activity models. We briefly outline this technique developed for the global characterization of motion content and specify it to the case of a given spatial area (further details can be found in [6]).

Let $\{x_k\}$ be the sequence of quantized motion-related quantities for the processed shot and k_0 the frame number of the selected key-frame, $\mathcal{R}$ the region of interest in the image k_0 and $x^{\mathcal{R}} = \{x_{k_0}^{\mathcal{R}}, x_{k_0+1}^{\mathcal{R}}\}$ the restriction of $\{x_{k_0}, x_{k_0+1}\}$ on the spatial support of region R. We assume that the pair $x^{\mathcal{R}} = \{x_{k_0}^{\mathcal{R}}, x_{k_0+1}^{\mathcal{R}}\}$ is the realization of a first-order Markov chain:

$$
P_{\Psi}(x^{\mathcal{R}}) = P_{\Psi}(x_{k_0}^{\mathcal{R}}) \prod_{r \in \mathcal{R}} P_{\Psi}(x_{k_0+1}^{\mathcal{R}}(r) | x_{k_0}^{\mathcal{R}}(r)) \tag{2}
$$

where Ψ refers to the scene activity model associated to area $\mathcal{R}$ and $P_\Psi(x_{k_0}^{\mathcal{R}})$ to the a priori distribution of $x_{k_0}^{\mathcal{R}}$. We will consider in practice a uniform law. In addition, $P_\Psi(x_{k_0+1}^{\mathcal{R}}(r)|x_{k_0}^{\mathcal{R}}(r))$ is expressed using an equivalent Gibbsian formulation as:

$$P_\Psi\left(x_{k_0+1}^{\mathcal{R}}(r)|x_{k_0}^{\mathcal{R}}(r)\right) = \exp\left[\Psi\left(x_{k_0+1}^{\mathcal{R}}(r), x_{k_0}^{\mathcal{R}}(r)\right)\right] \qquad (3)$$

with the normalization constraint:

$$\forall \nu' \in \Lambda, \quad \sum_{\nu \in \Lambda} \exp\left[\Psi(\nu, \nu')\right] = 1 \qquad (4)$$

This modeling framework is causal since we only evaluate temporal interactions i.e. cooccurrence of two given values at the same grid point at two successive instants. The advantages are two-fold. On one hand, it allows us to handle certain kinds of temporal non-stationarity. On the other hand, it ensures an exact computation of the conditional likelihood of a sequence of motion-related quantities w.r.t. a model. This is of key importance to achieve model estimation in an easy way and to define an appropriate measure of motion-based similarity from the Kullback-Leibler divergence. More precisely, the conditional likelihood $P_\Psi(x^{\mathcal{R}})$ can be expressed according to an exponential formulation (Gibbs model):

$$P_\Psi(x^{\mathcal{R}}) = \exp\left[\Psi \bullet \Gamma^{\mathcal{R}}\right] \qquad (5)$$

$\Gamma^{\mathcal{R}} = \{\Gamma^{\mathcal{R}}(\nu, \nu')\}_{(\nu,\nu')\in\Lambda^2}$ is the cooccurrence measurements defined by:

$$\Gamma^{\mathcal{R}}(\nu, \nu') = \sum_{r \in \mathcal{R}} \delta(\nu - x_{k_0+1}^{\mathcal{R}}(r)) \cdot \delta(\nu' - x_{k_0}^{\mathcal{R}}(r)) \qquad (6)$$

where δ is the Kronecker symbol. $\Psi \bullet \Gamma^{\mathcal{R}}$ is the dot product between the cooccurrence distribution $\Gamma^{\mathcal{R}}$ and the potentials specifying Ψ:

$$\Psi \bullet \Gamma^{\mathcal{R}} = \sum_{(\nu,\nu')\in\Lambda^2} \Psi(\nu, \nu') \cdot \Gamma^{\mathcal{R}}(\nu, \nu') \qquad (7)$$

In fact, this modeling approach is non-parametric in two ways. First, it does not correspond to 2D parametric (affine or quadratic) motion models [12]. Second, from a statistical point of view, it does also not on parametric distributions (Gaussian) to model the law $P_\Psi(\nu|\nu')$.

Furthermore, the ML (Maximum Likelihood) estimation of the model $\widehat{\Psi}^{\mathcal{R}}$ fitting to the motion distribution attached to the region $\mathcal{R}$ reveals straightforward. It simply comes to perform an empirical estimation of the distribution $\{P_{\widehat{\Psi}^{\mathcal{R}}}(\nu, \nu')\}_{(\nu,\nu')\in\Lambda^2}$. Therefore, the potentials of the model $\widehat{\Psi}^{\mathcal{R}}$, which verifies $\widehat{\Psi}^{\mathcal{R}} = \arg\max_\Psi P_\Psi(x^{\mathcal{R}})$, are given by [6]:

$$\widehat{\Psi}^{\mathcal{R}}(\nu, \nu') = \ln\left(\Gamma^{\mathcal{R}}(\nu, \nu')/\sum_{\vartheta\in\Lambda}\Gamma^{\mathcal{R}}(\vartheta, \nu')\right) \qquad (8)$$

4   Spatial segmentation based on scene activity

Given a video shot, we aim at extracting areas of interest in its key-frame in an automatic way. Here, meaningful entities are assumed to correspond to areas comprising pertinent scene activity. Hence, we exploit the statistical scene activity modeling introduced in the previous section. A prominent advantage of such an approach is to provide within the same framework the extraction and the characterization of particular areas to perform video retrieval with partial query.

In the sequel, we assume that a primary partition of the image is available. In practice, we consider a block-based partition of the image. The goal is to build meaningful clusters from this initial set of blocks based on motion content. To this end, we have first to define an appropriate measure of content similarity (subsection 4.1). Second, we exploit this similarity measure to create a hierarchical classification from the initial set of spatial regions (subsection 4.2).

4.1   Statistical measure of motion-based activity similarity

We exploit again the statistical scene activity modeling framework described in Section 3. We start from the initial elementary blocks, and we progressively merge neighboring blocks. Let us note $\mathcal{B}_i$ a current block. The point is to decide to merge it or not to another block $\mathcal{B}_j$. We compute the ML estimate of the scene activity model $\Psi^{\mathcal{B}_i}$ associated to block $\mathcal{B}_i$ using relation (8). Then, as explained in [6], we consider an approximation of the Kullback-Liebler divergence to evaluate the similarity between two probabilistic models. More precisely, for two blocks $\mathcal{B}_i$ and $\mathcal{B}_j$, the similarity measure $D(\mathcal{B}_i, \mathcal{B}_j)$ is defined by:

$$D(\mathcal{B}_i, \mathcal{B}_j) = \frac{1}{2} \left[KL(\mathcal{B}_i \| \mathcal{B}_j) + KL(\mathcal{B}_j \| \mathcal{B}_i) \right] \tag{9}$$

where KL is the Kullback-Liebler divergence approximated as (see [6]):

$$KL(\mathcal{B}_i \| \mathcal{B}_j) \approx \frac{1}{|\mathcal{B}_i|} \ln \left(P_{\Psi^{\mathcal{B}_i}}(x^{\mathcal{B}_i}) / P_{\Psi^{\mathcal{B}_j}}(x^{\mathcal{B}_i}) \right) \tag{10}$$

where $x^{\mathcal{B}_i}$ is the sequence of quantized motion-related measurements for block $\mathcal{B}_i$, and $\mathcal{B}_i$ the size of the block $\mathcal{B}_i$. Since $\Psi^{\mathcal{B}_i}$ is the ML estimate of the scene activity model associated to the block $\mathcal{B}_i$, $KL(\mathcal{B}_i \| \mathcal{B}_j)$ is positive and equals 0 if the two statistical distributions are identical. In fact, this ratio quantifies the loss of information occurring when considering $\Psi^{\mathcal{B}_j}$ instead of $\Psi^{\mathcal{B}_i}$ when characterizing motion information within $\mathcal{B}_i$. Using the exponential expression of the law $P_{\Psi^{\mathcal{B}_i}}$ (Eq.5), $KL(\mathcal{B}_i \| \mathcal{B}_j)$ is rewritten as:

$$KL(\mathcal{B}_i \| \mathcal{B}_j) \approx \frac{1}{|\mathcal{B}_i|} \left(\Psi^{\mathcal{B}_i} \bullet \Gamma^{\mathcal{B}_i} - \Psi^{\mathcal{B}_j} \bullet \Gamma^{\mathcal{B}_i} \right) \tag{11}$$

with $\Gamma^{\mathcal{B}_i}$ the matrix of temporal cooccurrence values of motion-related quantities for area $\mathcal{B}_i$ given by relation (6).

4.2   Hierarchical graph labeling

We need now to design a merging procedure relying on this similarity measure to extract relevant areas from the initial set of elementary blocks. Ascendant hierarchical classification is an attractive and flexible tool to supply a hierarchical representation of video sets and to facilitate the discrimination of different types of global dynamic content [6]. Our idea is to adopt this kind of approach, usually applied to classification problems, to solve the considered segmentation issue. This will allow to design a simple but efficient segmentation method able to handle quite various types of situations. Nevertheless, we must also take into account the spatial relations between the different regions of the image partition since we cope with a segmentation problem. Hence, we have developed a method exploiting the adjacency graph of these spatial regions.

It is first required to define the similarity measure D not only between elementary blocks but also between two regions $\mathcal{R}_1$ and $\mathcal{R}_2$. The similarity measure is then extended as follows:

$$D(\mathcal{R}_1, \mathcal{R}_2) = \max_{(B_1, B_2) \in \mathcal{B}_{\mathcal{R}_1} \times \mathcal{B}_{\mathcal{R}_2}} D(B_1, B_2) \tag{12}$$

where $\mathcal{B}_{\mathcal{R}_i}$ is the set of elementary blocks belonging to region $\mathcal{R}_i$. Using D, an ascendant hierarchical classification can be conducted as follows. As initialization, each elementary blocks of the primary image partition forms a leave in the hierarchy. At each step, we merge the two closest regions $\mathcal{R}_1$ and $\mathcal{R}_2$ according to D to form a new region at level $l + 1$ of the hierarchy. Besides, a similarity constraint is introduced to prevent from merging $\mathcal{R}_1$ and $\mathcal{R}_2$ if they are not enough similar:

$$\text{if } D(\mathcal{R}_1, \mathcal{R}_2) > D_{max}, \ \mathcal{R}_1 \text{ and } \mathcal{R}_2 \text{ are not merged.} \tag{13}$$

where D_{max} is a given threshold. For two regions $\mathcal{R}_1$ and $\mathcal{R}_2$, $\exp\left[-D(\mathcal{R}_1, \mathcal{R}_2)\right]$ is expressed as an average of two likelihood ratios comprised in $[0, 1]$ (relation 9). As a consequence, the parameter D_{max} is set as $D_{max} = -\ln \mu$ where μ is a threshold in $[0, 1]$. The threshold μ indeed quantifies the information loss we tolerate in terms of accuracy of description of motion distributions when substituting models attached to $\mathcal{R}_1$ by those attached to $\mathcal{R}_2$, and reciprocally.

Besides, to cope with the segmentation of the image into connected regions, this hierarchical classification is performed under a connectivity constraint. It consists in merging only regions which are connected. It simply comes to substitute for the similarity measure D in the merging constraint (13) a new similarity measure D^* defined by:

$$\begin{cases} D^*(\mathcal{R}_1, \mathcal{R}_2) = D(\mathcal{R}_1, \mathcal{R}_2), & \text{if } \mathcal{R}_1 \text{ and } \mathcal{R}_1 \text{ are connected} \\ \\ D^*(\mathcal{R}_1, \mathcal{R}_2) = D_{max}, & \text{otherwise} \end{cases} \tag{14}$$

In order to extract entities of interest, we select a level in the extracted hierarchy. In practice, we take level $L - 1$ where level L is the root of the binary tree since the goal is usually to segment one relevant area from the background but other choices could be easily considered if required. This results in the extraction of at least two spatial areas, i.e. the entity of interest and background.

4.3   Separation of entities of interest from static background

The last step of the extraction of entities of interest within the considered key-frame consists in selecting the relevant areas in the set of regions $\{\mathcal{R}_i\}$ determined by our scene activity segmentation approach. We aim at identifying the areas that do not correspond to the static background.

To this end, we also resort to the statistical modeling framework introduced in Section 3. More precisely, dynamic contents attached both to the static background and to the set of potential regions of interest $\{\mathcal{R}_i\}$ are described by means of a temporal Gibbsian model. Given a region $\mathcal{R}_i$, the associated model $\Psi^{\mathcal{R}_i}$ is estimated using relation (8). Besides, we can infer the prior model Ψ_{static} relative to the static background denoted as $\mathcal{R}_{static}$ since it theoretically corresponds to a distribution involving only null motion-related measurements in the warped sequence. As a consequence, the associated temporal cooccurrence histogram Γ_{static} is given by:

$$\forall (\nu, \nu') \in \Lambda^2, \quad \begin{cases} \Gamma_{static}(\nu, \nu') = 0, \ \text{if } (\nu, \nu') \neq (0,0) \\ \\ \Gamma_{static}(0,0) \ = 1 \end{cases} \tag{15}$$

and the ML model Ψ_{static} is then defined as:

$$\forall (\nu, \nu') \in \Lambda^2, \quad \begin{cases} \Psi_{static}(\nu, \nu') = \quad\quad -\log|\Lambda|, \quad\quad \text{if } \nu' \neq 0 \\ \\ \Psi_{static}(\nu, 0) = \quad\quad \log \epsilon, \quad\quad\quad \text{if } \nu \neq 0 \\ \\ \Psi_{static}(0, 0) = \log\left(1 - (|\Lambda| - 1)\epsilon\right), \quad \text{otherwise} \end{cases} \tag{16}$$

where ϵ refers to a set precision (typically, $\epsilon = 10^{-6}$). It prevents from computing $\log(0)$ and correspond to the weight given to cooccurrence configurations that never appear in the temporal cooccurrence distribution.

Then, we compute the set of similarity measures $(D(\mathcal{R}_{static}, \mathcal{R}_i))$ computed between the static background $\mathcal{R}_{static}$ and the potential regions of interest $(\mathcal{R}_i)$ using relation (9). The area relative to the lowest similarity measure is assumed to be associated to the static background. Therefore, for indexing purpose, we finally store all the regions $(\mathcal{R}_i)$ except the latter region in a base of entities of interest. Besides, for each selected region $\mathcal{R}_i$, we also store its associated model $\Psi^{\mathcal{R}_i}$ as a representation of its dynamic content used in the retrieval stage. Besides, for storage issues, we can achieve a model complexity reduction by evaluating likelihood ratios as described in [6].

5   Retrieval with partial query

5.1   Partial query

We now tackle retrieval with partial query by example. The first step consists in creating an indexed base comprising a set of meaningful entities extracted from the processed video set. Thus, each video is segmented into shots [2] and we then apply the scene activity segmentation scheme described in Section 4. This framework supplies us automatically and simultaneously with the extraction of meaningful entities and the associate characterization with regard to scene activity. The introduction of an entity is at last manually validated in order to sometimes reject areas which are not relevant for indexing purpose such as logos or score captions.

On the other hand, once a video query is provided by the user, we extract automatically from the submitted video sample local relevant entities and the user specifies if one of them represents an element of interest in order to perform the retrieval of similar examples from the indexed video base.

5.2   Bayesian retrieval

Similarly to [6, 15], the retrieval process is formulated as a Bayesian inference issue according to the MAP criterion. Given a video query q and a region $\mathcal{R}_q$ as partial query, the retrieval over a base of entities $\mathcal{D}$ of samples similar to partial query $\mathcal{R}_q$ comes to solve for:

$$d^* = \arg\max_{d \in \mathcal{D}} P(d|\mathcal{R}_q) = \arg\max_{d \in \mathcal{D}} P(\mathcal{R}_q|d)P(d) \qquad (17)$$

The distribution $P(d)$ allows us to express *a priori* knowledge on the video content relevance over the database. It could be inferred from semantical description attached to each type of video sequences or from relevance feedback by interacting with the user in the retrieval process [10]. In the current implementation of our retrieval scheme, we will set no a priori ($P(d)$ distribution is uniform).

In our case, a statistical model of scene activity Ψ_d is attached to each entity d of the database. Furthermore, we have also determined the sequence of motion-related measurements $x^{\mathcal{R}_q}$ for the partial query $\mathcal{R}_q$. Therefore, the conditional likelihood $P(\mathcal{R}_q|d)$ is formally expressed as $P_{\Psi_d}(x^{\mathcal{R}_q})$ and criterion (17) is given by:

$$d^* = \arg\max_{d \in \mathcal{D}} P_{\Psi^d}(x^{\mathcal{R}_q}) \qquad (18)$$

From the exponential expression of the law P_{Ψ^d} (relation (5)), we further deduce:

$$d^* = \arg\max_{d \in \mathcal{D}} \left[\Psi^d \bullet \Gamma^{\mathcal{R}_q} \right] \qquad (19)$$

with $\Gamma^{\mathcal{R}_q}$ the cooccurrence distribution within $\mathcal{R}_q$ computed using relation (6). Otherwise, the computation of the conditional likelihoods $\{P_{\Psi^d}(x^{\mathcal{R}_q})\}_{q \in \mathcal{D}}$ also supplies us with a ranking of the element d of the base $\mathcal{D}$ since it evaluates how the different statistical models Ψ^d fits to the motion-related measurements computed in the query area $\mathcal{R}_q$.

6   Results

6.1   Extraction of entities of interest

We have first carried out experiments for the extraction of entities of interest based on scene activity. We have processed different kinds of sport videos. Two main classes of shots can be distinguished: the first one involves close-up of a particular area of the play field, and the second one displays a global view of the scene. In the first case, the entities of interest are obviously the tracked players, whereas in the second case these are not a single player but rather a group of players or a particular area of the play field.

Figure 1 contains eight examples corresponding to these two different cases. In all these situations, our method extracts areas of interest which are relevant and accurate enough in the context of video indexing and retrieval.

This scheme for scene activity segmentation appears effective for motion-based indexing since it requires about 0.15 second of CPU time to process three successive 160×120 images (for a Sun Creator workstation 360MHZ).

6.2   Retrieval operations with partial query

At a second stage, we have conducted retrieval operations with partial query. We have considered a set of one hundred video shots involving different dynamic contents. We have focused on sport sequences such as rugby, football, basketball and hockey. In Figure 2, we report three examples of retrieval operations. The three best replies are given for each query. For all the processed examples, the system provides relevant replies in terms of motion properties. To appreciate the relevance of the replies, we give for each reply d the value of the conditional likelihood $P_{\Psi_d}(x^{\mathcal{R}_q})$. To further quantify the similarity between the retrieved entities of interest and the query, we have also determined the value of the similarity measure D computed between the probabilistic scene activity models estimated within the query area and those attached to the retrieved ones.

7   Conclusion

We have presented in this paper an original approach for motion-based video retrieval handling partial query. It relies on an automatic and efficient extraction of entities of interest from a video sequence based on scene activity characterization. Motion information is expressed as non parametric statistical scene activity models able to deal with a large range of dynamic scene content. This statistical framework can then be straightforwardly exploited to solve the retrieval process using a Bayesian framework.

In future work, we plan to evaluate our approach on a larger video base and to address the tracking of the extracted entities of interest in video shots.

References

1. P. Aigrain, H-J. Zhang, and D. Petkovic. Content-based representation and retrieval of visual media : A state-of-the-art review. *Multimedia Tools and Applications*, 3(3):179–202, September 1996.
2. P. Bouthemy, M. Gelgon, and F. Ganansia. A unified approach to shot change detection and camera motion characterization. *IEEE Trans. on Circuits and Systems for Video Technology*, 9(7):1030–1044, 1999.
3. R. Brunelli, O. Mich, and C.M. Modena. A survey on the automatic indexing of video data. *Jal of Vis. Comm. and Im. Repr.*, 10(2):78–112, 1999.
4. S.-F. Chang, W. Chen, H.J. Meng, H. Sundaram, and D. Zhong. VideoQ- an Automatic content-based video search system using visual cues. In *Proc. ACM Multimedia Conf.*, Seattle, November 1997.
5. R. Fablet and P. Bouthemy. Motion-based feature extraction and ascendant hierarchical classification for video indexing and retrieval. In *Proc. of 3rd Int. Conf. on Visual Information Systems, VISUAL'99*, LNCS Vol 1614, pages 221–228, Amsterdam, June 1999. Springer.
6. R. Fablet, P. Bouthemy, and P. Pérez. Statistical motion-based video indexing and retrieval. In *Proc. of 6th Int. Conf. on Content-Based Multimedia Information Access, RIAO'2000*, pages 602–619, Paris, April 2000.
7. A.K. Jain, A. Vailaya, and W. Xiong. Query by video clip. *Multimedia Systems*, 7(5):369–384, 1999.
8. A. Mitiche and P. Bouthemy. Computation and analysis of image motion: a synopsis of current problems and methods. *Int. Journal of Computer Vision*, 19(1):29–55, 1996.
9. M.R. Naphade, T.T. Kristjansson, B.J. Frey, and T. Huang. Probabilistic multimedia objects (Multijects) : a novel approach to video indexing and retrieval in multimedia systems. In *Proc. of 5th IEEE Int. Conf. on Image Processing, ICIP'98*, pages 536–5450, Chicago, October 1998.
10. C. Nastar, M. Mitschke, and C. Meilhac. Efficient query refinement for image retrieval. In *Proc. of IEEE Conf. on Computer Vision and Pattern Recognition, CVPR'98*, Santa Barbara, June 1998.
11. R. Nelson and R. Polana. Qualitative recognition of motion using temporal texture. *Computer Vision, Graphics, and Image Processing*, 56(1):78–99, July 1992.
12. J.M. Odobez and P. Bouthemy. Robust multiresolution estimation of parametric motion models. *Jal of Vis. Comm. and Im. Repr.*, 6(4):348–365, 1995.
13. J.M. Odobez and P. Bouthemy. Separation of moving regions from background in an image sequence acquired with a mobile camera. In *Video Data Compression for Multimedia Computing*, chapter 8, pages 295–311. H. H. Li, S. Sun, and H. Derin, eds, Kluwer, 1997.
14. N. Vasconcelos and A. Lippman. A Bayesian framework for semantic content characterization. In *Proc. of IEEE Conf. on Computer Vision and Pattern Recognition, CVPR'98*, pages 566–571, Santa-Barbara, June 1998.
15. N. Vasconcelos and A. Lippman. A probabilistic architecture for content-based image retrieval. In *Proc. of IEEE Conf. on Computer Vision and Pattern Recognition, CVPR'2000*, Hilton Head, June 2000.
16. V. Vinod. Activity based video shot retrieval and ranking. In *Proc. of 14th Int. Conf. on Pattern Recognition, ICPR'98*, pages 682–684, Brisbane, August 1998.
17. H. Wactlar, T. Kanade, M. Smith, and S. Stevens. Intelligent access to digital video: The informedia project. *IEEE Computer*, 29(5):46–52, 1996.

Figure1. Examples of segmentation based on motion-based activity. Entities of interest are delimited in white.

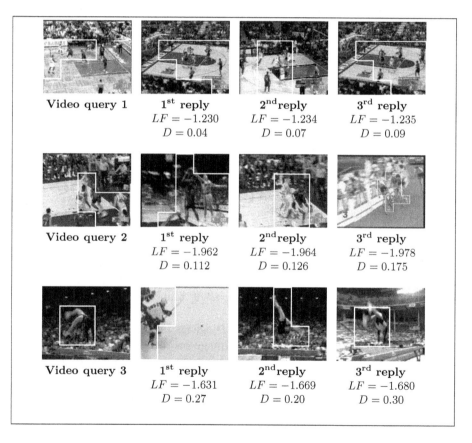

Figure2. Examples of retrieval with partial query. we give for each reply d the value LF of the log-likelihood $\ln\left(P_{\Psi^d}\left(x^{\mathcal{R}_q}\right)\right)$ corresponding to video query q. To a posteriori evaluate the relevance of the replies, we have also estimated model Ψ^q for the query and we report the distances D between $\Psi^{\mathcal{R}_q}$ and the different retrieved models Ψ^d.

Experiments in Using Visual and Textual Clues for Image Hunting on the Web*

Yuksel Alp Aslandogan and Clement T. Yu

Department of EECS, University of Illinois at Chicago
Chicago, IL 60607, USA

Abstract. In this paper we describe our experiences with Diogenes, a web-based search agent for finding person images. Diogenes[1] implements different ways of combining visual and textual information for identifying person images. The sources of visual information are a face detection and a face recognition module. The textual information is obtained by analyzing the HTML structure and full text of web pages. Four different ways of combining these pieces of information are evaluated experimentally: (1) Face detection followed by text/HTML analysis, (2) face detection followed by face recognition, a linear combination of (1) and (2) and finally, a Dempster-Shafer combination of (1) and (2). We also compare the performance of Diogenes to those of research prototype and commercial image search engines. We report the results of a set of experimental retrievals for 20 persons examining over 30,000 URLs. In these retrievals Diogenes had the best average precision among the search engines evaluated including WebSEEk, AltaVista, Lycos and Ditto.

1 Introduction

In this paper, we consider the problem of finding images on the web based on their contents. In particular, we evaluate strategies and systems to retrieve person images from the web. We compare various search strategies implemented by **Diogenes**, a web-based image search agent [2], and commercial search engines that have the image search capability.

Starting from an initial list of URLs, Diogenes retrieves web pages and associates a person name with each facial image on those pages. To accomplish its goal, Diogenes relies on two types of evidence: Visual and textual. A face detection module examines the images on the web page for human faces. A face recognition module identifies the face by using a database of known person images. A text/HTML analysis module analyzes the body of the text with the aim of finding clues about who appears in each image. The outputs of the face detection, text/HTML analysis and face recognition modules are merged using different evidence combination mechanisms to classify each image.

---

* Research supported in part by NSF grants ISR-9508953 and IIS-9902792

[1] After philosopher Diogenes of Sinope, d.c. 320 B.C. who is said to have gone about Athens with a lantern in day time looking for an honest man.

R. Laurini (Ed.): VISUAL 2000, LNCS 1929, pp. 108–119, 2000.
Springer-Verlag Berlin Heidelberg 2000

To answer to need to index the vast multimedia content available on the web, a number of web image search engines have been been built: These include research prototypes such as WebSeer [12], WebSEEk [11], ImageScape[5], Amore [6], WebHunter [7], ImageRover [13], and PicToSeek [3] as well as commercial ones such as Ditto. Commercial web text search engines such as Lycos, AltaVista and Yahoo have also been offering image search facilities. The search engine Ditto is particularly tuned for person image searches on the web. We will look into some of these systems more closely due to their similarity in purpose and scope to Diogenes.

WebSEEk indexes its images visually for similarity queries but relies on the words found in the image path/URLs and alternate texts (the piece of text that serves as a place-holder for an image in a text only browser) to classify images into conceptual categories. A user interested in people images is directed to the "people" category. **Diogenes** on the other hand uses both the image path/alternate text and the *full text* of the web pages. The commercial image search engines, Lycos (http://www.lycos.com/picturethis/) and AltaVista (http://jump.altavista.com/st.im) apparently do not perform any image analysis, but rely heavily on the image path/URLs and alternate texts. The details of the workings of Ditto (http://www.ditto.com) were not known. WebSeer goes one step further in image classification by integrating a face detector. Consequently its accuracy is much better than WebSEEk in people queries. Diogenes uses both a face detector and a face recognition module in analyzing images visually. To the authors' knowledge, the retrieval performance of WebSeer was not reported in the literature and no web interfaces were available as of this writing.

A feature of Diogenes that is not in the systems mentioned above is the incorporation of face recognition and the use of Dempster-Shafer evidence combination method with object recognition and automatic, local uncertainty assessment. When a text/HTML analysis module or a visual analysis module assigns a degree of similarity between an image and a person name, there are degrees of uncertainty associated with both these values. In Diogenes' case, both of these modules produce numeric values indicating their degrees of uncertainty. These values are obtained *automatically* (without user interaction) and *locally* (separately for each retrieval/classification).

Key contributions of this paper are the following:

- Experimental evaluation of different evidence combination methods used by Diogenes. We measured the average precision in retrieving person images from the web with the following methods:

  1. *Face detection followed by text/HTML analysis:* Web pages retrieved by a crawler are first screened by a face detector module. If there is any image that contains a human face, then this page is further analyzed by the text/HTML analysis module.

  2. *Face detection followed by face recognition:* Images that contain a human face as determined by the face detection module are submitted to the face recognition module which assigns a degree of similarity between

the retrieved image and the images in our database whose names are mentioned in the text of the web page.

3. A linear combination of the evidence due to text/HTML analysis as described in (1) above and that due to face recognition as described in (2) above.

4. The combination of evidences due to (1) and (2) above by using Dempster-Shafer formula.

- Experimental, quantitative comparison of various search engines for person image retrieval from the web with the best results obtained by Diogenes. The former includes three commercial systems and a research prototype. Diogenes had significantly better average precision than the other three search engines.

In the rest of the paper we first give an overview of the system architecture of Diogenes in section 2. This section also introduces the visual and textual features used by the image classifier. In sections 3.1, 3.2 and 3.3 we describe the simple, Linear and Dempster-Shafer methods for evidence combination respectively and how each is applied to the image retrieval domain. The results of our experimental evaluation are given in section 4. Section 5 summarizes key points of the paper and explores future directions.

2   Overview

Diogenes is a web-based, automated image search agent designed specifically for person facial images [2]. It travels the web off-line and builds an index. Figure 1 shows a snapshot of Diogenes search results for "Steve Forbes" query. Diogenes works with the web pages that contain a facial image accompanied by a body of text. The approach is to take advantage of the *full text* and HTML structure of web pages in addition to the visual analysis of the images themselves and to combine the two pieces of information. We describe the visual and text/HTML features used by the classifier further below.

2.1   Visual Features

The visual features used by the classifier of Diogenes consists of the outputs of face detection and face recognition modules. The neural network-based face detection module [8] examines an image to find a human face. If a face is found, the location is indicated to an intermediate module which crops (cuts out) the facial portion and submits the page to text/HTML analysis and the image to face recognition modules. Diogenes uses a face recognition module which implements the eigen-face method [14]. This module uses a set of known facial images for training. Each of these training images has an associated person name with it. At recognition time, a set of distance values between the input image and those of the training set are reported. These distances indicate how dissimilar the input image is to the training images. In addition, a global distance value called "Distance From Face Space" or DFFS is also reported. This is the global distance of the input image from the facial image space spanned by the training images. Diogenes uses this latter value to determine the uncertainty of the recognition.

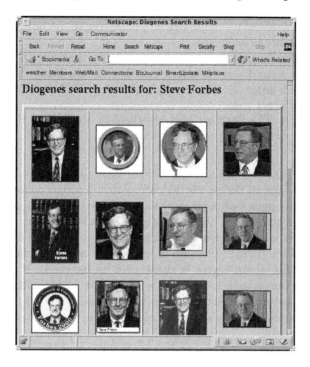

Fig. 1. A snapshot of the Diogenes results page for Steve Forbes.

2.2   Text/HTML Features

The text/HTML analysis module of Diogenes determines a degree of association between each person name on a web page and each facial image on that page. This degree of association is based on two factors: Page-level features and local (or structural) features. Page-level features such as frequency of occurrence and location-within-the-page (title, keyword, body text etc.) are independent of any particular image. Local/structural features are those factors that relate a name to an image. In an earlier work [1], we have shown that structured queries and image descriptions provide a better framework for matching different descriptions of the same phenomenon as opposed to free text descriptions. Diogenes takes advantage of the HTML structure of a web page in determining the degree of association between a person name and an image. The factors of interest include the following:

- *Frequency:* The significance of a name is proportional to its number of occurrences within the page and inversely proportional to its number of occurrences on the whole web. This is known as the $tf * idf$ (term frequency times inverse document frequency) formula [9, 15]. It captures the premise that if a rare word appears frequently on a page then it is very significant for that page. If a common word, on the other hand appears frequently on a page, it may not be as significant.

- *Name or URL Match:* A name that is a substring of the image path/URL is assigned a higher significance.
- *Shared HTML Tags:* Names that are enclosed in the same HTML tags with an image are more likely to be associated with that image. For instance, a caption for an image is usually put in the same HTML table on the same column of adjacent rows.
- *Alternate Text:* The alternate text identified by the "ALT" HTML tag generally serves as a suitable textual replacement for an image or a description of it.

The text/HTML analysis proceeds as follows: When a page is retrieved, a part-of-speech tagger tags all the words that are part of a proper name on the page. The occurrence frequency of these words are recorded. For each such word, and for each image on the page, a degree of association is established. The frequency of the word serves as the starting point for this score. Then the HTML analysis module analyzes the HTML structure of the page. If an image and a word share some common tags, their degree of association is increased. If the word is a substring of the image name or if the word is part of the alternate text for the image, the association is increased further. The formula for calculating the degree of association between an image and word can be summarized as

$$d(word, image) = \omega_{fr} * s_{fr} + \omega_{tag} * s_{tag} + \omega_{img} * s_{img} + \omega_{alt} * s_{alt}$$

where $d(word, image)$ is the degree of association between the word and the image; $\omega_{fr}, \omega_{tag}, \omega_{img}$, and ω_{alt} are the relative weights of word frequency, shared HTML tags, image name substring property and image alt text substring property respectively. The $s_{fr}, s_{tag}, s_{img}, s_{alt}$ are the corresponding scores for word frequency, number of shared HTML tags, whether the word is part of the image name, and whether the word is part of the alternate text, respectively. In the experiments reported in Section 4, these parameters were set as follows: $\omega_{fr} = 0.20$, $\omega_{tag} = 0.05$, $\omega_{img} = 0.35$, and $\omega_{alt} = 0.40$. The weights are assigned to emphasize local features more than the page-level features. Since the text/HTML analysis module assigns degrees of association to individual words, at the time of evidence combination, the scores of the two words (the first name and the last name) that make up a person name are averaged to get a single text/HTML score for the full name.

3   Evidence Combination

Once the visual and text/HTML features are computed for a particular web page, they can be combined in a number of ways. In the following we examine three approaches for evidence combination: Simple, Linear and Dempster-Shafer. These approaches have been implemented and evaluated experimentally.

3.1   Simple Evidence Combination

When a user issues a query like "Abraham Lincoln" two types of images may be retrieved: images of former US president Abraham Lincoln or the USS aircraft carrier Abraham Lincoln. Without further feedback from the user it is not possible to determine what type is the desired one. Hence some of the images returned may be very irrelevant to the user. For people image queries, Diogenes overcomes this problem by incorporating a face detector into its search mechanism.

When a page is retrieved together with any images on it, each image is analyzed by a face detector. If a face is found in one of the images on the page then the text of the page is submitted to the text/HTML analysis (TA) module.

In the next two sections, we will look into ways of combining the output of text/HTML analysis module with that of the face recognition module.

3.2   Linear Evidence Combination

A simple linear combination is a weighted sum of normalized individual features. Diogenes implements a feature-value combination scheme:

$$Score_{combined} = \omega_1 * Score_{FR} + \omega_2 * Score_{TA}$$

Where $Score_{FR}$ and $Score_{TA}$ are the numeric "degree of association" scores assigned to each pair of person name and facial image on a web page by the face recognition and text/HTML analysis modules respectively.

The simplest approach is to assigning weights to classifier inputs is to use constant weights. A more sophisticated approach might improve these weights by various learning algorithms. In the experiments reported in this paper we used a simple arithmetic average, i.e. $\omega_1 = \omega_2 = 0.5$.

3.3   Dempster-Shafer Evidence Combination

Dempster-Shafer Theory of Evidence (a.k.a. Mathematical Theory Of Evidence) is intended to be a generalization of Bayesian theory of subjective probability [10]. It provides a method for combining **independent** bodies of evidence using Dempster's rule.

For classifying person images obtained from the web, we rely on two sources of evidence: The output of a face recognition module (FR) which classifies the image and the output of a text/HTML analysis module (TA) which analyzes the text that accompanies the image. Both modules attempt to identify the person in the image based on different media. We assume that if more than one person appears in an image, identifying one of them is sufficient. We designate the two pieces of evidence as m_{FR} and m_{TA} respectively. By default, these two modules operate independently: The results of face recognition module does not affect the text/HTML score and vice versa. Hence the independence assumption of the Dempster-Shafer theory holds. The text/HTML analysis module determines a degree of association between every person name-facial image pair on the web page. It assigns numerical values to different person names for each image indicating this degree of association. The face recognition module assigns a distance value to each person in our database of known person images. We convert these values to similarity scores. We assume that for any person for which we have no stored image, the face recognition similarity score is zero. If we use Dempster's Rule for combination of evidence we get the following:

$$m_{FR,TA}(C) = \frac{\sum_{A,B \subseteq \Theta, A \cap B = C} m_{FR}(A) m_{TA}(B)}{\sum_{A,B \subseteq \Theta, A \cap B \neq \emptyset} m_{FR}(A) m_{TA}(B)}$$

Here $m_{FR,TA}(C)$ is the combined Dempster-Shafer probability for C. m_{FR} and m_{TA} are the basic probabilities assigned to sets A and B respectively by the two independent sources of evidence. A and B are sets that include C. A and B are not necessarily proper supersets and they may as well be equal to C. In this formula the numerator accumulates the evidence which supports a particular hypothesis and the denominator conditions it on the total evidence for those hypotheses supported by both sources.

In the case of classification of person images, it is possible to simplify this formulation. Our face recognition and text/HTML analysis modules give us information about individual images and the uncertainty of the recognition/analysis. This means we have only beliefs for singleton classes (persons) and the body of evidence itself ($m(\Theta)$). The latter is the belief that we can not associate with any hypothesis: It accounts for our "ignorance" about those subsets of Θ for which we have no specific belief. Thus, the basic probability assignment to Θ represents the *uncertainty* of the evidence:

$$m(\Theta) = 1 - \sum_{A \subset \Theta} m(A)$$

If in a body of evidence the basic probabilities assigned to proper subsets of Θ add up to 1, then this would make $m(\Theta) = 0$ meaning we have very high confidence in this body of evidence and no uncertainty.

For our image ranking problem, the Dempster combination formula can be simplified as follows:

$$rank(P_C) \quad \propto \quad m_{FR}(P_C) m_{TA}(P_C) + m_{FR}(\Theta) m_{TA}(P_C) + m_{FR}(P_C) m_{TA}(\Theta)$$

Here $\propto$ represents 'is proportional to" relationship. Later on, we shall replace "$\propto$" with "=". $m_{FR}(P_C)$ and $m_{TA}(P_C)$ are the beliefs assigned to person P_C by the face recognition and text/HTML analysis modules respectively. $m_{FR}(\Theta)$ and $m_{TA}(\Theta)$ represent the uncertainty in the bodies of evidence m_{FR} and m_{TA} respectively. More on this derivation can be found in [2] and [4].

The values of the uncertainties $m_{FR}(\Theta)$ and $m_{TA}(\Theta)$ are obtained as follows: For face recognition, we have a "distance from face space" (DFFS) value for each recognition. This value is the distance of the query image to the space of eigenfaces formed from the training images [14]. Diogenes uses the DFFS value to estimate the uncertainty associated with face recognition. If the DFFS value is small, the recognition is good (uncertainty is low) and vice versa. The following is Diogenes' formula for the uncertainty in face recognition:

$$m_{FR}(\Theta) = 1 - \left(\frac{1}{ln(e + DFFS)} \right)$$

For text analysis, uncertainty is inversely proportional to the maximum value among the set of degree of association values assigned to name-image combinations.

$$m_{TA}(\Theta) = \frac{1}{ln(e + MDA)}$$

Where MDA is the maximum numeric "degree of association" value assigned to a person name with respect to a facial image among other names. As described in section 2.2, each degree of association for an image name pair is a function of the frequency of occurrence of that name, location relative to the image, HTML tags shared with the image, etc. Both face recognition and text analysis uncertainties are obtained locally, i.e. for each retrieval and automatically without user interaction. This feature distinguishes Diogenes from other applications where the users provide the uncertainties [4].

4   Experimental Results

In this section we describe the process and the results of an experimental evaluation of Diogenes against other search engines. A set of experimental retrievals were performed where search engines were compared in terms of average precision in answering people image queries. Twenty popular person names were chosen randomly from among the people who appeared in the news headlines during the course of the development of Diogenes. Four search engines were available for this evaluation: WebSeek, AltaVista, Lycos (multimedia/picture search) and Ditto. Among the other systems mentioned in the introduction, WebSeer project was discontinued and hence the web interface was not available for this evaluation. Also, no web interface was available for WebHunter. The people images database of Yahoo Image Surfer (http://ipix.yahoo.com) was too limited to be included in this study. For AltaVista, the *image search* feature was used with the following options: Photos only, web only (no image collections), and no banners. It is worth noting that if proprietary image collections (such as Corbis^{TM}) are included in AltaVista image search, the average precision is significantly better than what is reported below. However, since our purpose in this work was to evaluate retrieval performance from the web, we have disabled this option in AltaVista and restricted its search domain to the web.

An image retrieved by a search engine was regarded as relevant if the person named in the query was clearly recognizable in the image. Images with multiple persons are accepted if they satisfy the same criterion. Banners were excluded and cartoons were counted as failures. It is important to note that not all systems mentioned here are tuned for finding images containing persons although they may be used for that purpose.

Since WebSEEk did not allow for multiple word queries, a convention was adopted: Only the last name of the celebrities were used and if there were multiple celebrities with the same last name, anyone was accepted as relevant. We report the performance of WebSEEk for the first ten queries separately in Table 1. Table 2 shows the results of the experiment where Diogenes was compared

Table 1. WebSEEk search results.

Srch. Eng.		Q1	Q2	Q3	Q4	Q5	Q6	Q7	Q8	Q9	Q10	Avg.
WebSEEk	prec.	.70	.55	.67	N/A	1.0	.05	1.0	.55	0	N/A	.57
	total	43	9	3	0	5	107	2	13	1	N/A	

with three commercial image search engines. In the table there are two numbers in each cell. The first number shows the average precision: the number of relevant images among the top 20 retrieved images. The number 20 was chosen based on the observation that the users typically do not browse beyond the top two pages of results and a typical results page contains 10 images. The second number which is shown in parentheses indicates the total number of images returned for the query. If the total recall number is less than 20, then the precision is computed over this total. In Table 2, the average precision of Diogenes (0.95)

Table 2. AltaVista, Lycos, Ditto and Diogenes search results for 20 queries.

Query	AltaVista	Lycos	Ditto	Diogenes
Q1: Bill Clinton	.60 (16112)	.60 (1234)	1.0 (622)	.90 (445)
Q2: Hillary Clinton	.40 (3786)	.90 (355)	.65 (426)	.90 (266)
Q3: Kenneth Starr	.40 (2304)	.75 (98)	.95 (79)	1.0 (124)
Q4: Monica Lewinsky	.70 (2146)	.80 (283)	.95 (385)	1.0 (285)
Q5: Madeleine Albright	.80 (568)	.85 (123)	.82 (17)	.95 (89)
Q6: Bill Gates	.65 (13864)	.90 (839)	.90 (307)	.85 (61)
Q7: Benjamin Netanyahu	.70 (1321)	.80 (72)	.50 (4)	1.0 (56)
Q8: Boris Yeltsin	.70 (650)	.65 (129)	.90 (44)	.85 (43)
Q9: Rush Limbaugh	.70 (1039)	.65 (89)	.95 (127)	1.0 (95)
Q10: OJ Simpson	.55 (1307)	.35 (27)	.50 (48)	.95 (113)
Q11: Al Gore	.45 (6664)	.90 (328)	1.0 (203)	1.0 (158)
Q12: Mikhail Gorbachev	.60 (153)	.70 (38)	.90 (10)	.95 (184)
Q13: Janet Reno	.90 (2794)	.95 (109)	.85 (25)	.95 (269)
Q14: Jesse Ventura	.70 (2129)	.90 (112)	.85 (87)	1.0 (237)
Q15: Kofi Annan	.90 (123)	.90 (135)	.60 (30)	.95 (118)
Q16: Bob Dole	.85 (13271)	.70 (140)	.65 (72)	.85 (235)
Q17: George Bush	.40 (13272)	.75 (357)	.80 (250)	1.0 (187)
Q18: Steve Forbes	.70 (14036)	.40 (41)	.65 (21)	1.0 (80)
Q19: Newt Gingrich	.75 (307)	.80 (144)	.80 (45)	.95 (274)
Q20: Slobodan Milosevic	.55 (132)	.85 (115)	.65 (48)	.85 (127)
Average	**.65**	**.77**	**.79**	**.95**

is higher than the average precision of each of the other three search engines. Due to the limited amount of time available to Diogenes to retrieve its images, its average recall was not as high as AltaVista but it was compatible with Lycos and better than Ditto for most queries. Diogenes has visited on the average 1500-2000 web sites per query, totaling more than 30,000.

Table 3 below shows how the different combinations implemented by Diogenes fare against each other. In Table 3 the number in each cell shows the average

Table 3. Performance comparison of search strategies implemented by Diogenes.

Query	FD/Text/HTML	Face Rec.	Linear	Dempster-Shafer
Q1: Bill Clinton	.90	.30	.85	.90
Q2: Hillary Clinton	.90	.65	.90	.90
Q3: Kenneth Starr	1.0	.25	1.0	1.0
Q4: Monica Lewinsky	1.0	.75	1.0	1.0
Q5: Madeleine Albright	.95	.55	.95	.95
Q6: Bill Gates	.95	.50	.85	.85
Q7: Benjamin Netanyahu	1.0	.40	1.0	1.0
Q8: Boris Yeltsin	.85	.30	.85	.85
Q9: Rush Limbaugh	1.0	.50	1.0	1.0
Q1: 0OJ Simpson	.85	.85	1.0	.95
Q11: Al Gore	1.0	.75	.95	1.0
Q12: Mikhail Gorbachev	.90	.70	.85	.95
Q13: Janet Reno	.90	.70	1.0	.95
Q14: Jesse Ventura	1.0	1.0	1.0	1.0
Q15: Kofi Annan	.95	.65	.90	.95
Q16: Bob Dole	.90	.65	.90	.85
Q17: George Bush	1.0	.70	1.0	1.0
Q18: Steve Forbes	1.0	.70	1.0	1.0
Q19: Newt Gingrich	.95	.45	.95	.95
Q20: Slobodan Milosevic	.90	.40	.85	.85
Average	**.95**	**.59**	**.94**	**.95**

precision over the top 20 retrieved images for a particular query. The column labeled "FD/Text/HTML" shows the retrieval results based on text/HTML evidence preceded by face detection. In other words, the page is analyzed by the text/html module only if it contained a facial image. The second column shows the results when the search agent relied on face detection and recognition alone. The third column is for linear evidence combination as described in section 3.2 and the fourth column is for Dempster-Shafer evidence combination approach.

The comparison of retrieval results in the above table for text/html analysis with face detection, linear combination and dempster-shafer combination reveals that neither of the combination strategies was able to provide any further improvement in precision beyond text/HTML analysis following face detection. Since the average precision of the face recognition module was significantly lower than that of the text/html analysis module, neither of the evidence combination mechanisms improved the performance any further.

To better analyze the effect of evidence combination, the text analysis module was modified to ignore the alternate text field for images. The last ten queries from the above set were re-run with this configuration. The following table shows the results. Each cell in the table shows the average precision of the method over the top 20 images. As can be seen in Table 4, the omission of the alternate text

Table 4. Performance of search strategies when text/HTML module ignored alternate text.

Retrieval Method	Q11	Q12	Q13	Q14	Q15	Q16	Q17	Q18	Q19	Q20	Avg.
Dempster/Shafer	1.0	.95	.95	1.0	.95	.85	1.0	1.0	.95	.85	.935
FD,Text/HTML	1.0	.80	.95	.95	.90	.90	.80	1.0	1.0	.85	.915
Face Recognition	.75	.70	.70	1.0	.65	.65	.70	.70	.45	.40	.72
Linear	1.0	.75	.95	1.0	.85	.95	.75	1.0	1.0	.90	.915

field by the text/HTML analysis module decreased the accuracy of the this module slightly but had less effect on the Dempster/Shafer combination results. These results indicate the potential benefits of the Dempster-Shafer combination mechanism over the other two methods. Further experiments are needed to identify the circumstances where this type of evidence combination is likely to be most beneficial.

5   Conclusion and Future Work

In this work we have described and provided an experimental evaluation of mechanisms of evidence combination for content based indexing of person images. These mechanisms are implemented in **Diogenes**, a person image search agent for the WWW. Although a number of web search engines have been reported in the literature for this purpose, precise description of their retrieval mechanisms or quantitative evaluation of their performances are rarely available.

The main contribution of this work is a quantitative evaluation of different methods and systems for indexing person images on the web. In this evaluation, Diogenes outperformed three other search engines including two commercial systems in average precision. A more thorough evaluation involving automatic learning of some parameters in text/HTML analysis is currently underway.

The techniques discussed and illustrated in this work are applicable to a number of other problems where multiple sources of evidence are available with different degrees of uncertainty. Example fields include medical diagnosis, corporate portals, stock photography sites, land-scape imaging systems and geographical information systems.

Acknowledgments

We would like to thank Matthew Turk (work done at MIT), Alex Pentland (MIT), Takeo Kanade (CMU) and Henry A. Rowley(CMU) for making software available for this project.

References

1. Y. Alp Aslandogan, Charles Thier, Clement T. Yu, Jun Zou, and Naphtali Rishe. Using Semantic Contents and WordNet(TM) in Image Retrieval. In *Proceedings of ACM SIGIR Conference*, Philadelphia, PA, 1997.
2. Y. Alp Aslandogan and Clement Yu. Multiple Evidence Combination in Image retrieval: Diogenes Searches for People on the Web. In *Proceedings of ACM SIGIR 2000, Athens, Greece*, July 2000.
3. Theo Gevers and Arnold W. M. Smeulders. PicToSeek: A Content-Based Image Search System for the World Wide Web. In *Proceedings of SPIE Visual 97*, 1997.
4. Joemon M. Jose, Jonathan Furner, and David J. Harper. Spatial Querying for Image Retrieval: A User Oriented Evaluation. In *ACM SIGIR*, pages 232–240, 1998.
5. Michael S. Lew, Kim Lempinen, and Nies Huijsmans. Webcrawling Using Sketches. In *Proceedings of SPIE Visual 97*, pages 77–84, 1997.
6. Sougata Mukherjea, Kyoji Hirata, and Yoshinori Hara. AMORE: A World Wide Web Image Retrieval Engine. *World Wide Web*, 2(3):115–132, 1999.
7. Olaf Munkelt, Oliver Kaufmann, and Wolfgang Eckstein. Content-based Image Retrieval in the World Wide Web: A Web Agent for Fetching Portraits. In *Proceedings of SPIE Vol. 3022*, pages 408–416, 1997.
8. Henry A. Rowley, Shumeet Baluja, and Takeo Kanade. Neural Network-Based Face Detection. *IEEE Transactions on Pattern Analysis and Machine Intelligence*, 20(1):23–38, Jan 1998.
9. Salton, G. *Automatic Text Processing*. Addison Wesley, Mass., 1989.
10. Glenn Shafer. *A Mathematical Theory of Evidence*. Princeton University Press, 1976.
11. J. R. Smith and S. F. Chang. Visually Searching the Web for Content. *IEEE Multimedia*, 4(3):12–20, July-September 1997.
12. Michael J. Swain, Charles Frankel, and Vassilis Athitsos. WebSeer: An Image Search Engine for the World Wide Web. Technical Report TR-96-14, University of Chicago, Department of Computer Science, July 1996.
13. Leonid Taycher, Marco LaCascia, and Stan Sclaroff. Image Digestion and Relevance Feedback in the ImageRover WWW Search Engine. In *Proceedings of SPIE Visual 97*, 1997.
14. M. Turk and A. Pentland. Eigenfaces for Recognition. *Cognitive Neuroscience*, 3(1):71–86, 1991.
15. Clement T. Yu and Weiyi Meng. *Principles of Database Query Processing for Advanced Applications*. Data Management Systems. Morgan Kaufmann, 1998.

Visualising Information: A Mosaic of Perspectives

Chaomei Chen

Department of Information Systems and Computing, Brunel University
Uxbridge UB8 3PH, UK
chaomei.chen@brunel.ac.uk

Abstract. Information visualisation has become a truly wide-ranging interdisciplinary endeavor. Researchers, practitioners, and end users are embracing the vibrant field from a variety of distinct but interrelated perspectives. As the field becomes increasingly diverse, one must address a number of fundamental questions. What exactly is information visualisation about? Where does it come from? Where is it going? This article highlights some of the most salient perspectives to information visualisation, including structural, spatial, temporal, semantic, behavioural, cognitive, social, ecological, and technological perspectives. Each of these perspectives is illustrated with representative works in the field. Interconnections among individual perspectives are also discussed in the broad context of information visualisation.

1   Introduction

Information visualisation has become a truly wide-ranging and interdisciplinary field of research and a vibrant global industry. There is a rapid growth in the literature of information visualisation [1-4]. As the field becomes increasingly diverse, one must address a number of fundamental questions. What is exactly information visualisation? Where does it come from? Where is it going?

This article highlights some of the most salient perspectives to information visualisation, namely structural, spatial, temporal, semantic, behavioural, cognitive, social, ecological, and technological perspectives. Each of these perspectives is illustrated with representative works in the field. The purpose of painting such a cross-perspective image of information visualisation is to foster more dynamic views on the role of information visualisation in problem solving and augmenting our ability to explore and analyse a wide range of types of data.

The rest of the article is organised as follows. Ten salient perspectives are introduced with illustrative examples from the literature. Some of these perspectives are well established, whereas others are rapidly evolving.

R. Laurini (Ed.): VISUAL 2000, LNCS 1929, pp. 120-126, 2000.
© Springer-Verlag Berlin Heidelberg 2000

2   Perspectives

A mosaic of ten perspectives of information visualisation are illustrated as follows to reflect the diversity of the fast growing field. These perspectives are certainly not isolated and independent from each other. What does each perspective contribute to the field of information visualisation? What are these perspectives in common? How do they fit into the field as a whole?

1. The Structural Perspective
2. The Spatial Perspective
3. The Temporal Perspective
4. The Semantic Perspective
5. The Behavioural Perspective
6. The Cognitive Perspective
7. The Perceptive Perspective
8. The Social Perspective
9. The Ecological Perspective
10. The Technological Perspective

Addressing these perspectives and their interrelationships will help us to clarify the driving force of information visualisation and also identify potentially prosperous directions of research as well as commercial developments. The mosaic of perspectives reflect the interdisciplinary nature of the field of information visualisation.

2.1   The Structural Perspective

In the structural perspective, the focal point of information visualisation is on the abstraction and visual representation of interrelationships of some sort. For example, the task by data type taxonomy for information visualisation as proposed by Shneiderman [5] includes commonly used data structures such as hierarchies and networks as abstract representations of a wide variety of information structures.

Botafogo's work [6] in structural analysis of hypertexts sets a good example of how the structural perspective can guide the analysis of hypertext as a graph. The structural perspective has the advantage that it can rely on a well-established body of knowledge in areas such as the graph theory. For example, minimum spanning trees have been used by several information visualisation systems in order to derive a simplified representation of a network structure. It plays an important role in association with the use of hierarchy-based visualisation models, such as cone trees. A number of more recent examples can be found in information visualisation of the World-Wide Web.

Although hierarchical structures and network structures are a popular choice in the majority of information visualisation systems so far, problems with navigating large networks have been well documented [7].

2.2 The Spatial Perspective

The spatial perspective emphasises the use of spatial properties of visualisation models to convey various types of information. Good examples include treemap visualisations and self-organised maps in two-dimensional models [8], and terrain relief maps and generic landscape maps in three-dimensional models [9].

What in common between visulisation models in the spatial perspective is the extended notion of maps from geographical maps. Within spatial models, users can explore and navigate through them.

2.3 The Temporal Perspective

The third perspective concentrates on the dimension of time. This perspective emaphsises changes over time in information being visualised. Examples in this perspective include weather forecast models, time series of financial data, and the evolution of websites.

The evolution of websites can be visualised over time to present the dynamics to the viewers more clearly [10]. Animations and simulations are usually closely related to this perspective.

2.4 The Semantic Perspective

The semantic perspective focuses on the extraction and representation of underlying and latent semantics. For example, latent semantic indexing [11] has been used as the basis of information visualisation [12, 13]. Pathfinder network scaling has been adapted as a means to visualising salient semantic structures [14, 15]. A common question one must address is that to what extent the salient semantics is preserved in the process and how one should interpret the semantics conveyed through visual-spatial representations.

The semantic perspective is also crucial to the success of other perspectives such as the behavioural perspective.

2.5 The Behavioural Perspective

The focus of the behavioural perspective is on the role of user behaviour in information visualisation. Chalmers et al. [16] describe a path model for visualising users' access records to the World-Wide Web.

Since late 1990s, there has been a growing interest in a central concept originated in Bush's visionary Memex [17] – the ability to create one's own threads of association in an ever-evolving information space. At the heart of this idea, an evolving information space like the Memex should make its users' trails persistent and accessible by others.

Threading through an information space is also known as trailblazing. A good example of how one may trailblaze the Web is Walden's Paths [18]. With Walden's Paths, teachers can effectively assembly a course of learning materials for young children based on existing documents on the Internet. Another example is the scent visualisation, to be explained later in the ecological perspective.

2.6 The Cognitive Perspective

The cognitive perspective is concerned with users. Factor-referenced cognitive tests are traditionally used to measure individuals' cognitive abilities. There are a large number of cognitive factors potentially related to information visualisation. More systematic and comparable experimental studies of information visualisations are needed.

Until recently, research in information visualisation has largely focused on the development of innovative computing techniques. George Robertson, the inventor of well-known information visualisation techniques such as Cone Trees [19], was among the first to draw our attention to the importance of empirical evaluation with his keynote speech in 1998 at the IEEE information visualisation symposium and more recently in 2000 at the IEEE conference on information visualisation. A pioneering special topic issue on empirical evaluation of information visualisations will be published later this year [20], which includes a collection of empirical studies of some classic information visualisations for the first time.

2.7 The Perceptual Perspective

Perception for design is the central theme of the recent book on information visualisation by Colin Ware [3]. He emphasises that there is a vast amount of literature on human perception and topics that would be valuable for designers of information visualisation. Unfortunately, this literature is very thinly spread out across many specialised disciplines and this has made it a very time consuming task for researchers and practitioners to locate useful information efficiently.

He stresses the significance of understanding the perceptual perspective. For example, the use of colours and textures in information visualisation is known to have a significant impact, but in many information visualisations to date such wisdom has not been utilised and probably even overlooked. The importance of the perceptual perspective is also in that it can lead to a more coherent integration of information visualisation design and evaluation.

2.8   The Social Perspective

The social perspective emphasises the essential role of social interaction in interpreting and understanding information visualisation between individuals. For example, one fundamental question from the social perspective is whether it is possible, or rather, meaningful, to generate a universally agreeable information visualisation. This question can be traced back to the long debate between social construction of knowledge and positivism views of knowledge.

Social navigation [21] is an example derived from the social perspective of information visualisation. The following example used to illustrate the ecological perspective can be also used to illustrate, from a different angle, the social perspective.

2.9 The Ecological Perspective

The ecological perspective takes into account the role of information visualisation in a broader context. Information foraging theory is one of the well-known examples taking an ecological perspective to the study of information seeking behavior [22]. Optimal foraging theory is originally developed in biology and anthropology in order to address how the tension between cost and effectiveness can be optimised. It is used to analyse various food-foraging strategies and how they are adapted to a specific situation. Information foraging theory is an adaptation of the optimal foraging theory in attempts to provide an analytic methodology to assess information search strategies in a similar approach. Like the original optimal foraging theory, it focuses on the trade-off between information gains and the cost of retrieval for the user. In information seeking, this involves instant estimation of the value of a document and cost of retrieving it.

A recent example is the so-called scent visualisation of a website [23], which is a system for analyzing and predicting information scent, usage, and usability of a web site. Several kinds of scent are made available to indicate the value of a particular document in the given website. Scent indicators are computed based on content similarity, hyperlinkage, and usage data. The magnitude of scent associated with a document is shown by the height of red bars on a tree visulisation, called the Dome Tree, of the website.

Scent visualisation is based on the notion of users' trails in an information space, which was proposed by Bush more than a half of century ago. At a much more ambitious level, Garfield [24] and Small [25] at the Institute for Scientific Information (ISI) have developed techniques to visualise the entire scientific literatures maintained in ISI's citation databases across a numerous number of disciplines. Their work is also known as science mapping, or scientography.

2.10 The Technological Perspective

The technical perspective is essentially driven by the advances in computer graphics and closely related areas. Its major concern is on the computational and algorithmatic approaches. For example, Jim Foley [26] recently listed the top ten problems for information visualisation. Most of these problems highlight technical challenges from the technological perspective. A recent survey on graph visualisation [4] also provides a summary of technical advances in information visualisations using algorithms related to graphs, especially graph drawing. More specifically focusing on graph drawing, algorithms for the visualization of graphs have been well documented [27].

3   Conclusion

In conclusion, information visualisation is interdisciplinary in nature. We will benefit from cross-disciplinary communication through the views of different perspectives. These perspectives are not independent to each other. On the contrary, they are interrelated and they reflect different aspects of information visualisation as a whole. The mosaic of perspectives can serve as a reference framework so as to foster interdisciplinary communication and advance information visualisation.

References

[1]   S. Card, J. Mackinlay, and B. Shneiderman, "Readings in Information Visualization: Using Vision to Think," : Morgan Kaufmann, 1999.

[2]   C. Chen, *Information Visualisation and Virtual Environments*. London: Springer-Verlag London, 1999.

[3]   C. Ware, *Information Visualization: Perception for Design*: Morgan Kaufmann Publishers, 2000.

[4]   I. Herman, G. Melancon, and M. S. Marshall, "Graph visualization and navigation in information visualization: A survey," *IEEE Transactions on Visualization and Computer Graphics*, vol. 6, pp. 24-43, 2000.

[5]   B. Shneiderman, "The eyes have it: A task by data type taxonomy for information visualization," presented at IEEEE Workshop on Visual Languages '96, 1996.

[6]   R. A. Botafogo, E. Rivlin, and B. Shneiderman, "Structural analysis of hypertexts: Identifying hierarchies and useful metrics," *ACM Transactions on Office Information Systems*, vol. 10, pp. 142-180, 1992.

[7]   S. G. Eick and G. J. Wills, "Navigating large networks with hierarchies," presented at IEEE Conference on Visualization, Los Alamitos, CA., 1993.

[8]   X. Lin, "Map displays for information retrieval," *Journal of the American Society for Information Science*, vol. 48, pp. 40-54, 1997.

[9]   J. A. Wise Jr., J. J. Thomas, K. Pennock, D. Lantrip, M. Pottier, A. Schur, and V. Crow, "Visualizing the non-visual: Spatial analysis and interaction with information from text documents," presented at IEEE Symposium on Information Visualization '95, Atlanta, Georgia, USA, 1995.

[10]   E. H. Chi, J. Pitkow, J. Mackinlay, P. Pirolli, R. Gossweiler, and S. K. Card, "Visualzing the evolution of web ecologies," presented at CHI'98, 1998.

[11]   S. Deerwester, S. T. Dumais, T. K. Landauer, G. W. Furnas, and R. A. Harshman, "Indexing by Latent Semantic Analysis," *Journal of the American Society for Information Science*, vol. 41, pp. 391-407, 1990.

[12]   C. Chen, "Tracking latent domain structures: An integration of Pathfinder and Latent Semantic Analysis," *AI & Society*, vol. 11, pp. 48-62, 1997.

[13]   C. Chen and M. Czerwinski, "From latent semantics to spatial hypertext: An integrated approach," presented at the 9th ACM Conference on Hypertext and Hypermedia (Hypertext '98), Pittsburgh, PA., 1998.

[14]   C. Chen, "Generalised Similarity Analysis and Pathfinder Network Scaling," *Interacting with Computers*, vol. 10, pp. 107-128, 1998.

[15]   C. Chen, "Bridging the gap: The use of Pathfinder networks in visual navigation," *Journal of Visual Languages and Computing*, vol. 9, pp. 267-286, 1998.

[16]   M. Chalmers, K. Rodden, and D. Brodbeck, "The order of things: Activity-centred information access," presented at Proceedings of WWW7, Brisbane, 1998.

[17]   V. Bush, "As we may think," *The Atlantic Monthly*, vol. 176, pp. 101-108, 1945.

[18]   R. Furuta, F. Shipman, C. Marshall, D. Brenner, and H. Hsieh, "Hypertext paths and the WWW: Experiences with Walden's Paths," presented at Hypertext '97, Southampton, UK, 1997.

[19]   G. G. Robertson, J. D. Mackinlay, and S. K. Card, "Cone trees: Animated 3D visualizations of hierarchical information," presented at CHI '91, New Orleans, LA, 1991.

[20]   C. Chen and M. Czerwinski, "Empirical evaluation of information visualisations: An introduction," *International Journal of Human-Computer Studies*, 2000.

[21]   C. Chen, L. Thomas, J. Cole, and C. Chennawasin, "Representing the semantics of virtual spaces," *IEEE Multimedia*, vol. 6, 1999.

[22]   S. Card, "Information visualization and information foraging," presented at the third Workshop on Advanced Visual Interfaces, Gubbio, Italy, 1996.

[23]   E. H. Chi, P. Pirolli, and J. Pitkow, "The scent of a site: A system for analyzing and predicting information scent, usage, and usability of a web site," presented at Proceedings of the CHI 2000 conference on Human factors in computing systems (CHI 2000), The Hague Netherlands, 2000.

[24]   E. Garfield, "Mapping the world of science," presented at the 150 Anniversary Meeting of the AAAS, Philadelphia, PA, 1998.

[25]   H. Small, "Visualizing science by citation mapping," *Journal of the American Society for Information Science*, vol. 50, pp. 799-813, 1999.

[26]   J. Foley, "Getting there: The ten top problems left," *IEEE Computer Graphics and Applications*, vol. 20, pp. 66-68, 2000.

[27]   G. Di Battista, *Graph Drawing: Algorithms for the Visualization of Graphs.* Upper Saddle River, NJ: Prentice Hall, 1998.

Spatial/Temporal Query Processing for Information Fusion Applications

Shi-Kuo Chang[1], Gennaro Costagliola[2] and Erland Jungert[3]

[1] Department of Computer Science
University of Pittsburgh -chang@cs.pitt.edu
[2] Dipartimento di Matematica ed Informatica
Università di Salerno -gencos@unisa.it
[3] Swedish Defense Research Institute (FOA) - jungert@lin.foa.se

Abstract. To support the retrieval and fusion of multimedia information from multiple sources and databases, a spatial/temporal query language called ΣQL was proposed. ΣQL is based upon the σ–operator sequence and in practice expressible in SQL-like syntax. ΣQL allows a user to specify powerful spatial/temporal queries for both multimedia data sources and multimedia databases, eliminating the need to write different queries for each. In this paper, we illustrate this approach by query processing examples for information fusion applications.

1. Introduction

To support the retrieval and fusion of multimedia information from multiple sources and databases in information fusion applications, a spatial/temporal query language called ΣQL was proposed [7, 6]. ΣQL is based upon the σ–operator sequence and in practice expressible in an SQL-like syntax. The natural extension of SQL to ΣQL allows a user to specify powerful spatial/temporal queries for both multimedia data sources and multimedia databases, eliminating the need to write different queries for each.

Query language for heterogeneous multimedia databases is a new research area and therefore the body of related work only just begins to grow. There has been substantial research on query languages for images and spatial objects [9, 3, 5]. Of these query languages, many are based upon extension of SQL, such as PSQL [15] and Spatial SQL [8]. Next come video query languages where the focus is shifted to temporal constraints [1] and content based retrieval [4]. Recent efforts begin to address query languages involving images, video, audio and text. Vazirgiannis describes a multimedia database system for multimedia objects that may originate from sources such as text, image, video [16]. The query language QL/G developed by Chan and Zhu supports the querying of geometric data bases and is applicable to both geometric and text data [2], but does not handle temporal constraints. An interoperable multi-database platform in a client/server environment using a common object model is described in [17], which can provide inter-operations between popular database systems. A related approach is to provide a database integrator (DBI) for

R. Laurini (Ed.): VISUAL 2000, LNCS 1929, pp. 127-139, 2000.
© Springer-Verlag Berlin Heidelberg 2000

customers who have data stored in multiple data sources, typically heterogeneous and/or non-relational, and want to view those data sources as a single logical database from the data and/or metadata perspective [10].

Several attempts to define data fusion, [18], exist and the most commonly used derive from the military context and in particular from the Joint Directors of Laboratories, Data Fusion Group. Their definition, [19], says that: "*Data fusion is a process dealing with the association and combination of data and information from single and multiple sources to achieve refined position and identity estimates for observed entities and to achieve complete and timely assessments of situations ...*". This somewhat shortened version of the definition deals basically with the aspect of fusion that is focused on in the query language presented in this paper where just lower levels of fusion are dealt with.

The paper is organized as follows. The basic concepts of the σ-operator are explained in Section 2 together with the usage of the various types of operators. Section 3 presents the architecture of the SIGMA system. Section 4 describes the data model, and Section 5 provides the detailed syntax of ΣQL with examples for information fusion applications. In Section 6, we conclude the paper and discuss further research.

2. Basic Concepts of the σ-Operator

The ΣQL query language is a tool for the handling of spatial/temporal information from multiple data sources, as most sensors generate spatial information in a temporal sequential manner. The ΣQL query language processor must be able to handle large volumes of data because most sensors can generate large quantities of data within short periods of time. Another aspect to consider is that questions asked by the end-users may include data from more than one sensor, leading to complex query structures, since the use of data from more than one sensor may require fusion of multiple sensor information. So far, no general solution exists to the fusion problem and most likely no such solution will be available for a long time to come. For this reason, it is natural to just try to solve the problem for a limited number of object types observed from a specific perspective by a limited number of sensors. One such application is to select sensors that are looking only at ground objects, primarily vehicles, from a top view perspective where the sensors are carried by a flying platform. The operators used by the ΣQL query language can be categorized with respect to their functionality. There are two major categories - transformational and fusion-oriented operators. These two categories will be called σ− and φ−operators, respectively. In this section we discuss the two operator categories with respect to their input and output data and their functionality.

2.1 σ–Operators

A σ-operator is defined as an operator to be applied to any multi-dimensional source of objects in a specified set of intervals along a dimension. The operator projects the source along that dimension to extract clusters [6]. Each cluster contains a set of objects or components whose projected positions falls in one of the given intervals along that dimension. As an example, let us write a σ-expression for extracting the video frame sequences in the time intervals t_1-t_2 and t_3-t_4 from a video source VideoR. The expression is $\sigma_{time}([t_1-t_2], [t_3-t_4])$ VideoR where VideoR is projected along the time dimension to extract clusters (frames in this case) whose projected positions along time are in the required intervals.

In case of uncertainty the components of the clusters may be associated with various probabilities or belief values. Input and output data may be of either qualitative or quantitative type although generally the later type is of main interest here. Thus, input data will be accessed from either some raw-data format, e.g. from some sensor, from structured data such as one or more databases, or from some internal representation such as qualitative strings. Generally, the output data correspond to clusters in relational representations that in practice may be available as qualitative strings of various types [3], e.g. as projection strings or object descriptions. The general formalism can thus be expressed in the following way:

$$\sigma_{dimension} (<intrv>)\{<src> \mid <clstr> \mid <clstr\_strns> \mid ...\} \Rightarrow \{<clstr> \mid < clstr\_strns> \mid ...\}$$

A large number of σ-operators may be defined, [7]. Many of these operators are in general fundamental in most spatial application. Examples are determination of various attributes and spatial relations, such as 'north-west-of' or 'to the left of'. For just simple inputs these operators may be described as:

$$\sigma_{attribute} (<attrb-vl>)<clstr\_strns> \Rightarrow <relat\_strns\_of\_(<attrib > < obj> <attrb vl>)>$$

$$\sigma_{relation} (<relat\_vl>)< clstr\_strns> \Rightarrow \{(<relat>(<relat\_vl> <obj>-i <obj>-j))\}$$

Instances to these operator types could be:

$$\sigma_{colour}(blue, red)(V:A < B) = (V:(colour\ A\ red) < (colour\ B\ blue))$$

$$\sigma_{direction}(north\_west)(U:A < B,V: B< A) = (direction\ (north\_west\ A\ B))$$

In case of uncertainties the input and output to the σ-operators includes an attribute corresponding to a specific belief value. The σ_{type}- and the σ_{motion}-operators may include this attribute. The σ_{type}-operator is concerned with matching between objects found in a sensor image and objects stored in a library database and where both objects are described in the same terms that may be either qualitative or quantitative. Traditionally matching has been a part of information fusion. Generally, however, the σ_{type}-operator and its result, i.e. a set of objects and their corresponding normalized belief values, can be expressed in the following terms when the input to the operator is a single cluster:

$$\sigma_{type} (type\_val) < clstr\_strns> \Rightarrow < clstr\_strns\_of\_ (<type\_val> <obj>-i <nbv>-i)>$$

where nbv corresponds to the normalized belief value which in practice becomes an attribute to the actual object. An instance of this is:

$$\sigma_{type} (car)(U:A < B < C) = (U:(car\ A\ 0.7) < (car\ B\ 0.1) < C)$$

The σ_{motion}-operator can be expressed as follows:

$$\sigma_{motion} (<motion\_value>)\{<clstr-seq> \mid <clstr>\} \Rightarrow \{(<motion\_value> <obj>-i)\}.$$

Again, this can be instantiated:

$$\sigma_{motion}(moving)(U:A < B < C) = (U: (moving\ A) < (moving\ B) < C)$$

2.2 φ-Operators

The φ-operators are far more complex than the σ-operators, since they basically are concerned with information fusion and related to problems which require more complex solutions as well as input data from multiple sources that may have been registered at different points in time.

The φ-operators perform fusion between information determined from at least two heterogeneous data sources that alternatively correspond to some kind of pattern or qualitative representation. The output will correspond to a normalized belief value. The operators must include solutions to the association problem [12]. The association problem is generally concerned with the problem on how to determine whether an object of a certain class observed at one time is the same object as is observed at a later time. The observations may be made by the same sensor or by different sensors of either the same or different types. This is a complex problem that normally requires probability-based approaches such as Baysian networks [13] or Demster-Shafer [14]. This problem has not yet been deeply addressed in this work but a study of the problem that can serve as a framework is presented in [12]. The general description of the functionality of this operator thus becomes:

$$\phi_{fusion} (\{<clstr> \mid < clstr\_strns> \mid ...\}_1, \{<clstr> \mid < clstr\_strns> \mid ...\}_2 \Rightarrow$$
$$\{(<same> <obj>\text{-}i ... <obj>\text{-}k <nbv>)\}$$

Finally, there is the $\phi_{similarity}$-operator that takes two images from either the same or from different sensors and transforms them into unified cluster data and then tries to establish the similarity between the two with respect to their contents. That operator can be described as:

$$\phi_{similarity}(<img\text{-}clstr>_1,<iag\text{-}clster>_2) \Rightarrow \{(<similar> < img\text{-}clstr >_1 < img\text{-}clstr >_2$$
$$<nbv>)\}.$$

This operator requires other methods than the earlier described above. One such method is described in [11] and is purely qualitative. Similarity retrieval has for a long time been part of image information retrieval and includes quiet often means for iconic indexing [6]. This type of operation is related to matching although in similarity retrieval the complete content of the images, instead of just single objects, is of concern. Another difference is that similarity retrieval is less concerned with the identity of the objects but with the classes of the objects, and their relationships and positions.

3. The Sigma System

Figure 1 shows the general architecture for information fusion systems. A *user* interacts with a user interface to produce a σ-*query*. This can be done directly or through a domain specific virtual environment customized to the user's level of expertise and described in the *user awareness subsystem*. Once a σ-query has been formulated, it can be compiled and its correctness and feasibility can be checked.

For a σ-query to be executable all the required operators must have been implemented in the system. The knowledge of what type of queries the system can execute is given in a knowledge base formed by the *Meta Database* and the *Applied operators*. The Meta Database contains a set of tables describing which operators are implemented in the system and how they can interact. The Applied operators are the set of algorithms that implement the operators. Once a query has been successfully compiled the *Sigma Query Engine* executes it against the *Distributed Multimedia Database* or directly against the *sensors input*. During the execution it applies *input filtering, indexing and data transformation* required by the application of the operators in the query. The sensors are controlled directly by the user through the user interface. The execution of a query produces (*Fused) Knowledge* that can then be used to modify the virtual environment in which the user operates providing useful feedback through appropriate *result visualizations*.

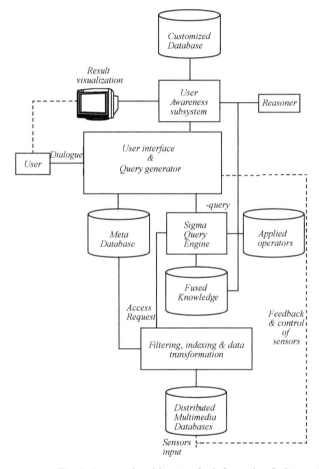

Fig. 1. A general architecture for information fusion systems.

The main characteristic of this architecture is that the same query language can be used to access any data source. This is possible due to the fact that the Meta Database and the Applied Operators hide the information to be processed, providing the ΣQL processor with a virtual data model, on which programmers base their queries.

In the next sections we show the underlying data model used by the ΣQL language and give some details of the language.

4. The Data Model

The ΣQL query language makes use of the Dimension Hierarchy Data Model (DHDM, for short) which allows a uniform structuring of heterogeneous data sources. In this data model, the structural schema to represent a data source is named *Representation Schema* while an instance of this schema is simply named *Representation*. A Representation Schema is a set of table schemas. Each table schema is described by a name and a list of fields: dim = [attr, dim_1, dim_2, ..., dim_k] (with k>=0) where attr is a proper attribute of dim, and dim_1, ..., dim_k are names of other table schemas.

Given a Representation Schema RS, a Representation is a set of instances of the table schemas in RS. An instance of a table schema *dim* will be referred to as a table of type *dim* and is composed by a possibly ordered set of rows (val_{attr}, $dval_1$, $dval_2$, ..., $dval_k$) where val_{attr} is a value for the attribute *attr* of *dim* and $dval_j$ is a reference to a table of type dim_j.

Let us give now an example showing how to represent a video clip according to DHDM. The main idea is to successively project or decompose the video clip along some dimensions. The type and number of dimensions strictly depends on the level of detail of the video clip representation we need to reach in order to get to the entities of interest occurring in the video clip. As an example, let us suppose we want to represent a video clip and are interested in representing the spatio/temporal position of the people shown in it. The dimensions we have to use are then the *time*, the *position* and the *type*. The resulting Representation Schema is given by the following table schemas: *source*=[Attr$_{source}$, time], *time*=[Attr$_{time}$, position],
position=[Attr$_{position}$, type], *type*=[Attr$_{shape}$].

Note that each dimension is directly coded into a table schema. The initial dimension *source* defines the sources to process (Attr$_{source}$) and the dimension (*time*) along which these are to be decomposed. Similarly the dimension *time* defines the temporal instances to be considered (Attr$_{time}$) and the dimension (*position*) along which to decompose the resulting entities. The dimension *type* does not refer to any other dimension since we are not interested in further details. It can be noted that the chosen Representation Schema actually defines a hierarchy of dimensions along which to decompose the source. The underlying hierarchy can be described by the string (*source* (*time* (*position* (*type*)))) where *source* is the root, *time* is its direct child and so on. Let us suppose that the video clip has 3 frames, each partitioned in 4x4 areas, and shows, among the others, four people, respectively, in the area position (3, 3) of the first frame, in the area positions (4, 3) and (4, 4) of the second frame, and in the area position (1, 3) of the third frame. Figure 2 shows part of the corresponding Representation. It can be noted that the table of type *source* has only one entity, i.e., the video clip under consideration. This entity refers to a table of type *time* containing three entities that, in our case, are the three frames of the video. Each frame refers to a table of type *position*, each containing a set of entities corresponding to the areas partitioning the frame. Finally, the tables of type *type* contain entities corresponding to the actually recognized types in each frame area.

Given a data source there are many ways of representing it. This means that a source can be represented with different Representation Schemas depending on which information in the data source needs to be represented. As an example, an alternative dimension hierarchy for representing a video clip is (*source* (*time* (*x* (*shape* (*type*))) *y* (*shape* (*type*))))). Here, again, we look at a video clip as a sequence of frames, but now each frame is seen as a set of separated rows and columns along the *x* and *y* directions, respectively. Moreover, each frame row or column is seen as a set of shapes of a certain type.

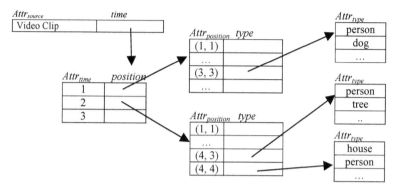

Fig. 2. A representation based on the dimension hierarchy (*source* (*time* (*position* (*type*)))).

5. The ΣQL Language

To write a ΣQL query on a given data source, a programmer must know which *Representation Schemas* are available on that source and, for each schema, he must know the corresponding dimension hierarchy. This is similar to SQL where a programmer has to know the table names and the table attributes of the relational database he wants to query. To better explain the behavior of a ΣQL query we first need to introduce the concept of "cluster" with respect to the DHDM model. Given a data source *Representation*, i.e., a set of instantiated tables representing a source, a *cluster* is a set of table rows from one or more tables with the same schema. Given a subset of tables ST in a *Representation*, with the term *clustering* we refer to the operation on ST of creating a cluster by deleting or simply not selecting some of the table rows in ST. Examples of clustering on the Representation of Figure 2, are: {time: *} that creates a cluster, on the table of type "time", with all the video frames; {time: 1, 3} that creates a cluster, on the table of type "time", with only the video frames with time stamps 1 and 3.

A clustering operation on a subset ST can work in *destructive mode* or *conservative mode*. In destructive mode all the table rows or entities that are not selected are deleted from ST; in conservative mode all the current table rows or entities that are not selected are kept in ST but not included in the cluster, i.e., they are virtually deleted - they are only needed to show the context of the cluster elements. Note that the destructive mode is the mode used in traditional relational databases.

On the other hand, a cluster can be **open** when the cluster, created by a clustering operation, is open to successive destructive clustering operations, i.e., the elements in the cluster can be deleted by successive clustering operations; or **close** when the elements in the cluster can only be virtually deleted by successive clustering operations.

Basically, a ΣQL query refines a source Representation by successively clustering it on some dimension under some constraints. The result of a query can be used by a nesting query to further refine the data source or can be output according to some presentation criteria. The following is a simple ΣQL query template:

```
SELECT dimension_list
CLUSTER clustering_op_list
FROM source [query_result [{ nested_query }]]
[WHERE condition]
[PRESENT presentation_method]
```

The FROM clause requires the specification of the input to the query: this can be either the name of the data source, or the result of a previously executed query or a nested ΣQL query. The SELECT clause requires the list of the dimensions along which to cluster the input. The CLUSTER clause requires a list of clustering operations, one for each dimension declared in the SELECT clause. The form of a clustering operation is as those shown above:

$\{dimension: [prot\_mode] \text{Val}^1_{dimension}, .., \text{Val}^n_{dimension}\}$ with the addition of the optional keyword "prot_mode" standing for one of the four protection modes: PUBLIC - if the clustering operation is to be *destructive* and the resulting cluster is to be *open*; PRIVATE- if the clustering operation is to be *destructive* and the resulting cluster is to be *close*; ALL&PUBLIC - if the clustering operation is to be *conservative* and the resulting cluster is to be *open*; ALL&PRIVATE .if the clustering operation is to be *conservative* and the resulting cluster is to be *close*.

The default protection mode is PUBLIC. Each $\text{Val}^i_{dimension}$ refers either to the wild character '*' indicating that all the dimension values must be considered, or to a constant value or to a variable whose constraints are to be set in the WHERE clause.

If the query is not nested in any other query it may not require any clustering and behave as a standard SQL query. In this case, the keyword CLUSTER is followed by the wild character '*'. The PRESENTATION clause requires the name of a presentation module that should have been defined 'ad hoc' for the presentation of the particular type of the query input.

Given the dimension hierarchy (*source* (*time* (*x* (*shape* (*type*))) *y* (*shape* (*type*))))). representing a video clip we now write a query to retrieve the columns of the second frame in a video clip, containing some people.

```
SELECT type          // Sub-query 4
CLUSTER *
FROM
          SELECT shape          // Sub-query 3
          CLUSTER {shape: *}
          FROM
                    SELECT x               // Sub-query 2
                    CLUSTER {x: *}
                    FROM
                              SELECT time       // Sub-query 1
                              CLUSTER {time: 2}
                              FROM Video
WHERE type = 'person'
```

The query must be read starting from the inner sub-query and proceeding with the closest enclosing ones. Sub-query 1 clusters the video source along the *time* dimension and extracts the frame with time stamp 2. Sub-query 2 extracts all the columns from the frame by clustering along the dimension *x*. For each column, sub-query 3 extracts all the shapes from all the columns by using the dimension *shape*. Sub-query 4 extracts all the people from all the shapes by asking for shapes of type = 'person'. The final result will then be only the columns of frame 2 containing shapes representing people while all the other shapes will be lost.

Note that sub-query 4 does not use clustering but, more likely to an SQL query, uses the WHERE clause to further refine the data. This is possible because sub-query 4 is not nested in any other sub-query. Given the hierarchy of dimension (*source* (*time* (*x* (*object* (*name, color*))), *y* (*object* (*name, color*)))))) we will now write two queries to retrieve information from a video clip whose simplification is given in Figure 3.

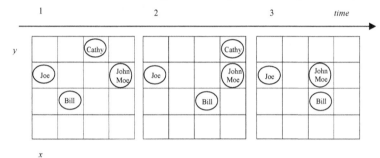

Fig. 3. A simplified video clip.

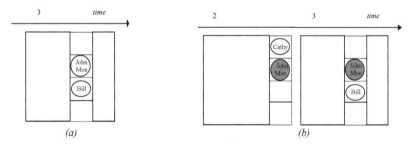

Fig. 4. Query results.

Example 1. Extract all the video frame columns containing entities with name John and entities with name Bill. The result is given by the frame column in Figure 4.a.

```
SELECT name
CLUSTER PUBLIC *
FROM
      SELECT x
      CLUSTER { x: PUBLIC * }
      FROM
                  SELECT time
                  CLUSTER { time: PUBLIC * }
                  FROM Video
      WHERE name CONTAINS 'John' AND name CONTAINS 'Bill'
```

Example 2. Extract all the video frame columns containing an entity with name Joe Moe. We want to know who else is in the same frame columns. The result is given in Figure 4.b.

```
SELECT name
CLUSTER  *
FROM
      SELECT object
      CLUSTER {object: PRIVATE *}
      FROM
               SELECT x
               CLUSTER {x: PUBLIC *}
               FROM
                        SELECT time
                        CLUSTER {time: PUBLIC *}
                        FROM Video
      WHERE name CONTAINS 'John' AND name CONTAINS 'Moe'
```

Note that because of the PUBLIC protection mode along the dimensions frame and column, all the frames and columns that do not respect the final query have been eliminated. However, because of the protection mode PRIVATE along the dimension object, all the objects have been kept both in the "SELECT object" and "SELECT name" subqueries. The final result shows the required objects in a highlighted form and also (non-highlighted) others forming their column context.

5.1 Information Fusion Using the Merge Operation

The merge operations are used to fuse information coming from two Representations to produce a new Representation. There are many possible merge operations and they strictly depend on the particular environment the query have to work in. A simple example of merge operation is the CARTESIAN_MERGE operation defined in the environment of the relational databases. Each operator con be defined on one or more distinct pairs of Representation schemata, but the same operator may not have different implementations for the same pair of Representation schemata. It is important to note that the merge operators may behave differently depending on the clusterings defined in the queries used in the operation. The template of an application of a merge operation is:

```
<MERGE OPERATOR>
<FROM>
      { select operation [merge operation]}
      ,
      { select operation [merge operation]}
```

Given the hierarchy of dimensions template for relational databases (*table* (*row* (*Attr$_1$, Attr$_2$, ..., Attr$_n$*))) and a relational database containing, among the others, a table "Names" with attributes *SSN* and *name* containing data about some people. Suppose we want to look for all web pages containing images about the people whose name is in the database. To do this, we first extract the table "Names" from the database by temporarily storing it in resultTable. This is done by using the following INSERT INTO clause:

```
INSERT INTO resultTable
{
    SELECT Table
    CLUSTER { Table: 'Names' }
    FROM DataBase
}
```

The final result is obtained through the following composed query:

```
MERGE_AND
FROM
        SELECT name
        CLUSTER {name: *}
        FROM resultTable
    ,
     SELECT pattern
     CLUSTER {pattern: *}
     FROM
                SELECT image
                CLUSTER {image: *}
                FROM
                        SELECT url
                        CLUSTER {url: PUBLIC *}
                        FROM WWW
```

In this query, the operator MERGE_AND returns a Representation made of the web documents containing images with the people whose names occur in the name field of the table "Names".

6. Discussion and Conclusion

As explained in previous sections, ΣQL can express both spatial and temporal constraints individually using the SELECT/CLUSTER construct and nested subqueries. Its limitation seems to be that constraints simultaneously involving space and time cannot be easily expressed, unless embedded in the WHERE clause. Although such constraints may be rare in practical applications, further investigation is needed in order to deal with such complex constraints.

We will also evaluate the effectiveness of the proposed spatial/temporal query language by studying several different applications. Formative evaluation will be carried out to improve the design, and summative evaluation will be carried out to conclude the experimental studies.

Acknowledgment

The authors would like to gratefully acknowledge the helpful discussions held with Dott. Francesco Orciuoli during this work.

References

[1] Ahanger, G., Benson, D. and Little, T.D., "Video Query Formulation," Proceedings of Storage and Retrieval for Images and Video Databases II, San Jose, February 1995, SPIE, pp. 280-291.

[2] Chan, E. P. F. and Zhu, R., "QL/G - A query language for geometric data bases," Proceedings of the 1st International Conf. on GIS in Urban Regional and Environment Planning, Samos, Greece, April 1996, pp 271-286.

[3] Chang, S.-K. and Jungert, E., "Symbolic Projection for Image Information Retrieval and Spatial Reasoning", Academic Press, London, 1996.

[4] Chang, S. K., "Content-Based Access to Multimedia Information," Proceedings of Aizu International Student Forum-Contest on Multimedia, (N. Mirenkov and A. Vazhenin. eds.), The University of Aizu, Aizu, Japan, Jul 20-24, 1998, pp. 2-41. (The paper is available at www.cs.pitt.edu/~chang/365/cbam7.html)

[5] Chang, S.-K. and Costabile, M. F., "Visual Interface to Multimedia Databases," in Handbook of Multimedia Information Systems, W. I. Grosky, R. Jain and R. Mehrotra, eds., Prentice Hall, 1997, pp 167-187.

[6] Chang, S.-K., Costagliola, G. and Jungert, E., "Querying Multimedia Data Sources and Databases", Procs of the 3rd International Conference on Visual Information Systems (Visual'99), Amsterdam, The Netherlands, June 2-4, 1999.

[7] Chang, S.-K. and Jungert, E.,"A Spatial/temporal query language for multiple data sources in a heterogeneous information system environment", The Intern. Journal of Cooperative Information Systems (IJCIS), vol. 7, Nos 2 & 3, 1998, pp 167-186.

[8] Egenhofer, M., "Spatial SQL: A Query and Presentation Language," IEEE Trans. on Knowledge and Data Engineering, Vol. 5, No. 2, 1991, pp. 161-174.

[9] Faloutsous, C., R. Barber, M. Flickner, J. Hafner, W. Niblack, D. Petkovic, and W. Equitz, "Efficient and Effective Querying by Image Content," Journal of Intelligent Information Systems, vol. 3, pp. 231-262, 1994.

[10] Holden, R., "Digital's DB Integrator: a commercial multi-database management system," Proceedings of 3rd International Conference on Parallel and Distributed Information Systems, Austin, TX, USA, Sept. 28-30 1994, IEEE Comput. Soc. Press, Los Alamitos, CA, USA, pp. 267-268.

[11] Lee, S.Y. and Hsu, F. J., "Spatial Reasoning and Similarity Retrieval of images using 2D C-string knowledge Representation", Pattern Recognition, vol. 25, no 3, 1992, pp 305-318.

[12] Jungert, E., "A Qualitative Approach to Reasoning about Objects in Motion Based on Symbolic Projection", in Procs. of the Conference on Multimedia Databases and Image Communication , Salerno, Italy, October 4-5, 1999.

[13] Jensen, F. V., "An Introduction to Bayesian Networks", Springer Verlag, New York, 1996.

[14] "Advances in Dempster-Shafer Theory of Evidence", Yager, Fedrizzi & Kacprzyk (Eds.), Wiley & Sons, 1994.

[15] Roussopoulos, N., Faloutsos, C. and Sellis, T., "An Efficient Pictorial Database System for PSQL," IEEE Transactions on Software Engineering, Vol. 14, No. 5, May 1988, pp. 639-650.

[16] Vazirgiannis, M., "Multimedia Data Object and Application Modelling Issues and an Object Oriented Model", Multimedia Database Systems: Design and Implementation, (Nwosu, K. C., Thuraisingham, B.and Berra P. B., Eds), Kluwer Academic Publishers, 1996, pp 208-250.

[17] Xu, X. B.; Shi, B. L. and Gu, N., "FIMDP: an interoperable multi-database platform," Procs of 8th International Hong Kong Computer Society Database Workshop. Data Mining, Data Warehousing and Client/Server Databases, Hong Kong, July 29-31 1997, SpringerVerlag Singapore, Singapore, pp 166-176.

[18] Waltz, E., Llinas, J., "Multisensor Data Fusion", Artec House, Norwood, MA, 1990.

[19] White, F. E., "Managing Data Fusion Systems in Joint and Coalition Warfare", Proceedings of EuroFusion98 - International Conference on Data Fusion, October 6-7, 1998, Great Malvern, UK, pp 49-52.

Metaphors for Visual Querying of Spatio-Temporal Databases

Christine Bonhomme, Marie-Aude Aufaure, and Claude Trépied

LISI – INSA and University of Lyon I
F- 69 621 Villeurbanne Cedex
Email: {Christine.Bonhomme, Marie-Aude.Aufaure,
Claude.Trepied@lisi.insa-lyon.fr}

Abstract. In recent years, citizen oriented applications have been developed with Geographic Information Systems (GIS). This is the reason why visual querying appears to be crucial. Many approaches for visual querying or browsing spatio-temporal data have been proposed recently. Geographic databases represent a spatio-temporal continuum. This is the reason why visual languages must integrate temporal data handling. We develop a visual language based on a query-by-example philosophy for spatial and temporal data. A query is formulated by means of predefined icons which map spatial and temporal objects and operators. New visual metaphors such as balloons and anchors are proposed in order to express spatial and temporal criteria. After a state of the art of visual querying for geographic databases, we define a spatio-temporal model. The visual language and its user interface are then explained. Samples are proposed upon a road risk management application. In this sample database both discrete and continuous temporal data are taken into account: moving points such as trucks, and life-cycle objects such as rivers. We then conclude about our future work.

Keywords. Spatio-temporal databases, Visual language, Geographic Information Systems, Metaphors.

1. Introduction

The main characteristics of Geographic Information Systems (GIS) are tied to the specificity of the spatial data they manage. GIS aims to store huge volume of data. They provide tools in order to manage these data. They often are used to handle applications coming from various domains such as urban and environmental planning, geomarketing, tourism and others general spatial applications.

Nowadays, the challenge is to consider together spatial and temporal data: the spatio-temporal data management is a rapidly growing field of research. Another important research domain still concerns ergonomic and friendly visualization of data. Spatial data are graphical by nature. Spatial relations are also expressed with a graphical manner. So, we can say that visual languages are well adapted to query spatial databases. Generally, spatial operators can be represented according to their mathematical visual representations which are well-known by users. We can notice that temporal operators can also be represented along a time axis.

R. Laurini (Ed.): VISUAL 2000, LNCS 1929, pp. 140-153, 2000.

This paper proposes an extension of the Lvis [2] language in order to support both spatial and temporal data. New metaphors are proposed to express spatial and temporal criteria. We introduce a spatio-temporal model.

In section 2, we present how to friendly visualize data. In Section 3, we define the concept of visual metaphor and give some examples of its usefulness. Section 4 deals with the state of the art on visual languages for the querying of spatial databases. We argue for the extension of such languages to spatio-temporal querying. In Section 5, we outline the spatio-temporal model proposed. In Section 6, we describe the language Lvis and its environment from the specification of a query to its translation into GIS host query language. In Section 7, we give some examples of Lvis queries. We conclude, in Section 8, with the summary of this paper and sketch future works.

2. Data Visualization

The evolution of man-machine communication in the field of Information Systems can be divided into two parts: firstly, the visualization of query results, and secondly, the use of methods to select relevant information in order to generate user-adapted answers.

The first point concerns information visualization [7][11]. Data are mapped onto visual structures such as a 3D visual structures which can be manipulated with rotation tools. The user selects the best vision angle in order to visually point out groups of points. In recent years, multidimensional methods have been developed. They can be classified into four categories: (1) pixel representations, (2) factorization methods, (3) parallel coordinates and (4) hierarchical methods. Pixel representation allows to associate to each variable a pixel with a color corresponding to its class. Factorization methods are used in order to bring together objects with a similar behavior. Parallel coordinates methods represent the main variables on parallel vertical axis. Variables are represented using broken lines and their position on each axis is determinate by the observed value on these axis. The hierarchical methods subdivide the multidimensional space into successive plans. In general, tools based upon hierarchical methods allow the user to navigate into the information and to visualize the information using different views (panoramic view, etc.).

In conclusion of this part concerning information visualization, we can say that many research efforts have been done during the last decade but it seems that two fields can be improved. Firstly, the ergonomic field which have to integrate 3-dimensional representations and animation. Secondly, the navigational field in order to allow the end-user to have different viewpoints about its data. In fact, a user can be interested by a particular information without having a global view, or can build a data set in order to identify objects close to this set, etc.

The second point concerns the selection of relevant information for an end-user. User profiles are generated and learning methods are performed (such as neural networks) in order to generate cooperative answers. User modeling have to be studied taking into account the adaptation and evolution of the end-users.

Next section describes the concept of visual metaphors.

3. Visual Metaphors

This section briefly recalls the concept of metaphor and describes its use for interacting with a spatio-temporal database.

3.1. The Concept of Metaphor

A *metaphor* is a cognitive process where a thing is understood in terms of another. It can be seen as a *mapping* from a *source domain* (the familiar concepts) to a *target domain* (the concepts that the user does not know, e.g., concepts in computer sciences) [20], [13], [9]. In order for a metaphor to be effective, the source domain must be by definition well known by the end user.

Use of metaphors in an interface allows to improve the user's level of understanding of the system. Moreover, when the tool is better understood, it seems easier to use, and finally allows work of greater efficiency. The success of the Macintosh interface depends mainly on the use of the desktop metaphor associated to the direct manipulation metaphor. These metaphors, applied to the concepts of a computer operating system, make quasi-intuitive the use of a computer (e.g., analogy between a 'file' and a 'document', a 'directory' and a 'folder', the 'deletion of a file' and the 'trashcan') and consequently, are very useful for novice users who are not familiar with computer terminology. Three classic problems can nevertheless be encountered [16]:

- Some concepts of the source domain (so well known by the end user) do not have corresponding elements in the target domain. The user could be frustrated.
- Some concepts of the target domain do not have corresponding elements in the source domain. In order to overcome this limitation, and consequently improve the usability of the system, it is possible to extend the metaphor by including those concepts that are not the source domain, and this without disrupting user's understanding of the metaphor [13].
- Some concepts exist in both domains but work differently, that can disturb the user. A smooth distortion is nevertheless possible whereas a strict respect of the metaphor generally can lead to a low-powered interface.

3.2. Use of Visual Metaphors in Human-Database Interaction

Concepts used in computer sciences are quite theoretical and cannot be supposed known by the end user. Therefore, it is interesting to also use metaphors in the field of database interfaces. A basis of a formal approach for the construction of metaphors in this field has been proposed [10] and allows us to clarify our vocabulary. Figure 1 describes the use of a visual metaphor in human-database interaction.

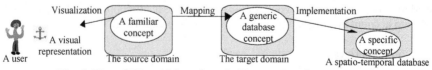

Fig. 1. Use of Visual Metaphors in Human-Database Interaction.

The three classic components of a metaphor are in the middle of the figure: the source domain, the target domain and the source-to-target mapping. Since there are still no standard data model and no standard query language for spatio-temporal databases, our target domain is a set of *generic* concepts (i.e. that exist in one form or another in most of existing models and languages). This genericity allows the metaphor to be independent of the implementation level and consequently to be used with several different systems. If the study concerned a specific system, it would obviously be possible to use the set of (specific) concepts of this system as target domain. Towards the end user, each concept of the source domain must be visualized. For this purpose we associate to each concept a *visual representation* (also called drawing [9] or cartographic object [24]) that can be displayed on a computer screen (e.g., text, symbol and icon).

Very few metaphors have been proposed in the field of spatial database interfaces but this way seems very promising. The map overlay metaphor [13] allows geo-referenced data to be represented onto a map displayed on the screen. Tools such as zoom and pan views are often associated to this metaphor in order to improve the properties of a paper map. Another example of visual metaphor, named the blackboard metaphor [21], is used in visual query languages. Its philosophy is to let users drawing the sketch of their query. The main advantage is that the resulting query is in accordance with the mental model of the user. Another advantage is that the end-user do not have to learn a new language.

Metaphors prove their usefulness in the field of interaction with Geographic Information Systems. We have to define new metaphors in order to take into account temporal and spatial data.

The next section describes the state of the art of visual languages dedicated to geographic information.

4. Visual Spatial Querying

The Lvis language is built on the state-of-the-art knowledge in visual spatial query languages. This section briefly describes three prominent visual spatial query languages seen in the literature, namely Cigales, *Sketch!* and Spatial-Query-by-Sketch, then summarizes their present limitations for querying spatio-temporal databases.

4.1. The Cigales Language

This language [19], [4], [6] can be seen as a precursor in the field of visual manipulation of spatial data. It allows us to express a visual query by means of a composition of static icons. The user interface contains two windows: one to express an elementary query (sub-query) and the other to resume the final query. An elementary query is usually built by defining the operands at first, then clicking on the spatial operator icon. The system answers by displaying the corresponding iconic composition. The database schema representation was initially textual then iconic in the latter versions [5] and its access is always contextual. A visual query is represented by an internal functional expression, which is next translated into an extended SQL query. A prototype is developed on a SUN workstation.

4.2. The *Sketch!* Language

This language [21] gives a greater freedom to the end user by means of the blackboard metaphor. A spatial query is expressed by drawing a sketch on the screen, which is later interpreted by the system. It means the spatial operators are directly derived from the sketch, but not chosen by the user, and then displayed on the screen. Moreover, a graphical language related to ER-diagrams is available. It allows the expression of the non-spatial part of the query (i.e. the part using non-spatial data) in a separated window. In both cases, the user consults a textual representation (menus) of the database schema. From the two parts of the query, the system builds a unique internal logical expression.

4.3. The Spatial-Query-by-Sketch Language

This language [14] looks like *Sketch!*, however, it is founded on a formal model for topological spatial relations (in 2D) and a computational model for the relaxation of sketched constraints. Spatial-Query-by-Sketch uses a touch-sensitive input device (e.g., a touch screen with a pen). The user interface is organized into three major interaction areas: (1) the control panel in which the user selects each object type he wants to use in the sketch of his query; (2) the sketch region in which the user draws an example of what he is looking for; and (3) the overview area which displays the sketch in its entirety. A visual query often contains constraints that the user did not intend to specify. To decide which constraints might be relaxed and which constraints should be followed, the query processor uses degrees of conceptual similarity between topological relations and the premise "if topology matters, metric refines", i.e. non explicitly specified metric constraints (e.g., distance, length and area) are just employed to sort the answers that fulfill the topological constraints. In conclusion, the query result is a close approximation of the topology drawn, but not necessarily of the metric.

4.4. The Present Limitations of Visual Spatial Query Languages

The languages we have just presented show considerable improvement in the field of visual spatial query languages. However, they also have currently some limitations:

- *The language is not associated to a visual representation of the database schema:* only textual representation (menus) of some concepts (e.g., object types and attributes) is usually provided. So database schema and queries are not represented with the same paradigm and a part of the semantics of the database schema (IS-A relationship, for example) is not taken into account by the end user.
- *Non-uniform handling of spatial and non-spatial objects:* even if the objects must be visualized in separated windows to avoid any ambiguity, they must be manipulated by means of the same language in order to avoid cognitive overload.
- *The specification of classical operators (e.g., Boolean operators and quantifiers) is not well studied:* it is sometimes difficult to express a disjunction (OR) and usually impossible to visually express a universal quantifier (ALL). We meet here the problem of visual specification of complex queries.

- *Certain spatial operators are not available*: it is often the case, for example, of directional operators (e.g., left of) and topological operators in 3D
- *Expressive power of the query language is unknown.* Its study needs to formalize the language and to define a notion of completeness.
- *The temporal aspects of spatial objects are not considered.* Depending on the type of time considered [15], it is sometimes necessary to take account of the fact that a spatial object (e.g., a river) can move, be modified or transform itself into an object of another type. Some *graphical* languages have been proposed [8], [12] but they all use too much graphical conventions to really be used by final user. We really believe that the best way is to define a *visual* language (i.e. using visual metaphors) associated to a *conceptual* model capturing the semantics of the *spatio-temporal* information. Very few data models of this kind have been proposed in the past [23], [25].

Our ultimate aim is to find a solution, even partial, to these problems. For the time being, we introduce a spatio-temporal conceptual model and its visual representation as a beginning of solution to the last problem. We also think that visual querying must be combined with navigation methods in order to build a user-friendly language. The language needs also to be adapted to the end-user, using profiles describing the user's preferences, in order to select only relevant information. The next section outlines the spatio-temporal model proposed.

5. Spatio-Temporal Model

Let us assume that, as far as applications of our interest are concerned, the time of transmission of information is insignificant (real-time updating). We consider a mono-temporal context where only valid time is taken into account and transactional time is left out.

5.1. Objects and Queries

In our model, each spatio-temporal *object* possesses an internal identifier (oid), a thematic identifier, a semantic identifier, a spatial location, a temporal location, a list of successive states and, if necessary, additional thematic attributes.

The thematic identifier of an object is associated to the type of this object. This object type represents a logical name (name of the relational table or the object class). The semantic identifier allows the user to point out an object as friendly as possible: it is composed of a sub-set of mono-valued or multi-valued attributes of the object. Let us assume that each object has a spatial location: mobile objects can be defined as punctual objects whose location often changes. In the same way, we consider that each object has a temporal location, that is [t, *now*] with t < *now*. This time interval represents the valid period for the current version of the object. Nevertheless, the value *no_change* can be attributed to some objects such as a geologic layer for which no change in time could occur and so for which the temporal validity is permanent. The list of successive states of objects contains an event list of its spatial evolution along time. Thus, in the case of moving objects, the position of the objects at given instants is saved; in the case of the evolution of cadastral parcels, for example, the shape of these objects is saved along its changes.

Queries can be classified as follows: thematic, spatial, temporal and spatio-temporal queries. Thematic queries do not include any spatial or temporal criteria. Spatial (temporal) queries are defined with one or more spatial (temporal) criteria. Spatio-temporal queries involve at least one spatio-temporal criterion or a combination of spatial and temporal criteria.

5.2. Basic Visual Elements

An object is visualized by an icon, a geometric shape and a color. This visual representation can be reinforced by textual elements and others visual metaphors such as balloons or anchors (See Figure 2).

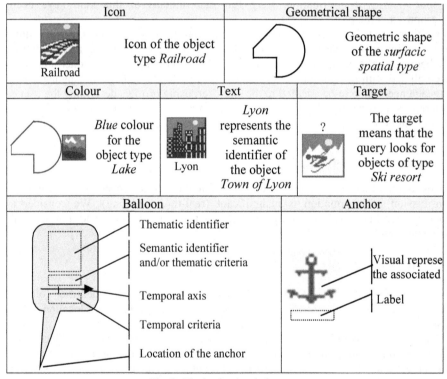

Fig. 2. The basic visual elements.

An icon models the thematic identifier of an object (i.e. its type). A geometrical shape is associated to each object of a query in order to represent its spatial type. The icon of an object is framed by a color. This same color is used to draw its associated geometrical shape. Thematic criteria of a query are expressed using text. The thematic criterion of an object is visualized by a textual chain located under its icon. When an object is the target of the query, a question mark is located above its icon. Temporal criteria of a query are expressed using the balloon visual metaphor. A balloon contains the specification of the criteria related to a given object. One or more anchoring pins are associated to a balloon (simple or multiple anchoring). The color of the balloon is an indication of the occurrence of an object involved in the query.

The use of colors can replace the use of variables. An anchor is the reduced representation of a balloon.

The spatial criteria of a query are expressed by means of the relative positions of the geometrical shapes of the objects of the query. Three spatial object types are handled by the model: *Point, Line* and *Polygon* (See Figure 3).

Fig. 3. Visual representations of spatial types.

The temporal criteria of an object are expressed by means of interval values onto a linear axis. The main temporal object type handled by the model is the *Interval*. A specific visual representation is associated with a period of null duration, called *Instant*. Figure 4 shows the visual representations of an interval or an instant.

Fig. 4. Visual representations of temporal types.

5.3. Visual Representations of Operators

Queries are composed of operands (objects of the query) and operators (logical, spatial, temporal or spatio-temporal). Figure 5 shows the visual representations of the set of the operators handled by the model.

Thematic queries consist in selecting objects or searching objects of a particular type, sub-type or complex type. Figure 6 shows examples of visual representations of thematic queries. They generally involve three basic visual elements: icons, textual chains and color. Logical operators are used to build complex queries (see Figure 5).
Spatial queries contain at least a spatial criterion. Spatial operators are topologic, metric, set and interactive selection ones. In this paper, we focus on topological and metric operators (see Figure 5). The following topological operators are supported by the spatial norm Spatial-SQL [17]: *intersection, inclusion, adjacency, disjunction* and *equality*. These operators can be applied upon spatial object types supported by our system: point, lines and polygons. The model can be extended to volumetric types. Objects or objects types are visualized using their thematic identifier (icon) and their spatial type.

Temporal queries include at least one temporal criterion. Temporal operators are based on those defined in [1]. Allen defines the following operators : *before, equals, meets, overlaps, during, starts* and *finishes* (see Figure 5). These operators are useful to compare two objects during time or one object vis-à-vis a reference period. So, these temporal operators may be unary or binary ones and are defined for the temporal object type *Interval*.

Logical operators	And		Or		Not

Spatial operators • Topological operators • Metric operators	Intersection	Inclusion	Adjacency	Disjunction	Equality
	Path	Distance	Ray distance		Buffer zone

Temporal operators • Allen operators	Before	Meets	Overlaps	During
	Equals	Starts		Finishes

Spatio-temporal operators • Life-cycle operators	Creation	Destruction	Merge
	Growth	Diminution	Split

Fig. 5. Visual representations of the Lvis language's operators.

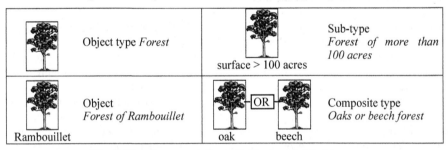

Fig. 6. Visual representations of objects and object types.

Spatio-temporal queries involve at least one spatial criterion and one temporal criterion. They can be perceived as being at the same time spatial and temporal queries. In concrete terms, these queries are thematic queries which include spatial and temporal criteria. They can also be the result of spatio-temporal specification criteria such as the evolution of spatial properties during time. We can specify six evolution operators: *creation, split, merge, growth, diminution* and *destruction*. (see Figure 5). They are used to memorize state changes and, in particular, form changes of spatial objects during time.

In the next section, we present the global architecture of our project. We emphasize the specifications of thematic, spatial, temporal and spatio-temporal queries.

6. Architecture

Lvis is a visual query language dedicated to spatial and temporal databases. This language is involved in a more global project which consists in associating this visual language to textual languages in order to express queries against any GIS platform.

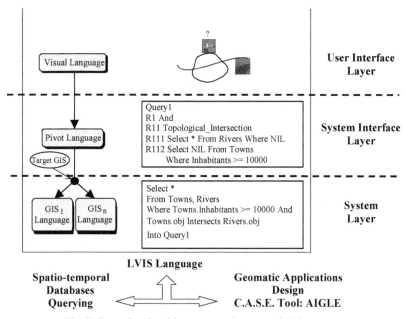

Fig. 7. From the visual language to the target GIS language.

A textual expression is associated to a visual query. This expression is based upon a pivot language. A query expressed in this pivot language is then translated into the host language of a GIS. Figure 7 shows the three levels of languages integrated in our system: visual, textual and target. It also underlines that Lvis can be used for spatio-temporal databases querying and also for applications design. Indeed, its visual characteristics have been reused in the marketed C.A.S.E. tool AIGLE [18] for the design of geomatic applications.

Lvis is based on a query-by-example philosophy and is an extension of the Cigales language [4]. A set of icons representing objects types stored in the spatio-temporal database is available. Operators like logical, spatial, temporal and spatio-temporal ones are also represented using icons. At the beginning, only spatial and logical operators are available.

The pivot language is the hearth of our system: it allows visual queries to be translated into the target language of a given GIS. At first, visual queries are stored using a tree structure. Then, they are translated into a textual expression according to the syntax of the pivot language. Last, textual queries are expressed in the target language of the GIS. The pivot language is based on a lexical parser that aims to be compatible with the standardized Spatial-SQL [17] for spatial operators and with TSQL2 [22] for temporal operators.

The validated query is computed and executed using a target GIS. When the user selects the *execute* command, the visual query is translated into the pivot language and then into the GIS target language. Objects which satisfies the defined criteria are then selected and visualized on a map. Two translation modules have been implemented: (1) Extraction of a textual representation (pivot language) from the structural representation of a given query; (2) Translation of the query from the pivot language to the GIS host language. We have chosen the marketed GIS MapInfo to perform tests on a example database.

The current work concerning our prototype is on one hand, the integration of the visual metaphors of balloons and anchors and on the other hand, the implementation of complex queries and of the graphical display of query results. Moreover a set of cognitive tests have been done [3]. Their major aims are to show that the icons of the language (especially spatial and logical operators) are well recognized by end-users. Both persons working with GIS and persons non expert in geography or in computing have been tested. The first results show that icons of the language are well accepted by the two populations. These tests could be extended to the new visual metaphors of balloons and anchors in order to test the recognition of visual representation of spatio-temporal queries. A Java version of the prototype is currently studying so as to test the usability of the language. Finally, ambiguities of visual representations of complex queries is another field of our actual research.

7. Example

In this section, we illustrate the specification of a query dedicated to a spatio-temporal database. The application concerns mobile and distorting objects.

Our sample database concerns the field of hazardous material transportation. It seems to be interesting in such an application to anticipate trucks route. We also have to take into account the evolution of the environment (growth of towns, floods, etc). We define four object classes: *Trucks, Roads, Rivers, Towns, Accidents* and *Floods*. *Towns* class contains the attribute *Number_inhabitants*, and *Accidents* class contains the attribute *Number_of_victims*

Query 1 (See Figure 8.a): Which paths from Paris to Vienna avoid towns of more than 1000 inhabitants?

This spatial query is built in two steps. The user first applies a metric operator (path) between two polygonal objects *Town of Paris* and *Town of Vienna* and specifies that the object type *Road* is the target of the query (route between *Paris* and *Vienna)*. The user then applies a topological operator (disjunction) to a linear object of type *Road* and to a polygonal object of type '*Towns of more than 1000 inhabitants*'.

Query 2 (See Figure 8.b): Where did crashes occur on the "National Road 7" during the month of December 1998?

We will use the balloon as new visual metaphor. To obtain this temporal query, two ways are possible. The first one consists in the application of a temporal operator of inclusion in the time interval *[01.12.1998, 31.12.98]* for a punctual object of type

Accident. The second one lets the user place a balloon on the pre-existant road "RN7" and directly enter the object type *Accident* and the temporal value *1998 December* into the balloon.

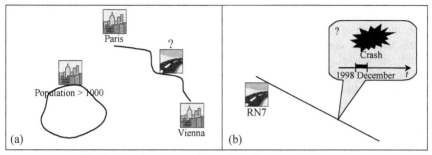

Fig. 8. Visual representations of: (a) Query 1; (b) Query 2.

Query 3 (See Figure 9): Which trucks did drive in a riverside expressway five hours before a flood?

This spatio-temporal query concerns a mobile track and the evolution of the life-cycle of objects. Two balloons (and anchors) are necessary to specify this query. First, the user applies a topological operator (adjacency) to a polygonal object of type *Road* and a polygonal object of type *River*. Next, he specifies the temporal criteria by means of two balloons .The first one is concerned with the flood event associated to a riverside object and the second one, with the passing of a truck five hours before the flood.

 The visual representation of this query can be split in two windows: *Spatial view* and *Temporal view*. The spatial view focuses on the spatial criteria of the query. In this representation, temporal criteria are visualized as anchors by default. The temporal view focuses on the temporal criteria of the query. Here, temporal constraints are represented in a chronological order. Each temporal criterion is represented by an icon (object type) and a label (reference to an anchor) Anchors may also be used to specify occurrences of events. The spatial and temporal views of the Query 3 are given in Figure 9.

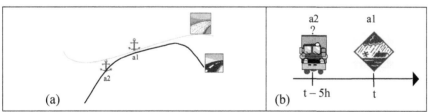

Fig. 9. Visual representation of Query 3: (a) Spatial view; (b) Temporal view.

8. Conclusion

In this paper, we present Lvis, an extension of the visual language Cigales devoted to spatio-temporal information systems. This language is based upon a query-by-example philosophy. We focus on the necessity for the language to be extended to deal with spatio-temporal querying and we propose a spatio-temporal model. This model includes on one side, the definition of spatio-temporal objects and on the other side the definition of spatial, temporal and spatio-temporal queries classes. Visual metaphors such as icons, balloons and anchors as well as visual representation of queries as a whole, are introduced. We then present the architecture of our project and the user interface of the language. We then illustrate the querying of a sample spatio-temporal database concerning the field of hazardous material transportation. Some examples of spatial, temporal and spatio-temporal queries involving mobile and distorting objects are presented.

A prototype has been developed according to the architecture of the project described in this paper. The current work concerning our prototype is the integration of the visual metaphors of balloons and anchors. The implementation of complex queries and of the graphical display of query results is studied too. We are also extending our language in order to allow the end-user to express queries using different modes (using pre-defined icons, the blackboard metaphor, etc.). This language will also integrate user profiles in the future which contains user preferences and information about how he uses the system.

9. References

[1]   J.F. Allen (1983) Maintaining Knowledge about Temporal Intervals, *Communications of the ACM,* Vol. 26, No. 11, pp 832-843.

[2]   M.-A. Aufaure-Portier, C. Bonhomme (1999) A High Level Visual Langage for Spatial Data Management, *Visual'99, 3rd International Conference on Visual Information Systems*, Amsterdam, The Netherlands, 2-4 June.

[3]   Aufaure M.-A., Bonhomme C., Lbath A., LVIS : Un langage visuel d'interrogation de bases de données spatiales, CIDE'99, *Second International Conference on the Electronic Document*, Syria, July 5-7, 1999. pp. .

[4]   M.-A. Aufaure (1995) A High-Level Interface Language for GIS, *Journal of Visual Languages and Computing*, Academic Press, Vol. 6, n°2, pp 167-182.

[5]   A. Brossier-Wansek & M. Mainguenaud (1995) Manipulations of Graphs with a Visual Query Language: Application to a Geographical Information System, *Proceedings of VDB-3 (Third Working Conference on Visual Database Systems, IFIP 2.6)*, Lausanne, Switzerland, pp 227-246.

[6]   D. Calcinelli & M. Mainguenaud (1994) Cigales, a Visual Language for Geographical Information System: the User Interface, *Journal of Visual Languages and Computing*, vol. 5, no. 2, pp 113-13.

[7]   S.T. Card, J.D. Mackinmay, B. Shneiderman (1999) Readings in Information Visualization: Using Vision to Think, Morgan Kaufmann

[8]   A.F. Cardenas, I.T. Ieong, R.K. Taira, R. Barker & C.M. Breant (1993) The Knowledge-Based Object-Oriented PICQUERY+ Language, *IEEE Transactions on Knowledge and Data Engineering*, vol. 5, no. 4, pp 644-657.

[9]   T. Catarci, M.F. Costabile & M. Matera (1995) Visual Metaphors for Interacting with Databases, *SIGCHI Bulletin (Special Interest Group on Computer-Human Interaction)*, vol. 27, no. 2, pp 15-17.

[10]   T. Catarci, M.F. Costabile, I.F. Cruz, Y. Ioannidis & B. Shneiderman (1995) Data Models, Visual Representations, Metaphors: How to Solve the Puzzle ?, *Proceedings of VDB-3 (Third Working Conference on Visual Database Systems, IFIP 2.6)*, Lausanne, Switzerland, pp 153-156.

[11]   C. Chen (1999) Information Visualization and Virtual Environments, Springer Verlag

[12] G. Congiu, A. Del Bimbo & E. Vicario (1995) Iconic Retrieval by Contents from Databases of Cardiological Sequences, *Proceedings of VDB-3 (Third Working Conference on Visual Database Systems, IFIP 2.6)*, Lausanne, Switzerland, pp 139-152

[13] M.J. Egenhofer & J.R. Richards (1993) Exploratory Access to Geographic Data Based on the Map-overlay Metaphor, *Journal of Visual Languages and Computing*, vol. 4, pp 105-125.

[14] M.J. Egenhofer (1996) Spatial-Query-by-Sketch, *Proceedings of VL'96 (IEEE Symposium on Visual Languages)*, Boulder, USA, pp 60-67.

[15] A.U. Frank (1998), Different Types of "Times" in GIS, In: *Spatial and Temporal Reasoning in Geographic Information Systems*, Eds. M.J. Egenhofer & R.G. Golledge, Oxford University Press, pp 40-62.

[16] D. Genter & J. Nielson (1996) The Anti-Mac Interface, *Communications of the ACM*, vol. 39, no. 8, pp 70-82.

[17] *ISO/IEC JTC1/SC21/N10441, SQL Multimedia and Application Packages, Part 3: Spatial*, 172 p. (1996)

[18] A. Lbath, M.A. Aufaure-Portier, R. Laurini (1997), Using a Visual Language for the Design and Query in GIS Customization, *VISUAL'97, 2nd International Conference on Visual Information systems*, San Diego, USA, pp. 197-204

[19] M. Mainguenaud & M.A. Portier (1990) CIGALES: a Graphical Query Language for Geographical Information Systems, *Proceedings of the 4th International Symposium on Spatial Data Handling,* Zurich, Switzerland, pp 393-404.

[20] D.M. Mark (1992) Spatial Metaphors for Human-Computer Interaction, *Proceedings of the 5th International Symposium on Spatial Data Handling*, Charleston, South Carolina, USA, pp 104-112.

[21] B. Meyer (1992) Beyond Icons: Towards New Metaphors for Visual Query Languages for Spatial Information Systems, *Proceedings of the first International Workshop on Interfaces to Database Systems*, Ed. R. Cooper, Springer-Verlag 1993, Glasgow, UK, pp 113-135.

[22] R. Snodgrass (Ed.). *The TSQL2 Temporal Query Language.* Kluwer Academic Publishers, 1995

[23] S. Spaccapietra, C. Parent & E. Zimanyi (1998) Modeling Time from a Conceptual Perspective, *Proceedings of CIKM'98 (International Conference on Information and Knowledge Management)*, Washington D.C., USA, Retrieved in February 1999 from the World Wide Web: http://lbdwww.epfl.ch/e/ publications/articles.ps/CIKM98.ps

[24] A. Voisard (1995) Mapgets: A Tool for Visualizing and Querying Geographic Information, *Journal of Visual Languages and Computing*, vol. 6, no. 4, pp 367-384.

[25] M.F. Worboys (1998), A Generic Model for Spatio-Bitemporal Geographic Information, In: *Spatial and Temporal Reasoning in Geographic Information Systems*, Eds. M.J. Egenhofer & R.G. Golledge, Oxford University Press, pp 25-39.

About Ambiguities in Visual GIS Query Languages: a Taxonomy and Solutions

Franck Favetta, Marie-Aude Aufaure-Portier

Laboratoire d'Ingénierie des Systèmes d'Information
INSA & UCBL Lyon
F-69 621 Villeurbanne
{ffavetta, maufaure}@lisi.insa-lyon.fr

Abstract. In visual query languages, especially in Geographic Information Systems (GIS), a query can lead to multiple interpretations for the system and for the user. An origin is that a unique working space is used to express different kinds of information. Another origin is that the user gives his own semantics to information. Ambiguities represent a big challenge in visual query languages because they are found at different levels and sublevels. Ambiguities depend on the action and on the interpretation of the user and on the representation of the system. We propose a taxonomy of ambiguities in visual GIS query languages in order to determine which case of ambiguity is met and at which level. We also propose different solutions to resolve the ambiguities we detected. A model has been made to solve a particular case of ambiguity in the Lvis [3] visual language. This model shows that the number of semantics in a spatial ambiguity can be very high. An extension of Lvis is currently implemented to test some resolution ways.

1 Introduction

The field of our research is the Geographic Information Systems (GIS). We propose here solutions to resolve problems in GIS domain, but the proposals made are more general and could certainly be extended to other research areas that are out of the scope of our studies, e.g., medical domain, etc. Many research works have been recently done in the domain of GIS, especially for data storage, new indexing methods, query optimization, etc. [10]. A main characteristics of GIS is to manage complex and large amount of data. A fundamental research area concerns the definition of high level user interface because GIS users are generally non-computer scientists. Many applications are concerned by spatial data: urban applications, geomarketing, vehicle guidance and navigation, tourism and so on. Humans implied in these applications are architects, engineers, urban planners, etc. In addition, GIS applications have recently migrated towards citizen-oriented applications. This makes crucial the definition of simple and user-friendly interfaces.

In most cases, the languages proposed by marketed GIS are very technical and dedicated to only one specific system. The consequence is the complexity for non-computer specialists to formulate queries. Visual GIS query languages have been proposed to solve this lack of user-friendliness. It exists different types of languages and different user profiles [7]. In visual languages, a query can lead to multiple *interpretations* for the system and for the user, spawning *ambiguities*. The origin is

R. Laurini (Ed.): VISUAL 2000, LNCS 1929, pp. 154-165, 2000.
© Springer-Verlag Berlin Heidelberg 2000

that a unique space is used to express different kinds of information and that the user gives his own semantics to information (user's mental model). The actions of the user may not represent his intentions and may lead to a wrong interpretation. The system may also represent information by different visual ways and has to choose one. So ambiguities are found at different levels: user's action and interpretation, system's interpretation and representation. In each level, several sublevels are also found, making the ambiguities one of the most important and difficult problem in visual GIS query languages. Only few research work has currently been done in this domain, and the ambiguities have not been completely detected. It would be difficult to exhaustively manage ambiguities in visual GIS Query languages.

Even if we can't be exhaustive, we propose a taxonomy of ambiguities in visual GIS query languages to better examine which case of ambiguity is met and at which level. We then propose solutions to resolve the detected ambiguities. A model has been made to solve a particular case of ambiguity in the Lvis [3] visual language. An extension of Lvis is currently implemented to test other ways of resolution. Section 2 firstly presents a brief state of the art of visual languages for spatial databases. Section 3 exposes the proposed taxonomy. Section 4 shows how to resolve the detected ambiguities, with a model adapted to a particular case of ambiguity. Section 5 presents our conclusion, perspectives and future work.

2 State of the Art

Many query languages have been proposed for Geographical Information Systems. We can summarise them in three categories: textual, diagrammatic and visual languages.

The *textual languages* are divided in two subcategories: the natural and formal languages. Natural languages seem user-friendly for end-users but present many problems of ambiguities. Formal languages like SQL are non-ambiguous, but present a technical barrier for users who are novices in computer science.

The *diagrammatic languages* offer a diagrammatic representation of the structure of the database, taking advantage of the two dimensions of the screen. We find three categories: the tabular languages, the languages using forms, and the graphical languages. Tabular approaches are defined as extensions of the QBE (Query-By-Example) language [15]. Thanks to the advent of graphical terminals, user-friendliness increased, allowing the use of forms and diagrams. The query expressed by forms is a metaphorical representation of the completion of an administrative form, filling textual fields and choosing attributes in lists. The graphical languages are a diagrammatic representation of the database structure [1]. The user-friendliness is strongly increased but, looking at GIS domain, the spatial criteria are still represented by textual variables and values. Besides, novice users don't need a precise representation of the structure of the database, and the manipulation of operators in a database structure is not intuitive.

Visual Languages use metaphors to model spatial objects and spatial relations between objects. A metaphor can be seen as a mapping from familiar concepts to concepts that the user does not know. For example, an icon can be viewed as a visual representation of a concept. This approach has been expanded very rapidly because of the evolution of the applications towards citizens and the requirements of user-friendliness. Two main approaches have been developed to design visual languages: (1) the end-user uses commands like buttons to display metaphorical patterns like icons or symbols (a constant set of defined lines) in a *command used* interface, and (2) the end-user makes a drawing directly on the screen using the *blackboard metaphor*. The first approach is illustrated by the *Lvis* language [3] (Fig. 1(a)) and the *Cigales* language [12]. Patterns are displayed in the working space which present icons corresponding to icon buttons (*icon selection*). The second approach is illustrated by the *Sketch!* [14] and *Spatial-Query-By-Sketch* [8] (Fig. 1(b)) languages. The user is free to draw by hand shapes or symbols on the screen, to express an objet or an operator. Hybrid languages have also been proposed which offer interfaces similar to the classical CAD or painting applications and including also textual inputs [13] [9]. The reader can refer to [2] to have more details about query languages for GIS. The main advantage of these two approaches comes from the fact that the user does not have any constraint to express a query and no new language to learn. Visual languages can be seen as precursors for visual querying in the GIS domain application. Nevertheless, many limitations still remain. The main limitation comes from the ambiguities of visual languages.

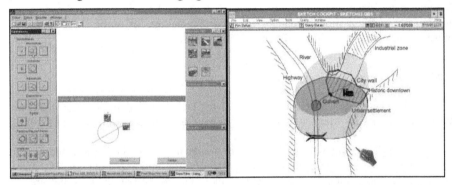

Fig. 1. Two visual GIS query languages. (a) *Lvis* [2] and (b) *Spatial-Query-By-Sketch* [8]

3 Taxonomy of the Ambiguities

In [5], a model has been formally defined for visual query systems which handles ambiguous interpretations of images. This formalism helps us to describe the whole visual query environment and to understand where ambiguities can be found. According to the authors, a *visual sentence* is a triple $<i,d,<int,mat>>$ where i is an *image*, d is a *description*, *int* is an *interpretation function* and *mat* a *materialization function*. Fig. 2 shows a representation of the formalism. The *image* is expressed by the means of a *pictorial language*. The *description* is expressed by the means of a *description language*. The functions *int* and *mat* link *images* with *descriptions*. Several *images* can *materialize* the same *description*. This formalism allows to manage multiple visual representations that convey the same meaning, as needed by different users for different tasks.

$$\text{description} \quad \text{description } d \xrightarrow[\text{interpretation } int()]{\text{materialization } mat()} \text{ image } i \quad \text{pictorial}$$
language   language

Fig. 2. Formalism of a visual query

We can use this formalism to describe the whole environment of a visual query system. The environment encapsulates a query language system and an interface. The user communicates through the use of a pictorial language (Fig. 3). The environment also provides, in the interface, commands like buttons and environment modifiers. The command part of the interface uses *materialization*, e.g., an icon button.

Fig. 3. Visual query environment

In the taxonomy, it is useful to classify ambiguities by what the system and the user may do, i.e., by the different *actions* of the user and by the different *images* the system can *materialize*. By this way, (1) when a user make an action, a visual GIS query system can know which ambiguities can occur and (2) when a visual GIS query system supplies a *materialization*, it can know how the user can *interpret* it. We will so classify ambiguities by user *actions* and system *materialization*. We need to describe which user *actions* and system *materialization* we can have.

In GIS environments, the user handles GIS objects, e.g., a town represented by a spatial attribute, and GIS operators, e.g., a topological intersection between a town and a river. Visual GIS query systems supply classical (*normal*) *actions* to the user: objets and operators of addition, selection, and unusually modification (Tab. 1). In GIS environments, we can so usually: add an object (addition object process), modify an object (modification object process), select an object (selection object process), add an operator (addition operator process), modify an operator (modification operator process), select an operator (selection operator process). When adding or modifying an operator, operands are needed. When adding or modifying an operator, the operator addition process and operator modification process can be seen as divided in two independent phases: first, a selection of objets or operators (*general* select phase: a *basic* selection of objet or operator), and second, an addition or a modification taking as operands the selected objets and operators (*general* add/modify phase: a *basic* addition or modification of objects or operators). For instance, in a *blackboard metaphor* interface, when the user draws a line representing a river on an already drawn polygon representing a town, the system (1) adds a river object, (2) selects the town object, (3) adds a topological intersection between the river and the town. That leads us to the taxonomy of user actions in Tab. 1. Modification of objects is rare and not taken into consideration.

Normal actions	*General* actions	*Basic* actions
a1 add object	aA select	ab1 select object
a2 add operator on selected objects/operators		ab2 select operator
a3 select objects/operators	aB add/modify	ab3 add object
a4 modify selected objects/operators		ab4 add operator
		(ab5 modify object)
		ab6 modify operator

Tab. 1 Possible *actions* that the user can do on the interface

The query system can execute on the interface the *materialization* summarised in Tab. 2. As for user actions, object modification is indicated but not taken into consideration.

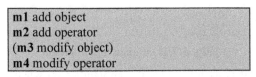

m1 add object
m2 add operator
(**m3** modify object)
m4 modify operator

Tab. 2 Possible *materialization* that the system can do on the interface

Fig. 3 shows that both the user and the system must *interpret* the interface. The ambiguity comes from the interpretation made in the user viewpoint as in the system viewpoint. For both of them, several interpretations are possible. But, which interpretation is the right one ? That leads us to classify ambiguities in two principal classes which are the several possible answers to the two following questions:

1. How must the system *materialize* objects and operators to be correctly *interpreted* by the user ? (MAT ambiguity)
2. How must the system *interpret* user actions ? (INT ambiguity)

In the MAT ambiguity, for each possible *materialization* of the system (m1, m2, m4 in Tab. 2), we find different ambiguities.

In the INT ambiguity, for each *action* of the user, we find different ambiguities. As shown in Tab. 1, we have two *general* actions of the user (aA and aB user action in Tab. 1) which correspond to two different phases in the *normal* actions of the user. That leads us to classify the INT ambiguity in two subclasses. In each subclass, for each *basic* action (ab1, ab2, ab3, ab4, ab6 in Tab. 1) of the user, we find different ambiguities.

In the taxonomy, for each class and subclass, we indicate the interface type in which the ambiguity can occur (the *blackboard metaphor* interface is indicated by ✍ and the *command used* interface by ▬).

3.1 MAT Ambiguity. How Must the System *Materialize* Objects and Operators to be Correctly *Interpreted* by the User ? (▬)

The *blackboard metaphor* interface (✍) does not meet ambiguities here because the shape drawn by the user constitutes the *materialization*. The aspect and the location of the *materialization* have been given by the user.

The detected ambiguities are the followings:

- *MAT1 ambiguity: add object (m1)*

Which *materialization* must be chosen by the system ? [12 §2.3.1.2] It can occur when objects and operators hold several possible *materialization*. Fig. 4 shows an example.

Fig. 4. MAT1 ambiguity. Which *materialization* must the system choose to *materialize* a town ?

- *MAT2 ambiguity: add operator (m2)*

(MAT11) **Which *materialization* must be chosen by the system ?** (MAT22) **Which *location* must be chosen by the system ?** [6] [12 §2.3.1.2, §2.3.1.3, §2.3.2.2, §2.3.3] [11] Location of *materialisation* carries semantics. Fig. 5 shows examples.

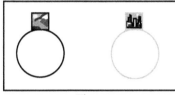 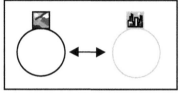

Fig. a   Fig. b

Fig. 5. MAT2 ambiguity. MAT21 ambiguity: to *materialize* a topological disjunction, which materialization must the system choose between an arrow (Fig. 5b) and no materialization (Fig. 5a) ? MAT22 ambiguity: In Fig 5a, the user can *interpret* the query "which are all the lakes and all the towns ?" or the query "which are the towns with a lake on its east side ?"

- *MAT3 ambiguity: modify operator (m4)*

Which *location* must be chosen by the system ? The example for MAT22 ambiguity is also valid here.

3.2 INT Ambiguity. How Must the System *Interpret* User Actions ?

We describe in the next two sections, the two subclasses corresponding to the two *general* actions of the user.

3.2.1 INTaA ambiguity. How must the system *interpret* selection of objects and operators ? (✎ , ■)

An important point to keep in mind is that the selection corresponds to the *normal* selection of the user but also to an implicit *basic* selection of operands when the user *normal* adds or modifies an operator.

The detected ambiguities are the followings:

- *INTaA1 ambiguity: select object/operator (ab1ab2)*

Does the object/operator selected by the system correspond to the selection intentions of the user ? For instance, a novice user can click on a logical conjunction of objets but he actually wants to express a topological intersection between objects. The user can click on a logical disjunction of objects but he actually wants to express a logical conjunction. The user desires to select a lake but he actually selects the shape which *materializes* a town.

- *INTaA2 ambiguity: select operator (ab2)*

Which operators are selected ? [12 §2.3.2.1] (▬),[6] (▬), [14] (✍). Fig. 6 shows examples.

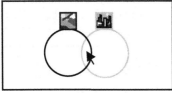

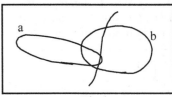

Fig. a   Fig. b

Fig. 6. INTaA2 ambiguity. (Fig. 6a) User selection: What does the user select: town∩lake, the town, the lake, town∪lake ? (Fig. 6b) ✍ Operand selection: with what the new added line is in topological intersection: a∩b, a, b, a∪b, Δ(b,a) ? Is the disjunction with Δ(a,b) important (logical *or* operator for a "don't care" relation [14]) ?

3.2.2 INTaB ambiguity. How must the system *interpret* user *basic* additions and modifications of objects or operators ?
The detected ambiguities are the followings:

- *INTaB1 ambiguity: add object, add/modify operator (ab3ab4ab6) (✍ ▬)*

Does the object/operator associated by the system to the materialization correspond to the object/operator that the user associates to the materialization (intention of the user) ? For instance, The user wants to express a logical disjunction operator (e.g. "I want all the objects which are either small towns *or* cities") and click on a logical conjunction operator (e.g. "I want all the objects which are small towns *and* cities" because of the query "I want the small towns *and* the cities" in his mental model). the user desires to express a city and draws the symbol of a small town. The user desires to express a topological disjunction between a road and a house, and draws an arrow which actually means a metrical distance operator.

- *INTaB2 ambiguity: add object/operator (ab3ab4) (✍)*

When several possible *interpretations* for a materialization exist, which *interpretation* must the system choose ? For instance, when the user draws a shape, does he mean the symbol of an object or the geometrical shape of an object ? In *command used* interfaces (■), this ambiguity cannot occur because each activated command correspond to a non-ambiguous *interpretation* for the system.

In INTaB2, the freedom of expression provided by the *blackboard metaphor* interface can lead to go beyond the expressive power of the visual language [14]. For instance, when the user draws a symbol which *materializes* an object or an operator, the system can know it is a symbol but does not recognise it. In *command used* interfaces (■), it can't happen because all the commands correspond to an existing object or operator.

Another final ambiguity is the confusion a novice user can make among the *actions* of addition, selection and modification in not well designed interfaces (INTc).

A general origin of the ambiguities is the knowledge level of the user on the expressive power of the pictorial language, of the description language, the database contents and the database access possibilities (expert or novice user ?).

The next section gives resolution ways for ambiguities in visual GIS query languages.

4 Ambiguities Resolution

The next two sections show a first resolution model and possible ways to resolve ambiguities.

4.1 First Resolution Model

As we have seen in the previous section, the ambiguities exist because we are often using several semantics. But, how many semantics exactly exist ? In order to have an idea of the number of possible semantics an ambiguity can spawn, we made a first determination of this number in a particular case of ambiguity. We proposed a resolution model for the Lvis language [3]. Lvis provides a *command used* interface and object types are lines and polygons. We realized a model to evaluate the number of possible topological configurations of objects (with only one relation between objects) with an increasing number of added objects and topological operators, which is the most common *interpretation* ambiguity in *command used* visual query languages (INTaA2). Our model is used to determine all the possible configurations and which default configuration must the system choose. Let's look at an example of query construction in the Lvis language: successively, the user adds a town object, a forest object with a topological intersection with the town, a river object with a topological intersection with the town. Several configurations are possible. The Fig. 7 shows three possible configurations.

Which towns are crossed by a river and have a forestry zone ? Three examples among several possible configurations.

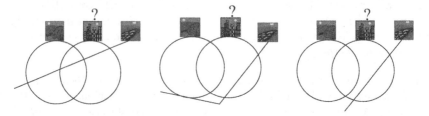

Fig. 7. An example of ambiguity in Lvis. The three visual configurations shown here correspond to three possible *interpretations* for the system.

The model is based on the intersection levels between objects involved in queries and is defined as a graph-type model including nodes and edges (Tab. 3 (a)). Nodes represent object intersections, and edges represent the topological equality. Nodes and edges can be either enabled or disabled according to spatial criteria of the query. The main advantage of this model is that the model for queries composed of a given number of objects is built only once, and is updated according to the spatial criteria of the other queries. When the user submits a visual query, the system searches for the set of possible configurations all over the graph of the query. If more than one possible configuration exist, the system decides which one will be the less ambiguous for the user using a weight scale for topological operators. For a query with n objects, the model contains 2^{n-1} nodes and $Card(2^{n-1},2) = 2^{n-1}!/(2!*(2^{n-1}-1)!)$ relations between the nodes.

Objects number	Nodes number	Possible configurations
1	1	2
2	3	4
3	7	19
4	15	167
5	31	7580
6	63	7 828 353
...	...	...

Tab. 3. Model for the detection of visual ambiguities. (a) The graph structure of the model. (b) The complexity of the model

A program explores the graph model to find the possible configurations. The results (Tab. 3 (b)) show how many possible configurations we found in the worst case: when object types are all polygons. We can conclude that:

- The number of configurations is very high for the system to choose itself the configuration the user wants. The probability for the system to choose the configuration that the user wants is very low.
- If, at the end of the query construction, we give the possibility to the user to choose himself on a list the configuration he wants, beyond 3 objects, the user will have to choose among over 167 possible configurations !

We need to find other solutions to resolve ambiguities.

4.2 Resolution Ways for Ambiguities

We describe now several solutions to resolve ambiguities.

4.2.1 General Resolution Ways for MAT and INT Ambiguities

Materialization must be well defined.

The grammar of the visual languages may be constrained to have a lower expressive power but, by the way, the grammar generates less ambiguities, e.g., defining one materialization for one object, splitting superposed metaphors and no negative expressions [14].

4.2.2 Resolution Ways for MAT Ambiguities

Objects materialization may be modified, geometrically deformed to respect the locations imposed by the operators [12].

Several windows may be used. Several windows can provide different views, e.g., one for alphanumerical data, and one for spatial data [14]. Windows can be encapsulated in the working window like comics' balloons and carry GIS information [4], they can also provide a way to visually express the parenthesis of operators, indicating operands.

4.2.3 Resolution Ways for INT Ambiguities

Senseless actions of the user may be avoided by disabling senseless inputs, e.g., a button may be disabled, a senseless selection may be ignored (for INTaA1, INTaB1, INTc ambiguities). Error messages may inform the user.

A text zone in the interface may express the query in a textual language (natural or formal), in order to give a possibility for more expert users to check the exact semantics [13]. We call this language the *clear language*. The *clear language* must be not or the less possible ambiguous. The added objects and operators (for INTaB ambiguity), the selection (for INTaA ambiguity), and the whole query (for INTaB ambiguity) may be shown in *clear language*.

Another way to resolve ambiguities which also presents the advantage of amply increasing user-friendliness, is to personalize the query environment to the profile of the user.

- The use of personalized *equivalents* for materialization can satisfy the user preferences, e.g., the user draws a symbol corresponding to a town in his mental model and another user draws another symbol corresponding to the same town in his mental model (for MAT, INTaA1, INTaB ambiguities).

- Semantics modes can be personalized in the interface, e.g., we can switch between a cardinal mode and a logical disjunction mode to change the system's interpretation of the location of materialization on the 2D window. [13] [6]

Another interesting resolution way is to establish a *dialog* with the user whenever an ambiguity occurs, e.g., the system shows all the available configurations and requests a choice. The *dialog* with the user is a succession of requests showing the possible *interpretations* of the system (see Fig. 8).

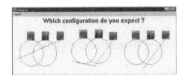

Fig. 8. The system establishes a *dialog* with the user. Whenever an ambiguity occurs, the system shows all the available configurations and requests a choice

For instance, in INTaB1 ambiguity, the system can ask the user which object or operator he wants to express. The system can show an error message if it does not exist in the database, and the system can show to the user which materialization can be used in order to get it. Such a feedback can become boring for the user [6], but the lists of requests can be ordered with a default semantics given in first position of the list. Requests can be personalized. The user can also disable the useless (according to him) semantics for later requests. A list can finally have only one enabled semantics that the system automatically chooses. A learning system may also infer the order of the list and the default semantics. Thanks to the feedback, *dialogs* with the user allow to build user profiles.

A conclusion on the resolution ways presented above is that the strategy to avoid ambiguities in most actual visual GIS languages is to define a non-fully visual, but hybrid languages, including a textual part and offering a constrained grammar with a low expressive power. They also take attention to supply well defined icons which are common to a large range of user types. Geometrical deformation of materialization is technically difficult to realize with an increasing number of objects and operators. The use of several encapsulated windows to materialize parenthesis gives a solution to express particular operators which generate important ambiguities problems as to express a logical disjunction (INTaB1 ambiguity). They also allow to have distinct views of the parts of the query. The disabling of senseless inputs of the user does not represent a technical difficulty and is more and more managed by applications. The *clear language* provides a way for more expert users to get a useful, permanent, and non-ambiguous feedback to check the construction of the query. The users, especially novice users, when getting started with the language, will certainly not take attention to that functionality, but, when building more and more complex queries, they will take more and more into consideration that non-ambiguous means to check their queries. The implementation of materialization's *equivalents* is technically difficult to realize but increases user-friendliness. Even if they can become boring for the user, *dialogs* with the user can be a means for the user to express to the system his choices and his preferences (adaptability). The feedback the system gets with *dialogs* is a means for the system to self-adapt itself to the user profile (adaptativity).

5 Conclusion and Future Work

We proposed a taxonomy, distinguishing ambiguities in visual GIS query languages. We also proposed ways of resolution for the detected ambiguities, and a model to solve a particular case of ambiguities. The model showed that the number of possible semantics in a spatial ambiguity can be very high. We can conclude that in visual GIS query languages, there is a compromise to make between user-friendliness (accessibility to a large range of end-user types) but ambiguous queries, and non-ambiguous queries but a lack of user-friendliness (accessibility to expert users only). A few research work has been carried out yet, offering great perspectives. To establish a *dialog* with the user seems to be an attractive way of resolution. An extension of the Lvis language is currently implemented. It will be adapt to integrate some modalities among user *dialog, clear language,* and *equivalents.* We plan to test some resolution ways with different types of users. We proposed here a taxonomy and resolution ways in GIS domain, but the proposals made are more general and could certainly be extended to other research areas, e.g., medical domain, etc.

References

1. Angelacio, B., Catarci, T., Santucci, G.: A Graphical Query Language with Recursion, IEEE Transactions on Software Engineering, Vol 16 (10), (1990) pp. 1150-1163
2. Aufaure-Portier, M.A., Trepied, C.: A Survey of Query Languages for Geographic Information Systems, Proceedings of IDS-3 (3rd International Workshop on Interface to Database), published in Springer Verlag's Electronic Workshops in Computer Series (1996) 14p (www.springer.co.uk/eWiC/Worshops/IDS3.html)
3. Aufaure M.-A., Bonhomme C., Lbath A., LVIS : Un Langage Visuel d'Interrogation de Bases de Données Spatiales, BDA'98, 14èmes Journées de Bases de Données Avancées, Hammamet, Tunisie, (1998) pp. 527-545
4. Bonhomme C., Trépied C., Aufaure M.-A., Laurini R., A Visual Language for Querying Spatio-Temporal Databases, ACM GIS99, Kansas City, USA, (1999) pp. 34-39
5. Bottoni, P., Costabile, M.F, Levialdi, S., Mussio, P.: Formalising visual languages, In Proc. IEEE Symposium on Visual Languages '95, (1995) pp. 45-52
6. Calcinelli, D., Mainguenaud, M.: Management of the Ambiguities in a Graphical Query Language for Geographical Information Systems, Advances in Spatial Databases, 2nd Large Spatial Database Symposium (SSD), Zürich, Switzerland, 28-30 Agust 1991, O. Günther. H-J Schek (Eds.), Proceedings, Lecture Notes in Computer Science, Vol 525, Springer, (1991) pp. 143-160
7. Catarci, T., Costabile, M. F., Levialdi, S., C.Batini: Visual Query Systems for Databases: A Survey, Journal of Visual Languages and Computing (JVLC), Vol 8 (2), (1997), pp. 215-260
8. Egenhofer, M. (1997), Query Processing in Spatial Query By Sketch, Journal of Visual Language and Computing, Vol 8 (4), pp. 403-424
9. Gaio, M., Buléon, P., Boursier, P.: L'Antéserveur Géographique, un Système Intuitif pour accéder à l'Information Géographique , actes des Journées Cassini 98, Revue Internationale de Géomatique, 8 (1-2), Université de Marne-la-Vallée , (1998) pp. 45-58
10. Laurini, R., Thompson D.: Fundamentals of Spatial Information Systems, The APIC series, Academic Press (1992)
11. Lbath, A., Aufaure-Portier, M-A., Laurini, R.: Using a Visual Language for the Design and Query in GIS Customization, 2nd International Conference on Visual Information Systems (VISUAL 97), San Diego, (1997) pp. 197-204
12. Lecocq-Carpentier, C.: La Gestion des Ambiguïtés dans un Langage Visuel: Application au Langage pour Bases de Données Géographiques CIGALES, Ph Dissertation, Université d'Evry Val d'Essone (1999)
13. Lee, Y., Chin, F. L.: An Iconic Query Language for Topological Relationships in GIS, The International Journal of Geographical Information Systems, Vol 9 (1), (1995) pp. 25-46
14. Meyer, B.: Beyond Icons : Towards New Metaphors for Visual Query Languages for Spatial Information Systems, Proceedings of the first International Workshop on Interfaces to Database Systems (R. Cooper ed.), Springer-Verlag (1993) 113-135
15. Zloof, M., M.: Query-By-Example: A Database Language, IBM Systems Journal, Vol 16 (4), (1977) pp. 324-343

Visualization of Dynamic Spatial Data and Query Results Over Time in a GIS Using Animation

Glenn S. Iwerks and Hanan Samet*

Computer Science Department, Center for Automation Research,
Institute for Advanced Computer Studies
University of Maryland, College Park, Maryland 20742
{iwerks,hjs}@cs.umd.edu

Abstract. Changes in spatial query results over time can be visualized using animation to rapidly step through past events and present them graphically to the user. This enables the user to visually detect patterns or trends over time. This paper presents several methods to build animations of query results to visualize changes in a dynamic spatial database over time.

Keywords: dynamic spatio-temporal data, visualization, animated cartography

1 Introduction

To help detect patterns or trends in spatial data over time, animation may be effective [10]. Alerters [2] or triggers [18] may be used to determine when a particular database state has occurred, but it may be desirable for the user to be aware of the events leading up to a particular situation. For example, a trigger can notify the user when vehicles enter a particular area of interest. When a trigger is fired the user knows that an event has occurred but does not know what led up to the event. In some cases it may be sufficient for the user to simply monitor the display as events occur, but if the amount of time between events is very long or very short, this may not be feasible. Depending on the situation, events may take hours, days, or even years to play out. This can make it difficult for the user to visually detect associations between events that occur far apart in time. One approach is to render spatio-temporal information in a static map [3, 10] but these can be confusing, and hard to read. Alternatively, the display output may be captured when data is processed and then sequenced into an animation. Using animation techniques, changes in spatial query results over time can be viewed, rapidly stepping through past events. This paper presents several methods to accomplish this result.

In this paper we address the display of 2D spatial features changing over time in a geographic information system (GIS). A GIS is a spatial database

* The support of the National Science Foundation under Grant EIA-99-00268 and IRI-97-12715 is gratefully acknowledged.

R. Laurini (Ed.): VISUAL 2000, LNCS 1929, pp. 166–177, 2000.
Springer-Verlag Berlin Heidelberg 2000

containing georeferenced data. A spatial database is defined here as a database in which spatial attributes, such as points, lines, and polygons can be stored using a relational data model. A table of related attributes is called a relation. A tuple in a relation is one instance of these related items. Base relations in a relational database are part of the relational data model. A view in a relational database is a query defined on base relations and made available to users as a virtual relation. A view may be materialized, or in other words, stored on disk so that the view need not be recomputed from the base relations each time it is used in further queries. Nevertheless, a materialized view must be updated when the base relations are modified by a transaction. Updating materialized views is also known as view maintenance [4]. A database transaction is a set of changes to a database state such that the database is left in a consistent state when the transaction is complete. If a transaction fails to complete, then the database reverts to the previous state just before the transaction began.

The remainder of this paper is organized as follows. Section 2 discusses background work in the area. Section 3 presents some algorithms for creating and viewing animations of spatial query results as they change over time. Concluding remarks and plans for future work are presented in Section 4.

2 Background

Most, if not all, previous applications of animation to this domain have been to visualize changes in base data rather than to database query results [3, 10, 17]. In general, most previous methods render spatial data in a bitmap. One bitmap is created for each discrete time step in a series. The bitmaps are then displayed in succession creating an animation, or in other words, animated maps. This is also known as animated cartography.

2.1 Animated Cartography

Visualization of georeferenced spatio-temporal data has been a topic of study for over 40 years [3]. One approach is to use static maps where temporal components are represented by different symbols or annotations on the map. Another approach is to use a chronological set of ordered maps to represent different states in time [11], sometimes known as strip maps. With the advent of more powerful computers and better graphics capabilities, animated maps are increasingly used. Animation is used in the presentation of meteorological data in weather forecast presentations to show changes over time [17]. Animated cartography is also used for decision support in disease control to visually detect patterns and relationships in time-series georeferenced health statistics [14, 13]. Animation is used in the study of remote sensing time-series data [15, 16]. In [9] animated cartography is used in the presentation of urban environmental soundscape information for environmental decision support. The use of animation of spatio-temporal data in non-cartographic fields is presented in [8] and [12] to visualize dynamic scientific spatio-temporal data. The effectiveness of animation techniques to present time-series cartographic data to a user is studied in [10]. The study concluded that animation may be able to help decrease the amount of time needed for a user to comprehend time-series spatial data and to answer questions about it compared with other methods.

2.2   The Spatial Spreadsheet

The Spatial Spreadsheet [7] serves as a testbed for the algorithms presented in this paper (see Figure 1). It is a front end to a spatial relational database. In the classic spreadsheet paradigm, cell values are non-spatial data types whereas in the Spatial Spreadsheet, cell values are database relations. The purpose of the Spatial Spreadsheet is to combine the power of a spatial database with that of the spreadsheet. The advantages of a spreadsheet are the ability to organize data, to formulate operations on that data quickly through the use of row and column operations, and to propagate changes in the data throughout the system. The Spatial Spreadsheet is made up of a 2D array of cells. Each cell in the Spatial Spreadsheet can be referenced by the cell's location (row, column). A cell can contain two types of relations: a base relation or a query result. A query result is a materialized view [4] defined on the base relations. The user can pose a simple query in an empty cell. For instance, a cell might contain the result of a spatial join between base relations from two other cells. Simple queries are operations like selection, projection, join, spatial join [5], window [1], nearest neighbor [6], etc. Simple queries can be composed to create complex queries by using the result of one simple query as the input to another. If a base relation is updated, the effects of those changes are propagated to other cells by way of the query operators.

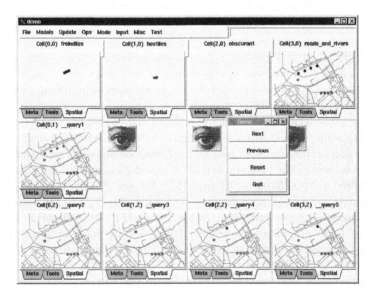

Figure 1: The Spatial Spreadsheet

3   Movie Mode

In the Spatial Spreadsheet, spatial attributes of a relation can be displayed graphically for each cell. When a base relation is updated, the change is propagated from cell to cell and the changes are reflected in each cell's display. To visualize changes over time, the display layers are saved and redisplayed in rapid succession like the frames of a movie. In the Spatial Spreadsheet, this is known as "movie mode". Each layer in the sequence is a movie animation frame. When contents of a base relation or a query result change, the old display layer is removed and saved, and then a new layer is rendered. When the user wants to play back the changes over time, layers are displayed successively in order from the oldest to the most recent.

3.1   Example Query

For the purpose of illustration, consider an example spatial join query in a spatial database. A join operation is a subset of the Cartesian product of two relations limited by a query predicate. The predicate is defined on the attributes of the two relations. For each tuple pair in the Cartesian product, if the query predicate is true, then the tuple pair is included in the result. A spatial join uses a query predicate defined on spatial attributes. An example spatial join query expressed in SQL is shown below.

```
SELECT *
FROM Observer, Target
WHERE Distance(Observer.Location, Target.Location) ≤ d
```

In this example, the schema of relations Observer and Target is (Name, Location) where Name is a string and Location is a point. The Distance() function returns the distance between two spatial attributes. The result of the query contains all the tuples joined from the two relations where attribute Observer.Location and attribute Target.Location are within distance d of each other.

Suppose at time t_0 relation Observer contains three tuples $\{(O1, (4, 1)), (O2, (3, 3)), (O3, (1, 2))\}$, and Target has one tuple $\{(T1, (4, 2))\}$ (see Figure 2a). Now consider the spatial join on these relations as expressed in the SQL query given above where d equals 1. The resulting output is shown in the first row of Figure 4 and graphically in Figure 3a. Now, suppose at time $t_0 + 1$ minute, the Target relation is updated by deleting tuple $(T1, (4, 2))$ and inserting tuple $(T1, (3, 2))$. The output of the recomputed spatial join is shown in the second row of Figure 4 and graphically in Figure 3b. Subsequently, suppose at time $t_0 + 4$ minutes the target at location $(3, 2)$ moves to location $(2, 2)$. The new spatial join output is shown in the third row of Figure 4 and graphically in Figure 3c.

3.2   Scan and Display

One can display results after a view is computed, or display results while the view is being computed. Function Scan_And_Display(), given below, is a simple

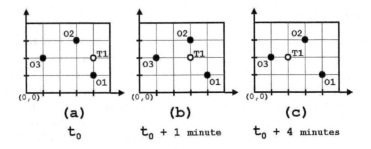

Figure 2: Graphical representation of spatial attributes in relations Observer and Target at different times. Point attributes of relation Observer are denoted by the • symbol and labeled Oi. Point attributes of relation Target are denoted by the ○ symbol and labeled Ti.

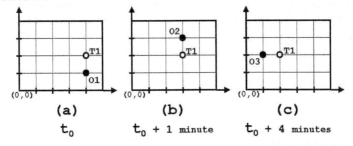

Figure 3: Graphical representation of the spatial join result between relations Observer and Target within a distance of 1 at different times. Point attributes of relation Observer are denoted by the • symbol and labeled Oi. Point attributes of relation Target are denoted by the ○ symbol and labeled Ti.

function for rendering a frame from a materialized view, or base relation after an update. Input parameter R is a relation to be displayed. Parameter *movie* is a sequence of animation frames. Each call to Scan_And_Display() adds a new frame to the animation.

In line 1 Create_New_Frame() creates a new animation frame. The outer **foreach** loop scans relation R tuple-by-tuple. The inner **foreach** loop renders each spatial attribute in a tuple. Procedure Render() invoked in line 6 is an

Time	Name1	Location1	Name2	Location2
t_0	O1	(4,1)	T1	(4,2)
t_0+1	O2	(3,3)	T1	(3,2)
t_0+4	O3	(1,2)	T1	(2,2)

Figure 4: Spatial join result between relations Observer and Target within a distance of 1 at different times.

implementation-specific procedure which performs the mechanics of rendering a spatial feature into a movie animation frame. Render() may also display the current animation frame to the user as it is drawn. The '|' operator, used in line 9, appends the new frame to the movie sequence. The modified *movie* sequence is the return value of Scan_And_Display().

```
function Scan_And_Display(R, movie): return movie sequence
    begin
1.       movie_frame ← Create_New_Frame()
2.       foreach tuple t in relation R do
3.          begin
4.             foreach spatial attribute a in tuple t do
5.                begin
6.                   Render(movie_frame, a)
7.                end
8.          end
9.       movie ← movie | movie_frame
10.      return movie
    end
```

3.3   Process Movie

Building an animation durring query processing adds processing overhead, but avoids rescanning the materialized view a second time. A movie frame is rendered durring processing using function Process_Movie() given below. Input parameter Q is a query to be processed. Parameter *movie* is a sequence of animation frames. Each call to Process_Movie() adds a new frame to the animation.

In line 1, a movie animation frame is created. Functions Process_First() and Process_Next(), in lines 2 and 9 respectively, process the query and return the next query result tuple. The **while** loop processes each query result tuple t until no more are generated. The **foreach** loop iterates through the spatial attributes in tuple t. Attributes are rendered in line 7. A new animation frame is appended to the sequence in line 11. The modified *movie* animation sequence is the return value of Process_Movie().

```
function Process_Movie(Q, movie) : return movie sequence
    begin
1.       movie_frame ← Create_New_Frame()
2.       t ← Process_First(Q)
3.       while( t ≠ ∅ ) do
4.          begin
5.             foreach spatial attribute a in tuple t do
6.                begin
7.                   Render(movie_frame, a)
8.                end
9.             t ← Process_Next(Q)
10.         end
11.      movie ← movie | movie_frame
12.      return movie
    end
```

3.4   Play Movie

Procedure Play_Movie(), given below, is used to play a movie created by either Scan_And_Display() or Process_Movie(). Parameter *movie* is a sequence of animation frames. The *frame_duration* input parameter controls the animation frame rate. The main loop iterates through the *movie* sequence and displays each frame. Procedure Show() is an implementation-specific procedure. It displays the *current_frame* to the user. Procedure Wait() halts the execution of Play_Movie() for the time period specified by *frame_duration*.

```
    procedure Play_Movie(movie, frame_duration)
        begin
1.          foreach current_frame in movie do
2.              begin
3.                  Show(current_frame)
4.                  Wait(frame_duration)
5.              end
        end
```

3.5   Variable Update and Playback Rates

The algorithms presented so far work well if updates occur at regular intervals. If updates occur at random intervals, then the perception of temporal relationships between events may be distorted durring playback. This occurs because procedure Play_Movie() displays each frame for the same amount of time. Function Process_Variable_Rate(), given below, creates variable rate animations to support irregular time intervals between updates.

```
    function Process_Variable_Rate(Q, movie, transaction_times)
        : return two sequences
        begin
1.          movie_frame ← Create_New_Frame()
2.          transaction_times ← transaction_times | Get_Last_Transaction_Time()
3.          t ← Process_First(Q)
4.          while (t ≠ ∅) do
5.              begin
6.                  foreach spatial attribute a in tuple t do
7.                      begin
8.                          Render(movie_frame, a)
9.                      end
10.                 t ← Process_Next(Q)
11.             end
12.         movie ← movie | movie_frame
13.         return movie and transaction_times
        end
```

Function Process_Variable_Rate() is similar to function Process_Movie(). One parameter is added and two lines are different. Parameter *transaction_times* is a sequence of numbers. Each element in *transaction_times* is associated with a *movie* animation frame representing the time at which a transaction took place resulting in the creation of the associated movie frame. The first element in *transaction_times* cooresponds to the first element in *movie*, and so forth. The time of the last transaction is returned by Get_Last_Transaction_Time() and is appended to the *transaction_times* sequence in line 2. The function return value is the modified *movie* sequence and the modified *transaction_times* sequence.

Procedure Play_Variable_Rate(), shown below, uses the *transaction_times* data gathered by Process_Variable_Rate() to determine the duration of animation frames durring playback. At playback, the time between frames is proportional to the time between update transactions. As an example, consider the query given in Section 3.1. An update transaction occurs after one minute and the next one occurs after another three minutes. The resulting animation has three frames. If the animation is played back so that the duration of the first frame is 0.5 seconds, then it follows that the duration of the second frame is 1.5 seconds. At this rate, playback is 120 times faster than realtime. The input parameter *dilation_factor* controls playback rate. A value greater than 0 but less than 1 is faster than realtime. A value greater than 1 is slower than realtime. If *dilation_factor* = 1, then playback will be close to realtime plus some added time for processing overhead. The algorithm could be made more precise by subtracting the processing overhead time from the computed *frame_duration* value. For simplicity, processing overhead was not considered here.

```
     procedure  Play_Variable_Rate(movie, transaction_times, dilation_factor)
        begin
 1.        current_time ← first(transaction_times)
 2.        transaction_times ← rest(transaction_times)
 3.        foreach next_time in transaction_times do
 4.           begin
 5.              frame_duration ← (next_time − current_time) * dilation_factor
 6.              current_frame ← first(movie)
 7.              movie ← rest(movie)
 8.              Show(current_frame)
 9.              Wait(frame_duration)
10.              current_time ← next_time
11.           end
12         current_frame ← first(movie)
13.        Show(current_frame)
        end
```

In procedure Play_Variable_Rate(), input parameter *movie* is a sequence of animation frames, and *transaction_times* is a sequence of times. The function first(*sequence*) used in line 1 returns the first element in a sequence. Function rest(*sequence*) used in line 2 returns a given sequence with its first element removed. The **foreach** loop iterates through the remaining elements of *transaction_times*. Each iteration of the loop displays an animation frame in the sequence. The frame durration is calculated by multiplying the time between transactions by the *dilation_factor* in line 5. Lines 6 and 7 extract a animation frame from the *movie* sequence. Procedure Show() in line 8 is an implementation-specific procedure that displays the *current_frame*. Procedure Wait() halts execution of the algorithm for a time period specified by $frame\_duration$. Lines 12 and 13 display the last frame of the $movie$ sequence.

3.6   Variable Update Rate and Fixed Playback Rate

At times, it may be desirable to export an animation using a standard fixed frame rate format for insertion into a web page, or for some other purpose. Function Convert(), shown below, converts a variable frame rate animation to a fixed frame rate animation. Basically, the algorithm sees how many times it can chop up each variable length input frame into fixed length output frames. A variable length interval is rounded off if the given output $frame\_duration$ does not divide evenly. The remainder is saved and added to the next frame time.

In the Convert() function, parameter $frame\_duration$ is the duration of each frame in the fixed rate output animation. Parameter $dilation\_factor$ controls the perceived rate of the output animation relative to realtime. The first seven lines of Convert() initialize local variables. In Line 7 the $transaction\_times$ sequence is artificially extended by one more value. The value is added so the last frame of the output animation sequence will have a duration. The duration of the last input animation frame is arbitrary. In our case, the last input frame is artificially calculated to be equal to the duration of the first input frame. The **foreach** loop iterates through all the remaining transaction times. Each iteration of the loop processes one variable length input frame producing zero or more fixed length output frames. It is possible that a frame may be droped if the duration of an input frame is less than the duration of an output frame. For simplicity, this case is assumed rare and is not considered here. Line 10 computes the dialated duration of an input frame. In line 11, the variable duration input frame is chopped up into fixed duration output frames. Function floor(x) in line 11 returns the integral portion of a decimal number x. In lines 12 through 17, the duration of the input frame is rounded off to a multiple of the output frame duration given by $frame\_duration$. The remainder is saved to be added back in durring the next iteration of the loop. The modulo funtion used in line 12 is as defined $\mathsf{mod}(x,y) \equiv x - \mathsf{floor}(x \div y)$. Lines 18 through 21 generate the output animation frames, and lines 22 through 24 move on to the next frame of the input animation. The resulting output animation is the return value of Convert(). The output animation can be played using procedure Play_Movie().

Figure 5 shows a trace of function Convert() on some example input. To see how this works, consider the example from Section 3.1. In the example the first update transaction occurs after one minute and the second update occurs after another three minutes. If time is measured in milliseconds, then the input parameter $transaction\_times$ is the sequence (0, 60000, 240000). Let input paramter $frame\_duration = 62.5ms$ (16 frames per second), and parameter $dilation\_factor = 0.01$. Parameter $dilation\_factor = 0.01$ corresponds to a speed increase factor of 100. The left column of Figure 5 shows at what line number the action for that row was performed. A number in a cell indicates a variable set to a new value. Boolean values indicate an expression evaluation result. Variables not affecting the control flow are not shown.

function Convert($movie, transaction\_times, frame\_duration, dilation\_factor$)
    : **return movie sequence**
    begin

```
1.   movie_out ← NULL
2.   remaining_delta ← 0
3.   current_frame ← first(movie)
4.   movie ← rest(movie)
5.   current_time ← first(transaction_times)
6.   transaction_times ← rest(transaction_times)
7.   transaction_times ← transaction_times | (last(transaction_times)+
                                    first(transaction_times) − current_time)
8.   foreach next_time in transaction_times do
9.     begin
10.       delta ← ((next_time − current_time) * dilation_factor)+
                                                     remaining_delta
11.       frame_count ← floor(delta ÷ frame_duration)
12.       remaining_delta ← mod(delta, frame) * frame_duration
13.       if remaining_delta > frame_duration ÷ 2 then
14.         begin
15.           frame_count ← frame_count + 1
16.           remaining_delta ← remaining_delta − frame_duration
17.         end
18.       for i ← 1 to frame_count do
19.         begin
20.           movie_out ← movie_out | current_frame
21.         end
22.       current_frame ← first(movie)
23        movie ← rest(movie)
24.       current_time ← next_time
25.     end
26.   return movie_out
      end
```

4   Conclusion

Procedure Process_Variable_Rate() is used to create a variable frame rate animation. Procedure Play_Variable_Movie() is used to play that movie. These two algorithms have an advantage in the Spatial Spreadsheet over other digital animation methods that use bitmaps or fixed frame rates. In the Spatial Spreadsheet, the frames are maintained as display layers. These layers are stored in an in-memory tree data structure that allows for zooming and panning. For each frame, the data structure is quickly traversed and the features valid for a given time are displayed. In this way, the user can play an animation of query results in the Spatial Spreadsheet, then stop the movie, pan and zoom, and then replay the movie from the new perspective without loss of fidelity. This allows for a more interactive animation. If the frames were mere bitmaps, then the image would become grainy when zooming in too close. A variable frame rate movie may be converted for export to a fixed frame rate format using the Convert()

line number	next _time	current _time	delta	remaining _delta	frame _count	remaining_delta > frame_duration ÷ 2
2				0		
5		0				
8	60000					
10			600			
11					9	
12			37.5			
13						true
15					10	
16			-25			
24		60000				
8	240000					
10			1775			
11					28	
12			25			
13						false
24		240000				
8	300000					
10			625			
11					10	
12			0			
13						false
24		300000				

Figure 5: Example trace of procedure Convert()

function described above. A minor difference between variable frame rate and fixed frame rate is the loss of timeing acuracy between frames in a fixed rate format.

The algorithms presented here require materialized views to be recomputed from scratch after each update to the view's base relations. This is acceptable if a sufficiently large percentage of the base relation tuples are altered during a transaction. In cases where only a few tuples in a base relation are changed, it is more efficient to use incremental view maintenance algorithms [4] to update materialized views. These algorithms calculate results using only the data that changed in the base relations to avoid recomputing the entire result from scratch. To accomplish this, many incremental view maintenance algorithms use differential tables. A differential table is a relation associated with a base relation used in the definition of a materialized view. A differential table contains all the tuples deleted or inserted into a base relation during the last transaction. Future work includes the development of movie mode algorithms to take advantage of incremental view maintenance differential tables to improve efficiency.

References

1. W. G. Aref and H. Samet. Efficient window block retrieval in quadtree-based spatial databases. *GeoInformatica*, 1(1):59–91, April 1997.

2. O. Buneman and E. Clemons. Efficiently monitoring relational databases. *ACM Transactions on Database Systems*, 4(3):368–382, September 1979.

3. C. S. Campbell and S. L. Egbert. Animated cartography: Thirty years of scratching the surface. *Cartographica*, 27(2):24–46, 1990.

4. A. Gupta, I. S. Mumick, and V. S. Subrahmanian. Maintaining views incrementally. In *Proceedings of the ACM SIGMOD Conference*, Washington, D.C., May 1993.

5. G. R. Hjaltason and H. Samet. Incremental distance join algorithms for spatial databases. In *Proceedings of the ACM SIGMOD Conference*, pages 237–248, Seattle, WA, June 1998.

6. G. R. Hjaltason and H. Samet. Distance browsing in spatial databases. *ACM Transactions on Database Systems*, 24(2):265–318, June 1999.

7. G. Iwerks and H. Samet. The spatial spreadsheet. In *Visual Information and information Systems: Third International Conference Proceedings, VISUAL '99*, pages 317–324, Amsterdam, The Netherlands, June 1999. Springer-Verlag.

8. B. Jobard and W. Lefer. The motion map: Efficient computation of steady flow animations. In *Proceedings of Visualization '97*, pages 323–328. IEEE, October 1997.

9. M. Kang and S. Servign. Animated cartography for urban soundscape information. In *Proceedings of the 7th Symposium on Geographic Information Systems*, pages 116–121, Kansas City, MO, November 1999. ACM.

10. A. Koussoulakou and M. J. Kraak. Spatio-temporal maps and cartographic communication. *The Cartographic Journal*, 29:101–108, 1992.

11. M. Kraak and A. M. MacEachren. Visualization of the temporal component of spatial data. In *Proceedings of SDH 1994*, pages 391–409, 1994.

12. K. Ma, D. Smith, M. Shih, and H. Shen. Efficient encoding and rendering of time-varying volumn data. Technical Report NASA/CR-1998-208424 ICASE Report No. 98-22, National Aeronautics and Space Administration, Langley Research Center, Hampton. VA, June 1998.

13. A. M. MacEachren, F. P. Boscoe, D. Haug, and L. W. Pickle. Geographic visualization: Designing manipulable maps for exploring temporally varying georeferenced statistics. In *IEEE Symposium on Information Visualization, 1998, Proceedings*, pages 87–94,156. IEEE, 1998.

14. A. M. MacEachren and D. DiBiase. Animated maps of aggregate data: Conceptual and pratical problems. *Cartography and Geographic Information Systems*, 18(4):221–229, 1991.

15. R. E. Meisner, M. Bittner, and S.W. Dech. Visualization of satellite derived time-series datasets using computer graphics and computer animation. In *1997 IEEE International Geoscience and Remote Sensing, 1997. IGARSS '97. Remote Sensing - A Scientific Vision for Sustainable Development*, pages 1495–1498, Oberpfaffenhofen, Germany, August 1997. IEEE.

16. R. E. Meisner, M. Bittner, and S.W. Dech. Computer animation of remote sensing-based time series data sets. In *IEEE Transactions on Geoscience and Remote Sensing*, pages 1100–1106, Oberpfaffenhofen, Germany, March 1999. IEEE.

17. F. Schroder. Visualizing meteorological data for a lay audience. *IEEE Computer Graphics and Applications*, 13(2):12–14, September 1993.

18. A. Silberschatz, H. F. Korth, and S. Sudarshan. *Database System Concepts*. McGraw-Hill, New York, third edition, 1996.

Upgrading Color Distributions for Image Retrieval Can We Do Better?

Constantin Vertan[1] and Nozha Boujemaa[1]

INRIA Rocquencourt, IMEDIA Project, BP105, 78153 Le Chesnay Cedex, France

Summary. Content-based image retrieval primarily used color distributions as descriptors of the image content; researches have since focused on the use of various color representation spaces, color and illumination invariance, color quantization and color matching. In order to overcome the many limitations of the description by a first-order distribution, several higher-order distributions have been introduced since (like autocorrelogram or color coherence vectors). Although they can perform better, their computational complexity is prohibitive and they require parameter setting. We propose to upgrade the first order color distribution (color histogram) by embedding for each color additional information about its perceptual or statistical relevance. Such information is obtained by using local activity measures such as the Laplacian, the entropy and others. We prove that the new color distribution family is compact, robust and easy to compute and provides a superior retrieval performance, independent with respect to the color representation.

1 Introduction

Content-based image retrieval (CBIR) became a must in the last decade. Powered by the explosive development of the Internet, Web and the continuously cheaper digital imagining devices and technologies, applications such as digital libraries, image archives, video-on-demand and specific image databases emerge as a real-life fact. The basic idea of the CBIR process is to compactly describe an image by a digital signature and then match the query image to the most resemblant image within the database according to the similarity of their signatures.

Traditionally, the content description is done (for either global or partial queries) according to the notions of color and texture. Thus the signatures are color distributions (histograms [1], color moments [2], color coherence vectors [3]), second-order, spatially constrained color distributions (color correlograms [4], edge correlograms [5]) or classical textural descriptors (Fourier coefficients [6], wavelet coefficients, Markov random field parameters, etc. [7]).

Starting with the works of Swain [1], the color distribution (histogram) became the main feature descriptor for image content. Given a color image

R. Laurini (Ed.): VISUAL 2000, LNCS 1929, pp. 178–188, 2000.
Springer-Verlag Berlin Heidelberg 2000

f, of size M by N pixels, characterized by the color c at location (i,j), i.e. $c = f(i,j)$, the color distribution (histogram) of the color set $\mathcal{C}$ is given by:

$$h(\mathbf{c}) = \frac{1}{MN} \sum_{i=0}^{M-1} \sum_{j=0}^{N-1} \delta\left(f(i,j) - \mathbf{c}\right), \quad \forall \mathbf{c} \in \mathcal{C} \tag{1}$$

In the equation above $\delta()$ is the unitary impulse function. We notice that the $h(\mathbf{c})$ values are normalized in order to sum to one. The value of each bin is thus the number of image pixels having the color $\mathbf{c}$, or, after normalization by MN, the probability that the color $\mathbf{c}$ appears in the image. Thus, in the classical histogram defined by (1), any pixel (regardless the color representation space) contributes with a constant weight (1 before normalization, or $1/MN$ after the probabilistic normalization), invariant with respect to the local image context.

Pixels having the same color are generally not similar (since they can represent corners, edges, uniform areas, etc.); according to this observation, Pass et al proposed in [3] to classify the pixels into two classes: coherent and contour. A coherent pixel is defined by the color uniformity of its neighbourhood, whereas the contour pixel is situated close to the separation lines between the image objects and thus it is characterized by a non-uniform neighbourhood. The color coherence vector (CCV) proposed in [3] is a separate counting of contour and coherent pixels, into two color distributions (histograms). Still, there is no further distinction for the pixels of any of the two classes, the contour/ coherent decision needs the definition of some parameters (that are not necessarily constant for different images) and the color distribution is twice the size of the classical histogram.

In this contribution we will revisit the use of color histograms from the perspective of embedding some local information about the statistical and visual relevance or importance of each pixel. In the following section we will describe the proposed modified histogram – the weighted color histogram and the various measures that describe the local behaviour of the colors. Section 3 will describe experimental results and section 4 will summarize the conclusions of this work.

2 The weighted histogram and weighting schemes

The approach proposed by the CCV [3] can be further refined by the classification of the image pixels in more than two classes, according to a local attribute (such as the edge strength). We can easely imagine a classification in three classes, consisting of pixels charaterized by a small, medium and high edge strength. The number of classes is thus related to the number of quantization level of the pixel attribute's. At the limit, since every pixel has acquired a supplementary, highly relevant characteristic, we can easely imagine a one pixel per class approach, which will certainly provide a very accurate description of the image, but will require a very important size.

In order to keep the balance between the histogram size and the discrimination between pixels we propose to adaptively weight the contribution of each pixel of the image into the color distribution. This individual weighting allows a finer distinction between pixels having the same color and the construction of a weighted histogram that accounts both color distribution and statistical non-uniformity measures. Thus, we will use a modified histogram, defined as:

$$h(\mathbf{c}) = \frac{1}{MN} \sum_{i=0}^{M-1} \sum_{j=0}^{N-1} w(i,j)\delta\left(f(i,j) - \mathbf{c}\right), \quad \forall \mathbf{c} \in \mathcal{C} \tag{2}$$

In the equation above $w(i,j)$ is the weighting coefficient of the color at spatial position (i,j). We may notice that, since $w(i,j)$ must be a scalar, we cannot use any color statistics (which are necessarily vector triples).

Intuitively the accounting within the color distribution of some local measures of each pixel could be considered as a way of integrating both color and texture, provided that the local measure have a textural background. In the following subsections we will describe the proposed weighting schemes: by the edge strength (Laplacian), by probabilistic measures and by fuzzy measures. Indeed, the probabilistic measures describe the local degree of chaos in the coloring; the fuzzy measures reveal the pertinence of the color of the current pixel with respect to its neighbourhood and the edge strength measures both the local non-uniformity and the presence of strong visual cues (as edges or corners).

Thus, the weighting is to be computed on a neighborhood of the current pixel and must quantify the color activity (or visual importance, or non-uniformity) of that neighbourhood. That implies that $w(i,j)$ is increasing with the color non-uniformity.

2.1   Laplacian-based measures

Visual perception studies have proven that edges in general, and corners in particular, are very important to scene analysis. Such information is provided by the image Laplacian $\Delta(i,j)$ [8]. The color Laplacian operator $\Delta(i,j)$ that we will subsequently use is the L_2 aggregation of the scalar Laplacian operators computed on each color component of the image.

A weighted histogram similar to (2) was presented in [9] as a tool for image thresholding; if $\Delta(i,j)$ is a Laplacian operator computed at location (i,j), the thresholding histograms were defined as:

$$\tilde{h}(\mathbf{c}) = \sum_{i=0}^{M-1} \sum_{j=0}^{N-1} \delta\left(f(i,j) - \mathbf{c}\right) \frac{1}{1 + \Delta(i,j)}, \quad \forall \mathbf{c} \in \mathcal{C}, \text{ or} \tag{3}$$

$$\tilde{h}(\mathbf{c}) = \sum_{i=0}^{M-1} \sum_{j=0}^{N-1} \delta\left(f(i,j) - \mathbf{c}\right) \Delta(i,j), \quad \forall \mathbf{c} \in \mathcal{C} \tag{4}$$

The relation (3) emphasizes the weight of pixels that belong to constant (uniform) regions: their Laplacian is very small, so they sum with an unitary weight; the pixels placed on the edges are characterized by an important Laplacian and thus their contribution to the corresponding $\mathbf{c}$ bin is very small. This behavior is thought to reduce the influence of the uncertain colors, situated at the border between different objects and is derived from the gray-scale image case of choosing the segmentation thresholds as the minima of the histogram. The relation from (4) corresponds to a dual behavior, counting the colors proportionally to their edge strength.

Since the edge information is highly relevant, we finally have chosen the weighting coefficient in (2) as the squared Laplacian:

$$w(i,j) = \Delta^2(i,j). \tag{5}$$

2.2   Probabilistic measures

Since the key factor in the evaluation of the local color activity is the color variability within some neighbourhood, the probability of occurrence of the current color $\mathbf{c} = f(i,j)$ within its neighbourhood could be a good estimate. If this probability is high, the neighbourhood include a significant uniform area, colored with $\mathbf{c}$ and thus the contribution of the color to the modified histogram must be reduced. If the probability of finding color $\mathbf{c}$ within its spatial neighbours is small, it follows that color $\mathbf{c}$ is rather singular (corner, isolated point), and thus its contribution to the modified histogram (2) must be increased.

Thus, we propose to use a weighting coefficient that is inverse proportional with the number of pixels $N_{ij}(\mathbf{c})$ having the same color $\mathbf{c}$ within the square window of size D, centered at the current location (i,j) (with $\mathbf{c} = f(i,j)$). We define $N_{ij}(\mathbf{c})$ as:

$$N_{ij}(\mathbf{c}) = \sum_{m=-D/2}^{D/2} \sum_{n=-D/2}^{D/2} \delta(f(i+m,j+n) - f(i,j)). \tag{6}$$

Thus, the weighting coefficient in (2) is:

$$w(i,j) = \frac{1}{N_{ij}(\mathbf{c})}. \tag{7}$$

Obviously the simple probabilistic approach defined by (7) measures the local non-uniformity form the current color's point of view. A global measure must take into account the occurrence probabilities for all the colors within the neighbourhood. The informational entropy could thus be used in order to measure the overall dissimilarity. Since the entropy is maximal when the probabilities are equal (and thus there are no identical colors within the neighbourhood) and is zero if the neighbourhood is absolutely uniform, we propose to use the informational efficiency (entropy to maximal entropy ratio) as a weighting coefficient of the colors:

$$w(i,j) = 1 - \frac{\sum_{\mathbf{c'} \in \mathcal{C}} N_{ij}(\mathbf{c'}) \log N_{ij}(\mathbf{c'})}{2D^2 \log D}. \tag{8}$$

2.3   Fuzzy measures

From a numerical point of view, the usual histogram h in (1) maps the color set $\mathcal{C}$ into the interval $[0, 1]$. According to Zadeh's [10] theory, such a function is a fuzzy set. In [11], Bezdeck further noticed that any such function can be a fuzzy set, but actually becomes a fuzzy set if and only if it fits a semantically plausible description for the properties of the object (the color in particular) within the universe (the color set $\mathcal{C}$). Thus, the normalized histogram from (1) cannot be a fuzzy set, as its semantical description is void from the uncertainty point of view. Digital images are mappings of natural scenes (sampled and quantized slices of 3-d reality) and thus have an important amount of uncertainty, in both value and location (spatial support) [12]. We will focus on the imprecise nature of the pixel values, since, in a complex, natural scene, most likely there is no perceivable difference between the gray levels of 99 and 100 (as suggested in [13]), or the colors – expressed as RGB triples – (201,100,199) and (200,100,199) (used for color image filtering, as suggested in [14]).

The simplest approach [15] is to normalize the usual histogram in (1) by the value of its largest bin, in such way that the most probable color will have a membership degree of 1 within the fuzzy set "image". The most predominant color can be thus considered as the most typical for the given image and the constructed fuzzy histogram (9) measures the typicality of a color within the image. For the entire image this leads to the fuzzy histogram h_1 [15], [16]:

$$h_1(\mathbf{c}) = \frac{h(\mathbf{c})}{\max_{\mathbf{c'} \in \mathcal{C}} h(\mathbf{c'})}, \ \forall \mathbf{c} \in \mathcal{C}. \tag{9}$$

The normalization by the mode from (9) allows us to assign the maximum, unitary typicality to the color that is dominant within the image, regardless its probability of appearance (which is not the case of the usual histogram).

The discussion from the previous subsection still holds if we are replacing, for the current color, the probability of occurrence within its neighbourhood by its typicality with respect to the same neigbourhood. If we denote by $N_{\max}$ the maximum number of pixels having the same color in the neighbourhood of pixel (i, j) (that is $N_{\max} = \max_{\mathbf{c'} \in \mathcal{C}} N_{ij}(\mathbf{c'})$), we have the following two expressions for the weighting coefficient $w(i, j)$:

$$w(i,j) = \frac{N_{\max}}{N_{ij}(\mathbf{c})}. \tag{10}$$

$$w(i,j) = \frac{D^2 \log N_{\max} - \sum_{\mathbf{c} \in \mathcal{C}} N_{ij}(\mathbf{c}) \log N_{ij}(\mathbf{c})}{N_{\max} \log D^2}. \tag{11}$$

Equation (10) is the fuzzy variant of (7). The weighting by the fuzzy entropy from (11) reduces to the entropy weighting from (8) if $N_{\max} = D^2$.

3 Experiments

The experiments performed in order to establish the retrieval capabilities of the proposed fuzzy histograms were conducted using the Surfimage software platform [17] developed at IMEDIA. We investigated both the objective and the subjective retrieval quality, on two different, heterogeneous, generalist image databases. A first, small, image database consists of 210 key frames from a television broadcast (part of the AIM corpus of INA), manually grouped into similarity classes; figure 1 presents some images within this database. A second image database consists of 792 color textures from both regular and irregular textures (part of the textures are from the Vistex database at MIT MediaLab); figure 2 presents some textures from this database.

We tested the retrieval capabilities of the proposed histograms for various color representation spaces. We finally selected the RGB, HSV and Lab color space as prototypical: RGB is the primarily acquisition space, HSV is the preferred natural-language color description mode and Lab models the perceptual inter-color difference by the L_2 metric. No color invariance models were considered for the moment, although some simple and powerful models have been proposed [18], [19].

Figures 1 and 2 show retrieval results within the used image databases; the weighted histogram performs clearly better (with increased recall and precision rates): in the case of textures it retrieves several textures from query image class (coffee beans), and in the case of broadcasting key-frames, it succesfully retrieves images containing the same character as the query image, but not necessarily within the same shot.

Figures 3, 4 and 5 show the precision-recall curves in the mentioned color spaces for the usual color distribution (1) and the weighting-updated color distributions (2). All the proposed weighting schemes perform well, providing an increased effectiveness with respect to the classical color distribution. The improvement is obtained regardless the color representation.

Figure 5 presents the typical performance variation of the weighting by the neighbourhood-based non-uniformity measures (probabilistic or fuzzy) with respect to the size of the squared, centered analysis window that models the neighbourhood. The performance increases as the analysis window is bigger (from 3 x 3 for $D = 1$ to 7 x 7 for $D = 3$). However, the size of the neighbourhood must be upper limited (with $D \le 3$), from both computational and statistical considerations.

Fig. 1. Image retrieval for the same query image (top left, blue contour highlighting) using the RGB uniformly quantized color space and L_1 metric. Upper picture block - retrieval by the usual histogram. Lower picture block - retrieval by the Laplacian weighted histogram, providing an increased accuracy. The images are presented in the order of decreasing similarity, from left to right and top to bottom. Thus, for the given query, the retrieval by the usual RGB histogram provides a 60 % accuracy, and the retrieval by the weighted histogram provides a 100 % accuracy. The keyframes of the television broadcast are available by courtesy of INA - Institute National de l'Audivisuel of France, who kindly provided the image database.

4   Conclusions

This contribution proposes the upgrade of the usual color distribution (histogram) by an adaptive weighting of each pixel's contribution. The weighting is related to a local measure of color non-uniformity (or color activity), computed within a neighbourhood of the pixel. The proposed non-uniformity measures are based on the evaluation of perceptual cues (corners and isolated colors, by the use of the Laplacian), statistical color area distribution (by the use of local probability of occurrence and informational entropy) and local color relevance (by a fuzzy typicality and fuzzy entropy). The magnitude of

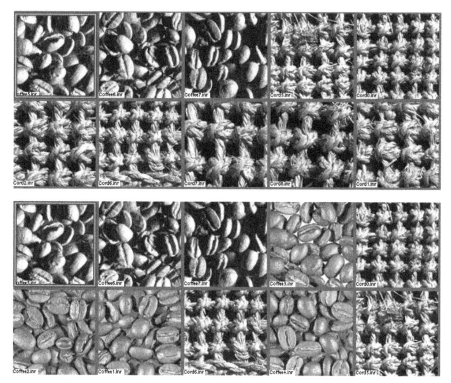

Fig. 2. Image retrieval for the same query image (top left, blue contour highlighting) using the RGB uniformly quantized color space and L_1 metric. Upper picture block - retrieval by the usual histogram. Lower picture block - retrieval by the Laplacian weighted histogram, providing an increased accuracy. The images are presented in the order of decreasing similarity, from left to right and top to bottom. Thus, for the given query, the retrieval by the usual RGB histogram provides a 30 % accuracy, and the retrieval by the weighted histogram provides a 70 % accuracy.

all these measures increases with the local color variability, being minimal for uniform regions.

The objective quality measures (precision-recall curves) show that the proposed approaches perform better than the usual color histogram, regardless the color representation space. The new histograms have the same size as the usual color distribution and can be compared by the same metrics and its computational complexity is not excessive. Thus we claim that the weighted histograms can be indeed a valuable upgrade to the traditionally color distribution based image retrieval.

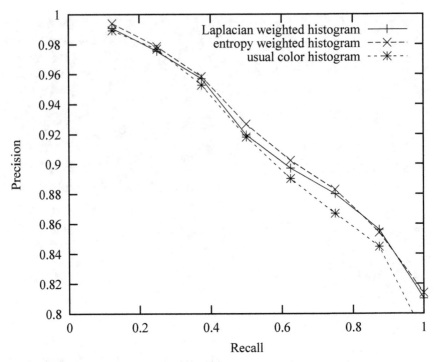

Fig. 3. Precision-recall curves for the retrieval within the texture image database, using *RGB* color representation, uniform 6 bins/ component quantization and various color distributions: usual color histogram (1), Laplacian weighted (5) histogram and entropy weighted (8) histogram. The later two curves significantly overcome the usual color distribution.

References

1. M. J. Swain and D. H. Ballard. Color indexing. *International Journal of Computer Vision*, 7(1):11–32, 1991.
2. B. M. Mehtre, M. S. Kankanhalli, A. D. Narasimhalu, and G. C. Man. Color matching for image retrieval. *Pattern Recognition Letters*, 16:325–331, Mar. 1995.
3. G. Pass and R. Zabih. Histogram refinement for content based image retrieval. In *IEEE Workshop on Applications of Computer Vision*, pages 96–102, 1996.
4. J. Huang, S. R. Kumar, M. Mitra, Zhu W.-J., and R. Zabih. Image indexing using correlograms. In *Computer Vision and Pattern Recognition CVPR '97*, San Juan, Puerto Rico, 17-19 Jun. 1997.
5. J. Huang, S. R. Kumar, M. Mitra, and Zhu W.-J. Spatial color indexing and applications. In *IEEE International Conference on Computer Vision ICCV '98*, Bombay, India, 4-7 Jan. 1998.
6. C. Vertan and N. Boujemaa. Color texture classification by normalized color space representation. In *Proc. of ICPR'2000*, Barcelona, Spain, 3-8 Sept. 2000.
7. A. del Bimbo. *Visual Information Retrieval*. Morgan Kaufmann, San Francisco, CA, 1999.

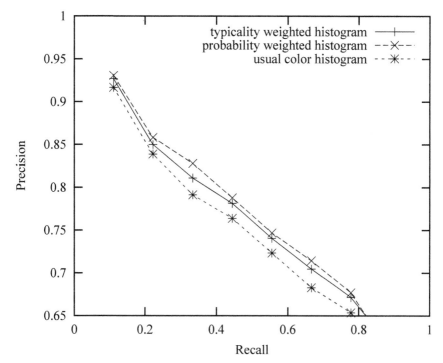

Fig. 4. Precision-recall curves for the retrieval within the key-frames image database, using *HSV* color representation, uniform 6 bins/ component quantization and various color distributions: usual color histogram (1), probability weighted (7) histogram and typicality weighted (10) histogram. The later two curves significantly overcome the usual color distribution.

8. A.K. Jain. *Fundamentals of Digital Image Processing.* Prentice Hall Intl., Englewood Cliffs NJ, 1989.
9. F. M. Wahl. *Digital Image Signal Processing.* Artech House, Boston, 1987.
10. L. Zadeh. Fuzzy sets. *Information and Control,* 8:338–353, 1965.
11. J. C. Bezdek. Fuzzy models - what are they and why ? *IEEE Trans. on Fuzzy Systems,* 1(1):1–5, Feb. 1993.
12. I. Bloch and H. Maitre. Fuzzy mathematical morphologies: a comparative study. *Pattern Recognition,* 28(9):1341–1387, Sept. 1995.
13. C. V. Jawahar and A. K. Ray. Fuzzy statistics of digital images. *IEEE Signal Processing Letters,* 3(8):225–227, Aug. 1996.
14. C. Vertan and V. Buzuloiu. Fuzzy nonlinear filtering of color images: A survey. In E. Kerre and M. Nachtegael, editors, *Fuzzy Techniques in Image Processing,* Heidelberg, Germany, 2000. Physica Verlag.
15. C. Vertan and N. Boujemaa. Using fuzzy histograms and distances for color image retrieval. In *Proc. of CIR'2000,* Brighton, United Kingdom, 4-5 May 2000.
16. C. Vertan and N. Boujemaa. Embedding fuzzy logic in content based image retrieval. In *Proc. of NAFIPS'2000,* pages 85–90, Atlanta, Georgia, 13-15 Jul. 2000.

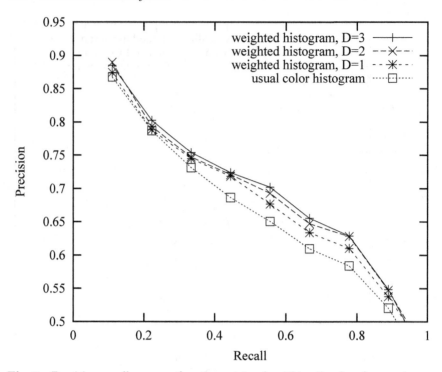

Fig. 5. Precision-recall curves for the retrieval within the key-frames image database, using *Lab* color representation, uniform 6 bins/ component quantization and various color distributions: usual color histogram (1) and probability (7) weighted histograms by increasing window sizes ($D = 1, 2, 3$). The retrieval by the weighted color distribution performs significantly better than the usual color distribution; an increased window size provides better accuracy.

17. C. Nastar, M. Mitschke, C. Meihac, and N. Boujemaa. Surfimage: a flexible content-based image retrieval system. In *ACM Multimedia '98*, Bristol, United Kingdom, 12-16 Sept. 1998.

18. B. V. Funt and G. D. Finlayson. Color constant color indexing. *IEEE Trans. on Pattern Analysis and Machine Intelligence*, 17(5):522–529, May 1995.

19. T. Gevers and A. W. M. Smeulders. A comparative study of several color models for color image invariant retrieval. In *First Inetrnational Workshop on Image Databases and Multimedia Search*, pages 17–26, Amsterdam, Holland, 1996.

Color Normalization for Digital Video Processing

Juan M. Sánchez and Xavier Binefa *

Computer Vision Center and Dpt. d'Informàtica
Universitat Autònoma de Barcelona, Edifici O, 08193, Bellaterra, SPAIN
{juanma,xavierb}@cvc.uab.es - http://www.cvc.uab.es/~juanma

Abstract. The color appearance of digital video imagery acquired from analog sources is affected by intrinsic device imperfections. Although the human visual system (HVS) is capable of perceiving color variations when comparing different acquisitions of the same video, it is able to identify the colors in an isolated image as well. Color based computer vision processes applied within digital video libraries do not have this capability and their performance is severely reduced. This paper presents a method for modeling the intrinsic color appearance given by acquisition devices. It is based on the approximation of the distribution of colors generated by a device using a mixture of Gaussians in RGB space. Its parameters are encoded in a specifically designed pattern, which provides a dense estimation of the distribution of colors along the whole RGB space. In this way, the model can be attached to every acquired video in order to put its original color appearance on record. The approximation by mixtures of Gaussians lets us define transformations between them that preserve the identity of colors. This fact is shown in the case of skin color segmentation, where the underlying concept of color is captured from samples obtained by a particular device. Other applications of color correction in digital video are pointed out in this paper as well.

1 Introduction

Although purely digital video is starting to be used, there are still lots of information in analog form being stored in digital video libraries. The devices taking part in the acquisition process significantly affect color appearance of digital video imagery. The HVS is able to identify the identity of and the relationships between the colors that appear in those images. Unfortunately, this capability is not present in computer vision processes, so that the performance of tasks within the digital libraries framework that directly rely on color information is limited by device caused variations. Indexing video databases by means of color histograms [17] or appearance based coding [16], skin color segmentation for face detection [18] and adult content filtering [6], or object recognition and tracking based on color models [13] are some examples of systems whose performance fully depends on the accuracy of color information. Although algorithms based

---

* This work was supported by CICYT grants TAP98-0631 and TEL99-1206-C02-02.

R. Laurini (Ed.): VISUAL 2000, LNCS 1929, pp. 189–199, 2000.
Springer-Verlag Berlin Heidelberg 2000

Fig. 1. Color variations caused by the devices involved in the video acquisition process.

on color models learned from data can consider variations caused by devices, it is not possible to take into account all possible combinations of VTR and video acquisition hardware in the model training process.

Similarly, video visualization and manipulation require a uniform appearance of colors as well. When the user of a digital video library reviews the result of a query such as "concatenate all shots showing Bill Clinton" [1], he probably expects Clinton's face to have a very similar tone, assuming a temporal coherence of colors. This coherence is also needed when images from different video sources are combined in space using basic *chroma-keying* or more sophisticated techniques [10]. The problems that may arise in these scenarios are clearly illustrated by the images in fig. 1[1]. A transformation between device color appearances is needed in order to keep visual coherence and improve the performance of digital video library tasks that rely on color.

Unfortunately, current color correction approaches based on recovering physical properties of surfaces and illuminants [2,8] have been shown to be not good enough for color based object recognition [7] and, in practice, are not appropriate for variations produced by video playback and acquisition devices. On the other hand, works on color calibration try to model sensor responses to different stimuli [20].

In this paper, we propose an automatic color correction procedure based on modeling color distributions by mixtures of Gaussians, which allows us to adapt the color appearance of images to the distributions inherent to different devices. The probabilistic combination of the transformations defined for the different Gaussian components preserves the identity of colors, as perceived by the HVS. The case of adapting the distribution of colors of an image into a known one lets us analyze the method. The global color distributions used in the general case are then encoded as a specifically designed pattern, which is enough for representing the transformation to be applied to every color in RGB space. The application of color correction is shown in the particular case of skin color segmentation.

2   Color appearance correction

The use of different devices in the video acquisition process causes significant non-linear variations in the distribution of colors in RGB space, i.e. the same

---

[1] Color figures will be available at http://www.cvc.uab.es/~juanma

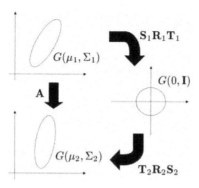

Fig. 2. Transformation of a data set in order to obtain a different Gaussian distribution.

color is not "seen" by different devices in the same position within this space. Our goal is to obtain a transformation between the variations produced by different devices in order to have coherent color appearances. Our representation of device-dependent colors is based on color naming. Color naming assigns a label or name to each different point of a color space. Usually, a model is defined for each label, and a color is assigned the label whose model is best suited. Lammens [12] used normalized Gaussian functions as color name models, thus assuming that a simple color concept[2] can be modeled by such function. In our case, a distribution of colors is assumed to be formed by a mixture of simple color concepts, and is thus approximated and parameterized by a mixture of Gaussians probability density function. A known and unique correspondence between the components of the mixtures that encode the shape and position of the color distributions given by different devices lets us define a transformation between them in terms of their parameters.

Considering the case of single Gaussian distributions, there is an affine transformation that can be expressed in terms of their means μ_1, μ_2 and the spectral decomposition of their covariance matrices Σ_1, Σ_2. The eigenvalues λ_{ij} of Σ_i are the variances of each distribution along their principal axis, which are given by their corresponding eigenvectors e_{ij}. Using these parameters, the final transformation matrix $\mathbf{A}$ is given by a composition of translation ($\mathbf{T}$), rotation ($\mathbf{R}$) and scaling ($\mathbf{S}$) matrices:

$$\mathbf{A} = \mathbf{T}_2\mathbf{R}_2\mathbf{S}_2\mathbf{S}_1\mathbf{R}_1\mathbf{T}_1 \tag{1}$$

where $\mathbf{T}_1$, $\mathbf{R}_1$, $\mathbf{S}_1$, $\mathbf{S}_2$, $\mathbf{R}_2$ and $\mathbf{T}_2$ are expressed in terms of μ_1, e_{1j}, λ_{1j}, λ_{2j}, e_{2j} and μ_2 respectively. Figure 2 shows the transformation process. The original distribution is first normalized by means of a traslation, rotation and scaling, and then reshaped to the target one. The transformation is completed in one step given by matrix $\mathbf{A}$.

---

[2] Simple color concepts are those related to basic colors such as black, red and green, opposite to complex color concepts like skin color.

The extension to the case $\{G(\mu_i^{(1)}, \Sigma_i^{(1)}), ..., G(\mu_i^{(n)}, \Sigma_i^{(n)})\}$ of n Gaussians in each mixture requires that:

- there exists a unique correspondence between the Gaussian components of both mixtures,
- and spatial relationships between mixture components in RGB space are kept in all distributions.

The full transformation is then expressed by the set of matrices $\{\mathbf{A}_1, ..., \mathbf{A}_n\}$ that transform each component of the mixture. Given a RGB color $x = (r, g, b, 1)^T$ to be corrected, the transformation matrix corresponding to the maximum probability component of the mixture should be applied:

$$x' = \mathbf{A}_j x, \quad j = \arg \max_{k=1..n} P(G(\mu_1^{(k)}, \Sigma_1^{(k)})|x) \tag{2}$$

where $P(G(\mu_1^{(k)}, \Sigma_1^{(k)})|x)$ is the posterior probability of the kth mixture component, given the sample x, computed using Bayes rule as:

$$P(G(\mu_1^{(k)}, \Sigma_1^{(k)})|x) = \frac{P(x|G(\mu_1^{(k)}, \Sigma_1^{(k)}))P(G(\mu_1^{(k)}, \Sigma_1^{(k)}))}{\sum_{k=1}^{n} P(x|G(\mu_1^{(k)}, \Sigma_1^{(k)}))P(G(\mu_1^{(k)}, \Sigma_1^{(k)}))} \tag{3}$$

Assuming the same prior probability for each Gaussian component, j is also obtained by maximizing their likelihood $P(x|G(\mu_1^{(k)}, \Sigma_1^{(k)}))$.

However, some undesirable effects appear in edges and color gradients due to the loss of continuity produced by the *maximum a posteriori* (MAP) classifier in eq. (2), which may assign different transformations to nearby colors. In order to keep the continuity in the transformed distribution, the contribution of the different parts of the transformation should be combined taking into account their probability of being applied:

$$x' = \sum_{j=1}^{n} P(G(\mu_1^{(j)}, \Sigma_1^{(j)})|x)\mathbf{A}_j x \tag{4}$$

The transformation as defined by eq. (4) preserves the joint distribution of the data set, i.e. the probability of each mixture component given a specific color is the same in all mixtures after applying the appropriate transformation. In terms of works in color naming [12], we could say that the identity of colors is preserved under this transformation, as far as the contributions of different "color models" are kept.

The final transformation given by eq. (4) requires the computation of n Gaussian probabilities and n 4×4 matrix multiplications. The implementation as a look-up table can be considered in order to allow real time processing in current home multimedia systems.

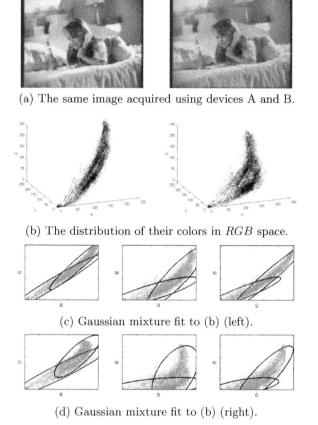

(a) The same image acquired using devices A and B.

(b) The distribution of their colors in RGB space.

(c) Gaussian mixture fit to (b) (left).

(d) Gaussian mixture fit to (b) (right).

Fig. 3. The same image acquired using different video devices shows a significant non-linear variation of its color distribution.

2.1 Single image correction

As an example of the proposed color correction method, the simple case of adapting color appearance of an image acquired using two different combinations of video devices, which we shall call A and B, in order to achieve color coherence is considered. The variation of the color distribution given by different devices can be visually assessed in fig. 3(a), showing a noticeable non-linear distortion, as seen in fig. 3(b). Each distribution was parameterized by a mixture of two Gaussians (figs. 3(c) and 3(d)), whose parameters were estimated from the data set using the EM algorithm [4]. The correspondence between components is straightforward. Note that the spatial relationships between the Gaussians are kept in both distributions as well, so that all requirements needed to obtain the transformation are fulfilled.

The transformation matrices that adapt the color appearance of the image acquired using B as if it had been acquired using A were obtained and applied

 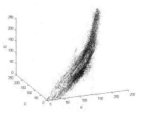

(a) Transformed image from devices B to A. (b) Transformed distribution of colors.

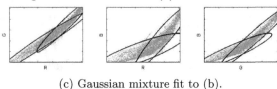

(c) Gaussian mixture fit to (b).

Fig. 4. Result of applying the transformation between the distributions in figs. 3.

as defined in eq. (4). The results are shown in fig. 4, where it can be seen that the corrected image from device B has acquired the color appearance of device A. The correction does not give exact results due to other device imperfections, like signal noise. However, the visual color appearance obtained is practically the same, and their color histograms are very similar as well.

2.2   Correction of the whole color space

The ideal transformation between color space variations should be given as a look-up table where every (r, g, b) triplet is assigned a unique transformed (r', g', b'). This approach has important practical problems, and can lead to ambiguities in the case of colors with multiple assignations.

The extension of our color correction to the general case requires modeling the distribution of all possible colors generated in RGB space that can be obtained using a particular combination of video devices. This distribution can be automatically learned from a pattern like the ones shown in fig. 5, which encodes the means and covariance matrices of a predefined mixture of Gaussians specifically designed to fill up the whole color space. Both requirements of the multiple Gaussians transformation are implicitly fulfilled by computing the parameters of each component from its corresponding region in the pattern. In this way, a parametric model of the color distribution generated by a particular device is obtained by acquiring the pattern and ambiguities are implicitly considered in the transformation defined by eq. (4).

The number and location of the mixture components are not imposed by the method, whenever the joint distribution considers all possible colors that can be generated by a device. The non-linearities of the transformations are better captured using as much Gaussians as possible, which also increases the computational cost of the correction process. We tested two different configurations:

Fig. 5. Patterns encoding the parameters of the mixture of Gaussians of the full RGB color space distribution, which are used to obtain device color models. Flat regions encode Gaussian means, while their covariance matrices are encoded in noisy ones.

(a) Images from fig. 1 corrected using configuration 1 (9 Gaussians).

(b) Images from fig. 1 corrected using configuration 2 (27 Gaussians).

Fig. 6. Image transformations using global models with different configurations.

1. 1 component in the middle of the RGB space (model for gray) and 8 equally spaced components in the periphery (models for black, white, red, green, blue, cyan, yellow and magenta), encoded by the pattern in fig. 5(left),
2. a $3 \times 3 \times 3$ grid of equally spaced components, encoded by the pattern in fig. 5(right).

Corrections using the first one showed fairly unnatural colors, which are very noticeable in fig. 6(a). On the other hand, the higher representation capability of the second configuration gave much better results, as can be seen in fig. 6(b). The quantitative evaluation of these results is not straightforward. Other variations caused by the acquisition process, i.e. noise and image misalignment, prevent us from using a pixel-based error measure. Most works on color mapping perform psychophysical evaluations [15, 3, 5, 14]. In this sense, the performance of our color correction algorithm improves using more Gaussian components in the representation. Therefore, color appearance as given by different devices can be adapted without prior knowledge about its final distribution in RGB space.

3   Skin color segmentation

Skin color segmentation is a very good example of the application of color correction in digital video. It is widely used within digital libraries as a preprocess for tasks like face detection and recognition [18], or adult content filtering [6]. Many works found in the literature are based on statistical models of skin and non-skin color distributions in RGB or other color spaces using histograms [11], single Gaussian distributions [18, 21] or Gaussian mixture models [9, 11]. The segmentation is performed in theses cases using the MAP classification rule.

The intrinsic variability of skin color from person to person makes its distribution to be better estimated using a mixture of Gaussians. These models are trained from a set of skin color samples using the EM algorithm. The use of color spaces other than RGB obtained by fixed global transformations does not affect the feasibility of fitting this kind of distribution to a learning data set. Other sources of variability in skin color values, such as illumination conditions, are supposed to be considered in the model training data set. However, the changes produced by the video acquisition process can not be taken into account in this way, as all possible combinations of video devices are not known during learning.

For the sake of simplicity, we have not defined a non-skin color model and the segmentation rule is given by thresholding the likelihood of candidate pixels by a suitable value. Using our color correction technique, we can deal with device caused variability following these steps:

1. Build a training data set of skin color values with samples from images acquired by a reference device R, whose color appearance is given by the Gaussian mixture M_R.
2. Train the skin color model in RGB space.
3. Obtain the color appearance model of the device used to acquire images to be segmented, M_D, and its transformation into the reference device model, A_{DR}.
4. For each pixel, correct its color using A_{DR} and apply the segmentation rule.

3.1   Experimental results

We have tested our approach on video imagery acquired using two different combinations of VTR and acquisition cards: (1) Mitsubishi M1000 + Matrox Marvel G200 TV, and (2) JVC BR-S822E + miroVideo DC30 Plus. Figures 7(a) and 7(b) show the same image acquired using both combinations of devices. The skin color model training data set was obtained from images acquired using the first one. Figures 7(d) and 7(e) show the skin color segmentation results of those images, when no correction at all was applied. The first one was correctly segmented, while the segmentation of the image from device 2 was absolutely wrong because the variability in skin color introduced by the change of device was not considered during training. On the other hand, fig. 7(c) corresponds to the result of transforming fig. 7(b) in order to adapt its color appearance to the first device. The correction makes skin color values to lie in the same region of

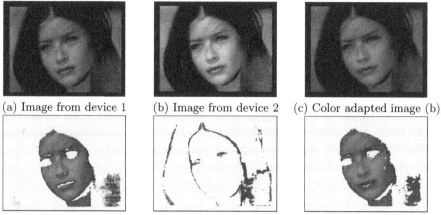

(a) Image from device 1   (b) Image from device 2   (c) Color adapted image (b)

(d) Skin segmentation of (a) (e) Skin segmentation of (b) (f) Skin segmentation of (c)

Fig. 7. Images used in the skin color segmentation experiments (see text).

the RGB space as in the reference device color model. Figure 7(f) shows the good segmentation results obtained in this case. Therefore, the transformations obtained using our method preserves the underlying identity of colors such as skin color. Matlab code is also available at http://www.cvc.uab.es/~juanma.

4   Other applications

Other applications where the use of color correction would be of great interest are:

Video indexing: Color histograms have been widely used for indexing image databases since its introduction by Swain and Ballard in [19]. They have been applied to video databases as well in order to index them from *keyframes* [17]. The color histogram of an image is significantly changed due to device color variations. Similarly, appearance based coding has also been used with this purpose [16]. However, it is very sensitive to changes of pixel values produced by different illumination conditions and color variations.

Object recognition: In the same way the concept of skin color was modeled in the previous section as a mixture of Gaussians in RGB space, McKenna et al. characterize objects from their colors in [13]. Samples that do not follow the model learned for a given object can easily appear when changing the acquisition device.

Video manipulation: Dealing with digital video allows us to easily manipulate it using basic *chroma-keying* techniques or more advanced ones. In this way, video imagery coming from different sources can be put together within the same space. One of the basic problems to be solved in this case is to obtain a seamless combination of images in order to offer a pleasant viewing experience to the audience [10]. Our color correction scheme provides a direct path to obtaining homogeneous color appearances in images acquired from different devices.

5   Conclusions

Color appearance variations of video imagery produced by the change of devices in the acquisition process strongly affect the performance of color based tasks such as indexing and recognition. Spatial and temporal coherence of colors expected by end users when viewing and manipulating digital video contents is corrupted as well. Taking theory into practice makes us notice of these effects, as it did during our previous works on automatic TV commercials recognition [16,17].

We propose color correction in order to obtain homogeneous color representations by automatically learning the appropriate transformation between color appearances given by different devices. The distribution of colors in RGB space produced by a particular device is modeled as a mixture of Gaussians, whose parameters are obtained from a color pattern and let us define affine transformations for each mixture component. These transformations are applied to each pixel to be corrected and are combined taking into account their probabilities in order to preserve its location in RGB space with respect to the final mixture components. In this way, the color appearance of acquired images can be adapted to different device appearances without prior knowledge of its own final distribution of colors in RGB space.

This correction technique has been shown to be very useful in the case of skin color segmentation. Its application allows us to stop worrying about the variability produced by the use of different acquisition devices. The results obtained suggest that many other color based tasks within digital video libraries can be improved by the use of color correction.

The attachment of the color pattern that encodes color appearance to digital video streams allows their automatic correction by software or hardware video players. We claim for the use of this method by including color correction patterns as metadata in standard video representations such as MPEG-7, at least during the transitional period towards full digitally acquired video. The device-dependent color pattern could be included in the description scheme as a color feature of video data, in the same way that other lens and camera parameters can also be specified. We are convinced that this is a necessary step to be given in forthcoming digital TV technologies.

References

1. A. Bibiloni. *Un sistema de edición vídeo por contenido aplicado a la creación de entornos hipervídeo dinámicos.* PhD thesis, Universitat de les Illes Balears, October 1999. (in Spanish).
2. D. H. Brainard and W. T. Freeman. Bayesian color constancy. *Journal of the Optical Society of America A*, 14(7):1393–1411, July 1997.

3. G. J. Braun and M. D. Fairchild. General-purpose gamut-mapping algorithms: evaluation of contrast-preserving rescaling functions for color gamut mapping. In *IS&T/SID 7th Color Imaging Conference*, pages 167–192, Scottsdale, 1999.
4. A. Dempster, N. Laird, and D. Rubin. Maximum likelihood from incomplete data via the EM algorithm. *Journal of the Royal Statistical Society B*, 39, 1977.
5. M. D. Fairchild and K. M. Braun. Investigation of color appearance using the psychophysical method of adjustment and complex pictorial images. In *AIC Color 97*, pages 179–186, Kyoto, 1997.
6. D. Forsyth and M. Fleck. Automatic detection of human nudes. *International Journal of Computer Vision*, 32(1):63–77, 1999.
7. B. Funt, K. Barnard, and L. Martin. Is machine colour constancy good enough? In H. Burkhardt and B. Neumann, editors, *Proc. of 5th European Conference on Computer Vision*, volume I, pages 445–459, Freiburg, Germany, 1998.
8. B. Funt and G. Finlayson. Color constant color indexing. *IEEE Trans. Patt. Anal. and Mach. Intell*, 17(5), May 1995.
9. D. Guillamet and J. Vitrià. Skin segmentation using non linear principal component analysis. In *Proc. 2 Congrés Català d'Intel·ligència Artificial (CCIA99)*, pages 224–231, Girona, Spain, 1999.
10. K. J. Hanna, H. S. Sawhney, R. Kumar, Y. Guo, and S. Samarasekara. Annotation of video by alignment to reference imagery. In *Proc. IEEE Intl. Conf. on Multimedia Computing and Systems*, volume 1, pages 38–43, Firenze, Italy, June 1999.
11. M. J. Jones and J. M. Rehg. Statistical color models with application to skin detection. *Cambridge Research Laboratory, Technical Report CRL 98/11*, December 1998.
12. J. M. Lammens. *A Computational Model of Color Perception and Color Naming*. PhD thesis, State University of New York at Buffalo, June 1994.
13. S. J. McKenna, Y. Raja, and S. Gong. Tracking colour objects using adaptive mixture models. *Image and Vision Computing*, 17(3-4):225–231, March 1999.
14. J. Morovic and M. Ronnier Luo. Cross-media psychophysical evaluation of gamut mapping algorithms. In *AIC Color 97*, pages 594–597, Kyoto, 1997.
15. J. Morovic and M. Ronnier Luo. Gamut mapping algorithms based on psychophysical experiment. In *IS&T/SID 5th Color Imaging Conference*, pages 44–49, 1997.
16. J. M. Sánchez, X. Binefa, J. Vitrià, and P. Radeva. Shot partitioning based recognition of TV commercials. *Multimedia Tools and Applications.* (in press).
17. J. M. Sánchez, X. Binefa, J. Vitrià, and P. Radeva. Local color analysis for scene break detection applied to TV commercials recognition. In *Proc. 3rd Intl. Conf. on Visual Information and Information Systems VISUAL'99*, pages 237–244, Amsterdam, The Netherlands, June 1999. Springer Verlag LNCS 1614.
18. S. Satoh, Y. Nakamura, and T. Kanade. Name-it: Naming and detecting faces in news videos. *IEEE Multimedia*, 6(1):22–35, January-March 1999.
19. M. J. Swain and D. H. Ballard. Color indexing. *International Journal of Computer Vision*, 7(1):11–32, 1991.
20. P. L. Vora, J. E. Farrell, J. D. Tietz, and D. H. Brainard. Image capture: Modelling and calibration of sensor responses and their synthesis from multispectral images. *Hewlett Packard Company, Technical Report, HPL-98-187*, November 1998.
21. J. Yang, W. Lu, and A. Waibel. Skin-color modeling and adaptation. In *Proceedings of the ACCV'98*, volume II, pages 687–694, 1998.

Multimedia Content Filtering, Browsing, and Matching Using MPEG-7 Compact Color Descriptors

Santhana Krishnamachari[1], Akio Yamada[2], Mohamed Abdel-Mottaleb[1], and Eiji Kasutani[2]

[1]Philips Research, 345 Scarborough Road, Briarcliff Manor, NY 10510, USA
santhana.krishnamachari@philips.com
mohamed.abdel-mottaleb@philips.com

[2]C&C Media Research Laboratories, NEC Corp.,
Miyazaki 4-1-1, Miyamae, Kawasaki 216-8555, JAPAN
{golgo, eiji}@ccm.cl.nec.co.jp

Abstract. This paper presents two compact color feature descriptors that have been accepted to the working draft of MPEG-7, the ongoing activity to standardize multimedia content descriptions. The need for content description arises from the increase in the number of broadcast channels and the availability of a large number of video content over the Internet. Without such descriptions, the average consumer would be left helpless with enormous amount of data and no viable tool to efficiently access the content. MPEG-7 is standardizing descriptions for audio-visual features such as color, shape, and texture, and as well as the higher level semantic features. Here we present two color descriptors that are very compact in size, namely, the compact color histogram descriptor and the compact color layout descriptor. These two descriptors capture complementary characteristics of the color content of images. The compact sizes of these descriptors result in minimal storage and transmission requirements of the image representation. We demonstrate the efficacy of these descriptors for video content filtering, image matching, sketch-based matching and browsing applications.

1 Introduction

The advent of digital broadcast television, proliferation of consumer electronic devices for creation and manipulation of digital multimedia content, and the growth of the Internet have made digital multimedia content ubiquitous. The increase in the number of video channels and the availability of large scale storage media in consumer devices have begun to enable the consumer to record and store large number of programs either manually or automatically based on the interest profiles. Therefore, it is necessary to empower the user with the capability to quickly and efficiently access the program or content of interest.

The convergence of television and the computer has opened up new ways in which the consumer interacts with multimedia content. Increasingly, viewers are not interested in just viewing a program in a linear fashion from start to end. Features that enable the user to browse through the program, selectively view sections of the program that he is interested in or even tailor sections of the program based on the user's profile will greatly enrich the viewing experience of the consumer. Such tools

R. Laurini (Ed.): VISUAL 2000, LNCS 1929, pp. 200–211, 2000.
 Springer-Verlag Berlin Heidelberg 2000

will not only increase the intrinsic value of the content for the content provider by increasing the viewers' interest in such content, but also play a major role in differentiating consumer electronics products from different manufacturers.

To enable the aforementioned features, the audio-visual content, be broadcast programs or video available over the Internet, has to be structured and the descriptions about the content should be made available.   Moreover, these descriptions have to be added in a standardized fashion that allows for the exchange, distribution of digital media and to prevent the obsolescence of consumer devices.

MPEG-7, the ongoing ISO activity to standardize the multimedia content descriptions, was started in October 1998 and is scheduled to be completed by September 2001. As of December 1999, the work on MPEG-7 has reached the stage of the working draft.   The description of audio-visual content includes low-level features that describe the signal characteristics, like the color, texture, shape, and motion trajectories of objects in an image or a video, as well as the high-level features that describe the semantics of the content. The descriptions represent the content in a way that a search engine can use these descriptions to find the material of interest to the user in a reasonable time. Although feature extraction and search engines are required for complete applications, these will be non-normative parts of the standard. The normative part of the standard will focus on the descriptions and their encoding. This will enable development of applications that will utilize the MPEG-7 descriptions without specific ties to a single content provider or search engine.

In this paper we present two compact color descriptors that were proposed to MPEG-7. These descriptors have been evaluated for various applications such as image matching, browsing, video segment matching and sketch based search and have been accepted to the working draft of MPEG-7. One of the compact descriptors is based on the Haar wavelet transformation of the color histogram and expresses the global color distribution in a compact fashion.   The second compact descriptor is based on DCT transformation of the image or video frame blocks and expresses the color layout. The need for compact descriptors is motivated in a later section.

This paper is organized as follows: In Section 2 the need for compact descriptors is presented. Section 3 presents the details of the compact color descriptors, the extraction methodology and the matching measures. Section 4 shows the use of the compact color descriptor for image/video matching and browsing applications. Section 5 concludes the paper.

2   Need for Compact Color Descriptors

Content-based search and retrieval techniques for multimedia content utilize various descriptors for different image features. The color content, being one of the easily computable features is often used in content-based search [1] and filtering [2] applications. MPEG-7 supports color related features that represent both the global color distribution [3] and the spatial distribution of colors [4]. The former is used to express color content of an image for similarity-based retrievals. Color histograms are often used for this purpose. The latter is used to represent the distribution and layout of the colors. This is accomplished by partitioning an image into multiple grids and representing the color content of each partition by one or more dominant colors.

Color histograms and grid-based dominant colors, in general, need relatively large number of bits for representation. Using such a representation may not pose a problem for applications with a large storage capacity and with ample computational resources. However for applications like content filtering, where the multimedia data and related descriptions are processed by a set-top box or a similar device with limited computational resource, limited bandwidth and real-time processing requirements, it is imperative to use a compact representation. Even for a database type application, histograms with a large number of bins pose difficult problems in indexing.

MPEG-7, at present, supports a hierarchy of color descriptors based on their size. At the bottom of the hierarchy are the detailed color descriptors, such as the color histograms and the grid-based dominant colors. The sizes of these color descriptors are fairly large, about 2048 bits, and they offer an excellent performance in terms of color-based search and filtering. These descriptors are useful for applications that have large storage capacity, sophisticated indexing schemes, large computational resource, and without acute bandwidth restrictions. At the top of the hierarchy are the compact color descriptors; the sizes of these descriptors are very small, typically less than 128 bits. These descriptors offer a very good performance, although arguably not as good as the detailed descriptors. Such descriptors are useful for applications where the computational resources are scarce and there is a need to stream the descriptors through a bandwidth-limited channel.

3   Compact Color Descriptors

In this section we present the details of the two compact color descriptors: the compact color histogram descriptor and the compact color layout descriptor. These two descriptors address complementary functionalities. The compact color histogram descriptor represents the global distribution of color in an image or video. This does not capture the spatial distribution of the color content. Such a representation is useful for applications where the specific color layout is not important. On the other hand, the compact color layout descriptor, as the name indicates, characterizes the spatial color distribution. Such a representation is necessary for applications where the color layout is important. It is conceivable to use color histogram descriptors on local grids. However this results in a descriptor that is not very compact in size, and also as the number of pixels in the local grids tends to be small, the computed histogram tends to be statistically less robust.

3.1 Compact Color Histogram Descriptor

As mentioned in the previous section, histograms are the most prevalently used descriptor to express color characteristics of images. Color histograms convey the quantitative characteristics of the color distribution. But for many applications, a more compact descriptor that expresses the qualitative characteristics is sufficient. In this section, a compact descriptor based on the color histogram is presented. This descriptor is obtained by applying the Haar wavelet transformation to a color histogram and binary quantizing the resulting coefficients of the transform. The resulting descriptor is 63 bits long and is therefore very compact. The simplicity of the Haar transform allows easy computation of the proposed descriptor. In spite of its compactness, the descriptor performs well for image, video search and browsing tasks. Objective measures developed by the MPEG-7 group to evaluate various representations show that this descriptor offers a superior performance when compared to other descriptors of comparable size. The binary nature of the descriptor allows simple matching metric based on Hamming distance and simple indexing scheme. The computationally inexpensive similarity metric associated with the descriptor makes it possible to perform very fast image search, and video segment search without any shot segmentation.

3.1.1 Descriptor Extraction

The extraction process for the compact color histogram consists of stages shown in Figure 1. The first stage is to obtain a color histogram using a suitable color space and quantization scheme. The histogram can be a one, two or three-dimensional histogram. The second stage is the computation of the Haar transform coefficients of the histogram. The second stage does not depend on the nature of the color space or the quantization table used in the first stage The Haar transform coefficients are obtained by taking the inner product of the basis functions with the given histogram. Each row in Figure 1(b) is a basis function for the Haar transform shown here for a length of 8. The third stage is the binary quantization of the resulting coefficients.

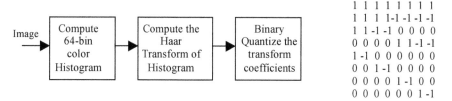

Fig. 1. (a) The compact color histogram extraction stages (b) The basis functions of the Haar transform of size eight.

The Haar wavelets are computationally very simple to implement, because the basis functions contain only values of $+1$, -1 and 0 as shown in Figure 1. Therefore, the computation does not involve any multiplication. The Haar coefficients capture the qualitative aspects of the histogram. For example, the second coefficient is positive if the sum of the left half of the histogram bins is greater than the right half and negative otherwise. Similarly, the third coefficient is positive if the sum of the first quarter of the histogram bins is greater than the second quarter and negative otherwise. In our descriptor, each of these coefficients is binary quantized to a 1 or 0, depending on whether their value is positive or not, and hence a binary representation is obtained. The motivation behind this descriptor is that for search and filtering applications, exact histogram values are not necessary, but a general qualitative description is sufficient. Also note that the first coefficient corresponds to sum of all probabilities in a histogram, it is always positive and is quantized to 1. Hence, this coefficient is not used in similarity matching. Therefore the effective length of the descriptor is 63 bits.

Two different color spaces have been used for computing the color histograms, the YCbCr and the HSV color space. We have used a 64-bin color histogram, but the technique is equally applicable to histograms of larger or smaller number of quantization bins. The quantized color centers were obtained based on the color probabilities of a selected set of images. The Haar transformation is applied on the resulting 64-bin histogram. More details on the implementation of the Haar transform can be found elsewhere [7].

3.1.2 Descriptor Matching

For the compact color histogram, the Hamming distance is used as the matching measure. The Hamming distance is computed by taking the XOR of the two 63-bit binary descriptors and computing the number of '1' bits in the result. This matching measure is extremely simple to compute and hence enables fast computation.

3.2 Compact Color Layout Descriptor

Compact color layout descriptors are designed to efficiently represent spatial distribution of colors, which is not supported by the compact color histogram. Color layout information is especially useful for retrieval applications that require visual structure of the contents. Hand-written sketch queries and video segment identification are the typical ones. Sketch-based retrieval can be used as an incremental search tool with very friendly interface, especially if the search is fast enough. Video segment identification requires a large number of similarity calculations and hence a fast search tool is necessary. Here a compact descriptor based on the grid-based dominant color is presented. This descriptor is obtained by applying the DCT transformation on a two dimensional array of local dominant colors. The resulting descriptor is only 63 bits long and enables very fast retrieval.

3.2.1 Descriptor Extraction

The descriptor extraction for the color layout consists of four stages, image partitioning, dominant color detection, DCT transformation, and non-linear quantization of the zigzag-scanned DCT coefficients as shown in Figure 2. In the first stage, an input picture is divided into 64 blocks. The size of the each block is W/8 x H/8, where W and H denote the width and height of the input picture, respectively. In the next stage, a single dominant color is selected from each block. Any method for dominant color selection can be applied. We use the simple average color as the dominant color in the following sections. This results in a compact image icon whose size is 8x8. In the third stage, each of the three color component is transformed by 8x8 DCT, so we obtain three sets of DCT coefficients. They are zigzag scanned and the first few coefficients, in the default case, 6 for luminance and 3 for each chrominance are quantized. The quantization is performed to match the characteristic of the human visual system. The number of coefficients may be increased to achieve resolution scalable representation. The number of quantization levels is 64 for DC coefficients and 32 for AC coefficients; so the total length of the color layout descriptor is 63 bits.

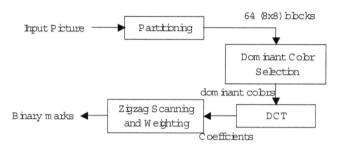

Fig. 2. The block diagram of the compact color layout descriptor extraction

3.2.2 Descriptor Matching

The matching measure used for the compact color layout descriptor is the weighted Euclidean distance. The distance of two color layout descriptors, CL {$Y0$, ..., $Y5$, $U0$, $U1$, $U2$, $V0$, $V1$, $V2$} and CL' is defined as follows.

$$D(CL,CL') = \sqrt{\sum_{i=0}^{5} \lambda_{Yi}(Yi - Yi')^2} + \sqrt{\sum_{i=0}^{2} \lambda_{ui}(Ui - Ui')^2} + \sqrt{\sum_{i=0}^{2} \lambda_{vi}(Vi - Vi')^2}$$

Lambda values in the distance definition denote the weighting for coefficients. In the frequency domain, the first coefficient is the most important and the contribution to the similarity of other coefficients should be reduced. The color layout description on a video segment is represented as a set of color layout descriptor values on individual video frames. Instead of using all frames, we select a subset of frames with fixed temporal interval. The distance of the two video segments with N selected frames, is defined as an average of the frame distance as follows:

$$D(\{CL\},\{CL'\}) = \frac{1}{N}\sum_{i} D(CL_i, CL_i')$$

If the temporal positions of the descriptors on two segments are different, interpolations of descriptor values are required. It should be noted that we simply compare all or a part of the frame descriptors without any shot detection. In general, most other conventional methods need key-frame detection because of constraint of the similarity calculation speed. The high-speed processing of this compact descriptor obviates the need for shot detection and offers more robust results.

4   Applications

In this section we demonstrate the efficacy of the compact color descriptors for content filtering, image matching, and browsing applications. Evaluation of these descriptors was performed both quantitatively and qualitatively during the MPEG-7 core experiment evaluation. To quantitatively evaluate the matching efficiency of various descriptors, MPEG-7 developed an objective measure called the Average Normalized Modified Retrieval Rank (ANMRR) [5]. Details of the ANMRR can be found in the Appendix at the end of this paper. The ANMRR measure combines the precision and recall measure to obtain a single objective value. The ANMRR is always in the range of [0, 1.0] and the smaller the value of this measure, the better the quality of retrieval. ANMRR values in the range of [0, 0.1] results in excellent retrieval performance and values in the range of [0.1, 0.3] results in good, acceptable performance.

4.1 Image Matching

The retrieval performance of the compact histogram descriptor is compared with the conventional 64-bit binary histogram. The conventional 64-bit binary histogram is obtained by computing the 64-bin histogram and binary quantizing each bin value. The same quantization centers were used in both cases. A database of 5466 diverse images is used and a set of 50 queries and ground truth sets are identified. The ANMRR measure was used as the objective measure. Table 1 shows the comparison of performances in two color spaces.

Table 1: Comparison of retrieval efficiency in two color spaces

	YCbCr	HSV
Compact Color Histogram Descriptor	0.207	0.241
Conventional Binary Histogram	0.423	0.487

The objective measure clearly shows the vastly improved performance of the compact color histogram compared with the conventional binary histogram of the same size.

The retrieval performance of the color layout descriptor is compared with the grid-based dominant color descriptor of the same size. Two different types of query are selected. In the first case, an image from the database is used as a query. In the second case, the user composes a query using a sketch. Figure 3 shows the comparison of the performance of color layout descriptor against the grid-based dominant colors for different grid sizes using the ANMRR measure. It clearly demonstrates that the proposed descriptor shows superior matching efficiency compared to the grid-based dominant color descriptors. The complexity of similarity calculation for the color layout descriptor is just about 1/7 compared to the simple 4x4 grid-based dominant color. The estimated similarity calculation speed for the compact layout descriptor is about 5 million times per second on 500MHz processor using Intel SSE instruction set when all the data is hit on processor cache [6]. Note that to obtain a given descriptor length for each case, the representation accuracy of the coefficients or dominant colors is varied using shift operations.

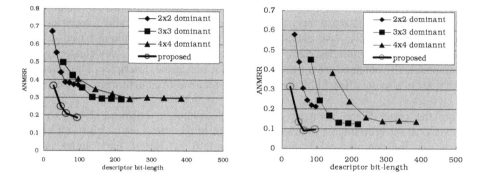

Fig. 3. Retrieval efficiency comparison for (a) Still Picture (b)Sketch Queries

4.2 Browsing

As the number of images or videos present in a collection increases, it is necessary to provide the user with tools to efficiently and rapidly browse through the content. Linear browsing of the content, like looking at the all the filenames in a directory in a computer system, is time consuming and laborious. For multimedia content, the browsing tool should allow the user to visually browse through the content.

4.2.1 Image Browsing

Most of the content-based search systems require the user to perform search by example, by choosing one of the existing images or video segments in the database as a query or by requiring the user to compose a query. Often users cannot present to the system good examples of what they are looking for without effectively browsing through the database. Hence an efficient browsing tool is essential to introduce the user to the contents of the database. After identifying an image or a video segment of interest through browsing, the user can perform content-based search to find similar entities from the database.

For databases with large numbers of images, it is not feasible to browse linearly through the images in the database. A desirable characteristic of a browsing system is to let the user navigate through the database in a structured manner. Browsing tools for video material are based on detecting shots and identifying key-frames corresponding to shots. The selected key frames are then grouped in temporal order or clustered based on content similarity to aid browsing. Browsing tools for large image databases have been presented using clustering techniques. The use of hierarchical clustering technique for fast image search and non-linear browsing has been shown [9]. An active browsing tool [8] that uses hierarchical clustering and relevance feedback has also been presented recently.

The drawbacks of the browsing techniques that use clustering techniques are: (1) they require computationally expensive clustering algorithms, (2) addition or deletion of content from the database may change the clusters considerably, requiring re-clustering periodically.   As detailed below, the browsing technique based on the compact color histogram descriptor presented here does not require any clustering and is automatically obtained from the compact color histogram descriptor. The proposed technique is also not affected by the addition or removal of content from the database.

From the given 63-bit compact histogram descriptor, a balanced 2^k-ary tree is constructed for browsing as follows. At the root of the tree, a set of k bits out of the 63 bits in the compact color histogram descriptor is chosen. Each image in the database can have one of 2^k values for these k bits. Depending on the values of these k bits, the entire database is divided in 2^k groups. Each of these groups is represented by a child node from the root of the tree. Each of these groups is further divided into 2^k groups, by considering another set of k bits. This process is repeated to build the entire tree. The number of levels in the tree is equal to the smallest integer large than $63/k$. A representative image is chosen at each node in the tree. In the first level of browsing at the root of the tree, the 2^k representative images corresponding to the first level of the tree are displayed. At the subsequent levels, the user traverses through the tree by selecting the representative image that is most similar to the image that he/she is looked for.   The selection of the k bits that are used to partition the database into groups at different levels of the tree can be selected in two ways: (1) selecting the most significant bits first followed by the least significant bits or (2) identifying the entropy of each of the 63 bits for a given database and selecting the bits in the decreasing order of the entropy values. The motivation behind the latter selection is that the bits with the largest entropy contain the most information and therefore are used to partition the database initially.

4.2.2 Visualization

One important distinction of the color layout descriptor is that it is generative, i.e., the content can be re-generated from this descriptor, albeit, only a very coarse version. Almost all of the descriptors attempt to concisely represent specific characteristics of the content, but it is not possible to generate the content back from the descriptor values. For example, using a color histogram values we cannot reconstruct an image. But the color layout descriptor contains sufficient information about the spatial color feature, so that we can generate a coarse representation of the original picture by transforming the descriptor values into the spatial domain. Three steps are requested to obtain the picture icons whose size are 8x8. The first step is to assign 0 values for the excluded DCT coefficients. The second step is the inverse quantization of the

DCT coefficients based on the quantization scheme used in the descriptor extraction. Then the IDCT process transforms the inverse-quantized coefficients into the icon. The derived icons of original pictures or selected video frames can be used for browsing and coarse visualization.

4.3 Content Filtering

In the query and search applications, the user is actively involved in selecting the query and possibly providing feedback to indicate the quality of retrieval. In content filtering applications, the multimedia content is automatically filtered by an agent in accordance with the user's interests and profile. For example, with the increasing number of available television channels, it is impossible for a user to manually flip through all the channels to find programs of interest.   However, by observing the user's watching habit, the system can automatically recommend programs or sections of programs for the user. By using the user profile, e.g., a child is not allowed to watch violent sections of a program, the system can automatically filter out the specific portions of a video. Many of the content filtering functionalities can be achieved with the textual annotation attached to the content. However, the low-level features can be used to draw certain semantic inferences for cases that are not covered by annotations or if the annotations are not present at all.

Video segment matching can be used to efficiently draw high level inferences: for example, a given news program can be broken up into anchor person shots leading to the partitioning of the news into different segments. Individual segments can be classified into different news categories based on audio-visual or close caption information and such a classification can be used to filter the content efficiently. Using the compact descriptors presented in this paper, we performed video segment matching without using any shot segmentation. Often shot segmentation is imprecise and difficult to generate. To compare video segments without shot detection, we extracted a key-frame every half a second from each video sequence. The key-frames corresponding to the desired query segment are compared with the key-frames of every other segment of the video in a time-overlapped fashion to obtain other similar segments. In Figure 4 identification of anchor shot sequences from a news program using the color layout descriptor is shown. Quantitative evaluation for video segment identification was again performed using the ANMRR measure resulting in a value of 0.015. This very low value of the achieved ANMRR implies that the proposed descriptor can detect almost all the identical or similar video segments. The compact nature of our descriptors allows searching over 24 hours of video in less than 2 seconds. The use of compact color histogram descriptor for similar video segment identification can be found in [7].

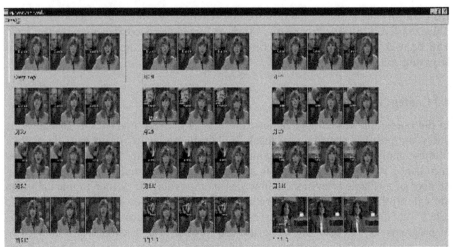

Fig. 4. Results of Anchorperson shot identification. Each segment is displayed using three frames, the first, and middle and last frames. The top-left corner is the query segment. The other retrievals are shown in the order of similarity.

5   Summary and Conclusions

We have presented two different compact color descriptors: the compact color histogram descriptor and the compact color layout descriptor. These descriptors represent the complementary aspects of the color content, the former represents the global color distribution and the latter represents the spatial color layout or distribution. The most important characteristic of these descriptors is the compact sizes of the resultant representation. Their compact sizes make these descriptors very attractive for applications that are bandwidth and computation resource constrained. The sizes of the descriptor, as presented in this paper, are 63 bits. The length of the description, in the case of the compact color histogram descriptor will depend on the size of the color histogram used and in the case of compact color layout descriptor will depend on the nature of the quantization and the number of the DCT coefficients. Quantitative and qualitative evaluation of the descriptor were conducted for different applications. The compact color histogram descriptor was shown to perform better than the conventional binary histogram and the compact color layout descriptor was shown to perform better than the grid-based dominant color descriptor. Various application scenarios, such as image matching, browsing and content filtering were demonstrated using these descriptors. Both these descriptors have been accepted to the working draft of the MPEG-7 based on their improved performance in comparison with other descriptors of comparable sizes. Currently there is an effort underway in MPEG-7 to generalize the Haar transformation of color histograms to build a scalable (non-binary) histogram descriptor.

References

1. W. Niblack, *et.al.*, "The QBIC Project: querying images by content using color, texture, and shape", In *Storage and Retrieval for Image and Video Databases I, Vol. 1908, SPIE Proceedings*, Feb. 1993.
2. N. Dimitrova, H. Elenbaas and T. McGee, "PNRS - Personal News Retrieval System", In *SPIE Conference on Multimedia Storage and Archiving Systems, SPIE Proceedings*, Sep. 1999.
3. F.Idris, "Review of Image and Video Indexing Techniques", *Journal of Visual Communication and Image Representation,* Vol. 8, No.2, June, pp.146-166 (1997)
4. "MPEG-7 Overview", ISO/IEC JTC1/SC29/WG11 N3158 (1999).
5. "Core Experiments on MPEG-7 Color and Texture Descriptors", ISO/IEC JTC1/SC29/WG11 N2929 (1999). [XM4] "MPEG-7 Visual part of eXperimentation Model Version 4.0", ISO/IEC JTC1/SC29/WG11 N3068 (1999).
6. A.Yamada *et.al.*, "Visual Program Navigation System based on Spatial Distribution of Color", *International Conference on Consumer Electronics 2000.*
7. S.Krishnamachari and M. Abdel-Mottaleb, "Compact Color Descriptor for Fast Image and Video Segment Retrieval", *Proc. of IS&T/SPIE Conference on Storage and Retrieval of Media Databases* 2000, January 2000
8. J-Y. Chen, C.A. Bouman and J. Dalton, "Active Browsing using Similarity Pyramids", In *Storage and Retrieval for Image and Video Databases VII*, Vol. 3656, SPIE Proceedings, Jan 1998.
9. S. Krishnamachari and M. Abdel-Mottaleb, "Image Browsing using Hierarchical Clustering", *In Proc. of the IEEE Symposium on Computers and Communications*, ISCC 99, Egypt, July 1999.

Appendix: ANMRR Computation

The details of the Average Normalized Modified Retrieval Rank (ANMRR) computations are presented here. First a set of query images and the corresponding ground truth images that are considered similar to the query are selected manually. The ground truth items are not ordered in any way, but all ground truth items were deemed to be equally relevant to the query. Let the number of ground truth images for query q be $NG(q)$. Let $K = \min\{4*NG(q), 2*GTM\}$ where GTM is $\max\{NG(q)\}$ for all queries. For each ground truth image, k, retrieved in the top K retrievals, compute the rank, $Rank(k)$, of the image, counting the rank of the first retrieved item as one. A rank of $(K+1)$ is assigned to each ground truth image that is not in the first K retrievals. Compute the *modified retrieval rank MRR(q)* for query q as follows:

$$MRR(q) = \sum_{k=1}^{NG(q)} \frac{Rank(k)}{NG(q)} - 0.5 - \frac{NG(q)}{2}$$

The normalized modified retrieval rank (NMRR) is then computed as:

$$NMRR(q) = \frac{MRR(q)}{K + 0.5 - 0.5 * NG(q)}$$

Note that NMRR(q) will always be in the range of [0.0,1.0]. Finally, the average of all NMRR values is computed over all queries to yield the ANMRR.

Shape Description for Content-Based Image Retrieval

E. Ardizzone[12], A. Chella[12], and
R. Pirrone[12]

[1] DIAI - University of Palermo, Viale delle Scienze 90128 Palermo, Italy
[2] CERE - National Research Council, Viale delle Scienze 90128 Palermo, Italy
{ardizzon, chella, pirrone}@unipa.it

Abstract. The present work is focused on a global image characterization based on a description of the 2D displacements of the different shapes present in the image, which can be employed for CBIR applications.

To this aim, a recognition system has been developed, that detects automatically image ROIs containing single objects, and classifies them as belonging to a particular class of shapes.

In our approach we make use of the eigenvalues of the covariance matrix computed from the pixel rows of a single ROI. These quantities are arranged in a vector form, and are classified using Support Vector Machines (SVMs). The selected feature allows us to recognize shapes in a robust fashion, despite rotations or scaling, and, to some extent, independently from the light conditions.

Theoretical foundations of the approach are presented in the paper, together with an outline of the system, and some preliminary experimental results.

1 Introduction

Images indexing and retrieval using content has gained increasing importance during last years. Almost all kinds of image analysis techniques have been investigated in order to derive sets of meaningful features which could be useful for the description of pictorial information, and a considerable effort has been spent towards the development of powerful but easy-to-use commercial database engines.

The most popular CBIR (content-based image retrieval) systems developed so far, like QBIC [5, 7] Photobook [9], Virage [8], model the image content as a set of uncorrelated shape, texture and color features. Queries are obtained either by manual specification of the weights for each feature or by presenting an example to the system, and they're refined by means of various relevance feedback strategies.

A more effective way to describe image content is to derive global descriptions of the objects, like in the approach followed by Malik et al. [2, 3]. In this way it's possible to obtain image indexing structures that are closer to the intuitive

R. Laurini (Ed.): VISUAL 2000, LNCS 1929, pp. 212–222, 2000.
Springer-Verlag Berlin Heidelberg 2000

descriptions provided by the end-user when he or she submits the query to the system.

Following this idea, we developed the recognition system presented in this work, which is aimed to extract global information about the shape of the objects in a scene and to provide a simple description of their 2D displacement inside the image under investigation. This, in turn, can be useful for content-based retrieval.

The proposed architecture is arranged as follows. Image is automatically searched in order to detect ROIs containing single objects. The objects' shape is described in terms of the eigenvalues of the covariance matrix computed from the pixel rows of the ROI: the eigenvalues are arranged as a single vector. We use a pool of suitably designed Support Vector Machines [13, 11] in order to classify different shape classes such as cubes, spheres, cones, pyramids, cylinders and so on.

The use of this particular feature is justified by theoretical analysis. First, it can be proven that, under the assumption of Lambertian surface, the eigenvalues vector is directly related to the change of surface normals of objects under investigation. Moreover, the eigenvalues vector are a very compact and efficient way to describe the statistical variance pattern of the shape profile, due to the complete de-correlation performed on the input patterns by the KL transform [6]. Finally, KLT allows comparisons between separate pixel rows populations, and therefore between different ROIs.

The rest of the paper is arranged as follows. In section 2 theoretical issues about the eigenvalues vector will be addressed. Section 3 will explain in detail the entire system performance, while the experimental results will be reported in section 4. Finally, conclusions will be drawn in section 5.

2   Theoretical Remarks

The use of KLT features for pattern recognition is a well known technique in the computer vision community [10, 12] but, in general, this transformation is applied to the image as a whole, and the transformed vectors are used directly for the classification task.

In our approach, KLT is implicitly applied to the scan-lines of a generic sub-image, and only the eigenvalues of their covariance matrix are taken into account. In other words, given a $N \times M$ rectangular region of an image, we compute the matrix:

$$\mathbf{C_r} = E\{(\mathbf{r_k} - \mathbf{r_m})(\mathbf{r_k} - \mathbf{r_m})^T\} = \frac{1}{N}\sum_{i=1}^{N}\mathbf{r_k}\mathbf{r_k}^T - \mathbf{r_m}\mathbf{r_m}^T, \text{ where } \mathbf{r_m} = \frac{1}{N}\sum_{i=1}^{N}\mathbf{r_k}.$$

In the previous equation $\mathbf{r_k}$ is the generic pixel row vector of the ROI under investigation, considered in column form. Then, we compute the vector:

$$\lambda = diag(\mathbf{C_q}) \qquad (1)$$

Here $\mathbf{C_q} = \mathbf{AC_rA}^T$, is the covariance matrix of the KL transformed vectors $\mathbf{q_k}$, while $\mathbf{A}$ is the transformation matrix whose rows are the eigenvectors of $\mathbf{C_r}$.

The matrix $\mathbf{C_q}$ is diagonal, so KLT performs total decorrelation of the input vectors. Moreover the mean value of the transformed vectors is always zero. These properties will be used in the rest of the section to reinforce our conclusions about the choice of λ as a global shape descriptor.

The first step towards the justification of the usability of λ, is the proof of the relation between λ and the actual shape of the object depicted in the selected ROI. In what follows we'll consider a weak perspective camera model and the Lambert law to model the light reflection process upon the object surface. These constraints are not so restrictive, and are widely used throughout computer vision to model perceptive processes. In particular, weak perspective is introduced only for simplicity in the mathematical passages, while the Lambertian surface constraint holds for most real objects.

If an object is imaged by a camera under the weak perspective assumption, each point $\mathbf{p_o} = (x, y, z)$ of the object, expressed in the camera coordinate system, is mapped onto an image point $\mathbf{p} = (u, v)$ where $\mathbf{p} = \mathbf{W_P p_o}$ is the perspective transformation. According to the Lambert law the image irradiance E in each point is equal to the image intensity value in the same point, and is expressed by:

$$I(i, j) = E(\mathbf{p}) = H \rho \mathbf{l}^T \mathbf{n}(\mathbf{p_o})$$

In the previous equation H is a constant value related to the lens model, ρ is the albedo of the object surface, $\mathbf{l}$ is the illuminant (constant) vector and $\mathbf{n}(\mathbf{p_o})$ is the surface normal at the point $\mathbf{p_o}$. The first equality takes into account the coordinate change from the image center to the upper-left corner, which is a linear transformation.

If we consider a vertical slice of the image, then each pixel row vector can be defined as:

$$\mathbf{r}_k = \{I(k, j) : j = 0, \ldots, M - 1\}^T, \; k = 0, \ldots, N - 1 \qquad (2)$$

Here the transpose symbol is used in order to define $\mathbf{r}_k$ as a column vector. If we substitute the expression of the generic pixel value $I(i, j)$ in equation 2 then we obtain:

$$\mathbf{r}_k = H \rho \{\mathbf{l}^T \mathbf{n}_{kj} : j = 0, \ldots, M - 1\}^T, \; k = 0, \ldots, N - 1 \qquad (3)$$

In equation 3 $\mathbf{n}_{kj}$ refers to the surface normal vector that is projected onto position (k, j) in the image plane.

Now, we want to derive an expression for the generic element $\mathbf{C}_r(i, j)$ of the pixel rows covariance matrix, using the equation stated above:

$$\mathbf{C}_r(i, j) = \frac{1}{N} \sum_k \mathbf{r}_{ki} \mathbf{r}_{kj} - \frac{1}{N^2} \sum_k \mathbf{r}_{ki} \sum_k \mathbf{r}_{kj} \qquad (4)$$

Substituting equation 3 in equation 4 we obtain:

$$\mathbf{C}_r(i, j) = \frac{H \rho}{N} \sum_k (\mathbf{l}^T \mathbf{n}_{ki})(\mathbf{l}^T \mathbf{n}_{kj}) - \frac{H \rho}{N^2} \left(\sum_k \mathbf{l}^T \mathbf{n}_{ki} \right) \left(\sum_k \mathbf{l}^T \mathbf{n}_{kj} \right) \qquad (5)$$

We can then rewrite equation 5, after some arrangements:

$$\mathbf{C}_r(i,j) = H\rho\mathbf{1}^T \left[\frac{1}{N} \sum_k \mathbf{n}_{ki}\mathbf{n}_{kj}^T - \frac{1}{N^2} \left(\sum_k \mathbf{n}_{ki} \right) \left(\sum_k \mathbf{n}_{kj} \right)^T \right] \mathbf{1} \qquad (6)$$

Finally, equation 6 can be rewritten in two different forms for diagonal and off-diagonal terms:

$$\mathbf{C}_r(i,j) = \begin{cases} H\rho\mathbf{1}^T \mathbf{C}_n^{(i)} \mathbf{1} & , i = j \\ H\rho\mathbf{1}^T \left(\mathbf{K}_n^{(ij)} - \mathbf{n}_m^{(i)} \mathbf{n}_m^{(j)T} \right) \mathbf{1} & , i \neq j \end{cases} \qquad (7)$$

The last equation states that diagonal terms of the pixel rows covariance matrix can be computed directly from the covariance matrices $\mathbf{C}_n^{(i)}$ of the object surface normals projecting themselves onto a single slice column. The off-diagonal terms of the same matrix can be computed from the difference between the correlation matrix $\mathbf{K}_n^{(ij)}$ of the normals related to two different columns minus the term obtained from the product of their mean vectors.

From the previous result we can argue that the matrix $\mathbf{C}_r$ is well suited to express the statistical variance pattern of the object surface shape along both rows (off-diagonal terms) and columns (diagonal terms) despite it is not referred to the entire slice, but it's computed starting from its rows. In this way we achieve a considerable reduction of computational time, without losing the expressiveness of the selected feature, because we've to compute only M eigenvalues, while the application of the KLT to the entire region involves the computation of $N \times M$ coefficients.

The use of the eigenvalues, allows us to transform our feature in a very compact way. The λ vector still expresses the rows variance pattern because it results from the covariance matrix (equation 1) of the KL transformed pixel rows that are completely uncorrelated.

Moreover, the λ vector allows performing comparisons between different regions in the same image or from different ones in order to search for similar shapes. In general, two different sets of rows cannot be compared directly, due to the presence of bias effects in the pixel values deriving from noise and/or local lighting conditions. The implicit application of KLT deriving from the use of λ implies that if we compare two different regions we refer to their transformed rows which have zero mean value: these can be correctly compared because they've the same mean value and no bias effect is present.

3   Description of the System

In this section, the complete structure of the presented system will be reported, starting from the considerations of the preceding section.

We've analyzed the histogram of the components of λ computed from several images both synthetic and real, depicting single shapes under varying attitudes and lighting (see figure 1). We've noticed that this histogram exhibits some dominant modes, whose relative position and amplitude depend on the shape observed. The amplitude and position of these histogram modes remain almost unchanged under rotation, translation, and scaling of the object. It can be noted from equation 7 that the light direction acts as a scaling factor for all the terms of $\mathbf{C}_r$, thus affecting in a uniform manner all the components of λ. From the experimental observation, we have noticed that varying $\mathbf{l}$ doesn't affect the histogram too much. Vectors for similar shapes tend to be similar, so we've set up a

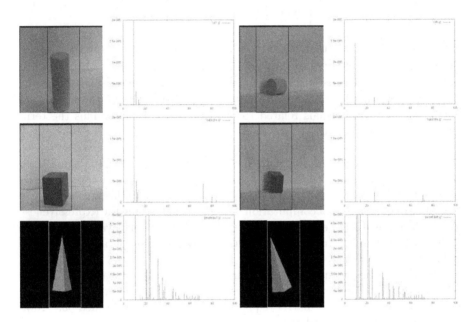

Fig. 1. Some shape examples together with the relative λ histogram. Selected ROIs are 256×100 wide. Comparing the couples along each row, it can be noted that changes in attitude and lighting don't affect the histogram too much.

classifier based on the use of a pool of suitably tuned SVMs that operate in the eigenvalues space.Moreover, a search algorithm for the automatic analysis of the test images has been derived, which is based on the maximization of correlation between the actual λ vector and some sample vectors from the different shape classes.

The complete system acts in the following way: first the image is scanned from left to right and from top to bottom by moving windows of fixed size in order to locate some possible regions of interest. Then the height of each window is resized in order to enclose at most a single complete object. Finally, all the selected regions are classified by the SVMs pool.

The rest of this section is arranged into two parts: the first one is devoted to the automatic search algorithm, while the second one provides some remarks on SVM and classification strategies.

3.1   Automatic Search Algorithm

The search algorithm we implemented is based on a two-pass strategy. The first step performs rough location of the ROIs both for the horizontal and vertical displacement. The second step defines the windows' dimensions for all the selected positions.

The search criterion is the correlation maximization between the λ vector of a fixed size slice and a sample of each shape class computed as the mean vector between those used as training set for the various SVMs. Scanning the image from left to right with a 256×100 fixed slice, all the correlation values are computed, one for each class sample, and the maximum is taken. This information is used only to detect if there's something without looking at a particular shape. Positive peaks of the correlation defined above vs. the position of the left side of the slice, the indicate a region of interest.

Relevant positions are selected as follows. The cumulative function of the correlation is computed, and the selected points are the zero crossings of its second order derivative: these are the slope inversion points of the cumulative function, that in turn correspond approximately to the correlation maxima (see figure 2). We found more convenient the use of the cumulative function in order to avoid noisy spikes that can be present near a peak when detecting maxima directly from the correlation plot.

For each selected ROI, single objects are detected using a 20×100 fixed slice that moves from top to bottom. Again the correlation maxima are computed with the previous strategy.

In the second step of the algorithm, we use the variance maximization as guiding criterion to resize windows' height in order to enclose a single complete object. Here the variance has to be intended as the maximum eigenvalue in the λ vector of the current slice. Starting from the position of each correlation peak, windows are enlarged along their height by a single row at a time, and the λ vector is computed, taking into account its maximum component. Positive peaks correspond approximately to the upper and lower edge of the object. Again we use the second order derivative of the cumulative function in order to avoid mismatches due to the presence of variance spikes near the actual maximum. Search results are depicted in figure 3.

3.2   Shape classification using SVM

SVMs have been introduced by Vapnik [13]. Here we will focus the attention on the most relevant theoretical topics on SVMs for pattern recognition: more detailed information can be found in [11].

In a typical binary classification problem we are given a set S of points $\mathbf{x}_i \in \mathbb{R}^N$, and a set of labels $y_i \in \{\pm 1\}$, $i = 1, \ldots, l$, and we want to find

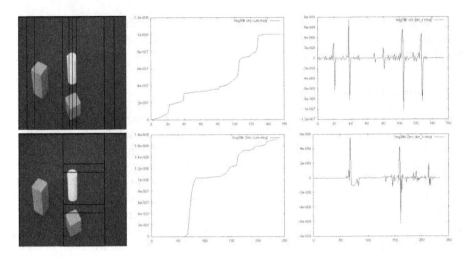

Fig. 2. an example of correlation maximization search. In the topmost row there is a sample with the slices corresponding to the correlation maxima, the cumulative function plot, and its second order derivative. Maxima have been found in position 21, 39, 105 and 128. In the lower row there are the vertical sub-slices of the ROI in position 105 along with the cumulative function and its second order derivative.

a function $f : \mathbb{R}^N \to \{\pm 1\}$ in order to correctly associate each point to the respective label.

Even if we find a function f that does well on all the training data, we are not ensured that it performs a correct generalization. Vapnik and Chervonenkis defined a measure of the generalization ability (the *capacity*) of a function class: the *VC dimension*, that is the largest number h of points that can be separated in all possible ways using functions of the selected class.

In order to obtain a correct generalization from the training data, a learning machine must use a class of functions with an adequate capacity. Vapnik and Chervonenkis considered the class of hyperplanes, and developed a learning algo-

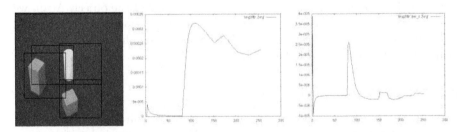

Fig. 3. an example of variance maximization search. On the left, final slices of the picture in figure 2 are depicted along with the plot of variance, and its second order derivative for the slice in position 105.

rithm for separable problems, finding the unique *Optimal Hyperplane* (OH) that separates data. This approach can be easily extended to non linearly separable problems.

The SVM in its original formulation is designed for two-class discrimination, so we used a particular training strategy, in order to cope with our multi-class task. Two different kinds of SVMs have been trained on six shape classes: cube, cylinder, pyramid, cone, ellipsoid, and box. First, six SVMs have been trained in a *one-versus-others* fashion, each of them being able to discriminate between a particular class and all other objects. Besides, a second pool of 15 SVMs have been trained using a *pair-wise* strategy: each SVM is trained to discriminate between a single pair of the desired classes, so for K classes we need $K(K-1)/2$ different machines.

The use of two learning strategies is related to the need to avoid mismatches in classification. Kreßel has demonstrated in [11] that a *one-versus-others* training leaves some uncertainty regions in the feature spaces where we're not able to decide correctly to which class belongs the actual sample. The *pair-wise* strategy provides a refinement of the boundaries between multiple classes.

In our experiments we've noticed that the use of *one-versus-others* or *pair-wise* strategy alone is not sufficient to obtain a correct classification. So, in the test phase, we use the first set of machines in order to provide a rough discrimination, which is then refined by the use of the second ones. The *one-versus-others* machines provide their own estimate in a *winner-takes-all* fashion: the distances between the object's λ vector and the optimal hyperplanes defining each shape class are computed, and the class with the highes positive distance is taken as the winner. In this way the class where the actual sample vector is more "inside" is selected.

In some cases this approach doesn't allow a very sharp classification, and the sample vector results inside two or more classes. The *pair-wise* machines are used in order to provide a disambiguation. In this case the result of testing the vector with each machine is accumulated for each class in a sort of round-robin challenge. The class with the highest score wins the tournament, and the sample vector is classified according to this outcome. In this way, each object belongs to a single class.

4   Experimental Setup

In order to set up the classifier a training set has been used, which consists of 118 images representing single objects belonging to all six classes. These images have been taken under varying lighting conditions, and they represent both real and synthetic shapes with different orientation and scaling.

The same training set has been used to train both *one-versus-others* and *pair-wise* SVMs in order to allow the second ones to act as a refinement of the boundaries between the various classes with respect to the first set of machines.

A 3×3 median filter is used to reduce noise and undesired mismatch due to artifacts in the background. Moreover all the input images are normalized with respect to the quantity $\sum_{i,j} I(i,j)^2$ that is a measure of the global energy content of the image. In this way we obtain that the λ vector components range almost in the same interval for all images.

Experiments have been carried on both images depicting single objects, and complex scenes with many objects even partialyy occluded. Some trys have been performed on some well known images from computer vision handbooks. Tables 1, 2, and 3, and figures 4, and 5 illustrate the results of some experiments.

Table 1. the performance of the system on the scene depicted in figure 3. The position values are referred to the upper left corner of each slice. In slice two the PW classification is incorrect, but it's not used to the high score obtained in WTA mode. PW refines the outcome of the WTA only in the last case.

Slice n.	Pos.	WTA (%)	PW
0	$(21, 91)$	box (87.03)	cube
1	$(39, 74)$	box (100)	box
2	$(105, 70)$	cylinder (89.52)	box
3	$(105, 152)$	box (68.67)	cube

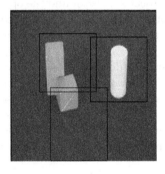

Fig. 4. an example of the performance of the system on a multiple objects image.

5   Conclusions and Future Work

The presented work is a first step in the direction of a more robust and general object recognition system, that can be a suitable extension to our image and video database system Jacob [4, 1]. Early results are satisfactory and provide us with many cues about future developments.

The use of a statistical approach makes the system quite robust with respect to noise, but the system fails in presence of textures. On the other hand one

Table 2. the output of the system for the slices in figure 4. It can be noted that for the first slice we obtain a weak correct response from the WTA machines, while the PW classification is almost wrong due to the closeness between the two shape classes. Many others slices, detected by the search algorithm, have been discarded by the classifier.

Slice n.	Pos.	WTA (%)	PW
0	$(52, 40)$	box (48.76)	cube
1	$(71, 132)$	box (69.87)	cube
2	$(141, 46)$	cylinder (100)	cylinder

Fig. 5. an example of the performance of the system on a real image, depicting the city of Venice.

Table 3. the output of the system for the slices in figure 5. Here, the slices have been selected interactively. Slice 1 is misclassified as a cone due to the strong similarity between one side of the actual pyramid and the background. Slice 3 is correctly classified by the WTA machine, and the PW response is not taken into account.

Slice n.	Pos.	WTA (%)	PW
0	$(1, 40)$	box (100)	box
1	$(15, 1)$	cone (57.10)	cube
2	$(118, 190)$	box (57.49)	box
3	$(118, 230)$	box (89.48)	box/cylinder

might think to specialize the system to the recognition of textures as a global feature, while shape could be argued using some other approach.

The influence of the illuminant direction has not yet exploited in detail, but our approach has proven itself not so much influenced by this parameter due to the fact that l affects all the elements of the covariance matrix in the same way. We are now studying the use of homomorphic filtering in order to strongly reduce the influence of the lighting conditions on the perceived scene.

Another possible development is the use of the approach in a 3D vision system, instead of a preprocessing stage for content based image indexing and retrieval. In this way the system should perform model recognition, thus providing a reconstruction layer with its information.

6   Acknowledgements

This work has been partially supported by the Italian MURST Project "Galileo 2000" and MURST-CNR Biotechnology Program l. 95/95.

References

1. E. Ardizzone and M. La Cascia. Automatic Video Database Indexing and Retrieval. *Multimedia Tools and Applications*, 4(1):29–56, January 1997.
2. S. Belongie, C. Carson, H. Greenspan, and J. Malik. Color- and Texture-based Image Segmentation using EM and its application to Content-based Image Rtrieval. In *Proc. of International Conference on Computer Vision*, 1998.
3. C. Carson, M. Thomas, S. Belongie, J.M. Hellerstein, and J. Malik. Blobworld: A System for Region-Based Image Indexing and Retrieval. In *Proc. of Third International Conference on Visual Information Systems VISUAL'99*, pages 509–516, Amsterdam, The Netherlands, June 1999. Springer.
4. M. La Cascia and E. Ardizzone. Jacob: Just a Content-based Query System for Video Databases. In *Proc. of IEEE Int. Conference on Acoustics, Speech and Signal Processing, ICASSP-96*, pages 7–10, Atlanta, May 1996.
5. M. Flickner, H. Sawhney, W. Niblack, J. Ashley, et al. Query by Image and Video Content: The QBIC System. *IEEE Computer*, 28(9):23–32, September 1995.
6. R.C. Gonzalez and P. Wintz. *Digital Image Processing*. Addison-Wesley, ii edition, 1987.
7. J. Hafner, H. Sawhney, W. Equitz, M. Flickner, and W. Niblack. Efficient Color Histogram Indexing for Quadratic Form Distance Functions. *IEEE Trans. on Pattern Analysis and Machine Intelligence*, 17(7):729–736, July 1995.
8. Hampapur et al. Virage Video Engine. *Proc. of SPIE, Storage and Retrieval for Image and Video Databeses V*, 3022:188–200, 1997.
9. A. Pentland, R. Picard, and S. Sclaroff. Photobook: Content-based Manipulation of Image Databases. *International Journal of Computer Vision*, 18:233–254, 1996.
10. A. Pentland and M. Turk. Eigenfaces for Recognition. *Journal of Cognitive Neuroscience*, 3(1):71–86, 1991.
11. B. Schölkopf, C. Burges, and A.J. Smola, editors. *Support Vector Learning*. Advances in Kernel Methods. The MIT Press, Cambridge, MA, 1999.
12. A. Talukder and D. Casaent. General Methodology for Simultaneous Representation and Discrimination of Multiple Object Classes. *Optical Engineering*, 37(3):904–913, March 1998.
13. V.N. Vapnik. *Statistical Learning Theory*. Wiley, New York, 1998.

Wavelet-Based Salient Points: Applications to Image Retrieval Using Color and Texture Features

Etienne Loupias[1] , Nicu Sebe[2]

[1] Laboratoire Reconnaissance de Formes et Vision,
INSA Lyon, France
loupias@rfv.insa-lyon.fr
[2] Leiden Institute of Advanced
Computer Science,
Leiden University, The Netherlands.
nicu@wi.leidenuniv.nl

Abstract. In image retrieval, global features related to color or texture are commonly used to describe the image. The use of interest points in content-based image retrieval allows image index to represent local properties of images. Classic corner detectors can be used for this purpose. However, they have drawbacks when applied to various natural images for image retrieval, because visual features need not to be corners and corners may gather in small regions. We present a salient point detector that extracts points where variations occur in the image, regardless whether they are corner-like or not. It is based on wavelet transform to detect global variations as well as local ones. We show that extracting the color information in the locations given by these points provides significantly improved retrieval results as compared to the global color feature approach. We also show an image retrieval experiment based on texture features where our detector provides better retrieval performance comparing with other point detectors.

1 Introduction

We are interested in content-based image retrieval in general image databases. The query is an image (*iconic search*), and the retrieved images should be *similar* to the query. We assume that high-level concepts (objects, feelings, etc.) cannot be extracted automatically from the image without specific knowledge, and so we use an *image similarity* based on low-level features (such as color, texture and shapes).

An image is "summarized" by a set of features, the *image index*, to allow fast retrieval. *Local features* are of interest, since they lead to an index based on local properties of the image. This approach is also attractive for sub-image search.

The feature extraction is limited to a subset of the image pixels, the *interest points*, where the image information is supposed to be the most important [9,2,11,1]. This

---

Guest period in Leiden University was supported by Région Rhône-Alpes (EURODOC grant)

R. Laurini (Ed.): VISUAL 2000, LNCS 1929, pp. 223–232, 2000.
Springer-Verlag Berlin Heidelberg 2000

paper focuses on the selection of points that are significant to compute features for indexing.

Corner detectors are commonly used for indexing [9,11]. They are usually defined as points where the gradient is high in multiple orientations. This definition leads to detectors based on local derivatives [6]. Corner detectors are in general designed for robotics and shape recognition and therefore, they have drawbacks when are applied to natural image retrieval.

Visual focus points need not to be corners: a meaningful visual feature is not necessarily located in a corner point. For instance in Fig. 1, the fur is too smoothed to be detected by a corner detector such as Harris' [6].

(a) Fox image   (b) 100 corners (Harris)

Fig. 1. Image with smoothed edges. No corners are detected in the fur.

Corners may gather in small regions: in various natural images, regions may well contain textures (trees, shirt patterns, etc.), where a lot of corners are detected (*cf.* Fig. 2). As the number of points is preset to limit the indexing computation time, most of the corners are in the same textured region.

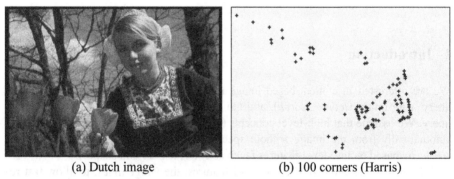

(a) Dutch image   (b) 100 corners (Harris)

Fig. 2. Image with texture in the Dutch dress. Corners are gathered in the textured region.

With corner detectors, both examples lead to an incomplete representation, where some parts of the image are not described in the index.

For these reasons, corner points may not represent the most interesting subset of pixels for image indexing. Indexing points should be related to any visual "interesting" part of the image, whether it is smoothed or corner-like. To describe different parts of the image, the set of interesting point should not be clustered in few regions.

From now on, we will refer to these points as *salient points*, which are not necessarily corners. We will avoid the term *interest points*, which is ambiguous, since it was previously used in the literature as *corner*. Wavelet representations, which express image variations at different resolutions, are attractive to extract salient points.

Previous point detectors make use of multiresolution representation. Chen *et al.* consider two different resolutions to extract corners [3]. In image retrieval context, contrast-based points are extracted in [2]. However, a lot of points are also extracted in textured regions because these regions are contrasted. Points are extracted with a specific wavelet in [1]. But since only a given scale is used, different resolutions features cannot be detected.

2 From wavelet transform to salient points

The wavelet transform is a multiresolution representation that expresses image variations at different scales. For wavelet theory, see [8].

A wavelet is an *oscillating* and *attenuated* function (its integral is equal to zero). We study the image f at the scales (or resolutions) $\frac{1}{2}$, $\frac{1}{4}$, ... 2^j, j Z and j -1. The wavelet *detail image* $W_{2^j} f$ is the convolution of the image with the wavelet function dilated at different scales.

Here we consider *orthogonal wavelets*, which lead to a complete and non-redundant representation of the image. A wavelet can also have a *compact support*: its value is zero outside a bounded interval. The simplest orthogonal compactly supported wavelet is the Haar wavelet, which is the discontinuous step function. Daubechies proposed wavelets, with any regularity p $(p > 1)$, that are also orthogonal and compactly supported [4].

The wavelet representation gives information about the variations in the signal at different scales. In our retrieval context, we would like to extract salient points from any part of the image where "something" happens in the signal at any resolution. A high wavelet coefficient (in absolute value) at a coarse resolution corresponds to a region with high global variations. The idea is to find a relevant point to represent this global variation by looking at wavelet coefficients at finer resolutions (as shown in Fig. 3).

Since we use wavelets with a compact support, we know from which signal points each wavelet coefficient at the scale 2^j was computed. We can study the wavelet coefficients for the same points at the finer scale 2^{j+1}. Indeed there is a set of coefficients at the scale 2^{j+1} computed with the same points as a coefficient $W_{2^j} f(n)$ at the scale 2^j

(see [7] for details). We call this set of coefficients the *children* $C(W_{2^j} f(n))$ of the coefficient $W_{2^j} f(n)$. The children set in one dimension[1] is:

$$C(W_{2^j} f(n)) = \{W_{2^{j+1}} f(k),\ 2n \le k \le 2n+2p-1\},$$

$$0 \le n < 2^j N \ (N \text{ is the length of the signal}, p \text{ the wavelet regularity}).$$

Fig. 3. Salient point extraction: spatial support of tracked wavelet coefficients

Each wavelet coefficient $W_{2^j} f(n)$ is computed with $2^{-j} p$ signal points. It represents their variation at the scale 2^j. Its children coefficients give the variations of some particular subsets of these points (with the number of subsets depending on the wavelet). The most salient subset is the one with the highest wavelet coefficient at the scale 2^{j+1}, that is the maximum in absolute value of $C(W_{2^j} f(n))$. In our salient point extraction algorithm, we consider this maximum, and look at its highest child. Applying recursively this process, we select a coefficient $W_{2^{-1}} f(n)$ at the finer resolution ½ (cf. Fig. 4). Hence, this coefficient only represents $2p$ signal points. To select a salient point from this tracking, we choose among these $2p$ points the one with the highest gradient. We set its *saliency value* as the sum of the absolute value of the wavelet coefficients in the track:

$$saliency = \sum_{k=1}^{j} \left| C^{(k)}(W_{2^j} f(n)) \right|, 0 \le n < 2^j N, \quad -\log_2 N \le j \le -1$$

The tracked point and its saliency value are computed for every wavelet coefficient. A point related to a global variation has a high saliency value, since the coarse wavelet coefficients contribute to it. A finer variation also leads to an extracted point, but with a lower saliency value. We then need to threshold the saliency value, in relation to the desired number of salient points. We first obtain the points related to global variations; local variations also appear if enough salient points are requested.

The salient points extracted by this process depend on the wavelet we use. Haar is the simplest wavelet function, so the fastest for execution. Some localization drawbacks can appear with Haar due to its non-overlapping wavelets at a given scale. This

---

[1] For clarity we use one-dimensional signals. Extension to two dimensions and signals with length not restricted to a power of 2, in addition to algorithm complexity, are discussed in [6].

can be avoided with the simplest overlapping wavelet, Daubechies 4. However, this kind of drawback is not likely in natural images.

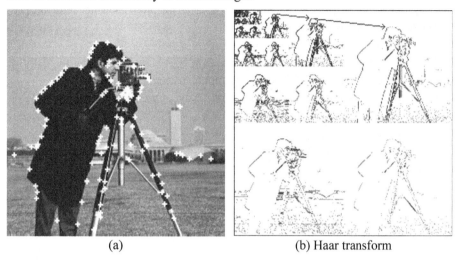

| (a) | (b) Haar transform |

Fig. 4. Haar transform. (a) 100 Haar salient points in the Cameraman image. (b) Tracked coefficients in the Haar transform of the Cameraman image

3   Examples

The salient points detected with the Haar transform are presented for the images used in Fig. 1 and Fig. 2 (*cf.* Fig. 5). Salient points are detected for smoothed edges (*cf.* Fig. 5.a) and are not gathered in textured regions (*cf.* Fig. 5.b). Hence they lead to a more complete image representation than corner detectors. Similar behavior can be observed with Daubechies 4 wavelets.

Repeatability of the detection under typical alterations is a common evaluation criterion for corner detectors. Repeatability of our detector is comparable to other detectors. However this criterion may not be relevant in our context, because features stability is more important than geometric stability for image retrieval.

4   Evaluation for image retrieval

The best way to evaluate points detectors for image retrieval is to compare the retrieval results[2]. In color indexing, global color distributions are mainly used to index images. We show in the next section that extracting the color information in the loca-

---

[2] The content-based image retrieval system can be accessed through **KIWI**, the Key points based Indexing Web Interface, from the URL **http://telesun.insa-lyon.fr/kiwi**

tions given by salient points improve the retrieval results as compared to the global color feature approach. Then we use salient points for image retrieval based on texture features and we show an experiment where our detector provides better retrieval performance comparing with other point detectors.

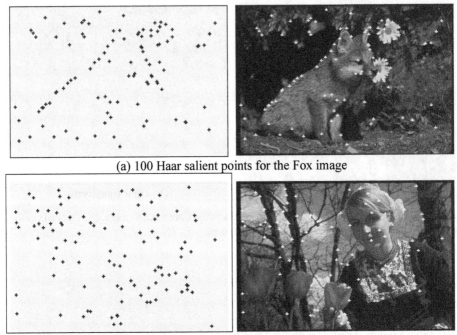

(a) 100 Haar salient points for the Fox image

(b) 100 Haar salient points for the Dutch image

Fig. 5. Haar salient points examples. We can notice that salient points are detected in smooth features like the fur and not gathered in textured region. For each image the detected points are superimposed on the original image to evaluate salient points location.

4.1   Color

The setup of our experiments was the following. First we extracted 100 salient points for each image in the database using *Haar* wavelet transform and the algorithm described in Section 2.

For feature extraction, we considered only the pixels in a 3 3 neighborhood around each salient point in forming an image signature. For each image signature we computed the color moments and stored them is a feature vector [10]. Since most of the information is concentrated on the low-order moments, only the first moment (mean), the second and the third central moments (variance and skewness) were used. We were working with the HSV color space and for each image in a database a 9-dimensional feature vector was considered. When the user selects a query, the system computes the corresponding feature vector and compares it with the feature vectors in the database. For benchmarking purposes we also considered the results obtained using color moments over the entire image.

In the first experiment we considered a database of 479 images of color objects such as domestic objects, tools, toys, food cans, etc [5]. As ground truth we used 48 images of 8 objects taken from different camera viewpoints (6 images for a single object). We expect the salient point method to be more robust to the viewpoint change because the salient points are located around the object boundary and capture the details inside the object, neglecting the noisy background. In Fig. 6 we present an example of a query image and the similar images from the database.

Query Image

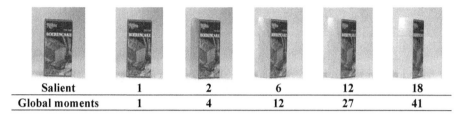

Salient	1	2	6	12	18
Global moments	1	4	12	27	41

Fig. 6. Example of images of one object taken from different camera viewpoints. The ranks of individual image were obtained using salient point information (Salient) and the global color moments method (Global moments)

The salient point approach outperforms the global color method. Even when the image was taken from a very different viewpoint, the salient points captured the object details enough so the similar image was retrieved with a good rank. When the global color moments were used the influence of the background became important so the retrieval results were worse.

In the next experiment, we used a database of 1505 various natural images. They cover a wide range of natural scenes, animals, buildings, construction sites, textures and paintings. As test set we considered 50 images which were grouped in 5 classes (10 images in a class): Airplane, Car, Flower, Lion, Bird. Fig. 7 shows an example of the retrieved images from a query using the salient point approach.

The salient points were able to capture the image details, even if the background was different and the position of the animal changed. In order to test the retrieval results for each individual class, we randomly picked 5 images from each class and used them as queries. For each individual class we computed the retrieval accuracy as the average percentage of images from the same class as the query which were retrieved in top 15 images. The results are given in Table 1.

Note that for classes where the background was complex (Car, Flower) the results were worse than for the other classes. However, the salient points captured the details of the foreground objects and therefore the results were significantly better than in the case of using global color moments.

Query Image

Fig. 7. Retrieved images from a query using the salient point approach. Match quality decreases from the top left to the bottom right

Class	Salient	Global
Airplane	94	88
Bird	88	82
Car	74	62
Flower	72	58
Lion	90	82

Table 1. Retrieval accuracy (%) for each individual class using 5 randomly chosen images from each class as queries

4.2 Texture

In the texture experiments, Gabor features are computed for regions around the extracted points (32 32) for 3 scales and 8 orientations. Features for each extracted point are used to build a set of 24 histograms (one histogram for each scale and orientation). We use two-dimensional histograms to take into account the spatial coherence in our representation, as described in [12].

We use the same database of 1505 various natural images as in the second color experiment. In this case we were not only interested to retrieve images with similar color (see Fig. 7), so we built another test set where each image belongs to an instinctive (and subjective) category (animals, flowers, landscapes, buildings, cities, etc). Very heterogeneous categories and images too different from the rest of the category were removed from the test set. Finally, we have a test set of 577 images in 9 classes.

For benchmarking purposes we compare the results obtained with different detectors. We considered two wavelet-based detectors (Haar and Daubechies4), the Harris corner detector [6], the contrast-based detector proposed in [2] and a detector based on random points. We present the recall-precision graph, computed from different numbers of return images n. The system retrieves r images that belong to the same class C as the query (r n). There are N_C images in the class C of the query. Then $P = r / n$ is the precision and $R = r / N_C$ the recall for this query. We use each test set image as a query, and use the average recall and precision for the graph (cf. Fig. 8).

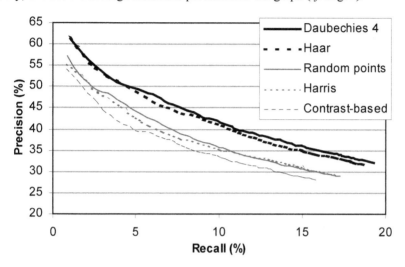

Fig. 8. Retrieval results with Gabor texture features for the database with 1505 natural images

We observe that the wavelet-based salient points perform better than other detectors for these features and this database. Daubechies 4 has better performances than Haar but is computationally more expensive. Random points are also used in the experiment: we randomly select points, and compute the Gabor features around these points. Their good result can be explained by their spreading in the image. For that reason they lead to a more complete representation of the image than some detectors. Obviously, the random points are very unlikely to be located in corners or edges point, but they are spread enough to represent these variations in the index. Good result of random points for indexing was observed with other databases and other local features [7]. These experiments show that the points spreading can be as important as the points location for image indexing (depending on the test set). However, wavelet-based salient points, which are simultaneously spread and located, perform better than random points.

5 Discussion

We presented a salient point detector based on wavelets. The wavelet-based salient points are interesting for image retrieval, because they are located in many visual features (whether they are corner-like or not), without gathering in textured regions. We presented an experiment of color retrieval where using salient points is an interesting alternative to global approaches, and another retrieval experiment with Gabor features where our method performs better than other point detectors from the literature.

We used the Haar transform for point extraction, which is simple but may lead to bad localization. Daubechies wavelets avoid this drawback, but are not symmetric. Since orthogonality is not required in our approach, we could extend it to other wavelets that are compactly supported and symmetric.

Since points performance for indexing depends on the image database, detector choice for a specific database should be investigated, as well as random points relevance for local features extraction. Wavelets are also attractive to extract image features for indexing. These local features would be more related to our salient points.

References

1. S. Bhattacharjee and T. Ebrahimi, "Image Retrieval Based on Structural Content ", *Workshop on Image Analysis for Multimedia Interactive Services*, Heinrich-Hertz-Institut (HHI) Berlin, Germany, May 31 - June 1 1999.
2. S. Bres and J.-M. Jolion, "Detection of Interest Points for Image Indexation ", *3rd Int. Conf. on Visual Information Systems, Visual99*, Amsterdam, The Netherlands, June 2-4 1999, pp. 427-434.
3. C.-H. Chen, J.-S. Lee and Y.-N. Sun, " Wavelet Transformation for Gray-level Corner Detection ", *Pattern Recognition*, 1995, Vol. 28, No. 6, pp. 853-861.
4. I. Daubechies, "Orthonormal Bases of Compactly Supported Wavelets ", *Communications on Pure and Applied Mathematics*, 1988, Vol. 41, pp. 909-996.
5. T. Gevers and A. Smeulders, "Color-based Object Recognition ", *Pattern Recognition*, 1999, Vol. 32, No. 3: pp. 453-464.
6. C. Harris and M. Stephens, "A Combined Corner and Edge Detector ", *Proc. of 4th Alvey Vision Conference*, 1988, pp. 147-151.
7. E. Loupias and N. Sebe, " Wavelet-based Salient Points for Image Retrieval ", *RR 99.11*, Laboratoire RFV, INSA Lyon, November 1999. http://rfv.insa-lyon.fr/~loupias/points/
8. S. Mallat, " A Theory for Multiresolution Signal Decomposition : The Wavelet Representation ", *IEEE Trans. on PAMI*, July 1989, Vol. 11, No. 7, pp. 674-693.
9. C. Schmid and R. Mohr, "Local Grayvalue Invariants for Image Retrieval ", *IEEE Trans. on PAMI*, May 1997, Vol. 19, No. 5, pp. 530-535.
10. M. Stricker and M. Orengo, "Similarity of Color Images ", *SPIE - Storage and Retrieval for Image and Video Databases*, 1995.
11. T. Tuytelaars and L. Van Gool, "Content-based Image Retrieval Based on Local Affinely Invariant Regions ", *3rd Int. Conf. on Visual Information Systems, Visual99*, Amsterdam, The Netherlands, 2-4 June 1999, pp. 493-500.
12. C. Wolf, J.-M. Jolion, W. Kropatsch and H. Bischof, " Content Based Image Retrieval Using Interest Points and Texture Features ", *to appear in Proceedings of 15th ICPR*, 2000.

Matching Shapes with Self-intersections

Sadegh Abbasi and Farzin Mokhtarian

Centre for Vision, Speech and Signal Processing
University of Surrey
Guildford, Surrey GU2 7XH
England
Email [S.Abbasi][F.Mokhtarian]@surrey.ac.uk
Tel +44-1483-876039
Fax +44-1483-876031

Abstract. We address the problem of 2D shape representation and matching in presence of self-intersection for large image databases. This may occur when part of an object is hidden behind another part and results in a darker section in the gray level image of the object. The boundary contour of the object must include the boundary of this part which is entirely inside the outline of the object.

In this paper, we study the effects of contour self-intersection on the Curvature Scale Space image. When there is no self-intersection, the CSS image contains several arch shape contours, each related to a concavity or a convexity of the shape. Self intersections create contours with minima as well as maxima in the CSS image.

An efficient shape representation method has been introduced in this paper which describes a shape using the maxima as well as the minima of its CSS contours. This is a natural generalisation of the conventional method which only includes the maxima of the CSS image contours. The conventional matching algorithm has also been modified to accommodate the new information about the minima. The method has been successfully used in a real world application to find, for an unknown leaf, similar classes from a database of classified leaf images representing different varieties of chrysanthemum. For many classes of leaves, self intersection is inevitable during the scanning of the image.

1   Introduction

A large number of shape representation methods have been introduced in the literature[2][4][7][8][9][10]. However, the problem of self-intersection has not been addressed properly. This may occur as a result of self-occlusion, when a part of an object is hidden behind another part. The resulting section of the image can be darker than its neighbourhood. If segmented properly, the boundary contour of the object intersects itself and this must be considered in the related shape representation method.

The Curvature Scale Space image of a shape is a multi-scale organisation of its inflection points as it is smoothed. For non-intersected shapes, the CSS image contains several arch shapes contours, each related to a concavity or a convexity of the shape. The maxima of these contours have already been used for shape representation in shape similarity retrieval [6]. For self-intersected parts of a shape, the CSS contours are different. They include a minimum as well as a maximum which convey information about the size and location of

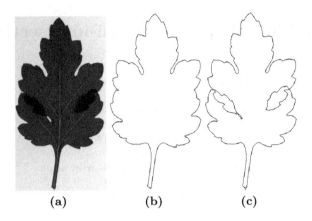

(a)   (b)   (c)

Fig. 1. An example of self-intersection. a) Gray level image. b) The boundary of object without considering self-intersection. c) The actual boundary of the object.

be used to represent a self-intersected contour. While a convexity or a concavity of the shape is represented by the maximum of its related arch shape contour in the CSS image, a self-intersected segment is represented by the locations of the maximum as well as minimum of the relevant contour of the CSS image.

The segmentation problem is always associated with the contour-based approach to shape representation. In the case of self-intersected shapes, segmentation is even more difficult [3] and may require user interaction.

We have used this representation in a real world application to find, for an unknown leaf, similar classes from a database of classified leaf images representing different varieties of chrysanthemum. For many classes of leaves, self intersection is inevitable during the scanning of the image. The task is to determine whether the unknown leaf belongs to one of the existing varieties or it represents a new variety. The system finds the most similar varieties to the input and allows the user to make the final decision.

We have tested our method on a prototype database of 120 leaf images from 12 different varieties. The results have indicated a promising performance of the system.

The following is the organisation of the remaining sections of this paper. In section 2 we explain the problem using several examples. The method of computing curvature scale space image, and the algorithm for finding maxima and minima of CSS image are described in section 3. The matching algorithm which is used to measure the similarity between the two CSS images is explained in section 4. The experimental results are presented in section 5. Concluding remarks are presented in section 6.

2   The problem of self-intersection

Fig. 1 shows how an intersection occurs. The actual boundary of the object of Fig. 1(a) has been partly hidden by some parts of the object. In order to extract the boundary of the object, one may ignore the hidden part and extract the

tion is missing in a trade-off which reduces the complexity of segmentation. A simple thresholding and a contour tracing algorithm extracts the boundary of the object. The actual boundary, as presented in Fig. 1(c) includes three points of self-intersection which need to be recovered interactively. During the process of contour tracing, the user should help the program to follow the contours inside the object rather than the boundary of it.

This contour must finally be represented by appropriate shape descriptors. The CSS image of the contour provides a good source of information which has been used to describe the shape. In the following section we briefly explain how the CSS image of a contour is constructed and how the useful information is extracted from this image.

3   The Curvature Scale Space Representation

The curvature of a curve is defined as the derivative of the tangent vector to the curve and can be expressed as:

$$\kappa(u) = \frac{\dot{x}(u)\ddot{y}(u) - \ddot{x}(u)\dot{y}(u)}{(\dot{x}^2(u) + \dot{y}^2(u))^{3/2}} . \tag{1}$$

There are several approaches in calculating the curvature of a digital curve [11]. We use the idea of *curve evolution* which basically studies shape properties while deforming in time. A certain kind of evolution can be achieved by Gaussian smoothing to compute curvature at varying levels of detail. If $g(u, \sigma)$ is a 1-D Gaussian kernel of width σ, then $X(u, \sigma)$ and $Y(u, \sigma)$ represent the components of *evolved* curve,

$$X(u, \sigma) = x(u) * g(u, \sigma) \qquad\qquad Y(u, \sigma) = y(u) * g(u, \sigma)$$

According to the properties of convolution, the derivatives of every component can be calculated easily:

$$X_u(u, \sigma) = x(u) * g_u(u, \sigma) \qquad\qquad X_{uu}(u, \sigma) = x(u) * g_{uu}(u, \sigma)$$

and we will have similar formulas for $Y_u(u, \sigma)$ and $Y_{uu}(u, \sigma)$. Since the exact forms of $g_u(u, \sigma)$ and $g_{uu}(u, \sigma)$ are known, the curvature of an evolved digital curve can be computed easily.

$$\kappa(u, \sigma) = \frac{X_u(u, \sigma)Y_{uu}(u, \sigma) - X_{uu}(u, \sigma)Y_u(u, \sigma)}{(X_u(u, \sigma)^2 + Y_u(u, \sigma)^2)^{3/2}} \tag{2}$$

As σ increases, the shape of Γ_σ changes. This process of generating ordered sequences of curves is referred to as the evolution of Γ.

Following the preprocessing stage, every object is represented by the x and y coordinates of its boundary points. To obtain a representation based on normalised arc length, we re-sample the boundary and represent it by 200 equally distant points. Considering the resampled curve as Γ, we can determine the locations of curvature zero crossings on Γ_σ, using the above mentioned formula.

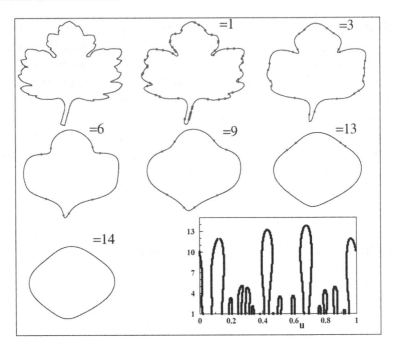

Fig. 2. Shrinkage and smoothing of the curve and decreasing of the number of curvature zero crossings during the evolution.

increases, Γ_σ shrinks and becomes smoother, and the number of curvature zero crossing points on it decreases. Finally, when σ is sufficiently high, Γ_σ will be a convex curve with no curvature zero crossings. The process has been shown in Fig 2. The original curve is represented in top left and the evolution has been shown through several values of σ.

If we determine the locations of curvature zero crossings of every Γ_σ during the evolution, we can display the resulting points in (u, σ) plane, where u is the normalised arc length and σ is the width of the Gaussian kernel. The result of this process can be represented as a binary image called CSS image of the curve (see bottom right of Fig. 2). The intersection of every horizontal line with the contours in this image indicates the locations of curvature zero crossings on the corresponding evolved curve Γ_σ. For example, by drawing a horizontal line at $\sigma = 9.0$, it is observed that there should be 8 zero crossing points on Γ_9. This fact is confirmed by the smooth curve with $\sigma = 9.0$ in the same Figure.

As shown in Fig. 2, the curvature zero crossings appear in pairs. Each pair is related to a concavity (or sometimes a convexity) on the boundary. As σ increases, the concavities are gradually filled and the related pair of zero crossings approach each other. The result on the CSS image will be two branches of a contour. Each branch conveys information on the locations of one of the zero crossings during the process. For a particular σ the concavity is totally filled and its pair of curvature zero crossings join each other. At this stage a contour of CSS image reaches its maximum. The $\sigma\_coordinate$ of the maximum is the relevant σ and the $u\_coordinate$ is the location of joined zero crossing

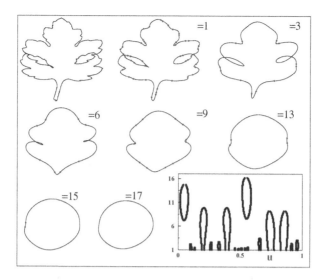

Fig. 3. Evolution for a shape with self-intersection.

If a local deformation occurs on the boundary, the shape of the contours on CSS image may change, but the location of the relevant maximum does not change dramatically. This is the main reason for selecting these points as our shape descriptors.

3.1 CSS image of self-crossed boundaries

An example of the evolution of such a shape is represented in Fig. 3. The original shape includes self-intersections and is seen in top left. For $\sigma = 1$, there are some inflection points inside the intersected loops due to small concavities in these areas which disappear in very early stages and before $\sigma = 3$. At this stage, there are no inflection points in these regions. However, the intersected loop gradually vanishes and a concavity appears in its place. This concavity, in turn, creates a contour in the CSS image which obviously does not start from $\sigma = 1$. The two branches of this contour are created from the moment that the intersected loop vanishes and the concavity is born. A minimum is then created in the CSS image at the relevant σ. It is obvious that the height of this minimum is proportional to the size of the intersected loop.

The location of a CSS minimum in the CSS image conveys information about the self-intersected loop of the shape. The horizontal coordinate of a minimum reflects the position of the loop on the shape, while the vertical coordinate shows the size of the loop.

We discovered that while we might expect a minimum to appear in the CSS image for every self-intersected region, this is not always the case in practice. In fact, if the size of the self-intersected loop is small, the minimum is expected to appear in early stages when the inflection points inside the loop have just disappeared. As a result, the maximum of the contour created by those small ripples joins the minimum of the contour created after the vanishing the loop.

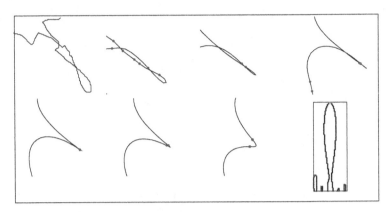

Fig. 4. Sometimes self-intersection does not create a minimum in the CSS image.

Fig. 5. To find a CSS maximum, we start from the top and scan each row of the CSS image, looking for a pair of black points with a small gap.

top left. As σ increases, all inflection points in the segment disappear except for one pair. When the loop disappears, this pair disappears but a new pair of inflection points is born. The result has been shown in the corresponding contour of the CSS image in the lower part of the Figure. The thin part of the contour is related to the moment when this event happens.

It should be noted that even if a minimum is created in such situations, due to its small height, its effect is not considerable.

3.2   Extracting maxima and minima of Curvature Scale Space Contours

We represent every image in the database with the locations of its CSS contour extrema For example, in Figure 3 there are six maxima and two minima. Therefore, the shape will be represented by 8 pairs of integer numbers. The locations of extrema are not readily available and must be extracted from the image. The CSS contours are usually connected everywhere except sometimes in a neighbourhood of their maxima as seen in Figure 5. We find the peaks of both branches of a contour in the CSS image and consider the middle point of the line segment joining the pair as a maximum of the CSS image. Starting from the top, each row of the CSS image is scanned for a black pixel. When found, the search continues in the same row to find another one in the neighbourhood. After finding a maximum of a contour, both branches of the contour are marked and at the same time, search for a possible minimum of the contour begins.

1. Start with scanning the second row. If a zero-crossing (black) point is found examine its neighbouring points. If there is no zero-crossing neighbour at the row just above and there is just one zero-crossing neighbour at the following row, go to step 3, otherwise go to step 2.
2. Scan the remaining points of the current row, and start scanning the next row if it is not the last one to be scanned. If a candidate is found go to step 3, and if this is the last row to be scanned , stop.
3. Scan the same row to find the same zero-crossing as described in step 1, in a reasonable distance. If the next candidate is not found, mark the first one and go to step 2. If it is found, do the following:
   - Consider the middle point of the line segment joining the pair as a maximum.
   - Mark (delete) all zero-crossings at both branches of the corresponding contour whose maximum has just been found.
   - When marking a branch, look for a minimum. A minimum is a point where there is no black point just below it.
   - If a minimum is found, go to step 2 immediately. Otherwise mark the contour down to the last row to be scanned and then go to step 2.

Note that usually the last few rows of CSS image represent some information about the existing noise on the actual image contour, so the last row to be scanned in step 2 has $\frac{1}{6}$ the height of the CSS image. Also note that if a candidate in step 2 is in first few columns, its couple may exist in last few columns of the same row and vice versa. In this case the search for next candidate must include the relevant interval.

4   Curvature Scale Space Matching

When there is no self-intersection in the boundary of the object, the CSS representation includes only the maxima of the CSS image contours. The algorithm used for comparing two sets of maxima, one from the input (also called *image*) and the other from one of the models, has been described in [6] and [5]. In this section, we first explain this algorithm briefly. Then we extend it to match the minima as well as the maxima.

The matching algorithm first finds any possible changes in orientation which may have been occurred in one of the two shapes. A circular shift then is applied to one of the image maxima to compensate the effects of change in orientation. The summation of the Euclidean distances between the relevant pairs of maxima is then defined to be the matching value between the two CSS images.

The following is a condensed version of the algorithm which includes the basic concepts.

- Apply a circular shift to all image maxima so that the *u_coordinates* of the largest maxima, one from the image and the other from the model become identical.
- Starting from the second largest maximum of the image, determine the

- Consider the cost of the match as the summation of the Euclidean distances between the corresponding maxima.
- If the number of the image and the model maxima differs, add the σ coordinates of the unmatched maxima to the matching cost.

4.1   Matching minima

A straight forward approach in taking into account the minima is to match the two sets of minima, one from the image and the other from the model exactly the same as the way we do with two sets of maxima. In this approach, the two sets of maxima are first matched and the corresponding matching value is found. Then the two sets of minima are matched and the resulting matching value is added to the latter to produce the final matching value between the two CSS image. In this approach, the shift parameter which is used to compensate the effect of change in orientation, may be different for the two parts of matching. In another approach, one may match the maxima and obtain the best shift parameter which is then used for matching the minima. The third approach is to match maxima and minima simultaneously. In other words, when two maxima are matched, their possible corresponding minima are also matched and the Euclidean distance of the minima is added to the Euclidean distance of the maxima. We examined these approaches and found out that the first approach leads to the best results which are presented in the following section.

5   Experimental results

In order to test our method, we used a database of classified leaf images representing different varieties of chrysanthemum. For many classes of leaves, self-intersection is inevitable during the scanning of the image.

In Britain, plant breeders who develop a new variety of plant are granted exclusive right to sell that variety for a period of time. One of the requirements imposed by current Plant Breeders Rights legislation is the distinctness of the new varieties. They should be different in at least one character from all existing varieties. The conventional CSS representation has already been used to find the most similar varieties to an unknown input leaf image [1], without considering the self-intersection.

We tested our method on a prototype database of 120 leaf images from 12 different varieties, both with and without considering the self-intersection. The task was to find out whether an unknown leaf belongs to one of the existing varieties or it represents a new variety. The system found the most similar varieties to the input and allows the user to make the final decision. The results indicated a promising performance of the new approach and its superiority over the conventional method.

5.1   Results

We tested the proposed method on a database of 120 leaf images from 12

consisted of just one object on a uniform background. The system software was developed using the C language under Unix operating system. The response rate of the system was much less than one second for each user query.

To evaluate the method, we considered every image in the database as an input and in each case, asked the system to identify the variety of the input, based on the first k similar images. Obviously, the first output of the system is identical to the input, but the system does not consider it in classification. In fact, for each sample we first pull it out of the database and classify it based on the remaining classified samples. The best varieties are then selected based on the number of their samples in the best k similar samples. The output of the system is the name of the first 3 classes.

We first used a simple automatic segmentation to recover the outline of the objects without considering the self-intersection (see Fig. 1). The resulting representations included only the maxima of the CSS images. We also used some global parameters to reject dissimilar candidates prior to the CSS matching [1]. The results for different values of k, the number of observed outputs for each query, has been presented in table 1. As mentioned before, in response to a query, the system returns the top 3 classes which are most similar to the input. The first row of table 1 shows the success rate of the system to identify the correct class as its first choice is 75.8% if the judgement is based on the first 5 outputs of the system. This figure is 77.5% for $k = 6$ and so on. The second row shows the success rate of the system to identify the correct class as its first or second choices, and so on for the third row.

As this table shows, for this particular database, one may get good results. However, as shown in table 2 even better results may be achieved by including the self-intersections in the process. It is interesting that the performance of the system is not sensitive to the value of k, specially when we consider the last row of this table. Overall, the superiority of the new method over the conventional one is seen in these two tables.

	$k = 5$	$k = 6$	$k = 7$	$k = 8$	$k = 9$	$k = 10$
1	75.8%	77.5%	78.3%	75.0%	72.5%	70.0%
<= 2	90.0%	88.3%	86.6%	87.5%	88.3%	89.1%
<= 3	91.6%	94.1%	94%	94.1%	95.8%	93.2%

Table 1. Results of evaluation for different values of k, old method.

	$k = 5$	$k = 6$	$k = 7$	$k = 8$	$k = 9$	$k = 10$
1	81%	85%	81.7%	79.2%	80%	78.3%
<= 2	94.3%	94.2%	93.4%	92.5%	91.7%	92.5%
<= 3	97.6%	97.5%	98.4%	97.5%	95.8%	95.8%

Table 2. Results of evaluation for different values of k, new method.

6   Conclusions

The problem of self-intersection was discussed in this paper. A shape representation method which can properly represent such shapes was introduced and explored. The Curvature Scale Space (CSS) image of a planar curve normally consists of several arch shape contours each related to concavity or a convexity of the curve. We observed that the shape of CSS contours change when the curve includes self-intersection. The arch shape of the contours is converted to a vertical ellipse. While the arch shape contours are represented by their maxima, the new contours of the CSS image include a minimum as well as the maximum.

In conventional form of CSS representation, a curve is represented by the locations of its CSS maxima. A new representation was introduced here which uses the minima as well of maxima of the CSS image. A method to extract extrema of the CSS image, as well as a matching algorithm to compare two sets of extrema and assign a matching value as the measure of similarity between the two curve were also introduced.

The method was tested on a prototype database of 120 leaf images from 12 different varieties of chrysanthemum with promising results. The performance of the method was also compared to the performance of the conventional method.

Acknowledgement Sadegh Abbasi is on leave from the University of Guilan Rasht, Iran. He is grateful to the Ministry of Science, Research and Technology of Iran for its financial support during his research studies.

References

1. S. Abbasi, F. Mokhtarian, and J. Kittler. Reliable classification of chrysanthemum leaves through curvature scale space. In *Proceedings of the Scale-Space'97 Conference*, pages 284–295, Utrecht, Netherlands, July 1997.
2. A. Del Bimbo, P. Pala, and S. Santini. Image retrieval by elastic matching of shapes and image patterns. In *Proceedings of the 1996 International Conference on Multimedia Computing and Systems*, pages 215–218, Hiroshima, Japan, June 1996. IEEE, Los Alamitos, CA, USA.
3. N. Katzir, M. Lindenbaum, and M. Porat. Curve segmentation under partial occlusion. *IEEE Transactions on Pattern Analysis and Machine Intelligence*, 16(5):513–519, May 1994.
4. R. Mehrotra and J. E. Gary. Feature-based retrieval of similar shapes. In *Proceedings of 9th International Conference on Data Engineering*, pages 108–115, Vienna, Austria, April 1993. IEEE, Los Alamitos, Computer Society Press, CA, USA.
5. F. Mokhtarian, S. Abbasi, and J. Kittler. Efficient and robust retrieval by shape content through curvature scale space. In *Proceedings of the First International Workshop on Image Database and Multimedia Search*, pages 35–42, Amsterdam, The Netherlands, August 1996.
6. F. Mokhtarian, S. Abbasi, and J. Kittler. Robust and efficient shape indexing through curvature scale space. In *Proceedings of the seventh British Machine Vision Conference, BMVC'96*, volume 1, pages 53–62, Edinburgh, September 1996.
7. D. Mumford. The problem of robust shape descriptions. In *First International Conference on Computer Vision*, pages 602–606, London, England,, June 1987.
8. W. Niblack, R. Barber, W. Equitz, M. D. Flickner, E. H. Glasman, D. Petkovic, P. Yanker, C. Faloutsos, and G. Taubin. The qbic project; querying images by content using color

9. E. Saber and A.M. Tekalp. Image query-by-example using region-based shape matching. In *Proceedings of SPIE - The International Society for Optical Engineering*, volume 2666, pages 200–211, 1996.

10. S. Sclaroff and A. P. Pentland. Modal matching for corresponding and recognition. *IEEE Transactions on Pattern Analysis and Machine Intelligence*, 17(6):545–561, June 1995.

11. D. Tsai and M. Chen. Curve fitting approach for tangent angle and curvature measurement. *Pattern Recognition*, 27(5):699–711, 1994.

A Novel Approach for Accessing Partially Indexed Image Corpora

Gérald Duffing and Malika Smaïl
E-mail : duffing@loria.fr / malika@loria.fr

UMR 7503 LORIA
Campus Sciences BP 239
54506 Vandoeuvre-Les-Nancy France

Abstract. This paper addresses the issue of efficient retrieval from image corpora in which only a little proportion is thematically indexed. We propose a hybrid approach integrating thematic querying/search with content-based retrieval. We show how a preliminary double clustering of image corpus exploited by an adapted retrieval process constitutes an answer to the pursued objective. The retrieval process takes advantage of user-system interaction via relevance feedback mechanism whose results are integrated in a *virtual image*. Some experimental results are provided and discussed to demonstrate the effectiveness of this work.

1 Introduction

It becomes very easy to gather large amounts of images into a corpus. When dealing with thousands of images, it remains however difficult to examine each picture to label it even with a few indexing terms. We think however that *partially indexed* corpora can be organised in a way that facilitates retrieval, provided the retrieval process is adapted.

Current existing image retrieval systems split into two main categories. Systems allowing only *keyword querying* will only consider the indexed part of the corpus, and performance will depend on the quality of indexing. The indexing structure varies between classical keyword vectors (RIVAGE [7], Cabri-n [19]), to complex data structures (VIMSYS [6], MMIS [5], MULTOS [16]). The difficulty of the indexing task varies accordingly. *Content-based retrieval* systems will allow retrieval by means of visual similarity comparison, but thematic relevance will probably be left aside. Of course computations must be performed off-line on each image to produce useful visual features. Let's cite TradeMark [23], Art-Museum [10], VisualSEEk [20] and SurfImage [11]. Hybrid approaches have been proposed that try to integrate both approaches. For example, in CHABOT [13], keywords are associated with a combination of visual predicates; in QBIC [12], the similarity measure relies on keyword, shape, colour and texture.

We believe however that content-based systems allowing visual retrieval give little attention to the thematic (semantic) part of the query. A complete indexing process has actually to be carried out to allow correct thematic retrieval.

R. Laurini (Ed.): VISUAL 2000, LNCS 1929, pp. 244–256, 2000.
Springer-Verlag Berlin Heidelberg 2000

Even if the corpus is not totally indexed, we think that keywords remain the best mediating object between users' desires and image content. To bridge the gap between text-based and visual-based queries without loss of high semantic search capabilities, we propose a new retrieval strategy based on a prior corpus organisation that takes into account both thematic and visual aspects. In this paper, we first examine how a corpus may be characterised and organised (§ 2). Then we show how a retrieval process can be designed to take advantage of this organisation (§ 3). Finally, current experimentations and results are presented and discussed (§ 4).

2   Corpus organisation

In our approach, images must be characterized on a thematic *and* visual point of view. Our first goal is then to select some relevant features, that can highlight image similarities, and be used thereafter for classification purposes.

2.1   Thematic description of images

We suppose that the collection of images is *partially* and *not finely* indexed. In other words, a limited amount of images are associated with textual description, and, when this indexation is available, three or four words only are assigned to the image.

We use WordNet [4] as a knowledge source to help dealing with synonyms, namely. In the lexical reference system WordNet, words are organised into synonym sets called "synsets". Each synset represents a lexical concept and is connected to other synsets with different kinds of semantic relationships that provides access, for example, to "generic", "specific", "antonyms" concepts. As a thematic similarity measure, classical vector model and cosine measure have been chosen [18]. This measure is useful for both clustering and retrieval.

2.2   Visual description of images

Each image can be characterised by a set of features computed by image analysis techniques. There are many possible features available in the literature, describing colour, texture or shape [15], but numerous problems remain. For example, it is well known that some features are particularly well adapted to a given domain, whereas they achieve poor results in an other one. Useful visual features are close to human perception, in order to take easily into account user judgements [14]. In our environment, we cannot assume domain-dependent knowledge that could help selecting relevant features, or defining specific ones, and thus we have to use "generic" features. We chose basic colour, texture and shape features. To improve localisation and to allow "layout" comparison, features are not only computed over the entire image (e.g. a colour histogram), but also on small image areas: a fixed grid is applied on the image, defining 32x32 pixels squares called *tiles*.

Colour and texture features are computed for each tile of each image in the corpus.

Texture is often computed on gray-scale images using statistical methods based on co-occurrence matrices: Haralick has proposed fourteen features at four different orientations [8]. We selected only four features, namely "angular second moment", "contrast", "correlation", and "entropy", and use the average value for all orientations. Our experiments show that those indices are powerful enough to provide a rough characterisation when images are tiled into 32x32 squares.

As a very general — though powerful — colour feature, we chose colour histogram [21], represented in L*u*v* colour space. L*u*v* is a device-independent and perceptually uniform colour model, thus well suited for comparisons. We considered three different colour spaces: RGB, L*u*v*, HVC. Not surprisingly, L*u*v* achieved the best results for colour comparisons.

A subset of 128 representative colours can be selected from the entire corpus, so that each image can be quantized according to this reduced colour map, and represented by a 128-components vector.

Shape characterisation is a difficult issue, as extraction of the "relevant" shape is not straightforward [1]. Thus, we defined shape feature as spatial organisation of visually homogeneous areas (according to colour and texture features), which is based on local characterization described above. Other approaches exist, but we think that they are more suited for object recognition purposes, that is when "known objects" have to be carefully characterised, before attempting to identify them in various images, or in homogeneous corpora, that is when images share some visual properties.

2.3   Classification-based corpus organisation

For corpus organisation purposes we focused on clustering techniques [3], which aim at grouping similar objects. They have been extensively used and studied in the field of Information Retrieval [9, 22]. No general conclusion may be made, however, concerning clustering techniques suitability for information retrieval. It is also worth noting that these techniques have been mainly applied to textual information organisation; we intend to use them for *image* classification too, based on visual features. In our approach, agglomerative hierarchical clustering (AHC) has been chosen to classify the corpus: a thematic and a visual classification are constructed based on features described in sections 2.1 and 2.2 above; the resulting structure, called "dendrogram", is reproduced on figure 1.

The advantage of hierarchical structure is that the cluster size can be controlled by a cut-off value (cf. fig. 1): at lower levels, clusters contain few, very similar images. The cluster size grows as we consider higher levels, and this suggests a simple way to balance precision against recall[1]. The cut-off value is determined during retrieval session, and is thus context-adaptive.

---

[1] *Precision* is defined as the proportion of the retrieved documents which are relevant, whereas *recall* is the proportion of relevant documents that are actually retrieved.

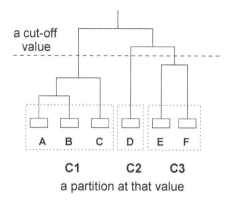

Fig. 1. The dendrogram: a hierarchic structure produced by Agglomerative Hierarchic Clustering.

3 Image Retrieval Process

3.1 Overall Process

Even if the visual aspect is important for image search, we believe that words often remain the best way for the user to launch a retrieval process. In fact, it is difficult to assume that the user has already found a good example of the image(s) he/she is looking for or that he/she is able to sketch the desired images.

Figure 2 shows the overall image retrieval process. The initial thematic query allows the retrieval system to propose a first set of images. An important characteristic of our approach is that this initial image set contains both thematically indexed and not indexed images. The user can then express his visual needs or preferences by providing precise feedback. This is performed by giving examples and counter-examples of what is relevant in respect with thematic aspect and visual aspect (colours, layout...). Indeed, users find it more comfortable to provide interactively examples of relevant and non relevant images. This feedback is exploited by the system in order to build a *virtual image* which gathers its understanding of the user's current need.

The vocabulary used in the query formulation step is limited to nouns from *WordNet*. A graphical interface allows user to pick words and to browse through synsets. Each selected item is then qualified : "absolutely", "rather" or "possibly" *present* or *absent* in the image.

Section 3.3 describes the cluster collecting aspect and our image ranking scheme. Section 3.2 explains how the virtual image constitutes a support for the relevance feedback mechanism (feedback criteria and modalities will be given). To improve the legibility of the paper, we present this section before the collecting and ranking section (since the latter operation, in the general case, assumes a visualisation phase and user's feedback gathering).

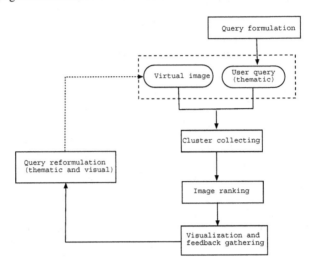

Fig. 2. The overall image retrieval process

3.2   Virtual image as a support for relevance feedback

After a visualisation step, it is important to gather information as precise as possible from user. Actually, images may have been judged relevant in only one point of view (thematic or visual): the system needs to know in what extent a retrieved image is relevant or not to the user. To achieve this, we propose a twofold judgement on each image.

The theme. – This kind of judgement is used to determine what themes are to be searched or avoided. A relevant image may feature new interesting themes that should be included in the next query, by means of reformulation.

The colour. – Colour has been chosen as the most representative among visual indices. It is a fundamental visual property of images, as users are very sensitive to colour; it has also a great discriminant power [21].

For each judgement type, user can "accept", "reject" or have "no idea" about each selected image. This vote can be moderated with a weight ranging from 1 to 10.

Furthermore, **the layout** seems to be an additional good criterion candidate, as it captures the whole "composition" of the image, and then some shape properties. In this work, "layout" refers to spatial localisation of blobs, each blob featuring some homogeneous visual feature. The user has the possibility to choose, among the proposed images, the most representative one (if any) according to the layout. This "typical" layout will be used for image ranking purposes at the next retrieval step. These restrictions are intended to facilitate the visual reformulation problem as well as the local visual similarity evaluation.

From this judgement data, the system derives a representation of its understanding of user's needs. Practically, we are looking for discriminating information : we will try to find both colours and themes that are in common in the set of accepted images, and then in the set of rejected ones.

To model this information, we introduce the **virtual image** concept. From the user feedback and from the features associated with displayed images, we can build two parts corresponding to wanted and unwanted image features, respectively. This applies both on thematic and visual features. The reformulation allows the "filling" of these different parts of the virtual image as follows:

- **thematic reformulation**: the thematic positive (resp. negative) feedback can be handled by a simple weighted averaging of the vectors representing the index of the user-relevant (resp. non relevant) images.

- **visual reformulation**: as image colours are also represented by vectors, the same method can be applied to handle the positive and the negative feedback on the colour aspect as for thematic reformulation.

3.3   Cluster collecting and image ranking

The retrieval process consists in searching the thematic dendrogram and the visual one in order to select some clusters likely to contain relevant images. The selected images are then ranked before being presented to the user.

Searching the thematic or visual dendrogram is done by an ascendant method which performs a constrained generalisation of the low level clusters (adapted from [17]). We use constraints that control the minimum/maximum size of the cluster, its dispersion rate, and the maximum distance. Depending on the collecting result, these constraints can be weakened.

−1− **Thematic dendrogram search**. — The thematic hierarchy is searched using the thematic part of the virtual image (cosine measure is evaluated between "positive" part of the query and the cluster centroid). Depending on clusters size, though, not all images may be equally relevant to the query: this motivates an additional thematic ranking process that will be used for the *tunnel* mechanism (see below). Let us suppose that cluster $C1$ is selected, in which image A is the best ranked.

−2− **Visual dendrogram search (direct)**. — The visual hierarchy is searched using the visual (colours) part of the virtual image (The "positive" part of the query and the cluster centroid are matched). This results in some likely interesting clusters.

−3− **Visual dendrogram search using tunnels**. — The corpus organisation process (§ 2) has led to two different images classifications, and we believe that links can be established between the thematic classification and the visual one, yielding to a thematico-visual synergy, which is based on the following hypothesis: "Thematic similarity and visual similarity are not independent". Figure 3 illustrates this thematico-visual cooperation called *tunnel*.

We assumed that image A from thematic cluster $C1$ is particularly relevant (step 1, above). The tunnel hypothesis tells us to consider visually similar images, which consists in locating image A in the visual dendrogram, and to consider that some "neighbourhood" around A as relevant. In our example, A also belongs to visual cluster $C2$, and all images in $C2$ will be selected as likely relevant (visually and thematically). Some of them are indexed whereas others are not.

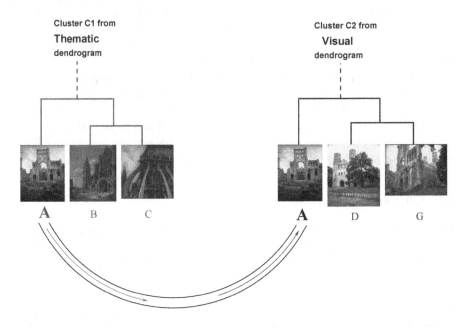

Fig. 3. The "tunnel" mechanism.

The overall advantage of this collecting process is that **non-indexed images have a chance to be retrieved** thanks to the tunnel mechanism even at the first retrieval attempt. Retrieved images in all the selected clusters can now be **ranked** in a unique list. The following formula is used to rank images:

$$S = w * S_t + (1 - w) * S_v.$$

where the visual score (S_v) and thematic score (S_t) may be weighted by the user (w factor) so that it is possible to give more or less importance to visual search against thematic search.

This ranking uses both positive and negative parts of the virtual image *i.e.,* what is wanted and unwanted by the user. Again, the cosine measure can be used for S_t and S_v after merging the positive and negative parts of the query in one vector (by affecting positive weights to wanted criteria and negative weights to unwanted ones).

Furthermore, if a typical layout has been chosen by the user, retrieval precision can be considerably improved by introducing a local visual matching (as opposed to the global colour-based matching). The term S_v above is then defined as a linear combination between a local term and a global term (the w_l factor gives less or more importance to the local visual term against the global one):

$$S_v = w_l * S_{l,v} + (1 - w_l) * S_{g,v}.$$

4 Experiments

4.1 Corpus characteristics and indexing

We used two different corpora (see table 1). In fact, almost every image is indexed, but experiments aims at evaluating the impact of partial indexing on retrieval in our approach. Therefore, we added to our prototype the facility to "hide" indexing, or, on the contrary, to make it visible to the retrieval process. In this context, indexing choices have been carried out randomly, or by hand. *Random indexing* consists in choosing randomly a certain amount of images (say, 20% of the total amount of images), and to make indexing keywords "visible" to the system. *Ad hoc indexing* relies on manual selection of images for which indexing should be visible. It is worth noting that *ad hoc* indexing concerns far less images than random indexing: this is on purpose, since we want to prove that our approach can achieve good performance, provided few images — chosen by hand — are indexed.

Corpus	Size	Indexing	Images
1	2470	Rand.: 20%, 40%; Hand: 5%	Heterogeneous: pictures, paintings, ...
2	1100	Hand: 5%	Building pictures and Fine Arts paintings

Table 1. Corpora characteristics.

4.2 Experiment description

In this work, we want the assess performance of the thematico-visual approach. To do so, we let the user conduct an entire session (i.e. consisting in as many iterations as he wants). Our goal is to determine whether the system allowed retrieval of interesting images, that is thematically and visually relevant images. As a retrieval session may return numerous images, and as each image is ranked according to its expected visual and thematic relevance, we say that a retrieval session is "successful" whenever a certain amount of best ranked images are thematically and visually relevant.

We assume that images are presented to the user by groups of n images. We consider only the k first groups for evaluation. Each of these $k \times n$ images is evaluated by the user from a visual and thematic point of view. Therefore, a symbolic grade is assigned to each image: A (very relevant), B (relevant), C (rather relevant), D (irrelevant), and E (totally irrelevant), according to its visual and thematic user-relevance. Our decision rules are as follows: an image visually and thematically relevant gets grade A; an image visually or thematically relevant only gets grade C; finally, an image that is not thematically nor visually relevant gets grade E (of course, other decision rules may be adopted, depending on a particular search context).

A set of 11 queries has been defined, in order to evaluate system performance on corpus 1. Table 2 lists these queries, along with a manual evaluation of the amount of potentially relevant images in the corpus.

Query Number	Query Formulation	Total nbr of relevant images
1	People at the airport	6
2	Military aircrafts	116
3	Sea birds	33
4	Boats	55
5	Soldiers in the desert	11
6	A cliff and a river	13
7	Cities views	70
8	Mountain sports	21
9	Trains or locomotives	43
10	Old cars	41
11	Fruits sales at the market	11

Table 2. A set of queries for evaluation.

Given the set of queries described above, retrieval sessions have been conducted in different indexing conditions, namely 20%, 40% and *ad hoc* indexing. Only the 10 first images are taken into account. As the user may tune visual against thematic weights to optimize the results, we also indicate the visual weight (in a range from 0 to 100). Table 3 shows the results corresponding to our 11 queries under different indexing conditions. The information provided in these tables corresponds to whole retrieval sessions, that is after possible feedback. It is organised as follows: for each query (col. 1), and under various indexing conditions (col. 2), relevance judgements are reported for the 10 best ranked images (col. 3 to 12): "T" stands for "thematically relevant", "V" for "Visually relevant". A session quality score Q is computed. Finally, the visual weight used to produce the reported results is given (col. 14).

4.3   Discussion

The impact of initial indexing Initial thematic indexing is of particular importance. We obtained the following average scores according to the three indexing conditions we considered: 35 at random 20%, 42 at random 40%, and 51 at *ad hoc* indexing. Not surprisingly, *ad hoc* indexing achieved the best results, even if far less images are actually indexed in this case. Moreover, indexing more images does not systematically lead to better results.

It is clear that retrieval techniques based on visual similarity evaluation only are not sufficient, since visual indices are often not powerful enough to characterize accurately *all* kind of images. In this situation, part of the corpus may be "invisible" to the system. Similar situation occurs when images are not indexed, and therefore not accessible from a thematic point of view. The thematico-visual approach tries to avoid both of these situations.

Similarity evaluation reliability In the thematico-visual approach, the *tunnel* mechanism has been devised to allow collaboration of thematic and visual retrieval techniques. Experiments show that, for each query, an interesting set of images has been retrieved, by means of thematic and/or visual similarity measures. However, these measures cannot always distinguish relevant from irrelevant images: *noise* seems to be the price to pay to obtain satisfactory recall.

Figure 4 shows how thematic (T), visual (V) and tunnel (U) techniques performed during this experiment on corpus 1. In this histogram, the average number of images retrieved using each technique is plotted. The lower part of the bar represent the number of images that are actually considered as thematically and visually relevant by user. We observe that the *tunnel* mechanism is fairly reliable: 62.5% of tunnel-retrieved images turned out to be relevant. Only 30% of images retrieved from visual techniques only proved to be relevant.

The hypothesis associated to the *tunnel* mechanism turned out to be verified: we observe that most of the images retrieved by means of *tunnel* have been judged as relevant by the user. In this way, the *tunnel* can be used to *confirm* image relevance. As a heuristic, we can say that an image retrieved by means of visual techniques *and* by means of *tunnel* is more likely to be relevant than another.

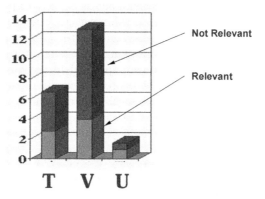

Fig. 4. Retrieval technique performance.

Query reformulation performance We shall focus here on visual reformulation, that permitted retrieval results improvement. Global colour-based reformulation allows the system to focus on a certain kind of images, namely those which are closer to the user's desires. As a complement, layout-based reformulation allows the system to refine image ranking.

Visual retrieval favours recall against precision. As a consequence, "noise" is the main drawback of this approach. We think, however, that this is necessary, as the corpus is not totally indexed. Actually, relevant images may not be indexed, and visual retrieval — combined with the *tunnel* mechanism — is the only chance we have to retrieve those images.

5   Conclusion and future work

We have presented an integrated method that allows thematic and visual image retrieval in a partially indexed corpus. Our strategy relies on a preliminary corpus organisation into two hierarchical structures by a clustering process. An adapted retrieval process was designed that takes advantage of the user-system interactions: precise feedback data are gathered and processed within a *virtual image*.

This approach for image retrieval is well adapted to large corpora in which a little proportion is thematically indexed: visual index is computed off-line, fast image filtering is allowed by hierarchical clustering, and new images may be easily added to the existing hierarchies...

First experimentation results confirm the relevance of our approach. We believe that it could be improved by efficient integration of other visual characteristics which will make possible to refine not only the user query but also the similarity measure by selecting the best characteristics according to the user and his preferences (as in [2, 14]).

Finally, we think that off-line session analysis is likely to produce interesting indexing hypothesises. Indeed, non-indexed images may have been retrieved during a session and user feedback is precise enough to allow us to determine if an image is relevant to a given query. Assuming some good properties of the query (such as compactness, i.e. few items are specified in the query), a temporary label can be attached to the image. Repeated successful retrievals of this image will increase the hypothesis confidence until it becomes a regular indexing item.

References

1. P. Aigrain, H. Zhang, and D. Petkovic. Content-Based Representation and Retrieval of Visual Media: A State-of-the-Art Review. *Multimedia Tools and Applications*, 3:179–202, 1996.
2. G. Ciocca and R. Schettini. A relevance feedback mechanism for content-based image retrieval. *Information Processing and Management*, 35:605–632, 1999.
3. R. Duda and P. Hart. *Pattern Classification and Scene Analysis*. John Wiley and Sons, 1973.
4. C. Fellbaum, editor. *WORDNET: An Electronic Lexical Database*. MIT Press, 1998.

5. C. Goble, M. O'Docherty, P. Crowther, M. Ireton, J. Oakley, and C. Xydeas. The Manchester Multimedia Information System. In *Lecture Notes in Computer Science, vol. 580*, pages 39–55. Springer, 1992.
6. A. Gupta, T. Weymouth, and R. Jain. Semantic queries with pictures: the VIMSYS model. In *Proceedings of the 17th int. conf. on Very Large Data Bases*, pages 69–79, Barcelona, septembre 1991.
7. G. Halin. Machine Learning and Vectorial Matching for an Image Retrieval Model: EXPRIM and the System RIVAGE. In J.-L. Vidick, editor, *ACM 13th Int. Conf. on Research and Development in Information Retrieval*, pages 99–114, Brussels (Belgium), septembre 1990. Presses Universitaires de Bruxelles.
8. R.M. Haralick, K. Shanmugam, and I. Dinstein. Textural features for image classification. *IEEE Trans. on Systems, Man, and Cybernetics*, SMC–3(6):610–621, 1973.
9. N. Jardine and C.J. van Rijsbergen. The use of hierarchical clustering in information retrieval. *Information Storage and Retrieval*, 7:217–240, 1971.
10. T. Kato. Database architecture for content-based image retrieval. In *Image Storage and Retrieval Systems*, volume 1662, pages 112–123, San Jose, CA, 1992. SPIE.
11. C. Nastar, M. Mischke, C. Meilhac, N. Boudjemaa, H. Bernard, and M. Mautref. Retrieving images by content: the surfimage system. In *Multimedia Information Systems*, Istanbul, 1998.
12. W. Niblack, R. Barber, W. Equitz, M. Flickner, E. Glasman, D. Petkovic, P. Yanker, C. Faloutsos, and G. Taubin. The QBIC project: querying images by content using color, texture and shape. In Wayne Niblack, editor, *Storage and Retrieval for Image and Video Databases*, pages 173–181, San Jose, CA, 1993. SPIE.
13. V. E. Ogle and M. Stonebraker. CHABOT: Retrieval from a relational database of images. *IEEE Computer*, 28(9):40–48, 1995.
14. R.W. Picard and T.P. Minka. Vision Texture for Annotation. *Multimedia Systems*, 3:3–14, 1995.
15. W.K. Pratt. *Digital Image Processing*. John Wiley & Sons, New York, second edition, 1991.
16. F. Rabitti and P. Savino. Querying semantic image database. In *Image Storage and Retrieval Systems*, volume 1662, pages 69–78, San Jose, CA, 1992. SPIE.
17. C.J. van Rijsbergen and W.B. Croft. Document clustering: an evaluation of some experiments with the Cranfield 1400 collection. *Information processing and management*, 11:171–182, 1974.
18. G. Salton and M.J. McGill. *Introduction to Modern Information Retrieval*. McGraw-Hill, 1983.
19. M. Smaïl. Case-Base Reasoning Meets Information Retrieval. In *RIAO 94: Intelligent Multimedia Information Retrieval Systems and Management*, page 133, 1994.
20. J. R. Smith and S.-F. Chang. Querying by color regions using the VisualSEEk content-based visual query system. In Mark T. Maybury, editor, *Intelligent Multimedia Information Retrieval*, pages 23–41. AAAI Press, Menlo Park, 1997.
21. M.J. Swain and D.H. Ballard. Color indexing. *International Journal of Computer Vision*, 7(1):11–32, 1991.
22. E. Voorhees. *The Effectiveness and Efficiency of Agglomerative Hierarchic Clustering in Document Retrieval*. PhD thesis, Cornell University, Ithaca, NY, Etats-Unis, 1985. Rapport Technique TR 85-705.
23. T. Whalen, E.S. Lee, and F. Safayeni. The Retrieval of Images from Image Databases. *Behaviour & Information Technology*, 14(1):3–13, 1995.

Query Number	Index Cond.	Image Ranks										Quality Score	Visual Weight
		1	2	3	4	5	6	7	8	9	10		
1	20	TV	TV	TV	V	TV			TV	TV		44	70
1	40	TV	TV	TV	TV	TV						40	100
1	AH	TV	TV	TV	TV	TV		TV				47	70
2	20	TV	TV	T	TV	T	T			T		24	60
2	40	TV	TV	TV	TV	TV	TV	T				49	70
2	AH	TV	TV	TV	TV	TV	T	T	T		T	48	90
3	20	TV	TV	TV	V	V	TV	T			V	31	90
3	20	TV	TV	TV	TV	V	TV	V	V			41	70
3	40	TV	TV	TV	TV	V	V		T			34	100
3	40	TV	TV	TV	TV	V	V	V		T	T	38	30
3	AH	TV	TV	T	TV	TV	T	T	T			36	40
4	20	TV	V	T	V	TV	V		V	TV		16	60
4	40	TV	T	T	TV	TV	T				T	24	50
4	AH	TV	TV	TV	TV	T		T	T	T	T	38	80
5	20	TV	TV	TV	TV	TV	V		TV			49	100
5	40	TV	TV	TV	TV				T			32	50
5	AH	TV	TV	TV	TV	TV	TV		TV	T	TV	63	70
6	20	TV	TV	TV	TV				TV			37	100
6	40	V	TV	TV	TV	V	V	TV	TV	V	V	40	100
6	40	TV	TV	TV	TV	TV	TV	V	V	V	TV	60	100
6	AH	TV	TV	TV	TV	TV	TV	T	V	V	V	55	60
7	20	TV	TV	V	TV	TV	V	T				34	90
7	40	TV	TV	TV	TV	TV					TV	47	100
7	40	TV	TV	TV	TV	T		TV		T	TV	46	60
7	AH	TV	TV	TV	TV	TV	TV	T	V	TV	V	60	60
8	20	TV	TV	TV	TV							26	60
8	40	TV	TV	TV		TV						26	70
8	AH	TV	TV	TV	TV	TV	TV	TV			TV	61	100
9	20	TV	TV	TV								12	60
9	40	TV	TV	TV	TV	T	T				T	34	75
9	40	TV	TV	TV	TV	TV		T			T	44	70
9	AH	TV	TV	TV	TV	T	TV		TV	T		46	20
10	20	TV	TV		TV	TV	TV			TV	TV	47	95
10	40	TV	TV	TV	TV	TV	TV	TV	TV			61	60
10	AH	TV	TV	TV	TV	TV	T	T	T		T	48	70
11	20	TV	TV	TV	TV		TV	V	V		V	39	15
11	20	TV	TV	TV	TV	TV	TV	V	T	V	V	55	90
11	40	TV	TV	TV	TV	TV		TV	TV			54	50
11	AH	TV	TV	TV	TV	TV	TV	TV		T	V	58	100

Table 3. Query results.

Show Me What You Mean!
PARISS: A CBIR-Interface
That Learns by Example

G Caenen[2], G Frederix[2,3], A.A.M Kuijk[1], E.J Pauwels[1,2*], B.A.M Schouten[1]

1. *Centre for Mathematics and Computer Science (CWI),*
   Kruislaan 413, 1098 SJ Amsterdam, The Netherlands
   {Eric.Pauwels, B.A.M.Schouten, Fons.Kuijk}@cwi.nl
2. *ESAT-PSI, K.U.Leuven, K. Mercierlaan 94,*
   B-3001 Heverlee, Belgium
   Geert.Caenen@esat.kuleuven.ac.be
   Eric.Pauwels@esat.kuleuven.ac.be
3. *Dept. of Mathematics, K.U.Leuven, Celestijnenlaan 200 B,*
   B-3001 Heverlee, Belgium
   Greet.Frederix@esat.kuleuven.ac.be

Abstract. We outline the architecture of a CBIR-interface that allows the user to interactively classify images by dragging and dropping them into different piles and instructing the interface to come up with features that can mimic this classification. Logistic regression and Sammon projection are used to support this search mode.

1 Introduction and Motivation

The explosive growth of digital multi-media repositories has created challenging new problems regarding indexing, access and retrieval of information. These challenges are particularly acute for image-databases as there is no canonical format for encoding the information encapsulated in an image. It is the explicit goal of *Content-Based Image Retrieval* (CBIR) to design algorithms and interfaces that will assist the user in this task [2, 5].

The **aim of this paper** is to outline the architecture of an interface that allows the user to interactively guide the search by manually rearranging or classifying images. A first version of this interface was introduced in [3], and baptized PARISS, short for *Panoramic, Adaptive and Reconfigurable Interface for Similarity Search.* This lengthy acronym refers to the following interface-characteristics:

- *Panoramic:* The relative location of images with respect to the rest of the database can be displayed;

---

* To whom all correspondence should be sent

R. Laurini (Ed.): VISUAL 2000, LNCS 1929, pp. 257–268, 2000.
Springer-Verlag Berlin Heidelberg 2000

- *Adaptive:* Relevance feedback (in the form of examples and counter-examples) is used to incrementally refine the probability measure that represents the accumulation of information during the search process;
- *Reconfigurable:* Similarities can be defined interactively through direct manipulation of images.

The idea of using a manipulation tool to define similarities interactively was first introduced by Santini [6]. However, his approach is based on modifying the Euclidean metric into a general Riemannian one to absorb the discrepancies between the user-defined similarities and the distance between the actual feature-vectors. The methodology proposed in this paper differs in that it concentrates on transforming the features themselves rather than the metric.

Formal statement of the problem   We assume that every one of the N images is represented by a K-dimensional feature-vector. In that sense, the database is represented by a $N \times K$ matrix where each row represents the numerical features of the corresponding image.

In abstract terms the CBIR-problem can be looked upon as an optimization problem for a function Φ that maps each image (or its feature-vector $\mathbf{x}$) to its user-defined numerical *relevance*. This relevance reflects the extent to which an image corresponds the user's goal, and for ease of argument we will assume that it can be assigned a numerical score ranging from *highly relevant* (1) to *not relevant at all* (-1):

$$\Phi : \mathbf{x} \in I\!R^K \longmapsto \text{relevance} \in I\!R$$

When conducting a *similarity* search Φ will be inversely proportional to the distance between the query image and the rest of the database; when *browsing* a catalogue looking for something interesting or beautiful, Φ will simply reflect the image's appeal. Clearly, this function is user-dependent, and each function-evaluation involves visual inspection of the image by the user.

Somewhat confusingly perhaps, we will refer to images as *relevant* for short, if they are either *highly relevant* ($\Phi \approx 1$, i.e. excellent examples of what we mean) or *highly irrelevant* ($\Phi \approx -1$, i.e. good counter-examples). For instance, if we are looking for images that are brightly red, then images that are predominantly red are highly relevant examples. However, images that are strikingly blue are also relevant in that they furnish the user with excellent counter-examples. Finally, an image exhibiting red patches could be said to be *partially relevant* as some of its aspects are informative to our query. The problem of extracting information from partially relevant images will be taken up in section 4 .

Different Search Strategies   The role of the interface is to use the available information (i.e. function evaluations based on visual inspection) and suggest to the user potentially interesting images for further evaluation. In mathematical parlance this amounts to a stepwise optimisation of Φ — a problem of considerable difficulty as our knowledge of the function is restricted to the few points at which it is evaluated (by visual inspection). To address such a problem, there are basically two strategies, both implemented in the current version of the interface (for more details we refer the reader to sections 2.2 and 2.3).

1. **Probabilistic search:** In this approach, the search space is sampled at different locations and the function evaluations are used to bias the next sample in an attempt to increase the probability of a high Φ-yield. More specifically, the next batch of points that are selected for evaluation will be made to cluster roughly about the point that yielded the best Φ-value.

   To enable this sort of probabilistic search in PARISS, we have implemented a **collection box** — for want of a better word — in which the user can collect relevant images. This collection of relevant images is continuously analysed by a module called the **inference engine** (see below) in an attempt to spot trends in the features-values that can direct the sampling procedure to more promising regions of the search space.

2. **Gradient ascent:** In gradient methods one determines how the function is changing near the current location and this gradient is then used to move to higher Φ-values. To assist the user in finding perceptually meaningful gradients we have designed a **manipulation window** that allows him to manually rearrange images according to his own appreciation of their relative similarity. Once this is done, the **projection engine** searches for a projection of the dataset that best reproduces this requested configuration. This form of manipulation allows the user to impose certain gradients by enforcing how the visual qualities change when moving from image to image.

In the next section we will elaborate in more detail how the interface has been designed to support a seamless combination of these two search modi.

2   The interface's architecture

2.1   Introduction

Even medium-size image databases contain at least several thousand images. The complexity of the retrieval problem is further compounded by the fact that, in order to capture the visual content, one needs to extract quite a large number (K) of features. Values for K ranging between 50 and 200 are typical, rather than exceptional. In the terminology introduced earlier this means that we are faced with the challenge of navigating through a large cloud of data-points in the high-dimensional space $I\!R^K$.

These astronomical sizes contrast starkly with the small number of images (20 to 50) that can simultaneously be displayed on screen. The fraction of the database that one is exploring at any given time is therefore tiny, and this myopic view entails that it is very easy to lose one's bearings while exploring the database. The proposed interface was designed to alleviate these problems and in what follows, we will therefore outline its architecture which, for the sake of clarity, is divided in **displays** and **computation engines**. The former are used to display images for different forms of relevance feedback, while the latter are invoked to translate the user's input into new search directions.

2.2   Display Windows

At all times, the interface shows three display-windows, between which the user can move seamlessly (for a schematic overview we refer the reader to Fig. 1).

1. **Sample display**

    This screen displays the by now standard matrix of images that are (initially randomly) sampled from the database and presented to the user for inspection. The user can select images that are deemed relevant whereupon they are transferred to the *collection box* (see below). Each time a "refresh button" is pressed, the sampling algorithm is activated and a new sample is generated for inspection. The sampling algorithm that is used to generate the new sample can be biased by the *inference engine* (cfr. section 2.3) to accommodate the preferences of the user.

2. **Collection box for relevant images**

    The second screen is used as a simple *collection box* in which there are two bins: one for the *examples* (i.e. similar or partially similar images), and one for the *counter-examples* (dissimilar images). Whenever the user comes across an image he considers relevant in that respect, it is transferred to the collection box. This box can be inspected at all times, and images that no longer seem relevant can be removed.

    The collection box should be thought of as reflecting the user's cumulative (qualitative) knowledge about the database. This information will be turned into more quantitative measures by the *inference engine* (see section 2.3).

3. **Manipulation window**

    This screen is used to manually redefine similarities between selected images. It therefore shows an xy-plot in which selected images (e.g. the ones that have been transferred to the *collection box*) are presented as thumbnails located at appropriate 2-dimensional xy-coordinates. The precise choice of these coordinates is altogether not very important as they will be changed during the search process, but to fix ideas we suggest to use the first two *principal component* coordinates (PC-coord) [1] as an initial choice.

    The really interesting feature of this window is that it can be **manipulated**. More specifically, when inspecting the displayed projection, the relative positioning of the images might strike the user as unsatisfactory. For instance, it might be the case that although image A is located near image B and quite far from image C, it's the user's understanding that this should be the other way round. He can then drag the thumbnail B to a location near C.

---

[1] Once all the K features have been determined for the N images in the database, one can compute the $K \times K$ covariance matrix and its eigenvectors. Using these eigenvectors as new coordinate system one can recompute the coordinates of all the points with respect to this new coordinate system. We suggest to use the coordinates that correspond to the eigenvectors associated with the two largest eigenvalues.

After rearranging the images, he can then instruct the interface to find a **transformation** that will project the original feature-space onto the screen in such a way that the resulting configuration better resembles the one that was manually defined (the computational details are explained in Section 2.3). The underlying rationale is that the manually defined arrangement of the images will reflect the preferences and tendencies that implicitly exists in the user's mind. Hence, constructing (new) features that are able to reproduce this configuration will probably reorganise the database along the same lines, and suggest directions (gradients if you will) in which to search next. For instance, if images with a fine-grained texture are dragged to the left part of the screen, while coarse-grained images are collected in the right part, one expects to find medium-grained images when exploring the middle part of the screen.

To enable this type of exploration, the manipulation window is also **clickable**: you can click at *any position* in the display (i.e. not just on an already displayed image) and the interface will look for the images the 2D-coordinates of which are closest to the selected point. If you consider any of these to be relevant, then you can add them to the *collection box*.

2.3   Computation Engines

Let us now take a peek under the bonnet and explain in some more detail the computational strategies that enable this type of interactivity.

1. **Projection Engine: Creating New Feature Combinations**

   The projection engine operates on the *manipulation window* and is activated to generate a transformation (A say) that yields features better conforming to the user's appreciation of the similarities. To keep things as simple as possible, we will assume that the transformation is *linear*, mapping the full feature space $\mathbb{R}^K$ onto a 2-dimensional display ($\mathbb{R}^2$):

   $$A : \mathbb{R}^K \longrightarrow \mathbb{R}^2$$

   A gradient descent method is used to determine the actual form of the linear transformation A and we will presently explain in more detail how we go about this. The reader who is not interested in the mathematics can proceed directly to the description of the *inference engine*.

   (a) Start by selecting a number (n say) of relevant or representative images in the database (e.g. images that have been amassed as examples or counter-examples in the collection box during an earlier exploration stage). These images are represented by their n feature-vectors $\mathbf{x}_i \in \mathbb{R}^K$.
   (b) Project the corresponding data-points onto a 2-dimensional subspace (selected manually or automatically) and show the result to the user (see also Fig.1). As explained above, this resulting 2-dimensional projection

is displayed in the *manipulation window*, in which the images are shown as thumbnails, each positioned at a location that corresponds to their projected (2D) coordinates $\mathbf{q}_i$ $(i = 1, \ldots, n)$.

(c) Next, allow the user to rearrange the thumbnails so that their new ("target") configuration $\mathbf{t}_i$ reflects more accurately the perceptual organization as perceived by the user. Once this is done, *the projection engine* is activated which attempts to find a linear mapping

$$A : \mathbb{R}^K \longrightarrow \mathbb{R}^2$$

(called *projection* for short) of the full feature space $\mathbb{R}^K$ onto a 2-dimensional space that, when applied to the selected points $\mathbf{x}_i$, best matches the user-defined configuration of the points $\mathbf{t}_i$.

The optimality is expressed with respect to *Sammon's metric stress* which is defined as:

$$S_M(A) = \sum_{i,j} \frac{(d(\mathbf{t}_i, \mathbf{t}_j) - d(A\mathbf{x}_i, A\mathbf{x}_j))^2}{d(\mathbf{t}_i, \mathbf{t}_j)}, \tag{1}$$

where d is the standard Euclidean metric on $\mathbb{R}^2$.

This Sammon-criterion can be minimized using *gradient descent*. Indeed, straightforward but tedious algebra shows that

$$\frac{\partial S_M}{\partial a_{kl}} = 2 \sum_{i,j} \left(1 - \frac{d(A\mathbf{x}_i, A\mathbf{x}_j)}{d(\mathbf{t}_i, \mathbf{t}_j)}\right) \cdot \frac{\partial d(A\mathbf{x}_i, A\mathbf{x}_j)}{\partial a_{kl}}$$

$$= 2 \sum_{i,j} \left(1 - \frac{d(A\mathbf{x}_i, A\mathbf{x}_j)}{d(\mathbf{t}_i, \mathbf{t}_j)}\right) \cdot \frac{[A(\mathbf{x}_i - \mathbf{x}_j)]_k [\mathbf{x}_i - \mathbf{x}_j]_l}{d(A\mathbf{x}_i, A\mathbf{x}_j)}$$

$$= 2 \sum_{i,j} \left(\frac{d(\mathbf{t}_i, \mathbf{t}_j) - d(A\mathbf{x}_i, A\mathbf{x}_j)}{d(\mathbf{t}_i, \mathbf{t}_j) \, d(A\mathbf{x}_i, A\mathbf{x}_j)}\right) \cdot \left[A(\mathbf{x}_i - \mathbf{x}_j)(\mathbf{x}_i - \mathbf{x}_j)^T\right]_{kl}$$

Hence, the gradient can be expressed explicitly as

$$\nabla_A S_M = 2A \sum_{i,j} \left(\frac{d(\mathbf{t}_i, \mathbf{t}_j) - d(A\mathbf{x}_i, A\mathbf{x}_j)}{d(\mathbf{t}_i, \mathbf{t}_j) d(A\mathbf{x}_i, A\mathbf{x}_j)}\right) (\mathbf{x}_i - \mathbf{x}_j)(\mathbf{x}_i - \mathbf{x}_j)^T \tag{2}$$

with corresponding gradient descent dynamics: $\partial A / \partial t = -\epsilon \nabla_A S_M$.

(d) Once the optimal transformation A has been found it is applied to all the elements in the database, i.e. not just to the original sample of size n on which the computation is based. This allows the user to have a fresh look at the database which now better reflects the user-defined (dis)similarity structure.

Extensions to quadratic (or higher order) transformations The use of a linear transformation immediately suggests the extension to quadratic and higher order transformations. However, such extensions are less straight-forward as they may appear at first sight, as the number of parameter increases dramatically (exponentially) when the order of the transformation is augmented.

We therefore propose to restrict the use of the higher order transformations to instances where further fine-tuning of the 2-dimensional display is called for. Hence, the mapping $A : I\!\!R^K \longrightarrow I\!\!R^2$ maps the full feature space onto a 2-D display space, whereupon a quadratic transformation $Q : I\!\!R^2 \longrightarrow I\!\!R^2$ is invoked to model the non-linear aspects in the approximation. This quadratic transformation is of the form $Q(\mathbf{y}) = \eta \in I\!\!R^2$ where $\eta = (\eta_1, \eta_2)$ satisfies:

$$\begin{cases} \eta_1 = \mathbf{y}^T \mathbf{Q_1} \mathbf{y} + \mathbf{p}^T \mathbf{y} + \alpha \\ \eta_2 = \mathbf{y}^T \mathbf{Q_2} \mathbf{y} + \mathbf{q}^T \mathbf{y} + \beta \end{cases}$$

It's important to notice that these equations are *linear* in the unknown parameters and optimisation we used for the original projection engine can therefore easily be adapted for this more complicated case.

2. Inference Engine: Biasing the Sample

As explained above, the *collection box* is used to collect both examples and counter-examples of the sort of images the user deems relevant. The reason for collecting them is to be found in the fact that this information can be used to bias the next sample favorably so that the fraction of interesting retrieved images increases over time. To this end we have implemented an *inference engine* that uses these data to generate an estimate of where interesting images can be found.

To cast this in a more formal setting, we denote by p the probability that an image is relevant. Hence, $p \approx 1$ would mean that it is highly similar, whereas $p \approx 0$ indicates that it is highly dissimilar. Strictly speaking, the probability measure p depends on the full feature vector $\mathbf{x} = (x_1, x_2, \ldots, x_K)$ and the images gathered in the collection box yield information on locations where the probability is markedly high or low. However, it is clear that reliably modelling the full probability density $p(\mathbf{x})$ on such scant information will in general prove to be an intractable problem, so we do the next best thing and model p as a function of each feature x_i separately.

Predicting similarity using logistic regression   In mathematical terms the problem boils down to this: the collection box contains a number of examples and counter-examples and for each single feature x_i (denoted x for short) we want to model the dependency of p on x through a function $p(x)$. The simplest case would be the one in which one can find a threshold value ($x^{(0)}$ say) that separates examples from counter-examples. Such information could then be fed back to the sampling procedure. However, in most cases the situation will be more complicated and trends will be less clear-cut. The best one can hope for is that one can correlate the probability p with the x-values so that trends become visible and can be harnessed to improve the efficiency of the search.

The standard way to handle such a situation is to invoke a *logistic regression model* (see [4])

$$\log \frac{p(x)}{1 - p(x)} = f(x) \tag{3}$$

where the logit-ratio of p in the left-hand side[2] is expressed as an appropriate function of the feature-value x. For the application we have in mind, we have opted for a *quadratic* logistic regression model:

$$\log \frac{p(x)}{1 - p(x)} = \alpha x^2 + \beta x + \gamma; \tag{4}$$

The parameters α, β and γ are determined by using *maximum likelihood estimation*, i.e. they optimize the probability of the actual configuration occurring. More explicitely, if we look up the x-value for each of the images in the collection box and then use eq.(4) to compute the probability p that they are in fact an example $(p > 1/2)$ or counter-example $(p < 1/2)$, then the parameters (α, β, γ) are chosen to optimize this prediction accuracy.

The reason for the choice of a *quadratic* function might need some clarification. If relevance is (directly or inversely) proportional to the feature value, then a linear model will suffice (i.e. we can put $\alpha = 0$); however there obviously are situations where for instance, only medium feature-values are acceptable, while extreme values (both larger and smaller) are unacceptable (have a look at Fig. 3). The quadratic model is the simplest model that can handle this sort of qualitative distinction.

Using regression diagnostics   The use of regression has the additional advantage that we can invoke standard regression diagnostics to judge the fit and predictive power of the model. This helps us to gauge the success of the feature in predicting relevance and can therefore be used to narrow down the feature-set. More precisely, if for a particular feature x_i, the prediction of the fitted model (4) fails to square up with the relevance feedback from the user, this indicates that that particular feature x_i does not feature prominently in the perceptual appreciation of the user. Hence, a uniform sampling regime for that feature is advisable, as there is no reason to narrow its sampling-range.

Conversely, if logistic regression yields a well-fitting model for a different feature x_j, we can conclude that the feature plays an important role in the user's appreciation of the image, and we are well advised to bias the sampling-procedure as to favour feature-values x_j that have high p-value. That way, the fraction of relevant features in each new sample (as displayed on the *sample display*) will gradually increase.

---

[2] The logit-ratio $\log(p/(1 - p))$ is introduced to transform the p-value, which is constrained to the interval $[0, 1]$, to a quantity that ranges over $\mathbb{R}$ and is therefore easier to link to a linear or polynomial regression model.

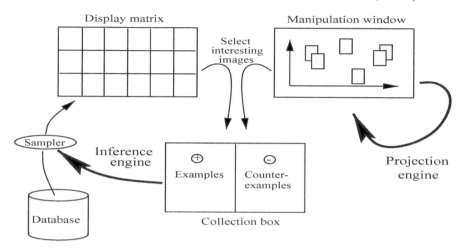

Fig. 1. Images are sampled from the database and presented for inspection on the *sample display* (top left). The ones relevant for the search (examples or counter-examples) are transferred both to the *collection box* (bottom) and the *manipulation window* (top right). Here their locations reflect their similarity. Moreover, the user can rearrange them to better match his similarity-perception and instruct the *projection engine* to compute features that match this ordering. Statistics of the images in the collection box are used by the *inference engine* and used to bias the next sampling procedure.

3   Using the Interface: An Interaction Scenario

After the detailed description of the different components that constitute the interface in the preceding paragraphs, we will now wrap up this section by concisely outlining what an interactive browsing session might look like.

The query-scenario we have in mind is one in which the user has a (more or less crisply defined) mental picture of a *target image* by which he can judge the relevance of the images encountered during the database exploration. For ease of argument we will assume that in a first exploratory stage, the user has been shown random (or representative) samples drawn from the database and that he has selected a number of images that in some respect are considered relevant for his search.

The database search now proceeds by mixing and iterating the following basic operations (for an animated version of this slightly complicated process, we refer to our website):

1. *Browse* the database by either inspecting the sampling display or by clicking in promising regions of the manipulation window;
2. *Add* interesting images to the *collection box* and *remove* the ones that are no longer relevant;
3. *Generate* "home-made" features by rearranging selected thumbnails and requesting the interface to come up with *new combinations of features* that are able to reproduce the user-defined ordering.

4. *Bias* the sampling procedure by fitting regression models to the underlying probability distribution.

4   Addressing the Problem of Partial Relevance

The learning done by the interface is reflected in a gradual fine-tuning of the probability density $p(\mathbf{x})$ (cfr.(4)) that models the relevance of images. At the start of the exploration, samples are drawn *uniformly* from the whole database, since the uniform distribution is the appropriate probability density to model the original "un-informed" state of the user. However, by transferring relevant images to the collection box and using these collection box statistics to bias the sampling procedure (as explained in subsection 2.3) there is a gradual shift from the original "uniform" (i.e. non-informative) prior probability to an "informed" density peaking around the *target image*.

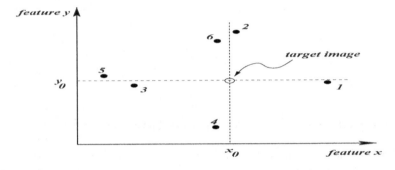

Fig. 2. Collecting partially relevant images 1 through 6 allows one to estimate the location of the target image at (x_0, y_0). See main text for more details.

However, this fine-tuning is compounded by the fact that most of images selected for inclusion in the collection box will only be *partially* relevant. For instance, if one is looking for images of *red circles*, then all images showing *circles* are relevant, as are all images that are predominantly *red*, for the target image belongs to the intersection of these two classes. The problem we have to address is how to convey to the system that this partial information is meant to be complementary.

Interaction modes to deal with partial relevance   As far as we can see, there are essentially two conceivable strategies to extract useful information from partially relevant images:

1. Either you can indicate for each partially relevant image, what *specific* feature is relevant for the search (e.g. the shape for image 1, and the colour for image 2). This is the approach championed by most interfaces. However, the

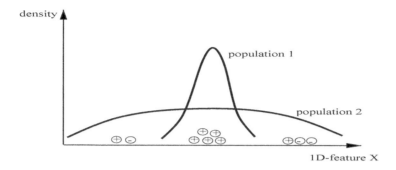

Fig. 3. Decomposing the density generated by (partially relevant) examples ($\oplus$) and counter-examples ($\ominus$) generates a mixture distribution; the peaked distribution (population 1) collects all the examples that are relevant for the x-feature that is plotted along the axis. The diffuse background distribution (population 2) collects the counter-examples as well as the examples that are relevant with respect to another feature.

requirement that features must be identified explicitly is a very restrictive one and in most cases not tenable. (After all, how would you inform the interface that you are looking for an image that is *just as colourful as this one, but as chaotic as that one?*)

2. The approach we propose is designed to circumvent this difficulty: there is no need to identify features, just point out additional images that are partially relevant. Over time, the statistics will automatically hone in on the relevant features. We will elaborate this proposal presently.

Integrating information from partially relevant images For clarity we will discuss the following caricature of the problem (see Fig 2): Assume that every image is characterized using two numerical features (x and y say); this means that every image can be represented as a single point $(x, y) \in \mathbb{R}^2$. Furthermore, assume that we are after the target image located at (x_0, y_0). While exploring the database we come across image 1 (with features x_1 and y_1, see Fig 2). Clearly this image is *partially relevant* to our search as it resembles the target image as far as the y-feature is concerned ($y_1 \approx y_0$). Because of this partial relevance it is added to the stack. Later on in the exploration, the user comes across image 2, which again is partially relevant, this time because of its x-feature ($x_2 \approx x_0$), and is therefore added to the stack. In the same vein images 3, 4, 5 and 6 are added, so that we end up with a stack containing 6 images, all of which are *partially*, but none of which is *completely* similar to the target image.

If we now project the six selected images on each of the two feature axes and construct the corresponding 1-dimensional densities, we would notice how in both cases the resulting density is in fact a mixture of two populations (see also Fig. 3). To fix ideas look at the projection on the x-feature: The first population comprises the images that are relevant with respect to x and therefore constitute a peaked density centered about the appropriate x-value.

The second population harbours the images that are relevant with respect to the y-feature. Their x-value therefore does not adhere to a narrow distribution and they are more or less uniformely distributed in the "background". Being able to tease apart these two distributions is key to efficiently locating the interesting region in the search space. Obviously, the quadratic logistic regression model (as specified by eq.(4)) is one important tool in this process. Using counter-examples is another, as will be explained next.

The importance of being negative Since counter-examples — by their very definition — indicate what you are not looking for, none of their projections on the feature axes will occur near the target values. Put differently, the projections of counter-examples will show up in the "background" density, rather than in the peaked "foreground" density (see Fig. 3). As a consequence, the peaked foreground contains examples only, whereas the diffuse background is a mixture of both examples and counter-examples.

In order to model this mixture-population in the background, the 1-D logistic regression model will further reduce its probability over the background regions but concentrate it near the peak-region, thus creating an even more pronounced delineation of the region of interest around the target-points x_0 and y_0.

Conclusion In this paper we outlined the architecture of a CBIR-interface that offers the user a graphical tool to create new features by *showing* (as opposed to *telling*!) the interface what he means. It allows him to interactively classify images by dragging and dropping them into different piles and instructing the interface to come up with features that can mimic this classification. For more details and an early proto-type, we invite the reader to visit our website: http://www.cwi.nl/~pauwels/pariss.html

Acknowledgments: E.P. and G.C. gratefully acknowledge partial support by the Belgian Fund for Scientific Research (F.W.O. Vlaanderen, Belgium), under grant G.0366.98. B.S. gratefully acknowledges support by NWO (The Netherlands).

References

1. B.A.M. Schouten, P.M. de Zeeuw. Image Databases, Scale and Fractal Transforms. To appear in Proceedings ICIP 2000
2. A.D. Del Bimbo: *Visual Information Retrieval*, Morgan Kaufmann Publishers, Inc., California, 1999.
3. G. Frederix, G. Caenen and E.J. Pauwels: *PARISS: Panoramic, Adaptive and Reconfigurable Interface for Similarity Search.* To appear in Proceedings ICIP 2000.
4. D W Hosmer and S Lemeshow: Applied Logistic Regression. Wiley 1989.
5. T. Kakimoto and Y. Kambayashi: *Browsing functions in three-dimensional space for digital libraries*, International Journal on Digital Libraries, (2):68-78, 1999.
6. S. Santini and R. Jain: *Beyond Query by Example.* Proceedings of ACM Multimedia'98, Bristol, UK.

Scale Summarized and Focused Browsing of Primitive Visual Content

Xenophon Zabulis[1,2], Jon Sporring[3], and Stelios C. Orphanoudakis[1,2]

[1] Foundation for Research and Technology – Hellas,
Vassilika Vouton, P.O. Box 1385,
GR-71110 Heraklion, Crete, Greece
{zabulis,orphanou}@ics.forth.gr
[2] Department of Computer Science,
University of Crete,
P.O. Box 1470,
GR-71409 Heraklion, Crete, Greece
[3] 3D-Lab, School of Dentistry,
University of Copenhagen,
Nørre Allé 20,
DK-2000 Copenhagen, Denmark
sporring@asters.lab3d.odont.ku.dk

Abstract. A study of local scale in images demonstrates that image features reside in different scales. Based on this observation a framework for the classification of features with respect to scale is proposed, linearly combining the visual impression of features at different scales. The proposed framework and a derived methodology are applied to typical feature extraction tasks, and in the generic case of estimating multiple scale feature distributions, as a tool for the identification of images of similar visual content. A possible formulation of queries for retrieving images by primitive visual content, taking scale into account, is also discussed.

1 Introduction

Structure in digital images resides somewhere between two scales, one defined by the sampling interval, and the other by image size. Thus, in order to focus attention at structures of different sizes, it is important to have the ability to select the appropriate scale. In general, scale selection finds application in almost all computer vision tasks such as image processing, feature detection, and image description. Therefore, it is central issue in the context of image retrieval by content.

[1] This research was carried out during Jon Sporring's term as a VIRGO postdoctoral fellow at ICS-FORTH and was funded in part by EC Contract No. ERBFMRX-CT96-0049 under the TMR Programme of the CEC. (http://www.ics.forth.gr/virgo)

R. Laurini (Ed.): VISUAL 2000, LNCS 1929, pp. 269–278, 2000.
Springer-Verlag Berlin Heidelberg 2000

It is possible and certainly useful to detect a single scale that matches the size of a structure. Nevertheless, several significant scales may be present at a single image point. Furthermore, the existing algorithms for singular scale selection are rather complicated and employ feature tracking at different scales [1,6], which may be intractable or at least unstable without a substantial number of scales used.

The application of feature extraction in the identification of images with similar primitive visual content is straightforward (but not simple), if context is neglected. The goal is to identify images that contain similar visual features or feature combinations, probably also taking into account their spatial arrangement. If features are classified with respect to their scale then more refined visual queries may be formulated. For example, a query could primarily aim at the retrieval of images of more abstract or dominant scene similarity, implying that feature comparison and matching should take place at coarse scales. Classifying features with respect to their scale should not only reduce similar feature retrieval time, but also support the formulation of more qualitative queries. In the same line of thought, feature scale may be used as a classification attribute in the perceptual grouping of image features into meaningful visual entities.

In the present work, Scale Summary Representation (SSR) and Scale Focusing (SF) are introduced, the first as a tool for representing feature information from all scales and the second as a classifier of features with respect to scale. The basic idea in SSR is the representation of information from all scales, into a single image, based on feature appearance intensity at each scale. SF smoothly restricts this process into a neighborhood of scales in order to extract features that reside only in these scales. Typically attention will be shifted to the dominant modes of scale observation, where the feature is best detected.

This paper is organized as follows: In Section 2, the theoretical definition of SSR and SF is defined along with details of how these tools may be applied to feature extraction. Section 3 presents experimental results from the domain of image feature extraction. In Section 4, the application of SSR to the estimation of feature distributions and image retrieval by content is discussed. Finally, conclusions and plans for future work are discussed in Section 5.

2   A Summary of Scale

Scale Summary Representation (SSR) is introduced as a method to summarize image features over scale for different classes of images. Such classes include the linear scale space (Gaussian smoothed images, see [6,12] for an overview), the families of angular content at various scales, etc.. The scale summarized image is defined as a weighted sum,

$$J(\boldsymbol{x}) = \sum_{\tau} w(\boldsymbol{x}, \tau) A[L(\boldsymbol{x}, \tau)], \tag{1}$$

$$\sum_{\tau} w(\boldsymbol{x}, \tau) = 1, \tag{2}$$

where $\tau = \log t$ is the logarithmic scale parameter, I the original image, A is a feature operator, L the image scale space (given by $L(x, \tau) = G(x, t) * I(x)$, with $G(x, t) = \exp(-|x|_2^2/(4t))/(\sqrt{4\pi t}))$, and w the probability of feature presence. The weight function w is henceforth called the scale selector. A simple scale selector for image edge related features (such as edges, orientation or corners) is the scale normalized square gradient $\mathrm{Grad}^2(x, \tau) = t(L_x^2(x, \tau) + L_y^2(x, \tau))$ [6]. Normalizing the sum yields the following scale selector:

$$w_{\mathrm{edge}}(x, \tau) = \frac{1}{k_{\mathrm{edge}}(x)} h\left(t\mathrm{Grad}^2(x, \tau)\right). \tag{3}$$

where the function $k_{\mathrm{edge}}(x) = \int_0^\infty h(t\mathrm{Grad}^2(x, \tau))\, d\tau$ is the normalizing function at each spatial point, and h is any strictly increasing function, chosen according to the nature of the feature detector. For simplicity, $h(x) = x$ is used throughout this paper. An example of a scale selector for intensity blob related features (such as gray level surfaces) is the scale-normalized Laplacian:

$$w_{\mathrm{blob}}(x, \tau) = \frac{1}{k_{\mathrm{blob}}(x)} h\left(t|L_{xx}(x, \tau) + L_{yy}(x, \tau)|\right), \tag{4}$$

where the normalization function is $k_{\mathrm{blob}}(x) = \int_0^\infty h(t|L_{xx}(x, \tau) + L_{yy}(x, \tau)|)\, d\tau$. Fig. 1 illustrates the SSR response of these two scale selectors, using them as the feature operator A in Eq. 1.

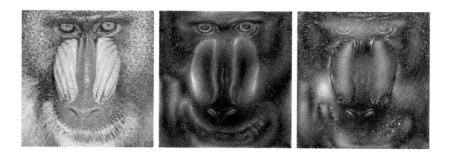

Fig. 1. An image (left) and the SSR scale selector response for edges (middle) and blobs (right).

For summarizing feature content restricted to a neighborhood of scales, Scale Focusing (SF) is introduced as the multiplication of the scale selector function with the Gaussian function at each pixel, as

$$w'_{m,s}(x, \tau) = \frac{1}{\sqrt{4\pi s(x)}} \exp\left(-\frac{(\tau - m(x))^2}{4s(x)}\right) \tag{5}$$

where m is the scale of interest and s the width of the scale neighborhood. A typical application of SF is the detection of the dominant scale at each pixel. In this case the Gaussian is centered at the maximum of the scale selector function.

Fig. 2 (top row) shows a synthetic image and the blob scale selector for the central dot (with the horizontal axis indicating scale). Three modes are observed corresponding to the three significant scales. The first three images of Fig. 2 (bottom row) illustrate the results of SF on these. The last image represents information from all scales in one image, using Eqs. (1) and (4). As observed, the response for fine scale dominates over the implicitly formed blobs at coarser scales. The importance of different scales may be defined by adjusting function h to reflect the bias.

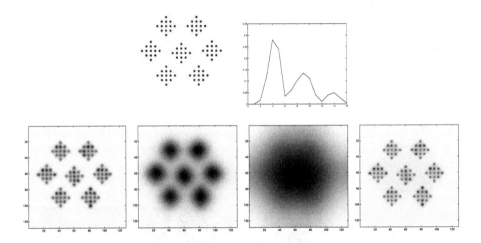

Fig. 2. An image and the blob scale selector for the image point corresponding to the central dot (top row). Three cases of SF and SSR of local scale for blob detection (bottom row, from left to right).

3   Feature Detection Applications

Summarizing feature detection information, carried out at all image scales, is expected to enhance the performance of methods operating at a fixed scale. The explicit selection of one scale for each image pixel is subject to computational instability because of noise and scale discretization, and typically yields unsmooth results.

The framework of SSR is applied to two categories of feature detection tasks: a) features derived from the image gradient, such as the detection of edges, linear feature orientation, and corners, and b) intensity blobs. In the latter category, SSR is applied to image smoothing as a representative case of blob detection.

3.1 Image Gradient Derived Features

By scale summarizing image gradients, a scaleless edge detection result is obtained, detecting edges at all scales. Using Eq. 3 as the feature operator A in Eq. 1 results in an image that scale summarizes edge information, as shown in Fig. 1 (middle image). To illustrate the effect of SF, as well as the discrimination among edges at different scales, Fig. 3 shows the results of SF on a fine and a coarse scale, where vertical edges are robustly detected at the higher scale. The last image shows the result of SSR.

Fig. 3. An image and the SF of its gradient on a fine and coarse scale. The last image shows the scale summarized gradients (from left to right). In the two middle images, when viewed in color, local orientation is linearly mapped to the color hues.

An important primitive visual feature is the local orientation of edges and linear features. A robust measure of local orientation is the direction of the eigenvector corresponding to the largest eigenvalue of the structure tensor [4]:

$$\mu(\boldsymbol{x}, \tau_1, \tau_2) = \begin{bmatrix} G(\boldsymbol{x}, \tau_2) * L_x(\boldsymbol{x}, \tau_1)^2 & G(\boldsymbol{x}, \tau_2) * L_x(\boldsymbol{x}, \tau_1)L_y(\boldsymbol{x}, \tau_1) \\ G(\boldsymbol{x}, \tau_2) * L_x(\boldsymbol{x}, \tau_1)L_y(\boldsymbol{x}, \tau_1) & G(\boldsymbol{x}, \tau_2) * L_y(\boldsymbol{x}, \tau_1)^2 \end{bmatrix} \quad (6)$$

The eigenvector corresponding to the largest eigenvalue will be robustly aligned along the gradient direction. As illustrated in Fig. 3, at fine scale a diagonal orientation dominates, while vertical dominates at a coarser scale. As scale increases, visual content with respect to orientation changes. Therefore, a full description of image content cannot be obtained by considering a single scale. In the two middle images local orientation is linearly mapped to the color hues. When viewed in grayscale, the scale focused gradient, upon which local orientation estimation is based, is shown.

Several measures exist for detecting corners in images. An overview of many of them may be found in [8]. Here the determinant divided by the trace of the structure tensor in Eq. (6) is used as the corner feature detector:

$$C(\boldsymbol{x}, \tau_1, \tau_2) = \frac{l_1(\boldsymbol{x}, \tau_1, \tau_2)l_2(\boldsymbol{x}, \tau_1, \tau_2)}{l_1(\boldsymbol{x}, \tau_1, \tau_2) + l_2(\boldsymbol{x}, \tau_1, \tau_2)} \quad (7)$$

where l_1, l_2 are the eigenvalues of $\mu(\boldsymbol{x}, \tau_1, \tau_2)$ and are functions are functions of $\boldsymbol{x}$, τ_1, and τ_2. A corner is an image feature, which depends on the existence of intensity or color edges and on the scale of investigation. For the computation, τ_1 is fixed at a fine scale and τ_2 is varied. Fig. 4 illustrates the detection of corners at a fine and a coarse scale, along with the SSR of corner information.

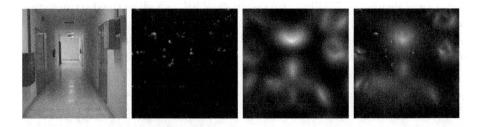

Fig. 4. An image and the detection of its corners at fine and coarse scale. The last image illustrates the scale summarized corner information (from left to right).

3.2   Blobs / Local Neighborhood Estimation

When summarizing blob information over scale, a scaleless blob detection result is obtained, detecting intensity regions at all scales. Using Eq. 4 as the feature operator A in Eq. 1 results in an image that summarizes blob information over all scales, as shown in Fig. 1 (right image). Estimation of features dependent on some intensity blob, is related to the size and content of that region. SSR, based on the blob detector, favors scales that adapt to image structure. This way the contribution of scales, where samples are taken from the neighborhood of interest, dominates over others. In this category of applications blob size is estimated by Eq. (4).

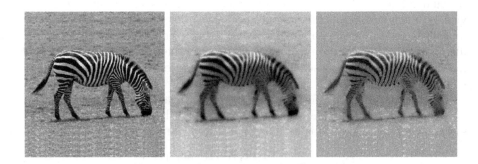

Fig. 5. Original image (left), SSR Smoothing (middle), Dominant SF Smoothing (right).

Fig. 5 demonstrates the application of SSR to image smoothing. The middle image illustrates the smoothing results obtained with SSR, using the local structure estimator given by Eq. (4). The image structure is retained, since SSR favors the contribution of those scales corresponding to local image structure. The right image illustrates SF at the dominant mode of the scale selector, applied at pixel. It is demontrated that the dominating blobs' spatial features are preserved while the variance of their luminosity content decreases.

Iterative application of SSR smoothing yields a scale space for which it can be proven that the minimum and maximum values are monotonic increasing and decreasing functions of n respectively. Qualitatively, the scale selector can be used to pick the next scale in linear scale-space. The family of images obtained with the iterative SSR or SF smoothing will decrease the variance of luminosity inside blobs while preserving their structure. Fig. 6 illustrates the evolution of an image over scale.

Fig. 6. Image evolution in scale space created by SSR smoothing (from left to right).

4   Studying Feature Distributions for Image Retrieval by Content

This section discusses the application of SSR and SF techniques in the generic study of spatial distributions of features and image retrieval by content. Through the multiscale estimation of feature distributions, a description of primitive visual content can be extracted in a statistically robust and stable way. SSR may be used for the dimemsionality reduction of the mutliscale feature distribution space, as well as for the normalization of similar distributions residing at different scales.

Estimation of local feature distributions is represented in a multidimensional scale space, where a local histogram is associated with each pixel neighborhood, for each image. Given the size s of some sampling neighborhood in an image and computing the local histogram $h_s(x)$ of some feature for each image element, the multidimensional image of local histograms can be obtained. For simplicity of representation, elements of each image are mapped into vectors of dimensionality equal to the number of bins in the histogram. By varying the size of the sampling area a scale space of such images images is defined as $H(x, \tau)$ [5], with τ indicating the scale index.

Summarizing the scale space into a single image of lower dimensionality is achieved with the use of Eq. (1), in the form of $J(x, \tau) = \sum_\tau w(x, \tau) H(x, \tau)$, while scale discrimination is achieved by focusing at the modes of the scale selector function which is chosen according to the feature sampled. The scale summarized data structure captures information from all scales with respect to the importance of each scale as defined by the scale selector. Similar feature distributions may be detected within the same image by clustering of distributions (using a suitable histogram distance function [3]).

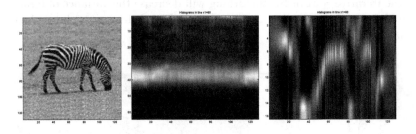

Fig. 7. An image and the visualization of the scale summarized feature distribution along the crentral line for luminosity (middle) and orientation (right).

The characterization of multiple feature distributions is a powerful que for identifying similar image regions in images. Fig. 7 (middle), shows the scale summarized histograms, vertically tiled, along the central image row. Notice that, due to the contribution of coarser scales and scale normalization, histograms from image column 30 to 110 are more similar, despite the local black / white variation (zebra stripes). Fig. 7 (right) illustrates the same information for the orientation feature. Distributions of small variance indicate a dominant direction, or parallelism. In the middle image of Fig. 8, intensity is inversely mapped with the variance of local orientation distribution, causing highly organized orientation distributions to stand out, as opposed to the right image, where luminosity is linearly mapped to the summarized gradient. Having in mind that visual content description is to serve the task of image retrieval by content, perceptual grouping rules [10] could also be incorporated into the clustering algorithm, so that clusters found would denote meaningful visual entities.

In an image retrieval by content application the system should search for clusters of similar distributions using multiple features. Judging the similarity of feature sets, in a perceptually correct and intuitive way, is critical for the appreciation of the retrieval result and an open issue [9]. Similarity of clusters may be judged afterwards by other criteria as well, such as spatial arrangement, size [11], etc.. Database queries may be formulated so that they would initially restrict search for similar distributions in coarse scales, where the image is abstract

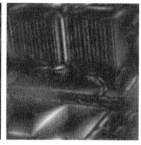

Fig. 8. An image (left) and the orientation distribution visualizations with using variance (middle) and scale summarized gradient (right). Color hue maps angular direction.

and dominant spatial features reside. Images that do not have a similar visual content at coarser scales may be disregarded, while the search could be continued for the rest of the images at a finer scale. This would result in a reduced computational cost for generic queries, under the assumption that large scales dominate image impression. Inversely, and depending on the field of application (e.g. texture similarity), detail may be primarily investigated by focusing at fine scale structure.

5   Conclusions - Future Work

In this work, scale was studied as a component of image feature detection and it was argued that task performance is enhanced if carried out in more than one scales. A framework was introduced for summarizing feature contributions from all scales, into a single scaleless representation, and a methodology was presented for the robust classification of features by scale of appearance.

The application of SSR and SF in the context of image retrieval by content was studied through the computation of feature distributions at multiple scales. The detection of dominating feature distributions gives a more qualitative description of an image's primitive visual content. Through scale classification of image features, queries may target more abstract scene content or image detail.

It is speculated that SSR and SF are compatible with neurophysiological results. Evidence of parallel multiscale analysis of structure is observed in primate vision, through spatial frequency selectivity in hypercolumns located in the striate cortex [7]. At a higher level, different spatial frequency responses are to be linearly (due to the computational nature of neurons) combined towards a single image perception. Focusing on certain scales for feature extraction is analogous to the attentional activation of winner-take-all networks [2].

Comparing the computational requirements of SSR and SF with scale space feature detection, it should be noted that the SSR approach does not require feature tracking, as employed in typical scale space methodologies [1,6]. The memory used by SSR techniques is simply proportional to the precision needed by the application. Computing multiscale feature information can be simultaneously parrallelized in two ways: (i) processing each scale's information independently (ii) processing separately local pixel information. Nevertheless, a serial methodology execution, of feature detection, in 256 x 256 image at eight different scales takes about half a minute, on an average personal computer.

Future work includes the study of color features, work on feature distribution clustering, the study of appropriate similarity measures, and the adoption of perceptual grouping rules for the formation of visual entities.

References

1. F. Bergholm. Edge focusing. *IEEE Transactions on Pattern Analysis and Machine Intelligence*, 9:726–741, 1987.
2. C. Koch D.K. Lee, L. Itti and J. Braun. Attention activates winner-take-all competition among visual filters. *Nature Neuroscience*, 2(4):375–381, 1999.
3. J. Puzicha et al. Empirical evaluation of dissimilarity measures for color and texture. In *Proceedings of the International Conference on Computer Vision*, 1999.
4. K. Kanatani. Detection of surface orientation and motion from texture by stereological technique. *Journal of Artificial Intelligence*, 23:213–237, 1984.
5. Jan J. Koenderink and Andrea J. van Doorn. The structure of locally orderless images. *International Journal of Computer Vision*, 31(2/3):159–168, 1999.
6. T. Lindeberg. *Scale-Space Theory in Computer Vision*. The Kluwer International Series in Engineering and Computer Science. Kluwer Academic Publishers, Boston, USA, 1994.
7. De Valois R. and De Valois K. *Spatial Vision*. Oxford Science Publications, Oxford, 1988.
8. Karl Rohr. Modelling and identification of characteristic intensity variations. *Image and Vision Computing*, 10(2):66–76, 1992.
9. S. Santini and R. Jain. Similarity matching. *IEEE Transactions on Pattern Analysis and Machine Intelligence*, 21(9):871–883, 1999.
10. S. Sarkar and K.L. Boyer. Perceptual organization in computer vision: A review and a proposal for a classificatory structure. *SMC*, 23:382–399, 1993.
11. J. R. Smith and S.-F. Chang. Integrated spatial and feature image query. *Multimedia System Journal. Springer-Verlag.*, 7(2):129–140, 1999.
12. J. Weickert, S. Ishikawa, and A. Imiya. On the history of Gaussian scale-space axiomatics. In Jon Sporring, Mads Nielsen, Luc Florack, and Peter Johansen, editors, *Gaussian Scale-Space Theory*, chapter 4, pages 45–59. Kluwer Academic Publishers, Dordrecht, The Netherlands, 1997.

Integrated Browsing and Searching of Large Image Collections [*]

Zoran Pečenović[1,2], Minh N. Do[1], Martin Vetterli[1], and Pearl Pu[2]

[1]Laboratory for Audio-Visual Communications
[2]Database/Human Computer Interaction Laboratory
Swiss Federal Institute of Technology Lausanne
CH-1015 Lausanne, Switzerland
{Zoran.Pecenovic, Minh.Do, Martin.Vetterli, Pearl.Pu}@epfl.ch

Abstract. Current image retrieval systems offer either an exploratory search method through browsing and navigation or a direct search method based on specific queries. Combining both of these methods in a uniform framework allows users to formulate queries more naturally, since they are already acquainted with the contents of the database and with the notion of matching the machine would use to return results. We propose a multi-modes and integrated image retrieval system that offers the user quick and effective previewing of the collection, intuitive and natural navigating to any parts of it, and query by example or composition for more specific and clearer retrieval goals.

1 Introduction

1.1 Searching and Browsing

The online availability of huge collections of images in digital form requires effective and efficient tools that allow users to search, browse and interact with such databases. There are two principal paradigms for retrieval from large image databases: direct search and browsing (or serendipitous discovery).

In the direct search environment, users present the system with a query (which can be an image, selected or constructed by painting and composition, or a keyword, or color characteristics of an image) and ask for the system to look for "more similar images" that match the query. One of the problems with direct search is that even with recursive query refinements and relevance feedback, users can be trapped in a small group of undesirable images. This fact arises from the typical large size of the search space and the local nature of any similarity measurements. Naturally, in this scheme, systems don't provide alternatives or images apparently not matching the user submitted query, thus forcing the user to slowly explore a small vicinity of the initial query. An additional problem is the construction of queries themselves as it can prove to be non-trivial for many users.

---

[*] This work was supported by the Swiss National Fund for Scientific Research, Grant no. 21-52439.97.

R. Laurini (Ed.): VISUAL 2000, LNCS 1929, pp. 279–289, 2000.
Springer-Verlag Berlin Heidelberg 2000

At the beginning of his interaction with an Image Retrieval System (IRS), the user is unable to know all of the data contained in the database, nor its structuring. Furthermore s/he can not know whether the desired type of data is present in the collection at all. A similar scenario occurs when a novice user starts using the system and feels insecure about the system's ability to evaluate similarity, or when the desired information is not clearly defined in the user's mind. In these cases, the browsing environment allows users to start from an overview of the collection and iteratively "zoom in" on the interesting parts until they can locate the desired image. Furthermore, the gathered images during the browsing process can be used as initial seed images to be modified into queries for finer retrieval using the search tools.

While the search environment is more popular and is extensively used in conventional retrieval systems, notably for *text retrieval*, the situation could be different for *image retrieval*. The reason lies in the fact that unlike in the text case where document relevance is difficult for users to grasp quickly, the relevance of an image to a specific query can be judged almost at a glance. Hence browsing and searching are complementary and necessary tools for effective image retrieval systems. In addition they share and rely on the major components of image retrieval systems: "good" extracted features from images and "good" similarity measurement between two images. While these two tasks are still open problems for study, we focus here on how to enhance the usability of underlying features and measurements and how to add an extra layer of interaction with image databases integrating both search and browse paradigms.

The main problem with image browsing is how to produce a visualization of the whole collection (or part of it) and how to provide an effective mechanism to navigate through that image database. One way of constructing the visualizing environments is to project images into a two or three-dimensional space where similar images are close to each other [7]. Experiments show that users preferred to view retrieved results in 2-D maps rather than in ranked lists by similarity in a "reading-order" where adjacency among retrieved images has little meaning. The operations on this projection map via continuously zooming and panning provide users with maximum freedom in navigating through the collection. However, without structure this becomes a burden to view and to display. Some systems proposed to organize images into hierarchical structures like self-organizing maps [5] or pyramids [1]. However in those systems, navigation is restricted to only "discrete" steps since images are positioned in tree-structured grids.

1.2   System Overview and Paper Organization

In this paper we will present our Content-based Image Retrieval and Consultation User System (CIRCUS), which offers the best from both worlds with seamless switching between modes. The main idea behind our approach is that dynamic and interactive visualizations of the data, *combined* with direct searching by queries, will help the user retrieve the desired information.

The typical scenario for a user of CIRCUS is the following: first the user would consult the tree structure for the overview of the image collection. For any particular interesting region they can use the browsing facility to pan or zoom in for more detail and see more images around that region. Finally, those images can be used as examples or can be modified to present as a new query in the search mode. In addition our system allows the incorporation of user's relevance feedback to adjust the similarity effectiveness.

In the next section, we describe the underlying building blocks of our system. Section 3 describes the visual interface taking advantage of those structures together with some examples. Section 4 provides some evaluation results together with discussion and outlook.

2   Underlying Building Blocks

The following computational tasks are performed *off-line* on image databases:

1. Extraction of d features from each of the n images. Those features allow similarity measurements between images to be computed.
2. Construction of a visual map of the image collection by projecting n feature vectors from $\mathbb{R}^d$ into 2-D spaces.
3. Hierarchical clustering of images and assigning representative images to result clusters.

For the completeness, we now briefly describe each of those building blocks.

2.1   Feature Extraction and Similarity Measurements

Our system is based on color features via color histograms [10] and moments [9], texture features via energies of the wavelet decomposition [8], and shape features via wavelet maxima moments [2]. Those features are normalized into a common range using deviations from medians of each component. If we denote the j-th feature from the i-th image by $\tilde{x}_i^j$ and n is the number of the images in the database then the normalization is performed by computing

$$x_i^j = \frac{\tilde{x}_i^j - m^j}{s^j},\tag{1}$$

where m^j is the median of $\{\tilde{x}_1^j, \tilde{x}_2^j, \ldots, \tilde{x}_n^j\}$ and $s^j = \frac{1}{n}\sum_{i=1}^{n}|\tilde{x}_i^j - m^j|$. Other popular normalizations replace m^j and s^j by the mean and standard deviation of the feature j, respectively. However those are known to be more affected by *outliers* — the features which due to uncontrollable causes deviate from the normal range.

Once the features are normalized, Euclidean distances on $\mathbf{x}_i$; $i = 1, 2, \ldots, n$ are used to estimate the dissimilarity between images.

2.2   Multivariate Data Projection

The purpose of this step is to construct a visualizable map of images so that adjacent images are similar. Given images can be indexed by feature vectors in a high dimensional space, this task amounts to a multivariate data projection. There are many methods for accomplishing this including: Principal Component Analysis (PCA), Sammon's projection (SP), and multidimensional scaling [4]. The SP is an non-linear projection method and is shown to be more adaptive to complex data sets so it is chosen in our system.

Given a set of n vectors $X = \{x_1, x_2, \ldots, x_n\}$ in $\mathbb{R}^d$, Sammon's method attempts to find a set $Y = \{y_1, y_2, \ldots, y_n\}$ in a lower dimensional projected space $\mathbb{R}^p$ (typically $p = 2$) such that the distance between pairs of vectors in X are preserved in their images in Y. Let us denote d_{ij}^* the Euclidean distances between x_i, x_j in the original space and d_{ij} the distance between their images y_i, y_j in the projected space. Sammon's algorithm tries to minimize the following error term:

$$E(Y) = \frac{1}{\sum_{i<j} d_{ij}^*} \sum_{i<j} \frac{(d_{ij}^* - d_{ij})^2}{d_{ij}^*} \tag{2}$$

Minimization of $E(Y)$ is an unconstrained optimization problem of $n \cdot p$ variables y_i^j ($i = 1, \ldots, n$; $j = 1, 2, \ldots, p$). Sammon's algorithm uses a gradient descent method to reconfigure Y so as to minimize $E(Y)$ in an iterative fashion.

One problem with the original SP is that it does not offer the generalization ability. When new images are inserted into the database, determining their positions in the existing map would require a re-run of the SP for the whole collection! For this, [6] proposed an interesting solution by modeling Sammon's projection using neural networks. In their model, the gradient descent optimization is converted into a back-propagation training.

Another problem with Sammon's projection is the large number of variables to optimize so that a good initial configuration is required to speed up convergence and to avoid local minima. To facilitate this, we first use a PCA projection map (which is linear transformation and can be computed relatively fast) as an initial configuration and then apply Sammon's iterations to refine the map.

2.3   Image Clustering

With the result of projection of feature sets into a 2-D space, images can be positioned in a visualization map. Our interface allows the user to continuously pan across this plane and zoom in on any particular regions (see Sec. 3.2). However with large collections, actual images only become visible when the user zooms in on a very small part of the map. Therefore we create an extra facility to organize images into hierarchical tree-structures.

To accomplish this we recursively cluster images in the higher dimensional *feature space* into regions that contain similar images. For each found region, we pick a representative image that is closest to the centroid of the cluster. This tree structure helps users efficiently navigate through the image collection.

At each level, the clustering step is done via a *K-means* algorithm with successive splitting of the centroids as in the LBG vector quantization [3]. Furthermore we enforce the constructed tree to be balanced by adding a heuristic constraint on the size of the clusters [1].

3 Interactive Visualization for Searching & Browsing

As hinted in the introduction, and relying upon the available retrieval and data structuring methods described in the previous section, we now present an integrated browsing & searching user interface.

3.1 The Searching Mode

The basic user interface of CIRCUS provides several query construction mechanisms along with several session management and data marking utilities. The primary query paradigm in most IRS's is the query by example — more complex scenarios require more complex queries. Our current experimental system can cope with the query types detailed below.

Query by Example (QbE) The user selects several example images (positive and negative for accommodating relevance feedback) and asks the system to retrieve similar ones (see Fig. 3 in Sec. 3.3).

Query by Text (QbT) The user can also specify keyword annotation either required to be present in the image or simply as additional desired property of the result. This type of query can be executed at any time by using the adequate field in the main tool-bar.

Query by Color (QbC) As a third possibility s/he can also construct a query specifying the color properties of the sought images, like proportions and general hues (see Fig. 1 below).

Query by Painting (QbP) Using the final and most flexible query tool, s/he can modify existing images or sketch new ones using elementary drawing, coloring and montage tools for copying & pasting. This new image can then be used as the example for a QbE (see Fig. 1 below).

Combined Query (CQ) Finally a query can be constructed using any combination of the above tools through operators familiar to most users like "OR", "AND" & "AND NOT". These queries are processed if possible jointly, if not then separately, and the results combined by the IRS into a single set.

In the searching mode, the user can operate with a set of tools to express the desired properties of the result. It is primarily adapted to users with a good knowledge of both the system and the underlying collection. Furthermore users must have a clear idea of what is being searched for, so as to express their needs in a precise way. The direct search mode is not adequate for explaining to the user the notion of similarity and match implemented in the IRS. Starting from these limitations we introduced the browsing mode[1] which is detailed below.

---

[1] A simple browsing of the collections by random samples is also available as part of the direct-search mode.

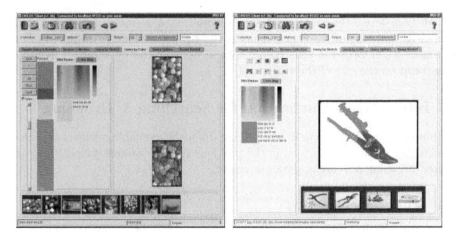

Fig. 1. The elementary query construction tools and some results. Left: (QbC). The proportion of several colors (picked from a palette or from existing images) was specified by dragging the colors in the left vertical area, at the bottom of the screen the user sees dynamically several results. Right: (QbP). The drawing area shows a simple sketch, with the user painting the pliers handles in a different color. Again a couple of best matches are shown below the drawing area, as the user draws.

3.2   The Browsing Mode

As a solution to the above expressed concerns, we argue that a fully interactive *real-time* display of a hierarchically clustered collection, projected into a two dimensional space can bridge the gap between the user and the system. By doing this we enhance the user's confidence, query specification ability and degree of acquaintance to the system. The human perceptual system offers a very high bandwidth channel for communication, and today the computing power on everyone's desktop allows for un-precedented possibilities for interaction. The demonstrated system runs as a JAVA application/applet on a Pentium II, 128Mb RAM system.

Based on the pre-computed results of the feature projection and hierarchical clustering steps detailed in Sec. 2, we display the 2-D browsable space in which images are presented using a semantic multi-resolution approach (Fig. 2). When examining the hierarchy at any level, the users see the representative images of each cluster displayed at the projection of the cluster centroid. Optionally several sub-levels can be displayed along with currently examined level; these sub-clusters are then rendered in a smaller size than their parents. The users can then zoom in, or pan around the display to bringing more images into focus or enlarging the images.

The display is linked with a progressive multi-resolution coding of the images, allowing the display of detail only when it becomes really necessary. It is also coupled with a semantic zoom both for single images and for clusters, i.e. when the zoom level becomes large that the images' symbolic annotation and meta-

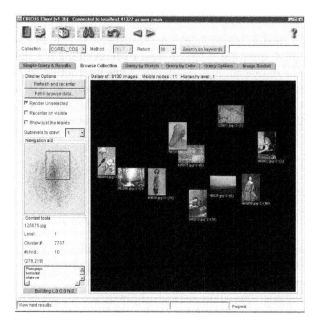

The user is descending the hierarchy tree and has reached an interesting cluster. By panning around s/he can view the cluster's neighborhood. By clicking on an image s/he can descend to the next level of hierarchy, or by clicking outside of an image climb to the parent level. All transitions from one view to an other are animated, by automatic panning and zooming.

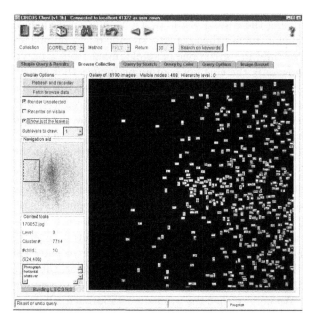

The user is examining the entire collection at a given level of the hierarchy (leaf level in this case). S/he can navigate through a galaxy, and — as far as the system resources permit it — images are rendered as thumbnails, if their number increases too much the system shows them as colored dots.

Fig. 2. Browsing the collection. In each example, the navigation aid — the overview map on the left with a small box indicating the current viewed region — helps the user know in which part of the space s/he is.

data becomes visible, and as the user moves in closer to a cluster, its sub-levels are automatically displayed. By clicking on an image, the display centers around it and if the image represents a cluster, it's sub-clusters are displayed. This multi-resolution scheme ensures for fast updating of the display, without ruling out the users ability to access any of the data available. At all ties, while interacting with the main display canvas, a smaller version of the entire space is represented in a side view with only the currently visible area highlighted. Consulting this view, the user can always know what part of the search space s/he is examining.

3.3   Seamless Integration

The integration of the searching mode with the browsing mode is achieved mainly through two mechanisms: first by a tight coupling of the browsing display with the query results, and second by direct manipulation and query specification in browsing mode. These two mechanisms allow users to browse and to perform different direct searches without ever leaving the browsing mode screen.

The first mechanism actually allows users to filter out the information displayed in the galaxy display using the results of the previous query or sequence of previous queries. For example if the user has issued a specific query on images containing the keyword "horse" and has given one example image from a previous search, the galaxy will show only the clusters containing images that satisfy those queries. The other images will be hidden (or grayed out). Thus iteratively, after specifying several queries, the size of the result set will be reduced and the display successively pruned of the undesired images and narrowed down to the desired ones. Figure 3 illustrates this principle by showing the restricted set of images returned by the described query as well as the QbE results in the linear-list "reading order" interface correspondingly.

The second mechanism allows users to specify new query constraints and new queries, directly from the galaxy display. For instance if the user right-clicks on an image in the display, a context-dependent menu allows him to launch a QbE on that image. Similarly, if the image is displayed with enough detail, a set of drawing tools appears in the context tools panel, allowing the user to paint directly in the galaxy display. This is depicted in Fig. 4. At any moment, the user can enter additional textual information for retrieving other images or restricting the already returned results. We believe that this *immersive* approach, allowing the user to navigate a space where the images "live" grouped by similarity, interact with them to specify new queries and immediately perceive the implications of his actions on the results is essential in an effective interactive IRS. Further allowing the user to change his mind, experiment "what-if" scenarios, and examine the results in a uniformly employed image space, helps her/im construct more intelligent future queries.

Viewing the results of a query by example in a ranked list displayed in "reading-order".

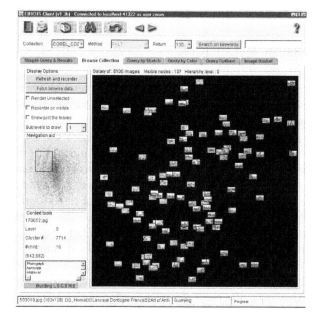

The same results displayed in the browsing view.

The actual query could have been initiated and can be refined from any of the two displays.

Fig. 3. Tight coupling of the browsing and searching facilities.

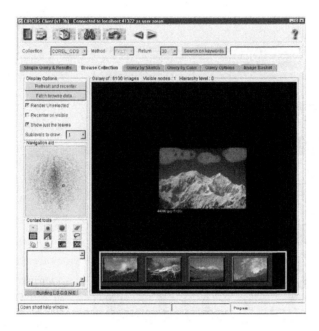

Fig. 4. Second integration mechanism. The user has zoomed in far enough to see only one image on the screen, the context tools then allow him to paint some "clouds" on the top of the original image, and the system responds with some candidate results.

4   Evaluation, Discussion & Outlook

Although we could not perform full scale usability testing, we did perform some experiments with several novice (4) and occasional users (2). We outline below some of the major conclusions.

In all of our experiments, the users had received a description of the task to perform and were observed during execution. Their comments and reactions were recorded. The major difficulty that was revealed was the discovery of the functionality (navigation, coupling) without prior explanation. Once acquainted with the controls, most users found the navigation natural and all of them found it beneficial to their search task. The more experienced users found the benefit to be lesser; justifying it by claiming that they already were familiar with the system's reactions and the database. This is by no means a surprise; it confirms our assumptions in Sec. 1.1. The novice users, on the other hand, grasped the idea of similarity, judging it somehow artificial (as one would expect). They greatly appreciated the synthetic overview the system was giving of the database comparing it to category-hierarchy search engines in text retrieval. Due to the lack of available testers and clear tasks associated with ground truth results, we could not perform comparative tests to measure the user performance increase when using the integrated browsing and searching mode. The information need clarification aspect we claim could thus not be investigated.

In brief, we have shown a working integrated system that enhances the user's ability to interact with an image retrieval engine. The two principal retrieval modes: searching and browsing have been merged into a seamless interaction model. The user thus gains insight in the organization of a large collection and can clarify his information needs and formulate more precise queries. The semantic navigation through a hierarchical representation of the data and the multi-resolution display (both for the image "signals" and their meta-data) enhance simultaneously the effectiveness and the speed of our system. The bottom line is that user satisfaction and ability to communicate with the machine are drastically enhanced.

We plan to solve some issues still pending, namely: (a) the enhancement of the map generation algorithms so as to accommodate projections and assignments of new images not yet in the collection; (b) increase the coupling between the search and browse modes, especially by integrating textual data into the browsing process; (c) enhance the multi-resolution rendering of the system, in the framework of slow communication channels between the IRS and the client applet.

References

[1] J. Chen, C.A. Bouman, and J.C. Dalton. Similarity pyramids for browsing and organization of large image databases. In *Proc. of SPIE/IS&T Conf. on Human Vision and Electronic Imaging III*, volume 3299, pages 563–575, 1998.

[2] M. Do, S. Ayer, and M. Vetterli. Invariant image retrieval using wavelet maxima moment. In *Proc. of 3rd Int. Conf. in Visual Information and Information Systems*, pages 451–458, 1999.

[3] A. Gersho and R. M. Gray. *Vector Quantization and Signal Compression*. Kluwer Academic Publishers, Boston, MA, 1992.

[4] A. K. Jain and R. C. Dubes. *Algorithms for Clustering Data*. Prentice-Hall, 1988.

[5] J. Laaksonen, M. Koskela, and E. Oja. Content-based image retrieval using self-organizing maps. In *Proc. of 3rd Int. Conf. in Visual Information and Information Systems*, pages 541–548, 1999.

[6] J. Mao and A. K. Jain. Artificial neural networks for feature extraction and multivariate data projection. *IEEE Trans. on Neural Networks*, 6:296–317, March 1995.

[7] Y. Musha, Y. Mori, A. Hiroike, and A. Sugimoto. An interface for visualizing feature space in image retrieval. In *Machine Vision and Applications*, pages 447–450, 1998.

[8] J. R. Smith and S.-F. Chang. Transform features for texture classification and discrimination in large image databases. In *Proc. of IEEE Int. Conf. on Image Processing*, 1994.

[9] M. Stricker and M. Orengo. Similarity of color images. In *Storage and Retrieval for Image and Video Databases III*, volume 2420 of *SPIE*, pages 381–392, 1995.

[10] M. Swain and D. Ballard. Color indexing. *Int. Journal of Computer Vision*, vol. 7(1), 1991.

A Rich Get Richer Strategy for Content-Based Image Retrieval

Lijuan Duan[1], Wen Gao, and Jiyong Ma

Institute of Computing Technology, Chinese Academy of Sciences,
Beijing, 100080 , China
Email: {ljduan, wgao, jyma}@ict.ac.cn

Abstract. A novel relevance feedback approach to image retrieval, Rich Get Richer (RGR) Strategy, is proposed in this paper. It is based on the general framework of Bayesian inference in statistics. The user's feedback information is propagated into the retrieval process step by step. The more promising images are emphasized by the Rich Get Richer (RGR) Strategy. On the contrary, the less promising ones are de-emphasized. The experimental results show that the proposed approach can capture the user's information need more precisely. By using RGR, the average precision improves from 5 to 20% for each interaction.

1 Introduction

The rapid development of WWW, the dramatically falling cost of data storage and the advancing in coding technology are generating a large amount of multimedia information and making information retrieval difficult and time-consuming. Consequently, there is an increasing requirement for advanced search techniques for multimedia information retrieval, especially for image retrieval [1-7].

In the past few years, content-based image retrieval (CBIR) has been a very active research area [1-7] and many CBIR systems have been developed [3-11]. At the early stage of CBIR, researches are focused primarily on exploring various feature representations, hoping to find a "best" representation for each visual feature. For example, for texture features, many representations have been proposed, including MRSAR, DCT, Wavelets, Tamura, Gabor filter, etc [4]. The corresponding system design strategy for early CBIR systems is as following. Firstly, each image is represented using a set of selected features (based on some definitions of "best features" or "most suitable for query"). Secondly, during the retrieval process, the user provides a query image or a set of feature values representing the query image and specifies a weight for each feature to assess the similarity between the query image and each image in the database. Finally, Based on the selected features and specified weights, the retrieval system tries to find images similar to the user's query.

However, the information that people tend to use in formulating their queries is usually related to high-level semantics, such as "cars", "sunset", and "birds". The

---

[1] The work reported in the paper was performed while the author was an intern at Microsoft Research China, Feb.-Apr. 2000.

R. Laurini (Ed.): VISUAL 2000, LNCS 1929, pp. 290-299, 2000.

features (color, texture, shape, etc.) and their associated weights used in assessing image similarity can not effectively model high-level concepts and user's subjective perception [4]. To resolve this problem, researchers have focused on relevance feedback. Relevance feedback is a powerful technique used in traditional text-based information retrieval systems. It is a process of automatically adjusting an existing query using the information fed back by the user about the relevance of previously retrieved objects such that the adjusted query is a better approximation to the user's information need [4]. First, the user submits a query and the system finds and displays a set of images relevant to the query. The user then informs the system of which images are relevant or irrelevant to the query. Like in text-based retrieval systems, most relevance feedback approaches focus on adaptively refining the user's query, ignoring histories of the previous selections of the user. The Rich Get Richer (RGR) strategy for relevance feedback proposed in this paper is based on Bayesian inference. It relies on belief propagation to integrate feedback provided by the user over a retrieval process. The user's feedback information is propagated into the retrieval process step by step and gradually the RGR approach gets more and more images relevant to the query.

The paper is organized as follows. Section 2 surveys the related work. Section 3 describes the basic framework and the related theorems. Section 4 describes the proposed method, Rich Get Richer strategy. Experimental results and conclusion are given in section 5 and section 6 respectively.

2 Related work

Previous researches on relevance feedback can be grouped into four categories: retrieval based on interactive image database annotation, retrieval based on modifying the query vector or the distance metric, retrieval based on updating image groups, and retrieval based on updating the probability distribution of the database. The interactive image database annotation originates from keyword annotation, which is a traditional information retrieval paradigm. Picard [12] proposed this technique for multimedia database annotation in 1995. Based on the examples provided by the user, the system tries to annotate similar image regions both within the image and across the images. Cox [13] used hidden annotation method to extend the image retrieval system PicHunter based on low-level features (such as color content, contrast, brightness, edge content, etc.). 134 semantic attributes were regarded as a boolean vector, combined with 18 low-level feature, and the search time was reduced by 28%-32%. However, we know that one person's annotation may not suit another person's perception, and the rich content in images could not be represented by several words exactly. Therefore, the effectiveness of the annotation method is limited.

To make the MIR system truly adaptive to different users, Rui et al. [3,4] and Gevers [14] applied the vector model used in text information retrieval to image retrieval. Based on the images that the user specified as being either relevant or irrelevant, the query feature vector is modified such that bigger weights are placed on the relevant terms and smaller weights are placed on irrelevant terms. This method has the effect of modifying the query vector closer to the cluster of positive examples and farther way from the negative examples. MARS designed by Rui et al. [3,4] introduced a re-weighting technique to estimate the ideal query parameters in image retrieval. The MinderReader system designed by Ishikawa [5] employed a more vigorous estimation method than MARS. Rui et al. [6] integrated the two methods into CBIR in 1999.

The third approach is based on updating image groups. The system designed by Lee et al. [7] is initialized by clustering images based on low-level image features. The correlation between two image clusters is then set equal to the inverse of the distance between the centroids of the two clusters. Through the selection of positive and negative examples for a given query, the semantic relationships between images are captured and embedded into the system by splitting/merging image clusters and updating the correlation matrix. Similar images are then retrieved based on the result of image clustering and the correlation matrix. Wood [15] employed the Learning Vector Quantization (LVQ) algorithm to cluster the images based on user's feedback. In this approach, the set of images closest to the interested image is selected and reclassified by the user. This iterative refinement continues until the user is satisfied with the results.

The fourth retrieval method is based on updating the probability distribution of the database. Cox [16] applied Bayesian learning to search target images. The goal of this approach proposed by Vasconcelos [17] is to minimize the probability of retrieval error. It uses Bayesian classifier as the following

$$g*(x) = \operatorname*{argmax}_i p(\omega_i | x) \tag{1}$$

where x is a sample provided by the user. ω_i is i^{th} class. $p(x|\omega_i)$ is class conditional probability density of ith class and $p(\omega_i)$ is the prior probability for i^{th} class.

When we have a sequence of t queries $\{x_1,......, x_t\}$ instead of a single query x, where t is time stamp. Bayesian rule is as following equation [17]

$$g*(x) = \operatorname*{argmax}_i p(\omega_i | x_1, x_2, ...x_{t-1}, x_t)$$

$$= \operatorname*{argmax}_i p(x_t | \omega_i, x_1, x_2, ...x_{t-1}) p(\omega_i | x_1, x_2, ...x_{t-1})$$

$$= \operatorname*{argmax}_i p(x_t | \omega_i) p(\omega_i | x_1, x_2, ...x_{t-1}) \tag{2}$$

It can be seen from Eq. 2 that the system's beliefs about the user's interests at time $t-1$ simply become the prior beliefs for time t. By taking logarithms and solving for the recursion, Eq.2 is written as the following [17]

$$g*(x) = \operatorname*{argmax}_i \{ \sum_{k=0}^{t-1} \log p(x_{t-k} | \omega_i) + \log p(\omega_i) \} \tag{3}$$

It is obvious that for a larger t the contribution of the new data provided by the user is relatively smaller compared to other terms. To avoid this limitation of the belief propagation mechanism as depicted by Eq.3, a decay factor α_{t-k} is introduced to penalizing older terms, and the Eq.3 becomes [17]

$$g*(x) = \underset{i}{\operatorname{argmax}} \{ \sum_{k=0}^{t-1} _{t\,k} \log p(x_{t\,k}| _i) + _0 \log p(_i) \} \tag{4}$$

The belief propagation mechanism proposed by Vasconcelos is based on weighting the *class conditional probabilities* of the sequence of t queries $\{x_1,......, x_t\}$, while the belief propagation mechanism proposed in this paper is based on Bayesian inference for each interaction. Instead of using of the *class conditional probabilities* of the sequence of t queries $\{x_1,......, x_t\}$, posterior probabilities of each image is updated using Bayesian rule, the difference between our approach proposed in this paper and that proposed by Vasconcelos is as follows:

- the class conditional densities $p(x| _i)$ in Vasconcelos's approach are not changed during the retrieval process, while they are updated continuously during the retrieval process in our approach.
- the belief propagation mechanism of this approach is different from that as shown Eq.4. Positive and negative examples are carefully chosen during each step of interactions between a user and the system. Two classes are trained by using the training samples, one for positive examples, the other for negative examples. Samples in the image database are classified according to the two training models. Posterior probabilities of image samples at the step t-1 are used as the prior probabilities at the step t. The detailed approach is shown in section 3 and section 4.

3 Basic Framework

In this section, we describe a general relevance feedback framework. The standard interaction paradigm for CBIR is so-called "query by example". First, the user provides the system with a query image, and the system retrieves images that are visually similar to the example. Second, the user informs the system which images are relevant or irrelevant to the query. Third, the system refines the query according to user's interaction, and returns reasonably accurate results. Repeat the last two steps, until the user is satisfied with the results. The problem can be formulated as classification. Two classes are trained by using the training samples, one for positive examples, the other for negative examples. Samples in the image database are classified according to the two training models. Posterior probabilities of image samples at the step is

$$p(^+|x) = \frac{p(x| ^+)p(^+)}{p(x| ^+)p(^+) + p(x|)p( )} \tag{5}$$

$$p(|x) = 1 - p(^+|x) \tag{6}$$

where x is an image in image database,   repesent two types of classes, one for positive examples, which are probably near to the query image, the other for negative examples, which are dissimilar to the query image. $p(x| \quad)$ are the two models trained by the positive examples and negative examples given by user. $p(\quad^+)$ is the prior probability of $^+$ class, $p(\quad)$ is the prior probability of   class. After each interaction, $p(\quad |x)$ are computed firstly, then images are sorted according to $p(\quad |x)$.

$p(\quad^+|x)$ and $p(\quad |x)$ are changed in feedback image retrieval system because of different examples provided by the user at different steps.

Due to the dynamic characteristic of feedback retrieval system, $p(\quad^+)$ and $p(\quad)$ are also changed after each interaction. We can get the prior probability $p(\quad)$ at time t according to user's   interaction at time t 1. Replacing $p(\quad)$ with $p(\quad(t))$, $p(\quad |x)$ with $p(\quad(t)|x)$ and $p(x| \quad)$ with $p(x| \quad(t))$, Eq.5 now becomes:

$$p(\quad^+(t)|x) = \frac{p(x| \quad^+(t))p(\quad^+(t))}{p(x| \quad^+(t))p(\quad^+(t)) + p(x| \quad(t))p(\quad(t))} \tag{7}$$

$$p(\quad(t)|x) = 1 \quad p(\quad^+(t)|x) \tag{8}$$

Eq.7 represents the posterior probability of image x at time t.

4 Rich Get Richer Strategy

In the preceding section, we have explained the basic framework of Bayesian inference. In the retrieval process, Eq.7 is not directly used to compute the posterior probability of a given image. Rich get Richer Strategy is proposed in this paper. Assume that responses of user are consistent during the feedback process, which means if an image is selected as a positive example, in the later interaction process, it should not be marked as a negative example. According to the above assumption, the larger the similarity of an image to positive examples in preceding interaction is, the larger the similarity of the image to positive examples in current interaction be. To emphasize the more promising images and de-emphasize the less promising ones, the Rich Get Richer (RGR) Strategy is proposed as the following.

The prior probability $p(\quad^+(t))$ in Eq.7 at time t is replaced with $p(\quad^+(t \quad 1)|x)$ to emphasize the more promising images (which have larger likelihood). Accordingly, the less promising (which have lower likelihood) images are de-emphasized. The Eq.7 becomes

$$p(\omega^+(t)|x) = \frac{p(x|\omega^+(t))p(\omega^+(t-1)|x)}{p(x|\omega^+(t))p(\omega^+(t-1)|x) + p(x|\omega^-(t))p(\omega^-(t-1)|x)} \tag{9}$$

Similar to the discussion about $p(\omega^+(t)|x)$, the posterior probability $p(\omega^-(t)|x)$ can be gotten as

$$p(\omega^-(t)|x) = 1 - p(\omega^+(t)|x) \tag{10}$$

In summary, the more promising images are emphasized and the less promising images are de-emphasized using Eq.9.

The detailed procedure based on the above discussion is summarized as the following.

(1) Give a query image q, and compute the similarity between it and other images. The similarity is obtained based on low-level features, and it is computed from weighting of six kinds of feature representations (color histogram, color coherence and color moments for color feature, MRSAR, Tamura coarseness histogram and directionality for texture feature). The similarity is used to approximate the class conditional probability density as the following

$$p(x|\omega^+(1)) = similarity(x,q) \tag{11}$$

For most feedback retrieval system, user doesn't provide negative examples at the first query. In the case of absence of negative examples at this time, $p(x|\omega^-(1))$ can be gotten as the following.

$$p(x|\omega^-(1)) = 1 - p(x|\omega^+(1)) \tag{12}$$

In general, we don't know which image the user is interested in and which images the user is not interested in before a query. In the absence of any prior information, it is assumed that $p(\omega^+(1)) = p(\omega^-(1)) = 0.5$. Therefore, $p(\omega^+(1)|x)) = similarity(x,q)$, and $p(\omega^-(1)|x) = 1 - p(\omega^+(1)|x)$.

(2) Rank the images by $p(\omega^+(t)|x)$, and display the images.

(3) After each interaction, the user provides positive examples and negative examples. Then the following computation is taken.
Firstly, compute $p(x|\omega^+(t))$ and $p(x|\omega^-(t))$, where $p(x|\omega^+(t)) = similarity(x,x_+)$, x_+ is the centroid of positive examples at time t; and $p(x|\omega^-(t)) = similarity(x,x_-)$, x_- is the centroid of negative examples at time t. If the user only provides positive or negative examples in an interaction, there is no new x_+ or x_-. The old x_+ or x_- is used in the current interaction.
Then, compute $p(\omega^+(t)|x)$ according to Eq.9.

(4) Repeat 2 to 3, until the user is satisfied with the retrieved results.

5 Experiment

We have implemented an image retrieval system based on the proposed strategy. This section presents the experiment results.

Tests are performed on commercial database Corel Gallery. It contains 1,000,000 images, being classified into many semantic groups. We create two test databases by randomly select images from Corel Gallery. One of it contains 800 images, which is composed of 32 categories of Corel Photographs (25 images in each category). The other contains 10,000 images, which is composed of 100 categories of Corel Photographs (100 images in each category).

The general way of performing subjective tests is to ask the user to evaluate the retrieval system subjectively. The user can browse through image database. Once the user finds an image of interest, that image is submitted as a query. Alternatively, the user may also submit images outside the database as a query. In Fig. 1, the query image is displayed at the upper left corner, and the best 19 retrieved images are displayed. Before any feedback, several "dogs" appear in the retrieval results. In the Fig. 2, the user gives positive examples and negative examples. After the user feeds back his interest in "model", more "models" are returned in next interaction (Fig. 3)

Fig. 1. Initial retrieval results   **Fig. 2.** User Interaction

Fig. 3. Retrieval results after the relevance feedback

Although we assume that the responses of user are consistent during the feedback process, the interaction processes are practically independent for the user. Even it is allowed that an image is selected as a positive example in the last interaction process, and marked as a negative example in next interaction process. RGR can continuously work, only converge speed will be decreased.

To evaluate the performance and the rate of convergence, a more complete experiment was carried out using the categories from the Corel database as the ground truth. 430 query images and 500 query images were respectively selected from each database. For each of these query images, 100 iterations of user-and–system interaction were carried out. In each interaction, the system examined the N (N=25 for first Database, N=100 for second database) most correlated images to the query images, and regarded them as positive examples, otherwise, as negative examples. The user's relevance feedback was automatically provided based on the ground truth. In other words, images from the same category as the query image are considered to be relevant, while images from different categories are considered to be irrelevant. The performance of the system was evaluated by its average precision in retrieving relevant images for each interaction. Precision is defined to be the ratio of the number of retrieved relevant images to the total number of examined images at each interaction.

In order to isolate the contribution of RGR, the comparison was performed against using RGR (Eq.9) and NO-RGR (Eq.7). Fig. 4 and Fig.5 show the performance of our system in terms of precision and recall. Since we have used exactly N (N=25 for the first database, N=100 for the second database) images as our ground truth for each query and we only actually retrieve N images, the value of precision and recall is the same. Fig. 4 shows the average precision of the system over 430 query images on first database. Fig. 5 shows average precision of the system over 500 query images on second database. It is obviously that RGR leads to a clear precision improvement and a fast convergence.

As shown in Fig. 5, the precision improves from 5 to 20% for every interaction by using RGR. The case in which the number of interaction is zero is based purely on retrieving images whose feature vectors were closest to the query feature vector. The average precision based only on feature vectors is 9.85%, while if the system incorporates relevance feedback from the user, the precision doubles to 19.9% after only one interaction and triples to 27.7% after 2 interaction by using RGR. The precision starts to converge after about 25 interactions. After 50 interactions, the average precision was 79%. At last interaction, the average precision was 86%.

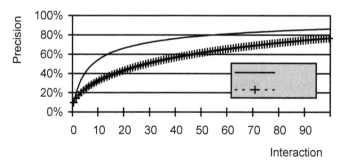

Fig. 4. Average performance of the image retrieval on first database. The y-axis represents the average precision over 430 retrievals. The x-axis represents the number of interaction.

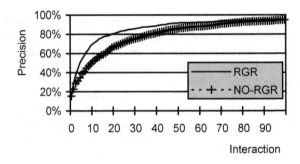

Fig. 5. Average performance of the image retrieval on second database. The y-axis represents the average precision over 500 retrievals. The x-axis represents the number of interaction.

6 Conclusion and Future Work

RGR is examined and evaluated for image retrieval. RGR demonstrates a performance advantage over the NO-RGR. This is due to the different retrieval algorithms based on the Bayesian framework. The user's feedback information is propagated into the retrieval process step by step in RGR. The more promising images are emphasized by RGR. On the contrary, the less promising ones are de-emphasized. RGR provides a new way of image retrieval with higher precision.

From the results, it seems that the user has to search for 25 times before the precision starts to converge. This may be too long for any average user. We will improve the convergence speed in the future work.

References

1. Rui, Y., Huang, T. S., Chang, S. -F.: Image Retrieval: Past, Present, and Future. Invited paper in Int Symposium on Multimedia Information Processing. Taipei, Taiwan (Dec. 1997).
2. Gudivada, V. N.: Content-Based Image Retrieval Systems. IEEE Computer, **28** (Sept. 1995) 18-22.
3. Rui, Y., Huang, T. S., Mehrotra, S.: Content-Based Image Retrieval with Relevance Feedback in MARS. In Proc. of IEEE Int. Conf. on Image Processing '97 (Oct. 1997) 815-818.
4. Rui, Y., Huang, T. S., Mehrotra, S., Ortega, M.: Relevance Feedback: a power tool for interactive content-based image retrieval. IEEE trans. Circuits and systems for video technology, **8** (Sep. 1998) 644-655.
5. Ishikawa, Y., Subramanya, R., Faloutsos, C.: Mindreaner: Query Databases Through Multiple Examples. In Proc. of the 24th VLDB Conference (1998).
6. Rui, Y., Huang, T. S.: A Novel Relevance Feedback Technique in Image Retrieval. ACM Multimedia'99 (1999) 67-70.

7. Lee, C., Ma, W. -Y., Zhang, H.: Information Embedding Based on User's Relevance Feedback for Image Retrieval. Technical report of HP Labs (1998).
8. Flickner, M., et al: Query by Image and Video Content: The QBIC System. IEEE Computer **28** (Sep. 1995) 23-32.
9. Pentland, A. P., Picard, R., Sclaroff, S.: Photobook: Content-based Manipulation of Image Databases. International Journal of Computer Vision **18** (June 1996) 233-254.
10. Smith, J., Chang, S. -F.: VisualSEEK: a fully automated content-based image query system. Proceedings of the Fourth ACM Multimedia Conference (1996) 87-98.
11. Ogle, V., Stonebraker, M.: Chabot: Retrieval from a Relational Database of Images. IEEE Computer **28** (Sep. 1995) 40-48.
12. Minka, T. P., Picard, R.: Interactive Learning Using a "Society of Models." Technical report 349, MIT Media Lab (1995).
13. Cox, I. J., Ghosn, J., Miller, M. L.: Hidden Annotation in Content Based Image Retrieval. IEEE Workshop on Content-Based Access of Image and Video Libraries (June 1997) 79-81.
14. Gevers, T., Smeulders, A. W. M.: The PicToSeek WWW Image Search System. IEEE International Conference on Multimedia Computing and Systems, **1** (June 1999) 264-269.
15. Wood, M . E . J., Thomas, B. T., Campbell, N. W.: Iterative Refinement by Relevance Feedback in Content-Based Digital Image Retrieval. In ACM Multimedia (Sep. 1998) 13-20.
16. Cox, I. J., Miller, M. L., Omohundro, S. M., Yianilos, P. N.: Pichunter: Bayesian relevance feedback for image retrieval system. In Intl. Conf. On Pattern Recognition (Aug. 1996) 361-369.
17. 17. Vasconcelos, N., Lippman, A.: Bayesian Representations and Learning Mechanisms for Content Based Image Retrieval. In SPIE Storage and Retrieval for Media Databases 2000.

MRML: A Communication Protocol for Content-Based Image Retrieval

Wolfgang Müller*, Henning Müller*, Stéphane Marchand-Maillet*,
Thierry Pun*, David McG. Squire', Zoran Pečenović'',
Christoph Giess''', Arjen P. de Vries[4]

*Computer Vision Group, Computer Science Department,
University of Geneva, Geneva, Switzerland.
'Computer Science and Software Engineering,
Monash University, Melbourne, Australia
''LCAV and Ergonomics Group,
Ecole Polytechnique Fédérale de Lausanne, Switzerland
''' Medical and Biological Informatics,
Deutsches Krebsforschungszentrum, Heidelberg, Germany
[4]CWI, Amsterdam, The Netherlands
Wolfgang.Mueller@cui.unige.ch
http://www.mrml.net

Abstract. In this paper we introduce and describe the Multimedia Retrieval Markup Language (MRML). This XML-based markup language is the basis for an open communication protocol for content-based image retrieval systems (CBIRSs). MRML was initially designed as a means of separating CBIR engines from their user interfaces. It is, however, also extensible as the basis for standardised performance evaluation procedures.

Such a tool is essential for the formulation and implementation of common benchmarks for CBIR. A common protocol can also bring new dynamics to the CBIR field — it makes the development of new systems faster and more efficient, and opens the door of the CBIR research field to other disciplines such as Human-Computer Interaction. The MRML specifications, as well as the first MRML-compliant applications, are freely available and are introduced in this paper.

Keywords: Multimedia retrieval, Communication protocol, Evaluation framework, Reusable software components

1 Introduction

During the past decade interest and research in CBIR has flourished. One of the attractions of CBIR research is that it is multidisciplinary. A wide range of research issues must be addressed: human perception, human-computer interaction, interface design, query representation for content-based search, feature extraction and representation, indexing structures, term-weighting schemes,

R. Laurini (Ed.): VISUAL 2000, LNCS 1929, pp. 300–311, 2000.
Springer-Verlag Berlin Heidelberg 2000

pruning strategies, performance evaluation and more. This richness is also one of the great challenges for CBIR research. At present, a researcher new to the field must build an entire system before he or she can address the aspect of the problem which interests him or her most. A researcher working alone or in a small team will have great difficulty constructing a state of the art system during the typical time-frame of a PhD or post-doc. MRML, the Multimedia Retrieval Markup Language, provides a framework in which components of CBIR systems can be built and exchanged interoperably. If state of the art components of CBIR systems are made MRML-compliant, all researchers will benefit from the opportunity to focus their investigations on their area of greatest interest and expertise.

Presently, almost every content-based image retrieval system (CBIRS) is a hard-wired connection between an interface and the functional parts of a program. Some programs provide easy-to-use web interfaces [1], while others need to be installed locally [2] and may be specific to particular operating systems. The reuse of components in CBIR, *e.g.* user interfaces, is thus very sparse. This is not only a time-consuming problem, since everything needs to be developed anew for each system, but it makes the sharing of user data and the comparison of system performances difficult.

In order to address these problems, Y.-C. Chang *et al.* [3] proposed a query taxonomy for multimedia databases. They proposed an initial formulation of the requirements for a system enabling communication between multimedia databases and clients. However, this approach is not yet translated into an extensible protocol.

In this paper we present MRML, an XML-based markup language for multimedia queries. MRML was designed to facilitate a bottom-up development approach, which separates the communication problem from the search for the best query language (e.g. [4],[5]) for multimedia databases. In other words, not only it is designed to fulfil the short-term needs of the image database research community, but it is also designed to cater for its long-term needs.

The development of standard query languages, together with standard methods for transmitting queries and data, can improve the interoperability of CBIRSs and thus increase the use and usefulness of multimedia databases. SQL and ODBC are examples of such developments for relational databases. The aim of MRML, however, is more similar to that of the DICOM protocol [6], which promoted the interoperability of medical imaging systems from different vendors. In summary, we address the urgent need for common tools which will facilitate the development and evaluation of multimedia database systems. By this means, we aim to facilitate the development of common benchmarks for CBIRS performance, similar those used for textual information retrieval [7].

The query-by-example (QBE) paradigm with relevance feedback (including browsing) is the search paradigm employed by most current CBIRSs. We therefore provide an extensible QBE facility within MRML. Further, some MRML-compliant tools have been developed and made freely available under the GNU Public License (http://www.mrml.net/download/). These are described briefly in Section 2, and include a CBIR search engine (*Viper*), which acts as a server, and an interface (SnakeCharmer), which acts as a client. Scripts (mostly Perl scripts) have also been made available, which might provide a basis for the creation of standard CBIRS benchmarks. An overview of various evaluation methods is given in [8], where the use of freely-available annotated image collections, such as [9], as test datasets is also advocated.

In order to be useful for research, MRML needs to be a "living standard": research groups will need to be able to test and use extensions without having to ask a committee for approval. We therefore employ a development model which permits phases of independent growth with subsequent code merging. In § 3, we present the main features of MRML and, in § 4, we show an example of how MRML can be extended to suit particular needs while staying coherent with the common standard.

2   *Viper*, CIRCUS and SnakeCharmer

MRML was initially designed to facilitate cooperation between research groups. The main programs for our testbed originate from the Ecole Fédérale Polytechnique de Lausanne (CIRCUS and SnakeCharmer) and from the University of Geneva (*Viper*). In this testbed, we use MRML to link a single interface (SnakeCharmer) to two different CBIRS (CIRCUS and *Viper*). A link to the MIRROR DBMS [10] is currently in development.

Viper [1] is an image search engine based on techniques commonly used in text retrieval and thus offers efficient access to a very large number of *possible* features (more than 80,000 simple colour and texture features, both local and global). Detailed descriptions of *Viper* may be found in [11, 12].

CIRCUS [2] is a server framework supporting multiple image retrieval methods and algorithms. Currently 4 methods based on LSI [13] and wavelet decomposition are supported.

SnakeCharmer is an MRML-compliant client application. It is written in JAVA for portability and offers query by multiple positive and negative examples, query history, multiple collection and algorithm selection, a scatter plot of the results according to various aspects of similarity and a basket for user-selected images.

3   Multimedia Retrieval Markup Language

MRML[3] is formally specified in [14]. It provides a framework that separates the query formulation from the actual query shipping. It is designed to markup multi-paradigm queries for multimedia databases. MRML enables the separation of interface and query engine and thus eases their independent development.

[1] http://viper.unige.ch/
[2] http://lcavwww.epfl.ch/CIRCUS
[3] http://www.mrml.net

MRML can be embedded into an existing system with little effort. First, it is XML-based, meaning that standard parsers can be used to process the communication messages. Further, the code for an example MRML-compliant CBIR system is freely-available and provides the basic implementation of both ends of an MRML-based communication toolkit. MRML is currently in a testing phase at several universities and further applications based on this protocol such as benchmark systems and meta-query engines are under development.

MRML is designed to allow extension by independent groups. By this means, it provides a research platform for extensions which later may become a part of common MRML.

3.1   Design goals of MRML

It is important for the following sections to keep in mind the priorities which we took into account during the design of MRML.

Interoperability: Interoperability is an obvious short term need of the CBIRS community. The fact that the interface between CBIRS client and server is not specified hampers research. Topics that could benefit from interoperability include:

- Meta-query engines query several "normal" query engines and assemble the results [15]. Constructing a meta-query engine would require to define a protocol abstraction layer corresponding to each of the different query embedded in the system. Using a common protocol would save a substantial amount of work.
- Human-computer-interaction aims at comparing the impact of different user interfaces on the performance of identical query engines, or test several engines with the identical interfaces. In this context, by ensuring the compatibility between engines and interfaces, MRML would ease this type of evaluation.
- Evaluation of query engines: Thanks to MRML, one can design a benchmark package that connects to a server, sends a set of queries and evaluates the results.

Extensibility without administration overhead: it was our goal to provide a communication protocol which can be extended without having to ask a standardisation body for permission. MRML enables independent development of extensions. As we will describe in Section 4.1 we invite MRML users to render their extensions accessible at http://www.mrml.net/extensions/. Later, stable extensions can be added to new common versions of MRML.

Common log file format: The whole area of CBIRS is craving for ground truth or other user data. MRML provides a common, human readable, easy to analyse, format for logging communication between CBIRS client and server. MRML contains a maximum of data which might be of interest for computer learning purposes. If needed, extensions of MRML can be designed in order to send additional data.

Simplicity of implementation: everything was designed so as to minimise the implementation overhead incurred when using MRML, while keeping a maximum of flexibility. MRML only uses a subset of the features of XML in order to maximise the number of tools that can use MRML.

3.2 Features of MRML

MRML-based communications have the structure of a remote procedure call: the client connects to the server, sends a request, and stays connected to the server until the server breaks the connection. The server shuts down the connection after sending the MRML message which answers the request. This connectionless protocol has the advantage of easing the implementation of the server. To limit the performance loss caused by frequently reconnecting, it is possible to send several requests as part of a single MRML message. The extension of MRML to a protocol permitting the negotiation of a permanent connection is also planned.

MRML, in its current specification (and implementation) state, supports the following features:

- request of a capability description from the server,
- selection of a data collection classified by query paradigm; it is possible to request collections which can be queried in a certain manner,
- selection and configuration of a query processor, also classified by query paradigm; MRML also permits the run time configuration of meta-queries.
- formulation of QBE queries,
- transmission of user interaction data.

The final feature reflects our strong belief that affective computing [16] will soon play a role in the field of content-based multimedia retrieval. MRML already supports this by allowing the logging of some user interaction data.

Graceful degradation: independent development on a common base Graceful degradation is the key to successful independent extension of MRML. The basic principles can be summarised as follows:

- servers and clients which do not recognise an XML element or attribute encountered in an MRML text should completely ignore its contents,
- extensions should be designed so that all the standard information remains available to the generic MRML user (see examples in Section 4).

These principles provide guidelines for independent extensions of MRML.

To avoid conflicts between differing extensions of MRML, and in order to we plan to maintain or promote a central database for the registration and documentation of MRML extensions. This would also facilitate the "translation" between user logs which contain extended MRML.

3.3   Logging onto a CBIR server

An MRML server listens on a port for MRML messages on a given TCP socket. When connecting, the client requests the basic properties of the server, and waits for an answer. Skipping standard XML headers, the MRML code looks like this:

```
<mrml>
 <get-server-properties />
</mrml>
```

The server then informs the client of its capabilities. This message is empty in the current version of MRML, but it allows for the extension of the protocol:

```
<mrml>
 <server-properties />
</mrml>
```

Goal of this tag is to provide a stub for negotiation which influences the whole communication, like e.g. the opening of a permanent, possibly encrypted connection.

Further negotiation between client and server may depend on the user, so before further negotiation we have to open a session for the user:

```
<mrml>
 <open-session user-name="A. User" session-name="a session" />
</mrml>
```

which will be answered by an acknowledgement signal containing the ID of the session just opened. We regard the concept of sessions as very important, as it allows multi-user servers and across-session learning. Of course, it is possible to close and rename sessions.

Now one can request a list of collections, which are available on the server user:

```
<mrml session-id="s-33">
 <get-collections />
</mrml>
```

The answer will be a list of collections, with a description of the ways the collection has been indexed, encapsulated in a `query-paradigm-list` tag.

Similarly, the client can request a list of algorithms (*i.e.* query methods), which can be used on the server. Each of the `algorithm` tags returned also contains a `query-paradigm-list` describing the way the algorithm can interact with the user, as well as which indexing methods are needed for employing the algorithm.

The user is now able to choose on his client an algorithm/collection combination which suits his needs, and in which the `query-paradigm-list`s of collection and algorithm have *match*. The matching of `query-paradigm-list`s is described in [14].

The client can then request property sheet descriptions from the server. Different algorithms will have different relevant parameters which should be user-configurable (*e.g.* feature sets, speed vs. quality). *Viper*, for example, offers several weighting functions [17] and a variety of methods for, and levels of, pruning. All these parameters are irrelevant for CIRCUS. Thanks to MRML property sheets, the interface can adapt itself to these specific parameters. At the same time, MRML specifies the way the interface will turn these data into XML to send them back to the server. The interested reader is referred to [14] for details.

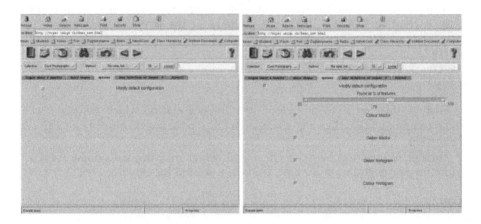

Fig. 1. Demonstration of property sheets in SnakeCharmer. The user has the choice to modify the default settings or not. If he decides to modify the default settings, widgets which enable him to do so pop up.

3.4   Query Formulation

The query step is dependent on the query paradigms offered by the interface and the search engine. MRML currently includes only QBE, but it has been designed to be extensible to other paradigms.

A basic QBE query consists of a list of images and the corresponding relevance levels assigned to them by the user. In the following example, the user has marked two images, the image 1.jpg positive (user-relevance="1") and the image 2.jpg negative (user-relevance="-1"). All query images are referred to by their URLs.

```
<mrml session-id="1" transaction-id="44">
<query-step session-id="1"
 resultsize="30"
 algorithm-id="algorithm-default">
 <user-relevance-list>
  <user-relevance-element image-location="http://viper.unige.ch/1.jpg"
                          user-relevance="1"/>
```

```
<user-relevance-element image-location="http://viper.unige.ch/2.jpg"
                        user-relevance="-1"/>
</user-relevance-list>
</query-step>
</mrml>
```

The server will then return the retrieval result as a list of images, again represented by their URLs.

Queries can be grouped into transactions. This allows the formulation and logging of complex queries. This may be applied in systems which process a single query using a variety algorithms, such as the split-screen version of *Tracking Viper* [18] or the system described by Lee *et al.* [19]. It is important in these cases to preserve in the logs the knowledge that two queries are logically related one to another.

4   Extending MRML

How to extend In order to demonstrate how easily MRML can be extended to other query paradigms, we give as an example QBE for images with user annotation. We assume that the user is invited to associate textual comments with images he or she marks as relevant or irrelevant. Since a tag for this purpose does not yet exist in MRML, we add an attribute `cui-user-annotation="..."` to the element. The prefix `cui-` is added to avoid name clashes with extensions from other groups which use MRML (namespaces are avoided here to keep things simple for old XML parsers).

```
<user-relevance-list>
 <user-relevance-element image-location="file:/images/1.jpg"
                         user-relevance="1"
                         cui-user-annotation="tropical fish"/>
</user-relevance-list>
```

It is important to note here that servers which do not recognise the attribute `cui-user-annotation` still can make use of the remaining information contained in the `user-relevance-element` element.

How *not* to extend As an example of how *not* to extend MRML, we give an extension with the same semantics but which does not respect the principle of graceful degradation:

```
<user-relevance-list>
 <cui-user-relevance-element image-location="file:/images/1.jpg"
                             user-relevance="1"
                             user-annotation="tropical fish"/>
</user-relevance-list>
```

Instead of adding an *attribute* to an existing MRML element (in this case, `user-relevance-element`), a new *element* was defined that contained the same kind of extension, namely `cui-user-relevance-element`. Consequently, servers which do not recognise this element will not be able to exploit any relevance information.

MRML and Binary data MRML's preferred mechanism for transferring binary data is to send the URL where the data can be found. Binary data is then retrieved using the URL. As it is a primary goal of MRML to enable the sharing of logging data we suggest to transfer big chunks of data as follows.

Binary data which stays constant over several sessions (*i.e.* images and other media items contained in the queried collection) should be transfered using their URL, as described above. This keeps log files relatively small, yet data is accessible for everyone.

Binary data which changes during the query process (*e.g.* a file containing an example image for a QBE query which is not accessible by the web) should be transferred using two attributes. One of the attributes should contain the base64-encoded binary data, the other one the corresponding MIME type.

However, in most cases, it is preferable to design proper extensions to MRML which provide the best accessibility and readability of the resulting logs.

4.1   The MRML development model

As it has been stated many times throughout this article, MRML allows each developer to extend MRML to his needs. In particular, these extensions can coexist, and a notification of a central body is not necessary for making these extensions work. However, to maximise the usefulness of MRML the authors are presently setting up a database which contains documentation of extensions to MRML. It is also intended to provide a forum for groups which want to extend MRML into similar directions.

We propose to develop extensions to MRML in the following fashion. Search first the page http://www.mrml.net/extensions/ for documentation of extensions which might already do what you want.

- If so,
    1. implement the existing extension
    2. double-check with the author of the existing extension that the documentation has been understood in the right way
    3. add your name and your affiliation to the list of people/groups who are using this extension which is kept on www.mrml.net.
- If not,
    1. implement the extension
    2. submit documentation for your extension along with your name and your affiliation to www.mrml.net.

The information contained on http://www.mrml.net/extensions/ will be useful both for analysing logs and for *merging* extensions, once an extension has proven more useful than others.

5 Further use of MRML

In this article, we have presented a stable, extensible and useful framework for the use in CBIRS and other multimedia retrieval systems. In the sequel, we shortly described tools that can be easily implemented using existing features of the MRML framework.

5.1 Meta query engines

We are currently conceiving a meta query engine which queries MRML compliant servers.

Meta query engines running under MRML will start a handshaking procedure, establishing for each of the attaches servers the available collections and algorithms. The meta query can then assemble this information into a property sheet that can be presented to the user via a standard MRML interface.

After configuration the meta query engine will pass arriving queries onto the attached servers, returning an assembled result. We plan to use methods similar to the ones described in [15].

5.2 Benchmarks

Only preliminary steps have been taken by the CBIR community towards developing common benchmarks – a comparison of evaluation techniques may be found in [8]. We are currently working on a more profound and flexible benchmarking system extending the results of this research. See figure 2 for a description of the structure of such a benchmark.

6 Conclusion

The development of MRML and the first MRML-compliant tools has established a common framework for the fast development of CBIR applications. To our knowledge, MRML is the first general communication protocol for CBIR actually implemented. The source code for the interface and the query engine is freely available. This should help developers of retrieval engines and developers of user interfaces to develop complete systems on the basis of existing components. Extensive tests have shown the stability of the protocol and our test components.

Since MRML is a free and extensible standard, the availability of more applications and tools supporting such a protocol will further facilitate the development of CBIR applications supporting a diversity of query paradigms.

More important, in our opinion, is the fact that the adoption of MRML will lead to the possibility of comparing different CBIR applications objectively. It will make it easy to develop common benchmarks for all MRML-compliant systems, similar to those which exist in the database and information retrieval communities.

Finally, the possibility of sharing MRML user logs will provide a useful tool for the sharing of user interaction data.

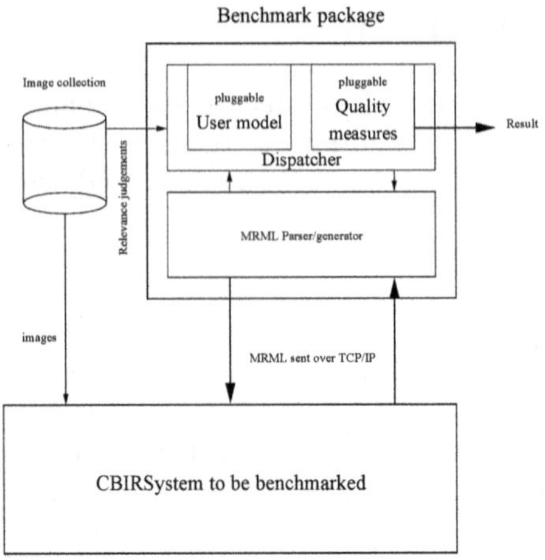

Benchmark package

Fig. 2. We propose a benchmark that relies on stored relevance judgements as a basis for the simulation of user feedback. We propose storing the relevance judgements done by several users for a set of identical queries in order to account for the fact that different users will judge relevance differently. The data in [20] have been obtained using this technique.

Acknowledgements

This project is supported by the Swiss National Foundation for Scientific Research under grant number 2000-052426.97. 10

References

1. Surfimage webdemo. http://www-rocq.inria.fr/cgi-bin/imedia/surfimage.cgi (1999)
2. QBIC^TM – IBM's Query By Image Content. http://wwwqbic.almaden.ibm.com/~qbic/ (1998)
3. Chang, Y.-C., Bergmann, L., Smith, J. R., Li, C.-S.: Query taxonomy of multimedia databases. In: Panchanathan *et al.* [21]. (SPIE Symposium on Voice, Video and Data Communications)
4. Li, J. Z., zsu, M., Szafron, D., Oria, V.: Moql: A multimedia object query language. In: *The Third International Workshop on Multimedia Information Systems*. Como, Italy (September 1997)
5. de Vries, A.: Mirror: Multimedia query processing in extensible databases. In: *Proceedings of the fourteenth Twente workshop on language technology (TWLT14): Language Technology in Multimedia Information Retrieval*. Enschede, The Netherlands (December 1998)
6. Revet, B.: DICOM Cook Book for Implementations in Madalities. Philips Medical Systems, Eindhoven, Netherlands (1997)
7. Vorhees, E. M., Harmann, D.: Overview of the seventh text retrieval conference (TREC-7). In: *The Seventh Text Retrieval Conference*. Gaithersburg, MD, USA (November 1998)

8. Müller, H., Müller, W., Squire, D. M., Pun, T.: Performance evaluation in content-based image retrieval: Overview and proposals. Tech. Rep. 99.05, Computer Vision Group, Computing Centre, University of Geneva, rue Gnral Dufour, 24, CH-1211 Genve, Switzerland (dec 1999)

9. Annotated groundtruth database. Department of Computer Science and Engineering, University of Washington, http://www.cs.washington.edu/research/imagedatabase/groundtruth/ (1999)

10. de Vries, A., van Doorn, M., Blanken, H., Apers, P.: The Mirror MMDBMS architecture. In: *Proceedings of 25th International Conference on Very Large Databases (VLDB '99)*. Edinburgh, Scotland, UK (September 1999). Technical demo

11. Müller, H., Squire, D. M., Müller, W., Pun, T.: Efficient access methods for content-based image retrieval with inverted files. In: Panchanathan *et al.* [21]. (SPIE Symposium on Voice, Video and Data Communications)

12. Squire, D. M., Müller, W., Müller, H., Raki, J.: Content-based query of image databases, inspirations from text retrieval: inverted files, frequency-based weights and relevance feedback. In: *The 11th Scandinavian Conference on Image Analysis (SCIA '99)*. Kangerlussuaq, Greenland (June 7–11 1999)

13. Pečenović, Z.: Image retrieval using Latent Semantic indexing. Final year graduate thesis, AudioVisual Communications Lab, Ecole Polytechnique Fédérale de Lausanne, Switzerland (June 1997)

14. Müller, W., Pečenović, Z., de Vries, A. P., Squire, D. M., Müller, H., Pun, T.: MRML: Towards an extensible standard for multimedia querying and benchmarking – Draft proposal. Tech. Rep. 99.04, Computer Vision Group, Computing Centre, University of Geneva, rue Général Dufour, 24, CH-1211 Genève, Switzerland (October 1999)

15. Beigi, M., Benitez, A. B., Chang, S.-F.: Metaseek: A content-based meta-search engine for images. In: *Symposium on Electronic Imaging: Multimedia Processing and Applications - Storage and Retrieval for Image and Video Databases VI, IST/SPIE'98, San Jose, CA* (1998)

16. Picard, R. W.: Affective Computing. MIT Press, Cambridge (1997)

17. Salton, G., Buckley, C.: Term weighting approaches in automatic text retrieval. Tech. Rep. 87-881, Department of Computer Science, Cornell University, Ithaca, New York 14853-7501 (November 1987)

18. Müller, W., Squire, D. M., Müller, H., Pun, T.: Hunting moving targets: an extension to Bayesian methods in multimedia databases. In: Panchanathan *et al.* [21]. (SPIE Symposium on Voice, Video and Data Communications)

19. Lee, C. S., Ma, W.-Y., Zhang, H.: Information Embedding Based on User's Relevance Feedback for Image Retrieval. In: Panchanathan *et al.* [21]. (SPIE Symposium on Voice, Video and Data Communications)

20. Squire, D. M., Müller, W., Müller, H.: Relevance feedback and term weighting schemes for content-based image retrieval. In: Huijsmans, D. P., Smeulders, A. W. M., eds., *Third International Conference On Visual Information Systems (VISUAL '99)*, no. 1614 in Lecture Notes in Computer Science. Springer-Verlag, Amsterdam, The Netherlands (June 2–4 1999)

21. Panchanathan, S., Chang, S.-F., Kuo, C.-C. J., eds.: Multimedia Storage and Archiving Systems IV (VV02), vol. 3846 of *SPIE Proceedings*, Boston, Massachusetts, USA (September 20–22 1999). (SPIE Symposium on Voice, Video and Data Communications)

An Integrated Multimedia System with Learning Capabilities

G. Ciocca, I. Gagliardi, R. Schettini, B. Zonta

Istituto Tecnologie Informatiche Multimediali
Consiglio Nazionale delle Ricerche
Via Ampere 56, 20131 Milano, Italy
e-mail: [ciocca, isabella, centaura, bruna]@itim.mi.cnr.it

Abstract. This paper describes the main features of the multimedia information retrieval engine of Quicklook^2. Quicklook^2 allows the user to query image and multimedia databases with the aid of sample images, or a user-made sketch and/or textual descriptions, and progressively refine the system's response by indicating the relevance, or non-relevance of the retrieved items. The performance of the system is illustrated with examples from various application domains.

1. Introduction

The need to retrieve visual information from large image collections is shared by many application domains [1]. This paper describes the main features of Quicklook^2, a system that combines in a single framework some approaches considered alternative for querying image databases: the alphanumeric relational query, the content-based image query exploiting automatically computed low-level image features (such as color and texture), and the textual similarity query exploiting any textual annotations attached to image database items (such as figure captions or textual cards...). These approaches are complementary: all of them may be useful in query session to deal with the different types of information that may be associated with images.

The evaluation of multimedia information is subjective in general, and that of visual and semantic information in particular. We can hope to have some chance of success in processing different types of queries, using a general purpose system, only if all available information, both visual and textual, is used in indexing, and if user feedback is considered in the retrieval process in order to understand what features the user has taken into account (and to what extent) in formulating this judgement. We have designed Quicklook^2 to address these issues. With Quicklook^2, the database can be queried with the aid of sample images, or user-made sketches, and/or textual image descriptions. When a query is submitted to the system, the retrieved items are presented in decreasing order of relevance, the user is then allowed to progressively refine the system's response by indicating their relevance, or non-relevance. To improve Quicklook^2 efficiency we implemented an indexing scheme based on triangle inequality [4], which reduces the number of direct comparisons between the feature vectors representing the query and those representing the database items (for the sake

R. Laurini (Ed.): VISUAL 2000, LNCS 1929, pp. 312–326, 2000.
Springer-Verlag Berlin Heidelberg 2000

of convenience we do not distinguish between feature comparison and image comparison here).

The paper is organized as follow: Section 2 is an overview of related studies and existing systems. In section 3 we describe how the visual and textual features are extracted and used in image indexing. Section 4 describes the relevance feedback algorithm implemented. In Section 5 we outline the overall system architecture, and report some experimental results.

2. Related works

In the framework of a visual information retrieval system, the integrated use of content-independent data is a rather straightforward affair: queries are generally made in standard query languages, such as SQL, to reduce the number of database items that must be further evaluated. General-purpose systems such as QBIC [14], VIR [3], and NETRA [22] employ this feature, as does our system. Much more challenging is the effective and efficient use of content-dependent data automatically extracted by the images themselves. Many special issues of leading journals have been dedicated to this topic, and several surveys have been published in recent years [1, 16, 30]. Notwithstanding the substantial progress made in this direction, this approach appears decisively feasible only for retrieving images from thematic databases, where the semantic content is limited to a specific domain. Although several general-purpose systems have been also developed in the last few years, the integrated management of the various image features remains complex and application dependent [3, 14, 22].

Much research has concerned the automatic assignment of significant terms to images in WWW pages on the basis of the different parts that can be identified through the use of HTML tags [17, 20, 26], and the definition of a similarity function among them. The basic idea of finding pieces of text similar to a given one has also been exploited in the framework of the hypertext for the automatic generation of the hypertextual link [19, 31]. Several experiments have been dedicated to the matter, but few prototypes have been produced for an integrated multimedia environment.

It is obvious that user feedback must be considered in the retrieval of multimedia information. The potentials of relevance feedback in textual information retrieval have been widely studied [32]. In image retrieval, it has been employed by Minka and Picard [24] and by Cox et al. [13] for target search, and by Rui et al. [29] and Sclaroff et al. [20] for similarity retrieval.

3. Image Indexing

3.1 Using Pictorial Features

Because perception is subjective, there is no one "best" representation of image contents. However, the features listed below constitute a general purpose library of low-level features which can be used in image indexing:

1. the ratio between the dimensions of the images;
2. the Color histogram and Color Coherence Vectors (CCV) in the CIELAB color space quantized in 64 colors [27];
3. the histogram of the transition in color (in a CIELAB color space quantized in 11 colors) [15];
4. the Spatial Chromatic Histogram (SCH), summarizing information about the location of pixels of similar color and their arrangement within the image [6];
5. the moments of inertia (mean, variance, skewness, and kurtosis) of the color distribution in the CIELAB space [34];
6. a histogram of opportunely filtered contour directions (considering only high gradient pixels) extracted by Canny edge detectors [11];
7. the statistical information on image edges extracted by Canny edge detectors [12];
8. the mean and variance of the absolute values of the coefficients of the sub-images at the first three levels of the multi-resolution Daubechies wavelet transform of the luminance image [9];
9. the Hu invariant moments [18];
10. the spatial composition of the color regions identified by the process of quantization in 11 colors [12];
11. the estimation of statistical features based on the Neighborhood Gray-Tone Difference Matrix (NGTDM) [2, 35];
12. the percentage of pixels that correspond to skin according to a detector trained on a large amount of labeled skin data [23].

SCH features are compared using the distance metric proposed in [6]. The city-block distance measure L_1 is used to compare all other features, as it is statistically more robust than the Euclidean distance measure L_2 [28]. The distance for a generic feature F_h, having c components, is therefore computed as follows:

$$D(F_h', F_h'') = \sum_{i=1}^{c} \left| F_h'(i) - F_h''(i) \right| \tag{1}$$

while, given two Spatial Chromatic Histograms H' and H'' having c bins, the distance is computed as follows:

$$D(H', H'') = \sum_{i=1}^{c} \min\left(h_{H'}(i) - h_{H''}(i)\right) \frac{\sqrt{2} - d\left(b_{H'}(i), b_{H''}(i)\right)}{\sqrt{2}} + \frac{\min\left(\sigma_{H'}(i), \sigma_{H''}(i)\right)}{\max\left(\sigma_{H'}(i), \sigma_{H''}(i)\right)} \tag{2}$$

where h(i) is the ratio of pixels having color i, b are the relative coordinates of the baricenter of their spatial distribution, and σ is the corresponding standard deviation.

When a new database has to be created the user chooses the features to use in indexing the pictorial contents of the images (Figure 1). When searching the database the user can select the set of features to use in evaluating the similarity, and decide whether these are referred to the global image and/or to sub-images obtained by dividing the original image in different ways.

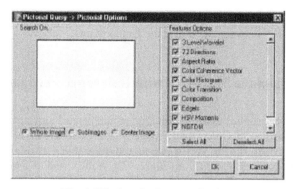

Fig. 1. Window for feature selection.

3.2 Using Textual Annotations

Images are sometimes accompanied by textual annotations describing their semantic contents. These annotations can be used in indexing and retrieving images if significant terms are automatically extracted from them to create a dictionary, and a suitable similarity function among sets of significant terms is defined [32, 33].

Generally speaking, dictionaries contain the sets of significant terms that can be used to index textual annotations, and they can be created automatically by IR process, or manually by experts. In our system, designed to be general purpose, the dictionaries are created automatically, and are composed of all the terms present in the textual annotations (excepting those on a standard Italian, stop-list). Each index term of a document is automatically assigned a weight TW reflecting its importance, on the basis of the number of times the term itself occurs in the document, as well as in the entire archive. For example, the weight TW of the term k in document i is computed as follows:

$$TW_{ik} = Freq_{ik}\ 1 + log\frac{n}{DocFreq_k} \tag{3}$$

where $Freq_{ik}$ is the frequency of term i in document k, n is the total number of documents in the database, and $DocFreq_k$ is the number of documents in which term k occurs at least once. The textual annotation associated with the generic image i is indexed therefore by a set of its relevant terms with the corresponding weights associated. We call such a set T_i. Text similarity, TS, between the textual annotations T_i and T_j, is defined as follows:

$$TS(T_i,T_j) = \frac{\sum_{k\ (T_i\ T_j)}(TW_{ik}TW_{jk})}{\sqrt{\sum_{k\ T_i}(TW_{ik})^2\ \sum_{k\ T_j}(TW_{jk})^2}} \tag{4}$$

TS can assume any value in the range of [0, 1]. The greater the value of TS, the greater the similarity between the two textual annotations.

4. Combing Distance Measures with Relevance Feedback

In this paragraph we introduce the function which is used to evaluate the similarity (i.e. the dissimilarity) between two images. Sub-vectors of visual features are indicated by X^i_h, where i is the vector index, and h the index of the feature; T^i is the corresponding textual annotation, if available; D_h is the distance associated with the feature h-th as defined in Paragraph 3; and TS, the similarity function associated to the textual annotations. The global metric used to evaluate the dissimilarity between two database items is defined as a linear combination of the distances between the individual features:

$$\text{Diss}(\mathbf{X}^i, \mathbf{X}^j) = \frac{1}{p}\sum_{h=1}^{p} w_h D_h(\mathbf{X}^i_h, \mathbf{X}^j_h) + w_T \left(1 - \text{TS}(\mathbf{T}^i, \mathbf{T}^j)\right) \tag{5}$$

in which p is the number of visual features considered, while w_h and w_T are weights.

4.1 Normalization of distances between visual features

The single distances may be defined on intervals of widely varying values: if we do not want one feature to overshadow the others simply because of its magnitude, we must normalize the distances to a common interval so that equal emphasis is placed on every feature score. To cope with this problem, we use the following normalization derived from the Gaussian normalization [25].

Assuming that the database contains n images, the average distance between the visual features of database items and the standard deviation are computed as follows:

$$\mu_h = \frac{2}{n(n-1)}\sum_{i=1}^{n}\sum_{j=i+1}^{n} D_h(\mathbf{X}^i_h, \mathbf{X}^j_h) \tag{6}$$

$$s_h = \frac{2}{n(n-1)}\sum_{i=1}^{n}\sum_{j=i+1}^{n} \left[D_h(\mathbf{X}^i_h, \mathbf{X}^j_h) - \mu_h\right]^2 \tag{7}$$

The vector of the normalized distance between two images having indices i and j respectively is:

$$\mathbf{D}(\mathbf{X}^i, \mathbf{X}^j) = \left[\frac{D_1(\mathbf{X}^i_1, \mathbf{X}^j_1)}{\mu_1 + K_1}, ..., \frac{D_h(\mathbf{X}^i_h, \mathbf{X}^j_h)}{\mu_h + Ks_h}, ..., \frac{D_p(\mathbf{X}^i_p, \mathbf{X}^j_p)}{\mu_p + K_p}\right]^T$$

$$= \left[d_1(\mathbf{X}^i_1, \mathbf{X}^j_1), ..., d_h(\mathbf{X}^i_h, \mathbf{X}^j_h), ..., d_p(\mathbf{X}^i_p, \mathbf{X}^j_p)\right]^T \tag{8}$$

where K is a positive constant that influences the number of out-of-range values. In our experiments K was set at 3. Any out-of-range values are mapped to the extreme values, so that they do not bias further processing. At this point our dissimilarity function has the following form:

$$\mathrm{Diss}(\mathbf{X^i},\mathbf{X^j}) = \frac{1}{p}\sum_{h=1}^{p} w_h\, d_h(\mathbf{X_h^i},\mathbf{X_h^j}) + w_T(1 - TS(T_i, T_j)) =$$

$$= \frac{1}{p}\sum_{h=1}^{p} w_h\, d_h(\mathbf{X_h^i},\mathbf{X_h^j}) + w_T d_T \tag{9}$$

4.2 Estimation of Weights

The weights of eqs. 5-9 are often to be set heuristically by the user, and this may be rather difficult, as there may be no clear relationship between the features used to index the image database and those evaluated by the user in a subjective image similarity evaluation. Quicklook[2] implement a dynamic updating strategy of the weights based on the user's images selection.

We let $\mathbf{R^+}$ be the set of relevant items selected by the user ($\mathbf{R^+}$ is usually only an approximation of the set of items relevant to the query in the whole database), d^+_h, the set of normalized distances (computed on the visual feature h) among the elements of $\mathbf{R^+}$, and μ^+_h, the mean of the values of d^+_h. Similarly, we let d^+_T be the set of normalized distances (computed on the textual indices) among the elements of $\mathbf{R^+}$, and μ^+_T, the mean of the values of d^+_T.

We define $\mathbf{R^-}$ as the set of non relevant items selected by the user to serve as negative examples, while d_h and d_T are the corresponding sets of distances. From $\mathbf{R^+}$ and $\mathbf{R^-}$ we can then determine whether the influence of a feature must be limited by reducing the corresponding weight in computing the dissimilarity: we let $\mathbf{R^{+-}}$ be the union of $\mathbf{R^+}$ with $\mathbf{R^-}$, and d^{+-}_h, d^{+-}_T the corresponding sets of distances among its elements. Since we can not make any assumptions about the statistical distribution of the features of non-relevant images by analyzing $\mathbf{R^-}$ (the selected non-relevant images may not be representative of all the non-relevant images in the database), we exclude set d_h from d^{+-}_h, and set d_T from d^{+-}_T obtaining two new sets of distances: $d^*_h = d^{+-}_h\backslash d_h$ and $d^*_T = d^{+-}_T\backslash d_T$. The weight terms w_h and w_T to use in the following Equations (x=h or x=T) are then updated:

$$w_x^+ = \begin{cases} 1 & \text{if } \left|\mathbf{R^+}\right| < 3 \\ \dfrac{1}{1 + \mu_x^+} & \text{otherwise} \end{cases} \tag{10}$$

$$
w_x^* = \begin{cases} 0 & \text{if } |\mathbf{R}^+| + |\mathbf{R}^-| < 3 \text{ or} \\ & |\mathbf{R}^-| = 0 \text{ or } |\mathbf{R}^+| = 0 \\ \dfrac{1}{+\mu_x^*} & \text{otherwise} \end{cases} \tag{11}
$$

$$
w_x = \begin{cases} 0 & \text{if } w_x^+ < w_x^* \\ w_x^+ \; w_x^* & \text{otherwise} \end{cases} \tag{12}
$$

where e and are positive constants, set in our experiments at 0.01 and 0.8 respectively. The term has been introduced to prevent features found in both negative and positive examples from being discarded entirely.

Looking at these formulas, we observe that if the user selects only relevant images, the weights are computed according to Equation (10). For any given feature, the w_x^+ term is large when there is some form of agreement among the feature values of the selected images. For any given feature the w_x^* term of Equation (11), is large when there is some form of agreement among the feature values of positive and negative examples. This should mean that the feature is not discriminant for the query; consequently its weight is decreased (Equation 12).

4.3 Query formulation

In visual querying one way to compute the query is to take a weighted average of query feature vectors and of relevant images. But in the case cited above, the algorithm can not provide for the fact that relevant images may differ from the original query with respect to some features. On the other hand processing all the relevant images as single queries, and then combining the retrieval outputs may create an unacceptable computational burden when the database is large. Our approach is to let $\mathbf{R}^+$ be the set of relevant images the user has selected (including the original query), while $\overline{\mathbf{Q}}$ is the average query, and $\overline{s}$, the corresponding standard deviation. We then proceed as follows:

$$
Y_h(j) = \left\{ X_h^i(j) \mid \left| X_h^i(j) - \overline{Q}_h(j) \right| \; 3\overline{s}_h(j) \right\} \quad h, i, \text{ and } j \tag{13}
$$

$$
\widetilde{Q}_h(j) = \frac{1}{|Y_h(j)|} \sum_{X_h^i(j) \; Y_h(j)} X_h^i(j) \tag{14}
$$

The query processing formulates a new visual query $\widetilde{Q}_h$ that better represents the images of interest to the user, taking into account the features of the relevant images, without allowing one different feature value to bias query computation.

A similar process is used for text: words found in relevant texts are added together to increase the weights associated with each word according to their relative frequency in the texts; instead, words present in both relevant and non relevant texts are discarded. Again, letting $\mathbf{T}^+$ be the set of the relevant texts and $\mathbf{T}$, the set of non relevant texts, the new textual query $\tilde{T}$ is computed as:

$$\tilde{T} = \bigcup_{T_i \ \mathbf{T}^+} T_i \ \setminus \ \bigcup_{T_j \ \mathbf{T}} T_j \tag{15}$$

4.4 Image Filtering

Since comparing a query Q with *every* image I in the database is a time-consuming task, we have implemented a method for filtering the database before the pictorial distances are actually computed. This method is based on a variant of *triangle inequality*, proposed by Berman and Shapiro [4], and has the advantage of being applicable to any distance measure that satisfies triangle inequality.

We let I represent a database image, Q the query, K a reference image called *Key*, and d a distance measure. The following inequality holds for every Q, K and I:

$$d(I,Q) \quad |d(I,K) \quad d(Q,K)| \tag{16}$$

Assuming that we have precalculated d(I,K) for all the images (I) in the database, to retrieve all the images such that distance d(I,Q) is not greater than a threshold S, we can use the previous inequality to filter the database as follows:

1. compute query Q
2. compute d(Q,K)
3. find all the images (I) having   d(I,K)   where   =d(Q,K)-S and   =d(Q,K)+S

Step 3 is a direct consequence of triangle inequality, adding the condition d(I,Q)   S. Since the distances d(I,K) have already been calculated, we can store them directly in the database, and a standard SQL query can be used to retrieve the correct images.

If distance d is a linear combination of distances d_i, as in our case, we can apply triangle inequality to each term of the measure, adjusting the threshold of each inequality as follows. Assuming that $d(I,Q)=w_1 d_1(I,Q)+\ldots+w_i d_i\ (I,Q)\ +\ldots+w_n d_n(I,Q)$, since we want d(I,Q)   S, we have $w_i d_i(I,Q)$ S for i=1…n, thus $d_i(I,Q)$ S/w_i. We have n conditions, similar to those in the previous case, that must be verified simultaneously, meaning that in the SQL query, they are and-ed together.

Since one image key K alone is not enough to discriminate the contents of the database, m keys are used. A good compromise between a suitable number of keys and limited data storage space is provided by a logarithmic function that increases the number of keys slowly:

$$m = \mathrm{Log}_{10} n \tag{17}$$

where n is the number of images in the database. The method based on triangle inequality, perform betters compared to the sequential search even when the keys are selected at random: we have chosen the keys in that way. The threshold S is updated according to the weights determined by relevance feedback using the equation:

$$S = S \frac{MaxDist}{1/e} \tag{18}$$

where MaxDist is the maximum value of the distance that can be obtained from the distance measure with the selected weights. The complete filtering method can be summarized as follows:

1. compute query Q and weights w_i
2. compute threshold S'
3. compute $d_i(Q,K_k)$ for i=1..n and k=1..m
4. find all the images (I) that

   $_{11} d_1(I,K_1) \quad _{11}$ and ... and $\quad _{1m} d_1(I,K_m) \quad _{1m}$ and

   ...

   $_{n1} d_n(I,K_1) \quad _{n1}$ and ... and $\quad _{nm} d_n(I,K_m) \quad _{nm}$

   with $\quad _{ij}=d_i(Q,K_j)-S'$ and $\quad _{ij}=d_i(Q,K_j)+S'$
5. compute the similarity d(I,Q) on the remaining images and rank them.

5. Implementation and Results

The Quicklook[2] system (Figure 2) has been implemented in Visual C++. It is composed of three independent subsystems. The first, the indexing module, which indexes the pictorial content of the images and the available textual information. The second is the retrieval module which applies relevance feedback to retrieve the desired images from the database, once a query (visual and/or textual) has been submitted. The third subsystem is the manager module which contains all the supporting utilities. In general the use of the system involves running all these modules.

When a new image database is fed into the system the corresponding thumbnails for display are computed, and the corresponding textual information, if available, is also imported. Then, the visual and textual indices are computed (see Section 2). All visual features or a subset can be used in indexing the images and these features are calculated on the global image and on the sub-images obtained by dividing the original image in different (Figure 1). Once the images have been indexed, the filter data archive and the dictionary data archive are automatically computed and stored.

At the beginning of a query session the user may modify the default retrieval strategy, which employs both visual and textual indices and the database filtering ("Pictorial Filter" in Figure 3). The user may also use standard SQL queries based on exact text matches to reduce the number of images to selected for further querying ("Textual Filter" in Figure 3).

To start a query session the user can:
- provide the system an example ready-made (image and /or text) of his information needs;
- sketch in an image and/or type in a text using the available tools;
- browse the database to find one, or more relevant images with which to begin.

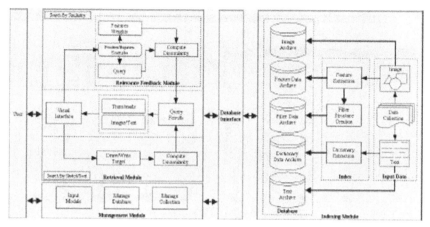

Fig. 2. Quicklook^2 system architecture

In the first two cases the relevance feedback mechanism does not modify the query representing the user's information needs, but only the weights used in the evaluation of similarity. When a query is submitted, the system rearranges the database images in order of decreasing similarity with respect to the query, and then shows the user the most similar images. The user is allowed to browse textual annotations, and may, in successive iterations, mark any of the retrieved items as relevant, or not relevant. A new query vector can then be computed, on the basis of the features of the relevant images, and the overall evaluation of the dissimilarity function updated, taking into account the features of both relevant and non relevant images. There is no limit to the number of images that can be selected or to the number of relevance feedback iterations. The user ends interaction with the system when he finds the desired images, or decides that they can not be found either because the system is unable to decipher his information needs, or the desired images are not present in the database.

The similarity retrieval features of the Quicklook^2 system has been tested on 15 different databases for a total of over 50,000 images. These databases were generated in the framework of feasibility studies of potential applications of the system, and include several collections of textiles, ceramics and trademarks, together with various archives of painting and photographs, both in color and in black and white. Relevance feedback improves the effectiveness of the retrieval considerably for all the databases by over 30% [7-12]. Figure 5 and 6 present two examples of the system's application for a database of approximately 12,000 images.

We have also tested the capability of our system in finding specific images (target search) in two, rather small catalogues of objects d'art, less then 2000 images, accompanied by textual cards [5, 21]. Textual descriptions are rather inhomogeneous in content; moreover, the image as shown does not always correspond exactly to the textual description primarily, because the image is bi-dimensional, while the description refers to a three-dimensional objects (Figure 4).

Fig. 3. Query setting interface

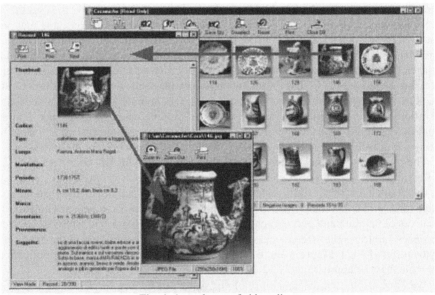

Fig. 4. A catalogue of object d'art

Our experiments were designed to compare the performance of the original pictorial-feature version of Quicklook^2 with that of the version incorporating textual annotations in finding specific images in the databases. Preliminary results indicate that the integrated use of textual and visual indices improves the retrieval performance significantly only when relevance feedback is applied. A more complete evaluation of the system's performance will be conducted on a much larger catalogue, currently under construction.

References

1. Aigrain O., Zhang H., Petkovic D.: Content-Based Representation and Retrieval of Visual Media: A State-of-the-Art Review. Multimedia Tools and Applications, 3 (1996) 179-182.
2. Amadasun M., King R.: Textural features corresponding to textural properties, IEEE Transaction on System, Man and Cybernetics, 19 (1989) 1264-1274.
3. Bach J.R., C. Fuller, A Gupta, A. Humpapur, H. Horowitz, R. Jain, C. Shu, The Virage image search engine: an opne framework for image management. Proc. SPIE Storage and Retrieval for Still Image and Video Database IV, S. Jose, 1996.
4. Berman A.P., Shapiro L.G., A flexible image database system for content-based retrieval. Computer Vision and Image Understanding, Vol. 75, Nos. 1/2, July/August, (1999) 175-195.
5. Carrara P., Della Ventura A., Gagliardi I., "Designing hypermedia information retrieval systems for multimedia art catalogues", The New Review of Hypermedia and Multimedia, vol. 2, pp. 175-195, 1996.
6. Cinque L., Levialdi S., and Pellicano' A., Color-Based Image Retrieval Using Spatial-Chromatic Histograms, IEEE Multimedia Systems 99, IEEE Computer Society, Vol. II, (1999) 969-973
7. Ciocca G., Gagliardi I., Schettini R Content-based color image retrieval with relevance feedback, Proc. International Conference on Image Processing, Kobe (Japan), Special session "Image Processing Based on Color Science", (1999).
8. Ciocca G., Gagliardi I., Schettini R., Quicklook: a content-based image retrieval system with learning capabilities, IEEE Multimedia Systems 99, IEEE Computer Society, Vol. II, (1999) 1028-1029.
9. Ciocca G., Gagliardi I., Schettini R.: Retrieving color images by content. In: Del Bimbo A., Schettini R. (eds.) Proc. of the Image and Video Content-Based Retrieval Workshop (1998)
10. Ciocca G., R. Schettini, A relevance feedback mechanism for content-based image retrieval, Information Processing and Management, 35 (1999) 605-632.
11. Ciocca G., Schettini R., Content-based similarity retrieval of trademarks using relevance feedback, Pattern Recognition, 2000 (in print)
12. Ciocca G., Gagliardi I., Schettini R, Interactive Visual Information Retrieval, 2000 IEEE International Symposium on Circuits and Systems, 28-31 may 2000 (Special Session on Digital Photography).
13. Cox I.J., M.L. Miller, S.O. Omohundro, P.N. Yianilos, PicHunter: Bayesian Relevance Feedback for Image Retrieval. Proc. ICPR'96, pp. 361-369, (1996)
14. Faloutsos C., Barber R., Flickner M., Hafner J., Niblack W., Petrovic D. Efficient and effective querying by image content, Journal of Intelligent Systems, 3 (1994) 231-262.
15. Gagliardi I., Schettini R.: A method for the automatic indexing of color images for effective image retrieval. The New Review of Hypermedia and Multimedia, 3 (1997), 201-224.
16. Gudivada V.N, Rahavan V.V.: Modeling and retrieving images by content. Information Processing and Management, 33 (1997) 427-452.
17. Harmandas V., Mark Sanderson, Mark D. Dunlop: Image Retrieval by Hypertext Links. SIGIR 1997: 296-303
18. Hu M., Visual pattern recognition by moment invariants, IRE Trans. Inf. Theory 8, 179-187, (1962).
19. Information Processing & Management, Vol. 33(2), 1997, Elsevier Science Ltd.
20. La Cascia M., S. Sethi, and S. Sclaroff Combining Textual and Visual Cues for Content-based Image Retrieval on the World Wide Web Proc. IEEE Workshop on Content-Based Access of Image and Video Libraries, June, 1998
21. La donazione Galeazzo Cora: ceramiche dal medioevo al XIX secolo, Museo Internazionale delle Ceramiche in Faenza, Gruppo Editoriale Fabbri, 1985, Milano.

22. Ma W.Y, B.S. Manjunath, Netra: a toolbox for navigating large image databases, Proc. IEEE International Conference on Image Processing, 1996.
23. Y. Miyake, H. Saitoh, H. Yaguchi, and N. Tsukada. Facial pattern detection and color correction from television picture for newspaper printing. Journal of Imaging Technology, 16:165-169, 1990.
24. Minka T., Picard R.W., Interactive learning with a "Society of Models". Pattern Recognition, Vol. 30(4), pp. 565-581, 1997.
25. Mood A.M, Graybill F.A., & Boes D.C: Introduzione alla statistica. McGraw-Hill (1988)
26. Mukherjea S., J. Cho, Automatically determining semantics for Word Wide Web multimedia information Retrieval, Journal of Visual Languages and Computing, Vol. 10, pp. 585-606, 1999.
27. Pass G., Zabih R., Miller J.: Comparing Images Using Color Coherence Vectors. Proc. Fourth ACM Multimedia 96 Conference (1996).
28. Rousseeuw P.J., Leroy A.M.: Robust regression and outlier detection, John Wiley & Sons (1987).
29. Rui Y., T.S. Huang, M. Ortega, S. Mehrotra, Relevance feedback: a power tool in interactive content-based retrieval, IEEE Transaction on Circuits and Systems for Video Technologies, Special Issue on Interactive Multimedia Systems for the Internet, Vol. 8(5), pp. 644-655, 1998.
30. Rui Y., T.S. Huang, Image retrieval: current technologies, promising directions, and open issues, Journal of Visual Communication and Image Representation, Vol. 10, pp. 39-62 (1999).
31. Salton G., A. Singhal, M. Mitra, C. Buckley, "Automatic text structuring and summarization", Information Processing & Management, Vol. 33(2), pp. 193-207, 1997, Elsevier Science Ltd.
32. Salton G., Automatic text processing, Addison-Wesley, 1989, New York.
33. Similarity in language, thought and perception, edited by Cristina Cacciari, Brepols, 1995.
34. Stricker M, Orengo M.: Similarity of Color Images. Proc. of the SPIE Storage and Retrieval for Image and Video Databases III Conference (1995).
35. Tamura H., S. Mori and T. Yamawaki, "Textural features corresponding to visual perception", IEEE Transaction on System, Man and Cybernetics 8, pp.460-473, 1978.

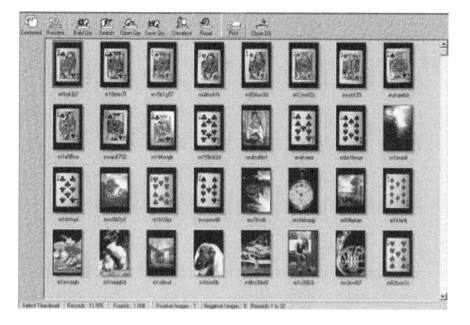

Fig. 5a. Initial retrieval results

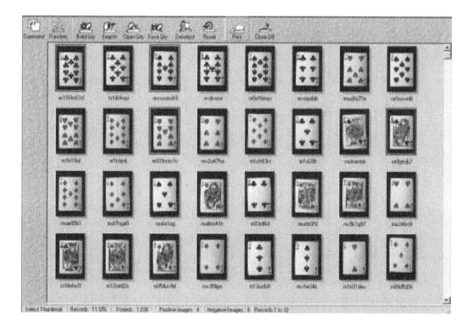

Fig. 5b. Retrieval results after the first iteration of relevance feedback

Fig. 6a. Initial retrieval results

Fig. 6b. Retrieval results after the first iteration of relevance feedback

Global Motion Fourier Series Expansion for Video Indexing and Retrieval

E. Bruno[1], D. Pellerin[1,2]

[1]Laboratoire des Images et des Signaux (LIS)
INPG, 46 Av. Félix Viallet 38031 Grenoble Cedex, France
[2]ISTG, Université Joseph Fourier, Grenoble, France
e-mail : bruno,pellerin@lis-viallet.inpg.fr

Abstract. This paper describes a new framework for global motion feature extraction and presents a video indexing and retrieval application. Optical flow between two frames is expanded, directly from the image derivatives, in a Fourier series. This technique provides a good global motion representation over a few Fourier components. These Fourier components are relevant to discriminate complex motions, such as human activities. Results of indexing and retrieval on a database of human activities sequences are presented.

1 Introduction

Video databases are growing so rapidly that most of the contained information becomes inaccessible. A valuable tool in the management of visual records is the ability to automatically "describe" and index the content of video sequences. Such a facility would allow recovery of desired video segments or objects from a very large database of image sequences. Efficient use of stock film archives and identification of specific activities in surveillance videos are usually cited as potential applications. While there is a lot of approaches to index static pictures, based on color, texture or shape, relatively little of them have focused on using motion to describe video sequences. A recent survey of image and video indexing could be found in [8].

An attractive approach consists in using global motion information to video indexing and retrieval [5, 10, 11, 13]. Without needing any prior motion segmentation or complete motion estimation, global motion feature allows to discriminate general types of motion situations. However these techniques remain unsuited to certain sequences when motions are complex, such as human activities.

In this paper we present a technique to extract global motion feature which are enough informative to discriminate complex global motions. It is based on motion Fourier series expansion. This kind of motion model has been used in the case of occlusion boundaries and moving bars estimation and detection [6]. We extend this approach to estimate the 2D Fourier series expansion of global optical flow between two frames. Such model allows to approximate a large range of motion in a compact form, and provides an efficient way to characterize

R. Laurini (Ed.): VISUAL 2000, LNCS 1929, pp. 327–337, 2000.
Springer-Verlag Berlin Heidelberg 2000

image sequences (in this work, each image sequence or sequence is considered as an elementary shot of video sequence). Global motion-based features (estimated Fourier components) are introduced in an *ascendant hierarchical classification* (AHC) in order to provide a hierarchical description of a video database [5].

This paper is organized as follows. Section 2 is concerned by the motion Fourier series expansion framework. Section 3 presents several types of motion with their Fourier model estimation. Section 4 describes the AHC procedure and results on a set of human activity sequences.

2   Global motion feature estimation

2.1   Motion Fourier series expansion

The Fourier series expansion is a powerful tool to get main characteristics of a function within some coefficients. Be $f(x)$ a periodic signal with fundamental period $T_0 = \frac{1}{\nu_0}$. If $f(x)$ is piecewise continuous and monotonic in $[-T_0/2, T_0/2]$ and if x_0 is a point of discontinuity of $f(x)$, where the right-limit and left-limit of $f(x)$ at the points x_0 exist, the Fourier series of $f(x)$ converges, and is:

$$f(x) = \sum_{k=-\infty}^{\infty} a_k e^{i2\pi k \nu_0 x}$$

with   (1)

$$a_k = \frac{1}{T_0} \int_{T_0} f(x) e^{-i2\pi k \nu_0 x} dx$$

The coefficients a_k denote the weights of each harmonic $e^{i2\pi k \nu_0 x}$ and characterize the function $f(x)$. In practical application, only a finite number of coefficients is computed in order to provide a function approximation by a trigonometric polynomial.

Let us consider $V(x, y) = (v_x(x, y), v_y(x, y))^T$ the 2D motion over a window Ω between two consecutive frames. We can write $V(x, y)$ components as a 2D periodic function, where period $T_{x_0} = \frac{1}{\nu_{x_0}}$ and $T_{y_0} = \frac{1}{\nu_{y_0}}$ are the Ω width and height respectively. In addition, we can consider that $V(x, y)$ is piecewise continuous and monotonic and, if singularities exist, their right-limit and left-limit exist too. Thus Fourier series approximation of $v_x(x, y)$ and $v_y(x, y)$ are:

$$v_x(x, y) \simeq \sum_{k,l=-N/2}^{N/2} a_x^{k,l} e^{i2\pi(k\nu_{x_0} x + l\nu_{y_0} y)}$$

$$v_y(x, y) \simeq \sum_{k,l=-N/2}^{N/2} a_y^{k,l} e^{i2\pi(k\nu_{x_0} x + l\nu_{y_0} y)}$$ (2)

For implementation ease, we have used real Fourier coefficients rather than complex Fourier coefficients. Obviously, complex and real Fourier expansions are

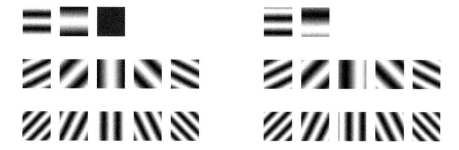

Fig. 1. Even and odd parts of the first 25 harmonics ($N = 4$) used to decompose $V(x, y)$.

equivalent. Figure 1 displays harmonics (even and odd part) corresponding to $N = 4$. Global motion is thus represented as a weighted sum of these patches.

At pixel $p(x, y, t)$, motion components are lying together by the *differential constraint equation* [7]:

$$I_x v_x(x, y) + I_y v_y(x, y) + I_t = 0 \tag{3}$$

with $I(x, y, t)$ the spatio-temporal luminance at pixel $p(x, y, t)$, $I_x = \frac{\partial I(x,y,t)}{\partial x}$, $I_y = \frac{\partial I(x,y,t)}{\partial y}$ and $I_t = \frac{\partial I(x,y,t)}{\partial t}$. Substituting relation (2) in equation (3) provides:

$$I_x \sum_{k,l=-N/2}^{N/2} a_x^{k,l} e^{i2\pi(k\nu_{x_0} x + l\nu_{y_0} y)} + I_y \sum_{k,l=-N/2}^{N/2} a_y^{k,l} e^{i2\pi(k\nu_{x_0} x + l\nu_{y_0} y)} = -I_t \tag{4}$$

Equation (4) is under-constrained since there are $P = 2(N + 1)^2$ unknowns. Then, using the fact that each location $p(x, y, t) \in \Omega$ satisfies equation (4), and using matrix notation, we obtain the system:

$$M\mathbf{a} = -B \tag{5}$$

where

$$M = \begin{pmatrix} I_x^{-N/2,-N/2}(p_1) & I_y^{-N/2,-N/2}(p_1) & \cdots & I_x^{k,l}(p_1) & I_y^{k,l}(p_1) & \cdots & I_y^{N/2,N/2}(p_1) \\ I_x^{-N/2,-N/2}(p_2) & I_y^{-N/2,-N/2}(p_2) & \cdots & I_x^{k,l}(p_2) & I_y^{k,l}(p_2) & \cdots & I_y^{N/2,N/2}(p_2) \\ \vdots & \vdots & & \vdots & \vdots & \ddots \\ I_x^{-N/2,-N/2}(p_m) & I_y^{-N/2,-N/2}(p_m) & \cdots & I_x^{k,l}(p_m) & I_y^{k,l}(p_m) & \cdots & I_y^{N/2,N/2}(p_m) \end{pmatrix}$$

$$\mathbf{a} = \left(a_x^{-N/2,-N/2}, a_y^{-N/2,-N/2}, \cdots a_x^{k,l}, a_y^{k,l}, \cdots, a_x^{N/2,N/2}, a_y^{N/2,N/2} \right)^T$$

$$B = \left(I_t(p_1), I_t(p_2), \cdots, I_t(p_m) \right)^T \tag{6}$$

with $I_{x/y}^{k,l} = I_{x/y}.e^{i2\pi(k\nu_{x_0}x+l\nu_{y_0}y)}$, $p_i = p(x,y,t) \in \Omega$ and $m = card(\Omega)$. Since $m > P$, system (5) is over-constrained and can be solved with the least-squares technique.

2.2   Least-squares solution by use of Singular Value Decomposition

In the case of an over-determined system, *Singular Value Decomposition* (SVD) produces a solution that is the best approximation in the least-squares sense [12]. We can write the non-square matrix M (since number of rows m is greater than number of columns P) as:

$$M = U \begin{pmatrix} w_1 & & & \\ & w_2 & & \\ & & \ddots & \\ & & & w_P \end{pmatrix} V^T \qquad (7)$$

U is an $m \times P$ column-orthogonal matrix, the $P * P$ diagonal matrix contains the *singular values* and V is an $P * P$ orthogonal matrix. It follows immediately that the inverse of M is:

$$M^{-1} = V[diag(1/w_j)]U^T \qquad (8)$$

Thus, the least-squares solution vector **a** is given by:

$$\mathbf{a} = -V[diag(1/w_j)]U^T B \qquad (9)$$

Column degeneracies in M (if exist) correspond to "small" or null w_j. To overcome this problem, one just needs to zero $1/w_j$ in relation (9). Then the solution corresponds to a subspace of vector B. In our case, this means that we zero one or more corrupted harmonic components without spreading roundoff errors to other components. Matrix M is numerically singular if the *condition number* of M, equal to $\frac{max(w_j)}{min(w_j)}$, is larger than a value, assumed 10^6 for floating precision. Thus, we consider "small w_j" as any *singular values* lower than $10^6 * max(w_j)$.

The Ω window, where **a** is estimated, has its lower size bounded by the number of harmonics used in relation (2). With this restriction, regression could be achieved on predefined blocks or on extracted areas resulting from a spatio-temporal segmentation when accurate description is needed. However for many types of motions and without any prior stage, a global estimation on the whole image will be close to real motion and able to extract some structure properties.

3   Optical flow results

In this section, we illustrate the Fourier model ability to represent a large range of motions. In this aim, we estimate motion Fourier components on both synthetic and real sequences. These sequences contain motion boundary, affine motion and natural complex motion. Results are represented in optical flow form in order to visualize the informative content of vector **a**.

3.1   Motion boundary

The estimation of motion boundary is an important problem in image sequences analysis. Fourier series expansion allows to model discontinuities. As an example the step function expansion is:

$$f(x,y) = \frac{4}{\pi}\left(\sin \nu_{x_0} x + \frac{1}{3}\sin 3\nu_{x_0} x + \frac{1}{5}\sin 5\nu_{x_0} x + \cdots\right) \qquad (10)$$

To test our technique on this type of function, we used a synthetic sequence which contains two opposite motions (Figure 2.a).

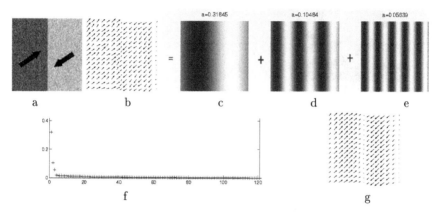

Fig. 2. Motion boundary with a) frame from sequence, b) estimated Fourier model motion with $N = 10$, c,d,e) the three highest harmonics for both v_x and v_y, f) plot of Fourier components $a_x^{k,l}$ in descending order and g) estimated Fourier model motion with $N = 4$.

Global motion was estimated with 121 harmonics ($N = 10$). Optical flow (Figure 2.b) is mainly a sum of the three highest components represented in Figure 2.c,d and e, since other terms in the sum have a very low contribution (Figure 2.f). As expected, the motion Fourier series expansion is conformed to expression (10).

However, using a large number of harmonics needs heavy computational cost and can introduce errors. Actually, the system (5) becomes less over-constrained when the number of unknowns are increasing. In order to reduce these problems, one needs to expand motion on fewer terms. A good compromise is reached with 25 harmonics ($N = 4$). For example, reconstructed optical flow (Figure 2.g) of the motion boundary sequence remains a close representation to real motion. For the rest of this section, we have chosen to expand motion on 25 harmonics. Lets note that 25 harmonics used represents 50 unknowns in equation (4).

3.2   Affine motions

Affine model is largely used in motion analysis. Most of motion induced by camera displacement can be modeled by an affine transformation (translation, zoom, rotation...). It is important to show how Fourier model deals with such motion.

Figure 3.a and 3.d represent two synthetic motion sequences used in [1]: Diverging Tree with pure diverging motion (Figure 3.b) and Yosemite with translating motion in the sky and diverging motion on the hills (Figure 3.e). Estimated

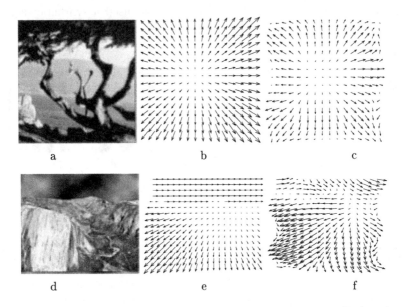

a   b   c

d   e   f

Fig. 3. (a,d) Frame from Diverging Tree and Yosemite sequence with (b,e) real optical flow and (c,f) reconstructed optical flow from **a** ($N = 4$)

global motion (Figure 3.c and Figure 3.f) are conform to reality. Nevertheless, using affine motion description will provide an accurate estimation for Diverging Tree. But such a model could not give a reliable description with Yosemite sequence, when Fourier motion model can take into account not only diverging motion on the hills, but also translating motion in the sky.

3.3   Complex motion

In the last example (Figure 4), the rotating Rubik cube sequence has a global motion more complex. Figure 4.b shows a dense optical flow estimated with algorithm presented in [2], close to the real image motion. Fourier model (Figure 4.c) is able to represent the rotating Rubik cube, but has failed to express motionless background. In this case, model limit is reached. In addition, the lack of textures in the background does not constraint enough system (9) to provide a more accurate estimation.

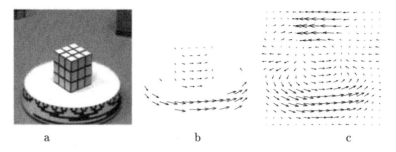

a   b   c

Fig. 4. Rubic with (a) frame from sequence, (b) optical flow dense estimation and (c) reconstructed optical flow from **a** ($N = 4$)

We have seen that Fourier series expansion allows to model a large range of optical flows. The number of harmonics used to model global motion will influence the description accuracy and the estimation robustness. Using a small number of Fourier terms allows to obtain relevant and robust information about global motion. This technique provides efficient motion-based feature for video indexing and retrieval.

4   Video indexing and retrieval using global motion Fourier components

In this section we are interested in motion-based indexing and retrieval using motion Fourier series expansion. Fourier components extracted from different sequences provide for each frame i of sequence S a motion Fourier vector $\mathbf{a}_S^i$. The motion-based feature vector associated to the sequence S is then defined as the center of gravity of all motion Fourier vectors of S.

$$\bar{a}_S = \frac{1}{N} \sum_{i=1}^{N} \mathbf{a}_S^i \tag{11}$$

4.1   Hierarchical indexing and retrieval

Once the entire database is characterized by (11), it is necessary to construct a hierarchical index representation which, given a query sequence described by a vector $\bar{a}_S$, directly points to classes of similar motion properties.

The *ascendant hierarchical classification* (AHC) [4] is an incremental clustering process used with efficiency for image and video database management [5, 9]. Let us consider the feature space containing database feature vectors. First, the AHC algorithm merges the closest pairs of vectors $\bar{a}_h, \bar{a}_k$ to form new clusters associated to their center of gravity. A sequence whose vector $\bar{a}_h$ is isolated from all the other ones, i.e. $min_k \parallel \bar{a}_h - \bar{a}_k \parallel > D_{max}$, where D_{max} is a predefined distance threshold, is kept as individual cluster. This procedure is iterated, until any clusters cannot be merged, for the lowest level to the upper one in the hierarchy.

Once the hierarchical index is constructed for the whole database, the retrieval with query by example procedure is as follow. First, the feature vector $\bar{a}$ is computed from the query sequence. The search starts from the upper level, where the retrieval algorithm selects the cluster which has the closest center of gravity to the query feature vector (according to the Euclidian norm). Then, the children node with the shortest distance to the query feature vector is selected. This process is repeated until the number of sequences represented by a node corresponds to the number of desired responses from the database.

4.2   Results

This approach has been validated with sequences representing six human activities (Figure 5): *up, down, left, right, come* and *go* . These sequences were acquired for activities recognition [3] (aquisition rate: $10Hz$). Each sequence includes ten frames and there are five sequences for each activity with different persons. So, video database contains 30 sequences.

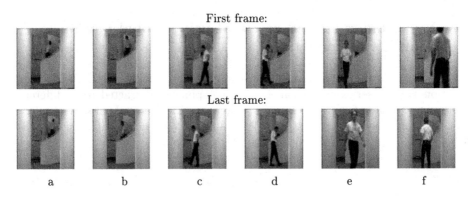

Fig. 5. First and last frame of human activities sequences: a) *"up"*, b) *"down"*, c) *"left"*, d) *"right"*, e) *"come"* and f) *"go"*

After computing motion-based feature vector for each sequence, AHC is applied to the database feature space. Figure 6 and 7 displays the center of gravity of each cluster with the associate sequences at the tree upper level for respectively a 18 dimension ($N = 2$) and a 50 dimension feature space ($N = 4$).

Classification with fewer features remains related to the main global motion properties of sequences (Figure 6). In fact, each cluster represents one type of activity. However, there is some misclassified sequences, such as the two sequences *down* which belong to the *go* class or some problems with *right* and *come* activities.

The six sequence classes proceeded from the 50 dimension feature space give a more efficient description of the different human activities present in the database (Figure 7). In particular, activity sequences *up*, *down*, *left* and *go* are perfectly classified. However, the activities *right* and *come*, which have close motion, belong to the same class. Obviously, in this case, the fact that we add more Fourier components to describe motion allows to remove some ambiguities between activities.

When the hierarchical index is constructed for the whole database, the retrieval stage with query by example compute, according to a maximum number of answers, the closest cluster in the tree. Figure 8 displays the first 3 answers according to a query *up* and a query *come*. According to the classification results (Figure 7), the retrieval process supplies accurate answers to the query *up*, whereas all answers for the query *come* are not relevant (Figure 8). However, all answers have the same right to left main motion.

5   Conclusion

We have presented a new framework to extract global motion features from video sequences. It is based on the optical flow Fourier series expansion between two consecutive frames. This kind of expansion has the advantage to model various types of motions and provides relevant information about motion structure. It is important to note that motion Fourier components are estimated directly from the image derivatives and do not require prior information of dense image motion.

We illustrated method abilities with an example of motion-based video indexing and retrieval. The mean of each frame Fourier components provides a relevant motion-based feature vector for the entire sequence. The AHC algorithm allows to build an appropriate database representation. Results of classification and retrieval using query by example are good and give a proof of motion-based Fourier descriptors efficiency.

Future work will explore two main issues. First, in the same way that we compute global motion components, it could be interesting to estimate local motion Fourier components to deal with more complex motion or to have an accurate motion estimation. Secondly, the motion-based feature vector definition (at present, the mean of each frame Fourier components) must be improved in order to better take into account Fourier components variation within a sequence.

References

1. J.L. Barron, D.J. Fleet, and S.S. Beauchemin. Performance of optical flow techniques. *International Journal of Computer Vision*, 1(12):43–77, 1994.

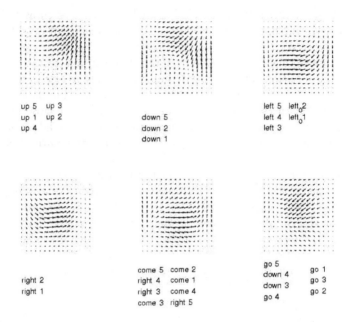

Fig. 6. Center of gravity of each cluster and associate sequences at the AHC hierarchy upper level. The dimension of the feature space is 18

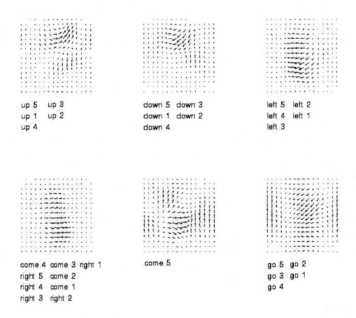

Fig. 7. Center of gravity of each cluster and associate sequences at the AHC hierarchy upper level. The dimension of the feature space is 50

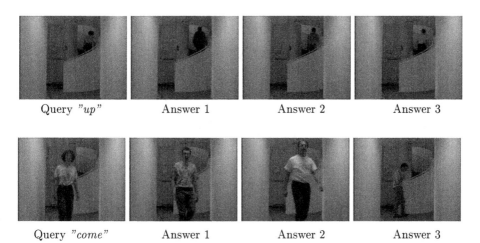

Query "up"   Answer 1   Answer 2   Answer 3

Query "come"   Answer 1   Answer 2   Answer 3

Fig. 8. The first 3 retrieval sequences to the queries *"up"* and *"come"* (only the first image of each sequence is displayed)

2. E. Bruno and D. Pellerin. Robust motion estimation using spatial gabor filters. In *X European Signal Processing Conference*, September 2000.
3. O. Chomat and J. Crowley. Probabilistic recognition of activity using local appearance. In *Conference on Computer Vision ans Pattern Recognition (CVPR)*, June 1999.
4. E. Diday, G. Govaert, Y. Lechevallier, and J. Sidi. Clustering in pattern recognition. *Digital Image Processing*, pages 19–58, 1981.
5. R. Fablet and P. Bouthemy. Motion-based feature extraction and ascendant hierarchical classification for video indexing and retrieval. In *Proc. of the 3rd Int. Conf. on Visual Information Systems, VISual99*, volume 1614, pages 221–228, June 1999.
6. D. J. Fleet, M. J. Black, and A. D. Jepson. Motion feature detection using steerable flow fields. In *IEEE Conf. on Computer Vision and Pattern Recognition, CVPR-98*, 1998.
7. B.K.P. Horn and B.G. Schunk. Determing optical flow. *Artificial Intelligence*, 17:185–204, 1981.
8. F. Idris and S. Panchantan. Review of image and video indexing. *Journal of Visual Communication and Image Representation*, 8(2):146–147, June 1997.
9. R. Milanese, D. Squire, and T. Pun. Correspondence analysis and hierarchical indexing for content-based image retrieval. In *ICIP'96*, September 1996.
10. R. Nelson and P. Polana. Qualitative recognition of motions using temporal texture. In *CVGIP: Image Understanding*, volume 1, July 1992.
11. K. Otsuka, T. Horikoshi, S. Suzuki, and M. Fujii. Feature extraction of temporal texture based on spatio-temporal motion trajectory. In *Proc. Int. Conf. on Pattern Recognition, ICPR'98*, August 1998.
12. W. H. Press, S.A. Teukolsky, W.T. Vetterling, and B.P. Flannery. *Numerical Recipies in C, Second Edition*. Cambridge University Press, 1992.
13. M. Szummer and R.W. Picard. Temporal texture modeling. In *ICIP'96*, September 1996.

Feature Driven Visualization of Video Content for Interactive Indexing

Jeroen Vendrig and Marcel Worring

Intelligent Sensory Information Systems, Department of Computer Science
University of Amsterdam, The Netherlands
Kruislaan 403, 1098 SJ Amsterdam
Tel/fax: ++31-20-525.7463/7490
{vendrig, worring}@wins.uva.nl

Abstract. When using visual video features in an interactive video indexing environment, it is necessary to visualize the meaning and impact of features to people that are not image processing experts, such as video librarians. An important method to visualize the relationship between the feature and the video is projection of feature values on the original video data.

In this paper, we describe the characteristics of video feature types with respect to visualization. In addition, requirements for the visualization of video features are distinguished. Several video visualization methods are evaluated against the requirements. Furthermore, for feature visualization we propose the backprojection method in combination with the evaluated video visualization methods.

We have developed the VidDex system which uses backprojection on various video visualization modes. By combining the visualization modes, the requirements for the feature characteristics identified can be met.

1 Introduction

For effective retrieval and interactive exploration of large digital video archives, it's necessary to index the videos using their visual, audio and textual data. We currently focus on the visual content of videos for indexing.

An important aspect of indexing of and navigation through digital video archives is the generation of video structure. Fully automatic interpretation of video content may be feasible in limited or well specified domains, e.g. TV sitcoms or broadcast news. In general domains, such as movies and documentaries, however, automatic interpretation of visual content still depends on the availability of human knowledge because of the "semantic gap". Therefore an image processing system and a human domain expert have to interact, requiring both partners to talk the same language. To achieve this, feature meanings have to be mapped to a form the viewer can relate to, since generally low-level visual features are hard to comprehend for humans. Feature driven visualization using backprojection on video summaries is an intuitive way to clarify to users the relationship between feature values and the original video data. Target users

R. Laurini (Ed.): VISUAL 2000, LNCS 1929, pp. 338–348, 2000.
Springer-Verlag Berlin Heidelberg 2000

are application developers and video content experts. The former want to evaluate the impact of their features and parameters. The latter are video librarians who want to navigate through a large amount of data to comprehend and index content quickly.

Once useful features for visualization on syntactic structure, the elementary level of visually and temporally coherent sequences, are found, the index system could be completed with high level structures to find semantic coherency. Examples of existing semantic structure detectors are Scene Transition Graphs [12] and Logical Story Unit segmentation [5].

This paper is organized as follows. First we describe the requirements for feature visualization. In section 3, we categorize feature types from a visualization perspective. Next, the backprojection method is introduced. In section 5, we systematically evaluate several methods for visualizing video content in relation to the backprojection method, the feature types and the visualization goals.

2   Visualization requirements

In this paper, we assume video segments correspond to shots, viz. "a strip of film produced by a single uninterrupted running of the camera" [2]. Shots are the building blocks for generation of syntactic video structure since they are "the finest level of descriptive granularity" [4].

For the purpose of assisting librarians in creating syntactic structure in large video sequences, we distinguish three shot feature visualization requirements:

- speed: the viewer has to be able to comprehend the content of the video and the associated feature value quickly.
- context: the viewer has to be able to establish the relationship between the video content and the feature values.
  - pictorial: the contribution of the video image data values to the feature value has to be visualized.
  - temporal: the viewer has to be able to evaluate differences and similarities between several video shots with respect to the feature values.
  - synchronization: the feature visualization and the visualization of the original video data have to refer to the same video sequence.
- general applicability: the feature has to be visualized on every type of video shot that can reasonably be expected.

The requirements ensure that the viewer is provided with a consistent feature visualization which can easily be related to the original video data. It allows to find structure in the pictorial content.

3   Pictorial video features

In this section, we establish *what, where/when* and *how* measurements are taken for visualization of video content. We first formalize aspects of video features in order to characterize them with respect to visualization. A video shot V consists of an uninterrupted sequence of T frame images $i_0..i_{T-1}$. Since visualization takes place on two levels, we introduce a video stream component C that can be either of type shot or of type frame. To characterize the visual content of a shot, visual shot features $f \in F$ are used. Generally, a feature f is an aggregation α^f (e.g. an average operator) over values measured by a measurement operation ψ^f on C (e.g. creation of a color histogram). The resulting feature value is denoted v^f. $\mathcal{I}^f$ is the range of valid values for v^f.

To characterize a shot feature based on video stream components, we distinguish three dimensions:

- measurement operation, the type of operation α that aggregates input values measured in video stream components into a value for the shot feature.
  - representation: $\mathcal{I}^f(\psi^f(C)) = \mathcal{I}^f(\alpha^f(\psi^f(C)))$.
  - abstraction: $\mathcal{I}^f(\psi^f(C)) \neq \mathcal{I}^f(\alpha^f(\psi^f(C)))$.

In the case of a representation operation, the feature value is a valid measurement value in the original video data domain. Hence, the output data type (of the feature value) is the same as the input data type (of the video data measurement). In the case of an abstraction operation, the feature value is an aggregation of measurement values from the original video data domain. Hence, the output data type differs from the input data type.

The representation measurement is data-driven and assumes no prior knowledge about the measurement values. It determines which value represents a shot best. Let us consider the example of the dominant color feature, based on a color histogram. If the blue bin is the most frequent color, it can be represented by the original values (all colors within the bin range) or by a static value for the bin (e.g. the median).

The abstraction measurement is model-driven. It assumes that only specific measured values are relevant for the feature value and considers just those for the feature value: how is a given value represented in a shot? For example, in [3] it is stated that the degree of action in a video is higher when the colors red and purple are significantly present. For such a feature, measurement values of other colors are ignored. This kind of feature typically is a count or average aggregation, e.g. the percentage of red and purple pixels in a frame.

The next dimension is defined as follows:

- measurement class, the type of video stream component on which a measurement operation is performed:
  - spatial: $v_t^f = \psi^f(i_t)$.
  - spatiotemporal: $v_t^f = \psi^f(i_t, i_{t+1})$.

For the sake of simplicity, the definition of the spatiotemporal class is limited to just two subsequent frames, but it could easily be extended to cope with a larger set of frames.

A value in the spatial class is based on pictorial data in one frame, e.g. a color histogram. For the spatiotemporal class the value is based on the relationship

Table 1. Examples of shot features in the 3 dimensions. For the measurement operation dimension, R=representation, A=abstraction.

	local	global
Spatial	R: object position [1]	R: dominant color
	A: size of object	A: number of recurring colors [3]
Spatiotemporal	R: object trajectory [7]	R: frame difference
	A: object's distance covered [7]	A: shot activity [8]

between pictorial data in several frames, e.g. an optic flow field. These measurements are also known in other contexts as intra-frame versus inter-frame [3] and instantaneous versus non-instantaneous [1] measurements.

Note that although spatial measurements of various frames are usually accumulated into a feature value for the entire shot, this operation is not done at the spatiotemporal measurement level since it ignores the relationships between frames. It can be described as $\alpha^f(\bigcup_{i\in I}\psi^f_{spatial}(i))$, where $I \subseteq V$. When a spatiotemporal feature uses spatial measurements to establish the relationship between frames, it can be described as $\psi^f_{spatiotemporal}(\psi^f_{spatial}(i_t), \psi^f_{spatial}(i_{t+n}))$.

The last dimension is defined as follows:

- measurement scope, the extent to which a video stream component is used for a measurement:
  - local: $v^f = \psi^f(C')$ where C' denotes a proper subset of C.
  - global: $v^f = \psi^f(C)$.

The value in the local scope is based on just a part of the video stream component, while in the global scope it is based on the entire component. For spatial measurements, the scope characterization is known from image processing. For spatiotemporal measurements the characterization needs further explanation. Since video streams contain huge amounts of redundant pictorial data, it is not always necessary to use all data available to compute a feature value. For example, if just a few frames are selected as representative for the entire shot, i.e. I is a proper subset of V, the measurement scope is local. If every frame in the shot is used for the computation of a feature, i.e. $I = V$, the scope is global.

In conclusion, features denote *what* is measured for visualization of video content. The measurement level and scope dimensions establish *where/when* measurements are taken, while the measurement operation dimension determines *how* is measured. In table 1 for all eight cells in the three dimensions feature examples are given.

4   Backprojection

Relating feature values to the original video content is of utmost importance to fulfill the requirements from section 2. Therefore, we use the *backprojection* method to visualize features in a way that allows the viewer to quickly relate values for a feature to the original video content. Backprojection determines how pixels in a frame are visualized by comparing their values for a specific feature and given values for the same feature. Examples are given in figures 2 and 3.

Our approach is comparable to the technique described in [9], but is not limited to one specific feature. Backprojection results in an image determined by visualization values v' for a pictorial data component p, typically a pixel.

$$v'^f(p) = \begin{cases} v'^f_{undefined} & \text{if } \psi^f(p) \notin \mathcal{I}(\psi^f(p)) \vee p \notin C' \\ v'^f_{active} & \text{if } \psi^f(p) = v^f; \\ v'^f_{inactive} & \text{if } \psi^f(p) \neq v^f. \end{cases} \tag{1}$$

The three possible values for v' are application dependent. Typically v'_{active} is equal to either v or to the original video data value. Usually, $v'_{inactive}$ and $v'_{undefined}$ are values that are not likely to appear in, or not part of, the domain of v'_{active}, e.g. very bright colors or gray values. $v'_{undefined}$ is used when no valid value is returned from ψ, e.g. gray values are undefined when measuring the hue of a color. Especially when the measurement scope is local, parts of the pictorial data can be undefined for a feature.

The measurement operation class has a big impact on the applicability of backprojection. For representation values, backprojection is trivial. Features based on abstract measurement, however, cannot be related to the original data directly, since they are defined for a shot in its entirety only. In this case there are two alternatives to comply with the context requirement from section 2.

The first alternative is to map the feature value to the domain of the video, e.g. by computing a gray value. The values then are in the same domain, albeit with different semantics. Such visualizations transfer little information to the user though, since they do not provide a pictorial and synchronization context.

The second alternative is to not visualize the feature value itself, but the measurement value it is based on. This is possible because both abstract and representation measurements do use the same measurement operations to compute feature values. Using the example of the action feature [3] again, not the actual feature value (e.g. the factual number "30% red and purple"), but the colors red and purple itself would be visualized. It is then left to the user to make the mapping from the representation to the abstraction. Hence, visualization behaves as a representation measurement operation. Then for abstract measurement, visualization on the original data tells the viewer what the feature value is based on. For representation measurement, it tells the viewer what the feature value is and what areas in the image have that value.

The measurement scope dimension has few impact on backprojection. The only consequence is that if measurements are local, the visualization has to show those local spots in the original video data as well. This is not always possible, since video summaries can be used, as will be shown in section 5. Only in the case of local measurements, it is required that the visualization shows the local spots in the original video data.

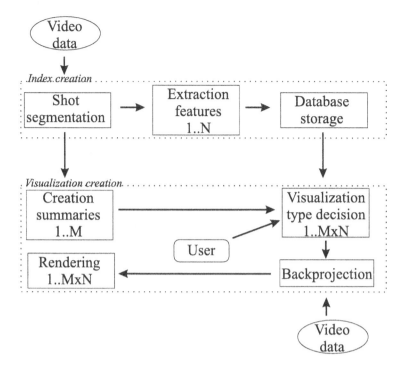

Fig. 1. Architecture of feature driven visualization system VidDex.

5 Video content visualization

The pictorial content of a video can be visualized in various ways. Showing the video as a stream is trivial. Alternatively, one can choose to see a video summary, which allows the viewer to evaluate large video sequences quickly. In this section, we evaluate the most important summary visualizations: key frames, mosaicking and slice summaries. The various visualization methods are evaluated with respect to backprojection. Table 2 summarizes to which degree the 4 visualization methods fulfill the visualization goals from section 2.

Backprojection on video summaries is implemented in the VidDex system described in figure 1. VidDex is based on the Microsoft DirectX Media Toolkit[1] for access to the video data and the Horus Image Library[2] for computation of feature values. In figures 2 and 3 example results from a feature film and a television series are shown.

5.1 Stream

For feature visualization the video stream method is very clear, since the backprojection is seen in every detail. The obvious disadvantage is the time needed

---

[1] http://www.microsoft.com/directx/
[2] http://www.wins.uva.nl/~horus/

Table 2. Feature visualization goals versus visualization methods

Method	speed	pictorial	temporal	synchronization	applicability
Stream	-	+	-	±	+
Key frames	±	±	±	+	+
Mosaicking	+	+	+	±	-
Slice summary	+	±	+	+	+

to evaluate a feature. The viewer is also forced to watch individual shots for a long time, while he has to establish differences between shots in a split second. Furthermore, the viewer is tempted to interpret visualization in one frame as visualization for the entire shot, making up for lack of synchronization. This may lead to confusion since the values really are abstractions of the underlying data. For example, blue may be the dominant color for a shot, but the color blue does not necessarily have to appear in each individual frame. The advantage of the visualization type is the possibility to evaluate specific details since everything is shown. It's especially suitable for fine-tuning in short video sequences.

5.2   Key frames

Key frames are frames from the video stream that represent its content. Since they're part of the original video stream, here too backprojection provides clear details, but only for the specific point in the stream. The problem is which and how many frames should be selected depending on the content. If too few frames are shown, the relationship between the feature value and the original content may not be obvious. If too many frames are shown, the viewer has to process much redundant data and is not able to relate shots. Key frames are especially suitable for visualizing static video shots, such as in dialog scenes, because the spatiotemporal aspect hardly plays a role then. In such cases one frame can easily represent the entire shot.

   In order to present key frames that best relate to the feature value being visualized, for each feature a different key frame is chosen to represent a shot, in contrast to using all available features for the selection process. At the moment, VidDex chooses the frame in a shot that has the feature value most similar to the shot feature value. Let δ_f be a function that computes the difference between the feature value of frame i and shot feature value v^f. Then a feature based key frame k^f for an image sequence is defined as follows.

$$k^f = \{i_j \in V \mid i_j = \operatorname*{argmin}_{j=0..T-1} \delta_f(\psi^f(i_j), v^f)\} \tag{2}$$

The amount of key frames selected could easily be extended to a dynamic number per shot for cases where visual content varies significantly within one shot. The use of distinct features allows a variable number of key frames for each feature. E.g. if there is a high variance in the values for feature A, it could use 5 key frames to represent the content, while for feature B only 1 key frame is needed. This reduces the information load for the user who is evaluating the video content.

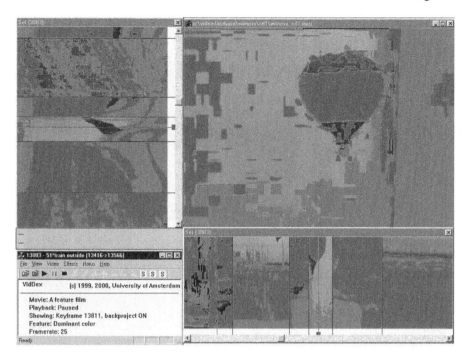

Fig. 2. The VidDex system with feature visualization. The dual slice summary shows the horizontal slice at the left and the vertical slice at the bottom, visualizing the dominant color feature. Pixels in the dominant color are shown in their original value, pixels with other colors are shown in green and colorless pixels are shown in gray. The red line indicates the current position in the video stream, blue lines denote shot boundaries. Clicking in the slices gives access to the key frame of the related shot, or to the related frames in the video stream (upper right). In this example, the background (blue sky) is the dominant color, the main object (a balloon) is green and the black window frame at the right is gray.

5.3   Slice summary

Slice summaries are very compact, two dimensional representations of a video. A slice is based on just one line of pixels of every frame, meaning the value for the vertical dimension is fixed in the case of a horizontal slice, which consequently has the size width*length of sequence, and vice versa for a vertical slice, which size is height*length. The fixed values are usually the center of the frame. Video slices were originally used for detecting cuts and camera movement [11], but they are now used for visualization as well, such as in the OM-representation [6]. The viewer can evaluate the relationship between shots quickly, e.g. in a dialog. Recurrent visual content can be spotted easily in a large amount of frames, typically 600 frames on a 15 inch screen. In special cases, a slice summary even gives a very exact representation of the visual content in a shot, so that a viewer immediately understands what is happening in the video and what kind of scene

Fig. 3. Visualization of a frame difference feature, based on hue histograms, in the context of the original dual slice summary. In this example, a yellow cab is moving and in the background parts of a building are visible because of a camera effect. Again, colors that are not contributing to the feature value are green, and pixels that are not defined for this feature (singular points) are gray.

a shot is part of. This does, however, require the object to move slowly relative to the camera in a direction perpendicular to the slice direction. The disadvantage of slice summaries is the assumption that relevant content is positioned in the slice areas. Although generally the region of interest is near the center of a frame, it's very well possible a slice summary misses action in the corners of a frame.

VidDex uses a dual slice summary that simultaneously shows both a horizontal and a vertical video slice[3]. The use of two directions increases the chance of showing a visually meaningful summary. The vertical slice provides most information about the video content since in practice it is more likely that the camera or object moves from left to right than from bottom to top. Dual slice summaries are very well suitable for backprojection since they include a part of every single frame in a shot. Note that a slice summary usually represents several subsequent shots in one image. In those cases, other than in mosaics and key frames, the parameters for the backprojection operation do not apply to the entire image. The slice summary must then be treated as a collection of separate images, each connected to one shot, on which the backprojections are performed.

---

[3] Examples available at http://carol.wins.uva.nl/~vendrig/samples/viddex/slices.html

Table 3. Suitable visualization methods depending on two dimensions of the video feature characterization.

Scope/Class	local	global
Spatial	keyframe, stream	keyframe, stream
Spatiotemporal	mosaicking	slice summary

5.4   Mosaicking

Mosaicking combines the pictorial content of several (parts of) frames into one image. Salient stills [10] are a noteworthy instance of mosaicking in which the output image has the same size as the input frames. The advantage of mosaicking is the visualization beyond frame borders and the visualization of events by showing the same object several times at different positions. The disadvantage is its dependence on uniform movement of camera or objects, making mosaicking only applicable in very specific situations. Also, the overlaying of visual information makes it harder for the viewer to synchronize video data and feature visualization. Mosaicking is well suitable for backprojection, but lacks general applicability. For this reason, mosaicking is not part of the VidDex system.

5.5   Discussion

Based on the findings in this section, we construct table 5.5 which shows which visualization methods perform best for different types of features. The performance is invariant under the measurement operation used. In the measurement class, mosaicking and slice summary are best able to visualize spatiotemporal features. Mosaicking is good for visualizing details at various time points. Hence, it performs best for features in the local measurement scope. Of course the general applicability problem noted before remains. A slice summary is not suitable for local features, because it captures just a small part of the video data. It is, however, very powerful for global features, since a slice summary is able to capture the general content of a video sequence well and it fulfills the temporal context requirement. If the measurement class is spatial, keyframes and the stream itself are sufficient to capture the details of the visualization. In this case it does not matter whether the measurement scope is global or local, since in both cases the entire picture will be visualized.

6   Conclusion and future work

Feature driven visualization of video data and video summaries using backprojection allows the viewer to quickly comprehend the meaning of a feature in the context of the particular video sequence. It helps developers to define and evaluate feature performance to fine-tune parameters. Furthermore, it allows the viewer to evaluate and compare video segments with respect to video features.

Using backprojection directly on video streams is useful to determine the expressive power of the values the aggregate feature is based on. Backprojection on video summaries is useful to determine the expressive power of the value of the aggregate feature itself, allowing video librarians to relate shots semantically based on visual characteristics.

Future research includes automatic pre-selection of features and scene determination based on consistence in shot feature values.

References

1. Z. Aghbari, K. Kaneko, and A. Makinouchi. Vst-model: A uniform topological modeling of the visual-spatio-temporal video features. In *Proc. of the 6th IEEE Int. Conf. on Multimedia Systems*, volume 2, pages 163–168, 1999.
2. J.M. Boggs and D.W. Petrie. *The art of watching films*. Mayfield Publishing Company, Mountain View, CA, 5th edition, 2000.
3. C. Colombo, A. DelBimbo, and P. Pala. Semantics in visual information retrieval. *IEEE Multimedia*, 6(3):38–53, 1999.
4. G. Davenport, T. Aguierre Smith, and N. Pincever. Cinematic principles for multimedia. *IEEE Computer Graphics & Applications*, pages 67–74, July 1991.
5. A. Hanjalic, R.L. Lagendijk, and J. Biemond. *Automatically segmenting movies into logical story units*, volume 1614 of *Lecture Notes in Computer Science*, pages 229–236. Springer-Verlag, Berlin, 1999.
6. H. Müller and E. Tan. Movie maps. In *International Conference on Information Visualization*, London, England, 1999. IEEE.
7. G.S. Pingali, Y. Jean, and I. Carlbom. *LucentVision: A System for Enhanced Sports Viewing*, volume 1614 of *Lecture Notes in Computer Science*, pages 689–696. Springer-Verlag, Berlin, 1999.
8. Y. Rui, T.S. Huang, and S. Mehrotra. Constructing table-of-content for videos. *Multimedia Systems, Special section on Video Libraries*, 7(5):359–368, 1999.
9. J.R. Smith and S.-F. Chang. Integrated spatial and feature image query. *Multimedia Systems*, 7(2):129–140, 1999.
10. L. Teodosio and W. Bender. Salient video stills: Content and context preserved. In *Proc. of the First ACM Int'l Conf. on Multimedia*, pages 39–46, 1993.
11. K. Weixin, R. Yao, and L. Hanqing. A new scene breakpoint detection algorithm using slice of video stream. In H.H.S. Ip and A.W.M. Smeulders, editors, *MINAR'98*, pages 175–180, Hongkong, China, 1998. IAPR.
12. B.-L. Yeo and M.M. Yeung. Retrieving and visualizing video. *Communications of the ACM*, 40(12):43–52, 1997.

Conceptual Indexing of Television Images Based on Face and Caption Sizes and Locations

Remi Ronfard *, Christophe Garcia †, Jean Carrive*

*INA, 4 avenue de l'Europe, 94366, Bry-sur-Marne, France
†ICS–FORTH, P.O.Box 1385, GR 711 10 Heraklion, Crete, Greece
Email: {rronfard,jcarrive}@ina.fr, cgarcia@ics.forth.gr

Abstract Indexing videos by their image content is an important issue for digital audiovisual archives. While much work has been devoted to classification and indexing methods based on perceptual qualities of images, such as color, shape and texture, there is also a need for classification and indexing of some structural properties of images. In this paper, we present some methods for image classification in video, based on the presence, size and location of faces and captions. We argue that such classifications are highly domain-dependent, and are best handled using flexible knowledge management systems (in our case, a description logics).

1 Introduction

Classifying shots based on their visual content is an important step toward higher-level segmentation of a video into meaningful units such as *stories* in broadcast news or *scenes* in comedy and drama. Earlier work on the subject has shown that shot similarity based on global features such as duration and color could be efficient in limited cases [20,1]. More recent work tends to highlight the limits of such techniques, and to emphasize more specific features, such as caption and face sizes and locations [17,18,12].

Captions and faces are powerful video indexes, given that they give generally a clue about the video content. In video segmentation, they may help to find program boundaries, by detecting script lines and to select more meaningful keyframes containing textual data and/or himan faces. Automatic detection of programs, such as TV Commercials or news, becomes possible using location and size of text.

One important issue that is not dealt with by previous work is the necessity of exploiting domain knowledge, which may only be available at run-time. In this paper, we establish a clear-cut separation between *feature extraction* which is based on generic tools (face detection, caption detection) and *classification*, which is based on heuristic, domain-specific rules. With examples drawn from real broadcast news , we ilustrate how such classes can be organized into taxonomies, and used as indexes in large audiovisual collections.

R. Laurini (Ed.): VISUAL 2000, LNCS 1929, pp. 349–359, 2000.
Springer-Verlag Berlin Heidelberg 2000

2   Description logic databases.

We use the CLASSIC Description Logics system [2] as a representation for both the image *classes* and the image *observations*, which are obtained through video analysis. CLASSIC represents classes as *concepts* which can be *primitive* or *defined*. Primitive concepts are only represented with necessary conditions. We use them to represent event classes which are directly observable: shots, keyframes, faces and captions. The necessary conditions determine the inferences which can be drawn in such classes - or instance, shots have at least one keyframe, and keyframes may have faces or captions. Defined concepts are represented with both necessary and sufficient conditions. Therefore, class membership can be inferred automatically for defined concepts. In this paper, we focus on defined concepts for keyframe and shot classes. Relations between concepts are called *roles*, and one important role between audiovisual events is containment (*part-of* role). Concepts and roles are organized in taxonomies such as the one shown in Figure 1, which is typical of a newscast applications.

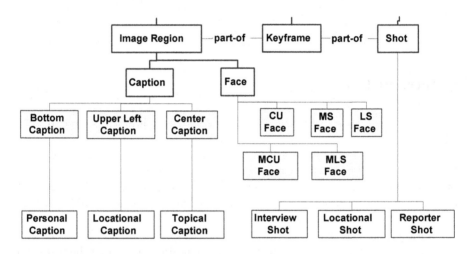

Figure1. A taxonomy of image regions, keyframes and shots. Image region, caption, face and shot are primitive concepts ; all other concepts are defined at runtime in terms of more generic classes, using subsumption and part-of links.

3   Feature extraction

In general, a shot can be represented synthetically by a small number of static keyframes. We select keyframes by clustering them based on their color content, and deciding on the right number of clusters, based on a local test performed during shot detection. The video segmentation and keyframe extraction tools of DIVAN have been described elsewhere [3], and we focus here on the techniques used to detect faces and captions.

3.1 Face detection

Faces appearing in video frames are detected using a novel and efficient method that we presented in details in [10]. The proposed scheme is designed for human faces detection in color images under non-constrained scene conditions, such as the presence of a complex background and uncontrolled illumination. Color clustering and filtering using approximations of the HSV skin color subspaces are applied on the original image, providing quantized skin color regions which are iteratively merged in order to provide a set of candidate face areas. Constraints related to shape and face texture analysis are applied, by performing a wavelet packet decomposition on each face area candidate and extracting simple statistical features such as standard deviation. Compact and meaningful feature vectors are built with these statistical features. Then, the Bhattacharrya distance is used for classifying the feature vectors into face or non-face areas, using some prototype face area vectors, acquired in a previous training stage. For a data set of 100 images with 104 faces covering most of the cases of human faces appearance, a 94.23% good detection rate, 20 false alarms and a 5.76% false dismissals rate were obtained.

3.2 Caption detection

Our method for caption detection is especially designed for being applied to the difficult case where text is superimposed on color images with complicated background and is described in [11]. Our goal is to minimize the number of false alarms and to binarize efficiently the detected text areas so that they can be processed by standard OCR software. First, potential areas of text are detected by enhancement and clustering processes, considering most of constraints related to the texture of words. Then, classification and binarization of potential text areas are achieved in a single scheme performing color quantization and characters periodicity analysis. First results using a data set of 200 images containing 480 lines of text with character sizes ranging from 8 to 30, are very encouraging. Our algorithm detected 93% of the lines and binarize them with an estimated good readability rate of 82%. An overall number of 23 false alarms have been found, in areas with contrasted repetitive texture.

4 Shot classification

The automatic detection of human faces and textual information provides users with powerful indexing capacities of the video material. Frames containing detected faces or text areas may be searched according to the number, the sizes, or the positions of these features, looking for specific classes of scenes. Number and size of detected faces may characterize a big audience (multiple faces), an interview (two medium size faces) or a close-up view of a speaker (a large size face). Location and size of text areas helps in characterizing the video content especially in news. But the mapping between structure (the sizes and locations of faces and captions) and meaning is inherently domain-specific. Different genres use different conventions, and even similar programs from different channels may each use their own vocabulary of captions and framings. We deal with this variability by encoding each collection of periodic television programs as a separate knowledge base, for example the TF1 newscast shown in Figure 2 or the France2 newscast shown in Figures 3 and 4. In this section, we explain in more details how such shot classes can be defined, and their instances recognized automatically, using specialized knowledge bases expressed in a Description Logic framework.

Figure2. Screenshot of our class browser and editor, as used for creating the knowledge base for the TF1 newscast. Person names and roles appear at the lower-left, and locations at the upper-left corner of the screen. Here, the concept of a reporter shot is defined as a medium close-up shot with a person name and a location.

4.1 Face classes

The first axis for shot classification is the apparent size of detected faces. Faces are an important semantic marker in images, and they also serve as a very intuitive and immediate spatial reference. With respect to the human figure, cinematographers use a vocabulary of common framings, called *shot values*, from which we selected five classes where the face can be seen and detected clearly. They range from the close-up (CU), where the face occupies approximately half of the screen, to the long shot (LS), where the human figure is seen entirely, and the face occupies around ten percent of the screen. Intermediate shot values are the medium shot (MS), the medium-close-up (MCU) and the medium-long-shot (MLS) [19].

Table1. Face sizes, distances and shot values (in 352 x 288 image).

Shot Value	CU	MCU	MS	MLS	LS
Face Width	176 ± 20	88 ± 10	58 ± 6	44 ± 3	35 ± 2
Distance	2	4	6	8	10
Range	$d \leq 4$	$2 \leq d \leq 6$	$4 \leq d \leq 8$	$6 \leq d \leq 10$	$8 \leq d$

Shot value classes are usually defined in relative and imprecise terms, based on the distance of the subject to the camera. In order to provide a quantitative definition, we use the fact that in television and film, the apparent size of faces on the screen vary inversely with their distance to the camera (perspective shortening). We therefore compute the quantity $d = \frac{FrameWidth}{FaceWidth}$ and classifiy the face regions according to five overlapping bins, based on a uniform quantization of d in the range of $[0, 12]$ (see Table 1). Note that this is consistent with the resolution used (MPEG-1 video with 22 macroblocks per line).

The five face classes follow immediately from the correspondance shown in Table 1, where we use overlapping ranges to accomodate the relative imprecision of the detected face regions. Given such classes, it is possible to define keyframe classes based on the number and size of their detected faces. When all faces are in a given class (for example, MCU-FACE) then the keyframe itself can be qualified (in that case, as MCU-FRAME). Note that in the case of multiple face classes, we do not attempt to classify the keyframe. But using overlapping face value classes allows us to automatically classify the frame into the common class of all its detected faces, in most practical cases.

4.2 Caption classes

While faces are classified according to their dimension, captions are best classified according to their position on the screen. In many contexts, such as broadcast news, the caption location determines the semantic class of the caption text. As an example, Figure 3 shows examples of two caption classes: person names (bottom right) and locations (bottom left) in the France2 newscast. The same classes can be defined in similar way in the TF1 newscast, as shown in Figure 2.

For classifying captions, we therefore define a small number of geometric caption classes based on simple tests for bottom, bottom-right, bottom-left, upper-left and upper-right captions, as we did with faces. But we propagate the class memberships from captions to frames and shots in a very different way from what did with shot values, because in this case the presence of a single center-left caption suffices to classify the frame as a *TOPIC-FRAME*, and the shot as a *TOPIC-SHOT*.

4.3   Shot classes

Shot classification immediately follows from keyframe classification in the case of *simple shots* (shots with exactly one keyframe). Shots containing more than one keyframe are qualified as *composite shots* and are only classified as CU, MCU, etc. when *all* their keyframes are in the same class. In all other cases, we leave them unclassified, for lack of more specific information. Curiously, this limitation coincides with limitations of CLASSIC itself, which can only handle conjonctions of role restrictions, but not negations or disjunctions. In the future, we will investigate other DL systems to overcome this limitation. As an alternative, we have developped a constraint-based temporal reasoning system which allows us to classify composite shots even in the case of camera motion, such as a *zoom in from MS to CU* [4,5,6].

In the context of a given collection of television programs, such as the eight o'clock newscast for a given channel, we can define more interesting shot classes, based on the knowledge of their filming styles and conventions. This is illustrated in this paper by examples for the evening news of TF1 (Figure 2) and France2 (Figure 4).

(a) Locational Shot   (b) Personal Shot (Inter- (c) Personal Shot (Reporter)
                           view)

Figure3. Examples of caption classes found in the France2 Evening News: locations and dates appear at the bottom-left, and person names at the bottom-right of the screen.

For instance, an *interview shot* can be defined as a one-shot which is both an MCU-shot and a personal-shot (as in Figures 3b, 3c, 6d and 6f. A reporter shot can be defined similarly, as a one-shot, MCU, locational shot (as in Figures 2 and 6e. And an anchor shot can be defined as a one-shot, MCU, topical shot (as in Figures 4 and 6c.

It should be noted that the class labels (interview, anchor, reporter) are th same in all knoledge bases. Only thir definitions are different. Therefore, although the class definitions are only valid within a particular context, they still allow useful inferences to be made for indexing, especially when dealing with large collections of very similar television broadcasts.

Figure4. A title shot in the France2 newscast can be defined as a medium close-up shot (MCU) with a title in the upper-right corner of the screen.

5   Experimental results and further work

Our shot classification system has been tested as part of the DiVAN prototype. DiVAN is a distributed audiovisual archive network which uses advanced video segmentation techniques to facilitate the task of documentalists, who annotate the video contents with time-coded descriptions. In our experiments, the video is processed sequentially, from segmentation to feature extraction, to shot classification and scene groupings, without human intervention, based on a precompiled shot taxonomy representing the available knowledge about a collection of related television programs. The results obtained on real examples of French evening news from TF1 and France2 are presented in Table 2. Examples of detected and missed faces are shown in Figure 5.

As Table 2 shows, real television broadcasts are more difficult than established benchmarks. Missed faces are easily explained by one of three factors:

Figure5. First line: correctly detected faces. Second line: missed faces. Third line: false detections. Such examples are collected for training enhanced classifiers and recognizers.

scale, illumination and angle. Most cases of false detections are caused by unusual light conditions. In the France2 example, a single news story showing fires and explosions accounted for 50% of false detections, due to the flesh-toned light effects in that sequence.

Table2. Experimental evaluation of recall and precision of face and caption detection.

FACES	Correct Detections	False Detections	Missed
TF1	51	31	43
France2	45	53	39
CAPTIONS	Correct Detections	False Detections	Missed
TF1	85	39	4
France2	57	39	18

In Figure 6, we present some results of the proposed face and text detection algorithms. The first line shows typical examples of multiple faces in the scene and close-up view of a face. The other examples illustrate the case of face and text detection appearing in the same frame, and the classifications results from various knowledge bases used for the DIVAN trials. In several examples, it can be noted that multiple or even conflicting interpretations (such as Interview and Reporter shot) are allowed. We believe that such ambiguities can only be resolved by adding more knowledge and more features into the system.

One way of adding such knowledge is to go from detection to recognition. Face and caption recognition enable more powerful indexing capacities, such as indexing sports programs by score figures and player names, or indexing news by person and place names. When detected faces are recognized and associated automatically with textual information like in the systems Name-it [16] or Piction [8], potential applications such as news video viewer providing description of the displayed faces, news text browser giving facial information, or automated video annotation generators for faces are possible.

In order to implement such capabilities, we are developing an algorithm dedicated to face recognition when faces are large enough and in a semi-frontal position [9]. This algorithm uses directly the features extracted in the detection stage. As an addition, our algorithm for text detection [11] includes a text binarization stage that makes the use of standard OCR software possible. We are also currently completing our study by using a standard OCR software for text recognition. With those capabilities, we will be able to extend the number of shot classes recognized by our system, to recognize shot sequences, such as shot-reverse-shots, and to resolve ambiguous cases, such as determining whether two keyframes contain the same faces or not (within a shot boundary).

6   Conclusions

Based on extracted faces and captions, we have been able to build some useful classes for describing television images. The description logic framework used allows us to easily specialize and extend the taxonomies. Classification of new instances is performed using a combination of numerical methods and symbolic reasoning, and allows us to always store the *most specific* descriptions for shots or groups of shots, based on the available knowledge and feature-based information.

Acknowledgements

We thank the Institut National de l'Audiovisuel (INA) for allowing us to reproduce the keyframes from the AIM corpus. The Class Browser and Editor shown in Figures 2 and 4 were implemented at INA by Yoann Blanchet and Nicolas Durut. DIVAN is an ESPRIT project which was supported by the European Commission from September 1997 to March 2000 (EP24956).

References

1. Aigrain, Ph., Joly, Ph. and Longueville, V.   Medium knowledge-based macrosegmentation of video into sequences Intelligent multimedia information retrieval, AAAI Press - MIT Press, 1997.
2. Borgida, A., Brachman, R.J., McGuiness, D.L., Resnick, L.A. 1989. CLASSIC: A Structural Data Model for Objects. ACM SIGMOD Int. Conf. on Management of Data, 1989.
3. Bouthemy, P., Garcia C. , Ronfard R. , Tziritas G. , Veneau E. Scene segmentation and image feature extraction for video indexing and retrieval. VISUAL'99, Amsterdam, 1999.

4. Carrive, J., Pachet F. , Ronfard R. Using Description Logics for Indexing Audiovisual Documents. Proceedings of the International Workshop on Description Logics, Trento, Italy, 1998.
5. Carrive, J., Pachet F. , Ronfard R. Clavis: a temporal reasoning system for classification of audiovisual sequences. RIAO, Paris, April 2000.
6. Carrive, J., Pachet F. , Ronfard R. A Language for Audiovisual Template Specification and Recognition Int. Conference on Constraint Programming, Singapore, September 2000.
7. Chan, Y. and Lin, S.H. and Tan, Y.P. and Kung, S.Y. Video shot classification using human faces. IEEE Intern. Conference on Image Processing, September 1996.
8. Chopra K. , Srihari R.K. . Control Structures for Incorporating Picture-Specific Context in Image Interpretation. in: *Proceedings of Int'l Joint Conf. on Artificial Intelligence*, 1995.
9. Garcia C. , Zikos G. , Tziritas G. . Wavelet Packet Analysis for Face Recognition. To appear in *Image and Vision Computing*, 18(4).
10. Garcia C. and Tziritas G. . Face Detection Using Quantized Skin Color Regions Merging and Wavelet Packet Analysis. *IEEE Transactions on Multimedia*, 1(3):264–277, Sept. 1999.
11. Garcia C. , Apostolidis X. . Text Detection and Segmentation in Complex Color Images. *IEEE International Conference on Acoustics, Speech, and Signal*, June 5-9 2000, Istanbul, Turkey.
12. Ide, I., Yamamoto, K. and Tanaka, H. Automatic indexing to video based on shot classification. Advanced Multimedia Content Processing, LNCS 1554, November 1998.
13. Jaimes, A. and Chang, S.F. Model-based classification of visual information for content-based retrieval Storage and Retrieval for Image and Video Databases, SPI99, San Jose, January 1999.
14. Patel-Schneider, P. and Swartout, B., KRSS Description Logic Specification from the KRSS Effort, http://www.ida.liu.se/labs/iislab/people/patla/DL/, January 1992.
15. Ronfard, R. Shot-level indexing and matching of video content. Storage and Retrieval for Image and Video Databases, SPIE, October 1997.
16. Satoh S. , Kanade T. . Name-it: Association of Face and Name in Video. in: *Proc. of Computer Vision and Pattern Recognition. IEEE Compu ter Society Press*, pp. 368-373, 1997.
17. Gunsel, B. and Ferman, A.M. and Tekalp, A.M. Video Indexing Through Integration of Syntactic and Semantic Features. WACV, 1996.
18. Ferman, A.M., Tekalp, A.M. and Mehrotra, R. Effective Content Representation for Video IEEE Intern. Conference on Image Processing, October 1998.
19. Thomson, R. Grammar of the shot. Media Manual, Focal Press, Oxford, UK, 1998.
20. Yeung, M. and Yeo, B.-L. Time-constrained Clustering for Segmentation of Video into Story Units International Conference on Pattern Recognition, 1996.

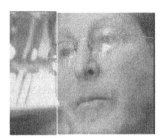

(a) CU

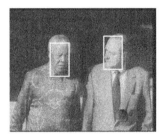

(b) MLS, MS

(c) MCU, MS, Topical, Anchor (from CANAL-INFO KB)

(d) CU, MCU, Personal, Interview (from TF1 KB)

(e) MCU, MS, Locational, Personal, Reporter, Interview (from TF1 KB)

(f) CU, MCU, Personal, Interview (from ARTE KB)

Figure6. Shot classification examples, based on face and caption detection. Examples (a-b) show the range of commonly found shot values (CU to MS). Examples (c-f) illustrate domain-specific classifications obtained with different knowledge bases created during the DIVAN trials.

SIMPLIcity: Semantics-sensitive Integrated Matching for Picture LIbraries*

James Z. Wang**, Jia Li***, and Gio Wiederhold†

Dept. of Computer Science, Stanford University, Stanford, CA 94305, USA

Abstract. We present here SIMPLIcity (Semantics-sensitive Integrated Matching for Picture LIbraries), an image retrieval system using semantics classification and integrated region matching (IRM) based upon image segmentation. The SIMPLIcity system represents an image by a set of regions, roughly corresponding to objects, which are characterized by color, texture, shape, and location. The system classifies images into categories which are intended to distinguish semantically meaningful differences, such as textured versus nontextured, indoor versus outdoor, and graph versus photograph. Retrieval is enhanced by narrowing down the searching range in a database to a particular category and exploiting semantically-adaptive searching methods. A measure for the overall similarity between images, the IRM distance, is defined by a region-matching scheme that integrates properties of all the regions in the images. This overall similarity approach reduces the adverse effect of inaccurate segmentation, helps to clarify the semantics of a particular region, and enables a simple querying interface for region-based image retrieval systems. The application of SIMPLIcity to a database of about 200,000 general-purpose images demonstrates accurate retrieval at high speed. The system is also robust to image alterations.

1 Introduction

The need for efficient content-based image retrieval has increased tremendously in many application areas such as biomedicine, military, commerce, education, and Web image classification and searching. Content-based image retrieval is highly challenging because of the large size of the database, the difficulty of understanding images, both by people and computers, the difficulty of formulating a query, and the problem of evaluating the results. Efficient indexing and searching of large-scale image databases remains as an open problem. The automatic

---

* This work was supported in part by the National Science Foundation's Digital Libraries initiative. We would like to thank the help of Oscar Firschein and anonymous reviewers. An on-line demonstration is provided at http://WWW-DB.Stanford.EDU/IMAGE/
** Also of Biomedical Informatics, Stanford University. Email: wangz@cs.stanford.edu
*** Research performed when the author was with Stanford University. Currently with the Xerox Palo Alto Research Center. Email: jiali@db.stanford.edu
† Also of Biomedical Informatics, Stanford University. Email: gio@cs.stanford.edu

derivation of semantics from the content of an image is the focus of interest for research on image databases. Image *semantics* has several levels: semantic types, object composition, abstract semantics, and detailed semantics.

Many content-based image database retrieval systems have been developed, such as the IBM QBIC System [9] developed at the IBM Almaden Research Center, the Photobook System developed by the MIT Media Lab [10], the Visualseek System [13] developed at Columbia University, the WBIIS System [18] developed at Stanford University, and the Blobworld System [2] developed at U.C. Berkeley. Content-based image retrieval systems roughly fall into three categories depending on the signature extraction approach used: histogram, color layout, and region-based search. There are also systems that combine retrieval results from individual algorithms by a weighted sum matching metric [4,9], or other merging schemes [12].

In traditional histogram-based systems [9, 11], an image is characterized by its global color histogram. The drawback of a global histogram representation is over-summarization. Information about object location, shape, and texture is discarded. Color histogram search is sensitive to intensity variation, color distortions, and cropping.

For traditional color layout indexing [9], images are partitioned into blocks and the average color or the color distribution of each block is stored. Thus, the color layout is essentially a low resolution representation of the original image. More advanced systems [18] use significant wavelet coefficients instead of averaging. By adjusting block sizes or the levels of wavelet transforms, the coarseness of a color layout representation can be tuned. The finest color layout using a single pixel block is merely the original image. We can hence view a color layout representation as an opposite extreme of a histogram, which naturally retains shape, location, and texture information if at proper resolutions. However, as with pixel representation, although information such as shape is preserved in the color layout representation, the retrieval system cannot perceive it directly. Color layout search is sensitive to shifting, cropping, scaling, and rotation because images are characterized by a set of local properties.

Region-based retrieval systems attempt to overcome the issues of color layout search by representing images at the object-level. A region-based retrieval system applies image segmentation to decompose an image into regions, which correspond to objects if the decomposition is ideal. Since the retrieval system has identified objects in the image, it is easier for the system to recognize similar objects at different locations and with different orientations and sizes. Region-based retrieval systems include the NeTra system [8], the Blobworld system [2], and the query system with color region templates [14].

The NeTra and the Blobworld systems compare images based on individual regions. Although querying based on a limited number of regions is allowed, the query is performed by merging single-region query results. Because of the great difficulty of achieving accurate segmentation, these systems tend to partition one object into several regions with none of them being representative for the object, especially for images without distinctive objects and scenes. Consequently, it is often difficult for users to determine which regions and features should be used for retrieval. Not much attention has been paid to developing similarity measures that combine information from all of the regions. One work in this direction is the querying system developed by Smith and Li [14]. The efficiency of their similarity measure depends critically on a pre-defined library of patterns, which are described only by color for the system in [14]. This measure is sensitive to object shifting, scaling, and rotation.

Although region-based systems attempt to decompose images into constituent objects, a representation composed of pictorial properties of regions is not ensured to be well related to its semantics. There is no clear mapping from a set of pictorial properties to semantics. An approximately round brown region might be a flower, an apple, a face, or a part of sunset sky. Moreover, pictorial properties such as color, shape, and texture of one object may vary dramatically in different images.

Despite the fact that it is currently impossible to reliably recognize objects in general-purpose images, there are methods to distinguish certain semantic types of images. The categorization of images into semantic types is one step towards filling the gap between pictorial representations and semantics. Information about semantic types enables a system to constrict the search range of images and improve retrieval by tuning a matching scheme to the semantic type in consideration. One example of semantics classification is the identification of natural photographs and artificial graphs generated by computer tools [5, 19]. Other examples include a system to detect objectionable images developed by Wang et al. [19], a system to classify indoor and outdoor scenes developed by Szummer and Picard [15], and a system to classify city scenes and landscape scenes [17]. Wang and Fischler [20] have shown that rough but accurate semantic understanding can be very helpful in computer vision tasks such as image stereo matching. Most of these systems use statistical classification methods based on training data.

In Section 2, the architecture of the SIMPLIcity system is presented. The region segmentation algorithm is provided in Section 3. In Section 4, the classification of images into semantics types is described. The similarity measure between images is described in Section 5. Experiments and results are provided in Section 6. We conclude in Section 7.

2   Architecture of the SIMPLIcity Retrieval System

The architecture of the SIMPLIcity system is described in Figure 1, the indexing process, and Figure 2, the querying process. During indexing, the system partitions an image into 4×4 pixel blocks and extracts a feature vector for each block. The k-means clustering algorithm is then applied to segment the image. The segmentation result is fed into a classifier that determines the semantic type of the image. An image is classified as one of the n pre-defined mutually exclusive and collectively exhaustive semantic classes. As indicated previously, examples of semantic types are indoor-outdoor, objectionable-benign, and graph-photograph

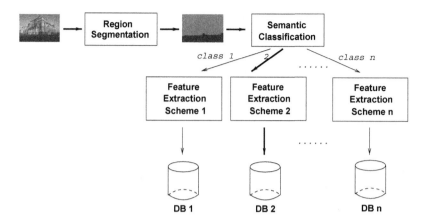

Fig. 1. The architecture of feature indexing module. The heavy lines show a sample indexing path of an image.

images. Although the classification is aimed at an image as a whole instead of individual regions, it is performed after the region segmentation so that the classifier may be assisted by information obtained from the segmentation. Features including color, texture, shape, and location information are then extracted for each region in the image. The features selected depend on the semantic type of the image. The signature of an image is the collection of features extracted from all of its regions. Signatures of images with various semantic types are stored in separate databases.

In the querying process, if the query image is not in the database, it is first passed through the same feature extraction process as was used during indexing. For an image in the database, its semantic type is first checked and then its signature is extracted from the corresponding database. Once the signature of the query image is obtained, similarity scores between the query image and images in the database with the same semantic type are computed and sorted to provide the list of images that appear to have the closest semantics.

The current implementation of the SIMPLIcity system provides several query interfaces: a CGI-based Web access interface, a JAVA-based drawing interface, a CGI-based Web interface for submitting a query image of any format anywhere on the Internet.

We allow the user to submit any images on the Internet as a query image to the system by entering the URL of an image. Our system is capable of handling any image format from anywhere on the Internet and reachable by our server via the HTTP protocol. The image is downloaded and processed by our system on-the-fly. The high efficiency of our image segmentation and matching algorithms made this feature possible[1]. To our knowledge, this feature of our system is

---

[1] It takes some other region-based CBIR system [2] several minutes CPU time to segment an image.

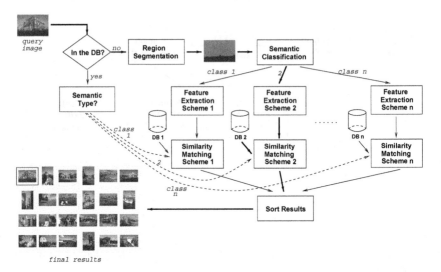

Fig. 2. The architecture of query processing module. The heavy lines show a sample querying path of an image.

unique in the sense that no other commercial or academic systems allow such queries.

3   Region Segmentation

This section describes the first component of the SIMPLIcity system: region segmentation. Our system segments images based on color and frequency features using the k-means algorithm For general-purpose images such as the images in a photo library or the images on the World-Wide Web (WWW), automatic image segmentation is almost as difficult as automatic image semantics understanding. To reduce the sensitivity to inaccurate segmentation, an integrated region matching (IRM) scheme is developed for defining a robust similarity measure.

To segment an image, SIMPLIcity partitions the image into blocks with 4×4 pixels and extracts a feature vector for each block. The k-means algorithm is applied to cluster the feature vectors into several classes each corresponding to one region in the segmented image. There are six features, three of which are the average color components in a 4×4 block. The well-known LUV color space is used, where L encodes luminance, U and V encode color information (chrominance). To obtain the other three features, a wavelet transform is applied to the L component of the image. After a one-level wavelet transform, a 4×4 block is decomposed into four frequency bands: the LL, LH, HL, and HH bands [3], each containing 2×2 coefficients. The square root of the second order moment of wavelet coefficients in each of the LH, HL, and HH bands is computed as one feature. Moments of wavelet coefficients in various frequency bands have proven effective for characterizing texture [1, 16]. The intuition behind this is that coefficients in different frequency bands show variations in different directions. For example, the HL band records activities in the horizontal direction. An image with vertical strips thus has high energy in the HL band and low energy in the LH band. This texture feature may not be the ideal feature. But it is a good compromise between computational complexity and effectiveness.

4   Image Classification

For the current implementation of the SIMPLIcity system, an image is first classified into artificial graph and photograph, which is then classified into textured and non-textured images. These three classes represent a high-level[2] categorization of images, for which the system is regarded as *semantics-sensitive*. Although we also developed a classifier to detect objectionable images, it is not integrated into the system presently because this type of images are not included in our database. By artificial graphs, we refer to synthetic images generated by computer tools, for example, clip-art images. Textured images are referred to images composed of repeated patterns that appear like a unique texture surface, e.g., a picture of lattices. Since textured images do not contain clustered objects, the perception of such images focuses on color and texture, but not shape, which is critical for understanding non-textured images. Thus an efficient retrieval system should use different features to depict those types of images. The algorithm for classifying textured and non-textured images is described in [6]. To distinguish artificial graphs and photographs, methods developed in [19,5] are used.

5   Integrated Region Matching (IRM) Similarity Measure

Besides using semantic classification, to reflect semantics more precisely by the region representation, the SIMPLIcity system exploits an image similarity measure determined by the properties of all the segmented regions. The motivation for fully using information about an image is that the co-existence of multiple regions often increases the confidence level of judging semantics. For example, flowers are usually present with green leaves, and boats with water. Therefore, a red region in a green background is more likely to be a flower than one in a white background. Compared with retrieval based on individual regions, the overall similarity approach reduces the influence of inaccurate segmentation. In addition to retrieval accuracy, an overall similarity measure allows a *simple* querying interface, which requires a user to specify only a query image to perform a search.

Mathematically, defining the similarity measure is equivalent to defining a distance between sets of points in a high dimensional space, i.e., the feature space. Every point in the space corresponds to the feature vector, or the descriptor, of a region. Although distance between two points in the feature space can be easily defined by the Euclidean distance, it is not obvious how to define a distance

---

[2] Here, we compare with low-level imagery features.

between sets of points that reflects a person's concept of semantic "closeness" of two images. A good distance is expected to take all the points in a set into account and be tolerant to inaccurate image segmentation.

To define the similarity measure, the first step is to match regions in two images. Consider the comparison of two animal photographs. The overall similarity of the two images should depend on the extent of analogousness between the animals and that between the background areas. The correspondence of objects in the images is crucial for judging similarity since it would be meaningless to compare the animal in one image with the background in another. Our matching scheme attempts to build appropriate correspondence between regions. Being aware that segmentation cannot be perfect, we "soften" the matching by allowing one region to be matched to several regions with significance scores. The principle of matching is that the closest region pair is matched first. This matching scheme is referred to as *integrated region matching* (IRM) to stress the incorporation of regions in the retrieval process. After regions are matched, the similarity measure is computed as a weighted sum of the similarity between region pairs, with weights determined by the matching scheme. Details regarding to the definitions of the IRM similarity measure and the distance between two regions are referred to [7].

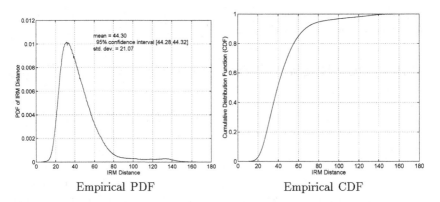

Empirical PDF   Empirical CDF

Fig. 3. The empirical PDF and CDF of the IRM distance.

To study the characteristics of the IRM distance, we performed 100 random queries on our COREL photograph data set. We obtained 5.6 million IRM distances. Based on these distances, we estimated the distribution of the IRM distance. The empirical mean of the IRM is 44.30, with a 95% confidence interval of [44.28, 44.32]. The standard deviation of the IRM is 21.07. Figure 3 shows the empirical probability distribution function and the empirical cumulative distribution function. Based on this empirical distribution of the IRM, we may give more intuitive similarity distances to the end user.

6 Experiments

The SIMPLIcity system has been implemented with a general-purpose COREL image database including about $60,000$ photographs and $140,000$ clip-art pictures, which are stored in JPEG format with size 384×256 or 256×384. These images were classified into graph, textured and non-textured types. For each image, the features, locations, and areas of all its regions were stored. Different types of images were stored in separate databases. An on-line demo is provided at URL: http://WWW-DB.Stanford.EDU/IMAGE/SIMPLIcity/

We compared the SIMPLIcity system with the WBIIS (Wavelet-Based Image Indexing and Searching) system [18] with the same image database. As WBIIS forms image signatures using wavelet coefficients in the lower frequency bands, it performs well with relatively smooth images, such as most landscape images. For images with details crucial to semantics, such as pictures containing people, the performance of WBIIS degrades because the multi-level wavelet transform in the system intends to smooth out details. In general, SIMPLIcity performs as well as WBIIS for smooth landscape images. For images composed of fine details, SIMPLIcity usually achieves significantly better results. For textured images, SIMPLIcity and WBIIS often perform equally well. However, in general, SIMPLIcity captures high frequency texture information better. The SIMPLIcity system also performs well on the clip-art pictures. Readers are referred to the demo web site for examples since we cannot provide many examples in this paper due to limited space.

Category	1	2	3	4	5	6	7	8	9	10
Average p	0.475	0.325	0.330	0.363	0.981	0.400	0.402	0.719	0.342	0.340
Average r	178.2	242.1	261.8	260.7	49.7	197.7	298.4	92.5	230.4	271.7
Average σ	171.9	180.0	231.4	223.4	29.2	170.7	254.9	81.5	185.8	205.8

Table 1. The average performance for each image category evaluated by precision p, the mean rank of matched images r, and the standard deviation of the ranks of matched images σ.

To provide numerical results, we tested 27 sample images chosen randomly from 9 categories, each containing 3 of the images. A retrieved image is considered a match if it belongs to the same category of the query image. Those categories are: sports and public events, beach, food, landscape with buildings, portrait, horses, tools and toys, flowers, vehicle. Most categories simply include images containing the specified objects. Images in the "sports and public events" class contain humans in a game or public event such as festival. Portraits are not included in this category. The "landscape with buildings" class refers to outdoor scenes featuring man-made constructions such as buildings and sculptures. The "beach" class refers to sceneries at coasts or river banks. For the "portrait" class, an image has to show people as the main feature. A scene with human beings as a minor part is not included.

Precisions are computed for both SIMPLIcity and WBIIS. Recalls are not calculated because the database is large and it is hard to estimate the total number of images in one category, even approximately. To account for the ranks of matched images, the average of precisions within k retrieved images, $k = 1, ..., 100$, is computed, that is, $\bar{p} = \frac{1}{100}\sum_{k=1}^{100} \frac{n_k}{k}$, where n_k is the number of matches in the first k retrieved images. This average precision is referred to as the weighted precision because it is equivalent to a weighted percentage of matched images with a larger weight assigned to an image retrieved at a higher rank. Except for the tools and toys category, in which case the two systems perform about equally well, SIMPLIcity has achieved better results measured in both ways than WBIIS. For the two categories of landscape with buildings and vehicle, the difference between the two system is quite significant—both precision and weighted precision differ by more than 0.4 on average. The average precision and weighted precision over the 27 images are 0.453 and 0.525 respectively for SIMPLIcity, but 0.226 and 0.253 for WBIIS.

The SIMPLIcity system was also evaluated based on a sub-database formed by 10 image categories, each containing 100 pictures. Within this small database, it is known whether any two images are matched. In particular, a retrieved image is considered a match if and only if it is in the same category as the query. This assumption is reasonable since the 10 categories were chosen so that each depicts a distinct semantics topic. Every image in the sub-database was tested as a query, and the retrieval ranks of all the rest images were recorded. Three statistics were computed for each query: the precision within the first 100 retrieved images, the mean rank of all the matched images, and the standard deviation of the ranks of matched images. The recall within the first 100 retrieved images was not computed because it is proportional to the precision in this special case since the total number of semantically related images for each query is fixed to be 100. The average performance for each image category in terms of the three statistics is listed in Table 1, where p denotes precision, r denotes the mean rank of matched images, and σ denotes the standard deviation of the ranks of matched images. For a system that ranks images randomly, the average p is about 0.1, and the average r is about 500.

Similar evaluation tests were carried out for color histogram match. We used LUV color space and a matching metric similar to the EMD described in [11] to extract color histogram features and match in the categorized image database. Two different color bin sizes, with an average of 13.1 and 42.6 filled color bins per image, were evaluated. We call the one with less filled color bins the Color Histogram 1 system and the other the Color Histogram 2 system. Figure 4 shows the performance as compared with the SIMPLIcity system. Both of the two color histogram-based matching systems perform much worse than the SIMPLIcity region-based CBIR system in almost all image categories. The performance of the Color Histogram 2 system is better than that of the Color Histogram 1 system due to more detailed color separation obtained with more filled bins. However, the Color Histogram 2 system is so slow that it is impossible to obtain matches on larger databases. SIMPLIcity partitions an image into an average of only 4.3

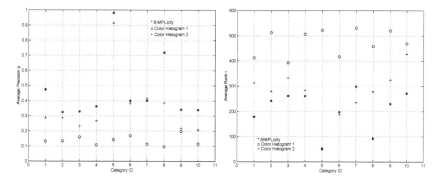

Fig. 4. Comparing with color histogram methods on average precision p and average rank of matched images r. *The lower numbers indicate better results for the second plot.*

Brighten 10%   Random spread 10 pixels

Darken 6%   Pixelize at 20 pixels

Blur with a 17 × 17 Gaussian filter   50% cropping

Sharpen by 70%   Horizontal shifting by 15%

20% more saturated   Rotate 45°

20% less saturated   Flip 180°

Fig. 5. The robustness of the system to image alterations. Best 5 matches are shown. The upper-left corner is the query image. Database size: 200,000 images.

regions. It runs at about twice the speed of the faster Color Histogram 1 system and gives much better searching accuracy than the slower Color Histogram 2 system.

We have performed extensive experiments to test the robustness of the system. The system has demonstrated exceptional robustness to image alterations such as intensity variation, sharpness variation, intentional color distortions, intentional shape distortions, cropping, shifting, and rotation. Figure 5 shows some query examples, using the 200,000-image COREL database.

The algorithm has been implemented on a Pentium Pro 430MHz PC with the Linux operating system. On average, one second is needed to segment an image and to compute the features of all regions. The matching speed is very fast. When the query image is in the database, it takes about 1.5 seconds of CPU time on average to sort all the images in the database using our similarity measure. If the query is not in the database, one extra second of CPU time is spent on processing the query.

7   Conclusions and Future Work

An important contribution of this paper is the idea that images can be classified into global semantic classes, such as textured or nontextured, indoor or outdoor, objectionable or benign, graph or photograph, and that much can be gained if the feature extraction scheme is tailored to best suit each class. We have implemented this idea in SIMPLIcity (Semantics-sensitive Integrated Matching for Picture LIbraries), an image database retrieval system that uses high-level semantics classification and integrated region matching (IRM) based upon image segmentation. The application of SIMPLIcity to a database of about 200,000 general-purpose images shows fast and accurate retrieval for a large variety of images. Additionally, SIMPLIcity is robust to image alterations.

We are working on integrating more semantic classification algorithms to SIMPLIcity. In addition, it is possible to improve the accuracy by developing a more robust region-matching scheme. The speed can be improved significantly by adopting a feature clustering scheme or using a parallel query processing scheme. The system can also be extended to allow an image being classified softly into multiple classes with probability assignments. We are also working on a simple but capable interface for partial query processing. Experiments with our system on a WWW image database or a video database could be another interesting study.

We use the disk storage to store all the feature vectors in the database. On average, 400 bytes are used to store the feature vector of an image. A database of 2,000,000 images takes less than 1.0 GB of space. To further speed up the system, we may store the feature data in the main memory.

References

1. J. Bigun and J. M. H. du Buf, "N-folded symmetries by complex moments in Gabor space," IEEE-PAMI, vol. 16, no. 1, pp. 80-87, 1994.

2. C. Carson, M. Thomas, S. Belongie, J. M. Hellerstein, and J. Malik, "Blobworld: A system for region-based image indexing and retrieval," *Third Int. Conf. on Visual Information Systems*, June 1999.
3. I. Daubechies, *Ten Lectures on Wavelets*, Capital City Press, 1992.
4. A. Gupta and R. Jain, "Visual information retrieval," *Comm. Assoc. Comp. Mach.*, vol. 40, no. 5, pp. 70-79, May 1997.
5. J. Li, R. M. Gray, "Text and Picture Segmentation by the Distribution Analysis of Wavelet Coefficients," *Int. Conf. Image Processing*, Chicago, Oct. 1998.
6. J. Li, J. Z. Wang, G. Wiederhold, "Classification of Textured and Non-textured Images Using Region Segmentation," *Int. Conf. Image Processing*, Vancouver, Canada, Sept. 2000.
7. J. Li, J. Z. Wang, G. Wiederhold, "IRM: Integrated Region Matching for Image Retrieval," *ACM Multimedia Conf.*, Los Angeles, 2000.
8. W. Y. Ma and B. Manjunath, "NaTra: A toolbox for navigating large image databases," *Proc. IEEE Int. Conf. Image Processing*, pp. 568-71, Santa Barbara, 1997.
9. W. Niblack, R. Barber, W. Equitz, M. Flickner, E. Glasman, D. Petkovic, P. Yanker, C. Faloutsos, and G. Taubin, "The QBIC project: querying images by content using color, texture, and shape," *Proc. SPIE - Int. Soc. Opt. Eng.*, in *Storage and Retrieval for Image and Video Database*, vol. 1908, pp. 173-87, 1993.
10. A. Pentland, R. W. Picard, and S. Sclaroff, "Photobook: Content-based manipulation of image databases," *SPIE Storage and Retrieval Image and Video Databases II*, San Jose, 1995.
11. Y. Rubner, *Perceptual Metrics for Image Database Navigation*, Ph.D. Dissertation, Computer Science Department, Stanford University, May 1999.
12. G. Sheikholeslami, W. Chang, and A. Zhang, "Semantic clustering and querying on heterogeneous features for visual data," *ACM Multimedia*, pp. 3-12, Bristol, UK, 1998.
13. J. R. Smith and S.-F. Chang, "Visualseek: A fully automated content-based image query system," *Proc. Int. Conf. Image Processing*, Lausanne, Switzerland, 1996.
14. J. R. Smith and C. S. Li, "Image classification and querying using composite region templates," *Journal of Computer Vision and Image Understanding*, vol.75, no.1-2, pp. 165-74, Academic Press, 1999.
15. M. Szummer and R. W. Picard, "Indoor-outdoor image classification," *Int. Workshop on Content-based Access of Image and Video Databases*, pp. 42-51, Jan. 1998.
16. M. Unser, "Texture classification and segmentation using wavelet frames," *IEEE Trans. Image Processing*, vol. 4, no. 11, pp. 1549-1560, Nov. 1995.
17. A. Vailaya, A. Jain, H. J. Zhang, "On image classification: city vs. landscape," *Proceedings IEEE Workshop on Content-Based Access of Image and Video Libraries*, pp. 3-8, Santa Barbara, CA, 21 June 1998.
18. J. Z. Wang, G. Wiederhold, O. Firschein, and X. W. Sha, "Content-based image indexing and searching using Daubechies' wavelets," *International Journal of Digital Libraries*, vol. 1, no. 4, pp. 311-328, 1998.
19. J. Z. Wang, J. Li, G. Wiederhold, O. Firschein, "System for screening objectionable images," *Computer Communications Journal*, vol. 21, no. 15, pp. 1355-60, Elsevier Science, 1998.
20. J. Z. Wang, M. A. Fischler, "Visual similarity, judgmental certainty and stereo correspondence," *Proceedings of DARPA Image Understanding Workshop*, Morgan Kauffman, Monterey, 1998.

Semantic Indexing for Image Retrieval Using Description Logics

Eugenio Di Sciascio, Francesco M. Donini, Marina Mongiello

Dipartimento di Elettrotecnica ed Elettronica
Politecnico di Bari
Via Re David, 200 - 70125 Bari
{disciascio,donini,mongiello}@poliba.it

Abstract. We propose an approach based on description logics for the semantic indexing and retrieval of images containing complex objects. We aim at providing a conventional content-based image retrieval system, which adopts low-level features extracted with image analysis, the ability to deal with the complex structure of objects in real images. Starting from a region based segmentation of images we provide a syntax for the description of complex objects as composition of simpler "basic" shapes. An extensional semantics allows to define reasoning services, such as retrieval, classification, and subsumption. A prototype system has been implemented to substantiate our ideas. First, encouraging, results are presented and discussed here.

1 Introduction

The availability of a huge amount of multimedia data, images and videos, calls for efficient methods and tools to index and retrieve such data types. The interest in this topic is witnessed by several special issues in journals, e.g. [16], [12],[10] and definitely by the currently "work-in-progress" MPEG-7 standard. Images and videos are typical unstructured documents so classical database techniques are not adequate to deal with such objects. Content-based techniques are needed, because they are able to extract relevant and "objective" features directly from documents. With particular reference to images, there are basically two approaches to the problem of indexing and retrieving: the first one adopts low-level or middle-level features, say color, texture, or shape of regions, that can be extracted using image processing techniques; the second one typically assumes knowledge of objects in images and concentrates on spatial relationships among domain objects. Each of these approaches is normally tailored on different domains of image contents. The first one has lately received greater attention because of the ability to cope with much more ample domains of images. Both these approaches, anyway, circumvent the problem of recognizing the semantic content of images. Yet high-level concepts are the most important cues humans use to judge similarity between images. Users of image retrieval systems generally want to find images based on the objects they contain, possibly in a determined scene, e.g. a boat in a harbor instead of a boat sailing in the sea. The

R. Laurini (Ed.): VISUAL 2000, LNCS 1929, pp. 372–383, 2000.
© Springer-Verlag Berlin Heidelberg 2000

first issue in content-based extraction of objects from an image is its segmentation. Segmentation is the process of subdividing an image into some partition meeting given requirements, e.g. homogeneous color or texture. The problem is that such a partition is into regions, not actual objects. Systems such as Netra [11] and Blobworld [3] automatically segment images and retrieve "regions" without any concern about the semantic meaning of regions. Another approach is to revert to classes of images where it is possible to reach somehow a foreground/background partition, which allows to select a principal region, which is assumed to be the principal object [4]. However, several images have not a homogeneous background, and in addition a single object can be composed by several regions, with different characteristics in terms of color or texture.

An effort is then needed to bridge the gap between low-level features extracted with image processing tools and the compound structure of objects; to this end we propose a structured language based on ideas borrowed from Description Logics. We start with a segmentation of regions as other approaches do, but use composition of regions to classify them as objects, using simple objects to gain the description of the complex object the simple ones are part of. The main advantage of this approach is the possibility to define a logical language that allows to manage the images as structured data. The proposed language is both a Definition and a Query Language; in fact, it allows to create new simple objects, to define the description of a new complex object combining elementary shapes and to query the image database. It is obvious that our query language has several limitations (e.g. the "or" clause is not implemented - but consider also the difficulty in expressing it in a sketch query -), but our research effort is aimed at building a working system, implementing a correct and complete reasoning algorithm. It is well known that too expressive query languages may lead to NP-complete or undecidable problems.

We anyway believe that the use of a language for describing parts of images can provide several benefits. First of all, it semantically clarifies the process of image retrieval (which we consider to be a recognition) as classification. Secondly, it allows to express complex queries to an image database, such as "retrieve all images with a portal between two smaller portals". Third, it allows a compilation of recognition (i.e., images are classified along known categories as soon as they are entered in the database), which can considerably speed up query answering.

We have implemented a simple prototype system, currently being tested and improved, that realizes the following reasoning services:

1. image classification: given a new image and a collection of descriptions, the new image is classified by finding the most specific descriptions it satisfies;
2. image retrieval: given a database of images and a shape description, retrieve all images that belong to the description;
3. description subsumption (and classification): given a (new) description D and a set of descriptions $D_i, i = 1, \ldots, n$, decide if D subsumes/is subsumed by each $D_i, i = 1, \ldots, n$.

We obviously build on foundations already posed by others. With reference to previous work on the subject, the use of structural descriptions of objects for the recognition of their images can be dated back to Minsky's frames. The idea is to associate parts of an object (and generally of a scene) to the regions an image can be segmented into. Structured descriptions of three-dimensional images are already present in languages for virtual reality like VRML or hierarchical object modeling [6]. However, the semantics of such languages is operational, and no effort is made to automatically classify objects with respect to the structure of their appearance. In [13] a formalism integrating Description Logics and image retrieval is proposed, but position of objects is not taken in consideration at all, while in [9] Description Logics are integrated with spatial reasoning and relative positions are taken in account using RCC8, which is too weak a logic to express how parts of an object are arranged. It follows that neither of the formalisms can be used to build representations of complex shapes. More similar to our approach is the proposal in [1], where parts of a complex shape are described with a Description Logic. However, the composition of shapes does not consider their positions, hence reasoning cannot take positions into account. Relative position of parts of a complex shape can be expressed in a constraint relational calculus as proposed in [2]. However, reasoning about queries (containment and emptyness) is not considered in that approach.

The remaining of this paper is structured as follows: next section presents the syntax and semantics of the proposed formal language; Section 3 presents a simple prototype system and proposes examples that illustrate distinguishing aspects of the approach; the last section draws some conclusions of the proposed work.

2   The formal language

Syntax. Our main syntactic objects are basic shapes, composite shape descriptions, and transformations. To be as general as possible, we initially introduce also colors and textures of shapes, although we will concentrate on shapes.

Basic shapes are denoted with the letter B, and have an edge contour $e(B)$ characterizing them. We assume that $e(B)$ is described as a single, closed 2D-curve in a space whose origin coincides with the centroid of B. Examples of basic shapes can be `circle`, `rectangle`, with the contours $e(\texttt{circle}) = \odot$, $e(\texttt{rectangle}) = \boxed{}$, but also any complete, rough contour — e.g., the one of a ship — is a basic shape.

The possible transformations are the simple ones which are present in any drawing tool: rotation (around the centroid of the shape), scaling and translation. We globally denote a rotation-translation-scaling transformation as τ. Recall that transformations can be composed in sequences $\tau_1 \circ \ldots \circ \tau_n$, and they form a mathematical group.

The basic building block of our syntax is a *basic shape component* $\langle c, t, \tau, B \rangle$, which represents a region with color c, texture t, and edge contour $\tau(e(B))$. With $\tau(e(B))$ we denote the pointwise transformation τ of the whole contour of B. E.g., τ could specify to place the contour $e(B)$ in the upper left corner of the image, scaled by $1/2$ and rotated 45 degrees.

Composite shape descriptions are conjunctions of basic shape components, each one with its own color and texture. They are denoted as

$$C = \langle c_1, t_1, \tau_1, B_1 \rangle \sqcap \cdots \sqcap \langle c_n, t_n, \tau_n, B_n \rangle$$

We do not expect end users of our system to actually define composite shapes with this syntax; this is just the *internal* representation of a composite shape. The system can maintain it while the user draws — with the help of a graphic tool — the complex shape by dragging, rotating and scaling basic shapes chosen either from a palette, or from existing images.

For example, the complex shape house-front could be defined as

$$\text{house-front} = \langle c_1, t_1, \tau_1, \text{rectangle} \rangle \sqcap \langle c_2, t_2, \tau_2, \text{trapezium} \rangle$$

with τ_1, τ_2 placing the trapezium as a roof on top of the rectangle, and textures and colors defined accordingly to the intuition (see Figure 3a).

In a previous paper [14] we presented the complete formalism, including a hierarchy of composite shapes, as it is done in hierarchical object modeling [6, Ch.7]. However, in this paper we just present two levels for simplicity: basic shapes and compositions of basic shapes. Also for simplicity, in what follows we do not consider color and texture.

Semantics. Shapes and components are interpreted as sets of images. An interpretation is a pair $(\mathcal{I}, \Delta)$, where Δ is a set of images, and $\mathcal{I}$ is a mapping from shapes and components to subsets of Δ. We identify each image I with the set of regions $\{r_1, \ldots, r_n\}$ it can be segmented into (excluding background). Each region r comes with its own edge contour $e(r)$. An image $I \in \Delta$ belongs to the interpretation of a basic shape component $\langle \tau, B \rangle^{\mathcal{I}}$ if I contains a region whose contour matches $\tau(e(B))$. In formulae,

$$\langle \tau, B \rangle^{\mathcal{I}} = \{I \in \Delta \mid \exists r \in I : e(r) = \tau(e(B))\}$$

The above definition is only for exact recognition of shape components in images, due to the presence of equality, but it can be immediately extended to approximate recognition: it is sufficient to define a similarity measure $sim(\cdot, \cdot)$ from pairs of contours into $[0,1]$ (where 1 is perfect matching). Then, a basic component would be interpreted as a function $\langle \tau, B \rangle^{\mathcal{I}}(I) = \max_{r \in I}\{sim(\tau(e(B)), e(r))\}$ from an image I into $[0,1]$. Note that sim depends on translations, rotation and scaling, since we are looking for regions in I whose contour matches $e(B)$, wrt the position and size specified by τ.

The interpretation of basic shapes, instead, includes the familiar translation-rotation-scaling invariant recognition. We define the interpretation of a basic shape as

$$B^{\mathcal{I}} = \{I \in \Delta \mid \exists \tau \; \exists r \in I : e(r) = \tau(e(B))\}$$

and its approximate counterpart as $B^{\mathcal{I}}(I) = \max_{\tau} \max_{r \in I}\{sim(\tau(e(B)), e(r))\}$. The maximization over all possible transformations $\max_{\tau}$ can be effectively computed by using a similarity measure sim' that is invariant wrt translation-rotation-scaling. Similarity of color and texture, if specified, can be added with a weighted sum. A basic shape B can be used as a query to retrieve all images from Δ which are in $B^{\mathcal{I}}$. Therefore, our approach generalizes the more usual approaches for single-shape retrieval, such as Blobworld [3].

Composite shape descriptions are interpreted as sets of images, which must contain all components, anywhere in the image, but in the described arrangement relative to each other. Unlike basic shapes, we did not include a "composite shape component" $\langle c, t, \tau, C \rangle$ — this would be necessary only if we used a composite shape description C as a (grouped) component in a more complex shape, see [14]. Let C be a composite shape description $\langle \tau_1, B_1 \rangle \sqcap \cdots \sqcap \langle \tau_n, B_n \rangle$ (again, for simplicity we drop color and texture which would introduce weighted sums).

In exact matching, the interpretation is the intersection of the sets interpreting each component of the shape:

$$C^{\mathcal{I}} = \{ I \in \Delta \mid \exists \tau : I \in \cap_{i=1}^{n} \langle (\tau \circ \tau_i), B_i \rangle^{\mathcal{I}} \} \qquad (1)$$

Observe that we require all shape components to be transformed within the image using the same transformation τ. This preserves the arrangement of the shape components relative to each other — given by each τ_i — while allowing $C^{\mathcal{I}}$ to include every image containing a group of regions in the right arrangement, wholly displaced by τ.

We can now formally define the recognition of a shape in an image.

Definition 1 (Recognition). *A shape C is recognized in an image I if for every interpretation $\mathcal{I}$ such that $I \in \Delta$, it is $I \in C^{\mathcal{I}}$. An interpretation $\mathcal{I}$ satisfies a composite shape description C if there exists an image $I \in \Delta$ such that C is recognized in I. A composite shape description is satisfiable if there exists an interpretation satisfying it.*

Observe that shape descriptions could be unsatisfiable: if two components define overlapping regions, no image can be segmented in a way that satisfies both components. Of course, if composite shape descriptions are built using a graphical tool, unsatisfiability can be easily avoided, so we assume that descriptions are always satisfiable.

Observe also that our set-based semantics implies the intuitive interpretation of conjunction "$\sqcap$" — one could easily prove that $\sqcap$ is associative, commutative and idempotent. These properties imply that the shape descriptions form a semi-lattice, with unsatisfiable descriptions as bottom element.

For approximate matching, we modify definition (1), following the fuzzy interpretation of $\sqcap$ as minimum, and existential as maximum:

$$C^{\mathcal{I}}(I) = \max_{\tau} \{ \min_{i=1}^{n} \{ \langle (\tau \circ \tau_i), B_i \rangle^{\mathcal{I}}(I) \} \} \qquad (2)$$

Observe that our interpretation of composite shape descriptions strictly requires the presence of all components. In fact, the measure by which an image I belongs to the interpretation of a composite shape description $C^{\mathcal{I}}$ is dominated by the least similar shape component (the one with the minimum similarity). Hence, if a basic shape component does not match any region in I, this brings near to 0

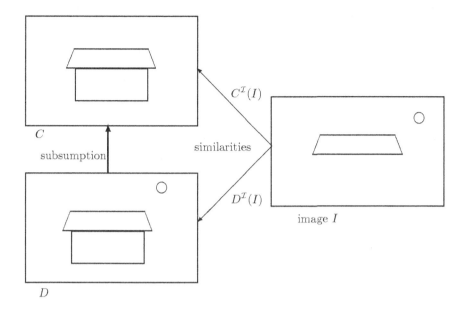

Fig. 1. In our approach, $C^{\mathcal{I}}(I) = D^{\mathcal{I}}(I) = 0$ (the rectangle is missing in I). In Gudivada & Raghavan's, it is possible that $D^{\mathcal{I}}(I) > threshold > C^{\mathcal{I}}(I) > 0$.

also the measure of $C^{\mathcal{I}}(I)$ (see Figure 3e for an example). This is more strict than, e.g., Gudivada & Raghavan's [8] or El-Kwae & Kabuka's [5] approaches, in which a non-appearing component can decrease the similarity value of $C^{\mathcal{I}}(I)$, but I can be still above a threshold.

Although this requirement may seem too strict, it allows us to prove the following important property of our formalism.

Proposition 1 (Downward refinement). *Let C be a composite shape description, and let D be a refinement of C, that is $D \equiv C \sqcap \langle \tau', B' \rangle$. For every interpretation $\mathcal{I}$, if shapes are interpreted as in (1), then $D^{\mathcal{I}} \subseteq C^{\mathcal{I}}$; if shapes are interpreted as in (2), then for every image I it holds $D^{\mathcal{I}}(I) \leq C^{\mathcal{I}}(I)$.*

Proof. For (1), the claim follows from the fact that $D^{\mathcal{I}}$ considers an intersection of components which strictly includes the one of $C^{\mathcal{I}}$. For (2), the claim analogously follows from the fact that $D^{\mathcal{I}}(I)$ computes a minimum over a superset of the values considered for $C^{\mathcal{I}}(I)$. □

The above property makes our language fully *compositional*. Namely, let C be a composite shape description; we can consider the meaning of C — when used as a query — as the set of images that can be potentially retrieved using C. At least, this will be the meaning perceived by an end user of a system. Downward refinement ensures that the meaning of C can be obtained by starting with one component, and then progressively adding other components (in any order). We remark that for other frameworks cited above [8, 5] this property does not hold. In fact, for Gudivada & Raghavan's approach it can be the case that an image I does not satisfy a description C, while it satisfies its refinement D because of a matched detail in D which raises the similarity sum weighted over all components. This is illustrated in Figure 1.

Downward refinement is a property linking syntax to semantics. Thanks to the extensional semantics, it can be extended to an even more meaningful semantic relation, namely, subsumption.

Definition 2 (Subsumption). *A description C subsumes a description D if for every interpretation $\mathcal{I}$, $D^{\mathcal{I}} \subseteq C^{\mathcal{I}}$. If (2) is used, C subsumes D if for every interpretation $\mathcal{I}$ and image $I \in \Delta$, it is $D^{\mathcal{I}}(I) \leq C^{\mathcal{I}}(I)$.*

Subsumption takes into account the fact that a description might contain a syntactic variant of another one, without both the user and the system knowing this fact. From the semantics, it is clear that we use "subsumption" as a (Description-Logics) synonym of *containment*. Intuitively , to actually decide if D is subsumed by C, we check if the sketch associated with D — seen as an image — could be retrieved using C as a query. Formal definitions follow.

Definition 3 (Prototypical image). *Let B be a basic shape. Its* prototypical image *is $I(B) = \{e(B)\}$. Let $C = \langle \tau_1, B_1 \rangle \sqcap \cdots \sqcap \langle \tau_n, B_n \rangle$ be a composite shape description. Its* prototypical image *is $I(C) = \{\tau_1(e(B_1)), \ldots, \tau_n(e(B_n))\}$.*

In practice, from a composite shape description one builds its prototypical image just applying the stated transformations to its components (and color/texture fillings, if present). Now subsumption can be decided exploiting the following general property relating subsumption to recognition of prototypical images:

Proposition 2. *A composite shape description C subsumes a description D if and only if C is recognized in the prototypical image $I(D)$.*

The notion of subsumption extends downward refinement. It enables also a hierarchy of shape descriptions, in which a description D is below another one C if D is subsumed by C. When C and D are used as queries, the subsumption hierarchy makes easy to detect *query containment*. Containment can be used to speed up retrieval: all images retrieved using D as a query can be immediately retrieved also when C is used as a query, without recomputing similarities.

3   Experiments with a prototype system

In order to substantiate our ideas we have developed a simple prototype system, written in C++ and Java.

The system structure is made up of four main components, as illustrated in Figure 2: the description classifier, the image features extractor, the image classifier and the image database management module. Some of the modules can be further decomposed into sub-components: the image features extractor contains an image segmentation module and a region data extraction one and

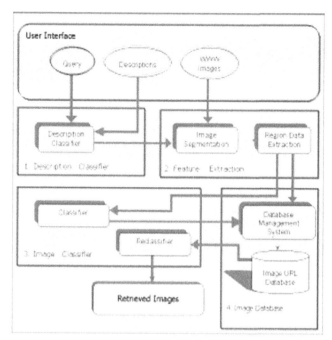

Fig. 2. Architecture of the proposed system.

the image classifier is composed by a classifier module and a module used in the image reclassification. Image segmentation is carried out with a simple algorithm that merges region growing and detected edges. Features are then extracted from detected regions (that have to comply with some minimal heuristics). We compute the shape feature as described in [4], color feature with a fragmentation weighted histogram [15] and texture feature with Gabor Filters. Each region has then three associated feature vectors.

Spatial relations among regions are determined with an algorithm based on Gudivada's [7] θ-R strings. The original algorithm has been modified in several ways, as it has already described in the previous section.

Similarity is computed in the range [0,1] as a weighted sum with properly defined weighting coefficients, allowing to account for non-exact matches.

The system can carry out two different processes: image insertion and description insertion; the two paths in Figure 2 highlight the two processes. The description classifier manages a graph that is used to represent and hierarchically organize shape descriptions: basic shapes, and more complex ones obtained by combining such elementary shapes and/or by applying transformations (rotation, scaling and translation). The real images are linked to the descriptions in the structure depending on the most specific descriptions that they are able to satisfy. The description classifier module is invoked when a new description must be inserted in the system or a new query is posed. The classifier performs a search process in the hierarchy to find the exact level in which the new description (a

Fig. 3. a) sketch based query; b)correctly retrieved image(sim=0.88; c)correctly retrieved image (sim=0.81); d) correctly retrieved image (sim=0.71); e)excluded image (sim=0.0)

simple or a complex one) must be inserted: the level is determined considering the descriptions that the new shape is subsumed by. Once the level has been found, the image reclassifier compares the new shape description with the images available in the database to determine those that satisfy the description; all the images that verify the subsumption algorithm are tied to the new description. This stage only considers the images that are tied to descriptions that are direct ancestors of the new inserted description. The image insertion process is carried out off-line: the image segmentation component segments and processes images to extract features from each detected region, which characterize the images in the database.

The image classifier carries out the classification process to link each real image to a particular description in the hierarchy. Notice that the query /retrieval process consists of a description insertion: a new query to the system is considered like a new description and added to the hierarchical data structure; all the images that are connected either to the query or to descriptions below the query in the hierarchical structure are provided as retrieved images. Both a query and a new description are hence treated as prototypical images that should verify the definition stated in the previous chapter. From a shape description one builds its prototypical image just applying the stated transformations and color/texture fillings to its components.

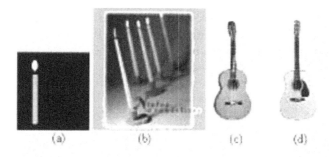

Fig. 4. A retrieval example: a) sketched query; higher rating retrieved images: b) sim=0.88; c) sim=0.78; d) sim=0.69.

Our prototype system avails of a simple user interface that allows to trace basic shapes as palette items, and properly insert and modify them, see Figure 3a. The system keeps track of the transformations corresponding to the user's actions, and uses them in building the (internal) shape descriptions stored with the previous syntax. The proposed system is currently being tested and needs further work. We are currently experimenting with a toy size database of 250 images. Largest part of them are synthetic, approximately one hundred are real images of variable size and quality. Images have been inserted off-line to create an initial knowledge base. First sets of experiments have been carried out to provide a preliminary validation of our approach, providing encouraging results. Example results presented here have no claim of exhaustivity. They only aim at showing distinguishing features of the proposed approach.

The first example, portrayed in Figure 3, shows an example of classification/retrieval process. A query, representing a simple house, is sketched in Figure 3a. Figures 3b, 3c, 3d show correctly retrieved images. Figure 3e shows what might appear, at a first look, a false negative, which is not. Observe that we are not dealing with image interpretation, with reasoning such as "there is a roof, hence there must be a house underneath". Here the system correctly segments the roof of the house, but is not able to extract a rectangular region under it. The presence of other regions/objects is accepted, as in other retrieved images, but not the lack of a region that was explicitly requested in the query. It should be anyway noticed that there is an enormous amount of available images, and at the current stage of research and technology no system can ensure a complete recognition; yet we believe that (differently from other information retrieval scenarios) the focus should be on reducing false positives, accepting without much concern a higher ratio of false negatives. In other words we believe it is preferable for a user looking for an image containing a house, e.g. using the sketch in 3a, that he/she receives as result of the query a limited subset of images containing almost for sure a house, than a large amount of images containing houses, but also several images with no houses at all.

The previous example can also be useful in clarifying the properties of our extensional semantics, which is compositional. Had the sketched query been just the trapezium, the image in Figure 3e would have been in the retrieved set, but adding details can only restrict the set of retrievable images.

The second example, in Figure 4, points out both a correct subsumption and retrieval process: the query represents a candle; the higher ranking retrieved image portrays some candles, which are correctly subsumed. The other two higher ranking images are guitars; they are retrieved as they contain a structure, in terms of both size and shape, which is quite close to the sketch. It should be noticed, by the way, that there was just one image with candles in the test images repository.

In order to better appreciate the system behavior in the subsumption process a further example is proposed in Figure 5. Here image a) shows the query, picturing a simple portal obtained combining two rectangles and an arch. The system correctly retrieves other scaled/rotated/translated portals (not shown here); correctly subsumes the image 5b, that includes three portals, but excludes the image in 5c, which has all parts of the previous image, but not in the correct positions.

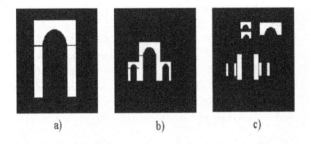

a)   b)   c)

Fig. 5. A subsumption example. a) query; b) correctly retrieved image (sim=0.92); c) correctly excluded image (sim=0.0).

4   Conclusions

We have proposed here a language based on description logics for the semantic indexing and retrieval of images containing complex objects. The proposed language is both a Definition language and a Query language. We start, as conventional image retrieval systems do, with the extraction from images of low-level features such as color, edges and texture, in order to define an image segmentation into regions. We then provide a syntax for the description of complex objects as compositions of simpler "basic" shapes. An extensional semantics allows to define reasoning services, such as classification and subsumption.

A prototype system has been built, implementing the proposed approach; first results appear encouraging.

Acknowledgements

This work has been supported by projects CNR-LAICO, CNR-DeMAnD, MURST 60 % "Sistemi Informativi di Immagini" and MURST-CLUSTER22.

References

1. E. Ardizzone et al. Hybrid computation and reasoning for artificial vision. In V. Cantoni, S. Levialdi, and V. Roberto, editors, *Artificial Vision*, pages 193–221. Academic Press, 1997.
2. E. Bertino and B. Catania. A constraint-based approach to shape management in multimedia databases. *Multimedia Systems*, 6:2–16, 1998.
3. C. Carson et al. Blobworld: A system for region-based image indexing and retrieval. In D.P. Huijsmans and A.W.M. Smeulders, editors, *LNCS*, volume 1614, pages 509–516. 1999.
4. E. Di Sciascio and M. Mongiello. Query by sketch and relevance feedback for content-based image retrieval over the web. *Journal of Visual Languages and Computing*, 10(6):565–584, 1999.
5. E.A. El-Kwae and M.R. Kabuka. Content-based retrieval by spatial similarity in image databases. *ACM Trans. on Information Systems*, 17:174–198, 1999.
6. J.D. Foley, A. van Dam, S.K. Feiner, and J.F. Hughes. *Computer Graphics*. Addison Wesley Publ. Co., Reading, Massachussetts, 1996.
7. V.N. Gudivada. θr-string: A geometry-based representation for efficient and effective retrieval of images by spatial similarity. *IEEE Trans. Knowledge and Data Engineering*, 10(3):504–512, 1998.
8. V.N. Gudivada and J.V.Raghavan. Design and evaluation of algorithms for image retrieval by spatial similarity. *ACM Trans. on Information Systems*, 13(2):115–144, 1995.
9. V. Haarslev, C. Lutz, and R. Moeller. Foundations of spatioterminological reasoning with descrition logics. In *Proc. of KR'98*, pages 112–123, 1998.
10. R. Jain. Special issue on visual information systems. *Comm. of the ACM*, 40(12), Dec. 1997.
11. W.Y. Ma and B.S. Manjunath. NETRA: A toolbox for navigating large image database. In *Proc. of IEEE ICIP*, 1997.
12. B. S. Manjunath, T. Huang, A. M. Tekalp, and H. J. Zhang (Eds.). Special issue on digital libraries. *IEEE Trans. Image Processing*, 09(01), 2000.
13. C. Meghini, F. Sebastiani, and U. Straccia. The terminological image retrieval model. In *Proc. of ICIAP-97*, number 1311 in LNCS, pages 156–163. Springer-Verlag, 1997.
14. E. Di Sciascio, F. M. Donini, and M. Mongiello. A description logic for image retrieval. In E. Lamma and P. Mello, editors, *AI*IA 99: Advances in Artificial Intelligence*, number 1792 in LNAI, pages 13–24. Springer-Verlag, 2000.
15. E. Di Sciascio, C. Guaragnella, and M. Mongiello. Color fragmentation-weighted histogram for sketch based image queries. In *Proc. of Eusipco-2000*, September 2000.
16. K. Sugihara and T. Shih Eds. Special issue on distributed multimedia systems. *Journal of Visual Languages and Computing*, 10(06), 1999.

An Iconic and Semantic Content Based Retrieval System for Histological Images

Ringo W. K. Lam[1], Kent K. T. Cheung[1], Horace H. S. Ip[1],
Lilian H. Y. Tang [2] and R. Hanka [2]

[1]Image Computing Group, Computer Science, City University of Hong Kong, HK.
email : cship@cityu.edu.hk

[2]Medical Informatics Unit, Medical School, University of Cambridge, United Kingdom

Abstract. This paper describes an intelligent image retrieval system based on iconic and semantic content of histological images. The system first divides an image into a set of subimages. Then the iconic features are derived from primitive features of color histogram, texture and second order statistics of the subimages. These features are then passed to a high level semantic reasoning engine, which generates hypotheses and requests a number of specific fine feature detectors for verification. After iterating a certain number of cycles, a final histological label map is decided for the submitted image. The system may then retrieve images based on either iconic or semantic content. Annotation is also generated for each image processed.

1. Introduction

Over the last few years, researchers have contributed a lot of efforts to propose and design computer systems for automatically analyzing and retrieving medical images, such as X-ray, ultrasound, CT and MRI. For examples, Chu et al. [1] made use of features including shape, size and texture, as well as spatial relationships among objects, to form a hierarchical structure to describe the image.

Concerning about retrieving image from the database, Petrakis and Faloutsos [2] proposed a method to handle approximate searching by image content in the databases. However, their experiment was based on manually segmented images. Besides, Korn et al. [3] used the distance transform and the mathematical morphology to retrieve similar medical tumor shapes from a large database. Their method was mainly concentrated on black and white image shape. As a result, the method is not able to identify features of similar shape but with different texture content. In other words, it is hardly used to analyze histological image.

Hou et al. demonstrated their content-based indexing idea in [4]. Although their technique was aimed at large image database, their experiment was only limited to much simpler MR chest images. Further research work was not published afterwards. On the other hand, Hamilton et al. [5] examined two kinds of features, respectively

R. Laurini (Ed.): VISUAL 2000, LNCS 1929, pp. 384-395, 2000.

the co-occurrence matrix and the number of low optical density pixels to identify abnormal tissues in the image. They claimed that 86% accuracy rate was obtained for classifying the training images by using two features only.

Recently, there is an ongoing project developed in the Pittsburgh Supercomputing Center of Carnegie Mellon University [14], however there is not much detail about their work published so far. Another well known project is under development in Purdue university [6] where they mainly focus on the computing tomography and have built an interface called ASSERT. In conclusion, the research on the histological image analysis is scarce. It is probably due to the wide variability and the subtle differences in visual appearance of the histological images [11]. In addition, there are other factors influencing the quality of the histological images during preparation, such as tissue cutting angle, tissue thickness, tissue deterioration, tissue orientation on the slide, slide preparation defect, patient disease, individual difference, capturing set up and staining, etc. Therefore, it is difficult to obtain satisfactory results even with tremendous computation time.

In this paper, we present a content-based image retrieval (CBIR) system for histological images. The images that we examined were extracted from six gastrointestinal (GI) tract organs. They are oesophagus, stomach, small intestine, appendix, large intestine and anus. The CBIR system is built upon a 5-tier framework and written in the object oriented programming language [12]. It links together with two databases, respectively DB2 and FoxPro. Where the DB2 is used to hold the image data and annotations, and the FoxPro is used to hold the patient information. The deployment of FoxPro in the system is to due to the reason that there is an existing FoxPro based Pathological Patient Information system used in the local hospitals. Therefore, our proposed CBIR system is ready to be linked to the other operational systems in hospitals. In section 2, we briefly introduce the features used in our system. Section 3 describes the fine histological feature detectors and the semantic analyzer. Section 4 is about the similarity measures used in our retrieval system and finally the performance of the histological image retrieval is presented in Section 5.

2. Feature Extraction

Depending on which scale a GI tract image is viewed, different details of the image can be observed. Generally, in a coarse scale, we may divide an image into 15 coarse regions such as lumen, mucosa and submucosa, with details given in Table 1. If viewing at a higher resolution (about x50 magnification), those 15 regions can be subdivided into a number of fine histological features. There are 76 such fine features [10] identified in our system. However, owing to the scarcity of some feature samples, 63 fine features are tested instead. In addition, some of 63 features actually come from the same kind of tissues but in different appearances, therefore we combine those 63 features into 45 groups after classifying.

As a matter of fact, the 76 features identified by our system do not cover all the histological features in the 6 GI tract organs. For example, blood sometimes spills

Coarse Region	Meaning
L	Lumen
M	Mucosa
S	Submucosa
E	Muscularis Externa
A	Serosa / Adventitia
I	Junction between Lumen and Mucosa
J	Junction between Mucosa and Submucosa
K	Junction between Submucosa and Muscularis Externa
O	Junction between Muscularis Externa and Serosa / Adventitia
U	Junction between Serosa and Outside
V	M, E
W	M, S
X	A, S
Y	E, M, S
Z	Every where

Table 1 : Coarse region of the histological images

over in the lumen that causes a junction between the blood and the lumen. Dirt and artifact sometimes occur in the image. Besides, some junctions are not yet defined, such as junction between fundus glands and lymph nodule, and junction between brunner's glands and other tissues, etc. As these features are not considered in our system, they may be wrongly classified into other features instead.

To enable the automatic analysis of the histological images, an image of 1123 x 870 pixels is first divided into 17 x 13 subimages, each of which has 64 x 64 pixels inside. For each subimage, two kinds of statistical features, namely coarse and semi-fine, are computed in the beginning. The coarse features include the RGB histograms and the gray histogram. These features are passed to a 3-layer MLP neural network to classify the subimage into one of the 15 coarse classes. Then, a set of semi-fine features including means, standard deviations of the gray and color level, as well as Gabor filters [7] are used to classify the subimage into one of the 63 fine features by a Bayes minimum risk classifier [8]. Since each fine feature actually corresponds to a coarse class, the coarse region derived from the semi-fine features is also used together with the coarse features (histograms) to classify the subimage into one coarse class. In other words, the coarse region of the subimage is determined by two kinds of information, the coarse results of the histograms and the semi-fine features.

The semi-fine Gabor and statistical features that we use are based on multiple-size windows. Except the boundary subimages, the semi-fine features of the other subimages come from two window sizes, 64 x 64 and 128 x 128. In total, there are 51 features (15 Gabor and 8 statistical features for window 64 x 64, 20 Gabor and 8 statistical features for window 128 x 128) used to decide the semi-fine histological label of the subimage. In our paper [13], we have discussed how the multiple window approach may increase the accuracy rate of the subimage classification. For subimages that are extracted from images about 90% the same as those used to create the training subimages but with different subimage areas, the classification accuracy rates of using double window sizes are respectively equal to 46.9% for 63 fine feature classes and 52.5% for 45 regrouped classes. For subimages that are extracted from images which have only about 10% the same as those used to extract the training subimages, the classification accuracy rates are respectively equal to 22.3% and 31.5% for 63 fine feature and 45 regrouped classes. Besides, the coarse classification accuracy rates are respectively equal to 65% and 75.6% for images containing and without containing training subimage samples.

3. Semantic Analyzing Process

After computing the semi-fine features, the semantic analyzer (SA) [9] goes through an iteration process to refine the fine histological feature label of each subimage. There are two kinds of iterations inside the process. The SA may decide whether to refine through a process involving the coarse and semi-fine features only, or to call the fine feature detectors for detailed analysis.

	Fine Detector
1	Anus : Stratified Squamous Epithelium
2	Junction between Lumen and Anus Stratified Squamous Epithelium
3	Appendix : Muscularis Externa
4	Blood
5a	Large Intestine : Long Colon Glands
5b	Large Intestine : Ovoid Colon Glands
5c	Large Intestine : Round Colon Glands
6	Lumen
7	Lymphocyte
8	Lymph Nodule
9a	Muscle : Fine Muscularis Mucosae
9b	Muscle : Loose Bundle
9c	Muscle : Loose Smooth In Mass
9d	Muscle : Tight Smooth In Mass
10	Oesophagus : epithelium
11	Junction between Oesophagus Epithelium and Lamina Propria
12a	Small Intestine : Cross Villi
12b	Small Intestine : Empty Villi
12c	Small Intestine : Flat Villi
12d	Small Intestine : Long Villi

Table 2 : Fine Feature Detectors

As the fine feature detectors are based on a set of morphological parameters such as shape, contour, distance to the lumen, neighbour configuration, etc. The detectors require much more computation effort than the statistical coarse and semi-fine features. At present, 12 main fine feature detectors, which may be further subdivided into 20 fine feature detectors have been built, as listed in Table 2. When calling the fine feature detector, the SA has a set of hypotheses. Based on the hypotheses, the SA passes a region of interest (ROI) to a set of detectors. Then, each detector will use different techniques to verify the ROI and return a confidence value to the SA after computing. At the end, the SA compares the returned confidence values from the detectors to verify its hypotheses. This process may go through several iterations before coming to a stable solution.

For example, when the SA hypothesizes that the region is probably an anus epithelium, it will ask the anus epithelium detector to determine the confidence value of the hypothesis. At present, the detector will start from a Gaussian filtered image and combine the ROI given by the SA to form a binary image according to a preset threshold value. Based on the binary image, the detector extracts every isolated island (groups of connected pixels) and examines its color content, size, boundaries with lumen and other tissues as well as its distance to the lumen. All these parameters have different weighting to the confidence value. After computing, it passes the confidence value back to the SA. Since the SA may request several detectors to verify the hypotheses, even the detector returns a very high confidence value to the SA, the SA may still reject the ROI to be that histological feature if there is another detector returning an even higher confidence value.

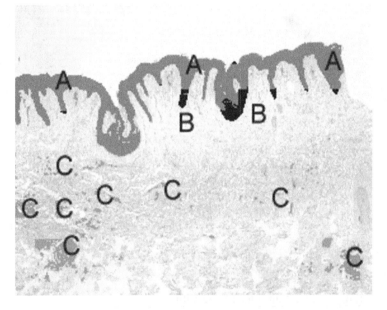

Fig.1 : Extracted Anus Stratified Squamous Epithelium (A), missing
area (B) by the fine detector and ROI (A + C) given by the SA.

As shown in Fig.1, the ROI given by the SA is the area marked by letter "A" and "C" (light color). Based on the ROI, the fine detector can cleverly extract most of the Anus Epithelium, which is indicated by letter "A" (light color). The amount of missing Anus Epithelium area indicated by letter "B" (dark color) is acceptable when compared to the whole epithelium layer. Since the area B has actually missed in the ROI, the ROI should be made as large as possible before passing to the fine detectors for decision. On the other hand, the detector rules out those areas not belonging to the epithelium, that is area "C".

To evaluate the iteration performance of the SA, we perform an experiment based on 50 images where 28 of them are never used to define the training histological features of the subimage. For each image, there should be 221 subimages. However, as there are some features inside the images not defined in our 73 or 63 histological feature labels, the actual number of subimages used in the experiment is equal to 10814. When the semi-fine features are used alone, a 42.2% accuracy rate is yielded for the regrouped 45 fine features. That accuracy rate is about the average of 52.5% and 31.5% in our previous test described in section 2. If the SA is invoked to run the iteration, a 53.1% accuracy rate of the features is obtained. It is about 25% higher than the result without invoking the SA. Although 52.5% accuracy rate is not very high but it can be better if we (a) implement more fine feature detectors, (b) better design those existing detectors, and (c) add more rules to the SA.

4. Similarity Measures

The system consists of two kinds of retrieval methods, semantic and iconic. After the semantic analyzer refines the histological labels, it retrieves the image according to (a) the frequency of predefined keyword of the histological features with equal weighting and (b) the identified GI tract organ of the image. If it concludes that the image is one of the GI tract organ, it will exclude the image shown in the other classes. To have better performance, future research work on the semantic similarity will be needed.

On the contrary, the iconic retrieval is solely based on the subimage histological labels classified by the semi-fine features. The system directly reads out the iconic data and compares with other images to find the most similar set of images. Three kinds of iconic similarity measures, namely Shape Similarity (SS), Neighbour Similarity (NS) and Subimage Frequency Distribution Similarity (SFDS), are implemented.

Concerning about iconic retrieval, SS is based on the 15 coarse histological regions of the image, which in fact roughly describes how the Lumen, Mucosa, Submucosa, junctions and etc. are distributed in the image. At the beginning, the 17 x 13 subimages are assigned to 16 overlapping windows each of which consists of 5 x 4 subimages. The occurrence frequencies of the 15 coarse histological regions are then ranked in each window, the system searches for images having the most similar coarse histological regions as the query image. Since we have not yet included rotation invariance in the SS. Therefore, it is likely that a rotated query image cannot be retrieved by the SS measure.

Shape Similarity (SS) is calculated based on the following procedures :

> *Similarity = 0*
> *For all windows do*
>   *winSimilarity = 1*
>   *Sort coarse labels of retrieved images by frequency.*
>
>   *For each coarse label of the retrieved image*
>   *if coarse label is the same as the most frequent coarse region of*
>   *the query image*
>   *winSimilarity =winSimilarity* c*
>   *End For Loop*
>   *Similarity += winSimilarity*
> *End For Loop*
>
> *Similarity = Similarity / number of windows*

Besides, *NS* uses a matrix to record the co-occurrence frequencies of the 63 histological labels of the 8-nearest neighbours against those of the center subimage. Each element *n(i, j)* of the matrix records how many times the center subimage being histological label *i* while the histological label of any one neighbour is equal to *j*, Since there are 63 histological labels employed in the system, the matrix size is 63 x 63. For each image in the database, the *NS* has to compare element by element in the two matrices, $n_q(i, j)$ of the query image and $n_r(i, j)$ of the candidate image; therefore, the computation time can be very long if the database has a lot of images inside.

Neighbour Similarity (*NS*) :

$$s_q, s_r = \frac{w_t}{w_t \quad w_L} \qquad\qquad eqn.(1)$$

$$similarity= \sum_{i=0}^{N_f} \sum_{j=0}^{N_f} |n_q(i, j)s_q \quad n_r(i, j)s_r| \qquad eqn.(2)$$

$$NS = \exp(\ similarity/W_N) \qquad\qquad eqn.(3)$$

Where w_L and w_t respectively are the numbers of Lumen and subimages in an image, N_f is the total number of fine histological labels, w_N is the number of subimages which have 8-connected neighbours. Finally s_q and s_r are the scaling factors to eliminate the influence of the number of Lumen in the query and retrieved images respectively.

Alternatively, *SFDS* directly counts the frequency of the 63 fine histological labels occurring in the image instead. For each image, the system only needs to compare the 63 entries, therefore the computation time is much shorter than the *NS*.

Subimage Frequency Distribution Similarity (*SFDS*) :

$$similarity = \sum_{i=0}^{N_f} |F_q(i)s_q \quad F_r(i)s_r| \qquad eqn.(4)$$

$$SFS = \exp(\ similarity \ /W_N) \qquad\qquad eqn.(5)$$

Where $F_q(i)$ and $F_r(i)$ are respectively the frequency of fine histological feature i for query and retrieved images, s_q and s_r have the same meaning as those in NS measure.

5. Histological Image Retrieval

To compare the performance of the semantic and iconic retrieval, an example is shown in Fig.2. Where a query image of Small Intestine is submitted to the system. After computation, four kinds of results corresponding to the (a) semantic retrieval, (b) iconic retrieval (SS), (c) iconic retrieval (NS) and (d) iconic retrieval ($SFDS$) are listed in the output window. Since the query image is not stored in the database, the system will only retrieve other most similar images; otherwise, the query image must be the most similar one. To have a clear visual comparison of the retrieval results, the first three retrieved images are displayed on the bottom with the most similar one on the left and the least similar one on the right. Besides, the query image is displayed on the left-top corner in the figure.

	Semantic	Iconic – SS	Iconic – NS	Iconic – $SFDS$
Anus	52.3%	18.2%	60.7%	59.6%
Appendix	59.3%	23.9%	62.9%	62.1%
Large Intestine	49.7%	16.4%	56.5%	58.5%
Oesophagus	59.9%	23.9%	58.0%	58.0%
Small Intestine	60.7%	33.3%	55.1%	55.4%
Stomach	59.1%	21.2%	63.0%	61.1%

Table 3 : Accuracy Rate of the first 5 retrieved images

	Semantic	Iconic – SS	Iconic – NS	Iconic – $SFDS$
Anus	69.2%	47.4%	94.7%	94.7%
Appendix	81.3%	56.3%	96.9%	96.9%
Large Intestine	71.4%	91.1%	96.7%	96.7%
Oesophagus	80.0%	54.8%	96.8%	96.8%
Small Intestine	100.0%	83.1%	91.5%	91.5%
Stomach	85.7%	71.1%	100.0%	97.8%

Table 4 : Accuracy rate of the first 5 retrieved images having at least one is correct

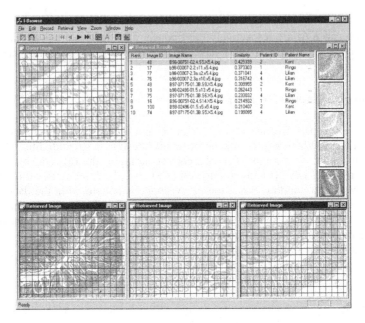

(a) Semantic Measure

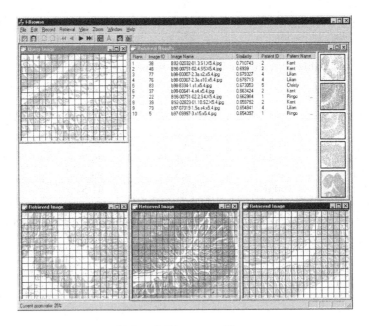

(b) Iconic Measure – Shape

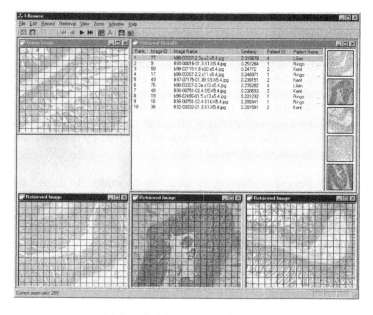

(c) Iconic Measure – Neighbour

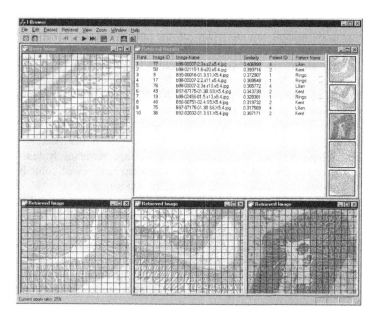

(d) Iconic Measure – Subimage

Fig.2 : Retrieved images based on four similarity measures for a small intestine query image sample

It can be seen that the images retrieved by the iconic retrieval is sometimes similar in appearance but actually the images do not always come from the same GI Tract organ as the query image. For example, in Fig.2(b), the most similar retrieved image (on the left most) by the iconic retrieval (*SS*) is a Large Intestine sample while the other two come from the Small Intestine. Similar results are obtained for iconic retrieval based on *NS* or *SFDS* where the second most similar image of Fig.2(c) and the third most similar image of Fig.2(d) come from the Large Intestine. On the other hand, the semantic retrieval does not return images similar to those of the Iconic retrieval. The retrieved images may also be wrong if the annotation given by the semantic analyzer is incorrectly identified as other GI tract organ.

A database of 89 images containing 13 anus, 16 appendix, 14 large intestine, 15 oesophagus, 17 small intestine and 14 stomach, is set up to compare the four retrieval methods. Table 3 illustrates the retrieval accuracy rates of these six GI tract organs by the four measures for the first 5 images excluding the query image. The *NS* and *SFDS* measures perform the best among all the methods, the *SS* measure gives very poor result because it is not designed for retrieving similar images of the same organ. Its purpose is only to retrieve images of similar coarse structure. The *NS* and *SFDS* measures yield nearly 60% accuracy for the first 5 retrieved images. On the other hand, the Semantic measure does not give a better result than the iconic measures even in Table 4, which shows the retrieval accuracy rates of the first 5 images having at least one correct. One of the main reasons is because the semantic retrieval excludes all those images when its annotation indicates another class. It causes the retrieval accuracy rate for that query image become so low that the average value is decreased by a significant amount. One of the interesting founding is about the retrieval accuracy rate of Small Intestine. The Iconic *NS* and *SFDS* measures perform the worst among all of the six GI tract organs; however, the Iconic *SS* and the Semantic measure gives the best retrieval rate for Small Intestine. These results show that the Semantic measure and the pure Iconic *NS*, *SFDS* measures do not correlate to a certain extent because of the SA iteration process.

6. Conclusions

An intelligent iconic and semantic content-based image retrieval system has been presented in the paper. By making use of the statistical features of color histograms and texture features, an image is first roughly classified to a label map. The histological features of the subimage array of the image are then refined through an iteration process where a semantic analyzer will generate a set of hypotheses. Based on the hypotheses, a set of fine feature detectors are called to determine the confidence level of the hypothesis. In addition, the retrieval system also implements four kinds of similarity measures, respectively based on one semantic and three iconic similarity measures. It is found by experiment that the iteration process may improve the accuracy rate of the histological features but the semantic similarity measure for image retrieval still needs improvement.

Acknowledgements

This project is funded by the Hong Kong Jockey Club Charities Trust. The authors would like to thank Dr. K. C. Lee for providing indispensable histological knowledge and images.

References

[1] W. W. Chu, C. C. Hsu, A. F. Cardenas and R. K. Taira, "Knowledge-Based Image Retrieval with Spatial and Temporal Constructs", *IEEE Transactions on Knowledge & Data Eng.*, vol. 10, no.6, pp. 872 – 888, 1998.

[2] E. G. M. Petrakis and C. Faloutsos, "Similarity Searching in Medical Image Databases", *IEEE Transactions on Knowledge & Data Eng.*, vol. 9, no.3, pp. 435 – 447, 1997.

[3] P. Korn, N. Sidiropoulos, C. Faloutsos, E. Siegel and Z. Protopapas, "Fast Effective Retrieval of Medical Tumor Shapes", *IEEE Transactions on Knowledge and Data Engineering*, vol. 10, no.6, pp.889 – 904, 1998.

[4] T. Y. Hou, P. Liu, A. Hsu and M. Y. Chiu, "Medical Image Retrieval by Spatial Features", *IEEE Inter. Conf. Systems, Man and Cybernetics*, vol.2, pp.1364 – 1369, 1992.

[5] P. W. Hamilton, P. H. Bartels, D. Thompson, N. H. Anderson, R. Montironi and J. M. Sloan, "Automated Location of Dysplastic Fields in Colorectal histology Using Image Texture Analysis", *Journal of Pathology*, vol. 182, pp. 68 – 75, 1997

[6] C. R. Shyu, C. E. Brodley, A. C. Kak, A. Kosaka, A. Aisen and L. Broderick, "Local versus Global Features for Content-Based Image Retrieval", *Proc. of IEEE Workshop Content-Based Access of Image and Video Libraries*, pp.30 - 34, 1998.

[7] A. K. Jain and F. Farrokhnia, "Unsupervised Texture Segmentation Using Gabor Filters", *Pattern Recognition*, vol.24, no.12, pp. 1167-1186, 1991.

[8] A. K. Jain, *Fundamentals of Digital Image Processing*, Prentice-Hall : Englewood Cliffs, 1989.

[9] L. H. Y. Tang, R. Hanka, R. Lam, H. H. S. Ip, "Automatic Semantic Labelling of Medical Images for Content-Based Retrieval", *Proceedings of Expersys '98*, pp. 77 - 82, USA, 1998.

[10] L. H. Y. Tang, R. Hanka, H. H. S. Ip, R.. Lam,"Extraction of Semantic Features of Histological Images for Content-Based Retrieval of Images", *Proceedings of SPIE Medical Imaging '99*, vol. 3662, pp. 360 - 368, USA, 1999.

[11] L. H. Y. Tang, R. Hanka, H. H. S. Ip, "A Review of Intelligent Content-Based Indexing and Browsing of Medical Images", *Health Informatics Journal*, vol. 5, no.1, pp. 40 - 49, March 1999.

[12] K. K. T. Chueng, R. W. K. Lam, H. H. S. Ip, L. H. Y. Tang and R. Hanka, "Software Framework for Combining Iconic and Semantic Content for Intelligent Retrieval of Histological Images", published in *Visual '2000*.

[13] R. W. K. Lam, H. H. S. Ip, K. K. T. Cheung, L. H. Y. Tang and R. Hanka, "A Multi-Window Approach To Classify Histological Features", published in *ICPR '2000*.

[14] A. Wetzel and M. J. Becich, "Content Based Image Retrieval and pathology Image Classification Image Processing," http://www.psc.edu/research/abstracts/becich.html, 1998.

Image Retrieval by Colour and Texture Using Chromaticity Histograms and Wavelet Frames

Spyros Liapis and Georgios Tziritas

Computer Science Department, University of Crete, Heraklion, Greece,
{liapis, tziritas}@csd.uch.gr,
WWW home page: http://www.csd.uch.gr/~tziritas

Abstract. In this paper the combination of texture and colour features is used for image classification. Texture features are extracted using the Discrete Wavelet Frame analysis. 2-D or 1-D histograms of the *CIE Lab* chromaticity coordinates are used as colour features. The 1-D histograms of the a, b coordinates were also modeled according to the generalized Gaussian distribution. The similarity measure defined on the features distribution is based on the Bhattacharya distance. Retrieval benchmarking is performed on textured colour images from natural scenes, obtained from the VisTex database of MIT Media Laboratory and from the Corel Photo Gallery.

1 Introduction

The current explosion in the generation rate of image archives necessitates the development of effective ways of managing (describing, indexing and retrieving) visual information by its content [2], since a textual description of the image content may be subjective and inadequate for automatic retrieval. In order to describe the image content, low level arithmetic features must be extracted that will be quantitatively comparable. The MPEG-7 working groups are aimed to define and standardize the image content description for automatic indexing.

Numerous features were proposed and used to describe quantitavily the visual information, like shape, colour, texture, motion etc... [2]. Also a lot of image retrieval systems were developed using all or some of these features, like QBIC [1], Photobook [9], Chabot [8], Virage [3].

In this work the combination of texture and colour features are used for image content description. Image classification is performed according to global features describing the texture and colour content for the whole image. It could be also possible to extract the same features for previously segmented objects.

In this paper, for texture feature extraction the Discrete Wavelet Frames (DWF) analysis is used [11] [5]. Texture characterization is obtained from spatial frequency decomposition into distinctive bands that differ in scale and orientation.

For colour features the *CIE Lab* colour system is chosen, which is designed to be perceptually uniform. Only the chromaticity coordinates (a, b) are used to

R. Laurini (Ed.): VISUAL 2000, LNCS 1929, pp. 397–406, 2000.
Springer-Verlag Berlin Heidelberg 2000

describe colour. In general, colour content is best described by the chromaticity distribution which is given by 1-D or 2-D histograms. The computational complexity is reduced if Gaussian or Laplacian models could be assumed for these distributions.

In order to compare texture and colour features a common distance measure is used. This measure is chosen to be the Bhattacharya distance for its good classification properties and because it allows the combination of different features in a simple way. The performance of the features is checked according to a retrieval benchmark proposed in [6]. Two data sets are considered. The first data set is obtained from the MIT Media Laboratory VisTex database [4], which contains images of scenes of physical colour textures. The second one is obtained from the Corel Photo Gallery.

2   Texture feature extraction

Texture analysis is performed with the use of Discrete Wavelet Frames. The aim of the analysis is to determine characteristics corresponding to each texture pattern, so that each texture pattern is uniquely defined. Such a distinction takes place in the frequency domain, where the input image is equivalently decomposed to different scale levels. The decomposition is performed with multichannel filtering. For this purpose a low pass filter $H(z)$ and its conjugate quadrature high pass $G(z)$ form the pair of prototype filters for generating the whole filter bank by upsampling with a factor of 2, so that the whole range of bands is covered. The fourth-order binomial filter and its conjugate quadrature filter are used,

$$\left. \begin{array}{l} H(z) = \frac{z^2 + 4z + 6 + 4z^{-1} + z^{-2}}{16} \\ G(z) = zH(-z^{-1}) \end{array} \right\} \tag{1}$$

in the frequency domain. In addition, the generated filters can form orthogonal wavelet base functions [7], so the input signal can be decomposed into discrete wavelet frame coefficients, each corresponding to a different frequency layer. The previous decomposition can be extended to 2-D signals (images), by forming wavelet bases which result from the cross product of separable bases in each direction. These four base functions deduce the following decomposition algorithm:

$$\left. \begin{array}{l} d_{1,i+1}(k,l) = [h]_{2^i}(k) * [g]_{2^i}(l) * s_i(k,l) \\ d_{2,i+1}(k,l) = [g]_{2^i}(k) * [h]_{2^i}(l) * s_i(k,l) \\ d_{3,i+1}(k,l) = [g]_{2^i}(k) * [g]_{2^i}(l) * s_i(k,l) \\ s_{i+1}(k,l) = [h]_{2^i}(k) * [h]_{2^i}(l) * s_i(k,l) \end{array} \right\} \tag{2}$$

where (k,l) is an image point, $[\ ]_m$ means upsampling by a factor of m, s_{i+1} the approximation of the decomposition, and $d_{1,i+1}, d_{2,i+1}, d_{3,i+1}$ are the details of the $i+1$ layer.

The previous analysis can be applied to texture images, yielding the following representative vector:

$$y(k,l) = < y_1(k,l), \ldots, y_{N-1}(k,l), y_N(k,l) > \tag{3}$$

where each element of $y(k,l)$ has been determined according to the analysis in (2) and the dimension of the vector is $N = 3I + 1$, composed of $3I$ detail components and the approximation at level I component.

The texture content is then characterized by the variances σ_i^2 of the $N - 1$ detail components of the representative vector $(i = 1, \ldots, N - 1)$. This characterization is based on the fact that the mean value of the details is zero, because $G(z)|_{z=1} = 0$, and the different components are uncorrelated, because the values of the covariance matrix except the diagonals are practically zero. In addition, the components of vector $y(k,l)$ could be assumed according to the generalized Gaussian distribution.

The main advantage of this analysis is that the coefficients are computed in a separable way, which makes it no computational expensive. Also DWF decomposition provides good feature localization. Each point has a representative vector of DWF coefficients, because the scale of input signal does not change, in contrast with Discrete Wavelet Transform [7].

3   Color features

In order to characterize the colour content of an image the *CIE Lab* colour space is used. The *Lab* colour coordinate system has the advantage that it is designed to be perceptually uniform, meaning that the same distance in the colour space leads to equal human colour difference perception. It also has the advantage that lightness L is distinct and independent from the other coordinates (a, b), which are the chromaticity coordinates. For colour image classification and retrieval it is more relevant to compare the chromaticity distribution of an image, disregarding the lightness component, *i.e.*, images which are perceptually similar have the same chromaticity components. This exclusion of lightness is enforced in our case by the fact that lightness is used to extract texture features.

In order to characterize the chromaticity content of an image the 2-D histogram of the (a, b) coordinates is used. A uniform quantization of the 2-D histogram down to 1024 chromaticity bins is performed, because otherwise it would be very large and very sparse $([-137, 96], [-99, 133]$ for (a, b) which yields 54056 bins). The number of chromaticities is so large because most of the values of these coordinates are very dense in a small region around zero. Higher absolute values are found only when the image contains pure colours such as high saturated red or blue. Empirically the values of (a, b) found in natural images are compact and occupy a small portion of the whole range of values.

This method has the advantage of describing exactly the 2-D distribution of the chromaticity coordinates. However has the disadvantage that needs 1024 floating point numbers for storage for each image. This size could be reduced if the coordinates are uncorrelated, in which case the 1-D histograms of each coordinate could be used. Thus colour feature could use the 232 and 233 bins of the (a, b) histograms respectively.

In order to reduce the number of the colour features we could assume a model for each coordinate distribution. In our case the Gaussian and Laplacian distribution are used as models, which require only the mean value and the variance of the image's colour coordinates. The storage demands are minimized and the comparison of colour features is accelerated. Detracting from this model's usefulness is that its assumptions are not always valid. This fact leads us to a constrained data set in which each image will contain chromaticities concentrated around a concrete value at each coordinate.

4   Dissimilarity measure

Measuring the dissimilarity between images is of central importance for retrieving images by content. Some different dissimilarity measures for colour and texture were empirically evaluated in [10]. In our work another dissimilarity measure, the Bhattacharya distance, was used in order to compare the extracted features and measure their dissimilarity. The definition of the Bhattacharya distance is

$$d_B(p_1, p_2) = -\ln \left(\int_x \sqrt{p_1(x)p_2(x)} dx \right) \tag{4}$$

where p_1, p_2 probability density functions of vector x of any dimension. This measure has the advantage that is designed to compare features for the two classes case. It is a special case of the Chernoff bound of the error probability in binary classification [12]. It is well known that the Chernoff information gives the highest achievable exponent for the error probability. The Bhattacharya distance has the symmetric property, $(d(p_1, p_2) = d(p_2, p_1))$. The triangle property is only satisfied for specific configurations.

In our case this distance should be defined on empirical probability distributions. The discrete expression is

$$d_B(h_1, h_2) = -\ln \left(\sum_i \sqrt{h_1(i)h_2(i)} \right) \tag{5}$$

where i is an index of the bins of the normalized histograms h_1, h_2.

In the case that we have a model for the histogram's distribution, a simpler expression of the Bhattacharya distance can be deduced. In this work we assume that some features might follow the generalized Gaussian distribution

$$p(y) = \frac{c}{2\sigma \Gamma(\frac{1}{c})} e^{-(\frac{|y-\mu|}{\sigma})^c} \tag{6}$$

where the parameter σ is directly related to the variance, and c with the sharpness of the probability density function. For $c = 2$ we have the Gaussian and for $c = 1$ the Laplacian distribution.

For example generalized Gaussian distribution is suitable for DWF coefficients [7]. Also we assume that each feature is uncorrelated to each other (e.g. for DWF coefficient which is practically true). The simplified expression assuming generalized Gaussian distribution and uncorrelated features is

$$d_B^{1,2} = \frac{1}{c} \sum_{i=1}^N \ln \frac{\sigma_{i,1}^c + \sigma_{i,2}^c}{2\sqrt{\sigma_{i,1}^c \sigma_{i,2}^c}} + \frac{1}{2c} \sum_{i=1}^N \frac{|\mu_{i,1} - \mu_{i,2}|^c}{\sigma_{i,1}^c + \sigma_{i,2}^c} \tag{7}$$

where N is the dimension of the feature vector and the parameters σ_1^c and σ_2^c are estimated from the data. In this work values $c = 2$ (Gauss) or $c = 1$ (Laplace) are used. For the texture features mean values are zero because the high-pass filters have coefficients with zero sum, which results in omitting the second term in formula (7). On the other hand for colour features both terms are used, because mean colour values, obviously, are not zero.

When texture features (variances) and colour histogram features (1-D or 2-D a, b histograms) need to be combined, the simpler expression (7) is used for texture features and the initial discrete expression (5) is used for histograms. The combined distance formula is formed by the independent sumation of the distance expression for each feature. This holds because all terms are depicted from the same initial expression and because features are assumed uncorrelated.

5   Benchmark

In order to exploit the capabilities of the texture and colour features a retrieval benchmark was performed [6]. The purpose of this classification experiment is to find out if the image features overcome the images inhomogeneities.

For this purpose all the images in the database are sectioned into an equal number of icons, all of the same size, provided that all the images in the database have the same size. A database of icons is obtained with a large number of items. Each small icon in the database is used to retrieve from the database the nearest (more similar) icons, except itself. The similarity between two icons is determined with the distance measure described in the previous section.

For each number of retrieved icons, we record the *recall*, *i.e.*, the number of relevant images retrieved relative to the total number of relevant images in the database. This result is presented graphically in a hit rate curve versus the number of retrieved images. It is obvious that this curve will be increasing, because as the number of the retrieved icons is increasing the *recall* rate is increasing.

We performed this experiment on a data set obtained from VisTex database of the Media Laboratory in MIT. From this database of homogeneous colour textures from natural scenes were chosen 55 images (512×512). These images contain wood, bark, food, sand, flowers, trees, tiles, fabric and other. In order to perform the retrieval experiment they were cut to 16 icons 128×128 each, yielding 880 icons.

The benchmarking experiment with this data set was performed with all the texture and colour features. Figure 1 shows the classification curve for all the combinations. For texture the DWF features are used. For colour are used the 2-D histogram of (a,b), the two 1-D histograms of a,b respectively, the parameters of a Gaussian and a Laplacian model. For the DWF analysis the levels of decomposition were 5, yielding 15 dimension feature vector. Also Laplace distribution modeling was used for texture features, because after experimental results has better performance than assuming Gauss.

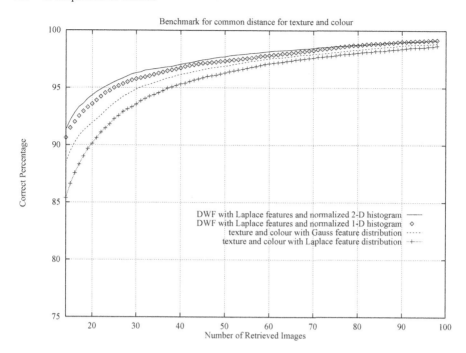

Fig. 1. Correct percentage curves using the combination of texture and colour features, for VisTex database

As expected the 2-D histogram has the best performance, even with small difference from 1-D histograms (91.3% against 90.6%). The modeling of the histograms distribution with Gauss and Laplace distribution provide good performance when combined with texture features yielding 88.5% and 85.3% of correct classification respectively. In practice a, b 1-D histograms are close to Gauss distribution in most of the cases. This is because most of the images are homogeneous which yields homogeneous chromaticities. Also Gauss modeling is enforced from Lab colour system which has chromaticity a, b coordinates very compact in a small range of all possible values.

Figure 2 shows the performance according to the benchmark using each texture or colour feature alone. Texture features have the best performance with 76.8%. Then the colour features follow, 2-D histograms, 1-D histograms, Gauss and Laplace modeling with 71.1%, 70.2%, 62.8%, 49.8% respectively. Texture features result in the best performance because the data set is texture oriented.

In Figure 3 are presented the results for the Corel Photo Gallery data set. The tested data set contains 350 images of 384 × 256 pixels. As for the VisTex data set, 128 × 128 subimages are considered. The total number of subimages is therefore 2100 belonging to 350 classes. Among these classes there are some similar in colour or in texture. Retrieving by only colour or only texture might give ambiguous results. The combination of both colour and texture gives much better classification rates. The benchmark is defined in the same way, as for the

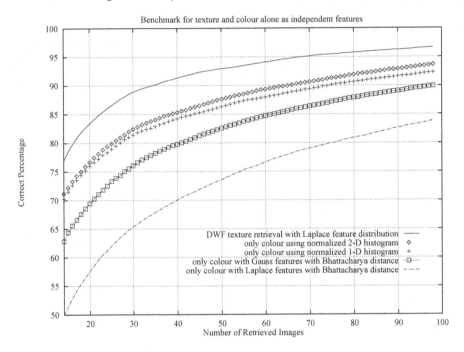

Fig. 2. Correct percentage curves using only texture or colour features, for VisTex database

VisTex data set, and the results show that the combination of texture and colour features gives a percentage of correct classification of the five first retrieved subimages equal to 93.6%. If only texture features are used the performance becomes 52.2%, and in the case of only colour features 83.5%. In Figure 4 are given the more inhomogeneous, in either colour or texture, images, for which the retrieval is less performant.

6   Summary

In this paper we presented texture and colour feature extraction methods. The Discrete Wavelet Frames analysis provides the texture features, which are the variances of the sub-bands. Color was described by the chromaticity distribution. These features were combined using a common distance measure, the Bhattacharya distance. The performance of the proposed image classification method was tested using a retrieval benchmark, where the performance is defined by the percentage of the correct for a given number of retrieved images. The data set was from nearly homogeneous natural colour textures from VisTex database and from Corel photo gallery.

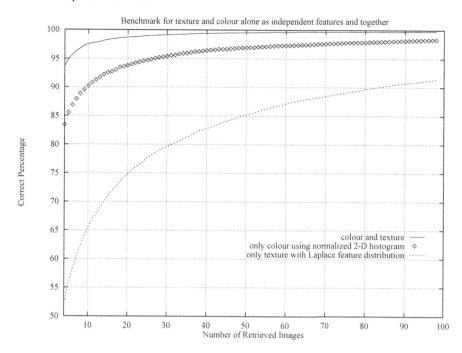

Fig. 3. Correct percentage curves for the benchmark on the Corel Photo Gallery data set

7 Acknowledgements

This work was funded in part by the PENED99 project, of the Greek General Secretariat of Research and Technology.

References

1. M. Flickner, H. Sawhney, W. Niblack, and J Ashley. Query by image and video content: the qbic system. *IEEE Computer*, 28(9):23–32, Sep 1995.
2. V. N. Gudivada and V. V. Raghavan. Content based image retrieval systems. *IEEE Computer*, 28, Sep 1995.
3. A. Gupta and R. Jain. Visual information retrieval. *Communicastions of the A.C.M.*, 40(5):70–79, May 1997.
4. MIT Media Laboratory. Vistex: Texture image database. *http://www-white.media.mit.edu/vismod/imagery/VisionTexture/vistex.html.*
5. S. Liapis, N. Alvertos, and G. Tziritas. Maximum likelihood texture classification and bayesian texture segmentation using discrete wavelet frames. *Intern. Conf. in Digital Signal Processing DSP97*, 2:1107–1110, July 1997.
6. F. Liu and R. W. Picard. Periodicity directionality and randomness wold features for image modeling retrieval. *Pattern Recognition*, 18(7):722–733, Jul 1996.
7. S. G. Malat. A theory of multiresolution signal decomposition: The wavelet representation. *IEEE Trans. on Pattern Analysis and Machine Intelligence*, 11:674–693, January 1989.

8. V. Ogle and M. Stonebraker. Chabot: Retrieval from a relational database of images. *IEEE Computer*, 28(9):40–48, Sep 1995.

9. A. Pentland, R. W. Picard, and S. Sclaroff. Photobook: Content-based manipulation of image databases. *M.I.T. Media Laboratory Perceptual Computing Technical Report No. 255*, November 1993.

10. J. Puzicha, J. Buhmann, Y. Rubner, and C. Tomasi. Empirical evaluation of dissimilarity measures for color and texture. *Intern. Conf. on Computer Vision*, Sep 1999.

11. M. Unser. Texture classification and segmentation using wavelet frames. *IEEE Trans. on Image Processing*, 4:1549–1560, November 1995.

12. T. Young and K.S. Fu. *Handbook of pattern recognition and image processing*. Academic Press, 1986.

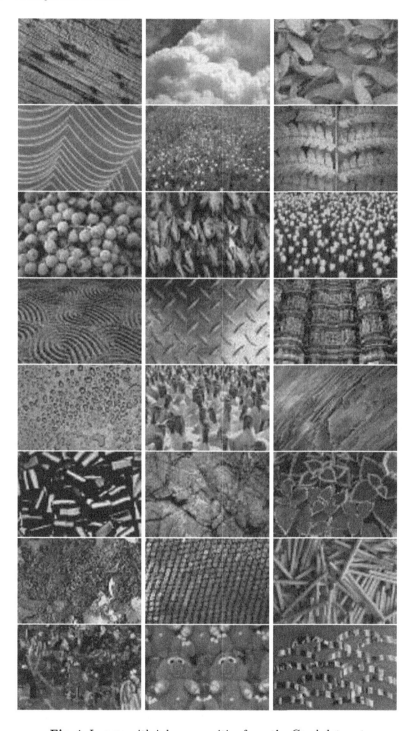

Fig. 4. Images with inhomogeneities from the Corel data set

Adaptive Multi-Class Metric Content-Based Image Retrieval

Jing Peng

Computer Science Department, Oklahoma State University, Stillwater, OK 74078, USA,
Email: jpeng@cs.okstate.edu
WWW home page: http://www.cs.okstate.edu/~jpeng

Abstract. Relevance feedback methods for content-based image retrieval have shown promise in a variety of image database applications. These techniques assume two (relevant and irrelevant) class relevance feedback. While simple computationally, two class relevance feedback often becomes inadequate in providing sufficient information to help rapidly improve retrieval performance. We propose a locally adaptive technique for content-based image retrieval that enables relevance feedback to take on multi-class form. We estimate a flexible multi-class metric for computing retrievals based on *Chi-squared* distance analysis. As a result, local data distributions can be sufficiently exploited, whereby rapid performance improvement can be achieved. The efficacy of our method is validated and compared against other competing techniques using a number of real world data sets.

1 Introduction

Relevance feedback methods for content-based image retrieval [9, 11] have shown promise in a variety of image database applications. These techniques use relevance feedback to compute flexible metrics for producing retrieval neighborhoods that are elongated along less relevant feature dimensions and constricted along most influential ones, as in [9], and to move the input query toward relevant retrievals and, at the same time, away from irrelevant ones, as in [11]. These techniques assume two (relevant and irrelevant) class relevance feedback that can be used to iteratively refine retrieval performance. While simple computationally, the assumption often becomes inadequate in providing sufficient information to help rapidly improve retrieval performance.

In this paper we propose a locally adaptive technique for content-based image retrieval that enables relevance feedback to take advantage of multi-class information. We estimate a flexible multi-class metric for computing retrievals based on *Chi-squared* distance analysis. As a result, local data distributions can be sufficiently exploited, whereby rapid performance improvement can be achieved. We demonstrate our technique and compare it against other competing methods using a number of real world data sets.

The rest of the paper is organized as follows. Section 2 describes related work addressing issues of feature relevance computation in the context of image

R. Laurini (Ed.): VISUAL 2000, LNCS 1929, pp. 407–418, 2000.
Springer-Verlag Berlin Heidelberg 2000

retrieval. Section 3 presents our adaptive multi-class metric approach to content-based image retrieval that exploits local data densities. Section 4 describes an efficient procedure for estimating our multi-class metric, hence local feature relevance. After that, we present in Section 5 experimental results demonstrating the efficacy of our technique using real-world data. Finally, Section 6 concludes this paper by pointing out possible extensions to the current work and future research directions.

2   Related Work

Friedman [3] describes an approach for learning local feature relevance that combines some of the best features of K-NN learning and recursive partitioning. This approach recursively homes in on a query along the most (locally) relevant dimension, where local relevance is computed from a reduction in prediction error given the query's value along that dimension. This method performs well on a number of classification tasks. In contrast, our method, inspired by [3], computes local feature relevance directly from the conditional probabilities, since in a retrieval problem the "label" of the query is known.

In our notations, the reduction in prediction error can be described by

$$I_i^2(\mathbf{z}) = \sum_{j=1}^{J} (\overline{\Pr}(j) - \overline{\Pr}(j|x_i = z_i)])^2, \tag{1}$$

where $\overline{\Pr}(j)$ represents the expected value of $\Pr(j|\mathbf{x})$. This measure reflects the influence of the ith input variable on the variation of $\Pr(j|\mathbf{x})$ at the particular point $x_i = z$. In this case, the most informative input variable is the one that gives the largest deviation from the average value of $\Pr(j|\mathbf{x})$.

The main difference, however, between our relevance measure (4) and Friedman's (1) is the first term in the squared difference. While the class conditional probability is used in our relevance measure, its expectation is used in Friedman's. As a result, a feature dimension is more relevant than others when it minimizes (4) in case of our relevance measure, whereas it maximizes (1) in case of Friedman's.

A recent work [11] describes an image retrieval system that makes use of retrieval techniques developed in the field of *information retrieval* (IR) for text-based information. In this system, images are represented by weight vectors in the term space, where weights capture the importance of components within a vector as well as importance across different vectors over the entire data set. The system then uses relevance feedback to update queries so as to place more weights on relevant terms and less weights on irrelevant ones. This query updating mechanism amounts to rotating the query vector toward relevant retrievals and, at the same time, away from irrelevant ones. One limitation of this system is that it is variant to translation and general linear transformation because of its use of the nonmetric similarity function [2]. Another limitation with the technique is that in many situations the mere rotation of the query vector is insufficient to achieve desired goals.

Peng et al. [9] present probabilistic feature relevance learning for content-based image retrieval that computes flexible retrieval metrics for producing neighborhoods that are elongated along less relevant feature dimensions and constricted along most influential ones. The technique has shown promise in a number of image database applications [10]. The main difference between the feature relevance measure proposed here and the one presented in [9] is that the former is based on a multi-class metric (2), while the latter is based on predicting class posteriors in a two-class setting.

The MindReader system described in [5] uses a multi-level scoring technique to adaptively compute a distance matrix and new query locations. While it provides a theoretical basis for MARS, it fails to analyze its working conditions. In addition, providing scores to retrieved images places burden on the user. In contrast, we exploit multi-class information to better predict the class posterior probabilities, hence local feature relevance.

PCF, *per category feature importance* [1], technique computes feature relevance based on conditional probabilities. This method estimates the conditional probability $p(c|f)$ for feature f in every category and uses it as a weight for f in category c. PCF assigns large weights to features having high correlation with the class. Clearly, feature importance as such is non-local, and therefore, insensitive to query locations. In addition, these global averaging correlation techniques do not work well on tasks that exhibit local feature differential relevance.

3   Adaptive Multi-Class Metric

In order to exploit local data densities effectively, we must first define a multi-class metric upon which to develop a theory of multi-class relevance feedback. We begin our discussion by introducing some classification concepts essential to our theoretical derivation [9, 12]. We state at the outset that this problem is opposite to typical classification problems based on lazy learning techniques [6], such as nearest-neighbor kernel methods. While the goal in classification is to predict the class label of an input query from nearby samples, the goal in retrieval is to find samples having the same "class label" as that of the query. Moreover, many lazy learning techniques for classification lend themselves to the kind of problems retrieval tasks may face. It is important to realize that, unlike classification problems, the notion of classes in image databases is a user-centered concept that is dependent on the query image. There is no labeling of images in the database. Nonetheless, the "class label" of an image is simply used here as a vehicle to facilitate the theoretical derivation of our feature relevance measure for content-based image retrieval. As we shall see later, the resulting relevance measure and its associated weightings are independent of image labels in the database and, thus, fit our goals nicely here.

Our technique is motivated as follows. In a classification problem, we are given J classes and N training observations. The training observations consist of q feature measurements $\mathbf{x} = (x_1, \cdots, x_q) \in \Re^q$ and the known class labels, L_j, $j = 1, \ldots, J$. The goal is to predict the class label of a given query $\mathbf{x}_0$.

In the one nearest neighbor classification rule, a single nearest neighbor $\mathbf{x}$ is found according to a distance metric $D(\mathbf{x}, \mathbf{x}_0)$. Let $\Pr(j|\mathbf{x})$ be the class conditional probability at point $\mathbf{x}$. Consider the *Chi-squared* distance [4, 8]

$$D(\mathbf{x}, \mathbf{x}_0) = \sum_{j=1}^{J} [\Pr(j|\mathbf{x}) - \Pr(j|\mathbf{x}_0)]^2 \tag{2}$$

which measures the distance between the query $\mathbf{x}_0$ and the point $\mathbf{x}$, in terms of the difference between the class posterior probabilities at the two points. Small $D(\mathbf{x}, \mathbf{x}_0)$ indicates that the classification error rate will be close to the asymptotic error rate for one nearest neighbor. In general, this can be achieved when $\Pr(j|\mathbf{x}) = \Pr(j|\mathbf{x}_0)$, which states that if $\Pr(j|\mathbf{x})$ can be sufficiently well approximated at $\mathbf{x}_0$, the asymptotic one nearest neighbor error rate might result in finite sample settings.

Equation (2) computes the distance between the true and estimated posteriors. Now, imagine we replace $\Pr(j|\mathbf{x}_0)$ with a quantity that attempts to predict $\Pr(j|\mathbf{x})$ under the constraint that the quantity is conditioned at a location along a particular feature dimension. Then, the *Chi-squared* distance (2) tells us the extent to which that dimension can be relied on to predict $\Pr(j|\mathbf{x})$. Thus, Equation (2) provides us with a foundation upon which to develop a theory of multi-class relevance feedback as well as feature relevance in the context of content-based image retrieval.

Based on the above discussion, our proposal is the following. We first notice that $\Pr(j|\mathbf{x})$ is a function of $\mathbf{x}$. Therefore, we can compute the conditional expectation of $p(j|\mathbf{x})$, denoted by $\overline{\Pr}(j|x_i = z)$, given that x_i assumes value z, where x_i represents the ith component of $\mathbf{x}$. That is,

$$\overline{\Pr}(j|x_i = z) = E[\Pr(j|\mathbf{x})|x_i = z] = \int \Pr(j|\mathbf{x})p(\mathbf{x}|x_i = z)d\mathbf{x} \tag{3}$$

Here $p(\mathbf{x}|x_i = z)$ is the conditional density of the other input variables. Let

$$r_i(\mathbf{z}) = \sum_{j=1}^{J} [\Pr(j|\mathbf{z}) - \overline{\Pr}(j|x_i = z_i)]^2 \tag{4}$$

$r_i(\mathbf{z})$ represents the ability of feature i to predict the $\Pr(j|\mathbf{z})$s at $x_i = z_i$. The closer $\overline{\Pr}(j|x_i = z_i)$ is to $\Pr(j|\mathbf{z})$, the more information feature i carries for predicting the class posterior probabilities locally at $\mathbf{z}$. Thus, (4) can be used as a measure of feature relevance for $\mathbf{x}_0$. (4) measures how well the class posterior probabilities can be approximated along input feature i within a local neighborhood of $\mathbf{x}_0$. Small r_i implies that the class posterior probabilities will be well captured along dimension i in the vicinity of $\mathbf{x}_0$. Note that (4) is a function of both the test point $\mathbf{x}_0$ and the dimension i, thereby making $r_i(\mathbf{x}_0)$ a local relevance measure.

The relative relevance, as a weighting scheme, can then be given by

$$w_i(\mathbf{x_0}) = (\bar{r}_i(\mathbf{x_0}))^t / \sum_{l=1}^{q} (\bar{r}_l(\mathbf{x_0}))^t. \tag{5}$$

where

$$\bar{r}_i = \max_j \{r(j)\} - r(i). \tag{6}$$

Here $t = 1, 2$, giving rise to linear and quadratic weightings, respectively. In this paper we use the following exponential weighting scheme

$$w_i(\mathbf{x_0}) = \exp(c\bar{r}_i(\mathbf{x_0})) / \sum_{l=1}^{q} \exp(c\bar{r}_l(\mathbf{x_0})) \tag{7}$$

where c is a parameter that can be chosen to maximize (minimize) the influence of r_i on w_i. When $c = 0$ we have $w_i = 1/q$, thereby ignoring any difference between the r_i's. On the other hand, when c is large a change in r_i will be exponentially reflected in w_i. In this case, w_i is said to follow the Boltzmann distribution. Exponential weighting (7) has demonstrated superior performance over both linear and quadratic weightings (5) on image databases we have experimented with. This is largely due to its sensitivity to changes in feature relevance (4).

(7) can then be used as weights associated with features for weighted distance computation

$$D(\mathbf{x}, \mathbf{y}) = \sqrt{\sum_{i=1}^{q} w_i(x_i - y_i)^2}. \tag{8}$$

These weights enable the neighborhood to elongate less important feature dimensions, and, at the same time, to constrict the most influential ones.

A justification for (4) and, hence, (5), may go as follows. Suppose that the value of $r_i(\mathbf{z})$ is small, which implies a large weight along dimension i. Consequently, the neighborhood gets shrinked along that direction. This, in turn, penalizes points along dimension i that are moving away from z_i. Now, $r_i(\mathbf{z})$ can be small only if the subspace spanned by the other input dimensions at $x_i = z_i$ likely contains samples similar to $\mathbf{z}$ in terms of the class conditional probabilities. Then, a large weight assigned to dimension i based on (7) says that moving away from the subspace, hence from the data similar to $\mathbf{z}$, is not a good thing to do. Similarly, a large value of $r_i(\mathbf{z})$, hence a small weight, indicates that in the vicinity of z_i along dimension i one is unlikely to find samples similar to $\mathbf{z}$. This corresponds to an elongation of the neighborhood along dimension i. Therefore, in this situation in order to better predict the query, one must look farther away from z_i.

4   Estimation

Since both $\Pr(j|\mathbf{z})$ and $\overline{\Pr}(j|x_i = z_i)$ in (4) are unknown, we must estimate them using retrievals with relevance feedback: $\{\mathbf{x}_n, y_n\}_{n=1}^{N}$. Here $y_n \in \{1, \cdots, J\}$. The quantity $\Pr(j|\mathbf{z})$ is estimated by considering a neighborhood $N_1(\mathbf{z})$ centered at $\mathbf{z}$:

$$\hat{\Pr}(j|\mathbf{z}) = \frac{\sum_{n=1}^{N} 1(\mathbf{x}_n \in N_1(\mathbf{z}))1(y_n = j)}{\sum_{n=1}^{N} 1(\mathbf{x}_n \in N_1(\mathbf{z}))}, \tag{9}$$

where $1(\cdot)$ is an indicator function such that it returns 1 when its argument is true, and 0 otherwise.

To compute $\overline{\Pr}(j|x_i = z) = E[\Pr(j|\mathbf{x})|x_i = z]$, we introduce a dummy variable g_j such that

$$g_j|x = \begin{cases} 1 \text{ if } y = j \\ 0 \text{ otherwise} \end{cases}$$

where $j = 1, \cdots, J$. We then have $\Pr(j|\mathbf{x}) = E[g_j|\mathbf{x}]$, from which it is not hard to show that

$$\overline{\Pr}(j|x_i = z) = E[g_j|x_i = z].$$

However, since there may not be any data at $x_i = z$, the data from the neighborhood of z along dimension i are used to estimate $E[g_j|x_i = z]$. This is the strategy adopted in [3, 9]. In detail, by noticing

$$g_j = 1(y = j)$$

the estimate can be computed from

$$\hat{\overline{\Pr}}(j|x_i = z_i) = \frac{\sum_{\mathbf{x}_n \in N_2(\mathbf{z})} 1(|x_{ni} - z_i| \le \Delta_i)1(y_n = j)}{\sum_{\mathbf{x}_n \in N_2(\mathbf{z})} 1(|x_{ni} - z_i| \le \Delta_i)}, \tag{10}$$

where $N_2(\mathbf{z})$ is a neighborhood centered at $\mathbf{z}$, and the value of Δ_i is chosen so that the interval contains a fixed number L of points:

$$\sum_{n=1}^{N} 1(|x_{ni} - z_i| \le \Delta_i)1(\mathbf{x}_n \in N_2(\mathbf{z})) = L. \tag{11}$$

Using the estimates in (9) and in (10), we obtain an empirical measure of the relevance (4) for each input variable i.

5   Empirical Evaluation

In the following we compare the probabilistic feature relevance learning (PFRL) method [9] and the adaptive multi-class metric (AMM) technique described above using a number of real data sets. In all the experiments, features are normalized to lie between 0 and 1. Also, 20 nearest retrievals at each iteration are used to provide relevance feedback. Procedural parameters for each method were determined empirically that achieved the best retrieval performance.

The first experiment involves Letter Image Recognition Data (LIRD) taken from [7]. It consists of a large number of black-and-white rectangular pixel arrays as one of the 26 upper-case letters in the English alphabet. Sample images are

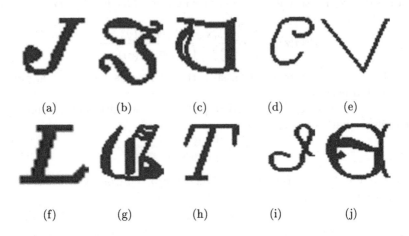

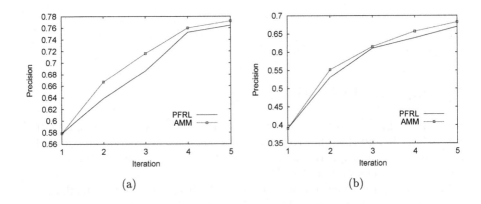

Fig. 1. Sample letter images.

shown in Figure 1. The characters are based on 20 Roman alphabet fonts. They represent five different stroke styles and six different letter styles. Each letter is randomly distorted through a quadratic transformation to produce a set of 20,000 unique letter images that are then converted into 16 primitive numerical features. Basically, these numerical features are statistical moments and edge counts. For this experiment we randomly select 100 letter images from each class. Thus, the data set consists of 2600 letter images. Each letter image is used as a query.

Fig. 2. Average retrieval precision as a function of iteration achieved by PFRL and AMM. Image class F; somewhat relevant class S. (b): Image class H; somewhat relevant class R.

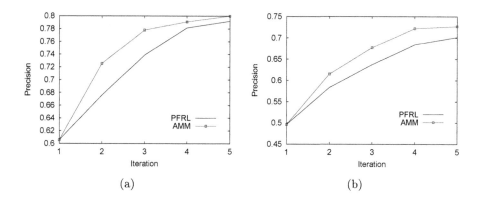

Fig. 3. Average retrieval precision as a function of iteration achieved by PFRL and AMM. (a): Image class J; somewhat relevant class K. (b): Image class Q; somewhat relevant class U.

For PFRL, retrieved images are grouped into relevant and irrelevant classes. For AMM, however, three class relevance feedback is provided. That is, retrieved images are grouped into three classes: relevant, somewhat relevant and irrelevant. Our goal here is to examine if more refined class information can help speed up performance improvement. Figures 2, 3 and 4 show the average retrieval precision as a function of iteration achieved by both PFRL and AMM on F, H, J, Q, W and Z letter classes, where S, R, K, U, O and I letter classes were marked as the somewhat relevant class, respectively. The results show that multi-class relevance feedback can indeed help achieve better retrieval performance. We obtained similar results on the rest of letter image classes.

Note that we use the letter image data to evaluate the performance of our multi-class relevance feedback technique because the precise nature of the problem our algorithm is facing is known. That is, we know precisely relevant, somewhat relevant and irrelevant retrievals for any given query. Thus, it allows us to reliably predict the strengths and limitations of the algorithm. Furthermore, numerical features representing letter images are similar, to a large extent, to features extracted from images to represent their content. Therefore, these data serve our goals nicely here.

The second experiment involves three data sets and is designed to test how AMM will behave when presented with simple, two class relevance feedback. The four data sets are: 1. Segmentation Data, taken from the UCI repository [7], consists of images that were drawn randomly from a database of 7 outdoor images. There are 7 classes, each of which has 330 instances. Thus, there are total 2310 images in the database. These images are represented by 19 real valued attributes; 2. Vowel Data, again taken from [7], has 10 input features and 11 classes. There is a total of 528 samples in this data set; 3. Image Data,

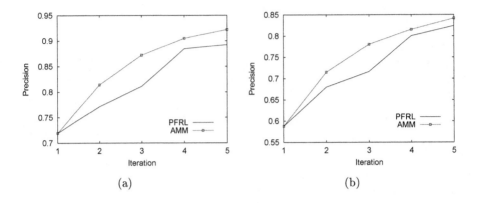

Fig. 4. Average retrieval precision as a function of iteration achieved by PFRL and AMM. (a): Image class W; somewhat relevant class O. (b): Image class Z; somewhat relevant class I.

taken from ftp://whitechapel.media.mit.edu/pub/VisTex, consists of 40 texture images that are manually classified into 15 classes. Each of these images is then cut into 16 non-overlapping images of 128×128, giving rise to a total of 640 images in the database. The number of images in each class varies from 16 to 80. The images in this database are represented by $q = 16$ dimensional feature vectors (8 Gabor filters: 2 scales and 4 orientations). The mean and the standard deviation of the magnitude of the transform coefficients are used as feature components, after being normalized by the standard deviations of the respective features, over the entire set of images in the database. Sample images are shown in Figure 5; and 4. LIRD data, similar to the one used in the first experiment, except that there are 400 letter images randomly taken from each class. Thus, this data set contains a total of 10400 letter images.

Figure 6 shows the average retrieval precision as a function of iteration achieved by PFRL and AMM on the four data sets. Again each image in the data sets was used as a query. Note that in this experiment both methods used two (relevant and irrelevant) class relevance feedback. The results show clearly that AMM can still achieve better retrieval performance using simple relevance feedback, although the improvement is not as pronounced as in the multi-class relevance feedback case. The improvement is particularly evident at earlier iterations, which can be considered highly desirable because acceptable results can be achieved with the minimum number of feedback cycles.

6   Summary

This paper presents a locally adaptive method for effective content-based image retrieval. This method estimates a flexible multi-class metric for producing

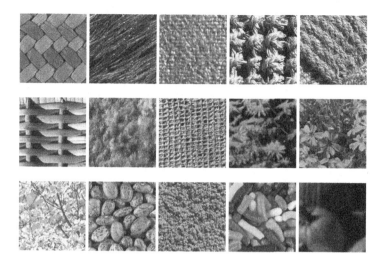

Fig. 5. Sample images from the Image database.

neighborhoods that are elongated along less relevant feature dimensions and constricted along most influential ones. Moreover, it is able to take advantage of multi-class relevance feedback, thereby sufficiently exploiting local data densities. The experimental results using real data show that the AMM algorithm can potentially improve the performance of PFRL and other two-class relevance feedback methods in many content-based image retrieval problems.

We have used three class relevance feedback to evaluate the performance of our adaptive multi-class metric retrieval technique. However, the technique is clearly applicable to image retrieval in more general settings, where relevance feedback is unrestricted. Here we have an apparent paradox. On the one hand, an image retrieval system that results from having multi-class relevance feedback can better exploit local data densities. On the other hand, insufficient data may impede the accurate estimates of class (conditional) probabilities (4), thereby making performance worse. We plan to examine this issue in our future research.

A potential extension to the technique described in this paper is to consider additional derived variables (features) for local relevance estimate, thereby contributing to the distance calculation. When the derived features are more informative, huge gains may be expected. On the other hand, if they are not informative enough, they may cause retrieval performance to degrade since they add to the dimensionality count. The challenge is to be able to have a mechanism that computes such informative derived features efficiently.

Acknowledgments

The author would like to thank Carlotta Demoniconi for helpful discussions. The author would also like to thank anonymous reviewers for constructive comments.

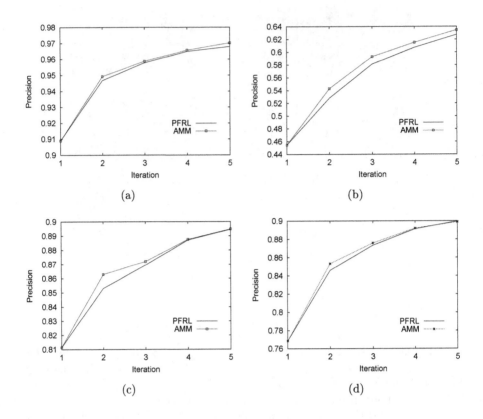

Fig. 6. Average retrieval precision achieved by PFRL and AMM. (a) Segmentation data set; (b) Vowel data set; (c) Image data set; (d) LIRD data set.

References

1. R.H. Creecy, B.M. Masand, S.J. Smith, and D.L. Waltz, "Trading Mips and Memory for Knowledge Engineering," *CACM*, 35:48-64, 1992.
2. R.O. Duda and P.E. Hart, *Pattern Classification and Scene Analysis*. John Wiley & Sons, Inc., 1973.
3. J.H. Friedman "Flexible Metric Nearest Neighbor Classification," Tech. Report, Dept. of Statistics, Stanford University, 1994.
4. T. Hastie and R. Tibshirani, "Discriminant Adaptive Nearest Neighbor Classification," *IEEE Trans. on Pattern Analysis and Machine Intelligence*, Vol. 18, No. 6, pp. 607-615, 1996.
5. Y. Ishikawa, R. Subramanya, and C. Faloutsos, "MindReader: Query databases through multiple examples," Proceedings of the 24th VLDB Conference, New York, 1998.
6. T. Mitchell, *Machine Learning*. McGraw-Hill, New York, 1997.
7. P.M. Murphy and D.W. Aha, UCI repository of machine learning databases.

http://www.cs.uci.edu/~mlearn/MLRepository.html, 1995.

8. J.P. Myles and D.J. Hand, "The Multi-Class Metric Problem in Nearest Neighbor Discrimination Rules," *Pattern Recognition*, Vol. 23, pp. 1291-1297, 1990.

9. J. Peng, B. Bhanu and S. Qing, "Probabilistic Feature Relevance Learning for Content-Based Image Retrieval", *Computer Vision and Image Understanding*, Vol. 75, No 1/2, pp. 150-164, 1999.

10. J. Peng and B. Bhanu, "Feature Relevance Estimation for Image Databases," Proc. of the 5th Int. Workshop on Multimedia Information Systems, pp. 12-19, 1999.

11. Y. Rui, T.S. Huang and S. Mehrotra, "Content-based image retrieval with relevance feedback in MARS", Proceedings of IEEE International Conference on Image Processing, pp. 815-818, Santa Barbara, California, October, 1997.

12. N. Vasconcelos and A. Lippman, "A Probabilistic Architecture for Content-Based Image Retrieval", Proceedings of IEEE Computer Society Conference on Computer Vision and Pattern Recognition," pp. 216-221, Hilton Head Island, South Carolina, 2000.

Integrating Visual and Textual Cues for Image Classification

Theo Gevers, Frank Aldershoff, Jan-Mark Geusebroek

ISIS, University of Amsterdam, Kruislaan 403
1098 SJ Amsterdam, The Netherlands
{gevers, mark}@wins.uva.nl

Abstract

In this paper, we study computational models and techniques to merge textual and image features to classify images on the World Wide Web (WWW). A vector-based framework is used to index images on the basis of textual, pictorial and composite (textual-pictorial) information. The scheme makes use of weighted document terms and color invariant image features to obtain a high-dimensional image descriptor in vector form to be used as an index. Experiments are conducted on a representative set of more than 100.000 images down loaded from the WWW together with their associated text. Performance evaluations are reported on the accuracy of merging textual and pictorial information for image classification.

1 Introduction

Today, a number of systems are available for retrieving images from the World Wide Web on the basis of textual or pictorial information [3], [4], for example. New research is directed towards unifying both textual and pictorial information to retrieve images from the World Wide Web [1], [3]. Most of these content-based search systems are based on the so-called query by example paradigm, and significant results have been achieved. A drawback, however, is that the low-level image features used for image retrieval often too restricted to describe images on a conceptual or semantic level. This semantic gap is a well-known problem in content-based image retrieval by query by example. To this end, to enhance the performance of content-based retrieval systems (e.g. by pruning the number of candidate images), image classification has been proposed to group images into semantically meaningful classes [5], [6], [7]. The advantage of these classification schemes is that simple, low-level image features can be used to express semantically meaningful classes. Image classification is based on unsupervised learning techniques such as clustering, Self-Organization Maps (SOM) [7] and Markov models [6]. Further, supervised grouping can be applied. For example, vacation images have been classified based on a Bayesian framework into city vs. landscape by supervised learning techniques [5]. However, these classification schemes are entirely based on pictorial information. Aside from image

R. Laurini (Ed.): VISUAL 2000, LNCS 1929, pp. 419–429, 2000.
 Springer-Verlag Berlin Heidelberg 2000

retrieval ([1], [3]), very little attention has been paid on using both textual and pictorial information for classifying images on the Web. This is even more surprisingly if one realizes that images on Web pages are usually surrounded by text and discriminatory HTML tags such as IMG, and the HTML fields SRC and ALT. Hence, WWW images have intrinsic annotation information induced by the HTML structure. Consequently, the set of images on the Web can be seen as an annotated image set. The challenge is now to get to a framework allowing to classify images on the Web by means of composite pictorial and textual (annotated) information into semantically meaningful groups, and to evaluate its expected added value, i.e. whether the use of composite information will increase the classification rate as opposed to the classification based only on visual or pictorial information.

Therefore, in this paper, we study computational models and techniques to combine textual and image features to classify images on the Web. The goal it to get to the classification of WWW images into photographical (e.g. real world pictures) and synthetical images (e.g. icons, buttons and banners). Classifying images into photo-artwork is a realistic application scenario as 80 % of the images on Internet are synthetic images and 20 % are photo's providing a significant image class division. Then, we aim at classifying photographical images into portraits-nonportrait (i.e. the image contains a substantial face or not at all). Portraits are one of the most favorite search scenario's among people. To achieve classification, a vector-based framework is presented to index images on textual, pictorial and composite (textual-pictorial) information. The scheme makes use of weighted document terms and color invariant image features to obtain a high-dimensional descriptor in vector form to be used as an index.

2   Approach

The Web-crawler down loaded over 100.000 images from the World Wide Web together with their associated textual descriptions appearing near the images in the HTML documents such as HTML-tags (IMG), and various fields (SRC and ALT). After parsing the text associated with an image, significant keywords are identified and captured in vector form. Then, salient image features (e.g. color and texture) are computed from the images in vector form. Then, the textual and visual vectors are combined into a unified multidimensional vector descriptor to be used as an index. The classification of an image is computed by comparing its composite feature vector to the feature vectors of a set of already classified images.

To be precise, let an image I be represented by its feature vectors of the form $I = (f_0, w_{I0}; f_1, w_{I1}; ...,; f_t, w_{It})$ and a typical query Q by $Q = (f_0, w_{Q0}; f_1, w_{Q1}; ...,; f_t, w_{Qt})$, where w_{Ik} (or w_{Qk}) represent the weight of feature f_k in image I (or query Q), and t image/text features are used for classification. The weights are assumed to be between 0 and 1. A feature can be seen as an image characteristic or a HTML keyword. Then, a weighting scheme is used to emphasize features having high feature frequencies but low overall collection frequencies. In this way, image features and key-words are transformed into numbers denoting the feature frequency (ff) times the inverse document frequency:

$$w_i = \text{ff}_i \log(\frac{N}{n}) \tag{1}$$

where n is the number of documents/images containing the feature on a total of N documents/images.

Depending on the content of the vectors, we will use different distance functions (e.g. histogram intersection for visual information and cosine distance for composite information). For general classification, the Minkowski distance is taken. To make the Minkowski distances comparable, normalization is obtained by dividing vectors by their standard deviation:

$$D_M(\boldsymbol{x}, \boldsymbol{y}) = \sqrt{\sum_{i=1}^{n} \frac{|\boldsymbol{x}_i - \boldsymbol{y}_i|^p}{\sigma_i}} \tag{2}$$

equalizing the length of the image vectors, where $\sigma_i^2 = \text{Var}[\boldsymbol{x}_i]$ i.e. is the standard deviation of the corresponding vector.

The classification scheme, used in this paper, is based on the Nearest Neighbor Classifier. In this scheme, the classification of an unknown image is computed by comparing its feature vector to the feature vectors of a set of already classified images. This is done by finding the nearest neighbors of the unknown image in the feature vector space. The class of the unknown image is then derived from the classes of its nearest neighbors.

3   Textual Information

HTML structure facilitates the extraction of information associated with an image. Firstly, an image is included on a Web page by its IMG-tag. This IMG tag contains the name of the file of the image to be displayed. In addition, the IMG tag contains fields such as SRC and ALT. Consequently, by using this tag and its fields, it is possible to identify textual information associated with an image. Note that text, appearing before and after a particular image, is not excerpted. From an informal survey of Web pages we came to the observation that, in general, these text blocks contain a large variety of words not very specific to the images nearby. A more elaborated survey on valuable HTML-tags can be found in [3]. In order to yield a robust, consistent and non-redundant set of discriminative words, HTML documents are parsed for each class during the training stage as follows:

- Class labeling: The class of WWW images is given manually such as photo, art, or portrait.
- Text parsing: Text fragments appearing in the IMG-tag and the SRC and ALT fields are excerpt.

- Eliminating redundant words: A stop list is used to eliminate redundant words. For example, to discriminate photographical and synthetical images, words such as image and gif, which appear in equal number in both classes, are eliminated.
- Stemming: Suffix removal methods are applied on the remaining words to reduce each word to its stem form.
- Stem merging: Multiple occurrences of a stem form are merged into a single text term.
- Word reduction: Words with too low frequency are eliminated.

In this way, a highly representative set of key-words are computed for each class during the supervised training stage. Then, weights are given to the key-words and represented in multidimensional vector space as discussed in Section 2.

4 Pictorial Information

In this section, visual cues are proposed to allow the classification of images into the following groups: photographical/synthetical images in Section 4.1, and portraits/non-portraits images in Section 4.2.

4.1 Photographic vs. Art

Classification of WWW images into photographic and synthetic (artwork) images has been addressed before by [2], for example. To capture the differences between the two groups, various human observers were asked to visually inspect and classify images into photo's and artwork. The following observations were made. Because artwork is manually created, it tends to have a limited number of colors. In contrast, photographs usually contain many different shades of colors. Further, artwork is usually designed to convey information such as buttons. Hence, the limited amount of colors in artwork are often very bright to attract the attention of the user. In contrast, photographs contain mostly dull colors. Further, edges in photographs are usually soft and subtle due to natural light variations and shading. In artwork, edges are usually very abrupt and artificial.

Based on the above mentioned observations, the following image features have been selected to distinguish photographic images from artwork:

Color variation: The number of distinct hue values in an image relative to the total number of hues. Hue values are computed by converting the RGB-image into HSI color space from which H is extracted. Synthetic images tend to have fewer distinct hue colors then photographs.

Color saturation: The accumulation of the saturation of colors in an image relative to the total number of pixels. S from the HSI-model is used to express saturation. Colors in synthetic images are likely to be more saturated.

Color transition strength: The pronouncement of hue edges in an image. Color transition strength is computed by applying the Canny edge detector on the H color component. Synthetic images tend to have more abrupt color transitions than photograph images.

To express these observation in a more mathematical way, we need to be precise on the definitions of intensity I, RGB, normalized color rgb, saturation S, and hue H. Let R, G and B, obtained by a color camera, represent the 3-D sensor space:

$$C = \int_\lambda p(\lambda) f_C(\lambda) d\lambda \qquad (3)$$

for $C \in (R, G, B)$, where $p(\lambda)$ is the radiance spectrum and $f_C(\lambda)$ are the three color filter transmission functions.

To represent the RGB-sensor space, a cube can be defined on the R, G, and B axes. White is produced when all three primary colors are at M, where M is the maximum light intensity, say $M = 255$. The main diagonal-axis connecting the black and white corners defines the intensity:

$$I(R, G, B) = R + G + B \qquad (4)$$

All points in a plane perpendicular to the grey axis of the color cube have the same intensity. The plane through the color cube at points $R = G = B = M$ is one such plane. This plane cuts out an equilateral triangle which is the standard rgb chromaticity triangle:

$$r(R, G, B) = \frac{R}{R + G + B} \qquad (5)$$

$$g(R, G, B) = \frac{G}{R + G + B} \qquad (6)$$

$$b(R, G, B) = \frac{B}{R + G + B} \qquad (7)$$

The transformation from RGB used here to describe the color impression hue H is given by:

$$H(R, G, B) = \arctan\left(\frac{\sqrt{3}(G - B)}{(R - G) + (R - B)}\right) \qquad (8)$$

and saturation S measuring the relative white content of a color as having a particular hue by:

$$S(R, G, B) = 1 - \frac{\min(R, G, B)}{R + G + B} \qquad (9)$$

In this way, all color features can be calculated from the original R, G, B values corresponding to the red, green, and blue images provided by the color camera.

Color Variation The number of distinct hue values in an image relative to the total number of hues. Synthetic images tend to have fewer distinct hue colors then photographs.

More precisely, a hue histogram $\mathcal{H}_H(i)$ is constructed by counting the number of times a hue value $H(R_x, G_x, B_x)$ is present in an image I:

$$\mathcal{H}_H(i) = \frac{\eta(H(R_{\boldsymbol{x}}, G_{\boldsymbol{x}}, B_{\boldsymbol{x}}) = i)}{N} \text{ for } \forall \boldsymbol{x} \in I \tag{10}$$

where η indicates the number of times $H(R_{\boldsymbol{x}}, G_{\boldsymbol{x}}, B_{\boldsymbol{x}})$, defined by eq. (8), equals the value of index (i). N is the total number of image locations.

Then the relative number of distinct hue values in an image is given by:

$$f_1 = \frac{1}{B}\eta(\mathcal{H}_H(i) > t_H) \tag{11}$$

where B is the total number of bins and t_H is a threshold based on the noise level in the hue image to suppress marginally visible hue regions.

Color Saturation The accumulation of the saturation of colors in an image relative to the maximum saturation. Colors in synthetic images are likely to be more saturated.

Let histogram $\mathcal{H}_S(i)$ be constructed by counting the number of times a saturation value $S(R_{\boldsymbol{x}}, G_{\boldsymbol{x}}, B_{\boldsymbol{x}})$ is present in an image I:

$$\mathcal{H}_S(i) = \frac{\eta(S(R_{\boldsymbol{x}}, G_{\boldsymbol{x}}, B_{\boldsymbol{x}}) = i)}{N} \text{ for } \forall \boldsymbol{x} \in I \tag{12}$$

where η indicates the number of times $S(R_{\boldsymbol{x}}, G_{\boldsymbol{x}}, B_{\boldsymbol{x}})$, defined by eq. (9), equals the value of index (i).

Then the relative accumulation of the saturation of colors in an image is given by:

$$f_2 = \frac{\sum_{i=1}^{B} i \, \mathcal{H}_S(i)}{B} \tag{13}$$

where B is the total number of bins.

Color Transition Strength The pronouncement of hue edges in an image. Color transition strength is computed by applying the edge detector on the H color component. Synthetic images tend to have more abrupt color transitions than photographs.

Due to the circular nature of hue, the standard difference operator is not suited for computing the difference between hue values. The difference between two hue values h_1 and h_2, ranging from $[0, 2\pi)$, is defined as follows:

$$d(h_1, h_2) = |h_1 - h_2| \bmod \pi \tag{14}$$

yielding a difference $d(h_1, h_2) \in [0, \pi]$ between h_1 and h_2.

To find hue edges in images we use an edge detector of the Sobel type where the component of the positive gradient vector in the x-direction is defined as follows:

$$H_x(\boldsymbol{x}) = \frac{1}{4}(d(H(x-1, y-1), H(x+1, y-1)) +$$

$$2d(H(x-1,y), H(x+1,y)) + d(H(x-1,y+1), H(x+1,y+1))) \tag{15}$$

And in the y-direction as:

$$H_y(\boldsymbol{x}) = \frac{1}{4}(d(H(x-1,y-1), H(x+1,y-1))+$$

$$2d(H(x,y-1), H(x,y+1)) + d(H(x-1,y+1), H(x+1,y+1))) \tag{16}$$

The gradient magnitude is represented by:

$$||\nabla H(\boldsymbol{x})|| = \sqrt{H_x^2(\boldsymbol{x}) + H_y^2(\boldsymbol{x})} \tag{17}$$

After computing the gradient magnitude, non-maximum suppression is applied to $||\nabla H(x,y)||$ to obtain local maxima in the gradient values:

$$\mathcal{M}(\boldsymbol{x}) = \begin{cases} ||\nabla H(\boldsymbol{x})||, \ \text{if} \ (||\nabla H(\boldsymbol{x})|| > t_\sigma) \ \text{is a local} \\ \text{maximum} \\ \\ 0, \ \text{otherwise} \end{cases} \tag{18}$$

where t_σ is a threshold based on the noise level in the hue image to suppress marginally visible edges.

Then the pronouncement of hue edges in an image is given by:

$$f_3 = \frac{1}{M} \sum_{i=1}^{M} \mathcal{M}(\boldsymbol{x_i}) \tag{19}$$

where M is the number of local hue edge maxima.

4.2   Portrait vs. Non-portrait

In the previous section, images are classified into photo/artwork. In this section, photo's are further classified into portrait-nonportrait type. We use the observation that portrait images are substantially occupied by skin-colors (color constraints) from faces (shape constraints). To that end, a two-step filter is used to detect portraits. Firstly, all pixels within the skin-tone color are determined resulting in blobs. Then, these blobs will be tested with respect to shape and size requirements.

It is known that when a face is folded (i.e. varying surface orientation) a broad variance of RGB values will be generated due to shading. In contrast, normalized color space rgb and $c_1c_2c_3$ are insensitive to face folding and a change in surface orientation, illumination direction and illumination intensity [2]. To further reduce the illumination effects, color ratio's have been taken based on the observation that a change in illumination color will affect c_1, c_2 and c_2, c_3 proportionally. Hence, by computing the color ratio's c_2/c_1 and c_3/c_2, and r/g and g/b, the disturbing influences of a change in illumination color is suppressed to a large degree. A drawback is that $c_1c_2c_3$ and rgb become unstable when intensity is very low near 5% of the total intensity range [2]. Therefore pixels with low intensity have been removed from the skin-tone pixels.

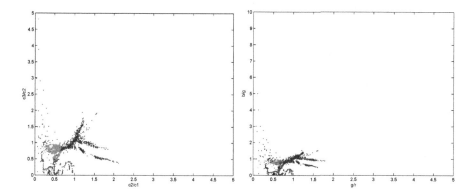

Fig. 1. *a. Skin (bright) and non-skin (dark) pixels plotted in the color ratio color space: c_2/c_1 and c_3/c_2. b. Skin (bright) and non-skin (dark) pixels plotted in the color ratio color space: r/g and g/b. The color ratio's achieve robust isolation of the skin-tone pixels.*

To illustrate the imaging effects on color ratio's, in Figure 1, pixels are plotted based on rgb and $c_1c_2c_3$ ratio's. As can be seen in Figure 1.a, the color ratio's achieve robust isolation of the skin-tone pixels. In fact, it allows us to specify a rectangular envelop containing most of the skin pixels. This rectangular envelop defines the limits of the c_2/c_1 and c_3/c_2 values of pixels taken from regions within the skin-tone. These limits have been set as follows: $c_2/c_1 = [0.35...0.80]$ and $c_3/c_2 = [0.40...0.98]$. These values have been determined empirically by visual inspection on a large set of test images. It has proved to be effective in our application.

The second step is to impose shape restrictions on these blobs to actually identify portraits. The reason is that still problems may occur when dealing with images taken under a wide variety of imaging circumstances. To this end, small blobs are removed by applying morphological operations. After removing small blobs, the remaining blobs are tested with respect to two criteria. First, blobs are required to occupy at least 5% of the total image. Further, at least 20% of the blob should occupy the image. This ensures that only fairly large blobs will remain.

5   Experiments

In this section, we assess the accuracy of the image classification method along the following criteria. In the experiments, we use two different sets of images. The first dataset consists of images taken from the Corel © Stock Photo Libraries. The second dataset is composed of the 100.000 images downloaded from the Web.

5.1   Photographical vs. synthetical

Test Set I:
The first dataset was composed of 100 images per class resulting in a total of 200 images. Hence the training set for each class is 100 images. The test set (query set) consisted of 50 images for each class.
Classification based on Image Features: Based on edge strength and saturation, defined in Section 4.1, the 8-nearest neighbor classifier with weighted histogram intersection distance provided a classification success of 90% (i.e. 90% were correctly classified) for photographical images and 85% for synthetical images. From the results it is concluded that automated type classification based on low-level image features provides satisfactory distinction between photo and artwork.

Test Set II:
The second dataset consists of a total of 1432 images composed of 1157 synthetic images and 275 photographical images. Hence, 81% are artwork and 19% photo's were provided yielding a good representative ratio of WWW images.
Classification based on Image Features: Images are classified on the basis of color variation, color saturation, and color edge strength. The 8-nearest neighbor classifier with weighted histogram intersection distance provided a classification success of 74% for photographical images and 87% for synthetical images.
Classification based on Composite Information: Images are classified on the basis of composite information. Therefore, the same image features are used: color variation, color saturation and color edge strength. Further, the annotations of the images have been processed on the basis of the HTML parsing method given in Section 3. Typical high frequency words derived from photo's were: photo -in different languages such as bilder (German) and foto (Dutch)-, picture and people. Typical high frequency words derived from artwork were: icon, logo, graphics, button, home, banner, and menu. Based on image features and keywords, the 8-nearest neighbor classifier with weighted cosine distance provided a classification success of 89% (i.e. 89% were correctly classified) for photographical images and 96% for synthetical images. From these results it is concluded that classification accuracy based on both text and pictorial information is very high and that it outperforms the classification rate based only on pictorial information.

5.2   Portraits vs. Non-portraits

Test Set I:
To classify images into portrait-nonportrait images, a dataset is used consisting of 110 images containing a portrait and an arbitrary set of 100 images resulting in a total of 210 images. The test set consisted of 32 queries.
Portraits vs. Non-portraits based on Image Features: Based on the skin detector, the 8- nearest neighbor classifier provided a classification success of 81% for images containing portraits.

Test Set II:
The second dataset is composed of a 64 images of which 26 were portraits and

32 non-portraits (arbitrary photo's).

Portraits vs. Non-portraits based on Image Features: Images have been represented by the skin feature in addition to 3 eigenvectors expressing color in the $c_1c_2c_3$ color space. As a consequence, the skin feature is used together with a global color invariant features for classification. Based on a 4-nearest neighbor a classification success of 72% for portrait images has been obtained and 92% for non-portrait images.

Portraits vs. Non-portraits based on Composite Information: HTML pages were parsed and relevant words were derived. Typical high frequency words derived for portraits were: usr, credits, team and many different names such as laura, kellerp, eckert, arnold, and schreiber. High frequency words derived for non-portraits were (see above): photo -in different languages such as bilder (German) and foto (Dutch)-, picture and tour. Based on image features and keywords, the 8-nearest neighbor classifier with weighted cosine distance provided a classification success of 72% (i.e. 72% were correctly classified) for portrait images and 92% for non-portrait images. From these results it is concluded that classification accuracy based on both textual and pictorial information is fairly the same with respect to the classification rate based entirely on pictorial information. This is due to the inconsistent textual image descriptions assigned to portrait images which we found on the Web. For example, different nicknames, surnames and family names were associated with portraits. The use of a list of names in the training set improved the classification rate of 87% for portrait images and 94% for non-portrait images. In the future, we research on other HTML-tags and word lists to improve portrait classification performance.

6   Conclusion

From the theoretical and experimental results it is concluded that for classifying images into photographic/synthetic, the contribution of image and text features is equally important. Consequently, high discriminative classification power is obtained based on composite information. Classifying images into portraits/non-portraits shows that pictorial information is more important then textual information. This is due to the inconsistent textual image descriptions for portrait images found on the Web. Hence only marginal improvement in performance is achieved by using composite information for classification. Extensions have been made by adding a list of surnames in the training set enhancing the classification rate.

References

1. Favella, J. and Meza,. V., "Image-retrieval Agent: Integrating Image Content and Text", *IEEE Int. Sys.*, 1999.
2. T. Gevers and Arnold W.M. Smeulders, "PicToSeek: Combining Color and Shape Invariant Features for Image Retrieval", *IEEE Trans. on Image Processing*, 9(1), pp. 102-120, 2000.

3. S. Sclaroff, M. La Cascia, S. Sethi, L.Taycher, "Unifying Textual and Visual Cues for Content-based Image Retrieval on the World Wide Web," *CVIU*, 75(1/2), 1999.

4. J.R. Smith and S.-F. Chang, "VisualSEEK: A Fully Automated Content-based Image Query System," *ACM Multimedia*, 1996.

5. A. Vailaya, M. Figueiredo, A. Jain, H. Zhang, "Content-based Hierarchical Classification of Vacation Images," *IEEE ICMCS*, June 7-11 1999, 1999.

6. H. -H. Yu and W. Wolf, "Scene Classification Methods for Image and Video Databases", *Proc. SPIE on DISAS*, 1995.

7. D. Zhong, H. j. Zhang, S. -F. Chang, "Clustering Methods for Video Browsing and Annotation", *Proc. SPIE on SRIVD*, 1995.

Evaluating the Performance of Content-Based Image Retrieval Systems

Markus Koskela, Jorma Laaksonen, Sami Laakso, and Erkki Oja

Laboratory of Computer and Information Science,
Helsinki University of Technology,
P.O.BOX 5400, Fin-02015 HUT, Finland
{markus.koskela,jorma.laaksonen,sami.laakso,erkki.oja}@hut.fi

Abstract. Content-based image retrieval (CBIR) is a new but in recent years widely-adopted method for finding images from vast and unannotated image databases. CBIR is a technique for querying images on the basis of automatically-derived features such as color, texture, and shape directly from the visual content of images. For the development of effective image retrieval applications, one of the most urgent issues is to have widely-accepted performance assessment methods for different features and approaches. In this paper, we present methods for evaluating the retrieval performance of different features and existing CBIR systems. In addition, we present a set of retrieval performance experiments carried out with an experimental image retrieval system and a large database of images from a widely-available commercial image collection.

1 Introduction

The recent development of computing hardware has resulted in a rapid increase of visual information such as databases of images. To successfully utilize this increasing amount of data, we need effective ways to process it. Content-based image retrieval (CBIR) utilizes the visual content of images directly in the process of retrieving relevant images from a database. The task of developing effective products based on CBIR has, however, proven to be extremely difficult. Due to the limitations of computer vision, the current CBIR systems have to rely only on low-level features extracted from the images. Therefore, images are typically described by rather simple features characterizing the color content, different textures, and primitive shapes detected in them.

Unfortunately, quantitative measures for the retrieval performance of an image retrieval system, or any single feature used in the process, are problematic due to the subjectivity of human perception. As each user of a retrieval system has individual expectations, there does not exist a definite right answer to an image query. Also, there exist no widely accepted performance assessment methods. As a result, objective and quantitative comparisons between different algorithms or image retrieval systems based on different approaches are difficult to perform. The discriminating powers of features also vary with different types of images. Therefore, we need to use a comprehensive set of diverse images to evaluate the

R. Laurini (Ed.): VISUAL 2000, LNCS 1929, pp. 430–441, 2000.
Springer-Verlag Berlin Heidelberg 2000

performance of different features and the systems employing them. Due to the lack of standard methods in this application area, the Moving Picture Experts Group (MPEG) has also started to work on a content representation standard for multimedia information search, filtering, management and processing called MPEG-7 or formally "Multimedia Content Description Interface" [9], expected to be completed in 2001.

2   Methods for Evaluating Retrieval Performance

The standard evaluation methods in information retrieval are precision and recall, which have been used also in evaluating different CBIR approaches. Although being objective measures of retrieval effectiveness, they suffer from certain shortcomings when used to evaluate image retrieval applications. CBIR applications are generally based on ranked lists of retrieved images. Therefore, precision and recall are usually calculated using a prespecified cutoff number M. Unfortunately, these measures are very sensitive to the choice of M. The simple adaptation of these methods also neglects the provided rank information [5].

The need for applicable evaluation criteria still persists. Reliable evaluation methods for performance would enable us to rate and rank different approaches and methods, and to find the best ones for a given task. For this purpose, a number of measures for evaluating image retrieval performance are presented in this section. First, a method for assessing the ability of various visual features to reveal image similarity is discussed. Second, a method for evaluating performance of whole retrieval systems is described.

Consider a database $\mathcal{D}$ containing a total of N images. First, we gather subsets of images which can be regarded as portraying a selected topic from the database. Such a set of images is called an image class $\mathcal{C}$. Image classes can include, for example images of aircraft, buildings, nature, human faces, etc. The process of gathering these classes is naturally arbitrary, as there are no distinct and objective boundaries between different image classes. If the images in the database already have reliable textual information about the contents of the images, it can be used directly; otherwise, manual classification is needed.

Now we have a database $\mathcal{D}$ containing a total of N images, and a class $\mathcal{C} \subset \mathcal{D}$ with N_C relevant images. The *a priori* probability ρ_C of the class $\mathcal{C}$ is

$$\rho_C = \frac{N_C}{N} .$$ (1)

An ideal performance measure should be independent of the *a priori* probability and the type of images in the image class.

2.1   Observed Probability

Let the images of $\mathcal{D}$ be ordered so that each has a unique index. For each image $I \in \mathcal{C}$ with a feature vector $\mathbf{f}^I$, we calculate the Euclidean distance $d_{L_2}(I, J)$ of $\mathbf{f}^I$ and the feature vectors $\mathbf{f}^J$ of the other images $J \in \mathcal{D} \setminus \{I\}$ in the database.

Then, we sort the images based on their ascending distance from the image I and store the indices of the images in a $(N-1)$-sized vector $\mathbf{g}^I$. We now have a vector $\mathbf{g}^I$ for each $I \in \mathcal{C}$ containing a sorted permutation of the images in $\mathcal{D} \setminus \{I\}$ based on their increasing Euclidean distance to I. By g_i^I, we denote the ith component of $\mathbf{g}^I$.

Next, for all images $I \in \mathcal{C}$, we define a vector $\mathbf{h}^I$ as follows

$$\forall i \in \{0, \ldots, N-2\} : \quad h_i^I = \begin{cases} 1, & \text{if } g_i^I \in \mathcal{C}, \\ 0, & \text{otherwise}. \end{cases} \tag{2}$$

The vector $\mathbf{h}^I$ thus has value one at location i, if the corresponding image belongs to the class $\mathcal{C}$. As $\mathcal{C}$ has $N_\mathcal{C}$ images, of which one is the image I itself, each vector $\mathbf{h}^I$ contains exactly $N_\mathcal{C} - 1$ ones. In order to perform well with the class $\mathcal{C}$, the feature extraction should cluster the images I belonging to $\mathcal{C}$ near each other. That is, the values $h_i^I = 1$ should be concentrated on the small values of i.

We can now define the *observed probability* p_i:

$$\forall i \in \{0, \ldots,, N-2\} : \quad p_i = \frac{1}{N_\mathcal{C}} \sum_{K \in \mathcal{C}} h_i^K. \tag{3}$$

The observed probability p_i is a measure of the probability that an image in $\mathcal{C}$ has as the i:th nearest image, according to the feature extraction $\mathbf{f}$, another image belonging to the same class.

In the optimal case, $p_i = 1$ if $i \leq N_\mathcal{C} - 2$, and $p_i = 0$ if $i > N_\mathcal{C} - 2$. This is equivalent to the situation where all the images in class $\mathcal{C}$ are clustered together so that the longest distance from an image in $\mathcal{C}$ to another image in the same class is always smaller than the shortest distance to any image not in $\mathcal{C}$. On the other hand, the worst case happens when the feature $\mathbf{f}$ completely fails to discriminate the images in class $\mathcal{C}$ from the remaining images. The observed probability p_i is then close to the *a priori* $\rho_\mathcal{C}$ for every value of $i \in [0, N-2]$.

2.2 Forming Scalars from the Observed Probability

The observed probability p_i is a function of the index i, so it cannot easily be used to compare two different feature extractions. Therefore, it is necessary to derive scalar measures from p_i to enable us to do such comparisons. As large values of p_i with small values i and small values of p_i with large values i correspond to good discriminating power, the scalar measure should respectively reward large values of p_i when i is small and punish large values of p_i when i is large.

We chose to use three figures of merit to describe the performance of individual feature types. First, good features should have high observed probabilities for the very first indices. Therefore it is justifiable to use a local performance measure based only on the first indices. A simple and straightly derived measure can be calculated as the average of the observed probability p_i for the first n retrieved images, i.e.:

$$\eta_{\text{local}} = \frac{\sum_{i=0}^{n-1} p_i}{n} \tag{4}$$

The η_{local} measure obtains values between zero and one. If $n \leq N_C - 2$, it yields the value one in the optimal case. For η_{local} to measure local performance, a suitable value for the parameter n could be approximately 1–5% of the size of the database. With the η_{local} measure, figures near one can be obtained even though the classes were globally split into many clusters if each of these clusters are separate from the clusters of the other classes. This measure can thus be regarded as an indicant for the local separability of a given image class with a certain feature extraction method. Note that η_{local} is dependent on the a priori probability ρ_C of the image class.

As mentioned above, the η_{local} measure may give high values even if the images are scattered into many small clusters in the feature space. This suggests using an appropriate weighting function, which would take global clustering into consideration. A general method to construct a scalar Φ from a function $f(x)$ is to use a weighting or kernel function $h(x)$ and integrate the product of $f(x)$ and $h(x)$ over the whole input space as in

$$\Phi = \int_{-\infty}^{\infty} f(x)\,h(x)\,dx \ . \tag{5}$$

By selecting a suitable weighting function $h(x)$ we can set the measure Φ to fit to our purposes.

In this case, the weighting function should reward large values of p_i in small indices and punish large values of p_i in large indices. One such weighting function is obtained by first defining a DFT-based complex-valued function $P(u)$ as follows:

$$P(u) = \sum_{i=0}^{N-2} p_i\,h(i) = \sum_{i=0}^{N-2} p_i\,e^{j\pi i/(N-1)} \ . \tag{6}$$

Now, the weighting function $h(i)$ rotates in $N - 1$ steps $\varphi = 0$ to $\varphi = \frac{N-2}{N-1}\pi$, which equals the upper half of the unit circle.

Finally, a global figure of merit, η_{global}, is obtained by considering the real part of $P(u)$ and normalizing the result with $N_C - 1$. Thus,

$$\eta_{\text{global}} = \frac{\text{Re}\left\{ \sum_{i=0}^{N-2} p_i\,e^{j\pi i/(N-1)} \right\}}{N_C - 1} \ . \tag{7}$$

Also η_{global} attains values between zero and one. It favors observed probabilities that are concentrated in small indices and punishes for large probabilities in large index values. To achieve high performance values, the features should cluster all the images belonging to C near each other, preferably into a single cluster.

The third value of merit, η_{half}, measures the total fraction of images belonging to C found when only the first half of the p_i sequence is considered,

$$\eta_{\text{half}} = \frac{\sum_{i=0}^{N'} p_i}{N_C - 1} \ , \tag{8}$$

where $N' = \text{int}(N/2)$. The η_{half} measure obviously yields a value one in the optimal case and a value half with the a priori distribution of images.

Overall, for all the three figures of merit, η_{local}, η_{global}, and η_{half}, the larger the value the better the discrimination ability of the feature extraction is.

2.3 τ Measure

Measuring feature performance is essential in order to find the set of features for CBIR applications which on the average perform as well as possible. Still, even more important task is to measure performance of different CBIR applications and approaches. In this section, we present one quantitative figure, denoted as the τ measure, for performance of CBIR systems. The measure can be applied to systems utilizing the relevance feedback [11] approach in some form.

Content-based image searches can be divided at least into three categories [4]: target search, category search, and open-ended browsing. In target search, the goal is to find a specific image from the database. The user may or may not know if the image actually exists in the database. In category search, the user is interested in one or more images from a category. This is a harder problem, as images in semantic categories can be visually very dissimilar. In the third search type, open-ended browsing, the user is just browsing the database without a specific goal in mind. System performance with the browsing approach is hard to measure objectively.

With the τ measure, it is assumed that the user is facing a target search task from a database $\mathcal{D}$ for an image I belonging to class $\mathcal{C} \subset \mathcal{D}$. Before the correct image is found, the user guides the search by marking all shown images which belong to class $\mathcal{C}$ as relevant images. Then, the τ value measures the average number of images the system retrieves before the correct one is found. The τ measure resembles the "target testing" method presented in [4], but instead of relying on human test users, the τ measure is fully automatic.

The τ measure is obtained by implementing an "ideal screener", a computer program which simulates the human user by examining the output of the retrieval system and marking the images returned by the system either as relevant (positive) or non-relevant (negative) according to whether the images belong to $\mathcal{C}$. This process is continued until all images in $\mathcal{C}$ have been found. The queries can thus be simulated and performance data collected without any human intervention.

For each of the images in the class $\mathcal{C}$, we then record the total number of images presented by the system until that particular image is shown. From this data, we form a histogram and calculate the average number of shown images needed before a hit occurs. In the optimal case, the system first presents all images in $\mathcal{C}$. The optimal value for the average number of images presented before a particular image in $\mathcal{C}$ is thus $\frac{N_{\mathcal{C}}}{2}$.

The τ measure for class $\mathcal{C}$ is then obtained by dividing the average number of shown images by the size of the database, N. The τ measure yields a value

$$\tau \in [\frac{\rho_{\mathcal{C}}}{2}, 1 - \frac{\rho_{\mathcal{C}}}{2}] \tag{9}$$

where $\rho_C = \frac{N_C}{N}$ is the *a priori* probability of the class C. For values $\tau < 0.5$, the performance of the system is thus better than random picking of images and, in general, the smaller the τ value the better the performance.

The number of new images the system presents each round, i.e., the cutoff number, is denoted as M. The selection of this parameter has also some effect on the resulting τ value.

3   PicSOM

The PicSOM image retrieval system is a framework for research on algorithms and methods for content-based image retrieval. The system is designed to be open and able to adapt to different kinds of image databases, ranging from small and domain-specific picture sets to large general-purpose image collections. The features may be chosen separately for each specific task and the system may also use keyword-type textual information for the images, if available. Image retrieval with PicSOM is based on querying by pictorial examples (QBPE) [2], which is a common retrieval paradigm in CBIR applications. With QBPE, the queries are based on reference images shown either from the database itself or some external location. The user classifies these example images as relevant or non-relevant to the current retrieval task and the system uses this information to select such images the user is most likely to be interested in. The accuracy of the queries is then improved by relevance feedback [11] which is a form of supervised learning adopted from traditional text-based information retrieval. In relevance feedback, the previous human-computer interaction is used to refine subsequent queries to better approximate the need of the user.

In PicSOM, the queries are performed through a WWW-based user interface and the queries are iteratively refined as the system exposes more images to the user. PicSOM supports multiple parallel features and with a technique introduced in the PicSOM system, the responses from the used features are combined automatically. This is useful, as the user is not required to enter weights for the used features. The goal is to autonomously adapt to the user's preferences regarding the similarity of images in the database.

In this section, a brief overview of the PicSOM approach is presented. A more detailed description of the system can be found in our previous papers, e.g. [8, 10]. The PicSOM home page including a working demonstration of the system is located at *http://www.cis.hut.fi/picsom*.

3.1   The Self-Organizing Map

The image indexing method used in PicSOM is based on the Self-Organizing Map (SOM) [6]. The SOM defines an elastic net of points that are fitted to the input space. It can thus be used to visualize multidimensional data, usually on a two-dimensional grid. The SOM consists of a regular grid of neurons where a model vector is associated with each map unit. The map attempts to represent all the available observations with optimal accuracy using a restricted set of models. At

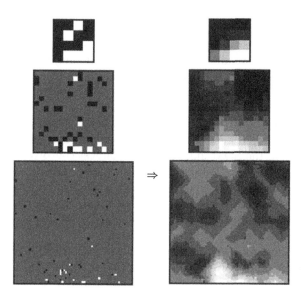

Fig. 1. An example of converting the positive and negative map units to convolved maps in a three-level TS-SOM. Map surfaces displaying the positive (white) and negative (black) map units are shown on the left. The resulting convolved maps are shown on the right.

the same time, the models become ordered on the grid so that similar models are close and dissimilar models far from each other. The PicSOM retrieval method can be described as a SOM-based implementation of relevance feedback.

In order to achieve a hierarchical representation of the image database and to alleviate the computational complexity of large SOMs, we use a special form of the SOM namely the Tree Structured Self-Organizing Map (TS-SOM) [7]. The TS-SOM is used to represent the database in several hierarchical two-dimensional lattices of neurons. Each feature is used separately to train a corresponding TS-SOM structure. As the SOM organizes similar feature vectors in nearby neurons, the resulting map contains a representation of the database with similar images according to the given feature located near each other. The tree structure of the TS-SOM, on the other hand, provides several map levels forming a set of SOMs with different resolutions.

3.2   Image Querying

In the beginning of a new query, the system presents the user the first set of reference images which are uniformly picked from the top levels of the TS-SOMs in use. The user then selects the subset of images which match her expectations best and to some degree of relevance fit to her purposes. Query improvement is achieved as the system learns the user's preferences from the selections made on the previous rounds.

The system marks the images selected by the user with a positive value and the non-selected images with a negative value in its internal data structure. These values are then summed up in their best-matching SOM units in each of the TS-SOM maps. Each SOM level is then treated as a two-dimensional matrix formed of values describing the user's responses to the contents of the map unit. Finally, the map matrices are low-pass filtered with symmetrical convolution masks in order to spread the user's responses to the neighboring units which, by presumption, contain images that are to some extent similar to the present ones. Starting from the SOM unit having the largest convolved response value, PicSOM retrieves from the database the image whose feature vector is nearest to the weight vector in that unit. If that image has not been shown to the user, it is marked to be shown on the next round. This process is continued with the second largest value and so on until a preset number of new images have been selected. This set is then presented to the user.

The conversion from the positive and negative marked images to the convolutions in a three-level TS-SOMs is visualized in Figure 1. First, a TS-SOM displaying the positive map units as white and negative as black is shown on the left. These maps are then low-pass filtered and the resulting map surfaces are shown on the right. It is seen that a cluster of positive images resides at the lower edge of the map.

A typical retrieval session with PicSOM consists of a number of subsequent queries during which the retrieval is focused more accurately on images resembling the positive example images. These queries form a list (or a tree of queries if the user is allowed to go back to previous query rounds and proceed with a different selection) in which all the queries contain useful information for the retrieval system.

3.3 User Interface

The PicSOM user interface used in our current WWW-based implementation in a midst of an ongoing query is displayed in Figure 2. First, the three parallel TS-SOM map structures represent three map levels of SOMs trained with RGB color, texture, and shape features, from left to right. The sizes of the SOM layers are 4×4, 16×16, and 64×64, from top to bottom. Below the convolved SOMs, the first set of images consists of images selected on the previous rounds of the retrieval process. These images may then be unselected on any subsequent round, thus changing their value from positive to neutral. In this example, a query with a set of images representing buildings selected as positive is displayed. The next images, separated by a horizontal line, are the 16 best-scoring new images in this round obtained from the convolved units in the TS-SOMs.

4 Experiments

We evaluated a set of features and the PicSOM approach with a set of experiments using an image collection from the Corel Gallery 1 000 000 product [3].

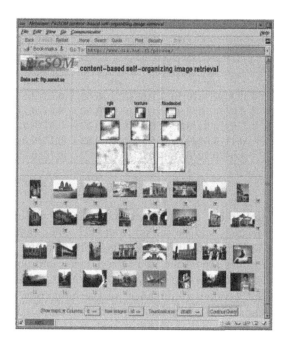

Fig. 2. The PicSOM user interface.

The collection contains 59 995 photographs and artificial images with a very wide variety of subjects. All the images are either of size 256×384 or 384×256 pixels. The majority of the images are in color, but there are also a small number of grayscale images.

4.1   Settings

Five different feature extraction methods were applied to the images and the corresponding TS-SOMs were created. The TS-SOMs for all features were sized 4×4, 16×16, 64×64, and 256×256, from top to bottom. The features used in this study included two different color and shape features and a simple texture feature. All except the FFT-based shape feature were calculated in five separate zones of the image. The zones are formed by first determining a circular area in the center of the image. The size of the circular zone is approximately one fifth of the area of the image. Then the remaining area is divided into four zones with two diagonal lines.

Average Color (*cavg* in Table 2) is obtained by calculating average R-, G- and B-values in five separate zones of the image. The resulting 15-dimensional feature vector thus describes the average color of the image and gives rough information on the spatial color composition.

Color Moments (*cmom*) were introduced in [12]. The color moment features are computed by treating the color values in different color channels in each

Table 1. Comparison of the performances of different feature extraction methods for different image classes. Each entry gives three performance figures ($\eta_{local}/\eta_{global}/\eta_{half}$).

features	classes		
	plane	face	car
cavg	0.06/0.16/0.59	0.05/0.10/0.56	0.03/0.21/0.63
cmom	0.06/0.16/0.59	0.05/0.10/0.56	0.04/0.21/0.63
texture	0.04/0.04/0.52	0.06/0.16/0.57	0.07/0.22/0.63
shist	0.11/0.62/0.84	0.10/0.54/0.82	0.13/0.34/0.68
sFFT	0.04/0.49/0.78	0.07/0.39/0.72	0.10/0.30/0.65

zone as separate probability distributions and then calculating the first three moments (mean, variance, and skewness) from each color channel. This results in a $3 \times 3 \times 5 = 45$ dimensional feature vector. Due to the varying dynamic ranges, the feature values are normalized to zero mean and unit variance.

Texture Neighborhood (*texture*) feature in PicSOM is also calculated in the same five zones. The Y-values (luminance) of the YIQ color representation of every pixel's 8-neighborhood are examined and the estimated probabilities for each neighbor being brighter than the center pixel are used as features. When combined, this results in one 40-dimensional feature vector.

Shape Histogram (*shist*) feature is based on the histogram of the eight quantized directions of edges in image. When the histogram is separately formed in the same five zones as before, a 40-dimensional feature vector is obtained. It describes the distribution of edge directions in various parts of the image and thus reveals the shape in a low-level statistical manner [1].

Shape FFT (*sFFT*) feature is based on the Fourier Transform of the binarized edge image. The image is normalized to 512×512 pixels before the FFT. Then the magnitude image of the Fourier spectrum is low-pass filtered and decimated by the factor of 32, resulting in a 128-dimensional feature vector [1].

To study the performance of the selected features with different types of images, three separate image classes were picked manually from the database. The selected classes were *planes*, *faces* and *cars*, of which the database consists of 292, 1115 and 864 images, respectively. The corresponding *a priori* probabilities are 0.5%, 1.9%, and 1.4%. In the retrieval experiments these classes were thus not competing against each other but mainly against the "background" of 57 724, i.e., 96.2% of other images. The used value for the parameter M was 20.

4.2   Results

Table 1 shows the results of forming the three scalar measures, η_{local}, η_{global}, and η_{half}, from the measured observed probabilities. The η_{local} measure was calculated for $n = 50$ first images. It can be seen that the η_{local} measure always is larger than the corresponding *a priori* probability. Also, the shape features *shist* and *sFFT* seem to outperform the other feature types for every image class and every performance measure. Otherwise, it is not yet clear which one of the

Table 2. The resulting τ values in the experiments.

features					classes		
cavg	*cmom*	*texture*	*shist*	*sFFT*	plane	face	car
×					0.30	0.35	0.39
	×				0.31	0.43	0.34
		×			0.26	0.26	0.34
			×		0.16	0.22	0.18
				×	0.19	0.22	0.18
×		×	×		0.16	0.21	0.18
×		×		×	0.17	0.23	0.18
×		×	×	×	0.14	0.21	0.16
	×	×	×		0.15	0.21	0.18
	×	×		×	0.18	0.22	0.19
	×	×	×	×	0.14	0.20	0.16
×	×	×	×	×	0.14	0.20	0.16

three performance measures would be the most suitable as a single measure of effectiveness.

The results of the experiments with the whole PicSOM system are shown in Table 2. First, each feature was used alone as the basis for the retrieval and then different combinations of features were tested. The two shape features again yield better results than the color and texture features, which can seen from the first five rows in Table 2. By examining the results with all tested classes, it can be seen that the general trend is that using a larger set of features yields better results than using a smaller set. Most notably, using all features gives better or equal results than using any single feature or subset of features. The implicit weighting of the relative importances of different features models the semantic similarity of the images selected by the user.

In the second and third sections of Table 2, the results of the experiment are presented when using first only one shape feature and then both features in the retrieval. It can be seen that the results are slightly better when using both shape features. These experiments thus also validate the overall trend that using more features generally improves the results. Therefore, it can be concluded that the PicSOM system is able to benefit from the existence of multiple feature types. As it is generally not known which feature combination would perform best for a certain image query, the PicSOM approach provides a robust method for using a set of different features and image maps formed thereof in parallel so that the result exceeds the performances of all the single features.

However, it also seems that if one feature vector type has clearly worse retrieval performance τ than the others, it may be more beneficial to exclude that particular TS-SOM from the retrieval process. For the proper operation of the PicSOM system, it is thus desirable that the used features are well balanced, i.e., they should on the average perform quite similarly by themselves.

5   Conclusions

In this paper, we have presented a set of methods for quantitative performance evaluations of different features and CBIR systems. The proposed τ measure is a general and automatic measure of a performance of retrieval systems based on the relevance feedback technique where the query is iteratively refined during multiple rounds of user-system interaction.

As a single visual feature cannot classify images into semantic classes, we need to gather the information provided by multiple features to achieve good retrieval performance. The results of our experiments show that the PicSOM system is able to effectively select from a set of parallel TS-SOMs a combination which outperforms single TS-SOMs in performance. The features used in the experiments are yet quite tentative and results suffer from the relative differences in performance between them. Therefore, we have started a series of experiments for selecting a proper and well-balanced set of features to be used in the PicSOM system in our future assessments.

References

[1] Sami Brandt, Jorma Laaksonen, and Erkki Oja. Statistical shape features in content-based image retrieval. In *Proceedings of 15th International Conference on Pattern Recognition*, Barcelona, Spain, September 2000. To appear.

[2] N.-S. Chang and K.-S. Fu. Query by pictorial example. *IEEE Transactions on Software Engineering*, 6(6):519–524, November 1980.

[3] The Corel Corporation WWW home page, http://www.corel.com, 1999.

[4] Ingemar J. Cox, Matt L. Miller, Stephen M. Omohundro, and Peter N. Yianilos. Target testing and the PicHunter bayesian multimedia retrieval system. In *Advanced Digital Libraries ADL'96 Forum*, Washington, DC, May 1996.

[5] Alexander Dimai. Assessment of effectiveness of content based image retrieval systems. In *Third International Conference on Visual Information Systems*, pages 525–532, Amsterdam, The Netherlands, June 1999.

[6] Teuvo Kohonen. *Self-Organizing Maps*, volume 30 of *Springer Series in Information Sciences*. Springer-Verlag, Berlin, 1997. Second Extended Edition.

[7] P. Koikkalainen and E. Oja. Self-organizing hierarchical feature maps. In *Proc. IJCNN-90, Int. Joint Conf. on Neural Networks, Washington, DC*, volume II, pages 279–285, Piscataway, NJ, 1990. IEEE Service Center.

[8] Jorma Laaksonen, Markus Koskela, and Erkki Oja. Content-based image retrieval using self-organizing maps. In *Third International Conference on Visual Information Systems*, pages 541–548, Amsterdam, The Netherlands, June 1999.

[9] MPEG-7: Overview (version 2.0). March 2000/Noordwijkerhout (The Netherlands) ISO/IEC JTC1/SC29/WG11 N3349.

[10] Erkki Oja, Jorma Laaksonen, Markus Koskela, and Sami Brandt. Self-organizing maps for content-based image retrieval. In Erkki Oja and Samuel Kaski, editors, *Kohonen Maps*, pages 349–362. Elsevier, 1999.

[11] G. Salton and M. J. McGill. *Introduction to Modern Information Retrieval*. Computer Science Series. McGraw-Hill, 1983.

[12] Markus Stricker and Markus Orengo. Similarity of color images. In *Storage and Retrieval for Image and Video Databases III (SPIE)*, volume 2420 of *SPIE Proceedings Series*, pages 381–392, San Jose, CA, USA, February 1995.

Benchmarking for Content-Based Visual Information Search

C. H. C. Leung* and H. H. S. Ip**

*School of Communications & Informatics, Victoria University of Technology,
Footscray Campus (FO119), P.O. Box 14428, Melbourne CMC, VIC 8001, Australia
Email: clement@matilda.vu.edu.au

**Department of Computer Science, City University of Hong Kong,
83, Tat Chee Avenue, Kowloon, Hong Kong
Email: cship@cityu.edu.hk

Abstract.
The importance of the visual information search problem has given rise to a large number of systems and prototypes being built to perform such search. While different systems clearly have their particular strengths, they tend to use different collections to highlight the advantages of their algorithms. Consequently, a degree of bias may exist, and it also makes it difficult to make comparisons concerning the relative superiority of different algorithms. In order for the field of visual information search to make further progress, a need therefore exists for a standardised benchmark suite to be developed. By having a uniform measure of search performance, research progress can be more easily recognised and charted, and the resultant synergy will be essential to further development of the field. This paper presents concrete proposals concerning the development of such a benchmark, and by adopting an extensible framework, it is able to cater for a wide variety of applications paradigms and to lend itself to incremental refinement.

1. Differences between Searching Text-Based Information and Searching Visual Information

Research in visual information search and retrieval has gained significant attention in recent times and many factors have contributed to this development. The capacity of today's computer hardware to store and deliver good graphical image at a relatively fast speed and cheap price [16], the development of good graphical software available on the Internet, the development of high speed computer networks are some of the factors. More importantly, it is driven by the need to manage and retrieve visual information in a growing number of image repositories, such as NASA's Earth Observing System, medical centres, art galleries/centres, film/video productions, etc. In addition, an image component is increasingly deployed in different varieties of document systems which relate to more general applications [14, 15]. To fully exploit future image databases, it is important to have efficient schemes to structure and represent image data by contents, and eventually to integrate image retrieval mechanisms into the Database Management System [1]. Visual Information System [20] is widely accepted to be the new paradigm for future computer-based information systems. Present day information systems are constrained by conventional technology and are mostly based on a *text in/text out* paradigm. They are principally geared to the processing of textual and structured information, sometimes augmented by diagrammatic, charting, and simple inter-media cross-referencing techniques.

R. Laurini (Ed.): VISUAL 2000, LNCS 1929, pp. 442-456, 2000.

A fundamental problem in any information processing system is the ability to search and locate the information that is relevant [1, 12, 13, 29, 32]. An important characteristic that originally led to the widespread adoption of conventional database systems was its ability to search and locate information much more efficiently than a manual approach. However, the problem of searching information in a conventional database was a comparatively straightforward one. Visual information search differs from conventional database search in the following respects.

1. Conventional database systems deal with highly structured information with a *well-defined ordering* among its components and data elements. In contrast, image objects are not directly indexable.

2. Every field in a conventional database only admits a finite number of possibilities. Given enough time, an exhaustive search will always be able to locate the required records. In an image of a given resolution, for example, although the number of possibilities is still finite (as determined by the number of pixels and the colour depth), it is not possible to identify images with the given objects no matter how much time is given to process the image, due to limitations in current algorithms in the recognition of image objects.

3. A normalised database insists that every record of the same type has a fixed number of fields. In contrast, an image can have a vast number of objects of interest, which may be of different size, partially hidden, or residing in the background. An image object may also be recursively decomposed into further meaningful constituent objects [23].

4. Conventional database access is generally concerned with information recovery, rather than information discovery. In an image query, one may have no notion as to what the target images would look like, how many of them are there or how many have been missed.

5. For given image objects, there are many ways of specifying them, and they can have many different ways of presenting themselves so that precise query specification resulting in precise answers are not possible. Some degree of manual intervention subsequent to query submission such as browsing and relevance feedback [10] is almost inevitable.

2. Benchmarks are Essential to Research Progress

The importance of the visual information search problem has given rise to a large number of systems and prototypes being built to perform such search. While different systems clearly have their particular strengths, they tend to use different collections to highlight the advantages of their algorithms. Consequently, a degree of bias may exist, and it also makes it difficult to make comparisons concerning the relative superiority of different algorithms. In order for the field of visual information search to make further progress, a need therefore exists for a standardised benchmark suite to be developed. By having a uniform measure of search performance, research progress can be more easily recognised and charted, and the resultant synergy will be essential to further development of the field.

The use of benchmarks in database search and performance is not new. The TPC suite of benchmarks for has been established for over a decade [34]. They were established with the aim of "bringing order out of chaos", and it is hoped that a similar objective may be achieved from the present effort. It is useful to note that, in these established benchmarks, they are not static but evolves as the field develops. One would expect that as the field of visual information search changes, the benchmarks will evolve and be augmented with additional features or characteristics. There are two key observations that may be noted from the TPC benchmark developments that the current development is likely to follow.

1. Incremental development and refinement

The TPC process originated with the batch-oriented TP1. It was followed by the DebitCredit benchmark, then the TPC-A benchmarks for gauging OLTP (Online

Transaction Processing) performance, and then the TPC-B benchmarks, which cut out the network and user interaction component of the TPC-A workload [9, 34]. TP1, TPC-A, TPC-B, TPC-C represent successive developments along the same line.

2.   *Caters for a variety of applications paradigms and new developments*
The TPC benchmarks cover a range of processing paradigms; e.g. TP1 is geared to batch processing, TPC-A is geared to OLTP, TPC-D is geared to decision support OLAP (Online Analytic Processing), and the TPC-W is geared to Web-based order processing.

In fact, other established benchmarks also exhibit similar patterns. For example, the SPEC benchmarks developed by the Standard Performance Evaluation Corporation, which started in 1988, have separate benchmarks for integer and floating point components for gauging machine performance. They also underwent successive refinement, e.g. SPEC89, SPECCPU95, SPECWeb96, SPECJVM98 [31]. In the related text retrieval field, the TREC collection [35] and associated conference provides a means of objective evaluation and comparison of systems performance. For each TREC Conference, the National Institute of Standards and Technology makes available a test set of documents and questions, where participants run their own retrieval systems on the data, and return to NIST a list of the retrieved top-ranked documents for evaluation. In image retrieval, a regular set of images tends to be widely used for comparing algorithm performance. Arguably, some degree of benchmark thinking already exists in this field.

3. Benchmarks Properties and Characteristics

Like the TPC benchmark for databases, what is needed is a series of standardised benchmarks for testing and comparing the retrieval competence of different algorithms. Such a series should have the following properties.

1.   *Parametric.* The benchmarks should allow the specification of a number of parameters, which may be selected according to different requirements. In particular, the size of the collection may be a parameter that can be adjusted.

2.   *Coverage of different types of visual information.* The mode of generation of different types of visual information may exhibit different characteristics and their databases may need to be searched differently (e.g. photographs may entail different methods for their indexing and identification from graphic art, and these accordingly have to be assessed in different ways). A benchmark suite consisting of a number of component sets geared to different requirements will be necessary.

3.   *Standard query set should be specified.* Apart from specifying the images for inclusion in the assessments, a standard set of queries ought to be applied to the component collections to enable uniform comparison of performance. These query sets should allow diverse functions and system capabilities to be tested. In particular, they should allow the weaknesses and strengths of the system under assessment to be highlighted.

4.   *The benchmarks should be purely content-based.* In certain image database systems, there is a component for the incorporation of secondary metadata. In regarding an image as an entity, secondary information such as the originator, date, and title may be regarded as identifying attributes of the image and entered into a relational database, which may be searched for correct image identification. Since these are unrelated to image content, the application of this approach, even in a limited way, should be excluded.

5.   *Speed is not of central concern.* Although most of the benchmarks in other areas of computing are preoccupied with speed and response time (e.g. TPC, SPEC), these will not play a central role in the present benchmark. While we clearly cannot ignore the speed of retrieval completely, it is primarily the software ability to identify visual information rather than the hardware efficiency that constitutes the main focus. Of course, search efficiency resulting from effectively pruning the search space has a direct bearing on the response time, and is a factor that needs to be taken into consideration.

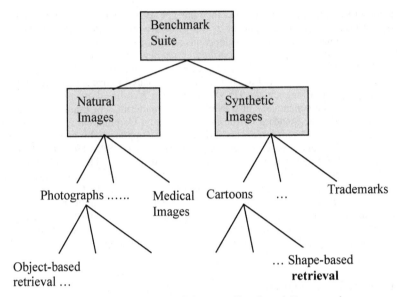

Fig. 1. An Extensible Image Benchmark Framework

6.. *Standard measures of retrieval performance should be provided.* Since it is the ability to identify relevant visual information that forms the main focus of the evaluations, it is suggested the established measures of *recall* and *precision* should form the basis of retrieval performance. Both of these measures hinge on the idea of a "relevant" image, which can be highly subjective. Thus, the set of relevant images corresponding to given queries should be pre-defined. This normally requires a manual process of going through *all* images in the database to extract the agreed set of relevant images, on which the size of the collection has a direct bearing. Other related measures may include *fallout* and *generality*. A systematic study of some of these measures may be found in [25].

As indicated above, the initial specification of relevant benchmarks need not, and should not, be fully complete and unchangeable. Here, we primarily focus on still images. This should not be regarded as a limitation, as frequently video streams are decomposed into a set of still images. The two main types of image benchmarks are:
1. naturally generated images,
2. artificially generated graphical images,

which we shall call Type I and Type II benchmarks respectively. Each of these may be subdivided further according to the different requirements and applications. A framework for these benchmarks is outlined in Figure 1.

4. Specifications of Type I Benchmarks for Object-Based Retrieval in Photographs

Depending on the applications, naturally generated images may be of arbitrary complexity. Photographs of different varieties are a dominant class within the category of naturally generated images. Much more information is generally contained in photographs than in synthetic images, since the amount of complexity and number of objects and characteristics in the latter are artificially pre-determined and controlled. Searching for particular characteristics or objects in photographs is harder, and their indexing mechanism in general does not readily lend itself to automatic processing.

4.1 Two Types of Image Contents

It is necessary to make a distinction between two main types of image contents for this type of benchmark, in order that search queries covering different aspects may be incorporated.

1. *Primitive.* Primitive image content is typically *semantically limited* and may include:
    *   a machine's view of the image including the raw elements from which the image is constituted (e.g. colour)
    *   those features of the image which can be recognised and extracted automatically by the computer (e.g. shapes, boundaries, lines); these normally form aspects or parts of an object without defining the complete object.

    Primitive contents are often quantitative in nature from which spatial relationships, positional, geometric or other quantitative properties may be extracted [3, 5, 6].

2. *Complex.* Complex image contents are *semantically rich* and they often correspond to the patterns within an image which are perceived as meaningful by human users. Complex contents are *object-based* in which entire objects within an image often form the basis of retrieval. Examples of objects are *car, child,* and *violin* (see Appendix). In addition, although complex contents are almost invariably built from objects, they need not be confined to isolated objects. Very often, *groups of objects* combined in specific ways may form higher-level concepts that may form the basis of meaningful retrieval; examples of these include *Christmas party celebration, riot,* and *concert* (see Appendix). In order to represent such semantics meaningfully, appropriate modelling of image contents data is necessary and this will have a direct bearing on the size of the benchmark database; more detailed analysis of such issues may be found in [11, 18, 19, 23, 30, 37]. Complex contents cannot normally be automatically identified by the computer and are often qualitative in nature, although their extraction may be, in a limited way, assisted by the identification of primitive contents. For example, if one were searching for the object *swimming pool*, then the appropriate use of colour and texture information would help to narrow down the search.

4.2 Size of the Benchmark Database

As indicated above, a central aim for the benchmark is to test the ability to retrieve images by contents rather than the speed of retrieval. Therefore, having a very large benchmark database is not critical. As one of the challenging problems in computer science is retrieval by *complex contents*, the ability to carry out this will be the primary concern here. Since retrieval by complex contents invariably will require some degree of manual indexing, it is impractical to have a very large database, since the cost of indexing the database or other preparation cost may be excessive. For example, it has been measured that the proper indexing of news stories type of images by content can require of the order of 10 minutes per image [17]. In many applications (e.g. those related to MPEG-7, MPEG-21 [24]), it is possible that some form of description is provided along with the contents. In addition, determining the correct answer will often require going through individual images within the collection. Having too small a database, on the other hand, will not be useful since to be qualified as a "database", it must consist of a significant number of items. It is felt that the initial benchmark should consist of N = 1,000 images. In subsequent developments, it would be necessary to scale this up to larger orders of magnitude. It is expected that later benchmarks will consist of N = 5,000 and N = 10,000 images.

4.3 Multi-Object Images

In many image collections, some kind of classification scheme is employed to group images into a number of classes. These classes are represented by class descriptors, and to search an image, one would go to a class based on the class descriptor. An image typically would belong to a single class. For some collections, this is often adequate because the images involved are typically single-object images (see Appendix).

It is relatively trivial to classify single object images since we can do so via standard schemes such as those used in thesaurus or encyclopaedia, and a single phrase is normally sufficient to completely describe the contents of single-object images. These images should not be of interest to the present benchmark. For multi-object images, a simple classification hierarchy is inadequate, since an image may have access from multiple paths. In addition to having multiple objects, the type of images selected for the benchmark should include object interactions together with rich attributes for the objects (see Appendix). Thus, to sum up, our benchmark database of images should be based on images with the following characteristics:

1. images should have multiple objects
2. images should include diverse relationships among the objects
3. the objects and/or relationships should include a variety of attributes that qualify them

It is evident from the above that a simple keyword approach will not be fully adequate, since keywords have no notion of relationships nor qualifiers, so that only a rather coarse level of semantic content may be represented.

4.4 Standard Queries

Although the benchmark database initially will have only 1,000 images, ultimately the algorithms will need to scale up to much larger databases. This means that a reasonably precise specification of contents is necessary. While a small database will tolerate a substantial fraction of images returned for browsing, large scale browsing is impractical for large databases. Current image search on the Internet is typically done through a combination of keywords and subject classification [4, 6, 28]. Although some degree of browsing seems unavoidable [10], these will have to be done in a limited way. In fact, this is a problem faced even by textual searches on the Web. Very often, searches carried out by common search engines return over thousands of candidate documents. Clearly, this will make it difficult for the users to obtain the target images. For instance, in the AltaVista Photo Finder [2], it supports searching both by keywords and visual similarity; e.g. a search for "Grand Piano" results in 8,846 images, spanning over 20 pages with 12 images per page, where three of the images in first page visually bearing no relationship with piano. Thus, for large image databases, a more precise retrieval than that provided by keyword description is necessary. Part of the work of MPEG-7 is aiming to provide a descriptive standard for visual information content [21, 22, 33].

In conventional database design, the selection of entities or relationships to include in the database is based on information that could form the basis of a meaningful query for the enterprise. The same principle for formulating standard queries may apply here. The queries must be sufficiently meaningful in terms of perception of image contents. In order to form meaningful averages and to allow a good cross-section of image contents to be searched, the following are recommended.

1. Queries must be reasonably precise with minimal ambiguity; the set of potential images returned for possible browsing should not be greater than 50 for the 1,000 item database
2. Queries must be meaningful in terms of human perception of complex image contents
3. Queries must include a good cross-section of image contents to be queried
4. The number of standard evaluation queries should be 20
5. For each query, there should be known answers that do not exceed 15 images.

Due to the lack of a suitable image query language, a query by example (QBE) approach is often adopted in searching for images by content. This makes use of visual similarity on the basis of primitive contents (e.g. colour, texture). It has been suggested [36] that this type of search is typically not sufficiently semantic rich nor meaningful. Consequently, it is felt that these types of queries in their isolated form should not be incorporated as part of this class of benchmark.

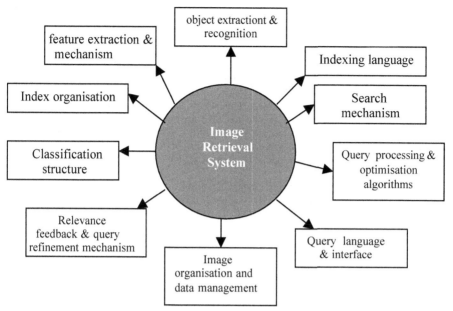

Fig. 2 Components of an Image Retrieval System

4.5 System Components Being Exercised
In evaluating the performance of the system, one is exercising a number of components of the system and testing out their individual as well as aggregate performance. Some of these components may include those indicated in Figure 2. A competent Image Retrieval System will require the different components to be individually competent, as well as their inter-working together in an efficient manner.

5. Measures of Performance

5.1 Basic Measures of Performance
By knowing in advance the characteristics and requirements of the benchmark, it is possible to design a search system or its indexing mechanism that specifically targets at these requirements, with the result that the system appears to perform better than it is. Indeed, for the TPC benchmarks, similar bias has been known to arise, where certain manufacturers designed into their production software special components (often called *benchmark special*) for specifically optimising and inflating TPC benchmark results.

Although there are a host of measures that may be used to measure retrieval performance [25,27], *recall* and *precision* are universally accepted to be the most important. Although other measures are sometimes used, most of them tend to be variants based on these, e.g. precision/recall after a certain number of images are retrieved. Both of these measures hinge on the concept of *relevance*. Unfortunately, unlike textual documents, there is no automatic way to determine relevance in an image collection for a given query. Thus, for each of the 20 standard queries specified, the 1,000 images will need to be manually processed so that the set of relevant images for each query may be precisely defined. A system that performs well will need to score high percentages in both the recall and precision measures. An ideal system will have the *results set* (the set of images returned by the system) coinciding with the *target set* (the set of correct answers). Sometimes the ranking of relevant images is used as a measure [8], which calculates the average rank of all images that are considered to be relevant. Here, we shall calculate a similar measure determined by the stage where a relevant image is retrieved.

Speed is important insofar as it tests the algorithm's ability to carry out efficient search. It should have minimal dependence on extraneous factors such as the network connection, disk bandwidth or processor speed. In fact, the TPC-B benchmark, which came as a refinement of the TPC-A benchmark, was designed to cut out some of these factors even though both of them use the same transaction type (banking transactions). In order to minimise hardware effects, it is advantages to have all of the 1,000 images loaded on to memory. This also means that some compression of the images are necessary. The JPEG format is widely used and seems appropriate, which for 1,000 images, should not take up more than 20-30 Megabytes. It is difficult to impose a strict requirement on the machine configuration. However, since this benchmark is not focused on speed, some variations may be tolerated, and certain numerical factors (e.g. CPU clock rate) may be applied to compensate any difference.

5.2 Performance Measures for Multi-Stage Image Retrieval

It is a characteristic of image retrieval systems that retrieval is done in stages. It is unusual to have systems that restrict retrieval to a single stage, without allowing further refinement of the query. Let there be M stages. At each stage of the retrieval, the following typically occurs.

1. *Browsing*. Browsing for image retrievals tends to be much more efficient than that for textual documents, since a quick glance at the image can normally determine its relevance to the query, while for textual documents, one would need to read through at least a portion of the document to determine its relevance. Thus presenting multiple images for browsing is not only feasible, but is an essential function of such systems.

2. *Selection*. Image selection normally follows browsing. The total collection of images selected from the different stages would form the *results set* S_k (Figure 3) for a given query k. Thus, if S_{ki} signifies the set of images selected as a result of selection in the ith stage, then the set of images retrieved as a result of this retrieval process is

$$S_k = \bigcup_{i=1}^{M} S_{ki} \ .$$

3. *Relevance Feedback and Query Refinement*. The images retrieved at one stage and those retrieved from the next stage are correlated via a relevance feedback or query refinement mechanism. In this paper, the term relevance feedback will also be used to include different types of query refinement. Some form of image similarity is normally associated with relevance feedback. For example, in the Virage search engine [2], it makes use of "visual similarity" based on four primary attributes: colour, composition, structure and texture. It is likely that similarity based on complex contents will be able to reduce the number of stages and considerably speed up the retrieval process.

The number of stages is determined by the query process, where a stage is considered to be final when the relevance feedback mechanism has no further scope for obtaining additional relevant images from the database. A multi-stage approach necessitates the basic measures of performance above to be modified. Let K be the number of queries in the benchmark (here $K = 20$), and we adopt the following notations:

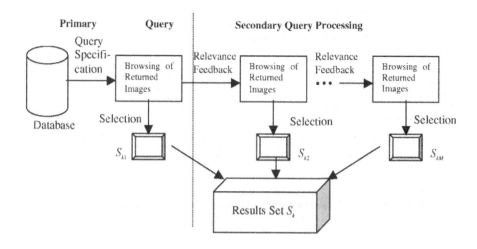

Figure 3. Multi-Stage Retrieval Process

Table 1 Summary of Notations

S_{ki},	set of images retrieved for query k at stage i,
I_{ki},	set of relevant images retrieved for query k at stage i,
n_{ki},	number of images retrieved at stage i for query k, $n_{ki} = \lvert S_{ki} \rvert$,
r_{ki},	number of relevant images retrieved at stage i for query k, $r_{ki} = \lvert I_{ki} \rvert$,
R_{ki},	recall of query k at stage i,
P_{ki},	precision of query k at stage i,
r_k,	number of relevant images in database for query k
N,	total number of images in database.

We have,

$$R_{ki} = \frac{r_{ki}}{r_k}, \qquad P_{ki} = \frac{r_{ki}}{n_{ki}} . \tag{1}$$

A good relevance feedback mechanism would play a dominant role in contributing to the retrieval performance of the system. Here, one would expect the precision curve exhibiting the characteristics of Figure 4, where each point represent the *non-cumulative* precision for a particular stage. It is possible that, when the relevance feedback mechanism works perfectly, then the curve would approach 100%, but most relevance feedback mechanisms are not capable of achieving this, particularly for image discovery where the number of relevant images are not known in advance, so that eventually, after most of the relevant images have been retrieved, the curve will tend to come down. Since most of the retrieval contribution comes from the second stage onwards, we would expect the following to hold.

$$P_{k1} < \text{Max} \, (P_{k2}, P_{k3}, ..., P_{kM}) . \tag{2}$$

A precision curve showing weak relevance feedback is given in Figure 5. As indicated in Figure 3, the first set of images returned S_{k1} has a special significance since it has not received any manual assistance from the mechanisms of browsing and relevance feedback. As such, it measures the system's ability to respond to the query language to produce the correct images.

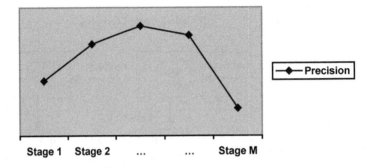

Stage 1   Stage 2   ...   ...   Stage M

Figure 4. Multi-Stage Precison Curve with Strong Relevance Feedback

It is useful to distinguish the entire query process into two parts, and these should be separately assessed. The first part can be called *primary query processing*, and is related to the images returned that are due entirely to the initial query specification – apart from the manual formulation of the query, this process is automatic, and is similar to query processing a conventional database. Unlike a conventional database query, the query in the present situation typically involves other modes of input in addition to a purely textual specification like SQL. For a system with powerful primary query processing capability, we should have

$$R_{k1} > \text{Max}\,(R_{k2}\,,\, \dots\,,\, R_{kM}), \tag{3}$$

which indicates that most of the relevant images are obtained from primary query processing. The second part can be called *secondary query processing*, and is related to the subsequent stages of query refinement as indicated in Figure 3, which consists of a fair degree of manual intervention. A situation where

$$R_{k1} < R_{k2} < \dots < R_{kM}\,, \tag{4}$$

suggests that the system relies heavily on manual browsing with limited primary query processing ability. In extreme cases, a system may have no primary query processing capability and relies entirely on some form of relevance feedback. In fact, some QBE systems may be regarded as falling within this category: no query formulation is required and the system randomly generates a set of images that form the basis for relevance feedback similarity retrieval.

Unlike the conventional single stage approach, recall and precision in the present situation may be measured in different ways. To measure the power of primary query processing recall R_k', we should simply use the results obtained from the first set of images returned, which we shall referred to as *primary recall*, i.e.

$$R_k' = R_{k1}. \tag{5}$$

To measure the effectiveness of relevance feedback, we should use the *secondary recall R_k''* related to secondary query processing

$$R_k = \frac{\left| \bigcup_{i=2}^{M} I_{ki} \right|}{r_k}\,. \tag{6}$$

which, in the important special case where the sets $\{I_{ki}\}$ are disjoint, equals

$$R_k = \frac{\sum_{i=2}^{M} r_{ki}}{r_k}\,.$$

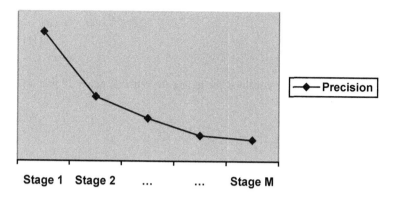

Figure 5. Multi-Stage Precision Curve with Weak Relevance Feedback

The combined recall measure R_k is determined by the total number of relevant images obtained from the entire process which, for disjoint sets equals, $r_{k1} + \ldots + r_{kM}$. Dividing this by the number of relevant images in the database for the given query, we have for the *aggregate recall* R_k for this situation,

$$R_k = R_{k1} + \ldots + R_{kM} = R_k' + R_k'' \ . \tag{7}$$

Similarly, the *primary precision* P_k' measures the precision related to primary processing, which for a given query k is simply

$$P_k' = P_{k1} \ . \tag{8}$$

Likewise, the *secondary precision* P_k'' measures the precision related to secondary processing, which for a given query k is

$$P_k = \frac{\text{number of relevant images retrieved in stages 2 to } M}{\text{total number of images retrieved in stages 2 to } M}$$

$$= \left| \bigcup_{i=2}^{M} I_{ki} \right| \Big/ \left| \bigcup_{i=2}^{M} S_{ki} \right| \ .$$

In the case where the sets $\{I_{ki}\}$ are disjoint, and also the sets $\{S_{ki}\}$ are disjoint, then we have

$$P_k = \sum_{i=2}^{M} r_{ki} \Big/ \sum_{i=2}^{M} n_{ki} \ . \tag{9}$$

The *aggregate precision* P_k gives the precision obtained from the entire process, and for the present situation is given by

$$P_k = \sum_{i=1}^{M} r_{ki} \Big/ \sum_{i=1}^{M} n_{ki} \ . \tag{10}$$

To compare the power of primary processing against that of secondary processing, we insist that most of the relevant images are obtained from primary query processing, and for the present situation, this is

$$r_{k1} > \sum_{i=2}^{M} r_{ki} \ . \tag{11}$$

Dividing both sides by r_k, our condition for testing the retrieval power of primary query processing becomes

$$R_{k1} > \sum_{i=2}^{M} R_{ki} \ . \tag{12}$$

This test guarantees that at least 50% of the images retrieved are done automatically by the primary query processing component of the system. We observe from the additivity of the components in (7) that, while browsing clearly improves recall, it need not improve precision. Even under the general situation where the sets $\{I_{ki}\}$ are not disjoint, improvement to recall performance should still be possible since normally

$$\left| \bigcup_{i=1}^{M} I_{ki} \right| > |I_{k1}| \ ,$$

Table 2: Measures of Benchmark Performance

Primary Recall:	$\displaystyle\sum_{k=1}^{K} \frac{r_{k1}}{r_k K}$,
Secondary Recall:	$\displaystyle\sum_{k=1}^{K} \sum_{i=2}^{M} \frac{r_{ki}}{r_k K}$,
Aggregate Recall:	$\displaystyle\sum_{k=1}^{K} \sum_{i=1}^{M} \frac{r_{ki}}{r_k K}$,
Primary Precision:	$\displaystyle\sum_{k=1}^{K} \frac{r_{k1}}{n_{k1} K}$,
Secondary Precision:	$\displaystyle\sum_{k=1}^{K} \sum_{i=2}^{M} \frac{r_{ki}}{n_{ki} K}$,
Aggregate Precision:	$\displaystyle\sum_{k=1}^{K} \sum_{i=1}^{M} \frac{r_{ki}}{n_{ki} K}$,
Effectiveness of Primary Query Processing	$\displaystyle\sum_{k=1}^{K} \frac{r_{k1}}{r_k} > \sum_{k=1}^{K} \sum_{i=2}^{M} \frac{r_{ki}}{r_k}$,
Effectiveness of Relevance Feedback	$\displaystyle\sum_{k=1}^{K} \frac{r_{k1}}{n_{k1}} < \mathbf{Max}\left\{ \sum_{k=1}^{K} \frac{r_{k2}}{n_{k2}} , \ \dots , \ \sum_{k=1}^{K} \frac{r_{kM}}{n_{kM}} \right\}$,
Average Number of Stages Required for Retrieving Relevant Images	$\displaystyle\sum_{k=1}^{K} \frac{k}{K}$.

giving $R_k > R_k'$. As indicated above, the ranking of the relevant images may also be used as a meaningful measure. Here, instead of calculating the average ranking of the relevant images, we use the average number of stages for retrieving the relevant images, which for a given query k is given by

$$_k = \sum_{i=1}^{M} ir_{ki} \Big/ \sum_{i=1}^{M} r_{ki} \quad .$$

So far, we have only concentrated on a single query, but the same derivation applies to the entire set of benchmark queries. Table 2 summarises the key measures and conditions averaging over all benchmark queries, and we have, for simplicity, assumed that the relevant sets under consideration are disjoint.

6. Summary and Conclusions

In order to enable the field of visual information search and retrieval to make further advances, it is essential to have a common yardstick by which the performance of different systems and algorithms may be compared and calibrated. Having a standard suite of benchmarks will provide an objective means of evaluating the search and retrieval performance of different systems. So far we have been concentrating on object-based retrieval in photographs, which, within an extensible framework for benchmark development, provides a useful starting point. Our recommendation consists of:

1. A suite of benchmarks that consist of a number of component sets that cater for different applications requirements should be developed
2. The initial number of images in the object-based photographs should be 1,000, which may be scaled up at a later stage.
3. The images should contain multi-object, with diverse relationships existing among the objects
4. Both the objects and relationships should include a variety of qualifying attributes
5. The 1,000 images should be in JPEG format
6. A set of 20 evaluation queries which cover a representative cross-section of contents should be designed against the 1,000 images
7. For each query, there should be known answers that do not exceed 15 images
8. Images returned for possible browsing should not be greater than 50 at any stage
9. Queries based solely on primitive contents should not be used
10. The measures given in Table 2 should be included for evaluating system performance
11. The average response time for the 20 queries may be used to measure system efficiency.

Such a suite will allow the strengths and merits of different methodologies to be identified and validated. In the long run, its dynamic and incremental nature will allow diverse categories of visual information to be incorporated.

References

1. D. Adjeroh, and K. C. Nwosu, "Multimedia database management   requirements and issues", *IEEE Multimedia*, Vol. 4, No. 4, 1997, pp. 24-33.
2. AltaVista, *http://image.altavista.com/*.
3. M. Campanai, Del Bimbo, A., and Nesi, P., "Using 3D spatial relationships for image retrieval by contents", *Proc. IEEE Workshop on Visual Languages*, 1992.
4. F. Chang, et. al., "Visual information retrieval from large distributed online repositories", *Comm. ACM*, Vol. 40, No. 12, 1997, pp. 63-71.
5. C. Colombo, A. Del Bimbo, and P. Pala, "Semantics in visual information retrieval", *IEEE Multimedia*, July-September, 1999.
6. Corbis, *http://www.corbis.com/*.

7. U. Gargi, and R. Kasturi, "Image database querying using a multi-scale localised colour representation", in *Proc. IEEE Workshop on Content-based Access of Image and Video Libraries*, Fort Collins, 1999.

8. M. Flickner, *et. al.*, "Query by image and video content: the QBIC system", *IEEE Computer*, Vol. 28, No. 9, September 1995, pp. 23-32.

9. J. Gray, "A measure of transaction processing power", *Datamation*, 1985.

10. W. I. Grosky, "Managing multimedia information in database systems", *Comm. ACM*, Vol. 40, No. 12, 1997, pp. 72-80.

11. V. N. Gudivada and V. Raghavan, "Modeling and retrieving images by content", *Information Processing & Management*, Vol. 33, No. 4, pp. 427-452, 1997.

12. A. Gupta and R. Jain, "Visual information retrieval", *Comm. ACM*, Vol. 40, No.5, 1997, pp. 70-79.

13. A. Gupta, S. Santini, and R. Jain, "In search of information in visual media", *Comm. ACM*, Vol. 40, No.12, 1997, pp. 35-42.

14. H. H. S. Ip, K. C. K. Law, and S. L. Chan, "An open framework for a multimedia medical document system", *J. Microcomputer Applications*, Vol. 18, pp. 215-232, 1995.

15. K. C. K. Law, H. H. S. Ip, , and F. Wei, "An abstract layered model for hypermedia document system", *Proc. IEEE International Conference on Multimedia Computing and Systems*, Florence, 1999, pp. 11-15.

16. G. Lawton, "Storage technology takes center stage", *IEEE Multimedia*, Vol. 32, No. 11, 1999, pp. 10-12.

17. C. H. C. Leung and D. Hibler, *Architecture of a Pictorial Database Management System*. British Library Research Report, London, 1991.

18. C. H. C. Leung and D. Sutanto, "Multimedia data modeling and management for semantic content retrieval", in *Handbook of Multimedia Computing*, B. Fuhrt (Ed.), CRC Press, 1999.

19. C. H. C. Leung and Z. J. Zheng, "Image data modelling for efficient content indexing", *Proc. IEEE International Workshop on Multi-media Database Management Systems*, New York, August 1995, IEEE Computer Society Press, pp. 143-150

20. C. H. C. Leung (Ed.) *Visual Information Systems*. Springer-Verlag Lecture Notes in Computer Science LNCS 1306, Heidelberg, 1997.

21. C. H. C. Leung, and A. M. Tam, "Validation experiment for structured annotation DS", *ISO/IEC JTC1/SC29/WG11 MPEG00/M5855*, Noordwijkerhout, NL, March 2000.

22. C. H. C. Leung, and A. M. Tam, "Workplan for CE on DSs for linguistic structure", *ISO/IEC JTC1/SC29/WG11 MPEG00/W3254*, Noordwijkerhout, NL, March 2000.

23. W. S. Li *et. al.* "Hierarchical image modelling for object-based media retrieval", *Data and Knowledge Engineering* 27, 1998, pp. 139-176.

24. MPEG *http://www.cselt.it/mpeg/*.

25. D. Narasimhalu, M. Kankanhalli, and J. K. Wu, "Benchmarking multimedia databases", *Multimedia Tools and Applications*, Vol. 4, 1997, pp. 333-356.

26. F. Pereira, "MPEG-7: A standard for content-based audiovisual description", *Proc. 2nd International Conference on Visual Information Systems*, San Diego , Dec 1997, pp. 1-4.

27. Salton, G. *Automatic Text Processing*. Addison-Wesley, Reading, MA,1989.

28. J. Smith and S. F. Chang, "Visually searching the Web for content", *IEEE Multimedia*, Vol. 4, No. 3, 1997, pp. 12-20.

29. W.W.S. So, C. H. C. Leung and Z. J. Zheng, "Analysis and evaluation of search efficiency for image databases", in *Image Databases and Multi-media Search* A. Smeulders and R. Jain (Eds.), World Scientific, 1997.

30. R. K. Srihari and Z. Zhang, "A multimedia image annotation, indexing, and retrieval system", *Proc. 1998 ACM SIGIR International Workshop on Multimedia Indexing and Retrieval*, Melbourne, August 1998, pp. 29-45.

31. Standard Performance Evaluation Corporation, *http://open.specbench.org/*.

32. A. M. Tam and C. H. C. Leung, "A multiple media approach to visual information search," *Proc. 1998 ACM SIGIR International Workshop on Multimedia Indexing and Retrieval,* Melbourne, August 1998, pp. 1-6.
33. A. M. Tam, and C. H. C. Leung, "Semantic content retrieval and structured annotation: beyond keywords", *ISO/IEC JTC1/SC29/WG11 MPEG00/M5738*, Noordwijkerhout, NL, March 2000.
34. Transaction Processing Performance Council, *http://www.tpc.org/.*
35. TREC *http://trec.nist.gov/.*
36. VIS '99 *3rd International Conference on Visual Information Systems*, Amsterdam, 1999, Panel Discussion.
37. L. Yang, and Wu, J., "Towards a semantic image database system," *Data & Knowledge Engineering*, Vol. 22, No. 3, May 1997, pp. 207-227.

Appendix: Illustration of Image Types

Objects: child, violin

Object group: concert

Multi-Object Images

Single Object Images

Video Content Representation Based on Texture and Lighting

Ivan S. Radev[1], George Paschos[2], Niki Pissinou[1], and Kia Makki[1]

[1] University of Louisiana
Lafayette, LA 70504
iradev@usa.net, pissinou@cacs.usl.edu, kia@usl.edu
[2] National University of Singapore
Singapore 117543
gpaschos@usa.net

Abstract. When dealing with yet unprocessed video, structuring and extracting features according to models that reflect the idiosyncrasies of a video data category (film, news, etc.) are essential for guaranteeing the content annotation, and thus the use of video. In this paper, we present methods for automatic extraction of texture and lighting features of representative frames of video data shots. These features are the most important elements which characterize the development of plastic (physical) space in the film video. They are also important in other video categories. Texture and lighting are two basic properties, or features, of video frames represented in the general film model presented in [12]. This model is informed by the internal components and interrelationships known and used in the film application domain. The method for extraction of texture granularity is based on the approach for measuring the granularity as the spatial rate of change of the image intensity [3], where we extend it to color textures. The method for extraction of lighting feature is based on the approach of closed solution schemes [4], which we improve by making it more general and more effective.

1 Introduction

Video annotation is a process in which, after the video segmentation, video characteristics are extracted, represented and organized guided by a model of the video application domain. Thus, before video data is available for use, it must be annotated (indexed) by content and its indices stored as metadata. The extracted features from the raw (unstructured) video data must be modeled in a way informed by the video data category (film, news, etc.). Hence, these types of models are essential for guarantee the content annotation of video data. However, there is considerable lack of such methodologies for video support, therefore, developing annotation models that adequately and successfully support the video annotation process and the subsequent video querying and navigation is essential for the effective use of video data.

The extraction and representation are the basic operations in which features from video data are extracted (guided by annotation models) for subsequent

R. Laurini (Ed.): VISUAL 2000, LNCS 1929, pp. 457–466, 2000.
Springer-Verlag Berlin Heidelberg 2000

retrieval of content information. These features are represented as text, strings, icons, etc. At the physical (pixel) level, features, such as texture and lighting, can be extracted automatically. There is a diversity of models for video indexing inherently based on extraction of various video features [6], [7], [9]. The features (texture, lighting, color, shape, size, spatio-temporal object relationships, etc.) are extracted based on the required information from the application domain (film video, news video, geographic video, etc.) which in general is organized in an annotation model.

The automatic extraction uses image processing techniques and tools developed for computer vision. Different types of feature extraction (and its associated similarity measure) are developed. One of the first methods for a proper image extraction despite changes in lighting and camera features, as angle and scale, is the color similarity measure. For a more precise definition of video objects, color extraction is often combined with spatial similarity. An example of a texture and shape analysis is presented in QBIC system [5].

All these methods are connected with extraction of low level visual features and establishment of similarity measure for retrieval and query execution. The higher level attributes (features) of a frame image and of a video structural unit (shot, scene, etc.) as a whole are concerned with semantic video content. Up until now an integrated system that covers the two levels of feature extraction and provides the whole scope of content-based video indexes has not been developed. However, the video indexing system with an underlying model, the general film model (GFM) presented in [12], proposes an effective approach for integration of both low-level, usually automatic indexing, and higher level, usually manual indexing in one video data category—film. In our paper, we propose methods of extraction of texture and lighting from video frames, which provide low level, automatic indexing. In [12], the higher level indexing approach is addressed.

As an example of the use of texture and lighting features in the process of video annotation, an annotation model (GFM) in one video category—film—will be considered in the paper. However, the same methods for texture and lighting processing can be apllied to other video categories. Texture and lighting are two basic properties, or features, of video frames represented in the GFM model. The texture feature of a video frame defines the texture granularity of the frame image. Lighting is the most important tool to support other features of a frame, such as color, form, direction, etc. by modifying their values, or codes. Lighting refers to the direction of the light source(s) in a given scene represented by a shot in a video. The method for extraction of texture granularity is based on the approach for measuring the granularity as the spatial rate of change of the image intensity [3], where we extend it to color textures, thus providing better human perception. The method for extraction of the lighting feature is based on the approach of closed solution schemes [4], which we improve by making it more general and more effective. The proposed methods for automatic extraction of the texture granularity and lighting features have been applied in processing a film video clip of 19 shots.

The rest of the paper is organized as follows. In Section 2, the basic GFM model characteristics are introduced. In Section 3, we present our methods for automatic extraction of the texture and lighting features for a representative frame of each shot. In Section 4, we present experimental evaluation of the methods. Finally, the conclusion provides some observations and some perspective for continuing our research.

2   Film Modeling

In this section, the elements of films, which can be visualized during their annotation (and subsequent visual querying), are briefly discussed, based on the major concepts of the general film model presented in [12]. The general film model provides representation of the basic structural, syntactic, and semantic elements and features contained in films, i.e., of the content of films. They can be captured using the knowledge and results from the film video domain proposed by the film analysis and theory [8]. The major groups of information, or

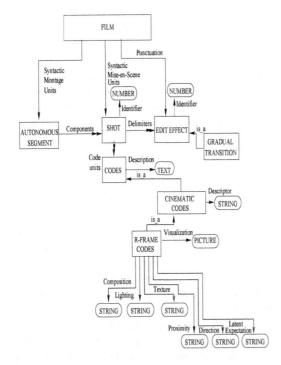

Fig. 1. (Partial) Syntactic Modeling of Film Video

modalities, about the film content represented in the general film model include the following film features (components): film statistical data, montage elements (editing, in the USA), mise-en-scene elements, meaning of the film sequences (called autonomous segment in the paper), screenplay, and film sound. These components reflect the types of queries which users typically tend to ask [13], such as queries on the bibliographic data, on structural data, on content data.

The main part of the general film model is the representation of a film. It presents objects that are cinema art products called films or motion pictures.

The three questions which filmmakers face during production of a film are: what to shoot, how to shoot it, and how to present the corresponding shot. The answers to the first two questions reflect the type of mise-en-scene represented through its corresponding shot, while the answer to the last question is determined by the process of film montage.

The film syntax is represented in the GFM model by a system of codes, or elements (Figure 1). The representations of the film mise-en-scene and montage are specified in the general film model by the set of all syntactic mise-en-scene units (actually, objects of class shot) and the set of all syntactic montage units (actually, objects of class autonomous segment) building up the plastic space and plastic time, respectively, of a particular film. The set of syntactic mise-en-scene units is built up from the properties of the shots of a film, while the set of syntactic montage units is built up from various structural parts of film footage called autonomous segments in the GFM model. The properties of each shot are represented by the set of codes characterizing the shot as a whole (shot codes) and the set of codes characterizing its individual frames (frame codes).

Thus, the film space is defined in the GFM model through the frame codes represented as properties of each *r-frame* (representative frame for a given shot), also called a *key frame*. The richness of the cinematic technique is represented in the GFM model using the combination of eleven properties of each r-frame with the properties of the camera work (shot properties) and edit effects. This combination allows not only the (Renaissance) perspective representation of reality to be presented in the film but also the film tone and atmosphere to be visually perceived by the spectators using such frame attributes as lighting, composition, and texture.

When a shot is considered as a whole, its properties, distance of framing, focus, angle, motion, and field depth, define its spatio-temporal relationships by manipulating the apparent distance for shooting of an object, the focus, the angle, and motion of the camera. Thus, these shot properties define the literal attitude of the director to the represented scene. All of these shot, or camera work, properties are represented in the GFM model as part of the film syntax.

Out of this exuberant variety of film features representing the space and time development in films, and described in the GFM model through the system of codes, we selected to investigate in detail the most important elements which the film director uses to manipulate the film space, or mise-en-scene, namely texture and lighting. These are two of the eleven properties of each r-frame represented in the GFM model. Texture defines the inherent texture of a subject in an r-frame and the texture, or grain, of the frame image as a whole. Lighting can modify many of the properties of an r-frame. Lighting effects are determined by the place and type of light source in the image. The light can be natural, artificial, or both. It can come from everywhere: in front, overhead, below, backside, alongside, and can highlight every detail. The lighting effects help define contrast in film.

The automatic extraction of these attributes and their representation in a video database during the annotation process with an underlying model, the GFM model, is, therefore, an effective way to describe the content of a film. In the next section, we describe our methods for automatic determination of the texture and lighting properties (values) of an r-frame.

3   Feature Extraction

Methods for the automatic extraction of texture granularity and lighting features from r-frames are described in the following two subsections.

3.1   Texture Granularity

Texture granularity refers to the size of the basic primitive(s) of a given texture. Small granularity means that the given texture consists of large primitives and vice versa—large granularity means that the texture consists of small primitives. In other words, small granularity implies a finer texture while large granularity implies a coarser texture. A texture with large primitives is fairly uniform over large areas compared to a texture with small primitives which exhibits more frequent changes in pattern over the image space. This leads to the idea of measuring granularity as the spatial rate of change of the image intensity, as proposed in [3]. In our approach, however, we extend this basic notion to color textures by measuring the total color rate of change over the image area. Assuming use of the RGB color space, we define the color difference, CD, between a pixel at image coordinates (i, j) and its neighboring pixels within a window $W \times W$ as follows:

$$CD_{ij} = \sqrt{(R_{ij} - R_{avg})^2 + (G_{ij} - G_{avg})^2 + (B_{ij} - B_{avg})^2} \qquad (1)$$

where (R_{ij}, G_{ij}, B_{ij}) is the color of pixel (i, j), and $(R_{avg}, G_{avg}, B_{avg})$ is the average color of the neighboring pixels. The local texture granularity within a given window centered at pixel (i, j) is defined as $\frac{1}{CD_{ij}}$, since a small color difference would imply high uniformity within the window and thus, large granularity for the image. Applying (1) at each pixel and averaging, we have the texture granularity, TG, for the entire image:

$$TG = \frac{1}{\frac{1}{(N-2W)(M-2W)} \sum_{i=W}^{N-W} \sum_{j=W}^{M-W} CD_{ij}} \qquad (2)$$

where N, M are the image dimensions (note that the pixels at the boundary of width W, all around the image, have been excluded, since an actual neighborhood does not exist for them). A value TG is the value of the *texture* (feature)

automatically extracted and represented as the texture granularity of a given
r-frame during the video annotation process.

Preliminary experiments with r-frame images have shown an advantage of
this method in capturing the granularity of a color texture as humanly perceived,
compared with the original intensity-only approach [3].

3.2   Lighting

Lighting refers to the direction of the light source(s) in a given scene. Here we will
assume that there is only one light source, located at infinity (i.e., far enough),
so that its direction is the same from any point in the scene. Also, surfaces are
assumed to be Lambertian (e.g., no highlights are taken into consideration).

Assuming a given 3-D cordinate system xyz, where z points to the direction
of the viewer (i.e., perpendicular to the image plane), the direction of the light
source is described by a vector $L = (x_L, y_L, z_L)$ from the origin toward the light
source. It can also be described by the two angles, tilt (t) and slant (s). Tilt
is the angle between L and the $x - z$ plane, while slant is the angle between
L and the positive z axis. Given t and s, L may also be represented as $L =
(\cos(t)\sin(s), \sin(t)\sin(s), \cos(s))$.

Several approaches have been proposed in the computer vision literature [4],
[11], [14], [15]. Some are based on iterative approximation [14], [15], and others
use closed-form solution schemes [4], [11]. Based on initial experimentation, we
have decided to follow Brooks and Horn method [4] but with two modifications:
normal vectors are not necessarily constrained to be of unit length, and initialization uses the image gradients as proposed by Worthington and Hancock [14].
We repeat the iterative scheme here for reference:

$$\bar{n}_{ij}^k = \frac{1}{4}(n_{ij+1}^k + n_{ij-1}^k + n_{i+1j}^k + n_{i-1j}^k) \tag{3}$$

$$n_{ij}^{k+1} = \bar{n}_{ij}^k + \frac{\epsilon^2}{2\lambda}(I_{ij} - n_{ij}^k \cdot L^k)L^k \tag{4}$$

$$L^{k+1} = [\sum_{i=1}^{N-2}\sum_{j=1}^{M-2} n_{ij}^{k+1}(n_{ij}^{k+1})^T]^{-1}\sum_{i=1}^{N-2}\sum_{j=1}^{M-2} I_{ij}n_{ij}^{k+1} \tag{5}$$

where n_{ij}^{k+1} is the current estimate of the normal vector at pixel (i, j), L^{k+1} is
the current estimate of the light source direction, T signifies vector transpose, λ
is a smoothing parameter, and ϵ is the distance between two adjacent pixels on
the image grid (typically $\epsilon = 1$). I_{ij} is the intensity at pixel (i, j) and is given
by the following formula:

$$I_{ij} = 0.299R_{ij} + 0.587G_{ij} + 0.114B_{ij} \tag{6}$$

For $k = 0$, we have set $L^0 = (0, 0, 1)$ (n_{ij}^0's are initiallized as described in [14]),
and $\lambda = 0.5$. As a stopping criterion we have used the minimization of the source
error, i.e., $\| L_k - L_{k-1} \| < \delta$, where $\| \cdot \|$ signifies vector norm, and $\delta = 0.001$.

To give a more intuitive way of specifying the direction of light in a scene, we use the specifications of the quadrants where the light sources reside, e.g., *left/upper/front* quadrant. Thus, given the final estimate for L supplied by the above method, we determine the major quadrant where the light source vector lies as follows:

```
if(z_L ≥ 0)
   if(y_L ≥ 0)
      if(x_L ≥ 0)   right/upper/front
      else    left/upper/front
   else if(x_L ≥ 0)   left/lower/front
        else   right/lower/front
else
   if(y_L ≥ 0)
      if(x_L ≥ 0)   right/upper/back
      else    left/upper/back
   else if(x_L ≥ 0)   left/lower/back
        else   right/lower/back
```

An identifier of a quadrant is the value of the *lighting* (feature) automatically extracted and represented as lighting of a given r-frame during the video annotation process.

4   Implementation and Results

The proposed methods for the automatic extraction of texture granularity and lighting features have been applied in processing a film video clip ("Pirates") that consists of 281 frames organized in 19 shots [2]. Our implementation extends the basic MPEG-1 player available at [1]. For video segmentation of the clip, or detection of shot cuts, we have used the method presented in [10]. All 18 cuts have been detected. Figure 2 shows the r-frames (first frame of each shot) along with their texture granularity and lighting values represented as pairs (*TG, lighting_source_quadrant_identifier*).

5   Conclusion

Automatic feature extraction methods for the representation of video content have been presented. The methods extract the texture granularity as well as the direction of the light source from each scene depicted in the video's key frames. The texture granularity method utilizes the color specification of pixels, thus, providing for the description of color texture in r-frame images. The lighting method utilizes one of the most successful existing light source detection algorithms with appropriate adaptations to make it more general and more effective. The results have been promising. The feature extraction mechanism has been

Fig. 2. R-frames of the 19 shots of the "Pirates" film video clip. The corresponding texture granularity and lighting values [pairs (TG, lighting_source_quadrant_identifier)], in left-to-right top-to-bottom order, are as follows: (0.041, left/upper/front), (0.038, left/lower/front), (0.061, right/upper/back), (0.076, left/lower/front), (0.031, left/lower/back), (0.029, left/lower/front), (0.053, left/lower/front), (0.034, left/upper/back), (0.039, right/upper/back), (0.054, right/lower/front), (0.041, left/lower/back), (0.046, left/lower/front), (0.084, right/upper/front), (0.048, left/upper/front), (0.061, left/lower/back), (0.030, right/upper/back), (0.022, right/upper/front), (0.031, left/lower/back), (0.040, left/lower/front)

implemented with an MPEG-1 decoder and can be used off-line for storage and later retrieval of the features, but also on-line while the video is decoded. The system is expected to be integrated with a complete database system at a later stage.

Using the automatic extraction of these two features for the key frames of video shots, the automatic determination of other features of a key frame and/or video shot taken as a whole can be investigated. For the film video category, for example, the automatic extraction and representation of other properties of the film syntax, represented via the general film model, such as form, distance of framing, motion and angle of the camera work, etc. can be pursued. This will provide a solid base for combined low-level and higher level indexing of film video data based on the GFM model. This in turn allows merging of all different types of multimodal information contained in a film in such a way that will greatly facilitate content-based access to the enormous variety and richness of film features and content.

References

[1] http://rnvs.informatik.tu-chemnitz.de/~ja/MPEG/MPEG_Play.html.

[2] www.fmc.edu/~paschos/pirates.mpa.

[3] M. Amadasun and R. King. Textural Features Corresponding to Textural Properties. *IEEE Transactions on Systems, Man and Cybernetics (SMC)*, 19(5):1264–1289, May 1989.

[4] M. J. Brooks and B. K. P. Horn. Shape and Source from Shading. *A.I. Memo 820, M.I.T.*, 1985.

[5] M. Flickner. Query by Image and Video Content. *IEEE Computer*, 28(9):23–32, September 1995.

[6] S. Gibbs, C. Breiteneder, and D. Tsichritzis. Audio/Video Databases: An Object-Oriented Approach. In A. Elmagarmid and E. Neuhold, editors, *Proceedings of 9th International Conference on Data Engineering (ICDE'93)*, pages 381–390, Vienna, Austria, April 1993. IEEE Computer Society Press.

[7] R. Hjelsvold and R. Midstraum. Modelling and Querying Video Data. In M. Maybury, editor, *Proceedings of 20th Conference on Very Large Databases (VLDB'94)*, pages 686–695, Santiago, Chile, September 1994. AAAI Press and The MIT Press.

[8] J. Monaco. *How to Read a Film: The Art, Technology, Language, History and Theory of Film and Media.* Oxford University Press, 1977.

[9] A. Nagasaka and Y. Tanaka. Automatic Video Indexing and Full-Video Search for Object Appearances. In E. Knuth and L. Wegner, editors, *Visual Database Systems, II*, pages 113–127. Elsevier Science Publishers B.V., 1992.

[10] G. Paschos and I. Radev. Video Sequence Cut Detection in Different Color Spaces. In *IASTED International Conference on Signal and Image Processing (SIP'99)*, Nassau, Bahamas, October 1999.

[11] A. P. Pentland. Finding the Illuminant Direction. *Journal of Optical Society of America*, pages 448–455, 1982.

[12] I. Radev, N. Pissinou, and K. Makki. Film Video Modeling. In *Proceedings of IEEE Workshop on Knowledge and Data Engineering Exchange (KDEX'99)*, Chicago, Illinois, November 1999.

[13] L. Rowe, J. Boreczky, and C. Eads. Indexes for Access to Large Video Databases. In W. Niblack and R. Jain, editors, *Proceedings of Conference on Storage and Retrieval for Image and Video Databases II (SPIE'94)*, volume 2185, pages 150–161, San Jose, California, February 1994. SPIE.

[14] P. L. Worthington and E. R. Hancock. New Constraints on Data-Closeness and Needle Map Consistency for Shape-for-Shading. *IEEE Transactions on Pattern Analysis and Machine Intelligence (PAMI)*, 21(12):1250–1267, July 1999.

[15] Q. Zheng and R. Chellapa. Estimation of Illuminant Direction, Albedo, and Shape from Shading. *IEEE Transactions on Pattern Analysis and Machine Intelligence (PAMI)*, 3(7):680–702, July 1991.

Shape Similarity Measures, Properties and Constructions

Remco C. Veltkamp and Michiel Hagedoorn*

Department of Computing Science, Utrecht University, The Netherlands
{Remco.Veltkamp,mh}@cs.uu.nl

Abstract. This paper formulates properties of similarity measures. We list a number of similarity measures, some of which are not well known (such as the Monge-Kantorovich metric), or newly introduced (reflection metric), and give a set constructions that have been used in the design of some similarity measures.

1 Introduction

Large image databases are used in an extraordinary number of multimedia applications in fields such as entertainment, business, art, engineering, and science. Retrieving images by their content, as opposed to external features, has become an important operation. A fundamental ingredient for content-based image retrieval is the technique used for comparing images. There are two general methods for image comparison: intensity-based (color and texture) and geometry-based (shape). A recent user survey about cognition aspects of object retrieval shows that users are more interested in retrieval by shape than by color and texture [26]. However, retrieval by shape is still considered one of the most difficult aspects of content-based search. Indeed, systems such as IBM's QBIC, Query By Image Content [21], perhaps one of the most advanced image retrieval systems to date, is relatively successful in retrieving by color and texture, but performs poorly when searching on shape. A similar behavior shows the Alta Vista photo finder [5].

There is no universal definition of what shape is. Impressions of shape can be conveyed by color or intensity patterns, or texture, from which a geometrical representation can be derived. This is shown already in Plato's work Meno, where the word 'figure' is used for shape. First the description "figure is the only existing thing that is found always following color" is used, then "terms employed in geometrical problems": "figure is limit of solid" [20]. In this paper too we consider shape as something geometrical, and use the term pattern for a geometrical pattern.

Shape similarity measures are an essential ingredient in shape matching. Matching deals with transforming a pattern, and measuring the resemblance with another pattern using some dissimilarity measure. The terms pattern matching and shape matching are commonly used interchangeably. The matching problem is studied in various forms. Given two patterns and a dissimilarity measure:

- (computation problem) compute the dissimilarity between the two patterns,
- (decision problem) for a given threshold, decide whether the dissimilarity between two patterns is smaller than the threshold,

* supported by Philips Research

- (decision problem) for a given threshold, decide whether there exists a transformation such that the dissimilarity between the transformed pattern and the other pattern is smaller than the threshold,
- (optimization problem) find the transformation that minimizes the dissimilarity between the transformed pattern and the other pattern.

Sometimes the time complexities to solve these problems are rather high, so that it makes sense to devise approximation algorithms that find an approximation:

- (approximate optimization problem) find a transformation that gives a dissimilarity between the two patterns that is within a specified factor from the minimum dissimilarity.

2   Properties

In this section we list a number of possible properties of similarity measures. Whether or not specific properties are desirable will depend on the particular application, sometimes a property will be useful, sometimes it will be undesirable. Some combinations of properties are contradictory, so that no distance function can be found satisfying them. A shape similarity measure, or distance function, on a collection of shapes S is a function $d : S \times S \to \mathbb{R}$. The following conditions apply to all the shapes A, B, or C in S.

1 (Nonnegativity) $d(A, B) \geq 0$.

2 (Identity) $d(A, A) = 0$ for all shapes A.

3 (Uniqueness) $d(A, B) = 0$ implies $A = B$.

4 (Strong triangle inequality) $d(A, B) + d(A, C) \geq d(B, C)$.

Nonnegativity (1) is implied by (2) and (4). A distance function satisfying (2), (3), and (4) is called a metric. If a function satisfies only (2) and (4), then it is called a semimetric. Symmetry (see below) follows from (4). A more common formulation of the triangle inequality is the following:

5 (Triangle inequality) $d(A, B) + d(B, C) \geq d(A, C)$.

Properties (2) and (5) do not imply symmetry.

Similarity measures for partial matching, giving a small distance $d(A, B)$ if a part of A matches a part of B, in general do not obey the triangle inequality. A counterexample is given in figure 1: the distance from the man to the centaur is small, the distance from the centaur to the horse is small, but the distance from the man to the horse is large, so $d(man, centaur) + d(centaur, horse) > d(man, horse)$ does not hold. It therefore makes sense to formulate an even weaker form [12]:

Fig. 1.   Under   partial matching,   the   triangle inequality does not hold.

6 (Relaxed triangle inequality) $c(d(A, B) + d(B, C)) \geq d(A, C)$, for some constant $c \geq 1$.

7 (Symmetry) $d(A, B) = d(B, A)$.

Symmetry is not always wanted. Indeed, human perception does not always find that shape A is equally similar to B, as B is to A. In particular, a variant A of prototype B is often found more similar to B than vice versa [27].

8 (Invariance) d is invariant under a chosen group of transformations G if for all $g \in G$, $d(g(A), g(B)) = d(A, B)$.

For object recognition, it is often desirable that the similarity measure is invariant under affine transformations, illustrated in figure 2. The following four properties are about robustness, a form of continuity. Such properties are useful to be robust against the effects of discretization, see figure 3.

9 (Perturbation robustness) For each $\epsilon > 0$, there is an open set F of deformations sufficiently close to the identity, such that $d(f(A), A) < \epsilon$ for all $f \in F$.

10 (Crack robustness) For each each $\epsilon > 0$, and each "crack" x in the boundary of A, an open neighborhood U of x exists such that for all B, $A - U = B - U$ implies $d(A, B) < \epsilon$.

11 (Blur robustness) For each $\epsilon > 0$, an open neighborhood U of $bd(A)$, the boundary of A exists, such that $d(A, B) < \epsilon$ for all B satisfying $B - U = A - U$ and $bd(A) \subseteq bd(B)$.

12 (Noise robustness) For each $x \in \mathbb{R}^2 - A$, and each $\epsilon > 0$, an open neighborhood U of x exists such that for all B, $B - U = A - U$ implies $d(A, B) < \epsilon$.

A distance function is distributive in the shape space if the distance between one pattern and another does not exceed the sum of distances between the one and two parts of the other:

13 (Distributivity) For all A and decomposable $B \cup C$, $d(A, B \cup C) \le d(A, B) + d(A, C)$.

The following properties all describe forms of discriminative power. The first one says that there is always a shape more dissimilar to A than some shape B. This is not possible if the collection of shapes is finite.

14 (Endlessness) For each A, B there is a C such that $d(A, C) > d(A, B)$.

The next property means that for a chosen transformation set G, the distance d is able to discern A as an exact subset of $A \cup B$. No $g(A)$ is closer to $A \cup B$ than A itself:

15 (Discernment) For a chosen transformation set G, $d(A, A \cup B) \le d(g(A), A \cup B)$ for all $g \in G$.

The following says that changing patterns, which are already different, in a region where they are still equal, should increase the distance.

16 (Sensitivity) For all A, B with $A \cap U = B \cap U$, $B - U = C - U$, and $B \cap U \ne C \cap U$ for some open $U \subset \mathbb{R}^2$, then $d(A, B) < d(A, C)$.

The next property says that the change from A to $A \cup B$ is smaller that the change to $A \cup C$ if B is smaller than C:

17 (Proportionality) For all $A \cap B = \emptyset$ and $A \cap C = \emptyset$, if $B \subset C$, then $d(A, A \cup B) < d(A, A \cup C)$.

Finally, the distance function is strictly monotone if at least one of the intermediate steps of adding $B - A$ to A, and $C - B$ to B is smaller than the two steps combined:

18 (Monotonicity) For all $A \subset B \subset C$, $d(A, C) > d(A, B)$, or $d(A, C) > d(B, C)$.

Fig. 2. Affine invariance: $d(A, B) = d(g(A), g(B))$.

Fig. 3. Discretization effects: deformation, blur, cracks, and noise.

3   Similarity Measures

3.1 L_p Distances, Minkowski Distance

Many similarity measures on shapes are based on the L_p distance between two points. For two points x, y in $\mathbb{R}^k$, the L_p distance is defined as $L_p(x, y) = (\sum_{i=0}^{k} |x_i - y_i|^p)^{1/p}$. This is also often called the Minkowski distance. For $p = 2$, this yields the Euclidean distance: $d(x, y) = (\sum_{i=0}^{k} (x_i - y_i)^2)^{1/2}$. For $p = 1$, we get the Manhattan, city block, or taxicab distance: $L_1(x, y) = \sum_{i=0}^{k} |x_i - y_i|$. For p approaching ∞, we get the max metric: $L_\infty = \lim_{p \to \infty} (\sum_{i=0}^{k} |x_i - y_i|^p)^{1/p} = \max_i(|x_i - y_i|)$. For all $p \geq 1$, the L_p distances are metrics. For $p < 1$ it is not a metric anymore, since the triangle inequality does not hold.

3.2   Bottleneck Distance

Let A and B be two point sets of size n, and $d(a, b)$ a distance between two points. The bottleneck distance $F(A, B)$ is the minimum over all $1 - 1$ correspondences f between A and B of the maximum distance $d(a, f(a))$. For the distance $d(a, b)$ between two points, an L_p distance could be chosen. An alternative is to compute an approximation $\tilde{F}$ to the real bottleneck distance F. An approximate matching between A and B with $\tilde{F}$ the furthest matched pair, such that $F < \tilde{F} < (1 + \epsilon)F$, can be computed with a less complex algorithm [11].

So far we have considered only the computation problem, computing the distance between two point sets. The decision problem for translations, deciding whether there exists a translation ℓ such that $F(A + \ell, B) < \epsilon$ can also be solved, but takes considerably more time [11]. Because of the high degree in the computational complexity, it is interesting to look at approximations with a factor ϵ: $F(A + \ell, B) < (1 + \epsilon)F(A + \ell^*, T)$ [25], where ℓ^* is the optimal translation.

3.3   Hausdorff Distance

The Hausdorff distance is defined for general sets, not only finite point sets.

The *directed* Hausdorff distance $\vec{h}(A, B)$ is defined as the lowest upperbound (supremum) over all points in A of the distances to B: $\vec{h}(A, B) = \sup_{a \in A} \inf_{b \in B} d(a, b)$, with $d(a, b)$ the underlying distance, for example the Euclidean distance (L_2). The Hausdorff distance $H(A, B)$ is the maximum of $\vec{h}(A, B)$ and $\vec{h}(B, A)$: $H(A, B) = \max\{\vec{d}(A, B), \vec{d}(B, A)\}$. For finite point sets, it can be computed using Voronoi diagrams [1].

Given two finite point sets A and B, computing the translation ℓ^* that minimizes the Hausdorff distance $H(A + \ell, B)$ is discussed in [8] and [18]. Given a real value ϵ, deciding if there is a rigid motion m (translation plus rotation) such that $H(m(A), B) < \epsilon$ is discussed in [7]. Computing the optimal rigid motion, minimizing $H(m(A), B)$, is treated in [17], using dynamic Voronoi diagrams.

3.4   Partial Hausdorff Distance

The Hausdorff distance is very sensitive to noise: a single outlier can determine the distance value. For finite point sets, a similar measure that is not as sensitive is the partial Hausdorff distance. It discards the k largest distances, for a chosen k. The partial Hausdorff distance is not a metric since it fails the triangle inequality. Computing the optimal partial Hausdorff distance under translation and scaling is done in [19, 16] by means of a transformation space subdivision scheme. The running time depends on the depth of subdivision of transformation space.

3.5   p-th Order Mean Hausdorff Distance

For pattern matching, the Hausdorff metric is often too sensitive to noise. For finite point sets, the partial Hausdorff distance is not that sensitive, but it is no metric. Alternatively, [6] observes that the Hausdorff distance of $A, B \subset X$ can be written as $H(A, B) = \sup_{x \in X} |d(x, A) - d(x, B)|$, and replaces the supremum by an average: $\Delta^p(A, B) = (\frac{1}{|X|} \sum_{x \in X} |d(x, A) - d(x, B)|^p)^{1/p}$, where $d(x, A) = \inf_{a \in A} d(x, a)$. This is a metric less sensitive to noise. This measure can for example be used for comparing binary images, where X is the set of all raster points.

3.6   Turning Function Distance

The cumulative angle function, or turning function, $\Theta_A(s)$ of a polygon A gives the angle between the counterclockwise tangent and the x-axis as a function of the arc length s. $\Theta_A(s)$ keeps track of the turning that takes place, increasing with left hand turns, and decreasing with right hand turns. Clearly, this function is invariant under translation of the polyline. Rotating a polyline over an angle θ results in a vertical shift of the function with an amount θ.

In [4] the turning angle function is used to match polygons. First the size of the polygons are scaled so that they have equal perimeter. The L_p metric on function spaces, applied to Θ_A and Θ_B, gives a dissimilarity measure on A and B:
$d(A, B) = \left(\int |\Theta_A(s) - \Theta_B(s)|^p \, ds \right)^{1/p}$, see figure 4.

In [28], for the purpose of retrieving hieroglyphic shapes, polyline curves do not have the same length, so that partial matching can be performed. Partial matching under scaling, in addition to translation and rotation, is more involved [9].

3.7   Fréchet Distance

The Hausdorff distance is often not appropriate to measure the dissimilarity between curves. For all points on A, the distance to the closest point on B may be
small, but if we walk forward along curves A and B simultaneously, and measure
the distance between corresponding points, the maximum of these distances may
be larger, see Figure 5. This is what is called the Fréchet distance. More formerly,
let A and B be two parameterized curves $A(\alpha(t))$ and $B(\beta(t))$, and let their parameterizations α and β be continuous functions of the same parameter $t \in [0, 1]$,
such that $\alpha(0) = \beta(0) = 0$, and $\alpha(1) = \beta(1) = 1$. The Fréchet distance is the minimum over all monotone increasing parameterizations $\alpha(t)$ and $\beta(t)$ of the maximal
distance $d(A(\alpha(t)), B(\beta(t)))$, $t \in [0, 1]$, see figure 5.

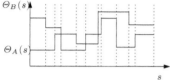

Fig. 4. Rectangles enclosed by $\Theta_A(s)$, $\Theta_B(s)$, and dotted lines are used for evaluation of dissimilarity.

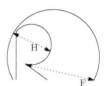

Fig. 5. Hausdorff (H) and Fréchet (F)
distance between two curves.

[3] considers the computation of the Fréchet distance for the special case of
polylines. A variation of the Fréchet distance is obtained by dropping the monotonicity condition of the parameterization. The resulting Fréchet distance $d(A, B)$
is a semimetric: zero distance need not mean that the objects are the same. Another variation is to consider partial matching: finding the part of one curve to
which the other has the smallest Fréchet distance.

Parameterized contours are curves where the starting point and ending point
are the same. However, the starting and ending point could as well lie somewhere
else on the contour, without changing the shape of the contour curve. For convex
contours, the Fréchet distance is equal to the Hausdorff distance.

3.8   Nonlinear elastic matching distance

Let $A = \{a_1, \dots, a_m\}$ and $B = \{b_1, \dots, b_n\}$ be two finite sets of ordered contour
points, and let f be a correspondence between all points in A and all points in
B such that there are no $a_1 < a_2$, with $f(a_1) > f(a_2)$. The stretch $s(a_i, b_j)$
of $(a_i, f(a_i) = b_j)$ is 1 if either $f(a_{i-1}) = b_j$ or $f(a_i) = b_{j-1}$, or 0 otherwise.
The nonlinear elastic matching distance $NEM(A, B)$ is the minimum over all
correspondences f of $\sum s(a_i, b_j) + d(a_i, b_j)$, with $d(a_i, b_j)$ the difference between
the tangent angles at a_i and b_j. It can be computed using dynamic programming
[10]. This measure is not a metric, since it does not obey the triangle inequality.

3.9   Relaxed Nonlinear elastic matching distance

The relaxed nonlinear elastic matching distance NEM_r is a variation of NEM,
where the stretch $s(a_i, b_j)$ of $(a_i, f(a_i) = b_j)$ is r (rather than 1) if either $f(a_{i-1}) =$

b_j or $f(a_i) = b_{j-1}$, or 0 otherwise, where $r \geq 1$ is a chosen constant. The resulting distance is not a metric, but it does obey the relaxed triangle inequality, property (6) above [12].

3.10 Reflection Distance

The *reflection metric* [15] is an affine-invariant metric that is defined on finite unions of curves in the plane. They are converted into real-valued functions on the plane. Then, these functions are compared using integration, resulting in a similarity measure for the corresponding patterns.

The functions are formed as follows, for each finite union of curves A. For each $x \in \mathbb{R}^2$, the *visibility star* V_A^x is defined as the union of open line segments connecting points of A that are visible from x: $V_A^x = \bigcup\{\overline{xa} \mid a \in A \text{ and } A \cap \overline{xa} = \varnothing\}$. The *reflection star* R_A^x is defined by intersecting V_A^x with its reflection in x: $R_A^x = \{x + v \in \mathbb{R}^2 \mid x - v \in V_A^x \text{ and } x + v \in V_A^x\}$. The function $\rho_A : \mathbb{R}^2 \to \mathbb{R}$ is the area of the reflection star in each point: $\rho_A(x) = \text{area}(R_A^x)$. Observe that for points x outside the convex hull of A, this area is always zero. The reflection metric between patterns A and B defines a normalized difference of the corresponding functions ρ_A and ρ_B:

$$d(A,B) = \frac{\int_{\mathbb{R}^2} |\rho_A(x) - \rho_B(x)| \, dx}{\int_{\mathbb{R}^2} \max(\rho_A(x), \rho_B(x)) \, dx}.$$

From the definition follows that the reflection metric is invariant under all affine transformations. In contrast with single-curve patterns, this metric is defined also for patterns consisting of multiple curves. In addition, the reflection metric is deformation, blur, crack, and noise robust.

3.11 Area of Overlap

Two dissimilarity measures that are based on the area of the polygons rather than their boundaries, are the area of overlap and the area of symmetric difference. For two compact sets A and B, the area of overlap is defined as $area(A \cap B)$. This dissimilarity measure is a not a metric, since the triangle inequality does not hold. The invariance group is the class of diffeomorphisms with unit Jacobi-determinant.

3.12 Area of Symmetric Difference, Template Metric

For two compact sets A and B, the area of symmetric difference is defined as $area((A - B) \cup (B - A))$. Unlike the area of overlap, this measure is a metric.

Translating convex polygons so that their centroids coincide also gives an approximate solution for the symmetric difference, which is at most $11/3$ of the optimal solution under translations [2]. This also holds for a set of transformations F other than translations, if the following holds: the centroid of A, $c(A)$, is equivariant under the transformations, i.e. $c(f(A)) = f(c(A))$ for all f in F, and F is closed under composition with translation.

3.13 Banach-Mazur Distance

For any two convex bodies A and B of the Euclidean plane, let $\lambda(A,B)$ be the smallest ratio s/r where $r, s > 0$ satisfy $rB' \subseteq A \subseteq sB''$, and B', B'' are some translates of B. Let $\tilde{B}$ denote class of bodies equivalent to B under translation and positive scaling (the homothets of B). The function $\tilde{\lambda}(\tilde{A}, \tilde{B}) = \log \lambda(\tilde{A}, \tilde{B})$ is a metric on shapes and is called the Banach-Mazur metric. It is invariant under affine transformations [13].

3.14   Monge-Kantorovich Metric, Transport Metric, Earth Mover's Distance

Given two patterns $A = \{(A_1, w(A_1)), \dots, (A_m, w(A_m))\}$ and $B = \{(B_1, w(B_1)), \dots, (B_n, w(B_n))\}$, where A_i and B_i are subsets of $\mathbb{R}^2$, with associates weights $w(A_i), w(B_i)$. The distance between A and B is the minimum amount of work needed to transform A into B. This is a form of the Monge-Kantorovich metric used in heat transform problems [22], which is also used in shape matching [14] and color-based image retrieval [23]. The discrete version can be computed by linear programming.

4   Constructions

In this section we discuss a number of constructions that can be used to manipulate similarity measures, in order to arrive at certain properties.

4.1   Remapping

Let $w : [0, \infty] \to [0, \infty]$ be a continuous function with $w(x) = 0$ iff $x = 0$, and which is concave: $w(x + y) \leq w(x) + w(y)$. Examples include $x/(1+x)$, $\tan^{-1}(x)$, $\log(x)$, $x^{1/p}$, for some $p \geq 1$, and $\min(x, c)$, for some positive constant c. If $d(A, B)$ is a metric, then so is $\tilde{d}(A, B) = w(d(A, B))$. In this way, an unbounded metric d can be mapped to a bounded metric. For the cut-off function $\min(x, c)$, the maximum distance value becomes c, so that property (14) above does not hold. It is used in [6] for comparing binary images. The $\log(x)$ function is used in the Banach-Mazur distance $\log \lambda(\tilde{A}, \tilde{B})$. Without the log it would not satisfy the triangle inequality, and therefore not be a metric.

4.2   Normalization

Normalization is often used to scale the range of values to $[0, 1]$, but it can also change other properties. For example, normalizing the area of overlap and symmetric difference by the area of the union of the two polygons makes it invariant under a larger transformation group, namely the group of all diffeomorphisms with a Jacobi determinant that is constant over all points [15].

4.3   From Semi-metric to Metric

Let S be a space of objects, and d a semimetric. Identifying elements A, B of S with $d(A, B) = 0$, and considering these as a single object yields another space S'. The semimetric on S is then a metric on S'.

4.4   Semi-metric on Orbits

A collection of patterns S and a transformation group G determine a family of equivalence classes S/G. For a pattern $A \in S$, the orbit is $G(A) = \{g(A) \mid g \in G\}$. The collection of all these orbits forms a space of equivalences classes. A semimetric d invariant under a transformation group G results in a natural semimetric on the orbit set: $\tilde{d} : S/G \times S/G \to \mathbb{R}$ defined by $\tilde{d}(G(A), G(B)) = \inf\{d(g(A), B) \mid g \in G\}$ is a semimetric on the space S/G. Rucklidge [24] used this principle to define a shape distance based on the Hausdorff distance.

4.5   Extension with empty set

A pattern space S not containing the empty set $\varnothing$, with metric d, can be extended with $\varnothing$, by defining $d'(A, B) = d(A, B)/(1 + d(A, B))$, $d'(\varnothing, \varnothing) = 0$, and $d'(A, \varnothing) = 1$ for $A, B \in S$. This gives a bounded metric pattern space such that the restriction of d' to S is topologically equivalent to d. In addition, the invariance group remains the same.

4.6   Vantageing

Let d be some distance function on a space S of patterns, $d : S \times S \to \mathbb{R}$. For some fixed $C \in S$ (vantage object), the function $\bar{d}_C(A, B) = |d(A, C) - d(B, C)|$ is a semimetric, even if d does not obey nonnegativity, identity, weak triangle inequality, and symmetry.

4.7   Imbedding patterns

Affine invariant pattern metrics can be formed by mapping patterns to real-valued functions and computing a normalized difference between these functions. Affine invariance is desired in many pattern matching and shape recognition tasks.

Let $\mathbf{I}(\mathbb{R}^2)$ be the space of real-valued integrable functions on $\mathbb{R}^2$. Define the L^1 seminorm on $\mathbf{I}(\mathbb{R}^2)$: $|\mathbf{a}| = \int_{\mathbb{R}^2} |\mathbf{a}(x)| \, dx$. For a diffeomorphism g the Jacobi-determinant is the determinant of the derivative of g at a given point. We use $j_g(x)$ to denote the absolute value of the Jacobi-determinant of g in x. For real-valued functions $\mathbf{a}, \mathbf{b} : \mathbb{R}^2 \to \mathbb{R}$, $\mathbf{a} \sqcup \mathbf{b}$ denotes the pointwise maximum. Define the *normalized difference* of two functions with non-zero integrals by $\sigma_n(\mathbf{a}, \mathbf{b}) = |\mathbf{a} - \mathbf{b}|/|\mathbf{a} \sqcup \mathbf{b}|$. This is a semimetric on the set of non-negative functions with non-zero integrals.

A large class of mappings from patterns in $\mathbb{R}^2$ to integrable functions result in invariant semimetrics based on the normalized difference σ_n. Namely, let S be a collection of subsets of $\mathbb{R}^2$. Let each $A \in S$ define a unique function $\mathbf{n}_A : \mathbb{R}^2 \to \mathbb{R}$ in $\mathbf{I}(\mathbb{R}^2)$, and let g be a diffeomorphism with constant Jacobi-determinant. If g determines a number $\delta > 0$ such that $\mathbf{n}_{g(A)}(g(x)) = \delta \mathbf{n}_A(x)$ for all $A \in S$ and $x \in \mathbb{R}^2$, then $\sigma_n(\mathbf{n}_{g(A)}, \mathbf{n}_{g(B)}) = \sigma_n(\mathbf{n}_A, \mathbf{n}_B)$ for all $A, B \in S$ [15]. This was used in the construction of the reflection metric.

References

1. H. Alt, B. Behrends, and J. Blömer. Approximate matching of polygonal shapes. *Annals of Mathematics and Artificial Intelligence*, pages 251–265, 1995.
2. H. Alt, U. Fuchs, G. Rote, and G. Weber. Matching convex shapes with respect to the symmetric difference. In *Proc. ESA*, pages 320–333. LNCS 1136, Springer, 1996.
3. H. Alt and M. Godeau. Computing the Fréchet distance between two polygonal curves. *International Journal of Computational Geometry & Applications*, pages 75–91, 1995.
4. E. Arkin, P. Chew, D. Huttenlocher, K. Kedem, and J. Mitchel. An efficiently computable metric for comparing polygonal shapes. *IEEE Transactions on Pattern Analysis and Machine Intelligence*, 13(3):209–215, 1991.
5. Alta Vista Photo Finder, http://image.altavista.com/cgi-bin/avncgi.
6. A. J. Baddeley. An error metric for binary images. In *Robust Computer Vision: Quality of Vision Algorithms, Proc. of the Int. Workshop on Robust Computer Vision, Bonn, 1992*, pages 59–78. Wichmann, 1992.

7. L. P. Chew, M. T. Goodrich, D. P. Huttenlocher, K. Kedem, J. M. Kleinberg, and D. Kravets. Geometric pattern matching under Euclidean motion. *Computational Geometry, Theory and Applications*, 7:113–124, 1997.

8. P. Chew and K. Kedem. Improvements on approximate pattern matching. In *3rd Scandinav. Workshop Algorithm Theory*, LNCS 621, pages 318–325. Springer, 1992.

9. S. D. Cohen and L. J. Guibas. Partial matching of planar polylines under similarity transformations. In *Proc. SODA*, pages 777–786, 1997.

10. G. Cortelazzo, G. A. Mian, G. Vezzi, and P. Zamperoni. Trademark shapes description by string-matching techniques. *Pattern Recognition*, 27:1005–1018, 1994.

11. A. Efrat and A. Itai. Improvements on bottleneck matching and related problems using geometry. *Proc. SoCG*, pages 301–310, 1996.

12. R. Fagin and L. Stockmeyer. Relaxing the triangle inequality in pattern matching. *Int. Journal of Computer Vision*, 28(3):219–231, 1998.

13. R. Fleischer, K. Mehlhorn, G. Rote, E. Welzl, and C. Yap. Simultaneous inner and outer approximation of shapes. *Algorithmica*, 8:365–389, 1992.

14. D. Fry. *Shape Recognition using Metrics on the Space of Shapes*. PhD thesis, Harvard University, Department of Mathematics, 1993.

15. M. Hagedoorn and R. C. Veltkamp. Metric pattern spaces. Technical Report UU-CS-1999-03, Utrecht University, 1999.

16. M. Hagedoorn and R. C. Veltkamp. Reliable and efficient pattern matching using an affine invariant metric. *Int. Journal of Computer Vision*, 31(2/3):203–225, 1999.

17. D. P. Huttenlocher, K. Kedem, and J. M. Kleinberg. On dynamic Voronoi diagrams and the minimum Hausdorff distance for point sets under Euclidean motion in the plane. In *Proc. SoCG*, pages 110–120, 1992.

18. D. P. Huttenlocher, K. Kedem, and M. Sharir. The upper envelope of Voronoi surfaces and its applications. *Discrete and Comp. Geometry*, 9:267–291, 1993.

19. D. P. Huttenlocher, G. A. Klanderman, and W. J. Rucklidge. Comparing images using the hausdorff distance. *IEEE Transactions on Pattern Analysis and Machinen Intelligence*, 15:850–863, 1993.

20. Plato. *Meno*. Perseus Encyclopedia, Tuft University, http://www.perseus.tufts.edu/Texts/chunk_TOC.grk.html#Plato, 380 B.C.

21. QBIC project, http://wwwqbic.almaden.ibm.com/.

22. S. Rachev. The Monge-Kantorovich mass transference problem and its stochastical applications. *Theory of Probability and Applications*, 29:647–676, 1985.

23. Y. Rubner, C. Tomassi, and L Guibas. A metric for distributions with applications to image databases. In *Proc. of the IEEE Int. Conf. on Comp. Vision, Bombay, India*, pages 59–66, 1998.

24. W. Rucklidge. *Efficient Visual Recognition Using the Hausdorff Distance*. LNCS. Springer, 1996.

25. S. Schirra. Approximate decision algorithms for approximate congruence. *Information Processing Letters*, 43:29–34, 1992.

26. L. Schomaker, E. de Leau, and L. Vuurpijl. Using pen-based outlines for object-based annotation and image-based queries. In *Visual Information and Information Systems*, LNCS 1614, pages 585–592. Springer, 1999.

27. A. Tversky. Features of similarity. *Psychological Review*, 84(4):327–352, 1977.

28. J. Vleugels and R. C. Veltkamp. Efficient image retrieval through vantage objects. In *Visual Information and Information Systems*, LNCS 1614, pages 575–584. Springer, 1999.

Leaf Image Retrieval with Shape Features

Zhiyong Wang, Zheru Chi, Dagan Feng and Qing Wang

Center for Multimedia Signal Processing
Department of Electronic and Information Engineering
The Hong Kong Polytechnic University
Hung Hom, Kowloon, Hong Kong
Email Address: enzheru@polyu.edu.hk
Tel: (852)2766 6219 Fax: (852)2362 8439

Abstract. *In this paper we present an efficient two-step approach of using a shape characterization function called centroid-contour distance curve and the object eccentricity (or elongation) for leaf image retrieval. Both the centroid-contour distance curve and the eccentricity of a leaf image are scale, rotation, and translation invariant after proper normalizations. In the frist step, the eccentricity is used to rank leaf images, and the top scored images are further ranked using the centroid-contour distance curve together with the eccentricity in the second step. A thinning-based method is used to locate start point(s) for reducing the matching time. Experimental results show that our approach can achieve good performance with a reasonable computational complexity.*

Keywords: Centroid-contour distance, Shape representation, Content-based image retrieval, Leaf image processing.

1 Introduction

Plant identification is a process resulting in the assignment of each individual plant to a descending series of groups of related plants, as judged by common characteristics. So far, this time-consuming process has mainly been carried out by botanists. Plant identification has had a very long history, from the dawn of human existence. Currently, automatic (machine) plant recognition from color images is one of most difficult tasks in computer vision due to (1) lack of proper models or representations; (2) a great number of biological variations that a species of plants can take; (3) imprecise image preprocessing techniques such as edge detection and contour extraction, thus resulting in possible missing features.

Since the shape of leaves is one of important features for charactizing various plants, the study of leaf image retrieval will be an important step for plant identification. In this paper, leaf image retrieval based on shape features is be addressed. In particular, we discuss two issues, shape feature extraction and shape feature matching. A number of shape representations such as chain codes, Fourier descriptors, moment invariants, and deformable templates [1, 2] as well as various matching strategies [3] have been proposed for shape-based image retrieval. There have been some successful applications reported [4–9]. In this paper, we first present a leaf shape representation with a centroid-contour distance

R. Laurini (Ed.): VISUAL 2000, LNCS 1929, pp. 477–487, 2000.
Springer-Verlag Berlin Heidelberg 2000

curve. It will be demonstrated that the representation can be scale, rotation and translation invariant after proper normalizations. Particularly, a thinning-based method is adopted to locate the start point(s) for reducing the computation time in image retrieval. In order to further reduce the retrieval time, we then propose a two-step approach which uses both the centroid-contour distance curve and the eccentricity of the leaf object for shape-based leaf image retrieval.

In Section 2, we define the centroi-contour distance curve and explain its invariant properties. A similarity measure with the distance curve is also discussed in the section. A leaf image retrieval scheme based on the eccentricity and centroid-contour distance curve is presented in Section 3. Experimental results and discussions are given in Section 4. Finally, concluding remarks are drawn in Section 5.

2   Center-Contour Distance Curve

2.1   Motivation

Tracing the leaf contour can be considered as circling around its centroid. The trace path from fixed start point represents a shape contour uniquely, that is to say, a contour point sequence corresponds to a shape uniquely if the start point is fixed. This is the basic idea for chain code representation of shape. As Figure 1 shows, a point P on the contour is determined by the centroid C, the distance R between the point P and the centroid C, and the angle α . In fact, it is not necessary that the object centroid has to be fixed in a coordinate system since the change of object centroid only leads to the translation of the object. The shape reconstruction can also be independent of the angle α given the fixed start point. Therefore, for the same start point, the object contour can be resonstructed with the centroid-contour distance curve. The distance between the object centroid and a contour point is termed as the centroid-contour distance. The contour can be represented by one dimensional curve, the centroid-contour distance curve.

2.2   Properties of Center-Contour Distance Curve

Generally, the properties of scale, translation and rotation invariance are expected for the shape feature based image retrieval. After some normalization, we can achieve these invariant properties with the centroid-contour distance curve.

Translation Invariant Property

The contour shape of an object is fully determined by the centroid-contour distance function and is nothing to do with the coordinates of the centroid position. Therefore, the distance curve is translation invariant. This is elaborated as follows. As shown in Figure 1,

$$|CP| = \sqrt{(x_C - x_P)^2 + (y_C - y_P)^2} \tag{1}$$

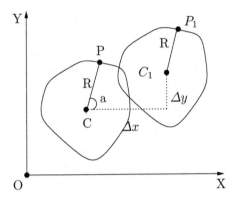

Fig. 1. Illustration of translation invariant property of the centroid-contour distance curve.

where (x_C, y_C) and (x_P, y_P) are the coordinates of points C and P respectively. And the object centroid (x_C, y_C) is defined as follows.

$$m_{pq} = \int\int_R x^p y^q dxdy, \quad x_C = \frac{m_{10}}{m_{00}}, \quad y_C = \frac{m_{01}}{m_{00}} \tag{2}$$

If the object is traslated by increasements Δx and Δy along x-axis and y-axis, repectively. The point P on the object contour is moved to point P_1 with its coordinates being $(x_P + \Delta x, y_P + \Delta y)$. According to Equation 2,

$$x_{C_1} = \frac{m_{10}^1}{m_{00}^1} = \frac{\int\int_{R^1} xdxdy}{\int\int_{R^1} dxdy} = \frac{\int\int_R (x + \Delta x)dxdy}{\int\int_R dxdy}$$

$$= \frac{\int\int_R xdxdy}{\int\int_R dxdy} + \frac{\int\int_R (\Delta x)dxdy}{\int\int_R dxdy} = x_C + \Delta x \tag{3}$$

where R^1 is the region of the new positioned object.

Similarly, $y_{C_1} = y_C + \Delta y$, that is, the new centroid point C_1 of the object is $(x_C + \Delta x, y_C + \Delta y)$. Obviously,

$$|C_1 P_1| = \sqrt{(x_{C_1} - x_{P_1})^2 + (y_{C_1} - y_{P_1})^2}$$

$$= \sqrt{(x_C - x_P)^2 + (y_C - y_P)^2}$$

$$= |CP| \tag{4}$$

The above equations show that the translation invariant property of the centroid-contour distance curve.

Scale Invariant Property

Let us consider a circle first. The centroid-contour distance of a circle object is a constant. For a larger circle, its distance is a larger constant and there are

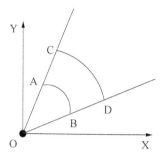

Fig. 2. Illustration of the scale invariant property of the centroid-contour distance curve.

more points on the contour. To make a matching possible, we should reduce the number of points on the contour of the larger object by down sampling. Figure 2 illustrate the situation that the arc AB of contour S_1 is scaled to arc CD of contour S_2 without any other change. We assume that $|OA| = s|OC|$, $|OB| = s|OD|$. For any point A on contour S_1, a correspondent point C can be found on contour S_2. In other words, we can represent shape S_2 with the same sample points of the shape S_1. The only difference is the distance. It is noticed that $|OA| = s|OC|$, $|OB| = s|OD|$. If the distance is normalized, the scale factor s will not exist any more. Therefore, the centroid distance curve of the scaled object contour S_2 is the same as that of the original object contour S_1 with sampling and normalizing processing. In our experiments, the centroid-contour distance is normalized to range $[0, 1]$.

As Figure 3 shows, with proper sampling and normalizing operations, the centroid-contour distancue curve is scale invariant.

Rotation Invariant Property

Rotation may be introduced in data acquisition such as picture grapping by a camera or scanner. If a shape feature is sensitve to the rotation, the same leaf rotated to an angle will not be retrieved with that shape feature, which is not desirable. As shown in Figure 4, an object contour with m points is rotated one pixel clockwisely. If the object contour is traced with the start position α, the centroid-contour distance sequences will be $(|OP_1|, |OP_2|, \ldots, |OP_m|)$ and $(|OP_m|, |OP_1|, |OP_2|, \ldots, |OP_{m-1}|)$ for the contour on the left and that on the right respectively. It is noticed that the only difference between the two sequences is the sequence of contour points. If the latter sequence is shift left one item wrappedly, the two sequences will be the same. Generally, for an arbitary rotation, we need to shift the sequence n items wrappedly. That is to say, the centroid-contour distance curve is rotation invariant after being shift n items wrappedly.

At the first sight of the Figure 5(b), the rotation invariant property is not be discovered, because it is not the same as Figure 3(d) at all. It is not difficult to find that the different start points cause the problem. This problem can be solved by shifting the curve wrappedly. As Figure 5 The centroid-contour distance curve

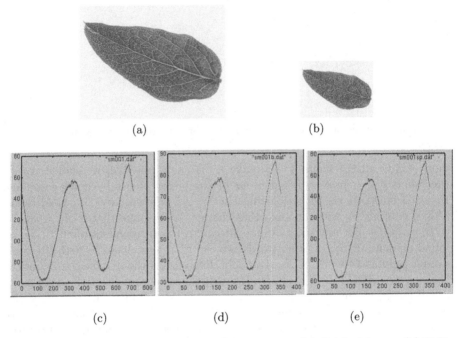

(a)   (b)

(c)   (d)   (e)

Fig. 3. Scale invariant property of center distance curve. (a) Original image; (b) Half-size image; (c) Centroid-contour distance curve for original image; (d) Centroid-contour distance curve for half size image; (e) Sampled center distance curve of original image.

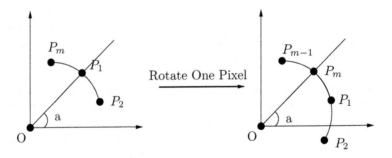

Fig. 4. Illustration of rotation invariant property of the centroid-contour distance curve.

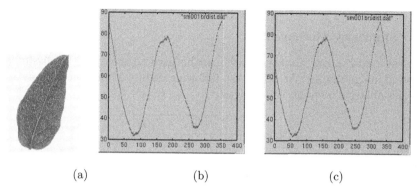

(a)   (b)   (c)

Fig. 5. Rotation invariant property of centroid-contour distance curve. (a) Rotated image; (b) Centroid-contour distance curve of rotated image; (c) Wrappedly shifted centroid-contour distance curve of rotated image.

shown in Figure 5(c) is generated by shifting that in Figure 5(b) 24 points to the left. The resulting curve is similar to that shown in Figure 3(d). Fourier transformation or correlation can be sued to locate the start point, however it is also computationally costly [3, 6]. A thinning-based start point(s) locating method is proposed to reduce the computation. First the binarized leaf image is thinned to obtain its skeleton. Several end-points are then located on the skeleton. The closest point for each end-point on the leaf contour is a possible start point. As shown in Figure 6, points A, B, C and D are the end-points, and points A_1, B_1, C_1 and D_1 are their closest points on the contour, repectively. Therefore, the distance curve is only needed to shift to those closest points during the matching process, which will reduce the computation greatly. Because of the quantization error, some neighbour points of the closest points will also be considered(5 neighbor points will be considered in our experiments).

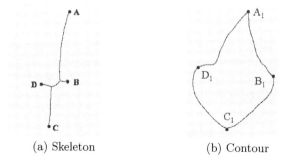

(a) Skeleton   (b) Contour

Fig. 6. Illustration of the thinning-based start point(s) locating method.

2.3   Similarity Measurement

The centroid-contour distance curve can be used to measure the dissimilarity between image shapes. We define the following distance function D to mearsure the dissimilarity between two images :

$$D = \sqrt{\frac{\sum_{i=1}^{n} |f_1(i) - f_2(i)|}{n}} \tag{5}$$

where $f_1(i)$ and $f_2(i)$ are the centroid-contour distances of the i-th point of two object contours, and n is the number of the sample points on the centroid-contour distance curve.

Rotation invariance is only true when we shift one of the curves by a number of points. In order to find the best matching result, we have to shift one curve n times, where n is the number of possible start points. The minimal distance D_{min} is recorded. We define the dissimilarity D_c between two object contours as

$$D_c = min\{D_1, ..., D_j, ..., D_n\}$$

where D_j is the distance between two object contours when one of the contours is shift by j points.

3   Leaf Image Retrieval with Feature Combination

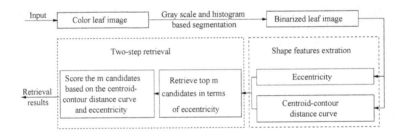

Fig. 7. Block diagram of our two-step leaf image retrieval approach.

In order to make leaf image retrieval more efficient, a computationally-simple feature is used to select top candidates first. We propose to use another shape parameter, the eccentricity of an object, for the first-stage leaf image retrieval. Eccentricity is defined with moments as [1]

$$e_I = \frac{(u_{20} - u_{02})^2 + 4u_{11}}{A}$$

$$u_{pq} = \int \int_R (x - x_C)^p (y - y_C)^q dx dy \tag{6}$$

where R is the whole region of an object and A is its area. and (x_C, y_C) is the object centroid which is the same as that used in computing the centroid-contour distance(Equation 2). It is easy to verify that the eccentricity is translation, scale and rotation invariant. The eccentricity dissimilarity D_e between two leaf images I and J is defined as

$$D_e(I, J) = |e_I - e_J| \tag{7}$$

The smaller D_e is, the more similar the leaf images I and J are.

Leaf shape is regular in some way. For example, for rough classification leaves can be classified into fat and round or thin and long type without considering the details of their contour (sawtooth or not). Eccentricity could be a good feature for the first-stage leaf image retrieval.

For the second-stage leaf image retrieval, the combination of two features, the eccentricity and centroid-contour distance curve, will be used to score the retrieved leaf images:

$$D_s(I, J) = \frac{w_1 D_e(I, J) + w_2 D_c(I, J)}{w_1 + w_2} \tag{8}$$

where I and J denotes two leaf images, and D_e and D_c are the distance measures with two features. w_1 and w_2 are used to weigh the relative importance of two features,which are determined by simulation tests.

Figure 7 shows the flow chart of our approach. In terms of the eccentricity measure, the top scored M images are retrieved from the image database. From these M images, the top scored N ($N < M$) images are selected based on $D_s(I, J)$ defined in Equation 8. In order to reduce search time furtherly, images in the database can be indexed with the eccentricity values of the images. When a query is submitted, the leaf image with the closest eccentricity value can be found with a fast search algorithm such as the half search algorithm. The top M leaf images with close eccentricity values can be easily found nearby. Since eccentricity is one dimensional feature, a multi-dimensional k-nearest search algorithm, such as the k-d tree approach [10], is not necessary.

4   Experimental Results and Discussion

In our experiments, two data set are used to test our approach. Data set 1 contains 135 320 × 240 color leaf images that seldomly come from the same plant. Data set 2 containing 233 color leaf images in arbitary sizes with about 10 samples collected from each plant. From Table 1 we can see that the thinning-based start point(s) locating method has reduced the shift-and-matching times greatly.

When a query request is submitted, the two-setp retrieval approach is performed. In the experiments, the top 30 closest images will be returned in the first step.

Figure 8 shows retrieval results for a query performed on the data set 1.The retrieved images are circularly except that the boundary of image Figure 8(f) are round. This result indicates that the features pay more attention to the global shape information. Another retrieval example performed on the data set 2 is

Table 1. Comparison of the average numbers of shift-and-matching operations.

	Contour points	Closest points
Data Set 1	806.0	5.4
Data Set 2	525.6	2.9

(a)

(b) 0.2128   (c) 0.2191   (d) 0.2282   (e) 0.2393   (f) 0.2592   (g) 0.2639

Fig. 8. A retrieval example for a sawtooth contour shape in the data set 1. (a) Query image; (b)-(g) Top 6 retrieved images with their D_s values.

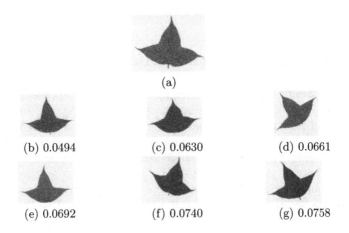

(a)

(b) 0.0494   (c) 0.0630   (d) 0.0661

(e) 0.0692   (f) 0.0740   (g) 0.0758

Fig. 9. A retrieval example for leaf image with stiff corners with the data set 2. (a) Query image; (b)-(g) Top 6 retrieved images with their D_s values.

shown in Figure 9. We can find the top six images are with the same plant. In these experiments, we set $w_1 = 0.4$, $w_2 = 0.6$ emperically.

These examples show that our approach can achieve retrieval results that are similar to the results from human visual perception. Table 2 shows the retrieval time for the above two examples when the exhaust search and our two-step search scheme are used. Our experiments are carried out on a Pentium 333 HZ PC. It is found that the two-step retrieval scheme can reduce the retrieval time significantly. The experimental results show that our approach is computationally more efficient.

Table 2. Comparison of retrieval time.

	Exhaust search (Sec.)	Two-step search (Sec.)
Example 1	13.32	2.82
Example 2	13.14	3.73

5   Conclusion

In this paper we present an efficient two-step leaf image retrieval scheme of using two shape features, the centroid-contour distance curve and eccentricity. It is shown that both features are scale, rotation, and translation invariant after proper normalizations. Our approach has been tested on two data sets with 135 and 233 leaf images respectively with good results. Compared with the exhaust search, our two-step approach is computationally more efficient. In addition, the identification of start point(s) using the skeleton of a leaf image reduces the matching time in image retrieval to a great extent. Since the proposed feature in this paper pay much attention to the global shape information, some local features will be adopted in our future work in order to improve the retrieval results.

Acknowledgment

The work described in this paper was substantially supported by a grant from the Hong Kong Polytechnic University (Project No. G-V780).

References

1. A. K. Jain. *Fundamentals of Digital Image Processing*. Prentice Hall, London, UK, 1989.

2. BV. M. Mehtre, M. S. Kankanhalli, and W. F. Lee. Shape measures for content based image retrieval: a comparison. *Information Processing & Management*, 33(3), 1997.
3. Xianfeng Ding, Weixing Kong, Changbo Hu, and Songde Ma. Image retrieval using schwarz representation of one-dimensional feature. In *Visual Information and Information Systems*, pages 443–450, Amsterdam, The Netherlands, June 1999.
4. C.W. Richard and H. Hemami. Identification of three-dimensional objects using Fourier descriptors of the boundary curve. *IEEE TRANS. on Systems, Man and Cybernetics*, SMC-4(4), July 1974.
5. S. A. Dudani, K. J. Breeding, and R. B. McGhee. Aicraft identification by moment invariants. *IEEE TRANS. on Computers*, C-26(1), Jan. 1977.
6. E. Persoon and K. S. Fu. Shape discrimination using Fourier description. *IEEE TRANS. on Systems, Man And Cybernetics*, SMC-7(3), Mar. 1977.
7. C. Chen. Improved moment invariants for shape discrimination. *Pattern Recognition*, 26(5), 1993.
8. A.K. Jain and A. Vailaya. Image retrieval using color and shape. *Pattern Recognition*, 29(8), 1996.
9. A.K. Jain and A. Vailaya. Shape-based retrieval:a case study with trademark image database. *Pattern Recognition*, 31(9), 1998.
10. R. Egas, N. Huijsmans, M. Lew, and N. Sebe. Adapting k-d trees to visual retrieval. In *Visual Information and Information Systems*, pages 533–540, Amsterdam, The Netherlands, June 1999.

A Software Framework for Combining Iconic and Semantic Content for Retrieval of Histological Images

Kent K. T. Cheung[1], Ringo W. K. Lam[1], Horace H. S. Ip[1],

Lilian H. Y. Tang[2] and Rudolf Hanka[2]

[1]City University of Hong Kong, Tat Chee Avenue, Kowloon Tong, Hong Kong
ktcheung@cs.cityu.edu.hk
[2]Medical Informatics Unit, Medical School, University of Cambridge, United Kingdom

Abstract. Content-based Image Retrieval (CBIR) is becoming an important component of a database system as it allows retrieval of images by objective measures such as color and texture. Nevertheless, retrieval of images intelligently by computer is still not common. In addition, different users might have different requirements so we need to address their needs by providing a more flexible retrieval mechanism. Finally, we might want to add CBIR functionality to existing system but none of the existing techniques is able to do this easily because they usually rely on one single environment. In this paper, we describe the design of a histological image retrieval system (I-Browse) that addresses the above three issues.

1. Introduction

Content-based Image Retrieval (CBIR) is becoming an important component of a database system as it allows retrieval of images by objective measures such as color and texture. In a typical CBIR system, an image to be stored in the database is usually processed to extract important features from it. The features can then be stored along with the image and other traditional data. On retrieval, an example image will be presented. The features of the example image will be extracted and then used to compare with those that are stored in the database to retrieval the most similar images. Retrieved images are usually ranked by a similarity function. An optional index structure might be present to index to the probable images before the similarity function is applied to rank the images for retrieval. A conceptual architecture was presented in [1].

There have been many techniques to extract salient features from an image. Color [2-5], shape [6-11], texture [12-13] and spatial relationships [14-18] are some examples of the techniques. In addition, some of the features might be combined to improve the retrieval results [1,19-21].

Despite the recent developments of CBIR techniques, CBIR systems usually suffer from the following weaknesses:

1. Only iconic image features are supported. Intelligent retrieval is not possible because image semantic is not included into the image features.

R. Laurini (Ed.): VISUAL 2000, LNCS 1929, pp. 488-499, 2000.
© Springer-Verlag Berlin Heidelberg 2000

2. Only one mode of retrieval is supported, i.e., only one kind of or even no index scheme and one similarity function is supported. However, different users may have different requirements. A flexible design to allow indexing and similarity schemes to be added is highly desirable.

3. Existing database cannot be adapted. There have been many image databases already existed. The ability to adapt such databases is very useful to provide CBIR to legacy image databases but current approaches usually enforce a single DBMS [19] which might not be the same as the existing database.

In this paper, we outline the design of a histological image retrieval system (I-Browse) that takes the above three issues into account. Item 1 is made possible by the framework architecture in [22-23]. I-Browse makes use of a framework (*CBIRFrame*) proposed in [24] to tackle items 2 and 3 above. Note that this paper focuses on the software design that tackles the above three general issues of CBIR systems. Please refer to [25] for the theory concerning histological image features and the similarity measurements.

Histological images are hard to tackle due to their high variability. Therefore, there are relatively few systems on this area. One system [30] is being developed by Pittsburgh Supercomputing Center of Carnegie Mellon University. However, not much information is disclosed in [30]. Aside from [30], there is not well known system that focuses on histological image retrieval.

There are retrieval systems for other kinds of medical images. In [31], KL Transform is used to extract the features of tomographic images. A shape retrieval technique is applied for tumor images in [32]. Both [31] and [32] operate on global shapes of the images. Shyu et al. [33] argues that global characterization is not enough for pathology bearing regions (PBR) images. An interface is built for the physician to delineate PBR regions for segmentation. In all these systems, no attempt is made to employ domain knowledge for an intelligent indexing and retrieval. In addition, only one mode of similarity or indexing is implemented. Therefore, flexible retrieval by different aspects is not possible.

In section 2, we describe the motivations of I-Browse and its important features. Section 3 gives a brief introduction to *CBIRFrame*. The system design of I-Browse is considered in section 4. Finally, the paper concludes in section 5.

2. The I-Browse Architecture

I-Browse is targeted to support *intelligent indexing and browsing of histological images based on iconic and semantic content*. In I-Browse, we try to capture the semantics as well as low level image features for indexing. As image semantics have been captured, intelligent retrieval is possible.

The conceptual architecture (Fig. 1) of I-Browse has been presented [22-23]. Disparate but complementary techniques are combined in the I-Browse architecture. Under the supervision of the semantic analyser, a number of visual feature detectors will be used to extract the necessary primitive features such as shape, texture, layout etc. from the input or query images. These feature detectors together form the visual feature detector. The extracted image features will be passed to a hypothesis generator together with some measure of certainty, which tell how likely the measurements represent specific histological meanings.

The hypothesis generator, with the help of a knowledge base (KB0) and a suitable reasoning mechanism, a set of hypotheses will be generated and sent to the semantic analyser. The semantic analyser will confirm or refute the hypotheses with another knowledge base (KB1) and generate high level descriptions for the images. In addition, it will produce feedback to the visual feature detector about which features need to be further confirmed by what kinds of specific feature detectors. After several iterations between visual feature detector and semantic analyser, we can further classify the images according to certain criteria such as the function organs or disease patterns etc. via a pattern classifier by the output of the semantic analyser.

We store the semantics of an image in an intermediate semantic representation structure called *Papillon* [26]. By comparing the structure generated for a query image and a stored image, we can assess the similarity of semantics of the images.

In addition, we also derive three similarity functions for comparing the iconic features. These functions are useful because sometimes we might be more interested in the image shapes and colors rather than the semantics. *CBIRFrame* has good support for choosing a similarity function at runtime to suit for different requirements of users.

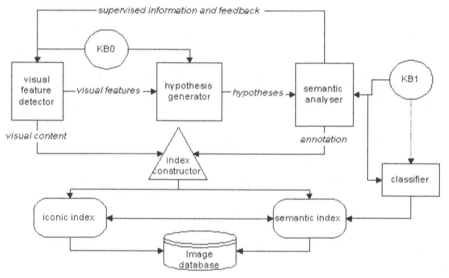

Fig. 1. I-Browse Conceptual Architecture

To allow faster retrieval, we index the database based on the keywords generated from the *Papillon* structure. Indexing then become the problem of searching text from a database, which can be done by a standard SQL statement. Similar to the case of similarity functions, the user might wish to search by iconic features and therefore disable this indexing feature at runtime. In section 4, we shall discuss the design of I-Browse to support these features.

3. A Framework for CBIR

Fig. 2 shows the 5-tier architecture in this framework. In this architecture, the domain component (DC) constitutes the modules for image feature extraction, and image construction from an image file, etc. It represents the knowledge within the domain, i.e., histological image features in I-Browse. The user interface component (UIC) includes all modules for manipulating user interface objects. The data management component (DMC) is the modules that interact with the DBMS.

Employing the Presentation and Application Logic pattern [27], we add a UI facade between the UIC and DC. Similarly, the use of the Database Interaction pattern [27] calls for the DM Facade between the DC and DMC. This architecture allows us to replace any single tier with little or no effect on other tiers of a CBIR system. We can thus achieve the independence of DBMS, running environment with the domain classes.

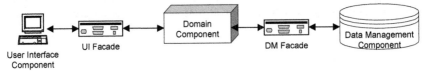

User Interface
Component

UI Facade

DM Facade

Data Management
Component

Fig. 2. 5-tier architecture

The independence among the tiers is important in several aspects. One of the advantages is that the DM Facade shields the DBMS from the rest of the system. We can thus provide a simplified view of the database(s) for the domain objects to adapt the system to run on top of existing databases by providing the database transparency within the DM Facade.

Another useful feature of the framework is that the domain objects are shielded from the user interface objects. We can then develop the user interface independently. In fact, some of our team members are good in developing image features while some are good for user interface. We can develop the modules independently and then integrate them with little effort. In addition, this flexibility allows different interfaces to be built for different applications based on the same CBIR engine. I-Browse has three different interfaces. This is discussed in section 4.3.

CBIRFrame defines a few classes such as Image, Feature and Content for a general framework of representing image and visual features in a typical CBIR system. For details on the design of *CBIRFrame*, please refer to [23].

4. System Design

In this section, we shall discuss the design of the middle three tiers in details. We shall not discuss the User Interface Component and the Data Management Component due to their relative simplicity.

Our notations are based on UML [28]. Also note that our classes are mostly derived subclasses of the classes defined in *CBIRFrame*. To save space and enhance clarity, we do not show these relationships in our object models.

4.1 Domain Component

I-Browse consists of a number of modules (objects) that are responsible for the user interface, image feature detection, semantic analyser based on an initial coarse classification of the image, then a number of fine feature detectors invoked by the semantic analyser for the final image classification. The following shows how these objects are related to one another. Fig. 3 shows the object model of the Domain Component, the UI Facade and the UI Component layers. The *Features class that associates with IBrowseContent represents a group of subclasses of Feature, which is a virtual class defined in *CBIRFrame*.

IBrowseImage is inherited from the CBIRFrame class Image that represents an image in the system. In the UI Facade, IbrowseImageFacade and IbrowseContentFacade are created to forward requests from the user interface classes to IBrowseImage and IBrowseContent. This shields the UI Component and the Domain Component to make them more independent.

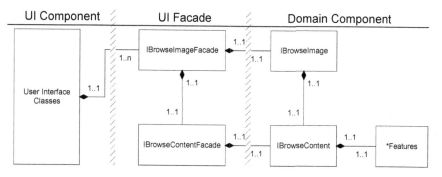

Fig. 3. Object Model of the Domain Component

The *Features are expanded and shown in Fig. 4. However, since there are many Feature classes that relate to the image features which may make the object model too complex, only the most important classes are shown.

In Fig. 4, all fine feature detectors inherit from FineDetector. FineDetector1, FineDetectorN and the dotted line between them denote the n fine feature detectors. These are visual feature detectors that are used to refine the histological feature classification during the iterations between the semantic anlayser and the visual feature detector in Fig. 1. Note that we do not allow image features to modify one another by calling mutable member functions among them. All image features values are set via their Extract() member function. This mechanism ensures that the values will not be modified incorrectly like the global variables in a large C program. However, the iterative approach adopted by I-Browse creates a problem for the *CBIRFrame*. We create two artificial feature class, Hypotheses and HypoResults to solve the problem. Hypotheses is the hypothesis generator in Fig. 1. It will be filled of the hypotheses by retrieving the values from the semantic analyser. The fine detectors then retrieve the hypotheses and perform the calculations when necessary. Finally, HypoResults observe the values in the fine detectors and construct the results that are retrieved by the semantic analyser.

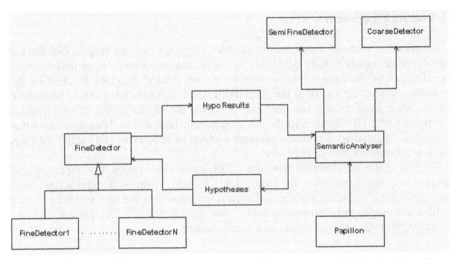

Fig. 4. Feature Dependency. CBIRFrame makes use of this graph to automatically determine the extraction order of image features.

As explained in section 3, we store the semantic content in a data structure called Papillon, which is also a Feature class. SemiFineDetector and CoarseDetector are two iconic feature classes that provide the initial image information for the semantic analyser to starts its analysis.

4.2 DM Facade

In section 1, we have discussed the failure of adapting existing databases as a weakness of current CBIR systems. In I-Browse, our prototype shows that we can adapt to an existing and running database from the hospitals in Hong Kong.

Fig. 5 shows the DM Facade and some corresponding entities in the Domain Component. In I-Browse, the Data Management Component (not shown) of I-Browse consists of two components, the DB2 database engine and the Visual Fox Pro database engine. In our prototype, we have two databases. The first one is the image database that is stored in a DB2 database. The other stores the patient information in a Visual Fox Pro database. The patient database is actually a simplified database of a histological information system called Pathos that is used in hospitals of Hong Kong. I-Browse can easily be integrated with Pathos to provide CBIR functionality to Pathos in our research prototype.

The novel technique is made possible by the fact that we have the DM Facade tier between the Domain Component and Data Management Component. By using suitable classes in the DM Facade, the Domain Component actually does not aware that there are in fact two different databases in the Data Management Component.

For any domain class, we make a derive class from it. For example, PersistPatient is derived from Patient to provide persistence to the Patient class. The persistent classes are also derived from PersistObj, a class that is defined in *CBIRFrame*. PersistObj requests for database operations by calling member functions to a broker class in the DM Facade, in our case, IBrowseBroker. As PersistObj knows only the broker class in the DM Facade, the domain objects do not care what databases exist in the Data Management Component. We therefore successfully implement the retrieval on top of the existing Pathos database.

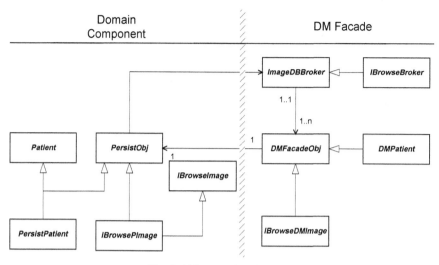

Fig. 5. Object Model of DM Facade

With the aid of the DM Facade, we have successfully hidden the details of the DBMS from the domain component. This can be very useful when we change the DBMS. For example, we might decide to upgrade the above FoxPro database to Oracle for better performance. In this case, we need only change the implementation of the corresponding DM Facade classes.

Note that the databases used are relational databases. In *CBIRFrame*, two pure virtual functions GetValue() and SetValue() are defined in the Feature class. The DM Facade calls these member functions to retrieval or assign feature values for database storage and retrieval. We design a few auxiliary data structures to map table names and column names to the feature values. Thus, the DM Facade can easily convert the feature values to the database schema, without knowing in advance how the domain feature objects are structured. This is very important in *CBIRFrame* since the domain objects might change dramatically in different applications while the design of the DM Facade should be relatively unchanged.

If object-oriented databases were used, the design in the DM Facade should be simpler. It is because the conceptual structure of the data in memory and the database is the same. In RDB, we have to convert the data of an object to a mapping of column names to their values. On the other hand, in OODB, there are usually functions to save or load an object directly in the DBMS.

4.3 UI Facade

The UI Facade shields the User Interface Component from the Domain Component. This is an important characteristic of CBIRFrame because it allows different user interfaces to be developed for I-Browse. Specifically, we build three running systems for I-Browse. The first one is a testbed for evaluating the feature extractors of I-Browse. The second one is used for populating the databases, i.e., the Patient Information Management System (PIMS).

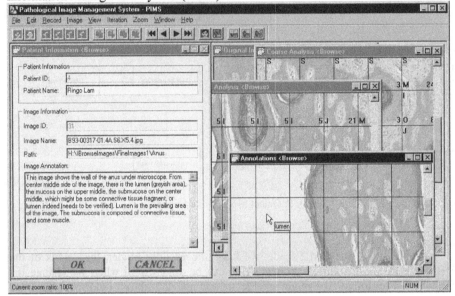

Fig. 6. PIMS – Patient Information Management System: we show image features along with patient information.

The third one is used for retrieval only. The retrieval system serves only as a small plug-in of Pathos to retrieve images and patient information by CBIR. Therefore, we separate database population and retrieval into two applications.

Fig. 6-7 show the interfaces of PIMS and the retrieval system. In each of the interface, we show the image along with the grids. We divide the image using these grids into sub-images and the image features are extracted according to each of the sub-image. The yellow label is the annotation of that sub-image, which shows the histological class of that sub-image.

In Fig. 6, an image has just been analysed and its features are shown in separate windows. Fig. 7 shows the image retrieval system interface that features and results list of the retrieved images. A selected image is shown in full size.

Fig. 8 shows the detailed design that has already been shown in Fig. 5. It actually shows three tiers, the User Interface Component, UI Facade and the Domain Component. In the object model, we separate objects for persistence from those that not. For example, IBrowsePContent inherits IBrowseContent to add persistence.

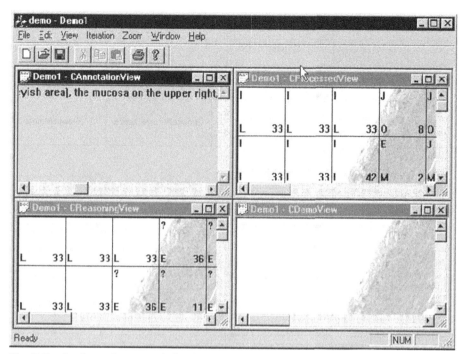

Fig. 7. Retrieval: we show a result list that shows image and patient information. The query image and a selected retrieved image can be viewed at full size.

4.4 Providing Multiple Modes of Searching

There need not be only one mode of searching an image database. In fact, based on different requirements, we may provide more than one mode of indexing and similarity functions to rank the retrieved images. This is also supported in *CBIRFrame* and I-Browse. As mentioned in section 1, this is not possible in many existing CBIR systems.

To support more than one index schemes and similarity functions, we make use of a feature of *CBIRFrame* that is not discussed in [24]. First of all, please note that IBrowseBroker is derived from a super class ImageDBBroker defined as a virtual class in *CBIRFrame*.

We identify that the index scheme and similarity function are two important parameters to the Search() member function of ImageDBBroker. Because of the variability of these parameters, we allow function objects to be passed into the function. A function object is an object that works as if it were an ordinary C function by overloading the function load operator (operator()). It may encapsulate other information such as thresholds or other runtime specified parameters. By writing a function object for each of these variations and pass it to the Search() function, we are able to provide a flexible software design that incorporates any kinds of index structure and similarity function.

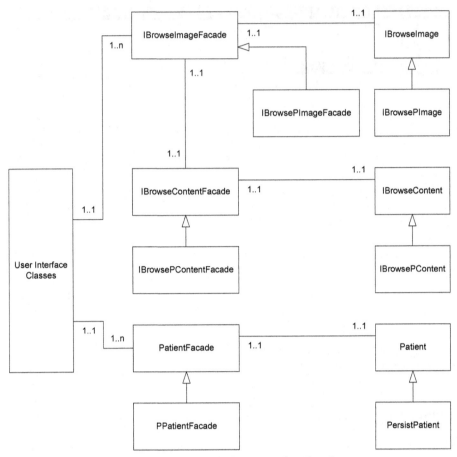

Fig. 8. Object Model of User Interface Facade

To ease the implementation problem of the framework user, we have also created two super classes for index scheme (IndexScheme) and similarity function (SimFunc) in the framework. These classes are written according to the Functoid pattern proposed in [29].

In I-Browse, we have only one index scheme, i.e., the one based on the keywords generated from the Papillon structure of an image. However, we have 4 similarity functions, three for iconic features and one for the semantic features.

5. Conclusion

The paper presents a software framework of a histological image retrieval system based on CBIRFrame. Our system is able to provide intelligent retrieval by capturing the iconic and semantic content within the images. It provides several indexing and similarity matching schemes in order to satisfy the requirements of different users. Finally, our system is able to run on top of an existing histological patient information system. These three features are usually missing from many CBIR systems as mentioned in section 1.

Acknowledgement

The *I-Browse* project is supported by the Hong Kong Jockey Club Charities Trust.

References

1. A. K. Jain and Aditya Vailaya, *"Image Retrieval Using Color and Shape"*, Pattern Recognition 29(8), 1233-1244 (1996).
2. M. Stricker and A. Dimai, *"Spectral Covariance and Fuzzy Regions for Image Indexing"*, Machine Vision and Applications, 10, 66-73 (1997).
3. Babu M. Mehtre, Mohan S. Kankanhalli, A. Desai Narasimhalu, Guo Chang Man, *"Colour Matching For Image Retrieval, Pattern Recognition Letters"*, 325-331(1995).
4. Michael J. Swain and Dana H. Ballard, *"Colour Indexing"*, Intl. Journal of Computer Vision, 7(1), 11-32(1991).
5. Mohan S. Kankanhalli, Babu M. Mehtre and Jian Kang Wu, *"Cluster-based Colour Matching For Image Retrieval"*, 29(4), 701-708(1996).
6. Alberto Del Bimbo and Pietro Pala, *"Visual Image Retrieval by Elastic Matching of User Sketches"*, IEEE Trans. on PAMI, 19(2), 121-132(1997).
7. Stan Sclaroff, *"Deformable Prototypes for Encoding Shape Categories in Image Databases"*, Pattern Recognition, 30(7), 627-641(1997).
8. Guojun Lu, *"Chain Code-based Shape Representation and Similarity Measure"*, in Visual Information Science, Lecture Notes in Computer Sceience 1306, ed. Clement Leung, Spinger-Verlag Berlin Heidelberg, Germany, pp. 135-150, 1997.
9. Kent K. T. Cheung and Horace H. S. Ip, *"Image Retrieval in Digital Library Based on Symmetry Detection"*, Proc. Computer Graphics International 1998, 22-26 Jun. 1998, Hannover, Germany, pp. 366-372.
10. A. D. Bimbo and P. Pala, *"Shape Indexing by Multi-scale Representation"*, Image and Vision Computing 17(1999), 245-261.
11. B. Huet and E. R. Hancock, *"Line Pattern Retrieval Using Relational Histograms"*, IEEE Trans. on PAMI, 21(12), 1363-1370(1999).
12. B. S. Manjunath and W. Y. Ma, *"Texture Features for Browsing and Retrieval of Image Data"*, IEEE Trans. on PAMI, 18(8), 837-842(1996).
13. E. Remias, G. Sheikoleslami, A. Zhang, T. F. Syeda-Mahmood, *"Supporting Content-based Retrieval in Large Image Database Systems"*, Multimedia Tools and Applications, 4, 153-170(1997).
14. Shi-Kuo Chang, Qing Yun Shi and Cheng Wen Yan, *"Iconic Indexing by 2-D Strings"*, IEEE Trans. on PAMI 9(3), 413-428 (1987).
15. S. K. Chang, C. W. Yan, Donald C. Dimitroff and Timothy Arndt, *"An Intelligent Image Database System"*, IEEE Trans. on PAMI 14(5), 681-688 (1988).
16. S. Y. Lee and F. J. Hsu, *"Spatial Reasonaing and Similarity Retrieval of Images Using 2D C-String Knowledge Representation"*, Pattern Recognition, 25(3), 305-318(1992).
17. P. W. Huang and Y. R. Jean, *"Spatial Knowledge and Similarity Retrieval for Image Database Systems based on RS-Strings"*, Pattern Recognition, 29(12), 2103-2114(1996).
18. C. C. Chang and C. F. Lee, *"Relative Coordiantes Oriented Symbolic String for Spatial Relationship Retrieval"*, Pattern Recognition, 28(4), 563-570(1995).

19. M. Flickner, H. Sawhney, W. Niblack, J. Ashley, Q. Huang, B. Dom, M. Gorkani, J. Hafner, D. Lee, D. Petkovic, D. Steele and P. Yanker, *"Query by Image and Video Content: The QBIC System"*, IEEE Computer, 23-32 (1995).

20. A. Pentland, R. W. Picard and S. Sclaroff, *"Photobook: Content-based Manipulation of Image Databases"*, IJCV 18(3), 233-254 (1996).

21. B. M. Mehtre, M. S. Kankanhalli and W.F. Lee, *"Content-based Image Retrieval Using a Composite Color-Shape Approach"*, Information Processing and Management, 34(1), 109-120 (1998).

22. Lilian H. Tang, Rudolf Hanka and Horace H. S. Ip, *"A System Architecture for Integrating Semantic and Iconic Content for Intelligent Browsing of Medical Images"*, Proc. of SPIE: Medical Imaging 1998, SPIE vol. 3339, Feb 1998, San Diego, USA, pp. 572-580.

23. L H Y Tang, Rudolf Hanka, R Lam, Horace H S Ip, *"Automatic Semantic Labelling of Medical Images for Content-Based Retrieval"*, Proc. of Expertsys'98, USA, 77-82(1998).

24. Kent K. T. Cheung, Horace H. S. Ip, Ringo W. K. Lam, R. Hanka, Lilian H. Y. Tang and G. Fuller, *"An Object-oriented Framework for Content-based Image Retrieval Using a 5-tier Architecture"*, Proc. Asia Pacific Software Engineering Conference 99, 7-10 Dec. 1999, Takamatsu, Japan, pp 174-177.

25. Ringo. W. K. Lam, Kent K. T. Cheung, Horace H. S. Ip, Lilian H. Y. Tang and R. Hanka, *"A Content-based Retrieval System for Histological Images"*, accepted for Visual' 2000, Lyon, France, Nov. 2000.

26. Lilian H Y Tang, Rudolf Hanka, Horace H S Ip, Kent K T Cheung, Ringo Lam, *"Semantic Query Processing and Annotation Generation for Content-based Retrieval of Histological Images"*, to appear at Proceedings of SPIE Medical Imaging '2000, San Diego, USA, February 2000.

27. M. Fowler, *"Analysis Patterns: Reusable Object Models"*, Addison Wesley, Reading, MA (1997).

28. M. Fowler and K. Scott, *"UML Distilled"*, Addison Wesley, Reading, MA (1997).

29. Konstantin Läufer, *"A Framework for Higher-Order Functions in C++"*, Proc. Conf. on Object-Oriented Technologies (COOTS), Monterey, CA, June 1995.

30. A. Wetzel and M. J. Becich, *"Content Based Image Retrieval and pathology Image Classification Image Processing"*, http://www.psc.edu/research/abstracts/becich.html, 1998.

31. G. Bucci, S. Cagnoni and R. De Dominics, *"Integrating Content-based Retrieval in a Medical Image Reference Database"*, Computerized Medical Imaging and Graphics, 20(4), 231-241 (1996).

32. P. Korn, N. Sidiropoulos, C. Faloutsos, E. Siegel and Z. Protopapas, *"Fast and Effective Retrieval of Medical Tumor Shapes"*, IEEE Trans. Knowledge and Data Eng., 10(6), 889-904 (1998).

33. C. R. Shyu, C. E. Brodley, A. C. Kak and A. Kosaka, *"ASSERT: A Physician-in-the-Loop Content-based Retrieval System for HRCT Image Databases"*, Comp. Vision and Image Understanding, 75(1/2), 111-132 (1999).

A Ground-Truth Training Set for Hierarchical Clustering in Content-based Image Retrieval

D.P. Huijsmans, N. Sebe and M.S. Lew

LIACS, Leiden University, P.O. Box 9512, 2300 RA Leiden, The Netherlands
huijsman,nicu,mlew@liacs.nl

Abstract. Progress in Content-Based Image Retrieval (CBIR) is hampered by the absence of well-documented and validated test-sets that provide ground-truth for the performance evaluation of image indexing, retrieval and clustering tasks. For quick access to large (tenthousands or millions of images) digital image collections a hierarchically structured indexing or browsing mechanism based on clusters of similar images at various coarse to fine levels is highly wanted. The Leiden 19th-Century Portrait Database (LCPD), that consists of over 16,000 scanned studio portraits (so-called Cartes de Visite CdV), happens to have a clearly delineated set of clusters in the studio logo backside images. Clusters of similar or semantically identical logos can also be formed on a number of levels that show a clear hierarchy. The Leiden Imaging and Multimedia Group is constructing a CD-ROM with a well-documented set of studio portraits and logos that can serve as ground-truth for feature performance evaluation in domains beside color-indexing. Its grey-level image lay-out characteristics are also described by various precalculated feature vector sets. For both portraits (near copy pairs) and studio logos (clusters of identical logos) test-sets will be provided and described at various clustering levels. The statistically significant number of test-set images embedded in a realistically large environment of narrow-domain images are presented to the CBIR community to enable selection of more optimal indexing and retrieval approaches as part of an internationally defined test-set that comprises test-sets specifically designed for color-, texture- and shape retrieval evaluation.

1 Introduction

So far a lot of effort in the CBIR community has been put into features, metrics and ranking (for our own effort see for instance [metric98] and [perfHuijsmans97]) but comparatively little effort has been put into performance evaluation (a theoretical example is [Dimai99] and a practical one [HP98]). The main obstacle for application of a sound statistical approach is not the lack of theory (see for instance [DeVijver82]), but missing ground-truth. Validated test sets like the Brodatz textures are hard to find; in most practical studies unvalidated ad hoc test cases are used that miss any ground. As to our knowledge no ground-truth test-set for hierarchical clustering exists in the CBIR domain.

R. Laurini (Ed.): VISUAL 2000, LNCS 1929, pp. 500–510, 2000.
Springer-Verlag Berlin Heidelberg 2000

Any content-based image retrieval task comes down to finding the right balance between grouping and separating images in like and unlike clusters. No general applicable way of image similarity clustering can be devised that provides the same answer to different vision tasks; the semantic clustering of human subjects may well overlap badly between different vision tasks and even be conflicting (one persons signal is the other persons noise and vice versa). This means that in a generally applicable image retrieval setting a learning or optimization stage like the one in [Kittler96] will be needed regularly or even on a search or goal image basis. Although the black box neural net approach would be a logic choice in this case, we prefer the use of a statistical approach, leaving most of the controls to us.

Image retrieval user interfaces should therefore present the user with tools to (fine)tune the indexing and retrieval mechanisms whenever the semantics of a task have changed. As databases get larger and larger an hierarchical clustering phase also becomes indispensable. Theory developed in the sixties and seventies of the last century (see [Hartigan75] and [survey83]) are being revived in efforts to visualize the information structure of very large information systems like Internet (for a recent overview see [specialissue98]). In a general CBIR system tools must be provided to spot the right information given a learning or design set or during an interactive dialog with the user to tune the indexing, retrieval and clustering methods for the task presented.

In our group two roads are explored to support the (fine)tuning phase:

- well-documented test-sets that provide ground-truth for (fine)tuning the feature selection in a large-scale well-defined static application using sound statistics.
- interactively used relevance feedback for small-scale (coarse) tuning within a dynamic search environment.

In this paper a well-documented ground-truth set of studio logos and portraits at various fine and coarse clustering levels for the first approach is described.

The relevance feedback approach is the topic of a recently started PhD research project. For relevance feedback a set-up was devised that should minimize the time spent in the learning stage. To quickly select and set weights for the contribution of specific indexes during retrieval, the user will be presented with a multi-dimensional ranking GUI (like the eight ranking lists in figure 1 around the central present best search or goal image, which might even be a random image at start). Images chosen for positive feedback will lead to the inclusion of specific feature vectors for the final one-dimensional ranking based on a weighted combination of indexes. Not only image features but real multi-media indexing using indexes for associated annotation and sound as well can be taken into account whenever feedback indicates this would be appropriate.

In addition, clustering may be a necessary tool for suppressing duplicates or near-duplicates in any interactive ranking stage; especially at the initial search phases and on Internet where many near-copies of original images might otherwise clutter the top of ranking lists.

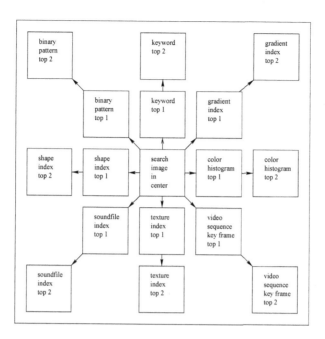

Fig. 1. Learning phase GUI with multi-dimensional ranking lists around present goal or search image: relevance feedback helps forming the specific classifier combination for final goal image delivery

2   Evaluation of content-based search for cluster members

2.1   (*Index*, *Retrieval*) pair performance

In general, CBIR approaches can be characterized by a specific (*index*, *retrieval*) pair used to produce a linear ranking $R_{i,r}$: *index* stands for any $feature - vector$ used to characterize content (from the raw digital pixel values to scale space, affine transform invariants, wavelet coeficients, etc.), whereas *retrieval* stands for any $distance - measure$ ($L_1, L_2, Mahalanobis$, etc.) calculated from (part of) the feature vector elements and used for sorting the similarities into a linear ranking order $R_{f,d}$. So: $R_{i,r} = R_{f,d}$.

Perfect ranking results For a cluster of m members embedded in a database of n images, a perfect ranking result would mean that the cluster members occupy the first $m - 1$ positions among the $n - 1$ ranked with each of the cluster members used in turn as the search image. When the feature vector of the search image itself is present in the database or compared with itself as well the first $m \in [1, n]$ positions would be occupied. So the ideal rank R_{id} for a cluster of m images within a database of n images ($n \geq m$) would be irrespective of database size:

$$R_{id} = R_{i,r} = R_{f,d} = m/2 \tag{1}$$

Imperfect ranking results In general, ranking results will show a less then ideal situation of dispersed cluster members; each cluster member $i \in [1, m]$ when using cluster member $j \in [1, m]$ as the search image, will end up at rank $k \in [1, n]$. Let m_{ijk} denote this rank. The average rank for a particular $(feature - vector, distance - measure)$ combination $R_{f,d}$ is obtained by averaging over i and j:

$$(\sum_i \sum_j m_{ijk})/(m \cdot m) = R_{f,d} \in [m/2, n - (m/2)] \tag{2}$$

Dividing R_{id} by $R_{f,d}$ gives a normalised performance measure $P_{f,d}$:

$$R_{id}/R_{f,d} = P_{f,d} \in [(m/2)/(n - (m/2)), 1]; P_{f,d} \in (0, 1] \tag{3}$$

for with $n \geq m$, $(m/2)/(n - (m/2)) \in (0, 1]; \lim_{n \to \infty} P_{f,d}(n) = 0$ and $P_{f,d}(n) = 1$ for $n = m$.

A plot of this performance against database size n will give a clear indication of the ranking strength of the $(index, retrieval)$ pair. The ideal $(index, retrieval)$ pair would show as a straight line at $P_{f,d}(n) = 1$ irrespective of n. Less ideal performances all start off at $P_{f,d}(m) = 1$, but will gradually fall away towards 0 for growing n. When more then 1 cluster is used to evaluate the performance of the $(index, retrieval)$ pair a weighted average of the individual cluster performances can be used instead (using the cluster sizes as weights).

In reality the best performing $(index, retrieval)$ combination will be the one that occupies the largest area under the $P_{f,d}(n)$ graph and thus performances of specific $(index, retrieval)$ or $(feature - vector, distance - measure)$ combinations can be compared using the single normalized qualifier:

$$(\int_m^n P_{f,d}(n)\, dn)/(n - m) = A_{i,r} = A_{f,d} \in (0, 1] \tag{4}$$

This comparison based on a single numeric normalized qualifier could also be used for the often used precision, recall graph by registering the area under the normalized precision, recall graph.

3   Cluster membership

3.1   Definition of a cluster

What specifically defines a cluster is often a very subjective grouping (when done by humans) or numerical harnass (like a k-means clustering) without being useful in general. Only in specific situations like (near-)copies can clustering be considered a well-defined task. The studio logos in the Leiden 19th-Century Portrait Database and the doubles and triples that exist from some portraits (that were once manufactured by the dozen from an identical glass negative) are cases of fine-level clustering that can be considered to be quite objective clusters. See for instance examples from identified cluster members in figures 2, 3, 4 and 5. Clearly members of these clusters were produced from the same printing plate made from a more or less artistic design.

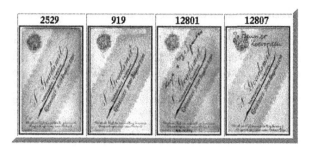

Fig. 2. Lowest level cluster 378 in LCPD showing annotation noise in c and d

Fig. 3. Lowest level cluster studio weyderveldt showing level noise and shift noise in c

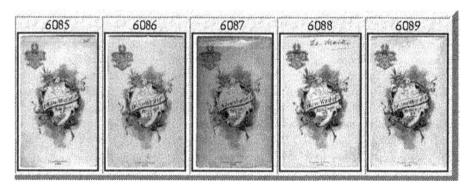

Fig. 4. Lowest level cluster of artistic design studio winsheym showing level noise in c and annotation noise in d

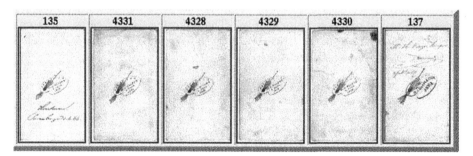

Fig. 5. Lowest level cluster 976 in LCPD showing annotation noise in a and f

3.2 Spread within a cluster: sources of noise

Several effects at the time of production and during conservation have altered the appearance of the images and are to be seen as added noise causing spread within clusters. Main causes for the studio logos of changed appearance are:

- *level − noise*, change in background intensity due to either manufacture or differences in daylight exposure;
- *contrast − noise*, different intensity distribution within normalised intensity range (bleached or faded copies)
- *rotation−noise*, mostly slight (but sometimes 180 degrees) misrotations that remain after normalizing orientation using the portrait on the front side
- *shift − noise*, small misalignments that remain after normalisation
- *condition − noise*, some images are better preserved, in terms of scratches, durt etc., then others
- *annotation − noise*, the addition of annotation (see figure 5) like person depicted, date of exposure and last but not least collection identifiers;
- *clip − noise*, change in size due to cutting off edges

These various noise sources that are found to be active within LCPD are representative for most cases of noise found in image collections. Some of the noise sources are symmetric, others are asymmetric in their effect upon noise distributions. *Level − noise, rotation − noise,* and *shift − noise* are examples of noise distributions symmetric around a mean noise level, whereas *contrast − noise, condition − noise, annotation − noise* and *clip − noise* show asymmetric distributions. Recognizing noisy members as belonging to a cluster is easier in the presence of symmetric then asymmetric noise. By working in gradient space many induced lighting variations can be minimized. By working with indexes obtained from low-resolution averages *condition − noise* can be kept small. For the clusters defined in the LCPD set *annotation−noise* will be the most difficult to cope with, for in gradient space its effect is even enlarged.

3.3 Representative member of a cluster

To represent clusters at a higher (coarser) retrieval level the concept of a *cluster−representative* becomes important. What is the most representative member according to the different noise sources? The following list indicates the representativity in terms of a statistical $MIN, MEAN, MEDIAN$ or MAX value of the associated noise distributions:

- *level − noise*, best by $MEDIAN$
- *contrast − noise*, best by MAX
- *rotation − noise*, best by $MEAN$
- *shift − noise*, best by $MEAN$
- *condition − noise*, best by $MEDIAN$
- *annotation − noise*, best by MIN
- *clip − noise*, best by MIN

One way to automatically select a representative of same images for a given $(feature - vector, distance - measure)$ is to take the highest ranking individual member, when ranking with $n = m$, for this identifies the member of the cluster closest to all the other members. However this can only be done easily when cluster membership is established. Especially in small clusters the members closest to all the others in the cluster may not be the one a user would pick as a representative. Because picking a $cluster - representative$ may not be easy, part of the clustering effort will be devoted to providing hand-picked ground-truth for that task as well.

3.4   Outliers of a cluster

Due to one or more noise sources the feature vector characterizations and distance measures obtained from them will be more or less succesful in clustering like images without wandering into nearby clusters. Clustering and choosing a representative from a cluster will be greatly enhanced when cluster members with the biggest noise contribution can be detected at an early stage and suppressed during specific stages. The next list tries to indicate those outliers per noise source:

- $level - noise$, worst by MIN, MAX
- $contrast - noise$, worst by MIN
- $rotation - noise$, worst by MIN, MAX
- $shift - noise$, worst by MIN, MAX
- $condition - noise$, worst by MIN, MAX
- $annotation - noise$, worst by MAX
- $clipnoise$, worst by MAX

For a given $(feature - vector, distance - measure)$ there is an easy way to isolate outliers automatically (again only when cluster membership is established!). By setting a threshold distance in the ranking results in case $n = m$ (ranking only applied to cluster members) outliers can easily be identified. However substantial overlap between clusters may remain for a certain threshold setting.

4   A hierarchy of clusters: superclusters

Although clustering above the lowest (fine)level clustering level in LCPD will be less objective we felt a strong need to define ground-truth for a hierarchy of cluster levels, to support initial browsing and to control the degree of likeness allowed in ranking lists.

4.1   Similar: between same and unlike

Grouping images for display purposes will have both a lower threshold on likeness (members treated as the same, undistinguished given the high amount of likeness) and an upper threshold on likeness (members still seen as similar but distinguishable).

Fig. 6. Supercluster of similar diagonal design with emblem top left while suppressing the printed character information

Fig. 7. Supercluster of same artistic design while suppressing printed character information

Fig. 8. Semantic OCR-level cluster of studio B. Bruining in Leiden when suppressing artistic design elements

4.2   Opposing views: OCR versus design

Our portrait database with scanned studio logos proves to present a particularly nice example of the different ways its information is indexed by various user groups: the content can be divided into three categories:

- printed characters (OCR recognizable part)
- artistic design
- added annotation (usually handwritten characters)

Collections can be characterized by the main key for sorting and storing these portraits: most collections (institutional and private) use the studio information (printed characters) as the main index; one private collector uses the artistic design as the main index; one institutional collection uses the added annotation (person depicted) as the main key. The studio and design index offer opposing views of the information contained in logos: the studio index demands complete suppression of artistic design elements, whereas the design index demands complete suppression of the printed character parts. For the extraction of information for the studio index from the printed characters a spotting method like Optical Character Recognition (OCR) is needed to suppress the more dominant artistic design signal; for the extraction of the design index it suffices to extract features from low resolution copies of the images. Annotation can be spotted by recording the difference of annotated backsides with an annotation-free cluster representative.

The LCPD directory (at http://ind156b.wi.leidenuniv.nl:2000/) uses the studio index as the main key and will use the design index as a second key.

Figures 6 and 7 show examples in our testsets of superclusters of artistic design elements. Figures 9 and 8 illustrate the effect of clustering when all the non-OCR recognizable patterns are treated as noise and part of the OCR recognizable information is used to form high-level semantic clustering of studio logos. Within the LCPD directory four clustering layers on the basis of printed characters (OCR recognizable information) is used to form superclusters in LCPD: photographer, photographer plus city, photographer plus city plus street, photographer plus city plus street plus streetnumber.

4.3   Supercluster in binarized gradient space

Most lighting noise sources can be effectively suppressed by extracting features from binarized gradient images. For photographs this transformation has a particularly attractive side-effect: positives and negatives of the same scene become highly alike, which makes it easy to trace back prints to original negatives; also in the LCPD studio logos many designs exist in both positive (black characters on light background) and negative (white characters on dark background) versions (see figure 9 a and b). In the LCPD ground-truth cluster definitions positive and negative versions are clearly indicated. An example of a supercluster based on gradient features in shown in figure 10.

Fig. 9. Semantic OCR-level supercluster of studio B. Bruining (Arnhem and Leiden combined) while suppressing artistic design elements

5   CD-ROM with LCPD ground-truth testsets for hierarchical clustering

Apart from an already available CD-ROM with about 500 testset pairs of portraits (originally contact-printed from a same glass negative) embedded in about 10,000 studio portraits and with a number of feature vector sets produced in December 1998, the ground-truth clustering effort undertaken for this paper will lead to a large test-set of about 2000 validated clusters and superclusters obtained from the logos at the back of 16,500 LCPD studio portraits. Researchers that would like to use this material for evaluation purposes should contact the first author in order to obtain a copy of the cluster CD-ROM at a minimal fee (covering copy and postage costs). The material on the CD-ROM can be used freely for non-commmercial activities.

6   Acknowledgements

We greatfully acknowledge support by a grant from Philips Research Laboratories in the Netherlands that made the construction of this ground-truth test-set for hierarchical clustering and performance evaluation of indexing and retrieval from large image databases possible.

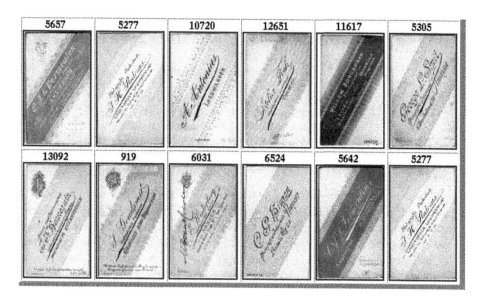

Fig. 10. Super cluster of diagonal design in gradient space where black on white (positives) and white on black (negatives) differences disappear

References

[specialissue98] Murtagh, F. (ed.): Special Issue on Clustering and Classification. The Computer Journal **41-8** (1998)

[survey83] Murtagh, F.: A Survey of Recent Advances in Hierarchical Clustering Algorithms. The Computer Journal **26** (1983) 354–359

[Hartigan75] Hartigan, J. A.: Clustering Algorithms. Wiley (1975)

[Dimai99] Dimai, A.: Assessment of Effectiveness of Content Based Image Retrieval Systems. Conf. Proc. Visual'99 LNCS **1614** (1999) 525–532

[HP98] Ma, W., Zhang, H.: Benchmarking of Image Features for Content-based Retrieval. IEEE (1998) 253–257

[DeVijver82] DeVijver, P.A., Kittler, J.: Pattern Recognition A Statistical Approach. Prentice-Hall (1982)

[Kittler96] Kittler, J., Hatef, M., Duin, R.P.W.: Combining Classifiers. IEEE Proc ICPR'96 (1996) **2B** 897–901

[metric98] Sebe, N., Lew, M., Huijsmans, D.P.: Which Ranking Metric is Optimal? With Applications in Image Retrieval and Stereo Matching. Conf Proc ICPR'98 (1998) 265–271

[perfHuijsmans97] Huijsmans, D.P., Lew, M.S., Denteneer, D.: Quality Measures for Interactive Image Retrieval with a Performance Evaluation of Two 3x3 Texel-Based Methods. Conf. Proc. ICIAP'97   LNCS **1311** (1997) 22–29

Query Models and Languages for Geographical Information Systems

Michel Mainguenaud

Laboratoire Perception, Systeme et Information
Institut National des Sciences Appliquees (INSA)
Site du Madrillet - Avenue de l'Universite
F76800 Saint Etienne du Rouvray - France
Fax : (+ 33) (0) 2 32 95 97 08
Michel.Mainguenaud@insa-rouen.fr

Abstract. This paper presents a synthesis on the query models and languages to manipulate a geographical database. We present the different classes of query languages : based on predicates, based on operators without composition and based on operators with composition. We analyze the consequences on the data model, on the expressive power and on the query modeling. The introduction of operators as query primitives requires the closedness of these operators on geographical data. The introduction of operators increases the expressive power allowing queries involving a composition of operators. As a path operator (with the same arguments) provides several answers and may appear several times in a query, the query modeling must provide such an opportunity. Depending on the required expressive power, we present the different classes of interfaces at the user's level.

1 Introduction

A lot of efforts are under progress to elaborate innovative solutions for the representation and exploration of complex database applications. Different research groups are simultaneously concentrating their works on Geographical Information Systems (GIS). GIS needs are very well known [11,12]. Nevertheless, several problems are still open. In this paper we focus on the analysis of a query modeling and the user interfaces of such systems.

Geographical data are defined with two major components : an alphanumeric part and a spatial representation. Conventional databases provide an efficient way to manage alphanumeric data. The spatial representation requires to extend the conventional data types (e.g., integer, string). With these new types, some basic manipulation primitives must be defined. The graphic representation of geographical data is very important. Geographical data are visual by essence. The user interface has a very important role in the acceptation of a new tool. Visual techniques may have a tremendous opportunity to play an important part in a query of a GIS database at the user's level. We distinguish two levels of manipulations. The first level involves the programmer of an application. The second level involves the end-user. The development of conventional database applications can be performed with two main

R. Laurini (Ed.): VISUAL 2000, LNCS 1929, pp. 511-520, 2000.

orientations. The first orientation is the introduction of database manipulation primitives in a conventional programming language (e.g., C, C++, Java). The second orientation is the use of a new development language (often named Fourth Generation Language - 4GL). A geographical application requires the same tools. These tools are a set of database manipulations and a set of programming constructors. The expressive power of the programming level (i.e., the class of queries a user can express) depends on the expressive power of the database geographical manipulations since pro-gramming constructors nowadays are very conventional (e.g., sequence, alternative, iteration). Graphical screens and graphical co-processors increased the opportunity to define new kinds of user interfaces. We distinguish the static querying and the dynamic querying. We define the static querying as the use of a predefined scenario of database manipulations (alphanumeric and spatial). This approach is very well adapted to define very repetitive queries. We define the dynamic querying as the full use of the visual nature of geographical data. A query is therefore represented with a drawing that expresses the semantics of a query. Obviously, the expressive power depends on the ability of the database to manage geographical operators. The user friendliness of a dynamic querying language must be favored whenever some degrees of freedom are required.

In part 2, we present the various philosophies of geographical database extensions to handle a spatial database. In part 3, we study the consequences of the introduction of a composition of operators as a query. In part 4, we study the associated user interfaces to handle an end-user query. The conclusion presents a synthesis and gives some research guidelines.

2 Query Model

The query model defines the way a query uses the notion of operators. We consider here the treatment applied on geographical data with a Data Base Management System. The treatment of the spatial representation outside the DBMS (i.e., a software component able to extract data from the database world, to apply a spatial operator and to re-introduce data inside the DBMS) is not considered here. The first step is the definition of geographical (i.e., in this way graphical) data. The simplest structure of operator is a predicate. The Boolean result of a predicate applied to geographical data can be use in a 'Where' clause of an 'SQL' statement. The expressive power is increased by operators. A querying language may or may not accept a composition of operators. In the first part, we introduce a sample database to illustrate the different examples used in this paper. In the second part, we study the introduction of predicates. In the third part, we study the notion of operators and in the last part, we study the notion of composition of operators.

2.1 Sample Database

Several formalisms [14] can be used to model a geographical database (e.g., an extended relational model with Abstract Data Types, an Object Oriented model). To simplify the presentation, let us use a complex object model defined with the aggregation [], the set {} and conventional types (e.g., integer, string, real). The spatial representation (or SR for short) is managed by an Abstract Data Type [13],

SpatialRepresentationType (or SRT for short). The aim of this part is to study the introduction of operators and its consequences. Therefore the retained data model used to define the sample database is not important. Let us use the following definitions to propose some queries :

```
TownType = [          Name : string, Population : integer, Mayor : string,
                      SpatialRepresentation : SpatialRepresentationType ]
ForestType = [        Name : string, Species : {string}, SR : SRT]
PollutedAreaType = [ Name : string, Reason : string, SR : SRT]
LakeType = [          Name : string, SpatialRepresentation : SRT]
RoadType = [          Name : string, Origin : TownType,
                      Destination : TownType, SR : SRT]
```

Let us define the following queries : (Q1) : I would like to know if a forest has a common part with a town named 'Paris'; (Q2) : I would like to know if a forest has a common part with a town named 'Paris' such as this part has a surface of 10 units or more ?; (Q3) : I would like to know if a road crosses a town named 'Paris' in its non-forest part; (Q4) : I would like to see the paths from the town named 'Paris' to the town named 'Nice' that border a lake and cross a forest in its non-urban part; (Q5) : I would like to see a road that crosses a forest for at least a 10 units length; (Q6) : I would like to see a road that crosses a polluted area for at least a 10 units length. If we consider query Q1, the aim is to obtain information about the town (may be about the forest) if an intersection occurs. The intersection itself is not important. If we consider query Q2, the query is similar to query Q1, but now the intersection is important since a property on this intersection is required (i.e., a surface of 10 units or more). If we consider query Q3, the query is similar to query Q2, but now a spatial operator (i.e., the spatial difference is applied to the town to extract the non forest part) is involved. A new operator (i.e., an intersection) is applied to the result of the previous operator (i.e., the spatial difference). If we consider query Q4, the query is similar to query Q3 (the non-urban part of a forest). The composition of operator is introduced by the fact the path(s) from Paris to Nice must border the lake and cross the non-urban part of the forest. Query Q5 and Q6 have the same semantics (i.e., an intersection between two database components under an aggregate constraint - 10 units long). The main difference is due to the fact that conceptually two forests do not have any reason to overlap but two polluted areas may overlap.

2.2 Notion of Predicates

From the historical point of view, the notion of predicate was the first extension to conventional database systems to manage spatial data. This solution is the simplest to introduce. The use of a predicate is reduced to the 'Where' clause of an Extended SQL statement. The result is built with the basic components of the database (i.e., attributes of base relations in an extended relational database or classes from an object oriented database). The first proposed models were based on the physical representation of geographical data (e.g., point, line). This option leads to a huge amount of predicates depending on the spatial representation of the data stored in the database. The introduction of Abstract Data Types to handle the geographical model reduced the number of predicates to a single predicate by semantics (e.g., intersection, bordering). The expressive power is very low since query Q2 cannot be expressed. This query required to manage the result of a spatial operator. The result as a Boolean answer is to weak to answer query Q2.

As an example, query Q1 in such a language would be expressed by :

Select	T.*
From	TownType T, ForestType F
Where	intersection (T.SR, F.SR)

One can remark that in this kind of language, the definition is tuple oriented.

2.3 Notion of Operators Without Composition

From the historical point of view, the introduction of operators is the second generation of extended databases to handle spatial properties. The expressive power is increased since a query may define some properties on the result of a spatial operator. Query Q2 can now be expressed since the result of the intersection is available. A function can be defined on this result and the property of a surface more than 10 units can be evaluated. Let us consider that we have already available an intersection operator (   ), a path operator (->), a border operator (<>) and a spatial difference operator (   ). We do not consider here the signatures to express constraints (e.g., on the path operator). The important is the fact that a path operator provides several paths as an answer of an evaluation from a given place to another one. As soon as a query requires the composition of operator (i.e., an operator applied on the result of another operator), this query cannot be expressed in a single order. As a consequence, query Q3 cannot be expressed since the intersection is applied on the result of a spatial difference. Such a query is therefore expressed with two database orders. The first one allows the evaluation of the spatial difference. The second one applies an intersection on the results of the spatial difference. Stating this fact, the final result is a sub-set of the result obtained during the evaluation of the first spatial operator. A forest that has an intersection with a town is retained in the first step but this forest may not have an intersection with a road. Therefore the result is the sub-set of the forests defined in the first step. Two main practices can be defined to keep only relevant data. The first one is the management of the history as soon as an operator is evaluated. The result of an operator has the history (that may be very long depending on the number of evaluated operators). One of the drawbacks is the lack of generality since the result of an operator is not a geographical object (an alphanumeric part and a spatial part) but a geographical object and its history. The second practice is to keep this history outside the definition of a geographical object and to define the result of a query as a set of database objects (from the database and the results of the operators) and a structure to manage the history. Whatever the retained practice, a software component must be developed (i.e., a Query Resolution Engine) to guarantee the correctness of the final result of a query. This solution can be considered as similar to the solution with the treatment of the spatial representation outside the DBMS since a software component is required. As an example, query Q2 would be expressed by :

Select	T.*
From	TownType T, ForestType F
Where	Surface ((T.SR, F.SR)) > 10

One can remark that in this kind of language the definition is tuple-oriented. Furthermore the operator is spatial representation oriented. The alphanumeric part of a geographical object is not considered. As soon as a query involves an operator in the select clause the alphanumeric part may be not relevant (e.g., Population) as it may be for the beginning of the expression of query Q3:

Select	T.Name, T.Population, T.Mayor, (T. SR, F.SR)
From	TownType T, ForestType F
Where	intersection (T.SR, F.SR)

Query Q3 must be cut into at least two orders to provide the part of the road that crosses the non-forest part of the town. In fact to provide a relevant answer to query Q3, the result must be defined as a geographical data (i.e., an alphanumeric part and a spatial representation). The alphanumeric part must be a subset of the data model of a town, of the forest and of the road [4,9][1]. The spatial representation is the result of the composition of an intersection applied on a spatial difference.

2.4 Notion of Operators With Composition

From the historical point of view, this approach received very few proposals [partially in 5, 6, 8]. A query language with the composition of operators allows defining a query with several spatial operators. The argument of an operator may be an operator. The expressive power is similar to the previous set of proposition if we consider the database management system as the query language and the software component required to guarantee the correctness of a result. Query Q3 can now be expressed since the spatial difference of the forest and the town is available within the same database order. The algebraic modeling of this query is a tree (see figure 2.1)

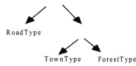

RoadType

TownType   ForestType

Fig. 2.1 Algebraic representation of query Q3

We define this composition as a vertical composition. Query Q4 illustrates an horizontal composition. Figure 2.2 presents an algebraic representation of query Q4. The path operator is used as an argument of the border operator and of the intersection operator. The path must verify the two properties (bordering a lake and having an intersection with a non-urban part of a forest). The algebraic modeling of this query is an acyclic graph (DAG).

As an example, query Q3 in such a language would be expressed by :

    Select   R.*, F.*,   (R.SR, (T.SR, F.SR))
    From   RoadType R, ForestType F, TownType T
    Where   intersection (F.SR, T.SR) and
                       intersection (R.SR, (T.SR, F.SR)) and T.Name = 'Paris'

A similar approach to the definition of query Q4 cannot be performed :

    Select   -> (T1.Name, T2.Name), L.*, F.*
    From   LakeType L, ForestType F, TownType T1, T2, T3
    Where   bordering [2] (-> (T1.Name, T2.Name), L.SR) and
              intersection (-> (T1.Name, T2.Name), (F.SR, T3.SR))
              and T1.Name = 'Paris' and T2.Name = 'Nice'

---

[1] In the following, we assume this rule is respected. * denotes the relevant attributes.

[2] To simplify the expression, we do not consider here the transformation from the logical point of view of a network (i.e., a graph and the transitive closure on this graph to evaluate a path) and its spatial representation.

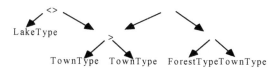

Fig. 2.2 Algebraic representation of query Q4

As soon as a path operator provides several answers as a result instead of a single one (e.g., a shortest path), there is no guarantee that the two path operators would represent the same path. Unfortunately a path operator with a single answer is not realistic. The evaluation of the path operator must provide several paths as an answer since the shortest one (in distance) may be far from being the most convenient, the less expensive may be very long, ... The problem is due to the fact that from two given instances (i.e., Paris and Nice) several paths (i.e., several results) are provided. The signature of the path becomes a set of paths as a result instead of being a path.

3 Composition of Operators

The composition of operator provides a very high expressive power. Conventional databases relies on the opportunity to combine a reduced set of operators. Relational databases provide the selection, the projection, the union, the difference and the Cartesian product as the basic operators. To provide an opportunity to define realistic queries some functions are provided such as the minimum, the maximum, the count, the average and the sum. Object oriented database query languages provide the opportunity to define some basic manipulations attached to a specific class. These manipulations can be used in the query language. Within the geographical context, several spatial operators are provided in the literature (e.g., intersection, bordering, spatial difference). These operators can be used in the extension of the query language to manipulate spatial data. The use of a composition of operators has two main consequences. The first one is the ability to use the same operator with the same arguments in a query. The second consequence is the ability to access to the result of the composition in the end-user query language.

3.1 The Use of the Same Operator

Several formalisms can be provided to formalize a query language. To illustrate the notion of composition, we adopt in this paper a simplified grammar of a functional query language (the choice of an other formalism - e.g., logic - does not change the raised problem). Let us define a simplified grammar (e.g., we do not consider the signature of the operators, we reduce it to binary operators) based on the following rules to illustrate the use of the same operator. The start symbol is "query". The terminals are DatabaseComponent (e.g., TownType), OID (i.e., an integer), spatialrelationship (e.g.,   ,   , ->)

    query::= composition (op , follow_op)
    op::= OID spatialrelationship(op,op) / DatabaseComponent OID
    follow_op::= op follow_op /

Query Q1 involves a predicate but can be generalized with an operator. Query Q2 is similar to query Q1 since we do not consider here the signature of the operator for the various constraints that can be expressed. Query Q3 is a vertical composition (similar to conventional functional languages).

Q1 = composition (3   (TownType 1, ForestType 2))
Q3 = composition (5   (RoadType 4, 3   (TownType 1, ForestType 2)))
Q4 = composition (3 -> (Towntype 1, TownType 2),
          5 <> (3 -> (TownType 1, TownType 2), LakeType 4),
          8   (ForestType 6, TownType 7)
          10   (3 -> (TownType 1, TownType 2),
                9   (ForestType 6, TownType 7)))

A path operator may be applied several times in the same query (e.g., two times). The semantics of the query may be : 'I would like two paths from a given place to another one' or 'I would like this path to verify two different properties' (this is different from the disjunction of the two properties). In the first case, the DBMS must consider these two paths as independent. This is possible since the path operator provides several paths as an answer. A path operator reduced to a single path as answer (e.g., a shortest path) cannot provide this expressive power. In the second case, the DBMS must consider these two path operators as the same one. To be able to distinguish between these two cases, the grammar must provide an OID to indicate that these paths are similar or independent. This technique is similar to the definition of an alias in a SQL statement.

3.2 Consequences on the User Interfaces

The composition of operators introduces the fact that several parts of a graphic representation are defined depending on the semantics of an operator. Let us use for example the spatial intersection. Figure 3.1 presents a symbolic representation of an intersection.

A   B

Fig. 3.1 - symbolic representation of an intersection

The application of the intersection provides (1) the intersection itself, (2) the part of A that does not intersect with B, (3) the part of B that does not intersect with A. The user interface based on a visual representation must provide the ability to precise the relevant part in a new subquery. Two queries with the same semantics must have the same visual expression. As an example a symbolic representation for query Q5 (or Q6 since they have the same semantics) is represented Figure 3.2 (we do not consider the way the drawing is performed - i.e. the type of user interface used to define such a query).

ForestType (resp. PollutedAreaType)

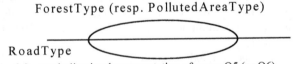

RoadType

Fig. 3.2 - symbolic visual representation of query Q5 (or Q6)

Since a user do not have to know the way data are stored in the database, the management of the overlap or not of the database components must not be handled at this level. The formal modeling of a query must be similar. The query must be formally represented by an expression like

composition (3   (ForestType 1, RoadType 2))
or   composition (3   (PollutedAreaType 1, RoadType 2))

The DBMS must be able to evaluate whether or not an overlap may occur or not since a wrong result may be obtained as soon as a tuple oriented philosphy is used for the query language. A SQL statement of query Q5 (or Q6) must be like :

Select   R.*,   (R.SR, F.SR)
From   RoadType R, ForestType F
Where   intersection (R.SR, F.SR)
Group by   R.name
Having   (length ((R.SR, F.SR)) > 10)

Figure 3.3 presents a symbolic representation of a data set. The strict application of such a query involves an inconstancy since the intersection of the road and the common part of the two polluted area is summed twice (in case of an overlap).

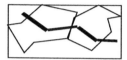 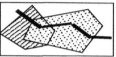

Fig. 3.3 - Symbolic representation of a data set

To provide a unique query formulation, the Data Definition Language must provide a supplementary clause managing the conceptual overlap or not between two instances of a type (relation or class depending on the data model). This precision can also be considered as an integrity constraint.

4 User Interfaces

An end user query language for GIS must emphasize the visual nature of geographical data. Numerous propositions [3, 7, 10] or studies on visual interfaces have already been performed [1, 2]. In this part, we consider the second level of manipulations (i.e., the end-user interface). Within the two kinds of querying, we consider the dynamic querying. A dynamic querying is based on the representation of the required spatial relationships as querying primitives. The drawing, modeling a query, may be provided by the end-user (with the problem of the interpretation of this query to express it with a formal language) or provided by the system using the user's directives (i.e., the required relationships). In both of them, ambiguities may appear depending on the allowed expressive power of the interface.

A database query language based on spatial predicates is not relevant for this kind of end-user interface. The operators are mandatory. Once operators are available, the problem is to determine whether they accept or not the composition. An underlying database query language, without composition and without the software able to simulate this composition reduces the expressive power since manipulations can only be performed on basic components of the database. The visual representation of a query is simplified since few ambiguities may appear. An underlying database query language without composition but with a software able to simulate it provides a better expressive power. This expressive power is similar to the one obtained with a query language allowing the composition. The level of ambiguity is closely linked to the existence or not of the spatial difference operator (since the number of relevant sub-parts of a query may be important - Figure 3.1).

A query language with a path operator between two given places providing a unique path as an answer (e.g., shortest path) or without a path operator can be designed upon a database extended with spatial (network) operators. As soon as the path operator provides several paths as an answer, the query language must be extended to allow the horizontal composition with identification of the path operator (since it may appear several times in the same query with the same arguments). Furthermore, the definition of a query with a path operator requires the introduction of aggregates (e.g., a cost less than 100 units). These aggregates are nearly mandatory to provide a realistic computational time and ... a realistic use of the results in the case of large databases. The aggregates may introduce also some ambiguities since the result of the path operator (i.e., a set of path) cannot be considered as a unique path.

5. Conclusion

The user-friendliness of a visual interface is one of the major argument for the acceptation of a new tool. The expressive power is a second one. Geographical data are by essence visual. A visual approach to query a geographical database seems a very promising solution. The expressive power of the geographical query languages varies depending on the query primitives. From the historical point of view, the introduction of spatial predicates was the first attempt. Its weakness is the very low expressive power. The second attempt was the introduction of spatial operators. The problem is then to allow or not the composition of operators. The composition of spatial operators is the best solution to provide a powerful database query language.

The user interface may rely on a 'click in a box' approach to a full freedom visual query language. The higher is the level of abstraction, the more difficult is the interpretation of a visual query. Ambiguities may be raised whenever a component of a query is selected or whenever a spatial relationship is visualized. From a visual query language to an alphanumeric database query language, the gap may be important. The composition of operators is a major requirement to define a realistic query language for geographical applications. A difference is introduced between a visual query language and a visual interface to a geographical DBMS. A visual query language must provide a higher level of abstraction than the query language of the DBMS is able to offer. A DBMS query language based on predicates leads to a very weak expressive power. A DBMS query language with a set of spatial operators but without composition requires a visual language allowing a composition and a software (applied in the middleware) to simulate the composition and to guarantee the consistency of final results. A DBMS allowing the composition (with the possibility to use several times the same operator with the same arguments in a query) would require now a sophisticated visual interface able to take into account the various components of the composition of operators. The definition of such an interface is therefore a challenge.

References

1. Aufaure M.A., Trepied C. : A Survey of Query Languages for Geographic Information Systems. Interfaces to databases (IDS-3), Napier University Edinburgh, 8-10 July (1996)
2. Batini C., Catarci T., Costabile M.F., Levialdi S.: Visual Query Systems: A Taxonomy, Visual Database Systems II, IFIP-TC2/WG2.6, Budapest, Hungary, IFIP Transaction A7, 30/9–3/10 (1991)
3. Calcinelli D., Mainguenaud M.: Cigales, A visual Query Language for geographical Information System : the User Interface, Journal of Visual Languages and Computing, Vol 5, Academic press, (1994), 113-132
4. Claramunt C, Mainguenaud M., : A Revisited Database Projection Operator for network Facilities in a GIS, Informatica, 23, (1999), 187-201
5. Guting, R. H., GRAL: An extensible relational database system for geometric applications. In Proceedings of the 15th International Conference on Very Large Data Bases, VLDB, 22-26 August Amsterdam, The Netherlands, (1989)
6. Haas, L., Cody, W. F., Exploiting extensible DBMS in integrated GIS. In Proceedings of the 2nd International Symposium on Large Spatial Database, Gunther, O. and Schek, H.-J. Eds, Springer-Verlag, Zurich, Lecture Notes in Computer Science, n° 525, (1991)
7. Egenhofer M., Spatial-Query-by-Sketch, IEEE Symposium on Visula Languages (VL), Boulder, Colorado, USA, 3-6 September, (1996)
8. Larue, T., Pastre, D. and Viémont, Y., Strong integration of spatial domains and operators in a relational database system. In Advances in Spatial Databases, Abel, D. J. and Ooi, B. C. Eds., Springer-Verlag, Singapore, Lecture Notes in Computer Science n° 692, (1993)
9. Mainguenaud, M., Consistency of geographical information system results. Computers, Environment and Urban Systems, Vol. 18, Pergamon Press, (1994), 333-342
10. Meyer B., Beyond Icons : Towards New Metaphors for Visual Query Languages for Spatial Information Systems. Ineterfaces to database Systems (IDS92), Glasgow, UK, 1-3 July (1992)
11. Peuquet DJ: A Concepetual Framework and Comparison of Spatial Data Models, Cartographica, Vol 21 (4), (1984) 66-113
12. Smith TR, Menon S, Star JL, Ester JE: Requirements and Principles for the Implementation and Construction of Large Scale GIS, Int. Journal of Geographical Information System, Vol 1, n°1, (1987), 13-31
13. Stemple, D., Sheard, T. and Bunker, R., Abstract data types in databases: Specification, Manipulation and Access. In Proceedings of the 2nd Int. Conference on Data Engineering, Los Angeles, USA, 6-8 Feb (1986)
14. Ullman JD: Principles of Database and Knowledge-base Systems, Computer Science Press, Maryland, (1988)

Content-Based Image Retrieval By Relevance Feedback [*]

Zhong Jin[1], Irwin King[2], and Xuequn Li

[1] Department of Computer Science,
Nanjing University of Science and Technology,
Nanjing, People's Republic of China
jinzhong@mail.njust.edu.cn
[2] Department of Computer Science and Engineering,
The Chinese University of Hong Kong,
Shatin, N.T., Hong Kong
{king, xqli}@cse.cuhk.edu.hk

Abstract. Relevance feedback is a powerful technique for content-based image retrieval. Many parameter estimation approaches have been proposed for relevance feedback. However, most of them have only utilized information of the relevant retrieved images, and have given up, or have not made great use of information of the irrelevant retrieved images. This paper presents a novel approach to update the interweights of integrated probability function by using the information of both relevant and irrelevant retrieved images. Experimental results have shown the effectiveness and robustness of our proposed approach, especially in the situation of no relevant retrieved images.

1 Introduction

Content-based image retrieval(CBIR) has become one of the most active research areas in the past few years [1]-[6]. Generally, a set of features (e.g. color, shape, texture, moments, etc.) is extracted from an image to represent its content. Successful content-based image retrieval systems require the integration of various techniques in the fields of image processing and information retrieval [7].

Relevance feedback in information retrieval is an automatic process for query reformulation [8]-[10]. In principle, relevance feedback is based on automatically changing the set of query terms as well as the weights associated with these terms. This is done in order to increase the weights of important query terms and to decrease the weights of unimportant ones. It is accomplished by investigating the set of documents initially retrieved, and increasing the weights of those terms that are in the relevant documents. Experiments show the relevance feedback techniques considerably improve the quality of the term-weighting retrieval system.

---

[*] This paper is supported in part by an Earmarked RGC Grant from the Hong Kong Research Grant Council # CUHK4176/97E.

R. Laurini (Ed.): VISUAL 2000, LNCS 1929, pp. 521–529, 2000.
Springer-Verlag Berlin Heidelberg 2000

Recently, relevance feedback based CBIR techniques have emerged as a promising research direction. MARS [7] introduced both a query vector moving technique and a re-weighting technique to estimate the ideal query parameter. MindReader [11] formulated a minimization problem on the parameter estimation process. Rui et al. [12] present a relevance feedback based interactive retrieval approach, which effectively takes into account the following two distinct characteristic of CBIR systems: the gap between high-level concepts and low-level features, and subjectivity of human perception of visual content. Rui and Huang [13] proposed a novel global optimization framework. Wood, Campbell and Thomas [14] described an image database query system(IDQS), which consisted of a set of radial basic function (RBF) networks.

Most relevance feedback based CBIR techniques have only utilized information of the relevant retrieved images and cannot deal with situations of no relevant retrieved images. They have not made great use of information of the irrelevant retrieved images, especially in the situation of there is less relevant retrieved images than irrelevant retrieved images.

In our opinion, both the relevant retrieved images and the irrelevant retrieved images contain much information of features used. This paper presents a novel update approach for interweights to . It is organized as follows. In section 2, some relevance feedback techniques are introduced. A novel update approach for interweights is proposed in section 3. In Section 4, performance experiments are conducted, and experimental results are discussed. Section 5 gives a conclusion.

2   Overall Similarity Function

Suppose an image databases DB is composed of c training images $\{I_1, I_2, \cdots, I_c\}$. For a query image Q, a retrieval decision can be made according to the overall similarity between Q and any image $I \in DB$. An image contains rich content, such as color, shape, texture and invariant moments of the object in the image, and each of these features(e.g. shape) can be characterized by a feature vector.

Feature Extraction For any image $I \in DB$, a feature extraction function F is defined as

$$F(I) : \Re^{|I|} \to \Re^n \qquad (1)$$

where $|\cdot|$ indicates the number of elements of a digital image matrix.

Suppose m feature vectors can be extracted for an image, the similarity for the ith feature between the query image Q and any training image $I \in DB$ can be defined as followings:

$$\Phi_i(I, Q) = (F_i(I) - F_i(Q))^T W_i (F_i(I) - F_i(Q)) \qquad (2)$$

where $F_i(I)$ and $F_i(Q)$ are the ith n_i-dimensional image feature vectors of the images I and Q, and W_i are the $(n_i \times n_i)$ intraweight matrix associated with the components of the ith feature vectors. Therefore, the overall similarity function between the query image Q and any training image $I \in DB$ can be defined:

$$D(I,Q) = \sum_{i=1}^{m} U_i \Phi_i (I,Q) \tag{3}$$

where U_i are the interweights associated with the ith feature vectors.

The images in the database DB are ordered by their overall similarities to the query image Q. The k most similar ones $\Re = \{R_1, R_2, \cdots, R_k\}$ are returned to the user, where k is the number of images the user wants to retrieve.

Optimization Approach Suppose for any retrieved image $R_j \in \Re$, π_j is the degree of relevance given by user. The following optimization problem was formulated by Y. Hui et al. [12]:

$$\min J = \sum_{j=1}^{k} \pi_j D(R_j, Q) \tag{4}$$

$$s.t. \begin{cases} \sum_{i=1}^{m} \dfrac{1}{U_i} = 1 \\ \det(W_i) = 1 \\ (i = 1, \cdots, m) \end{cases} \tag{5}$$

The optimal update for Q_i is

$$\hat{Q}_i = \frac{\sum_{j=1}^{k} \pi_j F_i(R_j)}{\sum_{j=1}^{k} \pi_j} \tag{6}$$

That is, the ideal query vector for the ith feature is nothing but the weighted average of the retrieved images for the ith feature.

The optimal solutions for W_i is

$$\hat{W}_i = \sqrt[n_i]{\det(C_i)}C_i^{-1} \tag{7}$$

where $C_i = \sum_{j=1}^{k} \pi_j \Delta_{ij} \Delta_{ij}^T / \sum_{j=1}^{k} \pi_j$, $\Delta_{ij} = F_i(R_j) - F_i(Q)$. The physical meaning of this optimal solution is that the optimal weight matrix is inversely proportional to the covariance matrix of the retrieved images.

The optimal update formula for U_i is

$$\hat{U}_i = \sum_{v=1}^{m} \sqrt{J_v / J_i} \tag{8}$$

where $J_v = \sum_{j=1}^{k} \pi_j \Delta_{vj}^T W_v \Delta_{vj}$ $(v = 1, \cdots, m)$. This formula tell us, if the total distance J_i of the ith feature is small, this feature should receive high weight and vice versa.

For the interweight updating formula (8), U_i are dealt only with the relevant retrieved images. This formula can not utilize any information of the irrelevant retrieved images, and does not work when all the retrieved images are regarded as irrelevant to the query by the user. This paper intends to make greater use of information of all the retrieved images.

Scoring Approach Suppose for any retrieved image $R_j \in \Re$, the user marks it as highly relevant, relevant, neutral, irrelevant, or highly irrelevant, according to his information need and perception subjectivity. Let $Score(R_j)$ be the relevance score fedback by the user for the jth retrieved image $R_j \in \Re$:

$$Score(R_j) = \begin{cases} 3 & \text{if highly relevant} \\ 1 & \text{if relevant} \\ 0 & \text{if no opinion} \\ -1 & \text{if irrelevant} \\ -3 & \text{if highly irrelevant} \end{cases} \tag{9}$$

Let $\Re^{(i)} = \{R_1^{(i)}, R_2^{(i)}, \cdots, R_k^{(i)}\}$ be the set containing the k most similar images to the query Q according to the similarity value $\Phi_i(I, Q)$ for the ith feature. The interweights U_i can be calculated with the following formula [13]:

$$U_i = \sum_{R_j \in \Re^{(i)}} Score(R_j) \tag{10}$$

It is noted that if $U_i < 0$, set it to 0 and the raw weights are needed to be normalized to make the sum of the normalized weights equal to 1.

3   Integrated Probability Function

Based on the posterior probability estimators, King and Jin [15] proposed an integrated probability function, which was successfully used as a new multi-feature combination decision rule in the Chinese cursive script characteristic image retrieval.

Integrated Probability Function The following integrated probability function can serve as the overall similarity function $D(I, Q)$ [15]:

$$D(I, Q) = \frac{\sum_{i=1}^{m} U_i P(F_i(I), F_i(Q))}{\sum_{i=1}^{m} U_i} \tag{11}$$

where $P(F_i(I), F_i(Q))$ is the estimator of the posterior matching probability between image I and image Q on the ith feature, which is determined according to the following formula:

$$P(F_i(I), F_i(Q)) = \frac{1}{c-1} \left(1 - \frac{\|F_i(I) - F_i(Q)\|}{\sum_{v=1}^{c} \|F_i(I_v) - F_i(Q)\|}\right) \tag{12}$$

where $\| \cdot \|$ indicates the common Euclidean distance.

Suppose for any retrieved image $R_j \in \Re$, the user marks it as **relevant**, **neutral**, or **irrelevant** according to his information need and perception subjectivity. Let S be the number of retrieved images in $\Re$ which are relevant to the query Q and T be the number of retrieved images in $\Re$ which are irrelevant to the query Q.

For the ith feature, Let s_i be the number of retrieved images in $\Re^{(i)}$ which are relevant to the query Q and t_i be the number of retrieved images in $\Re^{(i)}$ which are irrelevant to the query Q.

For the interweight updating formula (10), if the number of highly relevant or highly irrelevant retrieved images is supposed to be 0, U_i are dealt only with s_i and t_i. When S is much smaller than T, s_i have more probabilities to be less than t_i, and therefore U_i will be zero for each $i \in \{1, 2, \cdots, m\}$. For example, suppose that S be 1 and T be 9, then s_i will be in $\{0, 1\}$ and t_i will be in $\{0, 1, \cdots, 9\}$. However, it is easy to understand that in the above example, if for a given i, s_i be 1 and t_i be 2, the ith feature can be said to be more effective than all m features to be used with known interweights, i.e., U_i should be greater than 0, which is assigned according to the existing formula (10).

In our opinion, in order to make greater use of information of all the retrieved images, U_i should be dealt with the ratios of $\dfrac{s_i}{S}$ and $\dfrac{t_i}{T}$. Taking into account the situations of zero relevant retrieved images or zero irrelevant retrieved images, a novel updating formula of raw interweights U_i is presented as follows:

$$U_i(s_i, t_i) = \exp\left\{\alpha\left(\frac{s_i + 1}{S + 1} - \frac{t_i + 1}{T + 1}\right)\right\} \tag{13}$$

where $\alpha > 0$ is a constant.

Obviously, $U_i(s_i, t_i)$ will increase as s_i increases for a fixed t_i, and will decrease as t_i increases for a fixed s_i. If for any fixed i^{th} feature, $s_i = S$, and $t_i = T$, we have $U_i(S, T) = 1$, which means that the ith feature is as effective as all features. As we know, the exponential function $\exp(\cdot)$ changes slowly on the interval $(-1, 1)$, a large parameter α is needed in the formula (13). The raw weights are needed to be normalized to make the sum of the normalized weights equal to 1.

4   Experimental Results

In this section, we compare the retrieval performance between the proposed method and the scoring method.

There are 10 trademark images with 111×111 resolution [6]. For each trademark image, 10 deformed images and 10 hand draw images can be obtained, and these 21 images can be regarded as to be relevant images. The database is composed of 10 trademark images and their corresponding 10 deformed images for each. All the 110 images in the database DB are shown in Figure 1. In the experiment, we tested our system with 100 hand drawn images, which are divided into 10 groups and indexed from 1 to 100. Figure 2 shows these 100 hand drawn test images.

For an image, seven kinds of features are extracted. They are listed in Table 1. The first four kinds of features are from [6], and the last three kinds of features are computed on 55×55 low resolution images [15].

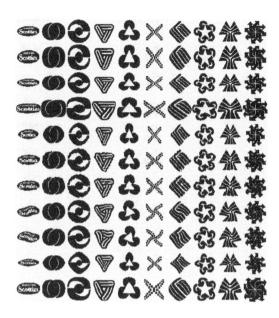

Fig. 1.   110 Images in the Database DB

The retrieval performance is measured using the following average retrieval precision:

$$Precision = \frac{relevant\ \ retrieved}{k} \times 100\% \qquad (14)$$

where $k = 10$ is the number of total retrieved images.

The initial interweights U_i ($i = 1, \cdots, 7$) are given to be equal. The parameter α is chosen to be 5. The average retrieval precisions for each test group and all the test images are summarized in Table 2. The symbol "rf" denotes how many iterations of relevance feedback.

From Table 2, the average retrieval precision increases from 74.7% to over 90% by relevance feedback techniques. Relevance feedback is a powerful tool for content-based information retrieval. Moreover, the proposed update formula (13) is more effective than the existing scoring formula (10).

For 74 samples out of all 100 test images, the same retrieval performances are obtained with these two methods. For the other 26 samples, two methods obtain different retrieval performances. These experimental results in detail are listed in Table 3.

From Table 3, the proposed novel method is shown to be more robust than the scoring method, especially for 33th sample. Moreover, it can make great use

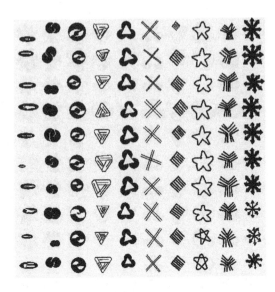

Fig. 2.   100 Hand Drawn Test Images

of information of both relevant retrieved images and irrelevant retrieved images, especially in the situations of no relevant retrieved images.

5   Conclusion

In this paper, a novel relevance feedback technique for updating the interweights has been proposed. Experimental results show that the proposed method outperforms the existing scoring method. Although our database is small, it is convincing that the proposed method can make great use of information of all the retrieved images to the user.

6   Acknowledgement

This paper is supported in part by a Earmarked RGC Grant from the Hong Kong Research Grant Council #CUHK4407/99E.

References

1. C. Faloutsos, R. Barber, M. Flickner, J. Hafner, W. Niblack, D. Petkovic, and W. Equitz. Efficient and effective querying by image content. *Journal of Intelligent Information Systems*, 3(3/4):231-262, July 1994.

Table 1. Seven Kinds of Features for an Image

No.	Description of Feature
1	1-dimensional eccentricity [6]
2	1-dimensional circularity of approximated boundary
3	7-dimensional invariant moment vector
4	63-dimensional Fourier descriptors of approximated boundary
5	36-dimensional pseudo Zernike moment vector $\{Z_{nk}(0 \le k \le n \le 7)\}$ [15]
6	30-dimensional Zernike moment vector $\{Z_{nk}(0 \le k \le n \le 8, \text{ and } n - k = \text{even})\}$
7	25-dimensional Legendre moment vector $\{\lambda_{mn}(0 \le m, n \le 4)\}$

Table 2. Average Retrieval Precisions in Percentage for Groups and for DB

Group	0 rf	Scoring 1 rf	Scoring 2 rf	Proposed 1 rf	Proposed 2 rf	Group	0 rf	Scoring 1 rf	Scoring 2 rf	Proposed 1 rf	Proposed 2 rf
1-10	100	100	100	100	100	51-60	100	100	100	100	100
11-20	81	100	100	100	100	61-70	50	97	100	92	100
21-30	17	60	60	63	81	71-80	63	91	92	95	95
31-40	98	94	99	99	99	81-90	78	81	85	87	90
41-50	96	100	100	100	100	91-100	64	77	77	83	85
Average Precision for DB							74.7	90	91.3	91.9	95

2. C. P. Lam, J. K. Wu, and B. Mehtre. STAR–A System for trademark archival and retrieval. In *2nd Asian Conf. on Computer Vision*, volume 3, pages 214-217, 1995.
3. Y. S. Kim and W. Y. Kim. Content-based trademark retrieval system using visually salient feature. In *IEEE Computer Society Cnf. on Computer Vision and Pattern Recognition*, pages 307-312, 1997.
4. A. K. Jain and A. Vailaya. Shape-based retrieval: A case study with trademark image databases. *Pattern Recognition*, 31(9):1369-1390, 1998.
5. J. P. Eakins, J. M. Boardman, and M. E. Graham. Similarity retrieval of trademark images. *IEEE Multimedia*, 5(2):53-63, 1998.
6. D. Y. M. Chan, I. King, D. P. Huijsmans et al. Genetic algorithm for weights assignment in dissimilarity function for trademark retrieval. In *Visual Information and Information Systems. Third International Conference, VISUAL'99. Proceedings (Lecture Notes in Computer Science Vol.1614)*, pages 557-565, The Netherlands, June 1999.
7. Y. Rui, T. S. Huang, and S. Mehrotra. Content-based image retrieval with relevance feedback in MARS. *Proceedings of IEEE International Conference on Image Processing*,pp815-818, Santa Barbara, California, October, 1997.
8. I. J. Aalbersberg. Incremental relevance feedback. *15th International ACM/SIGIR Conference on Research and Development in Information Retrieval*, Demark, June, 1992, pp11-22
9. C. Lundquist, D. A. Grossman, and O. Frieder. Improving relevance feedback in the vector space model. *Proceedings of the Sixth International Conference on Information and Knowledge Management. CIKM'97*, Las Vegas, Nevada, USA, Nov. 1997, pp16-23

Table 3. Average Retrieval Precisions in Percentage for 26 Samples

Sample	0 *rf*	Scoring		Proposed		Sample	0 *rf*	Scoring		Proposed	
		1 *rf*	2 *rf*	1 *rf*	2 *rf*			1 *rf*	2 *rf*	1 *rf*	2 *rf*
23	0	0	0	0	10	77	60	70	70	80	80
24	0	0	0	10	90	80	60	80	80	90	90
26	0	0	0	20	100	82	80	90	90	70	80
33	90	40	20	90	90	84	90	80	90	100	100
61	60	100	100	90	100	85	50	50	50	60	70
64	50	100	100	90	100	89	50	20	50	70	80
65	30	90	100	80	100	91	30	90	90	80	80
66	60	100	100	90	100	92	20	20	20	60	70
67	50	100	100	90	100	93	20	80	80	70	70
68	50	100	100	90	100	94	80	90	90	100	100
69	30	90	100	80	100	95	80	80	80	90	90
74	70	90	100	100	100	96	80	80	80	90	90
76	30	80	80	90	90	98	80	80	80	90	100
Average Precision for these 26 Samples							50	69.2	71.1	75.8	87.7

10. C Buckley and G. Salton. Optimization of relevance feedback weights. *18th International ACM SIGIR Conference on Research and Development in Information Retrieval* , Seattle, WA, USA, July 1995, pp351-357.

11. Y. Ishikawa, R. Subramanya, C. Faloutsos et al. Mindreader: querying database through multiple examples. *Proceedings of the Twenty-Fourth International Conference on Very-Large Databases*, New York, Aug. 1998, pp218-227.

12. Y. Rui, T. S. Huang, M. Ortega, and S. Mehrotra. Relevance feedback: a power tool for interactive content-based image retrieval. *IEEE Transactions on Circuits and Systems for Video Technology*, vol. 8, No. 5, pp644-655, 1998.

13. Y. Rui and T. S. Huang. A novel relevance feedback technique in image retrieval. *Proceedings ACM Multimedia '99(Part2)*,Orlando, FL, USA, 1999, pp67-70.

14. M. E. J. Wood, N. W. Campbell and B. T. Thomas. Iterative refinement by relevance feedback in content-based digital image retrieval. *Proceedings ACM Multimedia'98*, Bristol, UK, Sept, 1998, pp13-18

15. I. King, Z. Jin and D. Y. M. Chan. Chinese cursive script character image retrieval based on an integrated probability function, submitted to *the VISUAL 2000, 4th International Conference on Visual Information Systems*, Lyon, France, November 2-4, 2000

Chinese Cursive Script Character Image Retrieval Based on an Integrated Probability Function[*]

Irwin King[1], Zhong Jin[2], and David Yuk-Ming Chan[1]

[1] Department of Computer Science and Engineering,
The Chinese University of Hong Kong,
Shatin, N.T., Hong Kong
king@cse.cuhk.edu.hk
[2] Department of Computer Science,
Nanjing University of Science and Technology,
Nanjing, People's Republic of China
jinzhong@mail.njust.edu.cn

Abstract. Often in content-based image retrieval, a single image attribute may not have enough discriminative information for retrieval. On the other hand, when multiple features are used, it is hard to determine the suitable weighting factors for various features for optimal retrieval. In this paper, we present an idea of integrated probability function and use it to combine features for Chinese cursive script character image retrieval. A database of 1400 monochromatic images is used. Experimental results show that the proposed system based on Legendre moment feature, Zernike moment feature, and pseudo Zernike moment feature is robust to retrieval deformed images. Using our integrated probability function, ninety-nine percent of the targets are ranked at the top 2 positions.

1 Introduction

The last few years have seen an upsurge of interest in contend-based image retrieval (CBIR) — the selection of images from a collection via features automatically extracted from images themselves [1]-[6]. Chinese calligraphy is invaluable in the history of Chinese civilization. There are five styles of Chinese calligraphy. Among them, the cursive script style usually has a low level of legibility and most closely approaches abstract art. Figure 1 shows a page of Chinese cursive style calligraphy [7]. Therefore, it is challenging to develop a Chinese cursive script character image retrieval system. The goal is not to classify but to rank based on similarity.

The ultimate goal of designing information retrieval systems is to achieve the best possible retrieval performance for the task at hand. This objective traditionally led to the development of different retrieval schemes for any information

---

[*] This paper is supported in part by an Earmarked RGC Grant from the Hong Kong Research Grant Council # CUHK4176/97E and # CUHK 4407/99E.

R. Laurini (Ed.): VISUAL 2000, LNCS 1929, pp. 530–539, 2000.
Springer-Verlag Berlin Heidelberg 2000

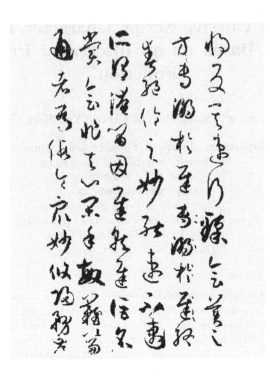

Fig. 1. A page of Chinese cursive style calligraphy

retrieval problem to be solved. The results of an experimental assessment of the different designs would then be the basis for choosing one as a final solution to the problem. It has been observed in such design studies, that different retrieval scheme design potentially offers complementary information which can be harnessed to improve the performance of the selected design.

One idea is not to rely on a single decision making scheme. Instead, all designs, or their subset, are used for decision making by combining their individual opinions to derive a consensus decision. This motivates the relatively recent interest in combining techniques. Cao et al. [8] presented to recognize handwritten numerals with multiple features and multistage classifiers. Kittler et al. [9] developed a common theoretical framework for combining classifiers and demonstrated that the combination rule — the sum rule — outperforms other classifier combination schemes. Recently, Chan and King [6, 10] proposed a weight assignment method in dissimilarity function using genetic algorithm.

This paper presents a combination technique of multi-feature based on the posterior probability estimators. Experiments with 6 kinds of features have been conducted on a database of 1400 Chinese cursive script character images. It is organized as follows. In section 2, a new combination technique is proposed. Section 3 performance experiments are conducted, and experimental results are discussed. Section 4 gives a conclusion.

2   Combination Technique

2.1   Problem Definition

Suppose an image database DB is composed of c distinct images $\{I_1, I_2, \cdots, I_c\}$ and there are K images $\{I_{q1}, I_{q2}, \cdots, I_{qK}\}$ for queries. For a query I_q, image retrieval decision can be made according to the dissimilarity between I_q and any image $I \in DB$. This dissimilarity can be called as a kind of decision function.

Definition 1 (Decision Function) A decision function between two images I and I_q is defined as

$$D(I, I_q) : \Re^{|I|} \times \Re^{|I_q|} \to \Re^1, \tag{1}$$

where $|\cdot|$ indicates the number of elements of a matrix.

Definition 2 (Training Pair) For any query I_{qj}, a training pair TP_j is defined as

$$TP_j = (I_{i(j)}, I_{qj}), \; j = 1, 2, \ldots, K, \tag{2}$$

where $i(j) \in \{1, 2, \cdots, c\}$, and $I_{i(j)} \in DB$ is the best matched image for I_{qj} defined by the user.

Definition 3 (Retrieval Position) Given a training pair $TP_j = (I_{i(j)}, I_{qj})$. The decision function values $\{D(I_i, I_{qj})\}_{i=1}^{i=c}$ can be computed for the given j with equation (1) and ranked according to the minimum rule. The target position of $D(I_{i(j)}, I_{qj})$ in the ranking, which is denoted by N_j, can be called the retrieval position of the training pair $TP_j = (I_{i(j)}, I_{qj})$.

Definition 4 (Average Position) An average position for a training pair set $TP = \{TP_j\}_{j=1}^{j=K}$ can be defined as follows:

$$\overline{N} = \frac{1}{k} \sum_{j=1}^{K} N_j. \tag{3}$$

2.2   Integrated Dissimilarity Function

In general, the dissimilarity of two images I_i and I_{qj} can be determined with their features.

Definition 5 (Feature Extraction) For any image I, a feature extraction function F is defined as

$$F(I) : \Re^{|I|} \to \Re^d, \tag{4}$$

which extracts a real-valued d-dimensional feature vector.

Definition 6 (Integrated Dissimilarity Function) Assume that there are M feature extraction functions $\{F_i\}_{i=1}^{i=M}$. The decision function $D(I, I_q)$ can be defined as the following integrated dissimilarity function:

$$D(I, I_q) = \frac{\sum_{i=1}^{M} w_i D(F_i(I), F_i(I_q))}{\sum_{i=1}^{M} w_i}, \tag{5}$$

where

$$D(F_i(I), F_i(I_q)) = \|F_i(I) - F_i(I_q)\| \tag{6}$$

is the Euclidean distance between the ith feature vector $F_i(I), F_i(I_q) \in \Re^{d_i}$, and the w_i is the weight assigned to the feature extraction function F_i.

2.3   Integrated Probability Function

Combination techniques in pattern recognition problems have been extensively investigated in recent years. Consider a pattern recognition problem where pattern Z is to be assigned to one of the c possible classes $(\omega_1, \omega_2, \cdots, \omega_c)$. Assume there are M distinct measurement vectors $\{x_i\}_{i=1}^{M}$. Kittler et al. [9] demonstrated that under some assumptions, the following combination rule — the sum rule — outperforms other classifier combination schemes:

$$Z \longrightarrow \omega_j \quad \text{with} \quad \arg\max_j \frac{1}{M} \sum_{i=1}^{M} P(\omega_j | x_i). \tag{7}$$

The most commonly used classifier is the minimum distance classifier.

Minimum Distance Rule Given a measurement vector x for the pattern Z and the representative measurement vectors x^j for the class ω_j ($j = 1, 2, \cdots, c$), the dissimilarity between two vectors x and x^j can be measured by the Euclidean distance. The minimum decision rule is

$$Z \longrightarrow \omega_j \quad \text{with} \quad \arg\min_j \|x - x^k\|, \tag{8}$$

where $\| \cdot \|$ indicates the Euclidean distance.

Generally speaking, the smaller the distance value $\|x - x^k\|$, the larger the posterior probability $\hat{p}(\omega_k | x)$. Thus, we can present an estimator of the posterior probability $P(\omega_k | x)$ as follows:

$$\hat{p}(\omega_k | x) = \frac{1}{c - 1}\left(1 - \frac{\|x - x^k\|}{\sum_{j=1}^{c} \|x - x^j\|}\right) \overset{\text{def}}{=} \hat{P}(x^k, x). \tag{9}$$

Therefore, it is obvious that the minimum decision rule (8) is equivalent to the following maximum decision rule:

$$Z \longrightarrow \omega_j \quad \text{with} \quad \arg\max_j \hat{P}(x^k, x). \tag{10}$$

Definition 7 (Integrated Probability Function) Assume that there are M feature extraction functions $\{F_i\}_{i=1}^{i=M}$. The decision function $D(I, I_q)$ can be defined as the following integrated probability function:

$$D(I, I_q) = \frac{\sum_{i=1}^{M} w_i \hat{P}(F_i(I), F_i(I_q))}{\sum_{i=1}^{M} w_i}, \tag{11}$$

where the w_i is the weight and $\hat{P}(F_i(I), F_i(I_q))$ is the estimator of the posterior matching probability between image I and image I_q on the feature extraction function F_i, which is determined according to Equation (9).

3   Retrieval Experiments

Our aim is to develop a Chinese cursive script image retrieval system that is insensitive to variations on image deformations. In experiments, we evaluate the performances of six shape features, which are the invariant moments [15], eccentricity [16], edge direction histogram [17, 18], Legendre moments, Zernike moments and pseudo-Zernike moments [19–21]. We also evaluate the performances of the various combination schemes of features according to the frequency of the retrieval positions and the average retrieval position.

3.1   Database

Our Database DB has 1,400 binarized Chinese cursive script character images. Each image is normalized to the size of 200 by 200 pixels. These images were scanned from the book [22] with the resolution of 150dpi. In experiments, we test the behavior of our image retrieval system in the presence of the deformation transformations as shown in Figure 2.

10 images in DB are used to generate a set of 100 deformed images, as shown in Figure 3.

The deformed images were submitted as query images to the retrieval system to examine whether the deformed images can retrieval their original images or not.

3.2   Feature Extracted

For an image, six shape features are extracted. They are listed in Table 1. The first three kinds of features are from [10], and the last three kinds of features are computed on 50×50 low resolution images.

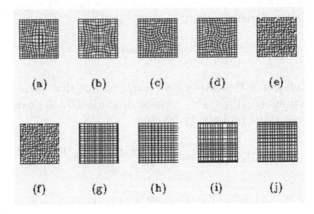

Fig. 2. Distortions include Pinch:(a) and (b); Twirl: (c) and (d); Ripple: (e) and (f); Horizontal Extension: (g) and (h); and Vertical Extension (i) and (j).

Table 1. Six Features for an Image

No.	Feature Description
x1	1-dimensional eccentricity [10]
x2	7-dimensional invariant moment vector
x3	30-dimensional vector of edge direction of the histogram
x4	36-dimensional pseudo Zernike moment vector $\{Z_{nk}(0 \leq k \leq n \leq 7)\}$
x5	30-dimensional Zernike moment vector $\{Z_{nk}(0 \leq k \leq n \leq 8, \text{ and } n - k = \text{even})\}$
x6	25-dimensional Legendre moment vector $\{\lambda_{mn}(0 \leq m, n \leq 4)\}$

3.3   Evaluation of Features

In order to evaluate the effectiveness of 6 features for Chinese cursive script character images, for any fixed j $(1 \leq j \leq 6)$, we can use the single feature x_j to conduct 100 queries with 100 training pairs. After 100 retrieval positions are obtained, the position frequency and the average position can be computed. These experimental results are listed in the Table 2.

From the Table 2, we have the following facts and discussions:

The 1-dimensional eccentricity and the 7-dimensional invariant moments are not effective features for Chinese cursive script character image retrieval since no less than 38% of the targets are ranked behind the top 70 positions. The dimensions of these two kinds of features are too small for our database. The low dimensional features do not have sufficient discriminative information for image retrieval on a large scale database.

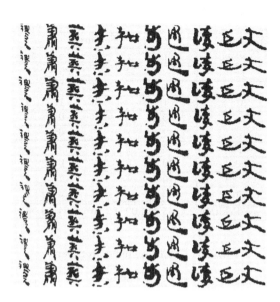

Fig. 3.   100 queries deformed from 10 character images for performance evaluation.

The 30-dimensional edge direction of histogram is not an efficient feature for Chinese cursive script character image retrieval as 21% of the targets are ranked behind the top 70 positions. As the histogram of an image is treated as a 1-D discrete signal, it can not have enough discriminative information for image retrieval on a large scale database.

The Legendre moments, Zernike moments, and pseudo Zernike moments are effective features for the Chinese cursive script character images, about 90% of the targets are ranked at the top 3 positions. But they are not very satisfactory as no less than 1% target was ranked after the top 70 positions. Generally speaking, moments can describe the global characteristic of an image. Therefore, high-order moments are required for image retrieval on a large scale database.

3.4   Combination Results

In order to evaluate the effectiveness of the integrated probability function, the following combination schemes are considered and listed in Table 3.

With each scheme, we can conduct 100 queries with 100 training pairs, and get 100 positions, with which the position frequency and the average position can be computed. The experimental results are listed in the Table 4.

From the Table 4, we have the following facts and discussions:

Table 2. Retrieval Results on Single Feature

Frequency of Positions	Features					
	x_1	x_2	x_3	x_4	x_5	x_6
1	2	33	27	89	81	94
2	4	3	7	5	7	2
3	1	5	5	1	3	0
4	0	0	4	0	0	0
5	2	1	1	0	1	1
(5,10]	3	7	7	2	2	1
(10,20]	10	6	7	0	1	0
(20,70]	16	7	21	1	4	1
>70	62	38	21	2	1	1
Average Position	200.65	114.09	62.76	5.64	4.58	4.31

Table 3. Seven Combination Schemes

No.	Scheme Description
C1	combining x_4 with x_5
C2	combining x_4 with x_6
C3	combining x_5 with x_6
C4	combining x_4, x_5 with x_6
C5	combining x_3, x_4, x_5 with x_6
C6	combining x_2, x_3, x_4, x_5 with x_6
C7	combining x_1, x_2, x_3, x_4, x_5 with x_6

With the proposed integrated probability function, the combination of features performs in general better than single feature does in decreasing the average position for retrieval.

Among seven combination schemes, the combination of Legendre moment, Zernike moment, and pseudo Zernike moment outperforms other combination schemes. Ninety-nine percent of the targets were ranked at the top 2 positions, and only one percent target was ranked at the fifth position. The combination of more than these three features cannot increase the effectiveness of image retrieval test. Therefore we proposed a retrieval system based on the combination of Legendre moments, Zernike moments, and pseudo Zernike moments.

The last column of Table 4 lists the retrieval results of [10]. It is obvious that our proposed system performs much better than the existing system.

4   Conclusion and Future Work

This paper presents an idea of using integrated probability function for retrieval of Chinese cursive script character images. It is based on the combination of Legendre moment, Zernike moment, and pseudo Zernike moment. Experiments

Table 4. Retrieval Results on Combination Schemes

Frequency of Positions	Schemes							Chan [10]
	C1	C2	C3	C4	C5	C6	C7	
1	89	98	96	97	97	97	95	43
2	3	0	1	2	2	2	2	
3	1	0	1	0	0	0	2	31
4	2	0	1	0	0	0	0	
5	0	0	0	1	1	1	0	
(5,10]	1	1	0	0	0	0	0	
(10,20]	1	1	1	0	0	0	1	20
(20,70]	2	0	0	0	0	0	0	
>70	1	0	0	0	0	0	0	6
Average Position	3.01	1.18	1.23	1.06	1.06	1.06	1.21	

show that the present system is superior to the existing system [10]. Ninety-nine percent of the targets are ranked at the top 2 positions in a database containing 1,400 images. Further work can be done with the feedback of the weight coefficients.

5   Acknowledgement

This paper is supported in part by a Earmarked RGC Grant from the Hong Kong Research Grant Council #CUHK4407/99E.

References

1. C. Faloutsos, R. Barber, M. Flickner, J. Hafner, W. Niblack, D. Petkovic, and W. Equitz. Efficient and effective querying by image content. *Journal of Intelligent Information Systems*, 3(3/4):231-262, July 1994.
2. C. P. Lam, J. K. Wu, and B. Mehtre. STAR–A System for trademark archival and retrieval. In *2nd Asian Conf. on Computer Vision*, volume 3, pages 214-217, 1995.
3. Y. S. Kim and W. Y. Kim. Content-based trademark retrieval system using visually salient feature. In *IEEE Computer Society Cnf. on Computer Vision and Pattern Recognition*, pages 307-312, 1997.
4. A. K. Jain and A. Vailaya. Shape-based retrieval: A case study with trademark image databases. *Pattern Recognition*, 31(9):1369-1390, 1998.
5. J. P. Eakins, J. M. Boardman, and M. E. Graham. Similarity retrieval of trademark images. *IEEE Multimedia*, 5(2):53-63, 1998.
6. D. Y. M. Chan and I. King. Genetic algorithm for weights assignment in dissimilarity function for trademark retrieval. In *Third International Conf. on Visual Information and Information Systems(VISUAL'99)*, volume 1614 of *Lecture Notes in Computer Science*, pages 557-565, The Netherlands, 1999. Springer.
7. K.C. Ma. *Shu Pu I Chu / Ma Kuo-Chuan I Chu*. Hong Kong: Shao-Hua Wen Hua Fu Wu She, 1977.

8. J. Cao, M. Ahmadi, and M. Shridhar. Recognition of handwritten numerals with multiple feature and multistage classifier, *Pattern Recognition*, 28(2): 153-160, 1995.

9. J. Kittler, R. Hatef, R. P. W. Dubin, and J. Matas. On combining classifiers. *IEEE Transaction on Pattern Analysis and Machine Intelligence*, 20(3):226-239, 1997.

10. D. Y. M. Chan and I. King. Weight assignment in dissimilarity function for Chinese script character image retrieval using genetic algorithm.

11. J. Ashley, R. Barber, M. Flickner, J. Hafner, D. Lee, W. Niblack, and D. Petkovic. Automatic and semiautomatic methods for image annotation and retrieval in QBIC. In *Proceedings of Storage and Retrieval for Image and Video Database III*, volume 2420, pages 24-35, February 1995.

12. J. K. Wu, B. M. Mehtre, Y. J. Gao, Chian-Prong Lam, and A. Desai Narasimhalu. STAR–A multimedia database system for trademark registration. In Witold Litwin and Tore Risch, editors, *Applications of Databases, First International Conf.*, volume 819 of *Lecture Notes in Computer Science*, pages 109-122, Vadstena, Sweden, 21-23 June 1994. Springer.

13. A. Soffer and H. Samet. Using negative shape features for logo similarity matching. In *14th International Conf. on Pattern Recognition*, volume 1, pages 571-573, 1998.

14. F. Mokhtarian, S. Abbasi, and J. Kittler. Efficient and robust retrieval by shape content through curvature scale space. In *First International Workshop on Image Databases and Multi-Media Search*, pages 35-42, Amesterdam, The Ntherlands, August 1996.

15. M. K. Hu. Visual pattern recognition by moment invariants. *IRE Transactions on Information Theory*, 8, 1962.

16. B. Jahne. *Digital Image Processing: Concepts, Algorithms and Scientific Applications*. Springer-Verlag, Berlin; New York, 4 edition, 1997.

17. J. Canny. A computational approach to edge detection. *IEEE Transactions on Pattern Analysis and Machine Intelligence*, 8(6):679-698, 1986.

18. A. K. Jain and A. Vailaya. Image retrieval using color and shape. *Pattern Recognition*, 29(8): 1233-1244, 1996.

19. S. X. Liao and M. Pawlak. On image analysis by moments. *IEEE Transaction on Pattern Analysis and Machine Intelligence*, 18(3): 254-266, 1996.

20. Cho-Huak Teh and R. T Chin. On image analysis by the methods of moments. *IEEE Transaction on Pattern Analysis and Machine Intelligence*, 10(4): 496-513, 1988.

21. R. R. Bailey and M. Srinath. Orthogonal moment features for use with parametric and non-parametric classifiers. *IEEE Transaction on Pattern Analysis and Machine Intelligence*, 18(4): 389-398, 1996.

22. H. H. Lu. *Han Tai Chien Tu Tsao Tzu Pien*. Shang-hai: Shang-hai Shu Hua Chu Pan She, 1989, 1 edition.

Author Index

Abbasi, S. 233
Abdel-Mottaleb, M. 200
Agnihotri, L. 62
Aldershoff, F. 419
Ardebilian, M. 74
Ardizzone, E. 212
Aslandogan, Y. A. 108
Aufaure-Portier, M.-A. 140, 154

Binefa, X. 189
Bonhomme, C. 140
Boujemaa, N. 178
Bouthemy, P. 96
Bruno, E. 327

Caenen, G. 257
Carrive, J. 349
Chan, D.Y.-M. 530
Chang, S.-K. 1, 127
Chella, A. 212
Chen, C. 120
Chen, D.-Y. 37
Chen, L. 74
Cheung, K.K.T. 384, 488
Chi, Z. 477
Ciocca, G. 312
Costagliola, G. 127

Delopoulos, A. 84
DeMenthon, D. 49
Di Sciascio, E. 372
Dimitrova, N. 62
Do, M. N. 279
Donini, F. M. 372
Duan, L. 290
Duffing, G. 244

Fablet, R. 96
Favetta, F. 154
Feng, D. 477
Frederix, G. 257

Gagliardi, I. 312
Gao, W. 290
García, C. 349

Geusebroek, J.-M. 419
Gevers, T. 419
Giess, C. 300
Grosky, W.I. 14

Hagedoorn, M. 467
Hanka, R. 384, 488
Huijmans, D.P. 500

Ip, H. H. S. 384, 442, 488
Iwerks, G.S. 166

Jin, Z. 521, 530
Jungert, E. 127

Kasutani, E. 200
King, I. 521, 530
Koskela, M. 430
Krishnamachari, S. 200
Kuijk, A.A.M. 257

Laakso, S. 430
Laaksonen, J. 430
Lam, R.W.K. 384, 488
Latecki, L.J. 49
Lee, S.-T. 37
Lee, S.-Y. 37
Leung, C. H. C. 442
Lew, M.S. 500
Li, J. 360
Li, X. 520
Liapis, S. 397
Loupias, E. 223

Ma, J. 290
Mahdi, W. 74
Mainguenaud, M. 511
Makki, K. 457
Marchand-Maillet, S. 300
Mokhtarian, F. 233
Mongiello, M. 372
Müller, H. 300
Müller, W. 300

Oja, E. 430

Orphanoudakis, S. C. 269

Paschos, G. 457
Pauwels, E.J. 257
Pecenovic, Z. 279, 300
Pellerin, D. 327
Peng, J. 407
Pirrone, R. 212
Pissinou, N. 457
Pu, P. 279
Pun, T. 300

Radev, I.S. 457
Ronfard, R. 349
Rosenfeld, A. 49

Samet, H. 166
Sánchez, J.-M. 189
Santini, S. 26
Schettini, R. 312
Schouten, B.A.M. 257
Sebe, N. 223, 500
Smaïl, M. 244
Smeulders, A. 26
Sporring, J. 269
Squire, D. McG. 300
Stanchev, P.L. 14

Tang L.H.Y. 384, 488
Trépied, C. 140
Tschepenakis, G. 84
Tziritas, G. 397

Veltkamp, R.C. 467
Vendrig, J. 338
Vertan, C. 178
Vetterli, M. 279
Vries, A. P. de 300
Vuilleumier-Stückelberg, M. 49

Wang, J. Z. 360
Wang, Q. 477
Wang, Z. 477
Wiederhold, G. 360
Worring, M. 26, 338

Xirouhakis, Y. 84

Yamada, A. 200
Yu, C. T. 108
Yuk-Ming Chan, D. 531

Zabulis, X. 269
Zonta, B. 312

Lecture Notes in Computer Science

For information about Vols. 1–1872
please contact your bookseller or Springer-Verlag

Vol. 1873: M. Ibrahim, J. Küng, N. Revell (Eds.), Database and Expert Systems Applications. Proceedings, 2000. XIX, 1005 pages. 2000.

Vol. 1874: Y. Kambayashi, M. Mohania, A M. Tjoa (Eds.), Data Warehousing and Knowledge Discovery. Proceedings, 2000. XII, 438 pages. 2000.

Vol. 1875: K. Bauknecht, S.K. Madria, G. Pernul (Eds.), Electronic Commerce and Web Technologies. Proceedings, 2000. XII, 488 pages. 2000.

Vol. 1876: F. J. Ferri, J.M. Iñesta, A. Amin, P. Pudil (Eds.), Advances in Pattern Recognition. Proceedings, 2000. XVIII, 901 pages. 2000.

Vol. 1877: C. Palamidessi (Ed.), CONCUR 2000 – Concurrency Theory. Proceedings, 2000. XI, 612 pages. 2000.

Vol. 1878: J.P. Bowen, S. Dunne, A. Galloway, S. King (Eds.), ZB 2000: Formal Specification and Development in Z and B. Proceedings, 2000. XIV, 511 pages. 2000.

Vol. 1879: M. Paterson (Ed.), Algorithms – ESA 2000. Proceedings, 2000. IX, 450 pages. 2000.

Vol. 1880: M. Bellare (Ed.), Advances in Cryptology – CRYPTO 2000. Proceedings, 2000. XI, 545 pages. 2000.

Vol. 1881: C. Zhang, V.-W. Soo (Eds.), Design and Applications of Intelligent Agents. Proceedings, 2000. X, 183 pages. 2000. (Subseries LNAI).

Vol. 1882: D. Kotz, F. Mattern (Eds.), Agent Systems, Mobile Agents, and Applications. Proceedings, 2000. XII, 275 pages. 2000.

Vol. 1883: B. Triggs, A. Zisserman, R. Szeliski (Eds.), Vision Algorithms: Theory and Practice. Proceedings, 1999. X, 383 pages. 2000.

Vol. 1884: J. Štuller, J. Pokorný, B. Thalheim, Y. Masunaga (Eds.), Current Issues in Databases and Information Systems. Proceedings, 2000. XIII, 396 pages. 2000.

Vol. 1885: K. Havelund, J. Penix, W. Visser (Eds.), SPIN Model Checking and Software Verification. Proceedings, 2000. X, 343 pages. 2000.

Vol. 1886: R. Mizoguchi, J. Slaney /Eds.), PRICAI 2000: Topics in Artificial Intelligence. Proceedings, 2000. XX, 835 pages. 2000. (Subseries LNAI).

Vol. 1888: G. Sommer, Y.Y. Zeevi (Eds.), Algebraic Frames for the Perception-Action Cycle. Proceedings, 2000. X, 349 pages. 2000.

Vol. 1889: M. Anderson, P. Cheng, V. Haarslev (Eds.), Theory and Application of Diagrams. Proceedings, 2000. XII, 504 pages. 2000. (Subseries LNAI).

Vol. 1890: C Linnhoff-Popien, H.-G. Hegering (Eds.), Trends in Distributed Systems: Towards a Universal Service Market. Proceedings, 2000. XI, 341 pages. 2000.

Vol. 1891: A.L. Oliveira (Ed.), Grammatical Inference: Algorithms and Applications. Proceedings, 2000. VIII, 313 pages. 2000. (Subseries LNAI).

Vol. 1892: P. Brusilovsky, O. Stock, C. Strapparava (Eds.), Adaptive Hypermedia and Adaptive Web-Based Systems. Proceedings, 2000. XIII, 422 pages. 2000.

Vol. 1893: M. Nielsen, B. Rovan (Eds.), Mathematical Foundations of Computer Science 2000. Proceedings, 2000. XIII, 710 pages. 2000.

Vol. 1894: R. Dechter (Ed.), Principles and Practice of Constraint Programming – CP 2000. Proceedings, 2000. XII, 556 pages. 2000.

Vol. 1895: F. Cuppens, Y. Deswarte, D. Gollmann, M. Waidner (Eds.), Computer Security – ESORICS 2000. Proceedings, 2000. X, 325 pages. 2000.

Vol. 1896: R. W. Hartenstein, H. Grünbacher (Eds.), Field-Programmable Logic and Applications. Proceedings, 2000. XVII, 856 pages. 2000.

Vol. 1897: J. Gutknecht, W. Weck (Eds.), Modular Programming Languages. Proceedings, 2000. XII, 299 pages. 2000.

Vol. 1898: E. Blanzieri, L. Portinale (Eds.), Advances in Case-Based Reasoning. Proceedings, 2000. XII, 530 pages. 2000. (Subseries LNAI).

Vol. 1899: H.-H. Nagel, F.J. Perales López (Eds.), Articulated Motion and Deformable Objects. Proceedings, 2000. X, 183 pages. 2000.

Vol. 1900: A. Bode, T. Ludwig, W. Karl, R. Wismüller (Eds.), Euro-Par 2000 Parallel Processing. Proceedings, 2000. XXXV, 1368 pages. 2000.

Vol. 1901: O. Etzion, P. Scheuermann (Eds.), Cooperative Information Systems. Proceedings, 2000. XI, 336 pages. 2000.

Vol. 1902: P. Sojka, I. Kopeček, K. Pala (Eds.), Text, Speech and Dialogue. Proceedings, 2000. XIII, 463 pages. 2000. (Subseries LNAI).

Vol. 1903: S. Reich, K.M. Anderson (Eds.), Open Hypermedia Systems and Structural Computing. Proceedings, 2000. VIII, 187 pages. 2000.

Vol. 1904: S.A. Cerri, D. Dochev (Eds.), Artificial Intelligence: Methodology, Systems, and Applications. Proceedings, 2000. XII, 366 pages. 2000. (Subseries LNAI).

Vol. 1905: H. Scholten, M.J. van Sinderen (Eds.), Interactive Distributed Multimedia Systems and Telecommunication Services. Proceedings, 2000. XI, 306 pages. 2000.

Vol. 1906: A. Porto, G.-C. Roman (Eds.), Coordination Languages and Models. Proceedings, 2000. IX, 353 pages. 2000.

Vol. 1907: H. Debar, L. Mé, S.F. Wu (Eds.), Recent Advances in Intrusion Detection. Proceedings, 2000. X, 227 pages. 2000.

Vol. 1908: J. Dongarra, P. Kacsuk, N. Podhorszki (Eds.), Recent Advances in Parallel Virtual Machine and Message Passing Interface. Proceedings, 2000. XV, 364 pages. 2000.

Vol. 1909: T. Yakhno (Ed.), Advances in Information Systems. Proceedings, 2000. XVI, 460 pages. 2000.

Vol. 1910: D.A. Zighed, J. Komorowski, J. Żytkow (Eds.), Principles of Data Mining and Knowledge Discovery. Proceedings, 2000. XV, 701 pages. 2000. (Subseries LNAI).

Vol. 1911: D.G. Feitelson, L. Rudolph (Eds.), Job Scheduling Strategies for Parallel Processing. VII, 209 pages. 2000.

Vol. 1912: Y. Gurevich, P.W. Kutter, M. Odersky, L. Thiele (Eds.), Abstract State Machines. Proceedings, 2000. X, 381 pages. 2000.

Vol. 1913: K. Jansen, S. Khuller (Eds.), Approximation Algorithms for Combinatorial Optimization. Proceedings, 2000. IX, 275 pages. 2000.

Vol. 1914: M. Herlihy (Ed.), Distributed Computing. Proceedings, 2000. VIII, 389 pages. 2000.

Vol. 1915: S. Dwarkadas (Ed.), Languages, Compilers, and Run-Time Systems for Scalable Computers. Proceedings, 2000. VIII, 301 pages. 2000.

Vol. 1916: F. Dignum, M. Greaves (Eds.), Issues in Agent Communication. X, 351 pages. 2000. (Subseries LNAI).

Vol. 1917: M. Schoenauer, K. Deb, G. Rudolph, X. Yao, E. Lutton, J.J. Merelo, H.-P. Schwefel (Eds.), Parallel Problem Solving from Nature – PPSN VI. Proceedings, 2000. XXI, 914 pages. 2000.

Vol. 1918: D. Soudris, P. Pirsch, E. Barke (Eds.), Integrated Circuit Design. Proceedings, 2000. XII, 338 pages. 2000.

Vol. 1919: M. Ojeda-Aciego, I.P. de Guzman, G. Brewka, L. Moniz Pereira (Eds.), Logics in Artificial Intelligence. Proceedings, 2000. XI, 407 pages. 2000. (Subseries LNAI).

Vol. 1920: A.H.F. Laender, S.W. Liddle, V.C. Storey (Eds.), Conceptual Modeling – ER 2000. Proceedings, 2000. XV, 588 pages. 2000.

Vol. 1921: S.W. Liddle, H.C. Mayr, B. Thalheim (Eds.), Conceptual Modeling for E-Business and the Web. Proceedings, 2000. X, 179 pages. 2000.

Vol. 1922: J. Crowcroft, J. Roberts, M.I. Smirnov (Eds.), Quality of Future Internet Services. Proceedings, 2000. XI, 368 pages. 2000.

Vol. 1923: J. Borbinha, T. Baker (Eds.), Research and Advanced Technology for Digital Libraries. Proceedings, 2000. XVII, 513 pages. 2000.

Vol. 1924: W. Taha (Ed.), Semantics, Applications, and Implementation of Program Generation. Proceedings, 2000. VIII, 231 pages. 2000.

Vol. 1925: J. Cussens, S. Džeroski (Eds.), Learning Language in Logic. X, 301 pages 2000. (Subseries LNAI).

Vol. 1926: M. Joseph (Ed.), Formal Techniques in Real-Time and Fault-Tolerant Systems. Proceedings, 2000. X, 305 pages. 2000.

Vol. 1927: P. Thomas, H.W. Gellersen, (Eds.), Handheld and Ubiquitous Computing. Proceedings, 2000. X, 249 pages. 2000.

Vol. 1928: U. Brandes, D. Wagner (Eds.), Graph-Theoretic Concepts in Computer Science. Proceedings, 2000. X, 315 pages. 2000.

Vol. 1929: R. Laurini (Ed.), Advances in Visual Information Systems. Proceedings, 2000. XII, 542 pages. 2000.

Vol. 1931: E. Horlait (Ed.), Mobile Agents for Telecommunication Applications. Proceedings, 2000. IX, 271 pages. 2000.

Vol. 1658: J. Baumann, Mobile Agents: Control Algorithms. XIX, 161 pages. 2000.

Vol. 1766: M. Jazayeri, R.G.K. Loos, D.R. Musser (Eds.), Generic Programming. Proceedings, 1998. X, 269 pages. 2000.

Vol. 1791: D. Fensel, Problem-Solving Methods. XII, 153 pages. 2000. (Subseries LNAI).

Vol. 1799: K. Czarnecki, U.W. Eisenecker, Generative and Component-Based Software Engineering. Proceedings, 1999. VIII, 225 pages. 2000.

Vol. 1812: J. Wyatt, J. Demiris (Eds.), Advances in Robot Learning. Proceedings, 1999. VII, 165 pages. 2000. (Subseries LNAI).

Vol. 1932: Z.W. Raś, S. Ohsuga (Eds.), Foundations of Intelligent Systems. Proceedings, 2000. XII, 646 pages. (Subseries LNAI).

Vol. 1933: R.W. Brause, E. Hanisch (Eds.), Medical Data Analysis. Proceedings, 2000. XI, 316 pages. 2000.

Vol. 1934: J.S. White (Ed.), Envisioning Machine Translation in the Information Future. Proceedings, 2000. XV, 254 pages. 2000. (Subseries LNAI).

Vol. 1935: S.L. Delp, A.M. DiGioia, B. Jaramaz (Eds.), Medical Image Computing and Computer-Assisted Intervention – MICCAI 2000. Proceedings, 2000. XXV, 1250 pages. 2000.

Vol. 1937: R. Dieng, O. Corby (Eds.), Knowledge Engineering and Knowledge Management. Proceedings, 2000. XIII, 457 pages. 2000. (Subseries LNAI).

Vol. 1938: S. Rao, K.I. Sletta (Eds.), Next Generation Networks. Proceedings, 2000. XI, 392 pages. 2000.

Vol. 1939: A. Evans, S. Kent, B. Selic (Eds.), «UML» – The Unified Modeling Language. Proceedings, 2000. XIV, 572 pages. 2000.

Vol. 1940: M. Valero, K. Joe, M. Kitsuregawa, H. Tanaka (Eds.), High Performance Computing. Proceedings, 2000. XV, 595 pages. 2000.

Vol. 1942: H. Yasuda (Ed.), Active Networks. Proceedings, 2000. XI, 424 pages. 2000.

Vol. 1943: F. Koornneef, M. van der Meulen (Eds.), Computer Safety, Reliability and Security. Proceedings, 2000. X, 432 pages. 2000.

Vol. 1945: W. Grieskamp, T. Santen, B. Stoddart (Eds.), Integrated Formal Methods. Proceedings, 2000. X, 441 pages. 2000.

Vol. 1948: T. Tan, Y. Shi, W. Gao (Eds.), Advances in Multimodal Interfaces – ICMI 2000. Proceedings, 2000. XVI, 678 pages. 2000.

Vol. 1954: W.A. Hunt, Jr., S.D. Johnson (Eds.), Formal Methods in Computer-Aided Design. Proceedings, 2000. XI, 539 pages. 2000.